The Communist International and US Communism

1919–1929

Historical Materialism Book Series

The Historical Materialism Book Series is a major publishing initiative of the radical left. The capitalist crisis of the twenty-first century has been met by a resurgence of interest in critical Marxist theory. At the same time, the publishing institutions committed to Marxism have contracted markedly since the high point of the 1970s. The Historical Materialism Book Series is dedicated to addressing this situation by making available important works of Marxist theory. The aim of the series is to publish important theoretical contributions as the basis for vigorous intellectual debate and exchange on the left.

The peer-reviewed series publishes original monographs, translated texts, and reprints of classics across the bounds of academic disciplinary agendas and across the divisions of the left. The series is particularly concerned to encourage the internationalization of Marxist debate and aims to translate significant studies from beyond the English-speaking world.

For a full list of titles in the Historical Materialism Book Series available in paperback from Haymarket Books, visit:
www.haymarketbooks.org/category/hm-series

The Communist International and US Communism

1919–1929

Jacob A. Zumoff

Haymarket Books
Chicago, IL

First published in 2014 by Brill Academic Publishers, the Netherlands

Published in paperback in 2015 by
Haymarket Books
P.O. Box 180165
Chicago, IL 60618
773-583-7884
www.haymarketbooks.org

ISBN: 978-1-60846-487-6

Trade distribution:
In the US, Consortium Book Sales, www.cbsd.com
In Canada, Publishers Group Canada, www.pgcbooks.ca
In the UK, Turnaround Publisher Services, www.turnaround-psl.com
In Australia, Palgrave Macmillan, www.palgravemacmillan.com.au
In all other countries, Publishers Group Worldwide, www.pgw.com

Cover design by Ragina Johnson.

This book was published with the generous support of
Lannan Foundation and the Wallace Global Fund.

Printed in the United States.

10 9 8 7 6 5 4 3 2 1

Library of Congress Cataloging-in-Publication data is available.

Contents

Acknowledgements vii
Abbreviations x

Introduction: History and Historiography of American Communism in the 1920s 1

1 The Formation of the Communist Party, 1912–21 24

2 The Fight for Legality 49

3 Communists and the Labour Movement 74

4 William Z. Foster and the Turn Towards the Labour Movement 98

5 The Farmer-Labor Party 112

6 The La Follette Fiasco, 1923–4 130

7 The Double-Edged Sword of 'Bolshevisation', 1924–6 152

8 The Foreign-Language Federations and 'Bolshevisation' 172

9 Factionalism and Mass Work, 1925–7 187

10 The Death of Ruthenberg and the Ascension of Lovestone, 1926–7 205

11 Lovestone Between Bukharin and Stalin, 1927–8 223

12 The 'Third Period', the Sixth Congress and the Elimination of Opposition, 1928–9 249

13 Lovestone Becomes a Lovestoneite, 1928–9 266

14 The 'Negro Question' to the Fourth Comintern Congress 287

15 The 'Negro Question' from the Fourth to the Sixth Congress 312

16 The Sixth Congress and the 'Negro Question' 330

17 'Self-Determination' and Comintern Intervention 352

Conclusion 365

Bibliography and Works Cited 369
Index 411

Acknowledgements

Any book is based not only on its author's efforts, but also the support of many others. This is probably especially true for this study, whose twenty-year gestation is twice as long as the time period it analyses. This book originated in an undergraduate term paper and senior thesis at Rutgers University for Norman Markowitz; parts were researched while the author was a student at the City University of New York Graduate Center, particularly in classes for Joshua B. Freeman, Dolores Greenberg, Hobart Spalding and Judith Stein. At the University of London, professors Rick Halpern (now at the University of Toronto) and Andrew Hemingway made sure I actually obtained my doctoral degree. For almost a decade the thesis gathered dust, until Sébastien Budgen from the Historical Materialism Book Series tracked me down and convinced me to revise and publish it.

In the latest round of research, many people have been helpful.

I am thankful to the history department at New Jersey City University, which provided financial and professional stability during what has been called 'the greatest economic crisis since the Great Depression': Jason Martinek, for reading earlier drafts and for sharing his own research; José Morales (*a quien le debo una finca cafetera puertorriqueña*); Rosemary Thurston, Timothy White, Rosamond Hooper-Hamersley and Patricia Catrillo.

The following scholars provided copies of their (often unpublished) research: Jordan Baev and Kostadin Grozev, Andrew Barbero, Bob Boughton, Carla Burnett, Tim Davenport, Maria Gertrudis Van Enckevort, Alex Goodall, Jessica L. Graham, Paul Heideman, John D. Holmes, Leslie Elaine James, Quincy R. Lehr, Minkah Makalani, Jason Martinek, Zebulon V. Milestsky, Eugene V. Orenstein, Fredrik Petersson, John Riddell, Thomas Sakmyster, Reiner Tosstorff, Andrew Kier Wise and Akito Yamanouchi. (My apologies to those I have left off the list, no doubt there are some). I must give special thanks to Mark Donnelly, who shared his research on Nicholas Hourwich, and to Andrei Nesterov in Moscow, who provided research assistance on Alexander Stoklitsky.

The following scholars answered my questions of all sorts: Hakim Adi, Marc Becker, Barry Carr, Stephen F. Cohen, Josephine Fowler, Richard Hudelson, Winston James, Dick J. Reavis and Daniela Spenser. I must also thank Miguel Álvarez for translation assistance in German, and Blandine Hauser Anwar for assistance in French. Extra thanks are due to Lisa Diamond, for invaluable assistance not only on the index, but for copy-editing the final manuscript.

The following people read portions of this manuscript, in various stages, and offered important advice: Don Andrews, Alison Dundy, Tim Davenport,

Michael Goldfield, George Kukich, Jason Martinek, Bryan D. Palmer, Mark Solomon, Jeff Taylor, Emily Turnbull, as well as the two anonymous readers at Brill. Of course, any and all remaining errors are my own.

If scientific research is based on laboratory experimentation, history is based on archival research. The study of history would not take place without the help of librarians and archivists. The staff at the Prometheus Research Library—a working Marxist archive in lower Manhattan—deserve special thanks. From my research as an undergraduate to the work on revising this manuscript, they provided political, archival and historical advice and guidance. It is fair to say that without the PRL, this book would not have been conceived, much less finished. I should like to especially thank Don Andrews, E. Benedict, Helene Brosius, Alison Dundy, Tim Marinetti, James Robertson, Caron Salinger and Emily Turnbull. Diana B. Kartsen and Carl Lichenstein, without whom this book could not have been written, died before it was published. This loss is still sorely felt.

The core of this book is based on the archives of the Comintern—in the Russian State Archive of Socio-Political History (RGAPSI)—and I am grateful for the help of the archive's staff in Moscow when I visited in 2001. Dale Reed of the Hoover Institution at Stanford University was indispensable, both in my original fortnight there while a doctoral student and with my subsequent inquiries.

The Tamiment Institute at New York University was also necessary for this work, and I wish to thank the staff, including Jillian Cuellar, Daniel Eshom, Peter Filardo and Michael Nash (whose untimely death occurred while I was finalising the manuscript); the staff of the European Reading Room at the Library of Congress, and Erika Hope Spencer in particular, put up with me while I parked myself in their space to use the Comintern files there (and they kindly refilled the paper and toner in the printer, repeatedly). The Interlibrary Loan staff at several libraries—Sawyer Library at Suffolk University; O'Neill Library at Boston College; the Santa Catarina and Campus Monterrey libraries at the Tecnológico de Monterrey; the Quinn Library at Fordham University Lincoln Center; and the Guarini Library at New Jersey City University—put up with repeated esoteric requests for material from all over the world. A key turning point for the Communist Party was the Passaic strike. I would like to thank the Julius Forstmann Library in Passaic, NJ, and the American Labor Museum/Botto House in Haledon, NJ, for helping me use their collections on the strike.

In one of my favourite short articles by Lenin from 1913, 'What Can Be Done for Public Education', the Bolshevik leader contrasts the access granted by the New York Public Library to the difficulty of obtaining books in tsarist Russia. In fact, I benefited greatly from the holdings and expertise of the NYPL—including its main research branch and the Schomburg Center in Harlem. Unfortunately, one hundred years after Lenin wrote that article, in capitalist America many great libraries are, like much of society, private property designated for exclusive use. In light of this, I am thankful to the various friends, colleagues, and acquaintances who helped make it possible to consult material at different university libraries. In particular, I wish to express my everlasting thanks to the unnamed student worker at Harvard's Lamont Library who explained how somebody without a Harvard ID could access the library's amazing microfilm collections. I am also thankful to the Rutgers Alumni Association for allowing all alumni borrowing privileges.

There are, of course, many more people who have contributed to this project through discussion and support. As Marx wrote, 'it is necessary to educate the educator himself'. I owe much to those who have helped in my understanding of the issues raised by the Communist movement. Rather than name each one, I will collectively thank everybody in Boston, Chicago, London, Los Angeles, Mexico City, New Jersey/New York, the San Francisco Bay Area, and Toronto. Elizabeth Jackson encouraged me to take up the project again when it was posed; Paul Cooperstein also deserves special note, not only for his extensive knowledge of the Sacco and Vanzetti case, but also for his extensive expertise on the juniper plant; Skye White was also crucial. As I was in the last stages of preparing the manuscript, Tweet Carter died. Although not directly involved in this project, she never stopped encouraging my research; I only hope that the book reflects at least some of her keen insight on the American left.

Finally, I must thank those who, although having little to do with the actual writing of this book, provided help in infinite ways: my parents Mary and Robert Zumoff, and my partner Bleida (*para quien no hay palabras*).

∴

I would like to thank the Columbia University Oral History Research Office for allowing me to quote from the Max Shachtman Reminiscences (in the Socialist Movement Project) and the Charles E. Taylor Reminiscences. I would also like to thank the editors of the following journals, in which portions of this work have been published in different forms, for allowing me to incorporate it in the present study: *The Journal of Caribbean History*; *Cercles*; *The Journal for the Study of Radicalism*. The Royal Historical Society and the Graduate School of University College London provided funding for a trip to Moscow.

Jacob A. Zumoff
New York, NY

Abbreviations

ABB	African Blood Brotherhood
ACWA	Amalgamated Clothing Workers of America
AFL	American Federation of Labor
ANLC	American Negro Labor Congress
CCE	Central Cooperative Exchange
CCLP	Cook County Labor Party
CEC	Central Executive Committee
CFL	Chicago Federation of Labor
CI	Communist International, Comintern
CIO	Congress of Industrial Organizations
CLA	Communist League of America
CLP	Communist Labor Party
CP	Communist Party
CPA	Communist Party of America
CPC	Communist Party of Canada
CPGB	Communist Party of Great Britain
CPPA	Conference for Progressive Political Action
CPUSA	Communist Party USA
ECCI	Executive Committee of the Communist International
FBI	Federal Bureau of Investigation
FFLP	Federated Farmer-Labor Party
FLP	Farmer Labor Party
FSF	Finnish Socialist Federation
FSR	Friends of Soviet Russia
FWF	Finnish Workers Federation
GEB	General Executive Board (of IWW)
IFWU	International Fur Workers Union
ILD	International Labor Defense
ILGWU	International Ladies' Garment Workers' Union
IRA	International Red Aid
ITUC-NW	International Trade Union Commission of Negro Workers
IWO	International Workers Order
IWW	Industrial Workers of the World
JSF	Jewish Socialist Federation
KUTV	University for the Toilers of the East
LDC	Labor Defense Council
LO	Left Opposition, split from CPA in 1921–2

MOPR	Russian acronym for International Red Aid
NAACP	National Association for the Advancement of Colored People
NEC	National Executive Committee (of SP)
RILU	Red International of Labour Unions, Profintern
SLP	Socialist Labor Party
SP	Socialist Party
SPL	Socialist Propaganda League
TUEL	Trade Union Educational League
TUUL	Trade Union Unity League
UBCJA	United Brotherhood of Carpenters and Joiners of America
UCP	United Communist Party
UFC	United Front Committee (in Passaic strike, 1926–7)
UFEL	United Farmers Educational League
UMWA	United Mineworkers of America
UNIA	Universal Negro Improvement Association
UTW	United Textile Workers
WC	Workers' Council
WDU	Workers Defense Union
W(C)P	Workers' (Communist) Party
WP	Workers' Party
YCL	Young Communist League

Introduction: History and Historiography of American Communism in the 1920s

In November 1917, the Bolsheviks in Russia seized state power amid the devastation of the World War, announcing that they were proceeding to build socialism. As the American Socialist John Reed put it, the Bolshevik Revolution 'shook the world' by making a workers' state flesh and blood instead of a goal. In Europe, Asia, Africa and the Americas, left-wing militants rallied to the Revolution and to the new Third or Communist International (Comintern) that Lenin, Trotsky and other Bolshevik leaders initiated in early 1919. The Bolsheviks envisioned the Comintern as a new, genuine, revolutionary International able to create Communist parties from those socialist militants who rejected the 'social-chauvinism' (support to militarism or imperialism using socialist rhetoric) and parliamentary reformism that had caused the social-democratic Second International to collapse in the face of the War. By summer 1919, the American Communist movement was born, its enthusiasm matched only by its divisions.

This book is a political history of the first decade of the American Communist Party (CP).[1] Above all, this study examines how the early Communists, inspired by the first successful workers' revolution in history, sought to forge a party in the United States capable of making a revolution in that country. In particular, this work analyses the 'Americanisation' of Communism: how Communists understood and applied the lessons of the international Communist movement to American society. Although historians of Communism are divided, there is broad agreement that this 'Americanisation' was counterposed to the 'interference' of the Communist International. This book, on the other hand, argues that in the early 1920s the Comintern helped the early Communists come to grips with American society. By the end of the decade, reflecting the political degeneration of the Russian Revolution under Stalin, the Comintern's interventions were more negative.

Two questions come to mind: why study American Communism in the 1920s? And why do we need *another* study? In much of the world in the

1 As described below, the American Communist movement underwent several splits in its early years, and when it unified in the early 1920s, it first called itself the Workers' Party and Workers' (Communist) Party, and only in 1929 did it become the Communist Party, USA. For the sake of simplicity, the term CP is used to describe the entire party during this period.

1920s, the question as to which class would rule society seemed immediately posed. From 1919–29, Communists in Central Europe repeatedly faced revolution. In England, Communists played a key role in the 1926 General Strike. Communists led revolutionary movements in Indonesia and China. If American Communists avoided the massive repression faced by their international comrades, it is only because they lacked these opportunities. In the popular imagination, American radicalism, after a brief upsurge during the First World War and in the heady days after the Bolshevik Revolution, was beaten back by Red Scare repression and 'roaring twenties' prosperity, enduring what a recent study of the American left labelled 'a dark decade of myopia and division'. Only with the Depression did Communism recover and 'bloom in the sunlight of a New Deal majority'.[2]

Judged by numbers alone, this appears correct. While at its birth in 1919 as a split from the Socialist Party (SP), the Communist Party counted tens of thousands of members, it soon atrophied—growing only a decade later during the Great Depression. In 1938, the party had 55,000 members, and in 1945 it had 65,000. Even in 1955, at the height of the Cold War, the FBI estimated that there were almost 23,000 members—almost twice the membership in 1928.[3]

Yet the importance of Communism in the 1920s is greater than its declining membership. There are several reasons why the Communists of the 1920s are important to study. First, if the child is father of the man, then understanding the 'mature' Communist Party of the 1930s requires examining its formative years. (Not just Wordsworth, but Mordecai Richler's description of Duddy Kravitz should be kept in mind when considering the evolution of the CP: 'A boy can be two, three, four potential people, but a man only one. He murders the others').

Second, while the 1920s were not the high point of Communist influence, this was a reflection of the period as much as of the party. F. Scott Fitzgerald described the 1920s as 'cynical rather than revolutionary', and observed that it was 'characteristic of the Jazz Age that it had no interest in politics at all'. Amid this reactionary period, the Communists were the most important left-wing component of the labour movement. The American Federation of Labor

2 Kazin 2011, p. 161.

3 Glazer 1961, pp. 92–3; Communist International 1928a, p. 20. Membership figures—for both the American Communist Party as well as parties in other countries—are notoriously inexact, reflecting fluctuating dues payments, changing definitions of membership, as well as manipulation and biases of party leaders, the press or the government agencies reporting them. Thus any numbers should serve as a general indication of party strength and not an exact census.

(AFL), prostrate in the face of anti-labour attacks, offered no alternative to 'prosperity' politics. When John L. Lewis was not fighting Communists in the miners' union, he was supporting Republican presidents Coolidge and Hoover. Communists played crucial roles in the major labour struggle of the decade, organising textile workers in Passaic, NJ, New Bedford, MA, and Gastonia, NC. Communists were key in the fight to save Italian anarchists Nicola Sacco and Bartolomeo Vanzetti, which symbolised the struggle against injustice in America.[4]

Traditional Historiography of American Communism

The study of American Communism is at once the study of Communists and previous studies of American Communism. The classic debate, as much political as historical, emphasises the question of how 'foreign' (dependent on the Soviet Union) or 'American' (rooted in American radical and labour history) was the Communist movement. The standard Cold War anti-Communist perspective portrayed Communism as a creation of the Soviet Union. Long time head of the Federal Bureau of Investigation (FBI), J. Edgar Hoover, who built America's anti-Communist repressive apparatus, declared that the archetypal Communist, 'Even though he lives in the United States ... is a supporter of a foreign power, espousing an alien line of thought. He is a conspirator against his country'.[5]

Anti-Communist assumptions motivated many historians. Among these, the historian who stands out, for the depth of his research and analysis and for the clarity of his argument, is former *Daily Worker* writer Theodore Draper (1912–2006). At the height of the Cold War, Draper wrote a two-volume history of the Communist Party in the 1920s. Draper's 1957 book *The Roots of American Communism* and his 1960 work *American Communism and Soviet Russia* are superb studies and remain standard works. Draper interviewed or corresponded with many veterans of the early Communist movement, and collected scattered archival sources. It is impossible to deal with the early Communist Party without taking into account Draper's work.[6]

For Draper, the central question was 'the relation of American Communism to Soviet Russia'. This 'has expressed itself in different ways ... But it has always

4 F. Scott Fitzgerald, 'Echoes of the Jazz Age', cited by Currell 2009, p. 4; Dubofsky and Van Time 1986, pp. 83, 111.

5 Hoover 1959, p. 4. For a recent account of the FBI's spying, see Weiner 2012.

6 Draper 1985; Draper 1986.

been the determining factor, the essential element' in the CP's history. The conclusion of *American Communism and Soviet Russia* answers the question posed by its title: 'even at the price of virtually committing political suicide, American Communism would continue above all to serve the interests of Soviet Russia'. This cut it off from 'other forms of American radicalism such as the open, democratic, pre-World War I Socialist party, the farmer-labor movement, or the syndicalist movement, all of which were far more indigenous and independent than the American Communist party'.[7]

In Draper's analysis, then, a Chinese Wall separated 'American' radicalism and 'foreign' Communism. The Comintern was the extension of Soviet domination that imposed itself on American soil, ignoring or disregarding earlier American radicalism, preventing Communism from becoming an authentically 'American' radical movement. Draper discounted the possibility that the Bolsheviks or other Comintern leaders may have had a *positive* influence on American Communism.

In the 1970s and 1980s, younger historians (often referred to as 'New Left' historians because many had been politically active) fought Draper with a vehemence that may have made him recall the factionalism described in his studies. These 'revisionist' historians did not focus on the 1920s. Instead, they examined times and areas of Communist work that appeared more sympathetic and more successful, for example, work among blacks in the 1930s, during World War II, or among car workers. Influenced both by 'social history' that examined 'history from the bottom up', and by the New Left perspective that 'the personal is political', these historians de-emphasised the 'line' of the party leadership. Instead, using oral history, they emphasised the lived experience of Communists themselves, often lower or mid-level cadres, including 'how activists ... sustain[ed] their morale in an essentially conservative political culture'. (That agreement with the politics of the Communist Party might have helped members sustain their morale seems to have been overlooked).[8]

They downplayed 'Soviet control', depicting the party as having sprouted from native soil. A Communist was not Hoover's foreign agent, but an 'American radical', as proclaimed by the title of a memoir by Steve Nelson, a Communist organiser in Pittsburgh. Social historians insisted that the American Communists were not dependent upon the Soviet leaders, and

7 Draper 1986, pp. 5, 441, 446.

8 Paul Lyons's letter in *New York Review of Books*, 23 June 1994; Important 'New Left' revisionist histories include Isserman 1995 (on World War II); Keeran 1980 (on car workers); Naison 2005 (on black Communists in Harlem); Solomon 1998 (on black Communists); memoirs edited by New Left historians include Healy and Isserman 1980; Nelson, Barrett and Ruck 1981.

that local Communists often acted independently of Communist directives from New York. The most innovative and subtle study was Robin D.G. Kelley's analysis of black Communists in Alabama during the Depression. He demonstrated that while Moscow-influenced politics played a role in Communist policy, rank-and-file Communists on the ground interpreted these broadly and enjoyed wide local autonomy.[9]

In the 1980s, Draper and his opponents crossed swords in the *New York Review of Books*.[10] Although there was no love lost between Draper and his critics, both *accepted* the same framework. The division between 'American' and 'foreign' in American Communism remained undisputed, with the Soviet/Comintern influence unquestionably negative. New Leftists inverted Draper's scheme: they argued that the 'American' traditions were more prominent than Draper allowed.[11] By this time, a 'traditionalist' school had developed that agreed with Draper's argument about the American party's relationship to Moscow. Led by Harvey Klehr, this school saw itself as extending Draper's analysis into the 1930s, which Draper had intended to explore but never did.[12]

The present work rejects this concept of Americanisation as counterposed to Comintern guidance. Leninism, as understood by the early Comintern, did not represent a set of formulae or dogmas, but rather the understanding of the need for a political struggle not only against the bourgeoisie but also the social-democratic leadership that had shown its bankruptcy through parliamentarianism and support to the slaughter of World War I. Lenin held that Bolshevism's basic principles, learnt through decades of struggle, were valid to revolutionaries throughout the world: an emphasis on class struggle and working-class independence, instead of opportunism and class-collaborationism; organising a workers' state, instead of reforming the bourgeois state; internationalism and opposition to one's own capitalist rulers, instead of social-imperialism or social-chauvinism; the need for a revolutionary socialist party, instead of unity with opportunists and chauvinists. In 1924, Trotsky identified as the 'essential aspect' of Bolshevism 'such training, tempering, and organization of the proletarian vanguard as enables the latter to seize power, arms in hand' when presented with a revolutionary situation.[13] Yet Lenin and Trotsky realised that

9 Kelley 1990.

10 Draper's two articles in the *New York Review of Books* (9 May 1985 and 30 May 1985) have been reprinted as the 'Afterword' to Draper 1986; Draper's critics responded in the *New York Review of Books* (15 August 1985 and 26 September 1985).

11 See Naison 1985.

12 See Klehr 1971; Klehr 1978; Klehr 1984. Klehr had the benefit of Draper's research materials.

13 Trotsky 1987, p. 24.

each country had its own history and conditions that required different revolutionary *tactics*.

It would be foolish to deny the importance of Bolshevik influence on the early Communist Party. As party leader C.E. Ruthenberg put it in 1922: 'Without the Russian revolution there would have been no Communist movement in the United States'. Rather than have Communist parties ape the Bolsheviks, however, the early Comintern wanted them to learn the political lessons of the Bolsheviks and apply them to the conditions of each society. At the Third Comintern Congress in 1921, Lenin stated that 'the revolution in Italy will take a different course from that in Russia'. Although the Comintern's 'fundamental revolutionary principles' were the same everywhere, these 'must be adapted to the specific conditions in the various countries'. Although Lenin insisted on splitting from reformists—which put him at odds with Giacinto Serrati at the Congress—he accepted that it 'would have been stupid' for Italian Communists 'to copy the Russian revolution'. Only later, under Stalin (and in the context of a fight in the American Communist Party), did the Comintern argue that capitalist societies were essentially the same throughout the world; differences were at most superficial.[14]

Forging a Bolshevik Party in the US did not mean transplanting the Russian experience wholesale to America (or worse, pretending that Russia and America were the same).[15] As will be explored in the following chapters, the Leninist Comintern compelled the American Communists to move beyond their origins as foreign-language-federation-dominated illegal groups, work within the labour movement and address racial oppression. This was done not because the Comintern leadership believed they knew more about America than Americans did, but because without understanding American history or society, it would be impossible to make a revolution there. In fact, the Comintern's Americanisation efforts were often realised in alliance with American Communists who sought to Americanise their party. Among historians in the US, and society at large, there is a provincial prejudice that Americans are best equipped to understand American society. Often this is true. However, leftists from a particular society are also more likely to overlook and succumb to national pressures. Representatives from the international

14 Ruthenberg 1922; Lenin 1965b, pp. 464–5; on Stalin's view of the relationship between world and national capitalism, see Chapter 13 below.

15 That Lenin understood that there was a vast difference between the US and Russia can be seen in his short piece, written in 1913, on the New York Public Library; Lenin 1977, pp. 277–9.

movement may be better able to recognise this, as most clearly demonstrated on the 'Negro question'.

It is also important to underscore the difference between this meaning of Americanisation and what became known as 'Eurocommunism' in the 1970s and 1980s, that is, the idea that Communists in Western capitalist democracies should seek guidance in national traditions and not Soviet Communism. Schooled by international Communism in its Stalinist form, this trend shared with Draper and the New Left historians the view that there existed what one leading Eurocommunist labelled 'a certain contradiction between the objective conditions with which workers' movements in western countries had to contend, and the adoption of the "Russian model" as a doctrinal and political base for Communist parties'.[16]

Post-Soviet Historiography

Capitalist counterrevolution and the destruction of the Soviet Union in 1991–2 affected this historiography in two ways. First, and most immediately, it led to the opening of archives in Moscow, including those of the Comintern.[17]

16 Azcárate 1978, p. 16.

17 Comintern archives are cited here by *fond*, *opisi* and *delo* (for example, 515:1:356). This will allow the researcher who travels to Moscow to locate the file. When this project was begun more than a decade ago, it was necessary to travel to Moscow to consult the files. Since that time, copies have been made for consultation in the United States, including in the European Reading Room of the Library of Congress, the Tamiment Institute at New York University, and the Prometheus Research Library. Since the unfamiliar often have misperceptions, it is important to understand that the files seem to be a testament to the archival practice of 'more product, less process'. Comprising correspondence, draft reports, newspaper clippings, motions, covering letters without enclosures, stenographic reports, handwritten notes and other similar materials—often with the intended recipient's name written on top—the archives at times seem to be based on the personal files of the people involved. Often a discussion or debate will be carried out over several different files. Former German Communist Wolfgang Leonhard helped evacuate the files during the Second World War. He described them as winning 'first place for chaos and confusion' since they contained 'not only whole bundles of Party documents which had been simply stuffed in without even a file-cover being put around them, but also the remains of cinema advertisements, old numbers of the *New York Times*, broken pencils and every kind of rubbish that had not the slightest connection with the archives'; Leonhard 1979, p. 233. Along with the Comintern practice of using pseudonyms, as well as generally sloppy secretarial practices such as not signing or dating documents, this has left the authorship or date of many documents in question. In cases where this is

Second, it led to a view among the bourgeoisie that capitalism was triumphant, and among the left and labour movement to a retrogression of political consciousness. Thus today, amid a global capitalist depression, the idea that capitalism can be replaced with a social system based on collective ownership and production for use is seen as obsolete or impossible by most intellectuals, workers and oppressed peoples.

The historiography of Communism reflected this widening of archival sources combined with the narrowing of political vision. Klehr, along with John Earl Haynes, published numerous studies after the destruction of the Soviet Union that seized upon the Comintern archives to prove, once and for all, that American Communism was nothing more than an appendage to Soviet totalitarianism. Coming full circle to J. Edgar Hoover, much of this literature has tried to show that Communists were often spies. (Ironically, this school, in its own way, is guilty of the same crime of which Draper accused his New Left opponents: by emphasising espionage, they downplay the political essence of the party).[18]

In response, several former 'revisionists' capitulated to the 'traditionalist' argument, particularly concerning the role of Soviet espionage and American Communism. Declaring 'facts are stubborn things', Maurice Isserman announced in the *New York Times*: 'about the involvement of several score (perhaps as many as 300) American Communists as accomplices of Soviet espionage during World War II, there are no longer grounds for serious disagreement'.[19]

---

clear by context, I have placed the information in square brackets; where I am only fairly certain, I have indicated this by adding a question mark. Since many documents are in more than one location—as well as contained in non-Comintern archives—I have also given the author, title and date of the document where appropriate. In these and other archival sources, I have rendered names as they appear (e.g., 'Losovsky', 'Zinovieff'), even if this contradicts modern-day usage. (For those unable or unwilling to use the original documents, Tim Davenport's Early American Marxism website has a good selection of important documents, especially up to 1924; see <www.marxisthistory.org/subject/usa/eam/>. On the archives themselves, see Naumov 1996; Shchechilina 1996; Firsov 1989.

18 See Haynes 1996; Haynes 2000; Klehr, Haynes and Firsov 1995; Klehr, Haynes and Anderson 1998; Klehr and Haynes 2003.

19 Isserman 1999. It will be noticed that the present work does not deal with espionage. In part, this is because I do not believe that spy-hunting and the study of the politics of American Communism are the same. More importantly, I have found no evidence of espionage in the 1920s, mainly because I was not looking, but also because, as even Haynes and Klehr assert: 'So far as we know, until the final years of the 1920s Soviet intelligence

At the same time, a new historiography has emerged, one that attempts to draw on the strengths of both the 'traditionalist' and the 'revisionist' schools, while transcending their 'narrow focus on the party and its members that both these groups largely share' (in the words of Jennifer Uhlmann). This perspective 'should embed the party story in the life and culture of the United States', focusing on 'the CP's influence on American life' instead of 'histories of the CPUSA'.[20] If the revisionists were New Left historians, this school can be called 'No Left' historians, because it is informed by the collapse of any sense of a socialist alternative to capitalism.

Many of their studies are marked by a focus on the *culture* of Communism instead of *politics*. In this they extend a trend of the revisionists: Paul Buhle, a leading scholar of the culture of radicalism, had earlier complained that leftists inspired by the October Revolution emphasised politics and 'culture vanished from the foreground of Marxists' concerns'. And the New Left politicisation of the personal has been applied with a vengeance. Studies have illuminated the personal lives of Communists (and highlighted the fact that sexism was often engrained in the functioning of the party at various levels).[21] The lived experiences of Communists are a legitimate subject of historical investigation, and provide a fuller account of American Communism, especially in a society in which Communists are seen perhaps as slightly less repellent than cannibals. It is easier to victimise people who have no names or faces, so the humanisation of Communists is significant. As one labour historian has observed in reference to standard anti-Communist historiography, 'it is possible to accept this portrait only if one is so influenced by the anti-Communist atmosphere that one considers the men and women who worked in the plants and belonged to the Communist Party as abstractions rather than people'.[22]

While many of the new historians have claimed to place American Communism in a broader context, they deepen the New Left trend of depoliticising Communism, which obscures the broader history of the party and its importance in American politics. Communism becomes merely one of a long

agencies had only a transitory and limited presence in the United States'; see Haynes and Klehr 2006.

20 Uhlmann 2009, p. 24.

21 Brown 1996; Brown and Faue 2000; Hurewitz 2007; McDuffie 2011. It will be noticed that there is not much on the party and the issue of women's oppression. To a large degree, this is because, unlike the party's changing attitude on racial oppression, there seems to be little evidence of the party's attention in the 1920s beyond what one researcher has labelled 'minimal and tokenistic'; see Weigand 2001, pp. 15–20.

22 Buhle 1987, p. 116; Pricket 1975.

line of reformist, radical or millennial movements. According to James Barrett, the Popular Front 'was *not* only a strategy dictated by the Comintern', but also 'a broad political formation based on mass social democratic politics of which the CPUSA was but one part'. Or as Michael Kazin has argued, the 'popularity of the Popular Front culture owed much to a tradition of democratic radicalism which flowered long before the 1930s'. Of course, this echoes the party's own view during the popular-front era that, in the words of then party leader Earl Browder, 'Communism is the Americanism of the twentieth century'.[23]

This misses the point of Communism; it poses the danger that Geoff Eley had described in 1986 as writing the 'history of communism with the Communism left out'.[24] Rather than trying to fit into a litany of radical movements, early Communists sought to destroy American capitalism and replace it with soviet power, that is, the rule of the working class. The issue of the popular front must be judged not only by how it relates to 'democratic radicalism', but also by whether it advanced the goal of achieving workers' power. (Thus Leon Trotsky criticised the popular front—Communist alliances with non-working-class parties—as a criminal betrayal by Stalin.)

The present book is *not* a social history of the Communist Party of the 1920s. No doubt, such a history would be valuable. As one researcher remarked to me, while spinning reel after reel of the *Daily Worker*, one's mind naturally wanders to the advertisements for restaurants, dentists and doctors. One wonders about the lives of the Communists who read the paper. Be that as it may, since the Communist Party was a political organisation comprising dedicated members, it is necessary to first understand the politics of the organisation. As such, this book emphasises what Barry Carr has labelled 'the politics of the Central Committee'. There are worthwhile specialised studies awaiting their historians, but these will only make sense once the overarching political significance of American Communism is clear.[25]

The Contribution of the Present Work

To return to the original question: why write another book on the history of the early years of American Communism when Draper's books are excellent? Draper's books contain two weaknesses that warrant a new study. The first is

23 Barrett 2003, p. 181; Kazin 2011, p. 158; Browder 1936.

24 Eley 1986, p. 92.

25 Carr 2007, p. 522. For example, the current author is planning a study of Communism in New Jersey, but such a study would have little value by itself, despite its inherent interest as a topic.

analytical. While rightly insisting on the importance of the Comintern to the early years of American Communism, Draper saw this as negative. Instead, as will be shown in the following chapters, Comintern intervention was crucial in forcing the American party to 'Americanise'. Draper also did not distinguish between the Comintern in the early 1920s and in the later 1920s. The Comintern in this period became Stalinist, reflecting the political degeneration of the Soviet Union. Thus the Comintern's intervention by the late 1920s, as a general rule, prevented the American party's development into a revolutionary force.

In themselves, such historiographic disagreements do not warrant a new study, especially when similar arguments have already been made, particularly by Bryan Palmer, and earlier by Michael Goldfield, as well as in a collection of early Communist Party documents by Cannon published by the Prometheus Research Library.[26]

The main justification for a new study is that in the more than fifty years that have passed since Draper's studies, new sources have come to light. The present study makes use of manuscript collections, memoirs and other sources (such as FBI files) that Draper could not have used. The most important of these are the Comintern archives in the former Soviet Union. Such sources present the historian with the opportunity and obligation to test old hypotheses. These archives—comprising reports, correspondence, presentations, publications, minutes and other documentation of the early Communist Party—are immense. The 'temporary registry' for only *fond* 515—that dealing with the CPUSA from 1919 to 1943—is 85 pages, comprising a listing of 325 microfilm reels. Other material is scattered throughout the files of the Comintern itself, its various divisions and other parties.[27]

Historians have published scores of studies using the Soviet archives, which taken together present a fuller picture of American Communism. Yet their narrowness is striking. There have been studies of black Americans and the Communist Party; Yiddish speakers and Communism; Chinese and Japanese immigrants and the Communist movement; regional studies of Communism in parts or all of Alabama, California, Georgia, Illinois, Maryland, Montana, New York, North Carolina and Pennsylvania; biographies of George Andreytchine, Ella Reeve Bloor, Earl Browder, James P. Cannon, William Z. Foster (two), Otto Huiswoud, Lovestone, M.J. Olgin and John Pepper.[28]

26 See Palmer 2003; Palmer 2009; Introduction to Cannon 1992; Goldfield 1985.

27 The registry can be found at <http://www.brill.com/sites/default/files/downloads/31721 Guide.pdf>.

28 The extensive studies of blacks and Communism will be dealt with in the relevant chapters below, but for a start, see Gilmore 1998; Makalani 2011; McDuffie 2011; Solomon 1998; Turner 2005; on Jewish immigrants, see Michels 2005; on Japanese and Chinese

Each of these studies is welcome; it goes without saying that each has a different perspective. But none has attempted a synthetic history of the party in the 1920s, such as Draper wrote. The closest and most successful is Palmer's biography of Cannon. Although Palmer successfully places Cannon in the context of the broader party in the 1920s, a biography is by definition narrow. (That Cannon was expelled in 1928, when Lovestone was still in power, also limits its breadth). The present work attempts to use the Comintern's archives, along with other sources, to provide a case study of the Comintern's interventions into the American party. At the same time, it provides a means to re-examine Draper's basic approach. While my differences with Draper should be clear to the reader, so should my debt to him. At bottom, the Comintern archives provide nuance and detail to the history of early American Communism, but they do not change the broad outline of Draper's history.[29]

An important contribution by Palmer was his appreciation of Stalinism in the American Communist movement. 'Stalinism', of course, is a contested term without any consensus of definition. For anti-Communists, the term refers to all things bad about the Soviet Union and Communism. These include centralisation, political violence and dogmatism. Of course, Stalin did not invent these, and the Comintern under his leadership was not the first context in which such actions were employed by the left. The German Social Democracy, for example, was more than capable of directing violence against the left, for example, in the murder of Rosa Luxemburg and Karl Liebknecht.

Hermann Weber, in the context of the German Communist Party, defined Stalinisation as 'the transformation of communism', that is, 'a change from a party exercising internal democracy to a rigidly disciplined organization with a strictly centralized power structure, making it monolithic and hierarchical', as well as 'ruled by the top echelon of the party' with 'party policy ... implemented exclusively in the spirit of the Stalinist CPSU, in line with its directives'. This certainly describes the American Communist Party at the end of the present study, after the expulsion of pro-Trotsky (led by Cannon) and pro-Bukharin

immigrants, see Fowler 2007; on Alabama, see Johnson 2010 and Johnson 2011; on California, see Cherny 2002; Hurewitz 2007; on Georgia, see Lorence 2006; on Illinois, see Storch 2007; on Maryland, see Pedersen 2001 and Skotnes 1996; on Montana, see McDonald 2010; on North Carolina, see Taylor 2009; on Pennsylvania, see Howard 2004; on Andreytchine, see Baev and Grozev 2008; on Bloor, see Brown 1996; on Browder, see Ryan 1999; on Cannon, see Palmer 2007; on Foster, see Barrett 1998 and Johanningsmeier 1994; on Huiswoud, see Enckevort 2001; on Lovestone, see Morgan 1999; on Olgin, see Michels 2011; on Pepper, see Sakmyster 2012.

29 Palmer 2007.

(led by Lovestone) groupings and the ending of factionalism; however, until this point, the party was not 'monolithic', no matter how much its leaders wished for it to be so.[30]

Another definition of Stalinism refers to the rise of Stalin himself. Certainly, in the debates within the Comintern in the 1920s, there were 'Stalinists' who supported Stalin and his perspective. V.V. Lominadze, A. Lozovsky and V.M. Molotov were stalwarts of Stalin in this time (although each would in turn fall out of favour). Yet Stalinism as a political phenomenon extended beyond the vision of its namesake. In this work, Stalinism refers to the ideological reflection of the degeneration of the Comintern (Stalinisation) starting in 1924. In this period, as revolutions in Europe (primarily Germany) were defeated, Soviet Russia was left isolated and backward, and a bureaucracy came to power through a political counterrevolution. It was marked by the anti-internationalist concept of 'socialism in one country', as well as increasing violence and repression, above all aimed at Communist critics.

This process, which Trotsky labelled the Soviet 'thermidor', left important gains of the Revolution intact—the economic collectivisation, centralised planning and the monopoly of foreign trade—but the workers' state increasingly degenerated. Stalin came to personify this, and, of course, of the leading Bolsheviks at the time of the October Revolution, almost he alone survived. Other important leaders—including Bukharin, Kamenev, Zinoviev—were integral to the degeneration of the Bolshevik Revolution (Stalinisation), although they were not part of the 'Stalin faction'. The Comintern also became Stalinised, as the goal of forging Communist parties that would be capable of leading the working class to power was abandoned. Instead, as a corollary to 'socialism in one country', the Comintern's sections in essence became tools to pressure the capitalist governments for policies favouring the Soviet Union.

Stalinisation did not occur overnight, nor was it smooth or inevitable; its full extent and importance were not obvious to all those who experienced it. To borrow from grammar, in the 1920s, this degeneration was best described in the imperfect and not the preterite. Parties underwent Stalinisation at different rates and in different ways, reflecting pressures from the Comintern and from their own national terrain. In the US, the party became Stalinist in part through adopting the ideology of Stalinism and the organisational dictates of the Stalinist Comintern.

A key contribution of Palmer's study of Stalinism in American Communism was his insistence that if the relationship between the Comintern and the

30 Weber 2008, p. 22.

American party remained crucial in the 1920s, the content of this relationship changed. The present work draws heavily on this framework (which, as Palmer would be the first to acknowledge, owed much to Cannon's Trotskyist critique of the American party). The Comintern in the early 1920s helped ground its American followers in Communist theory *and* American reality. Early chapters focus on the first splits from the Socialist Party; the fight over a legal or underground party; work in the 'reactionary' AFL; and the farmer-labour movement. Most important, the Comintern fought with the American party to address racial oppression, a bedrock of American capitalism.

However, by 1924–5, the nature of the intervention began to change. The insistence that the party split from Robert M. La Follette's 'third-party' milieu, if abrupt, saved the party from political liquidation. Subsequently, as the American party descended into factionalism, the Comintern's intervention focused on creating a pliant party loyal to the dominant faction in Moscow. This is explored in the chapters dealing with 'Bolshevisation' and factionalism. This reached a culmination in the expulsion of Cannon's and Lovestone's groups, and the installation of Earl Browder as the head of the party. For more than a decade, Browder was loyal to Moscow.

As Palmer has pointed out, it is the changing (or better, degenerating) nature of this intervention that Draper overlooked. Both traditionalist and revisionist scholars reject the fact that the Comintern in 1930 was different from the Comintern in 1920. James Barrett has written that 'it is difficult to ignore earlier instances of Soviet intervention and manipulation', pointing to 1925, while John Earl Haynes argues that this manipulative intervention began much earlier. Similarly, in regards to German Communism, Hermann Weber locates the 'prehistory' of Stalinisation in 1921–2. While not pretending that the early Comintern was perfect and turned everything it touched to gold, the present study examines the change in Comintern intervention over time—the Stalinisation of the Comintern itself.[31]

The early Comintern rarely imposed its will without consulting and discussing with American Communists. Haynes recognises this, but asserts that such consultation was the exception that proved the rule: 'On matters where their own views were tentative or nonexistent, Soviet leaders did welcome advice and dialogue from Western radicals. But this period was only transitional; once they gained their footing and were more confident of their power, dialogue ended'. This confounds the *power* of the Bolsheviks within the Comintern and the *firmness of their opinion*; it also mixes questions of principle—such as

31 Barrett 2003, p. 182; Haynes 2003, pp. 188–9; Weber 2008, p. 23.

splitting from 'social chauvinists' or centrists—on which the Bolsheviks were insistent, and tactics, on which the Comintern leaders were more flexible.

The example that Haynes cites is indicative. In 1921, at the Third Comintern Congress, Nicholas Hourwich, 'one of the leading figures in the founding of the American party', had the 'temerity to argue with Lenin', and as a result was sent down, 'simply not allowed to leave the Soviet Union and disappeared from the history of American Communism'. Historians often cite Hourwich—leader of the Russian federation and a former Bolshevik activist in Russia—as an example of the Russian domination of the early party. More importantly, Haynes ignores the essence of the dispute. In the same article, to show that the Bolsheviks could not have much of value to teach their American comrades, Haynes argues that 'What American Communists needed was advice on operating in a democratic polity'. But this was what Lenin was trying to drive home to Hourwich and other American Communist leaders: Lenin was fighting to get his American comrades to organise legally and publish a newspaper, while Hourwich wanted an illegal party, believing that the Red Scare had not ended. In other words, Lenin was trying to get American Communists to understand the difference between Russia and America.

Lenin was not applying Russian fiat, but was responding to the struggle by American Communists, such as Max Bedacht and Cannon, to have the party seize the opportunity offered by American conditions. In other words, this episode demonstrates how the Comintern *Americanised* Communism in the United States, in response to pressure by American Communists. (The unaware might think that Hourwich paid dearly for his transgression, but he was transferred to the Soviet Communist Party and spent most of the rest of his life as a university lecturer in Moscow before dying of a heart attack in 1934). As this example indicates, there was a dialectic at work between 'Moscow' and 'America' in the relationship between the two parties.[32]

Factionalism in the early Communist movement, while wrenching, was to a large extent simply natural 'growing pains'. Although early Communists were united by their desire to forge a revolutionary party in the United States, they shared neither a common understanding of what this meant, nor a view of how to realise it. Added to the divergent origins of early Communists, these differences inevitably led to political fights—over legality, unification, the trade unions, the role of foreign-language federations, and black oppression. These

32 Haynes 2003, pp. 188–9. The fight with Hourwich is dealt with in Chapter 2 below. One can speculate that the cause of Hourwich's death was less benign than a heart attack, as was the case with many foreign Communists in Russia during the Stalinist purges of the 1930s. Even if this was the case, this could not be laid at Lenin's feet.

tensions led to continuous pressures towards sterility (such as remaining an illegal party longer than necessary) or opportunism (such as the attempt to find a get-rich-quick scheme through the Farmer-Labor movement).

If painful, these fights were not unhealthy. Although it exasperated the Comintern leadership and many American Communists, this factionalism gave the American party a vitality that other, calmer parties lacked. (The British Communist Party did not experience such factionalism, but rather than a sign of health, this reflected a sterility resulting in part from the failure of early British Communism to recruit some of the most revolutionary, internationalist elements of the socialist movement, such as Sylvia Pankhurst).[33]

The early Comintern attempted to help guide their American comrades, and assimilate the lessons of the Bolsheviks' own development. The early interventions were not perfect, but they did help the party chart a rough course.

By the mid-1920s, this relationship had changed. The Comintern did not pause in imposing policies or leaders upon the American party. In 1924, the Comintern prevented the party from tailing La Follette. This was a necessary intervention, but it was carried out in an abrupt and confusing manner. By 1925, however, the Comintern's intervention had begun to be less salutary, as the party was 'suspended by cables' from Moscow. This was Stalinisation. (In this sense, Barrett is correct that the roots of Stalinisation precede Stalin's personal rise).

Palmer is right to emphasise this process. However, as Cannon pointed out, the Stalinisation of American Communism was not only 'made in Moscow', but also reflected pressures in the US. For the American party, a key part of Stalinisation was social-democratisation. Despite the interlude of the 'ultra-left' Third Period, the full flowering of Stalinism in the United States was achieved when the party tailed the pro-Democratic Party bureaucracy of the Congress of Industrial Organizations (CIO) in the Great Depression and supported the war aims of US imperialism during World War II. To be sure, these followed the line worked out in Moscow, but the anti-Soviet Socialists took similar positions. In the case of the 1920s, 'Stalinism' took the form of adapting to the 'prosperity' of American capitalism. Revolution ceased to be on the agenda. An important prelude to the political Stalinisation of American Communism was the strong impulse to tail the movement around Robert La Follette in the 1924 presidential election. American Communists did not need Moscow to tell them to do this—they came up with it on their own. As Jürgen Rojahn has stressed, 'Stalin and those siding with him emerged as victors from the conflicts taking place simultaneously' within the Comintern and foreign

33 See Foster 1985 for analysis of the 'stillborn' character of early British Communism.

parties. Many foreign Communists supported Stalin's concept of 'socialism in one country' in the 1920s, not just (or mainly) because they were forced to, but because they saw in Stalinism an answer to the problems their parties faced in remaining revolutionary in a non-revolutionary period. (That this 'solution' proved illusory did not diminish its appeal).[34]

Furthermore, the internal situation of the party led to its leadership embracing Stalinist centralisation and control. In this sense, Haynes is correct that 'factionalism of the 1920s demonstrated the movement's organic readiness for Stalinism'. But this is because the factionalism was so debilitating that it made many Communists eager for a solution from Moscow. (Other parties that were less factional, such as the British or the Canadian parties, did not avoid Stalinisation).

This study hopes to contribute to a broader understanding of the Stalinisation of the Comintern itself, addressing several of what Kevin McDermott labelled in 1998 'the major controversies in Comintern history'. These include the relationship between the Leninist and Stalinist periods of Comintern history; the relationship between the Comintern in Moscow and the national parties; and 'the crucial issue' of Communist relations to other forces in the labour movement 'to win over a majority of the organised working class for revolutionary perspectives in an essentially non-revolutionary era'.[35]

It must be cautioned, however, that this is a study of the relationship between the Comintern and its section in the United States. Although the present study attempts to situate the development of American Communism within a broader context, it is not a general history of the Comintern, nor is it an organisational history of the Comintern apparatuses that dealt with the United States (such as the Anglo-American Secretariat). In the 1920s, the Bolsheviks (in addition to party and governmental issues in the Soviet Union) focused on countries with mass Communist Parties and palpable struggles; American Communism was on the periphery of the Comintern, and one assumes that letters to American Communists occupied a small portion of the time of the Comintern leaders.

Day-to-day work was often left to lesser functionaries, many of whom were recent converts to Bolshevism. (Two prominent examples are Max Goldfarb—also known as Petrovsky or A.J. Bennett—and Boris Reinstein). These functionaries in Moscow operated under the broad supervision of the top Comintern leadership. In contrast, Comintern representatives sent to the US—also often lower-ranked, and drawn from other sections—were sometimes a blunt

34 See Rojahn 1996, p. 41.

35 McDermott 1998, pp. 31–2.

instrument. The most famous of these was an exiled Hungarian, József Pogány, who (under the name 'John Pepper') assumed wide powers in the American party, to disastrous effect.[36]

In 1921, the American representative to the Comintern used the parlance of the underground party to bemoan 'the little esteem that the general office has for the American business in general', and to complain that 'the main office considers the American branch more as a nuisance than as a bona fide business institution'. In 1926, of the 46 Communist Parties in the capitalist world, the American CP was the sixth largest. But the American party's 12,000–14,000 members paled in comparison to the 125,000 German, 12,000 British or 53,000 French Communists. By this time, Communists in these countries (all of which had much smaller populations than the United States) had seen major crises that in some cases had posed workers' revolutions.[37]

At the same time, the Comintern paid more attention to the American party than other small parties (such as Canadian Communists). This was to some degree because incessant factionalism required constant Comintern intervention to keep the party from disintegrating. More important, however, was that US imperialism's growing strength and international importance made the American Communist Party crucial in the struggle for world socialism. In September 1919, Zinoviev stressed this in a speech at the Petrograd Soviet:

> the birth of a Communist party in America, however young and weak it may be, is looked upon by the whole of the third International as one of the greatest events in world history...The world revolution can be established when it will be victorious not only in the European continent, but when it will also embrace America. The birth of the American Communist Party, and its growth, is the first swallow that foretells the coming of the world-wide spring.

Communist International ran articles about the American CP, first reprinted from the North American left-wing press, and then by leading American cadres. By the mid-1920s, Soviet leaders sat on the Comintern's American Commission. Stalin called the American Party 'one of those very few Communist parties of

36 On Pepper, see Sakmyster 2012. This situation was not quite so chaotic as the early Comintern approach to Mexico, reflected in the title of a recent study, *Stumbling its Way Through Mexico: The Early Years of the Communist International*; see Spenser 2011.

37 James Marshall [Max Bedacht] to 'Dear Friends', 25 April 1921; in the Comintern archives, 515:1:39. Membership figures are taken from Reese and Thorpe 1998, p. 2; Communist International 1928a, p. 30.

the world that are entrusted by history with tasks of decisive importance from the point of view of the revolutionary movement'.[38]

There was a gap between American Communists' 'decisive importance' and their actual role in American society. Their importance was not that the Comintern leadership expected them to make a revolution in the near future. Rather, they were important despite their weakness; a Communist movement in the strongest capitalist country in the world was necessary. Thus, an irony of American Communists was that the strength of US capitalism at once lessened their importance in American politics while raising their importance for the Comintern.[39]

Judging American Communism

Tied up with the historiographical debate is a basic question: how does one judge the Communist Party and its goals? Haynes and Klehr are openly anti-Communist and their writing oozes contempt for those who see anything of value in American Communism. In 2003's *In Denial*, they equate 'sympathy for the Communist project and distaste for attacking it' with Holocaust denial. Barrett, more sympathetic to the left, still asserts that the Communist Party was doomed to failure from the start: 'The tragedy of Communism in the United States came in its subordination to a powerful international vanguard, particularly with the rise of Stalinism'. This statement repeats two common assumptions that this work contests. First, that Stalinism was inevitable, and second, that Leninism and Stalinism were at most variations of one another. Similarly, there have been several attempts in the last period to argue that Leninism in fact does not exist as distinct from social democracy, or that at least Leninism was not an appropriate model for the left in the capitalist world.[40]

38 *Communist International*, October 1919; Stalin, taken from *Communist*, June 1930, cited in Starobin 1972, p. 44.

39 There was another, lesser reason for Comintern attention to the US. Many Russian and foreign Communist leaders had been active in the American left—including Goldfarb (Petrovsky), Sen Katayama, James Larkin, Reinstein, M.N. Roy, S.J. Rutgers and G. Serrati. To differing degrees, these foreign Communists followed American Communism. There were also numerous less important Communists with experience in the US. This subject (which could provide insights into early Soviet perceptions of the US) is waiting for its researcher; in the meantime, see Draper 1985, pp. 73–9; Gardner 1967, p. 402; Margulies 1968.

40 Klehr and Haynes 2003, p. 13; Barrett 2003, p. 182. Lars T. Lih is a prominent proponent of the view that Lenin added little to Kautsky's conception of social democracy; his most

The current work does not see the goals of the early Communists as wrong, misguided or at best quixotic. This book is written from a Marxist perspective. I am sympathetic to their goal of workers' revolution in the United States as part of a struggle for world socialism; indeed, this is a goal that, in my opinion, is still necessary today, as the world capitalist system is mired in what is now the sixth year of economic depression. This does not mean that I am uncritical of the early Communist Party (or the Comintern). However, it does mean that they must be judged by the yardstick of their goal.

In this way, there is a temptation to dismiss the early Communist Party as a failure, since they did not 'make' a revolution. Not seizing state power is not the failure of American Communists. Unlike in Europe or in Asia, there were no revolutionary situations in the US during the 1920s. (Had Communists acquitted themselves better in Germany in 1923, Britain in 1926, or China in 1927, this could have changed quickly; this is another, indirect manner in which the Stalinised Comintern damaged the American party).

On the other hand, several historians have argued that the value of Communism was to pressure bourgeois politics to the left. Especially in the labour movement and the fight for black rights, Communists deserve credit for struggling for goals that nobody else fought for, and for shifting the political discourse. Yet this view implicitly assumes that a workers' revolution in America was impossible, and that bourgeois pressure-politics was the best Communists could have achieved, following the social-democratic logic of popular-front Stalinism.[41]

Against anti-Communist dismissal and social-democratic embracing of reformism, from a Marxist perspective the only realistic task of the American Communists in the 1920s was to forge a revolutionary party with the cadres and programme that would have been able to seize the opportunity that war and crises inevitably bring. As this work will show, this is where the Communists failed. In the 1930s, amid a crisis of capitalism, the CP grew, but by then it had embraced Stalinism. It gained influence among black people, workers and intellectuals, but squandered this by building popular-front support for the Democratic Party's New Deal.

This failure was not inevitable. In the 1930s, the party embraced the same social-democratic perspective that its founders had rejected a decade earlier.

systematic exposition of these views is Lih 2006, while the most boldly stated is Lih 2009. For a recent article that implies Leninism is not appropriate for the West, see Kellogg 2009.

41 Prominent examples of this include Gilmore 2008 and Zaretsky 2012.

This reflects both the pressure of American capitalist society and the degeneration of the Comintern. This is an academic study, directed at all scholars interested in the topic. At the same time, it is the author's hope that socialists in today's world—one more reactionary than the 1920s—will draw lessons from the failure of the early Communists, since their task is now outstanding almost 100 years later.

Outline of the Book

The first part of the book examines the early years of the Communist Party, and the role of the Comintern in politically guiding the new movement. Chapter One analyses the growth of the left wing within the Socialist Party, and the birth of the Communist movement, divided into competing groups. The Comintern proved crucial in providing the political framework and organisational guidance to unify the party.

Chapter Two turns to the question of legality. The party was born amid the Red Scare; this drove the party underground. However, the United States as a norm allows a larger degree of freedom of press and organisation than many countries. Nonetheless, much of the leadership and membership of the party believed that illegality was necessary to be a real revolutionary movement, even if this hindered the party. The second chapter chronicles the role of the Comintern in backing up American leaders to grasp the opportunity of legality.

The next several chapters focus on the party's early work in the labour movement. Chapter Three examines the party's approach to the Industrial Workers of the World (IWW) and the American Federation of Labor. The Comintern insisted that the party work within the much larger AFL, even though it was conservative-led and anti-Communist. At the same time, the party attempted to recruit from the radical IWW. Chapter Four describes the recruitment of William Z. Foster, one of the leading labour radicals of the period. In part, this was due to the prestige of the Bolshevik Revolution and the earlier fight that the Comintern had waged to work in the AFL.

Chapter Five analyses the party's work in the Farmer-Labor movement. In the early years, the CP ignored the sentiment for a labour party. After the Comintern insisted, Communists intervened. By this time, however, the movement had lost much of its working-class centrality and became more imbued with agrarian radicalism. Under the guidance of John Pepper, who quickly became central to the leadership, the party began an opportunistic attempt to build a two-class movement, on a radical reformist programme. In doing so, the party alienated most of its allies in the labour movement, courting both political and organisational disaster. The factionalism that would last until the end of the decade originated in this debacle.

By the 1924 presidential elections, most of the farmer-labour movement had liquidated in support of the 'Progressive' Republican Senator Robert La Follette. The party came under intense pressure to support La Follette indirectly. Only the intervention of the Comintern—acting under pressure of Trotsky—prevented this, thus saving the party from political destruction. Nonetheless, by 1924 the party was isolated.

The next portion of the book examines the debilitating factionalism that raged until the end of the decade, and the changing Comintern intervention. Unlike the earlier stages, factionalism did not have a clear political basis, and Comintern intervention did not politically resolve the issues in play. Chapters Seven and Eight focus on the 'Bolshevisation' campaign. Comprising semi-autonomous, foreign-language groups, and divided by factions, the party had real problems. However, while 'Bolshevisation' promised to solve these problems, in reality it embedded factionalism more deeply in the party, as well as furthered the Stalinisation of the party.

Chapter Nine examines how the party demonstrated the strength of its programme and organisation through the 1926 textile strike in Passaic, NJ, and the fight to save Sacco and Vanzetti in 1927. These earned the party respect and prestige within the labour movement. At the same time, factionalism became ever more bitter, threatening to tear the party apart despite its impressive mass work.

The next portion of the book analyses the increasing factionalism. Chapter Ten looks at the rise of Jay Lovestone as a factional leader after the death of Ruthenberg in early 1927. At the same time that Lovestone was rising in power, the Stalinisation of the Comintern was proceeding more rapidly; despite his later falling out with Stalin, Lovestone was crucial in the process of Stalinisation of the American CP. Chapter Eleven examines Lovestone at the apex of his power, as he allied himself with Bukharin in the Comintern. This chapter pays special attention to Lovestone's assertion that American capitalism was still growing; although this would later be used as evidence for Lovestone's disloyalty to the Comintern, in 1927–8 this was in keeping with the general position of the Comintern.

The next two chapters examine the endgame of the factionalism. Chapter Twelve focuses on the Sixth Congress of the Comintern of 1928, the rise of Stalin and the fall of Bukharin. This chapter details the creation of an American section of the Left Opposition, under the leadership of James P. Cannon, who was expelled from the party in 1928. Chapter Thirteen focuses on Lovestone's fall from power, and the ending of factionalism in the party by the imposition of a pliable pro-Stalin leadership under Earl Browder. This completed the Stalinisation of the party's leadership.

The final section of the book examines the party's position and activity on the 'Negro Question'. This issue most clearly indicates the importance of Comintern guidance and assistance. Although black oppression was a bedrock of American capitalism, the early Communists continued the 'colour blind' tradition of the left-wing Socialist Eugene V. Debs. While anti-racist, like Debs, the early Communists saw racial oppression as another form of economic oppression, and not a unique type of oppression. Chapter Fourteen traces the party's approach to black oppression from its roots to the Fourth Congress of the Comintern of 1922. While the early Communists ignored black oppression, the Bolshevik Revolution inspired a group of black Caribbean radicals in Harlem, the African Blood Brotherhood (ABB). The chapter examines how the ABB was recruited to Communism, and the subsequent fight waged by the Comintern and the ABB to make the party address the Negro Question.

Chapter Fifteen describes the party's approach to the Negro Question from the Fourth Congress to the Sixth Congress of 1928. During this time, the Comintern repeatedly intervened in the American party, insisting that it address the issue. The party made its first attempts to win an audience among militant black Americans, including the 'Negro Sanhedrin' of 1924, and the American Negro Labor Congress of 1925. Neither succeeded in recruiting many black people, in part because of the factionalism in the party, but also because of errors in the work.

Chapters Sixteen and Seventeen examine the Negro Question and the Sixth Congress. This Congress was a turning point in the Communist approach to black oppression. On the one hand, the Comintern made clear that the American party had to pay more attention to the issue. On the other hand, it also developed the perspective that black Americans were an oppressed national group, with the right of self-determination, that is, to secede from the United States. These chapters examine the roots of this line, including the initial resistance by almost all black Communists. In the end, the party adopted the 'self-determination' line. However, the line was never central to the party's 'Negro work'. At the same time, after the Sixth Congress, the party carried out important and brave work among blacks in the North and the South. Thus, despite Stalinist degeneration, the Comintern in the late 1920s forced the party to fight black oppression, making Communists respected (and feared) for their fight for black liberation in the 1930s.

CHAPTER 1

The Formation of the Communist Party, 1912–21

The Bolsheviks envisioned the October Revolution as the first in a series of proletarian revolutions. The Communist or Third International was to be a new, revolutionary international born from the wreckage of the social-democratic Second International. They sought to forge this international with what they saw as the best elements of the international working-class movement, those that had not betrayed socialism by supporting the war. The Comintern was to be a complete and definite break with the social-democratic politics of the Second International. In the face of the support of World War I by many labour and social-democratic leaders, significant sections of the workers' movement rallied to the Bolsheviks.[1]

This was most pronounced in Italy and France, but in the United States as well the first Bolshevik supporters came from the left wing of the labour movement. In much of Europe, the social-democratic leaders either openly supported the militarism and imperialism of their 'own' ruling classes (such as when the German Social Democratic representatives voted for war credits on 4 August 1914) or (in the case of Karl Kautsky) provided 'left' cover to open social-chauvinists. In the United States, which entered the war late in the day, the party leadership as a whole opposed the war. However, the American socialist movement was still infected with electoral reformism, and a significant number of influential Socialists downplayed the party's official opposition to the war.

This chapter examines how the American Communist movement developed out of these antecedents. The Comintern and its Bolshevik leadership were crucial in cohering a unified party, first by supplying the ideological basis for a Communist Party (CP) and then by forcing its supporters into one organisation. The Comintern was essential in the creation of a revolutionary left in the United States in the 1920s: without its intervention and guidance, the American Communists would not have been able to unify and American Communism would have been stillborn.

1 Nation 1989.

 | DOI 10.1163/9789004268890_003

America's Revolutionary Heritage

Most American socialists were grouped around three organisations. Divisions among these groups were fluid; militants and leaders often belonged to more than one or switched membership more than once. The Communist movement would draw from and be influenced by all three. The oldest, most orthodox and smallest was the Socialist Labor Party (SLP), led by Daniel De Leon (who died in 1914). His lasting contribution to left socialism in the United States was opposition to 'palliative' reforms, and his emphasis on dual revolutionary unions counterposed to American Federation of Labor (AFL) craft unions. In 1900, Morris Hillquit and Job Harriman split from the SLP, and a year later merged with another group led by Eugene V. Debs and Victor Berger to form the Socialist Party (SP). By the 1910s, the SP was larger than the SLP, and comprised socialists of various types and tendencies.[2]

The third organisation was the Industrial Workers of the World (IWW), whose most visible leaders were William D. Haywood and Vincent St. John. The IWW was founded in opposition to the 'pure and simple' craft unionism (exemplified by the AFL's leadership under Samuel Gompers) that accepted capitalism and left many workers unorganised. Wobblies also opposed electoral reformism: although both De Leon and Debs were among the IWW's founders in 1905, by World War I the group espoused a version of syndicalism, opposing 'politics' in favour of militant unionism.[3]

The SP was a broad tent, and by the early 1910s a right wing had crystallised, represented by leaders such as Berger. Called 'sewer socialists' (for their emphasis on municipal reforms), right-wing Socialists supported electoral campaigns and reformism; leaders in several AFL unions supported this tendency. By 1912, the SP had 118,000 members, received 900,000 votes in the presidential election, and counted among its ranks more than a thousand office holders, including Berger (the Party's sole Congressman), several state legislators, 56 mayors and more than 300 aldermen.[4]

At the same time, an amorphous left wing in the American socialist movement had developed around the *International Socialist Review*, published by Charles H. Kerr. In 1910–13, the left- and right-wings of the Socialist movement

2 On De Leon and the SLP, see Buhle 1987; Coleman 1979; Herreshoff 1967, Chapter 5; Reeve 1972; Seretan 1979.

3 On De Leon and the IWW, see De Leon 1966; see also Coleman 1979, Chapter 5; Salerno 1989, pp. 66, 121.

4 Bell 1967, pp. 33–6, 61–4; Fine 1928, p. 214; Hillquit 1965, pp. 294–310; Shannon 1967, p. 5.

engaged in heated battles. The IWW was central to these disputes. Despite the anti-political perspective of the IWW, several prominent 'Wobblies', such as Haywood, belonged to the SP, and many left-wing SP members sympathised with the 'one big union'. Moderate and right-wing Socialists saw the IWW's militancy and radicalism as a threat.

During this time, Hillquit attacked Haywood for supposedly advocating illegal terrorist actions. In late 1911, Haywood was elected to the National Executive Committee (NEC) of the SP with more votes than Hillquit. After the IWW became more prominent during the 1912 textile strike in Lawrence, MA, Hillquit purged Haywood from the NEC in February 1913 for refusing to denounce violence and sabotage. Tens of thousands of members left the SP while the IWW surged. Although some of the leaders of this left wing would become Communists, the movements were distinct.[5]

The Development of the 1919 Left Wing

World War I caused the next polarisation in the SP. At the start of the war, the United States remained officially neutral. Amid widespread anti-war sentiment, the SP opposed the war, unlike most social-democratic parties in belligerent countries who supported their rulers' war aims. In 1915, the party refused to maintain membership in the Second International because of its failure to oppose the inter-imperialist war.[6]

5 On Kerr and the *International Socialist Review*, see Martinek 2010. On Haywood and the SP, see Haywood and Bohn 1911, p. 54; St John 1919, p. 45; Conlin 1967; Dubofsky 1987, pp. 50–94. The factionalism was exacerbated by the McNamara case in Los Angeles, involving two AFL ironworkers who were convicted of bombing the *Los Angeles Times* building during a strike. The McNamara brothers eventually pleaded guilty, and the SP was divided over how to react: see Bassett 1964, p. 13; Bell 1967, pp. 73–7; Johnson 2000. On the 1912 factionalism, see Esposito 1992, p. 312; Kipnis 1972; Mackson, pp. 29–30. On the aftermath of the purge from the SP, see Draper 1985, pp. 42–6; Salerno 1992, p. 78; Dubofsky 1987, pp. 78–9; Bell 1967, pp. 73–7; Kipnis 1972, p. 418. The exact membership decline in 1912 is impossible to ascertain. According to Conlin 1967, SP membership in May 1912 was 135,000, which fell to 100,000 with the adoption of the anti-sabatoge amendment, and then in the next four months fell again to 80,000. However, based on an analysis of SP internal figures, Tim Davenport cites a high figure of 118,000 in 1912 and a low figure of 81,000 in June 1913, which rose to 97,000 in October; see Davenport 2012. In any case, it is indisputable that the purge of Haywood overlapped with a significant decline in membership.

6 On the SP's response to the War, see Shannon 1967, pp. 86, 98. On 11 October 1918, Germer wrote to Hillquit claiming that the SP had not paid dues 'for several years' because the 'International has not functioned'; Hillquit papers, reel 2, document 803.

An anti-war left wing coalesced around *Class Struggle*, edited by left-wing attorney Louis Boudin, German American socialist Ludwig Lore, and a young Italian immigrant Louis Fraina. Boudin, a Russian Jewish immigrant whose writings on Marx were well known, was the better-known editor; the journal, whose first issue was dated May–June 1917, was an eclectic tribune for the party's left wing. S.J. Rutgers, a Dutch engineer who had been in the Dutch East Indies (the future Indonesia), was also active in the left wing as a publicist and a financial backer of *Class Struggle*. The Ohio affiliate of the SP, led by C.E. Ruthenberg and Alfred Wagenknecht, was another centre of the socialist left. While this left wing provided the soil for the development of American Communism, its politics were not what would come to be known as Leninist.[7]

In April 1917, the Socialists had a convention to deal with the war, and adopted the famous St. Louis Manifesto. According to Boudin, the convention 'showed a considerable excess of passion and resentment over clearly thought out principles and politics'. The convention's manifesto asserted the organisation's 'unalterable opposition to the war' and called upon 'the workers of all countries to refuse support to the governments in the wars'. Instead, 'The only struggle which would justify the workers in taking up arms is the great struggle of the working class of the world to free itself from economic exploitation and political oppression'.[8]

The St. Louis Manifesto, despite its left-wing rhetoric, was a compromise that hid political differences in the SP. It had been written by right-wingers such as Berger and Harriman, the centrist Hillquit, and left-wing leader Ruthenberg. It satisfied neither the right nor the left, but allowed the party leadership to maintain control. In *Class Struggle*, Boudin denounced it as 'nothing better than an ill-assorted collection of soap box immaturities and meaningless generalities; assertions which cannot be defended when taken literally, and which must therefore be taken with a mental reservation which renders them utterly worthless as a definite statement of position'. Many right-wingers ignored or downplayed their party's supposed anti-war stance when it became

7 On *Class Struggle*, see Buhle 1995, pp. 72–4. Boudin (but not *Class Struggle*) is discussed in Braudy 2003, pp. 4–5. Boudin's most influential works were on Marxism and on the First World War; see Boudin 1907 and Boudin 1916, respectively. Ruthenberg (whose full name was Charles Emil, but he was generally known only by his initials) is dealt with below. On Rutgers, see Voerman 2007; English summary of Yamanouchi 1996.

8 Boudin 1917a; the St. Louis Resolution is in *Class Struggle*, July–August 1917, as well as *Revolutionary Radicalism* 1920, I.

inconvenient. For Hillquit, his alliance with Ruthenberg undercut his left-wing critics, preventing them from organising an independent tendency.[9]

The SP's official stance on the war had important ramifications nonetheless. After the US entered the war, the government cracked down on the party. Using the 1917 Espionage Act, the Post Office refused to deliver leftist material, including SP journals such as the *Masses*, *Appeal to Reason*, and *International Socialist Review*. Scores of IWW members and leaders, including Haywood, and many Socialist leaders, left, right or centre, were arrested. Left-wing Socialist Rose Pastor Stokes was accused of violating the Espionage Act and held on a $10,000 bond. In September, Debs was convicted on three violations of the act and faced a prison sentence of twenty years and a $10,000 fine on each. (As a result, he lost his citizenship, which was only restored in 1976, fifty years after his death). While the persecution beheaded the IWW, most of the Socialist Party's prominent intellectual supporters quit—either out of support for the war or to avoid the fate of prominent pacifist intellectual Scott Nearing, who faced twenty years' imprisonment and a $10,000 fine.[10]

In the place of the intellectual deserters, thousands of new members, largely urban working-class East and Central European youth, joined because of the party's anti-war stance. In 1917, 125,000 people marched in the SP's annual May Day demonstration. Within two months of the St. Louis Manifesto, 12,000 new members joined. Hillquit's 1917 New York City mayoral campaign, on an anti-war platform, gathered 500 percent more votes than four years previously: 22 percent of voters throughout the five boroughs, and 31 percent in the Bronx, cast Socialist ballots. Ten Socialists were elected to the New York

9 Boudin 1917a; on the right wing, see Miller 1973, pp. 166–71; on the left wing, see Draper 1985, p. 93. On the superficial nature of the SP's opposition to the war, see Esposito 1992, pp. 364–5, 374. Max Bedacht, a left-winger from the German federation, in his unpublished memoirs claimed that the compromise was due to the fact that while the pro-war members were in control of the convention, they were split between those who supported the Central Powers and those who supported the Allies, and the latter supported the anti-war resolution to keep control of the organisation. See Bedacht's 'On the Path of my Life' [1968?], in Max Bedacht papers, folder 17, p. 196.

10 On the SP repression, see Lore 1917. The only significant leader not arrested was Hillquit, who spent 1918–9 in hospital for tuberculosis. On the Espionage Act, see Rabban 1997, Chapter 6. On the IWW, see Renshaw 1968; *New York Times*, 18 August 1918. On Stokes, see *New York Times*, 23 April 1918. On Debs, see *New York Times*, 1 July 1918 and 13 September 1918. On Nearing, see *New York Times*, 22 March 1918. On prosecution of the SP leadership, see Bell 1967, pp. 103–5. On Debs's citizenship, see *New York Times*, 4 July 1976. On intellectuals quitting the SP, see Bell 1967, p. 8; Foner 1988, p. 237; Sharp 1979, pp. 130–6. On Gitlow, see Lendler 2012, pp. 8–10.

State Assembly in 1917, including Benjamin Gitlow. Representative of the new Socialists was Bertram D. Wolfe, who recalled that he 'knew nothing about socialism except that it seemed to stand solid and brave against the war'. As many western and southern native-born Socialists left the party, immigrants in the industrial urban north joined, changing the SP's political and demographic weight. By 1919, foreign-language federations constituted some 53 percent of the party's 110,000 members. The Slavic federations alone comprised 20 percent of the membership.[11]

Émigrés and Social Democrats

Many of these immigrants had participated in the Russian revolutionary movement. Nicholas Hourwich, the son of prominent liberal Russian émigré Isaac Hourwich and a future American Communist, had joined the Russian Marxists in 1899, sided with Lenin, and then emigrated to the US in 1910. Alexander Stoklitsky, another future Communist, claimed to have been a Bolshevik in Lithuania in 1904–9. As early as June 1912, Lenin was in contact with a 'New York Group of Russian Social Democrats', although it is not clear whether this group supported the Bolsheviks or the Mensheviks. After World War I had destroyed the Second International, the Bolsheviks sought supporters among left-wing socialists, including in the United States, to build a new revolutionary international, even before the October Revolution. Alexandra Kollontai and Nikolai Bukharin, two important Bolshevik leaders, were in America during the war. The influence of these Russians on American socialism before the Bolshevik Revolution was minimal. Neither Bukharin nor Kollontai was active in the Socialist Party's English-speaking left wing; neither Hourwich nor Stoklitsky was prominent in the American socialist movement before the war. Lenin urged Kollontai to contact various left socialists in America. Left-wing publications in America, Lenin hoped, would reach socialists in Britain. Lenin's frustration indicates that this was not fruitful.[12]

11 Bassett 1964, pp. 274–6; Bell 1967, pp. 99–103; Draper 1985, pp. 94–5; Haverty-Stacke 2008, p. 88; Weinstein 1967, p. 182; Wolfe 1981, p. 162. On the centrality of the war to the New York City elections, see *New York Times*, 28 September 1917, 4 November 1917 and 5 November 1917.

12 Lenin to the 'New York Group of Russian SD', 4 June 1912, in Boris Nicolaevsky Collection, Hoover Institution; copy with English translation in Prometheus Research Library collection; information on Hourwich is taken from correspondence with Mark Donnelly, 23 June 2011. Donnelly is writing a biography of Hourwich, to whom he is related by

The most influential of the far-left Socialists with roots in the tsarist empire was the Boston-based Socialist Propaganda League (SPL), comprising mainly Latvian-speaking Socialists. Historian Paul Buhle described this as 'one of the smallest, most insular, and until the late 1910s surely one of the least important of the language groups'. Fricis Rozins, an SPL founder, had been a social-democratic militant in the Russian empire before emigrating to the US in 1913.[13]

In July 1915, after failing to gain control of the Massachusetts Socialist Party, Rozins and his followers founded the SPL. An 'open letter' that October denounced what they claimed was the SP's 'drift away from democratic, revolutionary tactics and toward those of bureaucracy and reform'. The SPL's goal was to win the SP 'uncompromisingly for Revolution, Democracy, Industrial Unionism, Political Action in the full acceptance of the term, Unity of Socialist Parties, True Internationalism and Active Anti-Militarism'. According to an article in the *International Socialist Review* in December 1916 by Rutgers, the SPL sympathised with the left wing of the international socialist movement, and set their sights above just Massachusetts. They decided 'to make a nationwide appeal and to support their action and their organization by a weekly paper'. These international aspirations (and their connections with Rutgers) explain why European leftists, including Lenin, saw their propaganda. The Bolshevik leader, in a 1915 letter to the SPL, saw the formation of the SPL as a positive development. He agreed that the SPL's open letter 'corresponds fully with the position our party ... has taken from the beginning of this war and has always taken during more than ten years'.[14]

---

marriage. The information originally comes from the Comintern archives in Moscow. Louis Fraina/Lewis Corey told the FBI several decades later that neither Hourwich nor Stoklitsky had been prominent on the Socialist left wing, but that he knew Hourwich had been a Bolshevik and that Stoklitsky may have been one. According to Comintern personnel files, in the late 1930s Stoklitsky claimed to have been a Bolshevik in Lithuania two decades earlier, but a leading Lithuanian Communist claimed this was not possible. Information in Comintern archives, 495:261:1085; research assistance provided by Andrei Nesterov. According to immigration records, Kollontai arrived in Ellis Island on 20 August 1916; see <www.ellisisland.org/search/matchMore.asp?LNM=KOLLONTAY&PLNM=KOLLONTAY&kind=exact&offset=0&dwpdone=1>. Bukharin arrived in New York in November 1916; Cohen 1980, p. 43. On Lenin's urgings to Kollontai, see, for example, Lenin 1966a; Lenin 1966b.

13 Buhle 1995, pp. 66–7; Draper 1985, pp. 67–8, 132; Weinstein 1967, p. 184. On Rozins and Marxism in Latvia before the Bolshevik Revolution, see Broks, Tabuns and Tabuna 2001, p. 54; on Latvian American politics and Rozins, see Zake 2010, pp. 18–19.

14 On the founding of the SPL, see Draper 1985, pp. 68–9. See also Rutgers 1916.

However, his letter (which he speculated had been lost to censors when he received no reply) highlighted several elements of left-wing immigrant politics in the US that would later become issues in the early Communist Party. Lenin criticised their refusal to fight for reforms. While '*no* reform can be durable, sincere, serious if not seconded by revolutionary methods of struggle of the masses', he admonished the SPL, claiming that 'a socialist party not uniting this struggle for reforms with the revolutionary methods of working-class movement can become a sect, can be severed from the masses, & that this is the most pernicious menace to the success of the clear-cut revolutionary socialism'. Lenin supported their opposition to the right-wing socialists: 'We do not preach unity in the *present* (prevailing in the Second International) socialist parties'. Lenin emphasised that 'we preach *secession* with the opportunists'. Yet he did not favour a loose party organisation: 'We defend always in our press the democracy in the party. But we never speak against the centralization of the party. We are for the democratic centralism. We say that the centralization of the German Labor movement is not a feeble but a strong and good feature of it'.[15] These issues—Communist participation in mass struggles and the need for a centralised party—would captivate the Communist movement for years.

In November 1916, the SPL issued a manifesto that 'strongly denounce[d] all brands of social patriots and social imperialists as opposed to the interests of the working class'. Asserting that a 'true revolutionary spirit and action has never been less in evidence among party leaders than during the period of war', it advocated 'a thoro [sic] reorganization of our party', solidarity with the left wing of the European socialist movement, and a revolutionary Third International. Except to declare that there was no qualitative difference between tsarist Russia and the United States, the letter ignored Russia.[16]

The Russian revolutions of 1917 made the Bolsheviks famous, but except for small groups of European émigrés like the SPL, few American socialists knew anything about them. Such émigré circles basked in the Bolshevik glory. J.B.S. Hardman (then known as Jacob Salutsky)—a leader in the SP's Jewish Federation who first opposed the formation of the CP, later joined it, and then was expelled in 1923—recalled that those immigrants, 'a good many [who]

15 SPL's open letter and Lenin's response are in Mason and Smith 1970, pp. 146–50. The text of Lenin's reply is taken from Lenin 1964a. In an interview in 1949 or 1950, Fraina (then known as Lewis Corey) told the FBI: 'I never saw that letter [by Lenin]. I don't even know if it was received by anyone'; 'FBI Interrogation of Lewis Corey, 1949–1950', in Lewis Corey papers, box 2, folder 5.

16 Manifesto of the Socialist Propaganda League of America, 26 November 1916, in *International Socialist Review*, February 1917.

worked in the revolutionary movement, in secret or underground' in Russia, 'were psychologically attuned to the promotion of a similar movement in the United States'. He remarked, 'A foreign-born Socialist, especially an emigrant from Russia, was somebody in 1919, and a Russian accent was a badge of distinction'.[17]

The final SPL manifesto, written in January 1918, hailed the Bolshevik Revolution and stated it was committed to waging 'a struggle on two fronts, inside and outside of the Socialist Party'. At the founding of the Comintern in March 1919, Rutgers had a consultative vote for the SPL as well as the Dutch Communists. In 1919, the SPL merged with the New York Left Wing. (After the Bolshevik Revolution, Rozins returned to Latvia to play an important role in Soviet politics, including heading a revolutionary government in Latvia, before dying in 1919).[18]

The SPL represented the left-wing urban immigrant roots of the Communist Party; C.E. Ruthenberg, a long-time Socialist organiser in Ohio and perennial candidate for Cleveland mayor, represented the more indigenous left-wing social-democratic elements. No less than the 'sewer socialists', Ruthenberg was involved in electoral politics. An article in the *Cleveland Press* about his campaign in 1911 was titled: '"Municipal Ownership" Is the Length, Breadth and Width of his Mayoralty Campaign'. A 1917 pamphlet highlighted his social-democratic politics: 'By taking control of the police and military establishment [the working class] can wrest powerful weapons out of the hands of the capitalists, and the legislative powers of the government are also of utmost importance to the working class in shaping industry in harmony with their needs'. Yet Ruthenberg opposed the war. In 1917, he received more than 20,000 votes for mayor of Cleveland, on an anti-war platform. Along with fellow Ohio Socialists

17 Hardman, 'Communism in America', undated [1930?] manuscript, in J.B.S. Hardman papers, box 14, folder 10, p. 28. For Hardman/Salutsky's attitude towards the Left Wing in 1919, see Michels 2005, p. 224; Orenstein 1978, especially Chapter 6.

18 Socialist Propaganda League, 'A Program For Revolutionary Socialism', in Johnpoll 1994, p. 7; on Rutgers at the First Congress, see Riddell 1987, p. 42. *Revolutionary Age*, 8 March 1919; Draper 1985, p. 423, n. 7; Klehr 1978, p. 29. In an introduction in the *Revolutionary Age*, left-wing editor Fraina not only claimed that the SPL had 'accepted the Bolshevik program long before the Bolsheviki conquered power', but that Kollontai and Bukharin had been members—something that Lenin's correspondence refutes. Decades later, when talking to the FBI, Fraina/Corey stated: 'I have no recollection of Kollontai or Bukharin ever being members of the Socialist Propaganda League. They may have been ... It was a loose thing'; 'FBI Interrogation of Lewis Corey', Corey papers, box 2, folder 5, p. 2.

Alfred Wagenknecht and Charles Baker, he was arrested for violating conscription laws by allegedly urging young men not to register.[19]

An attempt to fuse these left-wing trends occurred in January 1917, at the Brooklyn flat of Ludwig Lore, attended by Boudin, Bukharin, Fraina, Sen Katayama, Kollontai, Trotsky, V. Volodarsky and J.D. Williams (for the SPL), among others. They debated the future of the American left. Trotsky recalled the high hopes: 'America showed more steadfastness in this period than Russia, and many European countries as well'. Trotsky and Bukharin, along with other Russians, edited *Novy Mir*, a Russian-language publication which Trotsky claimed became 'the headquarters for internationalist propaganda' in all languages. According to Akito Yamanouchi's study, Bukharin and Trotsky published 35 and 47 articles, respectively, in *Novy Mir* during their brief stay in the US, as well as making left-wing speeches. The most important result of this meeting was that it helped pave the way for Trotsky's cooperation with the Bolsheviks. Shorn of the Russians, the meeting formed the basis for the editorial board of the journal *Class Struggle*, the focal point of the developing left wing.[20]

The Impact of the Bolshevik Revolution

Liberals and radicals of all shades hailed the February Revolution, which toppled the brittle tsarist autocracy and replaced it with the 'dual power' consisting of workers' soviets and the capitalist Provisional government. Pro-war liberals and Socialists supported the Revolution, in the words of historian Christopher Lasch, because it 'purified the Allied cause' and 'removed what for most liberals was the chief stumbling block to participation in the war on the side of the Allies'—tsarism itself. Except for small circles of émigrés like the

19 *Cleveland Press*, 7 July 1911, in C.E. Ruthenberg Collection, box 2, folder 1; Ruthenberg 1917, p. 40; Cleveland *Plain Dealer*, 16 August 1934, in Ruthenberg Collection, box 2, folder 2; on the trial, see Ruthenberg, Wagenknecht and Baker 1917.

20 Trotsky to Lore, 26 March 1930, in Exile Papers of Leon Trotskii, Houghton Library, Harvard University, reel 18, document 8938; Trotsky 1930, pp. 274–6. See Bukharin's autobiographical statement in Haupt and Marie 1974; Cohen 1980, pp. 43–4; Deutscher 1954, pp. 241–2; Draper 1985, pp. 80–6; Kublin 1964, pp. 240–4; Wolfe 1981, pp. 182–3; Yamanouchi 1989, pp. 23–8. On *Novy Mir* see Buhle 1987, pp. 118–19. Katayama, who became a leading Japanese Communist, also would be on the Comintern's Anglo-American Secretariat, which oversaw American Communism. On his efforts in the early Japanese American Left Wing, see Fowler 2007, pp. 36–40, and the English summary of Yamanouchi 2009.

SPL, and their supporters like Fraina, most Americans (even socialists) knew little of Lenin or Trotsky and initially saw the October Revolution as an extension of the February Revolution.[21]

Left-wing socialists rallied to the October Revolution because it demonstrated the possibility of socialist revolution. In November 1917, radical journalist John Reed cabled the Socialist *New York Call* from Petrograd: 'This is the revolution, the class struggle, with the proletariat, the workmen, the soldiers and peasants lined up against the bourgeoisie'. In the *Liberator*, Reed declared: 'The real revolution has begun'. In November 1918, Fraina founded the first American Communist journal *Revolutionary Age*, observing that 'Mighty currents of ideas and of action are pulsing through the party, the germinal sap of new ideas producing a new life'. This increased left-wing dissatisfaction with the leadership of the Socialist Party for not 'measuring up to the opportunity'.[22]

Almost immediately after the Revolution, *Class Struggle* dedicated an issue to the Bolsheviks, publishing writings by Trotsky and Lenin. Soon enough, the Bolshevik Revolution would split the American left. What separated the left- and right-wings of American socialism was not support of the Revolution, but whether the Revolution was a democratic revolution in a far-off country worthy of solidarity, or a seizure of power by the working class that workers in the US should emulate. (This support by the left was not unanimous: Boudin criticised the Bolsheviks in an article called 'The Tragedy of the Russian Revolution'; he soon resigned from the journal).[23]

At the same time as the Bolsheviks (in Lenin's words) were building the socialist order, American workers and capitalists were engaged in bitter struggle. The roots of the post-war wave of strikes were in government wartime policy. While repressing anti-war voices in the labour movement, the government rewarded unions that supported the war. Government agencies like the National War Labor Board recognised unions, raised wages, and shortened the working week. By June 1919, union membership had swelled by more than two million people, reaching a peak in 1920 that was double the 1915 figure. After the war, capitalists wanted to reverse these gains, attack unions and enshrine the 'open shop'. In 1919, more than four million workers struck, including meat

21 Foner 1967, p. 15; Lasch 1962, pp. 26–9, 57, 121–2; in summer 1917, Fraina wrote an article for *Class Struggle* supporting Lenin, probably the first English-language pro-Bolshevik article in America; see Fraina 1917.

22 Hornberger and Biggart 1992, pp. 69, 74; *Revolutionary Age*, 30 November 1918.

23 *Class Struggle*, November–December 1917; the headline of the issue was 'Trotzky, Lenine, Kautsky on the Russian Revolution'; Boudin 1917b; Anderson 1942; Filene 1967, Chapter 6; Le Blanc 1996, pp. 169–71.

packers, telephone workers, steel workers, streetcar conductors, shipyard workers, and workers in many other trades and industries. Against the backdrop of Russia, the strikes seemed to indicate to eager socialists, as well as fearful capitalists, that Bolshevik-style revolution was approaching. For the government, this was a pretext for increased repression against the labour and socialist movement. A decade later Hardman (by then an official in a New York textile workers' union) recalled: 'The year 1919 was the banner year of radicalism in the United States. Revolution was seriously discussed among honest people'.[24]

The left-wing socialists rallied to the Third International after the Bolsheviks proclaimed it in March 1919. Reed's *New York Communist*, the 'official organ of the Left Wing, Socialist Party, Greater New York Locals', declared in its first issue's lead editorial: 'We take our stand with the Russian Communist Party (Bolsheviki), with the Spartacides [sic] of Germany, and the Communists of Hungary and Bavaria, believing that only through the Dictatorship of the Proletariat can the Socialist order be brought about'. As the left wing's strength increased, the battles within the party deepened. Arne Swabeck recalled decades later that the Bolshevik Revolution 'shook the Socialist Party to its foundation and brought new lessons and inspirations to the left wing'. In 1919, Fraina drafted a left-wing manifesto that opposed the party leadership and spelled out the left's determination 'to secure control of the Party, to conquer the Party for revolutionary Socialism and impose upon it a consistent proletarian-Bolshevik policy'.[25]

The left won 12 of 15 seats in the elections for the SP's NEC in March 1919. Reed defeated Berger for the position of international delegate, and the left defeated Hillquit in his bid for international secretary. By April 1919, the Boston, Bronx, Brooklyn and Queens locals supported the left wing, and Cleveland, Philadelphia, Rochester and Seattle were moving towards the left. In response, Hillquit pushed through a resolution at an Albany meeting of the New York State party to purge locals sympathetic to the left. The leadership 'reorganised' 16 Kings County (Brooklyn) locals and purged the Bronx and Buffalo organisations.[26]

24 On union membership, see *New York* Times, 8 June 1919; Van Giezen and Schwenk 2001; Hardman 1928, p. 9. On the strikes see Foner 1988, pp. 1–3, 237–56; Johanningsmeier 1994, pp. 88–149; Leuchtenberg 1958, pp. 40, 70; Strouthous 2000, pp. 7–8.

25 *New York Communist*, 19 April 1919; *Revolutionary Age*, 8 February 1919, 22 March 1919, 17 May 1919; Swabeck 1969, p. 30. See also Bassett 1964, p. 297; Lendler 2012, pp. 13–14. This Manifesto was to serve as the basis for the prosecution of Benjamin Gitlow, Jim Larkin and Harry Winitsky for criminal anarchy in New York.

26 Seyler 1952, pp. 331–5; Bassett 1964, p. 304.

In May 1919, Berger filed a complaint with the NEC against Ohio left-winger and national officer Alfred Wagenknecht for 'wilfully and maliciously' attacking the Wisconsin right-winger. A few days later, SP Executive Secretary Adolph Germer circulated a memo to the NEC, decrying the party's 'abnormal and unhealthy condition'. He highlighted that more than half of its membership was in foreign-language federations, which he accused of organising a 'concerted movement to capture the party and subject it' to their rule.[27]

The left wing sought to convince Debs, the most authoritative Socialist leader, but he refused to take sides in internal struggles. At the time of the New York left-wing convention in February 1919, Debs—who was to enter federal prison in April—claimed 'sympathy with the radical tendencies' in the party. However, he stressed:

> the changes that are necessary can all be made and should be made within the party. I am opposed to splitting the party and I refuse to get into the squabble the New York comrades may have between themselves. I have no time for that sort of business.[28]

That same month, leftists Jim Larkin, Rose Pastor Stokes, John Reed and Maximilian Cohen forwarded to Debs a copy of their manifesto, seeking his endorsement. A few days later, Fraina and Ruthenberg cabled Debs, urging him to accept their nomination as international secretary, claiming that 'the party's future demands it and you can also serve the radicals'. Debs replied: 'I have no stomach for factional quarrelling and I refuse to be consumed by it ... I can fight capitalists and not comrades'. James P. Cannon recalled later that if Debs had supported the left, 'there is no doubt he could have carried the majority with him'. Debs's ambiguous relationship with the left-wing Socialists, and later the Communists, continued until his death in 1926.[29]

27 Victor Berger to NEC, 22 May 1919, in Victor Berger papers, reel 15; Adolph Germer to NEC, 24 May 1919, enclosed in Germer to Victor Berger, 26 May 1919, in Berger papers, reel 15 (a copy is also in the Socialist Party Collection, Tamiment Library, IX:9).

28 Eugene V. Debs to Julius Gerber, 27 February 1919, in Tamiment Library Debs Collection, reprinted in Eugene V. Debs papers, microfilm edition, reel 2.

29 Jim Larkin, Rose Pastor Stokes, John Reed and Maximilian Cohen to Eugene Debs, 28 February 1919, in Debs Collection, Indiana State University, reprinted in Debs papers, reel 2. Louis C. Fraina and C.E. Ruthenberg to Eugene V. Debs, 6 March 1919, Debs Collection, Indiana State University, reprinted in Debs papers, reel 2; Debs to David Karsner, 30 April 1920, in *Labor Age*, June 1920; Cannon 1962, p. 267. When Ruthenberg visited Debs in prison in June 1920 to ask him to join the Communists, Debs declined. In his campaign for president in 1920 from federal prison, he spoke favourably of the

Hillquit 'Clears the Deck'

The Germer-Hillquit leadership engaged the growing left wing in fierce battle. While paying lip service to the Bolshevik Revolution, Hillquit derided the left wing as 'a sort of burlesque on the Russian Revolution' and advocated that the left- and right-wings of the party 'separate, honestly, freely and without rancor'. The leadership refused to accept the result of the NEC elections and began to expel the left. Hillquit declared that it was time to 'clear the decks' of the leftist menace within the Socialist Party. The lead-up to the upcoming Socialist Party convention, to open in Chicago on 30 August, would be key to deciding the balance of forces in the organisation.[30]

At the end of May, the NEC met for almost a week, dividing into a right-wing majority and a left-wing minority. The NEC began a wholesale purge of the left: they reorganised the Michigan group, expelling the leftists; suspended the New York City organisations; suspended seven language federations; and refused to count all the ballots for the upcoming national convention, claiming the left was organising a parallel party. These suspensions and expulsions 'cleared the deck' of one-third of the Socialist Party's membership. In the leadership, only left-wingers Wagenknecht and Katterfeld opposed this purge.[31]

By August, the purge had been extended to the Massachusetts and Ohio groups. Some two-thirds of the party's membership had by then been purged, declining from 111,000 at the start of the year to fewer than 40,000. A final split

---

Bolsheviks. In November 1921, the Communists speculated that Debs might join them, although he did not break with the Socialist Party. The Communists and Debs had fallen out by February 1922 over Soviet policies, and his former close friend, Communist Rose Pastor Stokes, dismissed Debs as 'not a proletarian revolutionist'. By March, however, Stokes, along with Cannon, Lovestone, Jack Carney and Wagenknecht, were seeking to meet with Debs. A year later, the Communists labelled Debs the 'revolutionary' wing of the SP. On the Communists' relation to Debs, see Ginger 1949, pp. 396–8. For Communist speculation about Debs, see *New York Times*, 27 November 1921. Rose [Pastor Stokes] to Dan [Kiefer], 1 February 1922, in Rose Pastor Stokes Papers, Socialist Party Collection, Tamiment Institute, XIX:15f. See also Zipser and Zipser 1989, pp. 233, 263; [Wagenknecht] to 'Comrade EV Debs', 23 March 1922, and EV Debs to 'Comrade Wagenknecht', 25 March 1922, both in Communist Party USA. Collection, Tamiment Institute, box 256, folder 2. On the CP's 1923 attitude towards Debs, see Pepper 1923, p. 35.

30 *New York Call*, 21 May 1919. The editorial was reprinted in pamphlet form, Hillquit 1919; quotes are from pp. 14–15; Pratt 1973, p. 142.

31 See the minutes of the SP NEC, 24–30 May 1919, in Johnpoll 1994, pp. 75–121. For a detailed description of the purge, see Seyler 1952, pp. 336–58. On the Michigan group, see Davenport 2010, pp. 10–11.

was inevitable. The question for all sides was not how to prevent a split, but on whose terms and under whose control was the split going to occur. To maintain control of the party apparatus, the NEC majority under Germer and Hillquit was willing to trample any semblance of organisational democracy. A while later Wagenknecht underlined that 'the main point around which these "expelling" acts of the former national executive committee revolve, is one of principle rather than one of party autocracy or democracy'. The expelled left wing, he continued, '*demanded* that the Socialist Party affiliate with our Russian comrades, change the tactics of the Socialist Party in cinformity [sic] with lessons taught us by the Russian revolution and the fiasco of the Scheidemanns in Germany and therefore make sure that our party would not run up a blind alley at the crucial moment'.[32]

Meanwhile, the left wing had been organising. In June 1919, 'about seventy five delegates—some as far west as the Pacific Coast', in Ruthenberg's words, arrived in New York for a National Left Wing Conference 'to create a revolutionary working class movement in America'. The delegates opposed parliamentary strategies, declaring that 'the workers can only win the state power by extra parliamentary action which must have its basis in the industrial mass action of the workers'. The delegates eschewed reformist strategies, arguing that when capitalists accept reforms, they 'have as their object and their result the further exploitation and deception of the workers'.[33]

Rather than forming a united tendency, the leftists split over their relationship to the Socialist Party in what Ruthenberg described in a letter to his wife as 'a bitter fight about staying in the party in the [upcoming national] convention or organizing a new party at once'. On one side were most of the American-born or more Americanised leftists such as John J. Ballam, Cannon, Fraina, Benjamin Gitlow, Larkin, Reed, Ruthenberg and Wolfe. This group advocated staying in the SP through the convention to avoid a premature split. As the *Revolutionary Age* argued in May: 'We refuse to turn over the Socialist Party to

---

32 *New York Call*, 19 April 1919; Bell 1967, p. 111; Draper 1985, p. 158; Foner 1988, p. 242; Wolfe 1981, pp. 193, 199. On the right wing, see the *New York Call* and the *Socialist* of the period; see also Bassett 1964, p. 315; Miller 1996, pp. 230–40. On how this split affected individual locals, see Miller 1995; Shaffer, pp. 283–300; Shaffer 1967; Wagenknecht, circular 'To All National Convention Delegates', 19 August 1919, in Comintern archives, 515:1:4.

33 C.E. Ruthenberg to Rose Ruthenberg, undated letter, postmarked 22 June 1919, in Ruthenberg Collection, box 2, folder 3. In a detailed report on the convention, *Revolutionary Age* (5 July 1919) claimed 'over 90 delegates from 20 different states', while Draper stated that there were 94 delegates; Draper 1985, p. 166. Political descriptions take from 'Left Wing Section of the Socialist Party: Report of the Labor Organization Committee', in John S. Reed papers, Houghton Library, Harvard University, bms Am 1091:1449.

the moderates. We shall not abandon the struggle to revolutionize the Party, for the bulk of the membership is overwhelmingly revolutionary'.[34]

The other group consisted of members of the Russian federation, led by Hourwich and Stoklitsky, and the expelled Michigan Socialist groups. They advocated organising a Communist Party immediately. Noting the NEC's 'expulsion of nearly half of the membership', the self-styled National Office of the Organization Committee issued a 'Call for a National Convention for the Purpose of Organizing a Communist Party in America'. This argued that 'the time has passed for temporizing and hesitating', while urging 'those who realize that the capturing of the Socialist Party as such is but an empty victory' to 'not hesitate to respond to this call and leave the "right" and "center" to sink together with their "revolutionary" leaders'. Further complicating matters, on 28 July, a majority of those who had favoured going to the SP convention, including Ruthenberg, Fraina, Wolfe and Ballam, changed their minds and advocated an immediate foundation of a new party. Gitlow and Larkin maintained their position against a hasty split.[35]

Shortly before the Chicago convention, the NEC defended the expulsions as necessary to maintain a centralised and unified party as part of 'our clear duty, as the trustees of the party, to do all we could to preserve the integrity of the party'. The left was not resting either. A circular by Wagenknecht, a left-wing member of the old NEC, announced a caucus the day before the convention, for left-wing delegates to 'discuss the necessary steps to take when the national convention convenes', and to arrive at decisions that 'should make it possible to effect a policy which will be to the best interests of International Socialism'.[36]

The Comintern and Early American Communism

The early Comintern sought to unite all socialists who had broken from the Second International into a new revolutionary movement. In the United States,

34 C.E. Ruthenberg to Rose Ruthenberg, undated letter, postmarked 22 June 1919, Ruthenberg papers; *Revolutionary Age*, 24 May 1919.

35 Dennis E. Batt, S. Kopnagel, D. Elbaum, J. Stilson, O.C. Johnson, Alexander Stoklitsky and John Keracher, 'Call for a National Convention', July 1919, enclosed in a letter from Adolph Germer to Morris Hillquit, 14 July 1919, Morris Hillquit papers, reel 2, document 858; Draper 1985, pp. 168, 175.

36 James Oneal, A. Shiplacoff, Victor L. Berger, George H. Goebel, Dan Hogan, John M. Work, Seymour Stedman and Frederick Kraft, 'Supplementary Report of the National Executive Committee' to the Special 1919 Convention, in Socialist Party papers, Duke University, series I, part D.

this was no easy task. The left was fragmented, and the 'red scare' repression had driven it underground. While the former Socialists were the most prominent, the Bolsheviks also appealed to left-wing elements of the SLP and the IWW. Lenin had urged Kollontai to find supporters in America. In the 1919 call for a Third International, the Bolsheviks had listed four US groups among those invited to Moscow, including the SP left wing—'in particular the group represented by Debs and the League for Socialist Propaganda', the IWW, the SLP, and De Leon's Workers International Industrial Union. A Comintern circular urged the formation of an American Communist Party from the 'left elements' of different left groups, on the basis of the 'recognition of the necessity for the proletarian dictatorship, that is, Soviet power, through revolutionary mass action (strikes and insurrections) which destroys the old machinery of the capitalist state and creates a new proletarian state, transforming the organs of mass action (Soviets of Workers Deputies) into organs of power over the resisting bourgeoisie'. For the Bolsheviks, these political points, not organisational baggage, were crucial.[37]

Much of the SLP remained aloof from the Bolsheviks, in part because they rejected the 'dictatorship of the proletariat' in the United States. The most prominent SLP leaders to join the Communists were Boris Reinstein, the Russian immigrant in Buffalo, who joined the Comintern at the First Congress, and (indirectly) Fraina. By 1919, Fraina had already quit the SLP, and Reinstein had no official mandate.[38]

Most Comintern effort was expended on consolidating its self-styled supporters in the competing Communist parties. Fraina, Ruthenberg and Wolfe formed the Communist Party of America (CPA), which supported immediately leaving the SP, while Gitlow and Reed organised the Communist Labor Party (CLP), which advocated struggling within the SP. The issue was resolved when the SP leadership barred CLP supporters entry to the August convention, but the two organisations hardened into hostile groups. As Theodore Draper has commented, 'Few things left a deeper and more lasting mark on the American Communist movement than this seemingly unnecessary split'. The main dif-

37 Degras 1956, I, p. 4; Bucharin and J. Bersin (Winter) for the Bureau of the Communist International, 'Parliamentarism, Soviet Power and the Creation of a Communist Party of America: Thesis of the Executive Committee of the Third International', undated [1919?], in Comintern archives, 515:1:1. Presumably the ASP is the American Socialist Party, that is, the SP.

38 See Wheeler 1953, p. 20; cf. Reinstein 1929. Fraina told the FBI that the SLP 'repudiated' Reinstein for his support for Lenin; 'FBI Interrogation of Lewis Corey, 1949–1950', Corey papers, Columbia University, box 2, folder 5, p. 27. On Reinstein, see Wise 2011.

ference was not programmatic, but in composition. The CPA's militants were mainly East European immigrants, often with years of political experience, but little connection to broader American society. The smaller CLP consisted of more native-born or 'Americanised' (that is, English-speaking) militants who often lacked their counterparts' theoretical sophistication, but were more rooted in American society.[39]

Each group published a paper called the *Communist*[40] that swore loyalty to the Bolshevik Revolution and denounced its counterpart. If this gives the modern-day researcher a migraine, it could not have left contemporaries much clearer. In his memoirs written in the 1960s, Max Bedacht derided the differences as 'wortklauberei', or quibbling. 'In our debates', he wrote, 'it became obvious that some new concepts were still rather hazy in our minds'. One bitter dispute was whether 'mass action' or 'action of the masses' was the revolutionary alternative to the Socialist Party's parliamentarism.[41]

The first issue of the CPA's *Communist* described the larger CLP as '[r]endered impotent by the conflicting emotions and lack of under-standing' of those who pursued the 'centrist' policy of trying 'to capture the old party machinery and the stagnant elements which have been struggling for a false unity, who are only ready to abandon the ship when it sinks beneath the waves of reaction'. Another article denounced the CLP as a 'fetid swamp'.[42]

With no obvious political differences, this division baffled observers. Henry Kuhn, a leader of the post-De Leon SLP, wrote to Reinstein (in Russia) that 'the two [Communist] formations came about largely because of rival leadership; there is little else to divide them'. Such histrionics must have alienated thousands of sympathetic socialists. As Cannon put it, 'Nobody knows how many thousands of American radical socialists—potential communists—were lost and scattered'. While two-thirds of the SP's 104,000 members supported the left wing, only a much smaller number joined either Communist organisation.[43]

39 Cannon 1962, pp. 40–2; Laidler 1920; Ruthenberg 1926b; *Communist* (CP), July 1921; Draper 1985, pp. 158, 169.

40 In the footnotes, each *Communist* is identified by the name of the organisation that issued it, for example, *Communist* (CPA). For a more detailed description, see Draper 1985, p. 432, n. 21, p. 451, n. 4.

41 Bedacht, 'On the Path of My Life', p. 216, folder 17.

42 *Communist* (CPA), 19 July 1919.

43 Henry Kuhn to comrade Reinstein, 9 December 1919, in Comintern archives, 515:1:4. Cannon 1962, p. 50. In testimony during his trial after the 1922 Bridgman raid, Ruthenberg claimed that 'about one-third of the Socialist Party came into the Communist Party of America' by January 1920, comprising about 50,000 members. By the Bridgman Convention, membership had fallen 'to about five thousand'; Testimony of C.E. Ruthenberg,

These groups engaged in a complicated ritual of fissions and fusions that confused and alienated all who beheld it. Untold energy was wasted on this fight. One Communist sympathiser in Pittsburgh complained: 'Comrades, I really don't know with who [sic] to agree. In a fact, we are now in a big mess, and at the present it is hard to tell who is right and who is wrong. It seems to me we are all right and wrong in same time'.[44]

In December 1919, most of the Michigan group, led by John Keracher and Dennis Blatt, split from the CPA to form the Proletarian Party. For its part, the CLP advocated unity of the two main factions from the beginning. In 1919, its *Ohio Socialist* had run an editorial, 'Communists Unite!', which noted: 'The rank and file of both sections see no fundamental differences between the two parties' because the 'programs of both parties are based upon the programs of the Third International formed at Moscow … What differences exist in tactics and inner party construction are not of such a nature as should create a permanent division of the two sections'. One Communist organiser predicted that 'unless unity between the two communist parties comes soon, we will lose all the membership' because of frustration over the split. According to the CPA, in October–December 1919, their average membership was 23,744; by January–April 1920, it had dropped to 5,584. Repression against the left weakened the Communists, but frustration with this factionalism also diminished the ranks.[45]

The CPA split in 1920. A majority insisted that the CLP was 'centrist', and labelled their unity campaign as being 'deliberately started and … being carried out in order to create discord and disintegration in our party'. A minority, led by Ruthenberg ('Damon'), including many of the CPA's English-speakers, fused with the CLP, forming the United Communist Party (UCP). According to the rump CPA, Ruthenberg, who had been the group's national secretary, took with him three other members of the 13-strong Central Executive Committee

26 April 1923, in Lovestone papers, box 207, pp. 549, 552–3. On Reinstein, see Falkowski 1994; Hardy 1956, pp. 135–6; Kearns 2011; Wise 2011.

44 'Report to the Secretary of the CPA', 10 [13?] July 1920, in Comintern archives, 515:1:30; James Oneal *et al.*, 'Supplementary Report of the National Executive Committee', in Socialist Party papers, Duke University, series I, part D; [PE Stankovich?] to John Reed and Ben Gitlow, 19 August 1919, in Comintern archives, 515:1:4.

45 Draper 1985, pp. 158–9. On the Proletarian Party, which remained for decades a small sect in Michigan, see Oakley Johnson, fragment of untitled, undated autobiographical manuscript in William W. Weinstone papers, box 19, folder 3, pp. 10–12; Draper 1985, pp. 210–11. (Draper gives the date of separation from the CPA as January 1920); its background is described in Davenport 2010; see also Lewis Corey to Granville Hicks, 30 December 1935, in Corey papers, box 1; *Ohio Socialist*, 29 October 1919; organiser quoted in letter from E.F. to Damon [Ruthenberg], 24 April 1920, in Jay Lovestone papers, box 195, folder 11.

and some 28 percent of the membership. This split increased hostility between the two groups, in what one participant later described as 'a most bitter factional battle'. The CPA denounced the CLP's 'meaningless pleading for Communist unity' and declared that the 'Communist Labor Party has no vestige of principle, Communist or any other kind'. The CPA asserted that 'Unity with the U.C.P. as a party of centrists is impossible' except 'on the basis of our principles, program, and tactics'.[46]

Ruthenberg's letters to his wife evidence frustration and predicted 'nothing but personal squabbles for months to come'. At one point, he mused: 'I am sick and tired of the whole business and only wish I could drop out without leaving people who are depending on me in the lurch'. Two months later, upon moving to Chicago, Ruthenberg described the situation as 'drifting and general unsatisfactory'.[47]

Before bolting the CPA, Ruthenberg put forward a motion in its leading body, the Central Executive Committee (CEC), advocating unity with the CLP. It warned against becoming an SLP-style sect:

> There never was any division between the C.P. and the C.L.P. on fundamental Communist principles ... The differences between the two party programs are differences merely in the form of expression ...
>
> Unity with the C.L.P. would aid in bringing the Communist movement into contact with the American workers. For instance, the C.P.[A.] has hardly any English-speaking membership, and no prospects for doing any organization work west of the Mississippi.

In the spring of 1921, the UCP claimed 5,927 members organised into 771 groups. Of these members, 3,566 paid dues. There were 14 districts with 12 paid organisers and three paid sub-district organisers. It published 35 monthly journals in eight languages, including English, with a circulation of over 1.6 million. The CPA, for its part, claimed 6,328 dues-paying members organised into six districts, each with a paid organiser, and four sub-district organisers. It published, also in eight languages, 19 papers with almost one million monthly readers.[48]

46 *Communist* (CPA), 4 October 1919, 22 November 1919, 1 May 1920, 1 July 1920, 1 August 1920; *Communist* (CP), July 1921; Report to the Secretary of the CPA, 10 [13?] July 1920, in Comintern archives, 515:1:30.

47 C.E. Ruthenberg to Rose Ruthenberg, Ruthenberg collection.

48 Minutes of 17, 18, 19, 20 March 1921 CEC of CPA, in Comintern archives, 515:1:51; *Communist* (CP), July 1921. According to Davenport, in 1921 the Socialist Party claimed some 25,000 members in January, which fell to 13,500 later in the year; see Davenport 2012.

Unity from the Comintern

Only the Comintern could force its American followers to transcend such squabbles by focusing on the political basis for unity. In January 1920, Grigory Zinoviev wrote to the CPA and CLP. 'The split has rendered a heavy blow to the Communist movement in America. It leads to the dispersion of revolutionary force, to a harmful parallelism, an absurd partition of practical work, and senseless discussions and an unjustifiable loss of energy in interfactional quarrels'. He underlined 'that the split has not been caused by any profound differences of opinion as regards programme'. The letter demanded immediate unity. In Moscow, Reed of the CLP and John Anderson, a Latvian representative of the CPA, signed an agreement in January 1920 for unifying their two parties, but this did not happen. A similar letter was sent by the ECCI in June. Since there were 'no serious differences in the programs of the two parties', it argued, the split 'must by all means be liquidated'. The only way 'to create a strong Communist party in America' was the 'immediate realization' of unity. Continued division was 'absolutely not allowed'.[49]

Foreign-Language Federations

One divisive issue was the role of more than a dozen foreign-language federations, which comprised a large portion of the CPA. In fact, English-speakers were a distinct minority in the early American Communist movement, especially among the rank and file. These federations had originated in the Socialist Party. Between 1904 and 1921, eleven federations joined the SP. Their relationship to the broader Socialist movement was uneasy, and the

49 Zinoviev, 'To the Central Committees of the American Communist Party and the American Communist Labour Party', 12 January 1920, in Comintern archives, 515:1:17; John Reed and John Anderson, 'Agreement for the Unification of the American Communist Party and the American Communist Labour Party', 12 January 1920, in Comintern archives, 515:1:21; *Communist* (UCP), 17 July 1920, 15 August 1920 (excerpted in Degras, I, 1956). Presumably the failure to realise the unity agreement was related to the failure of Reed and Anderson to realise another Comintern assignment. Both were entrusted with Comintern jewels to bring to their respective parties. Reed was arrested in Finland trying to smuggle them, and never returned to the US. Anderson decided not to try to bring the jewels to the US, and did not rejoin the Communist movement upon his return; see Charles Dirba, 'An Investigation by the Communist Party of America', 14 April 1921, Comintern archives, 515:1:61).

federations often affiliated to the national organisation instead of local or state branches.[50]

The federated nature of the socialist movement in the US reflected the fact that the working class itself had been created by successive waves of immigration. The First International in the United States had also been organised into national sections, which had led Friedrich Engels to note to Friedrich Sorge in 1893 that the working class was divided into native-born and foreigners, and the latter into numerous sectors, including 'many small groups, each of which understands only itself'. 'To form a single party of these requires quite unusually powerful incentives' and even then 'the dissimilar elements of the working class fall apart again'. The IWW had experimented with foreign-language federations to reach foreign workers. Non-radical organisations that recruited among workers faced similar issues: between 1880 and 1918, 34 of 61 new Catholic parishes in Manhattan were 'national' or ethnic churches.[51]

In 1908, 71 percent of the SP membership were born in the United States, and an additional 17.5 percent were born in northern or western Europe. By 1919, 53 percent of the 108,000 dues-paying Socialists belonged to a language federation. Socialist leaders criticised the federations for hindering the development of a unified Socialist movement; this was true of future Communists, such as Ruthenberg and Ella Reeve Bloor, as well as right-wing and centrist leaders.[52]

The Communist Party in the United States was not the only section of the Comintern with language federations. The Communist Party of Canada (CPC) had a *greater* percentage of its membership in federations, while the Communist Party of Argentina had 19 language groups (which comprised 54 percent of Communists in Buenos Aires as late as 1928). Communists in Brazil and Uruguay were organised by language, and the French Communist Party between 1924 and 1945 organised 15 language groups. As in the US, the

50 Seyler 1952, pp. 341–2. The number and membership of Communist federations fluctuated. According to the report at the Fourth National Convention of 1925, in 1922 there were 15 non-English federations, ranging in membership from 33 (the Scandinavian) to 5,846 (the Finnish); in 1923, there were 17 non-English federations, ranging from 59 members (the Armenian) to 6,583 (the Finnish); in 1924, there were the same number of federations, ranging in membership from 61 (Armenian) to 7,099 (Finnish); by 1925, there were 18 non-English federations, ranging in size from 14 (the Slovenian) to 6,410 (the Finnish); the Armenian group had grown to 132 people, and the Scandinavian had grown to 211; *Fourth National Convention* 1925, pp. 28–40.

51 Marx and Engels 1953, p. 258; McEnroe 1960, pp. 425–8; Cohalan 1983, p. 217.

52 Brown 1996, p. 164; Buhle 1987, p. 112; Johnson 1957, p. 66; Leinenweber 1968, pp. 203–10.

immigrant nature of the working class in these countries made language groups necessary.[53]

There was nothing inherently left wing or pro-Bolshevik about the federations, although their propaganda often reflected a European sophistication and familiarity with Marxist theory that eluded many American radicals. Some—like the Latvian SPL—were left wing, but others—like the much larger Finnish and Jewish federations—were more moderate. By 1919, as many European workers became radicalised amid the post-war revolutionary wave, many immigrants in the US were radicalised as well. When *Revolutionary Age* began publishing in November 1918, with Fraina as editor, its motto was 'a chronicle and interpretation of events in Europe', and in fact not until its third issue did it run an article about the US.[54]

Several of these federations were prominent in the fight between the left- and right-wings of the Socialist Party in 1919, making it appear as if the issue was one of foreign-language federations versus the American party, rather than one of clearer political issues. At the time of the split, right-wing Socialist leader Adolph Germer posed the question whether the SP should remain

> the organization of the Socialist movement in the United States, including the various nationalities which make up the population of the country, or ... be reduced to the tail of certain Foreign Federations, engaged in a special form of propaganda made to suit the peculiar conditions of the countries of their origin.[55]

It was not the federation organisation itself that made some of them left wing, but rather the radicalisation of sections of the immigrant working class.

The CPA, which largely consisted of such groups, wanted them to play an important role in the new party, while the UCP did not. For the Comintern, the issue was not 'turf', but how to best position the Communist Party to intervene in the political life of the country. The Bolshevik Party's fight for democratic-

53 Zumoff 2009, pp. 187–8. On Argentina, see Camarero 2007, Chapter 5; Pasolini 2007.

54 *Revolutionary Age*, 16 November 1918; the first article about the US was on Tom Mooney, in *Revolutionary Age*, 23 November 1918.

55 Adolph Germer, Report to the NEC, 24 May 1919, in Socialist Party Collection, Tamiment Institute, IX:9; also in Victor Berger papers, State Historical Society of Wisconsin, reel 15; for the justification of the expulsion of the left-wing language federations, see James Oneal, A. Shilacanoff, Victor L. Berger, George H. Goebel, Dan Hogan, John H. Work, Seymour Stedman and Frederick Krafft, 'Supplementary Report of the National Executive Committee' to the Special 1919 Convention, in the Socialist Party papers, Duke University, series I, part D.

centralism and against the Yiddish-speaking Bund predisposed them against a party federated by language.[56]

Furthermore, while intersecting immigrant workers was important, English was the dominant language of the labour movement in the United States. Small foreign-language sects did not have the ability to win the mass of American workers to communism. Lenin wrote a preface to Engels's letters in 1907, highlighting that 'What Marx and Engels criticise most sharply in British and American socialism is its isolation from the working-class movement'. Although Russian-speakers had replaced Germans by 1920, the importance of learning English and aiding the development of the American labour movement had not changed.[57]

The January ECCI letter warned against the isolation of the language federations from American life and the Reed-Anderson agreement stressed that the federations must be put under party control and that there be one federation per language. It is indicative that a 'protocol' for unity between the two parties put organisational questions before political issues. It acknowledged the necessity of language federations, but emphasised that they should be made redundant by requiring their members to learn English and participate in the English-language party. The 'center of gravity in the American Communist movement must be in the English-speaking branches', the protocol stressed. The ECCI's June letter underlined that the federations must 'amalgamate as closely as possible with the organization of the American party'. It continued: 'The language federations may reserve their autonomy regarding the work of propaganda in their respective languages, but in the case of political and economic struggles they must be subordinated to the regular party organ'.[58]

Responding to such prompting from the Comintern, the CPA and UCP convened a unity convention that, after two days of debate, adopted a unity

56 Zinoviev's history of Bolshevism stressed that 'We could not agree to fragment our organization into separate national sections'; Zinoviev 1973, p. 87.

57 Lenin 1972, p. 363. In the 1880s, Engels had criticised German American socialists for remaining aloof from American society at the time of massive working-class turmoil. If German-speaking socialists, Engels wrote of the socialist movement in February 1887, 'join it, in order to help it or to hasten its development in the right direction, they may do a great deal of good and play a decisive part in it. If they stand aloof, they will dwindle down into a dogmatic sect and be brushed aside as people who do not understand their own principles'; Marx and Engels 1953, p. 169.

58 'Protocol: Unity of Communist Labor Party with Communist Party', undated, in Comintern archives, 515:1:21; Zinoviev, 'To the Central Committees of the American Communist Party and the American Communist Labour Party', 12 January 1920, in Comintern archives, 515:1:17; *Communist* (UCP), 15 August 1920.

constitution. Ruthenberg noted that despite this wrangling, 'No compromise was needed on either side to reach agreement on principles. The discussion soon showed that on program there was practically unanimity of opinion'. This was true, but despite this unanimity, organisational unity was only achieved, as the party recognised, 'in accordance with the mandate of the Executive Committee of the Communist International'. The *Communist* announced that the 'Third International has spoken and its mandate could no longer be postponed'. Still, it took not only the Bolshevik programme, but also what Arne Swabeck later described as 'some effective prodding from the Communist International' to create a unified Communist Party in the United States.[59]

59 *Communist* (CP), July 1921; Swabeck 1969, p. 38.

CHAPTER 2

The Fight for Legality

By 1921, the Bolsheviks had held onto power, but at a tremendous cost: a destructive civil war and an economy in shambles amid isolation and backwardness. This highlighted the importance of world revolution for the Bolsheviks who believed no ultimate solution within Russia itself was possible. Yet the wave of European revolution after the Bolshevik Revolution had receded, the capitalist system had stabilised, and the traditional trade-union and social-democratic leaders of the working class had begun to recover from the fiasco of the war. Of all the revolutions in 1919–20, only the Bolsheviks survived victorious. For the Bolsheviks, the situation underscored the need for the Communist International to codify the lessons of the October Revolution and impart them to its sections.

The 'Theses' adopted at the Third Congress of the Communist International of 22 June to 12 July 1921 declared that since the Second Congress a year earlier, 'a series of working-class uprisings and battles have resulted in partial defeats'. They envisioned 'a long period of revolutionary struggle' because 'the world revolution is developing even more slowly than expected'. This was particularly due to the treachery of the 'strong workers organisations and workers parties, namely the social-democratic parties and trade unions, which were created by the proletariat to fight the bourgeoisie', but which had turned into 'organs of counter-revolutionary influence that ensnared the proletariat and are continuing to hold it in their grip'. The theme of the Third Congress was that member parties needed to gain influence in the working class, and win workers to Communist leadership away from social democracy.[1]

Most Communist Parties were not up to the task. In a letter to Zinoviev, Lenin observed that 'none of the Communist Parties anywhere have yet won the majority of the working class, not only regards organisational leadership, but to the principle of communism'. Thus, 'the tactics of the Communist International should be based on a systematic drive to win the *majority of the working class*, first and foremost *within the old trade unions*'. As part of this, the newly formed Communist Parties needed to assimilate the lessons of the Bolsheviks' struggles to forge a revolutionary party before the Revolution, as well as the lessons from the Revolution itself. Throughout this period, Lenin polemicised against what he labelled revolutionary impatience, or the belief

1 Trotsky 1980, pp. 184–5.

that a small party could take power without working-class support. One solution Lenin developed was the 'united front', a tactic of winning rank-and-file workers in mass social-democratic organisations, through proposing and carrying out joint actions.[2]

Many European workers were pro-socialist, and tactics such as the united front aimed to win them to Communism by demonstrating leadership of day-to-day economic and political struggles, often of a defensive character, for partial demands. That most American workers were not socialists did not stop American Communists from impatiently advocating revolution. In the summer of 1920, for example, workers went on strike at the Brooklyn Rapid Transit Company, demanding a closed shop, an eight-hour day, higher wages and better schedules. The CPA issued a leaflet that demanded: 'Broaden and deepen your strike. Make it a political strike. Get ready for armed revolution to overthrow the Capitalist Government and create a Workers Government—as your brothers did in Russia. Stop asking merely for a little more wages'.[3]

Communists and the 'Red Scare'

This leaflet highlighted the Communists' problems in intervening in the labour movement. The fundamental concern in implementing the lessons of the Third Congress was the question of illegality. The American Communist movement was born amid increased political repression. This had begun during the war, and intensified in the face of the revolutionary wave abroad begun by the Bolshevik Revolution. A series of real or attempted bombings in the spring of 1919, including of the house of Attorney General A. Mitchell Palmer, gave the government an excuse to wage war on radicals and immigrants. By that fall, the nascent Bureau of Investigation (predecessor of the Federal Bureau of Investigation) had files on some 60,000 suspected radicals. On 7 November 1919 (the second anniversary of the Bolshevik Revolution), the first 'Palmer raid' was carried out against the leftist Union of Russian Workers in Lower Manhattan and other cities. More than 250 were arrested. In December, 249 suspect radical aliens, including the anarchists Emma Goldman and Alexander Berkman, were deported to Soviet Russia aboard the *Buford*. While the Department of Justice took the lead, the Supreme Court, state and local police, and US Military

2 Lenin 1969b, pp. 320–1; Communist International 1988.

3 'BRT Strikers!', Comintern archives, 515:1:30. On the strike (which lost), see *New York Times*, 18 August 1920; Freeman 1989, p. 18.

Intelligence, all contributed to the 'Red Scare' war on radicals, often in competition with one another.[4]

The repression drove the fledgling Communists underground. In the summer of 1919, the police harassed the founding Communist conventions, forcing them to remove red flags from the platforms and arresting one delegate as 'seditious'. The *New York Times* noted after the formation of the movement that 'the fact that there are in the United States those who advocate and organize for revolution and social destruction is not to be ignored'.[5]

The Department of Labor declared it 'mandatory...to take into custody aliens who are members' of the CP and 'deport them'. By the end of December 1919, some 3,000 arrest warrants were issued for supposed Communists. By early January 1920, the federal government rounded up another 4,000 radicals in 23 states. According to historian Robert Murray, 'practically every leader of the [Communist] movement, national or local, was put under arrest'. In California, thirteen Communist leaders were arrested within a month of the founding of the state's party. In Chicago and New York, dozens of suspected Communists were rounded up, and, in Murray's words, 'brutality was practiced to an excessive degree'. Repression targeted leading foreign-born Communists, such as Irish labour leader James Larkin, as well as prominent American Communists, like New Jersey born Ben Gitlow. By early 1920, 250 members of the CPA were under indictment for criminal syndicalism, criminal anarchy or conspiracy charges. This included all national officers, the entire CEC, and all Translator-Secretaries of the language federations.[6]

This repression made sustained legal work impossible. Max Bedacht, a target of repression in California and Illinois, recalled: 'Publicity for meetings had to be avoided. Ordinary get togethers had to be given the form of outings, or of other innocuous gatherings'. Members expected raids and arrests at any time, and distrusted outsiders and strangers. Members were instructed to not only hide internal documents and addresses, but to avoid openly claiming membership. Max Shachtman described going to 'Trotsky Circle', a well known

4 Above information taken from Murray 1964, pp. 194–213. See also Schmidt 2000; Preston 1994; on Military Intelligence, see Talbert 1991.

5 *New York Times*, 31 August 1919, 1 September 1919, 2 September 1919, 4 September 1919.

6 *House Immigration*, pp. 2–3; Mackson 1996; Murray 1964, pp. 211–30; Uhlmann 2007, p. 34. See Lendler 2012; on Larkin, see O'Riordan 1998; Larkin 1990, Chapter 10; Draper 1985, p. 206. On the Red Scare in individual cities, see Jaffe 1972; Pedersen 2001, Chapter 1; Pfannenstiel 2003; Shaffer 1962, pp. 300–29; Siener 1998. On the Red Scare and blacks, see Ellis 1994; Kornweibel 1998. On the 'red scare' after the Haymarket events, see Avrich 1986, Chapter 15. The Department of Immigration was part of the Department of Labor from 1913 to 1940, when it was moved to the Department of Justice.

radical hangout at the intersection of 110th Street and Fifth Avenue in Manhattan, trying to join the underground movement, only to find members 'exceedingly cagey' of his accent-free English and refusing to recruit him.[7]

Capitalist state repression was expected by radicals throughout the world. The Comintern insisted that parties, particularly those from the West, maintain an illegal apparatus. Excessive legalism, including an obsession with trade-union positions and parliamentary seats, had been a hallmark of many of the parties of pre-war Social Democracy. There had been periodic waves of repression in the United States going back to at least the Haymarket police riot of 1886. In a circular to American Communists in 1919, the ECCI had emphasised 'the necessity of creating illegal underground machinery side by side with the legally functioning apparatus'.[8]

If at the party's founding, illusions in American capitalist democracy were not an immediate danger, by the fall of 1920 the Red Scare had largely ended. The party entered what Bedacht described in his memoirs as a 'semi-legal existence'. Repression did not abate entirely, especially in New York City, where the anti-Communist 'Lusk Committee' continued 'investigating' radicals for several years. However, the Republicans won the White House with the promise of 'normalcy'; Palmer (a Democrat) retired, and the government tired of wholesale persecutions. Even the bombing of Wall Street in September did not reignite Palmer-style raids. Political repression is a regular but not constant feature of American capitalism. (After the Red Scare, J. Edgar Hoover retrenched and professionalised his Bureau's repressive apparatus, creating a durable apparatus of repression in the form of the FBI, ready for future use).[9]

Trying to become a legal party became one of the first battlegrounds to 'Americanise' the Communist movement. Many early Communists in the foreign-language federations believed that the Red Scare was the norm rather than the exception. For them, a legal party would violate Communist principles. Bittelman recalled that the irrational fears of the government during the Red Scare fed many underground Communists' own unfounded belief that

7 Bedacht, 'On the Path of My Life', p. 240, folder 17. Reminiscences of Max Shachtman, Socialist Movement Project, Columbia University Oral History Collection, pp. 6–7. See the CPA's Central Executive Committee, 'Rules for Underground Party Work', and 'Pointers on Defense to Members of the Communist Party of America', both undated [1920?], in Comintern archives, 515:1:34.

8 N. Bucharin and J. Bersin (Winter), 'Parliamentarism, Soviet Power and the Creation of a Communist Party of America', undated [1919?], in Comintern archives, 515:1:1.

9 Bedacht, 'On the Path of My Life', p. 289, folder 20; on the 1920 bombing, see Gage 2009. On continued repression in New York, see Jaffe 1972; Pfannenstiel 2003; Schmidt 2000, p. 18. On Hoover in the post-Red Scare period, see Goodall 2006, pp. 43, 51–4.

revolution was nigh, making them 'feel considerably more important'. On the other hand, many native-born or Americanised cadres, including Bittelman, Earl Browder, Cannon, Jay Lovestone and Ruthenberg, sought to establish 'living contact' with the masses through increased legal work and to defend the Communists' legal rights to organise. Cannon recalled later that the 'labor party policy, the development of the trade union work, and the whole process of Americanizing the party were subsumed under the overall issue of legalizing the party'. Without a strong legal apparatus, almost no other work could be accomplished, and the Party would remain an isolated sect of foreigners. By helping Communist leaders like Cannon, Bittelman and Ruthenberg to realise these goals, the Comintern helped 'Americanise' Communism.[10]

The Bolsheviks' experience underground made them appreciate the need for legal and illegal work. Before their Revolution, the Bolsheviks had taken advantage of all opportunities for legal work, including standing candidates for the Duma. The Comintern *Guidelines* voted at the Third Congress criticised parties that neglected illegal work, but also assailed the opposite tendency in underground parties and 'often insufficient understandings of the possibilities for exploiting legal activity and for building a party organization in living contact with the revolutionary masses'. This led to party activity tending 'to remain a fruitless Sisyphean labor or impotent conspiracy'.[11]

In early 1921, Zinoviev wrote to the CP leadership claiming that any delay in creating a legal party would be 'a *very great mistake* ... We are very late with this matter in America, and every week of further tardiness brings the greatest harm'. Although not advocating an immediate legal party, he stressed that 'it is necessary to make use of every inch of the ground' towards this end, since 'it would be the greatest mistake to lock ourselves in amongst ourselves'. He emphasised that this was the 'unquestionable instruction of the Comintern', and threatened those in America who sabotaged it, 'particularly the Russian comrades'. At about the same time, Bukharin, Karl Radek and Otto Kuusinen for the ECCI sent another note. They accepted that 'Under existing circumstances it is impossible for the Communist Party in the United States to be a legal party'. At the same time, they stressed the need to establish a legal apparatus, especially an English-language press.[12]

10 Bittelman, 'Things I Have Learned', folder 13, p. 335; Cannon 1962, p. 58.

11 Communist International 1988, p. 52.

12 Zinoviev to CPA, marked 'NOT for publication', 9 February 1921, in Comintern archives, 515:1:32; N. Bukharin, K. Radek and O. Kuusinen for the ECCI, 'Concerning the Next Tasks of the CP of A', 1921, in Comintern archives, 515:1:38; also reprinted in CEC 'Special Bulletin on Party Situation', May 1922, in Comintern archives, 515:1:28.

At the Third Congress, the leadership of the Comintern prodded their American comrades. Hourwich opposed becoming a legal party, as did many Russian-born American Communists. Bedacht, a delegate, reported that he and Hourwich 'had repeated personal talks' with Zinoviev, Radek and Lenin. During these discussions, 'each one of these comrades invariably brought up the question of the necessity of going into extensive legal activities and, for that purpose, the creation of a legal organization, a legal party'. American Communism, Bedacht noted, 'was considered as dominated by leftism and by a sectarian spirit and not at least in conformity with the conceptions of the Communist International'. In his memoirs, Bedacht recalled that Lenin was concerned that American Communists be able to relate to American workers. When the German-born Bedacht asked Lenin if they should speak in German, the main language of the Comintern, Lenin insisted Bedacht 'should speak in the language of the land whose Party [he] represented', something that Lenin thought was a requirement of leadership.[13]

Lenin organised a conference with the American delegation on 7 July 1921. Two contemporary reports exist of this meeting. One by Charles Wallace, a delegate, stressed that it was Lenin's opinion that 'the American comrades do not utilize all the opportunities of struggle', and that he 'considers a daily legal newspaper in the English language the most essential necessity for spreading our propaganda'. Wallace continued that Lenin 'advised us to take the necessary steps to establish a legal Communist organization' to recruit workers unable to join an illegal party. Bedacht recalled that Lenin called a legal party an 'absolute necessity' along with a daily press. In his memoirs, Bedacht stressed Hourwich's obstinacy, noting that 'toward the end of the Conference [with the American delegates], Lenin's patience visibly tired'. The Russian Americans' opposition was neutralised when most of them, including Hourwich, remained in Russia and transferred their membership to the Soviet Party. (After spending two years in Ukraine, Hourwich and his family settled in Moscow, where he was a university lecturer in Marxism until his death in 1934).[14]

---

13 James Marshall [Max Bedacht], 'To Central Executive Committee of the CPA' [1921], in Comintern archives, 515:1:56; Bedacht, 'The Paths of My Life', p. 262, folder 20.

14 'Report of Charles Wallace', undated [1921], Comintern archives, 515:1:51; Marshall, 'To Central Executive Committee of the CPA', Comintern archives, 515:1:56; see also Charles Wallace, answers to 'Question to International Delegates', 13 October 1921, Comintern archives, 515:1:39. Cf. Hardy 1956, pp. 135–6. Bedacht, 'Paths of My Life', pp. 277–89, folder 20. Information on Hourwich from correspondence with Mark Donnelly, 23 June 2011, based on information in Comintern archives.

The Workers' Council and the Workers' Party

The issue of establishing a legal party divided Communists into complicated groupings. The immediate cause of the first division was the party's relationship to the Workers' Council (WC), which had originated in a pro-Comintern group within the Socialist Party. Despite expelling the Left Wing, the SP leadership had moved to the left in 1919–20 in response to the popularity of the Bolshevik Revolution. The convention's manifesto (written by Hillquit, the closest American equivalent to Kautsky) opposed imperialist war and pledged support for the revolutions in Russia, Germany, Austria and Hungary. By a vote of 56 to 26, the convention declared that 'the Second International is no more', and solidarised with the Bolsheviks and German Spartakists.[15]

Rhetorical support for the Bolsheviks was easy because it was popular and meaningless. Joining the Comintern was more divisive, since this would have required a decisive break with the social-democratic politics that animated much of the SP leadership. In March 1920, the SP formally applied to join the Comintern. Two months later, in response to opposition to the Comintern, a grouping led by J. Louis Engdahl advocated a resolution reaffirming its attempted affiliation to the Comintern. Another minority, led by Berger, advocated that the SP eschew the Comintern altogether. A centrist compromise, supported by Hillquit, was passed, advocating affiliation to the Comintern provided 'no formula such as "The Dictatorship of the Proletariat in the form of Soviets" or any other special formula for the attainment of the Socialist commonwealth be imposed or exacted as condition of affiliation with the Third International'.[16]

The minimal hopes of the SP's joining the Comintern were dashed when the Second Congress of the Comintern (July–August 1920) approved the 21 conditions for any party wishing to join it. These were designed to deepen the split in the international socialist movement and form a revolutionary left purged of what the Bolsheviks saw as remaining opportunists, careerists and centrists. Condition 7 listed Hillquit as one of the leaders who needed to be purged for

15 *New York Times*, 31 August 1917; Morris Hillquit, typescript of 'Manifesto of the Socialist Party Emergency Convention', 4 September 1919, in Hillquit papers, reel 6, document 112. Bell 1967, p. 111; Leavell 1962, pp. 28–30; Shannon 1976, pp. 150–1.

16 Report of the SP Committee on International Relations, September 1919, Morris Hillquit papers, reel 6, document 905; *Labor Age*, June 1920. See also Ottini 1948, p. 56. On the split with the Second International, see Shannon 1967, p. 86; N.F. Pratt 1973, pp. 165, 167.

their organisations to join the Comintern. The SP National Committee refused, and in November the Comintern rejected the SP's application.[17]

Over the next period, increasing numbers of SP members left in sympathy with the Bolsheviks. These included the 'Workers' Council' group, comprising Socialists like William F. Kruse, J. Louis Engdahl, Moissaye J. Olgin, J.B. Salutsky (also known as Hardman)[18] and Alexander Trachtenberg, and counting on the support of a third of the membership. Olgin and Salutsky had been in the leadership of the Yiddish-language Jewish Socialist Federation (JSF), which split in the autumn 1921 after a majority of its leadership voted to disaffiliate from the SP. They appeared an unlikely pro-Bolshevik duo. In 1917, Olgin, along with Max Goldfarb, had opposed the JSF's endorsement of the Zimmerwald anti-war manifesto *from the right*. In November 1917, Goldfarb returned to Russia and worked with the Bolsheviks (under the name Petrovsky), but Olgin was hostile to Bolshevism. Olgin, an academic expert on Russia, so opposed the October Revolution that Abraham Cahan, editor of the right-wing Socialist *Forward*, had to tone down his articles' criticisms of Lenin; in December 1917, Olgin published an anti-Bolshevik article in the *New York Times*.

For his part, Salutsky was the editor of the JSF's paper, *Naye Welt*. According to Eugene Orenstein's study of the JSF, after the February 1917 Revolution Salutsky 'insisted that the only way to preserve the Russian Revolution and thus democracy in Europe and the world was to support the war aims of President Woodrow Wilson and the British Labor Party'. With Olgin he orchestrated the purge of Jewish left-wing Socialists in 1918. This was a 'most intense and bitter' faction fight, according to Alexander Bittelman, one of the left-wing leaders. While Salutsky would remain wary of Bolshevism, even while a member of the Communist Party, Olgin's visit to Soviet Russia in 1920–1 had won him over to Bolshevism. Trachtenberg and Kruse were active in the Rand School and the Socialist youth organisation, respectively. Engdahl and Kruse had waged a fight at the 1920 SP New York Convention to push the party to the left. While Hillquit was willing to apply for membership to the Comintern, he was not willing to accept their conditions, and the SP's application was rejected.[19]

17 On the SP's attempt to affiliate with the Comintern, see note by NEC on relations to Communist International, 1920, in *Revolutionary Radicalism* 1920, II, pp. 1815–21; Bell 1967, pp. 113–14; Degras 1956, I, p. 170.

18 According to his obituary in the *New York Times* of 31 January 1968, 'in 1922 he assumed the nom de plume J.B.S. Hardman and legalized it shortly afterward'; Orenstein 1978. 'Hardman' was Salutsky's pseudonym in the Russian underground before emigrating to America.

19 On the split in the JSF, see *New York Times*, 6 September 1921; Michels 2005, Chapter 5; Orenstein 1978, Chapters 5 and 6 (quote on p. 201). On Goldfarb and Olgin's opposition to the Zimmerwald manifesto, see Orenstein 1978, pp. 144–6; on Goldfarb's return to Russia,

By the 1921 Socialist convention in Detroit, the SP's old-guard leadership was openly anti-Bolshevik. In pre-conference discussion, Engdahl complained, 'For two years now the party officialdom has been busy expelling and driving out of the party those comrades who have taken a stand with the Third International'. When Kruse submitted a resolution for Comintern affiliation, 31 delegates voted against, while only four supported it.

The old-guard SP leadership also opposed the term 'dictatorship of the proletariat'. Kruse and Engdahl put forward a motion that asserted the right of the proletarian dictatorship to prevent 'anything to stand in the way of [the workers] being the ruling class'. This was defeated. So was Hillquit's compromise to define the dictatorship of the proletariat as 'the political rule of the working class in the period of the transition from the capitalist system to the socialist order', while asserting that 'it is not necessarily associated with a restraint of the political rights of opponents or with violence or terror'. Berger opposed any use of the term, arguing, according to the *New York Times*, that 'the Terror is inseparable from the dictatorship of the proletariat'. Hillquit's motion reflected his desire to maintain control of the SP despite the leftward pressure of its membership. Salutsky recalls being told by Berger that he forthrightly opposed Bolshevism and would not obscure the issue like Hillquit: 'Look', Salutsky claims Berger confided to him, 'you can call me a reactionary, it's all right with me. But I'm not a faker'.[20]

After their defeat, Kruse, Engdahl and their followers organised the Committee for the Third International along with the left wing of the JSF. In their resignation statement from the SP, they claimed to have waged a three years' long 'constant struggle' to 'place the Socialist Party in the front ranks of the international labor movement, in the vanguard of the world struggle for Socialism', but that by 1921 the SP had 'become a hindrance rather than aid to working class progress'. They predicted 'the early demise of the Socialist Party and call[ed] upon all those who read the future as we do, to get ready to quit the ship that does not sail the flag of working class Socialism'. Their journal, *The Workers' Council*, declared that it stood 'uncompromisingly and

see *New York Times*, 30 November 1917. Orenstein's study deals with Goldfarb, Olgin and Salutsky throughout. On Olgin, see Epstein 1959, p. 383; on Salutsky, see Holmes 2008, p. 87; *New York Times*, 2 December 1917; the characterisation of JSF faction fighting is from Bittelman, 'Things I Have Learned', folder 13, p. 312. See also pp. 272–4 for a sense of Salutsky and Olgin's role in the JSF. Olgin's trajectory is discussed in Michels 2011 and Soyer 2005.

20 J. Louis Engdahl, 'There Is But One Issue', in National Office of the Socialist Party, Press Service Circular, 11 June 1921, Comintern archives, 515:1:89. Cf. the responses in the Circular for the SP leadership's response; *Going to the Masses* 1921; *New York Times*, 27 June 1921; J.B.S. Hardman, interview with Arthur A. Goren, 19 July 1966.

unreservedly with the Third (Communist) International and its principles'. They advocated an 'attempt to carry agitation into working class circles that have never been reached before'.[21]

The WC remained aloof from the underground CP, and tirelessly advocated a legal Communist movement. They declared three principles: support of the Third International; the dictatorship of the proletariat; and 'political action', that is, 'participation in all political activities, as well as electoral campaigns'. They attacked the Communists' insistence on illegality as 'not only an obvious mistake, but a violation of the conditions laid down by the Communist International'. The American Communists' refusal to surface from the underground left the 'revolutionary movement in the United States ... not only weaker than that of other countries' but also 'hopelessly divided'. Thus, 'illegality becomes the end and aim instead of a necessity'.

The WC wished to work with the official underground Communists to forge 'a sound communist movement in harmony with the present conditions in this country'. The title of the WC's two manifestos left no room for misunderstanding: 'The open Communist Party—the task of the hour' and 'We want an open Communist Party'. Legality was the 'only question' dividing the illegal Communist Party from the Workers' Council, in the latter's eyes.[22]

The CP saw things differently. No doubt this reflected some disdain toward figures who had been important parts of the SP apparatus and had refused to split in 1919, whom Cannon later called 'a group of second-line, second-grade Communists'. In August 1921, the CEC wrote a letter to the WC that reasserted the CP's status as the Comintern affiliate in the US and the Communist position that any unity would be on the CP's terms and programme. 'The underground organization is an absolute necessity for the performance of revolutionary communist work in this country', the letter asserted. Furthermore, the CP was 'decidedly opposed to the formation of any organization uniting seceding sections of the S.P.' The letter proposed, in effect, that the Communist Party take over the WC wholesale.[23]

21 *Workers' Council*, 1 April 1921; *Going to the Masses* 1921; Draper 1985, pp. 327–34; Lincove 2004, pp. 90–3; Pratt 1973, pp. 170–3. See also Leavall 1962, pp. 32, 44–6, 48, 50–4; Ottini 1948, pp. 34–44, 47–56. On the evolution of the Socialist Party after the expulsion of the left wing, see Routsila 2009; Shannon 1967, Chapter 7.

22 *Workers' Council*, 1 May 1921, 15 June 1921, 15 October 1921, 15 November 1921; *Go to the Masses* 1921.

23 J. Carr for the CEC to 'Dear Comrades', 1 August 1921, Hardman papers, box 38, folder 3; Cannon 1972, pp. 173–4.

The Comintern continued to pressure American Communists to realise 'the immediate construction of a legal party on a national scale', even at the cost of 'the program of the legal party [being] somewhat restricted'. Communists came to see the Workers' Council as a tool to fulfil the Comintern's instructions. In 1921, a recently formed legal Communist front organisation, the American Labor Alliance, and the WC negotiated the formation of a legal party, the Workers' Party (WP). The resulting organisation, with some 25,000 members, was dedicated, in Engdahl's words, 'to wage the open struggle for communism in the United States'.[24]

The 'Convention Call' in late 1921 to form the new party supported the Comintern and announced its desire to 'not only valiantly defend the workers but ... also wage an aggressive struggle for the abolition of capitalism'. The call did not mention the 'dictatorship of the proletariat'; instead, its first point advocated 'the abolition of capitalism through the establishment of a government by the working class and for the working class—a *Workers' republic in America*'. The second point pledged 'to participate in political activities, including electoral campaigns, in order to utilize them for the purpose of carrying our message to the masses'.[25]

The *Communist* described the formation of the Workers' Party in cryptic underground parlance: the underground Communist Party was called 'Number 1' and the legal Workers' Party, 'Number 2'. The CP's CEC voted:

> To organize No. 2 with the purpose of building a mass movement in this country and win the majority of workers to our program. To maintain our No. 1 machinery, making merely adjustments just now and final adjustments at our next Party convention.

The motion continued by noting the importance of the legal party:

> With the more or less exclusive and static membership of No. 1 we can not reach out to the broad masses and exercise a directing influence over

24 Bukharin, Radek and Kuusinen, 'Concerning the Next Tasks of the CP of A', Comintern archives, 515:1:38; CEC minutes, 3–9 November 1921, in Comintern archives, 515:1:51; Cannon 1962, pp. 44–5; Engdahl 1922; Hardman 1928, p. 22.

25 'Convention Call to Organize the Workers' Party of America', signed by the American Labor Alliance and Affiliated Organizations, the Workers' Council, and the Jewish Socialist Federation, Comintern archives, 515:1:77.

> them ... The CP is underground and only reaches the outskirts of the Labor Movement.[26]

The motion underlined the importance of the Comintern. The CP sought discussion with 'those who state that they are willing to follow the direction of our Main Directing Body', that is, the Comintern. The formation of the WP was 'in conformity with the needs of the workers in America', as well as 'in accordance with the instructions of our Main Directing Body'.[27]

According to Bryan Palmer, around 108 delegates attended the founding convention of the Workers' Party on 23–6 December 1921 in Manhattan. Cannon presided over the formation of the WP and was its first chairman. His keynote speech stressed that the new organisation 'brought together into one convention practically every left wing element in America', even if they 'have come here from different roads'. They 'came to submit in the name of unity, and sealed and guaranteed our pledge to present a unified movement to the workers of America'. Cannon emphasised the Comintern's importance: 'every man and woman in this hall will say with me that we look for our guidance to the inspirer, the organizer and leader of the world proletariat, the Communist International'.[28]

Cannon urged his comrades to 'take out of our minds the last bit of personal malice' and 'in the true spirit of revolutionary comradeship, join together in this work'. Some twenty years later, Cannon was more blunt and described the new Workers' Party 'not as a self-sufficient party, but as a cover for the underground movement and as one step in our fight for legality'. The WP was 'completely under the domination of the Communist Party' as its 'legal expression'. Melech Epstein, an official in the JSF and later the Communist Party, described the convention as 'not a smooth affair'. In his book (written after he was expelled from the CP), he quoted Salutsky as follows: 'on the first day of the convention, the old [underground Communist] crowd was not only in evidence but in control'. According to a report at the time by Ludwig Katterfeld, the Workers' Party had a 17-member executive committee, of whom 12 were from the illegal Communist Party.[29]

26 *Communist* (CP), January 1922.

27 Ibid.

28 Cannon 1992, pp. 90–3; a typescript of the speech is also in Comintern archives, 515:1:72. Speeches from the convention were also printed in *Voice of Labor*, 6 January 1922; Palmer 2007, p. 135.

29 Cannon 1992, p. 94; Cannon 1972, pp. 173–4; Epstein 1959, p. 100; 'Report 2', by Carr [Katterfeld], 18 January 1922, Comintern archives, 515:1:93.

The two elements of the Workers' Party distrusted each other. Bittelman recalled that the WC leadership 'didn't seem very happy' about joining the CP. Fearing the domination of the erstwhile CPA, whom he termed 'subway Communists' for their underground habitat, Salutsky had proposed to abort the entire fusion in the midst of the founding convention, but was overruled by his comrades in the WC. In an interview in 1966, Salutsky called the fusion 'the worst crime of my life', and recalled telling his comrades: 'This is my political cemetery, I am doing this against my judgement ... I have no confidence in the Bolsheviks'. He claimed to have gone along with the fusion out of loyalty to the Workers' Council, and to salvage the existence of the JSF. Be that as it may, almost immediately after the fusion, the JSF leadership felt duped by the CPA over the liquidation of the illegal apparatus, and battled their new comrades over the next several years for control of the JSF apparatus, especially its newspaper.[30]

For the CPA's part, the *Communist* described the WP as having a 'revolutionary program that needs only to be lived up to by a well organized and disciplined party to create the real beginning of an independent political movement of the American working class'. The CPA saw itself as 'the most revolutionary' element in the new group, and having provided 'the moving spirit and backbone of the whole affair'. The *Communist* complained, 'the same can not be said for the Workers' Council group, particularly its leadership'. The paper's editors referred to the WC leadership's 'old sins against the Communist Party of America and the Communist International'. The underground Communists saw the former WC leaders as cynical centrists; the latter, for their part, saw their CPA counterparts as immature and unrealistic romantics. Only the Comintern was able to provide enough cohesiveness to ensure that this concoction remained together long enough for the Communist movement to emerge from the underground. In the upshot, there was truth in both sides' assessments of the other. Some underground Communists refused to accept legal work, and some Workers' Council leaders—particularly Salutsky—became anti-Communists. However, some of the WC leaders—such as Engdahl, Kruse, Olgin and Trachtenberg—went on to become important Communists.[31]

Adding to the stew was the recruitment of another pro-Bolshevik grouping of ex-Socialists that had opposed an illegal organisation, the Finnish Socialist Federation (FSF). Finns played an important role in American radicalism.

30 Bittelman, 'Things I Have Learned', folder 13, p. 352; J.B.S. Hardman, interviewed by Arthur A. Goren, 19 July 1966; Epstein 1959, Chapters 11 and 12; Michels 2005, pp. 236–50.

31 *Communist* (CP), January 1922; Michels 2005, pp. 236–50; Bittelman, 'Things I have Learned', folder 13, p. 352.

In the seven years after its founding in 1907, the FSF had mushroomed from fewer than 3,000 members to almost 14,000. By 1914, between a quarter and a third of Finnish Americans were Socialists—roughly the same proportion that supported the Finnish American Church. The FSF was the first language section to affiliate with the SP, and had created an entire 'hall socialist' culture, replete with newspapers, and some sixty-five to seventy meeting halls valued at $600,000 in 1913. Although a majority of the some 10,000 Finnish American Socialists supported the Bolshevik Revolution, with few exceptions (such as Santeri Nourteva) most maintained their distance from the left wing. Instead, the Finns hoped to pressurise the SP to support the Comintern and adopt a revolutionary programme. FSF leaders feared that illegality would be ineffective and jeopardise the FSF's assets, including its network of halls. In December 1920, the FSF voted to split from the SP, but it still remained aloof from the illegal Communist Party. When the Workers' Party was formed, the FSF unanimously voted to join—bringing in some 7,000 Finns. At this time, the Communists claimed about 10,000 members.[32]

Continued Struggles Over Legality

The creation of the WP did not end the internecine factionalism within the Communist Party over legality, but rather complicated the issue further. The former members of the Workers' Council, now the 'Right Opposition' within the WP, continued to advocate total legality. A 'Left Opposition', consisting of 'Henry, Curtis, Dow' (pseudonyms of CEC members George Ashkenudzie, John J. Ballam and Charles Dirba) split to form an illegal organisation.

They issued a proclamation that defended their split as part of 'a struggle to prevent the liquidation and destruction of the Communist Party as planned by those centrist and semi-centrist elements within the communist movement in this country'. They denounced the former WC leaders as warmed-over social democrats who 'for more than two years' had been 'seeking to stab the young communist movement in the back'. Fusion with the WC had been the greatest treachery because it 'unit[ed] in one camp all the menshevik elements in the American movement'. For clarity, this new group chose the same name as the official CP, issued a paper called the *Communist*, and adopted the same constitution as the CP, with the additional claim that it was 'an underground

32 Kolehmainen 1952, p. 396; Kostiainen 1978, p. 32; Palmer 2007, p. 101; on Nourteva, see Ahola 1981, pp. 6–13, and Kostiainen 1983. Membership estimation taken from Draper 1985, p. 353.

and illegal organization'. They dedicated themselves to 'carry on the fight to expose and destroy the Workers' Party as completely as we smashed to bits the Socialist Party of America'. This needed to be done quickly, they warned, since the majority's 'agents were busy in Moscow' duping the Comintern.[33]

Once again, the Comintern rescued the party, helping it find tactics appropriate to American conditions. This split, although tiny, threatened to sacrifice American Communism upon the altar of factionalism. In November 1921, after hearing of the split, the Comintern cabled the CEC: 'Full board directors yesterday officially unanimously confirmed president's stand unreservedly endorsing new corporation, demanding all salesmen immediately comply'. When Henry, Curtis and Dow refused, the CEC suspended them from that body and the party. In March 1922, Kuusinen communicated the ECCI's agreement with the minority's suspension for their 'serious and intolerable breach of discipline'. He urged the CEC to create 'as little permanent disorganization as possible', and to try to convince the minority to rejoin the party and accept party discipline.[34]

Underscoring the Comintern's importance, both sides dispatched representatives to Moscow to argue their case before the American Commission. The hefty composition of the commission—including leaders such as Heinrich Brandler, Mátyás Rákosi, Reinstein and Boris Souvarine, as well as Kuusinen—indicates the efforts that the ECCI expended on the troublesome American party. At first, Ballam (now using the name 'Moore') was unrepentant. He issued a missive that decried the 'haphazard' nature of the commission, and claimed that 'the entire question has been misrepresented'. In his testimony to the commission, he claimed the support of 5,000 comrades and announced: 'We will stay outside the Communist International if we must, but within one year the Communist International will recognize the Communist Party of America which I represent, or they will recognise nobody'.

Despite this defiance, the commission unanimously supported the 'right' leaders, Bedacht and Katterfeld, on the necessity of a legal party, and 'refuse[d] recognition' to the 'split-off faction'. The ECCI 'severely reprimand[ed]' the splitters for their 'refusal to abide by the decisions of the C.I. and their

33 For the splitters' opposition to legalisation, see the CEC minutes of 3–9 November 1921; for their suspension from the CEC and the party, and their rebuke by the Comintern, see 28 November 1921. Both in Comintern archives, 515:1:51; *Communist* (LO), February and March 1922. See also DC [District Committee], 'To All Members', 26 November 1921, for an example of their denouncing the WP, in Cannon papers, reel 47, frame 35.

34 CEC minutes, 28 November 1921, in Comintern archives, 515:1:51; O.W. Kuusinen for the ECCI to the CPA CEC, received 9 May 1922, in Comintern archives, 515:1:128.

destructive breach of Communist discipline'. Rather than destroy Henry, Curtis and Dow, the ECCI 'demand[ed] of all members of the faction ... that they rejoin the C.P. of A. as soon as possible'. If they did, the ECCI promised 'full membership rights'. If they did not accept the ECCI's decision within 30 days, they would be 'expelled from the Communist International, and [could] not be readmitted to any section of the Third International, except as new members'.[35]

The cryptic cable announcing the decision is worth quoting in full, if only to give a flavour of Comintern directives:

> HENRY CURTIS DOW COMPANY INSTRUCTED QUIT USING OUR FIRM NAME AND TRADEMARK STOP THEY MUST DISSOLVE AND REJOIN OUR COMPANY IMMEDIATELY OR LOSE THEIR STOCK JOHN IS WRITING THEM TO QUIT COMPETING AND ATTACKING OUR BUSINESS STOP YOU MUST ACCEPT THEM WITHOUT PREJUDICE AND POSTPONE STOCKHOLDERS CONFERENCE UNTIL THEY CAN PARTICIPATE.[36]

The American Commission ordered the 'left opposition' to return to the party, and instructed the party to call a convention to work out the relationship between the legal and illegal organisations. A representative of the American party in Moscow wrote to his supporters saying that Ballam 'has capitulated completely, although he did make one hell of a roar while he was at it'. Within days, Ballam rejoined the party and accepted its discipline, declaring, 'I cannot oppose ... the policies of the Comintern'. He attempted to convince his followers to return to the party. By June, according to Ballam, only 30 percent of 'Henry, Curtis, Dow' supporters had returned—leaving some 3,000 former oppositionists, mainly non-English speakers, outside the party.[37]

35 'Report of the International Delegate to the Conference of the CPA', June 1922; Moore's protest to ECCI, 18 March 1922; statement by Moore, 18 March 1922, all in Comintern archives, 515:1:128; Letter from Mátyás Rákosi for the American Commission of the CI to the American CP, *Communist* (LO), June 1922; 'To All Members of the Communist Party of America', March or April 1922, in Comintern archives, 495:1:26, published in Klehr, Haynes and Anderson 1998, p. 19; Draper 1985, p. 356.

36 Cable from 'Block and Company', Comintern archives, 515:1:39.

37 Moore to Zinoviev, 'In Re: American Situation', 24 March 1922; J. Carr [Katterfeld] and John Moore, 'Declaration' on the Party Situation, 25 March 1922, both in Comintern archives, 515:1:128. This file also contains a letter from L.C. Wheat [Lovestone] for the CEC to Curtis, Dow, Henry, 11 April 1922, inviting them back into the party; as well as a 'Special Bulletin on Party Situation', issued by the CEC in May 1922, that contains several relevant documents. Description of Bellam's capitulation taken from J. Carr's 'Dear Friends', 1 April

The Comintern had forced the American party to pursue legalisation, but was still dissatisfied. A May 1922 ECCI letter to the American Communists noted that it had 'for the last two years … been following with deepest concern the strife in the Party in America, which presents constant obstacles to the creation of a strong revolutionary Party'. This letter 'reassert[ed] in the most emphatic manner' the ECCI's support for a legal party. It denounced the minority's conception of the party as a 'religion for the chosen ones', and ordered the opposition to return. Yet the letter introduced a new element: besides calling for a convention, the Comintern also announced it was sending a 'plenipotentiary representative'. It warned: 'We already had to contend with even greater differences than yours in some countries, and we have learned to overpower them'.[38]

The convention that took place at Bridgman, Michigan, in August 1922 is best known for being the scene of the last overt repressive attack against Communists in this period. Federal agents and local police hid in the forest, awaiting the start of the convention. They then raided the gathering and seized documents. More than thirty Communists were eventually arrested, including Ruthenberg and William Z. Foster.[39] Jacob Spolansky, head of the Bureau of Investigation's Chicago office, later declared that the raid had less to do with any threat posed by the Communists than with anti-radical panic created by an ongoing national railway strike. Nonetheless, virtually the entire leadership of the party faced arrest or indictment, and the party posted $100,000 surety.[40]

It is necessary to examine the role of the Comintern's representative to understand the Bridgman Convention and the relationship between the American party and the Comintern. The main representative was Henryk Valetski (or Walecki)—the revolutionary pseudonym of Maksymilian Horwitz, a Jewish mathematician and former Bundist from Poland. He was assisted by Boris Reinstein, the Russian American dentist who had been a member of the SLP in Buffalo and who represented the Red International of Labour

---

1922; membership figure taken from 'Report of John Moore, Delegate of the Minority Faction of the CPA, to the Comintern, to the CEC', 27 June 1922; both in Comintern archives, 515:1:93.

38 'ECCI to the Communist Party of North America', 30 May 1922, Comintern archives, 515:1:128.

39 C.E. Ruthenberg, Josef Pogány and A. Jakira, 'The General Party Situation', report to Enlarged ECCI, 11 April 1923, in Comintern archives, 515:1:201. Foster's recruitment to the party is examined in the next chapter. A selection of the seized documents was published in Whitney 1924.

40 *Menace of Criminal Syndicalism*, undated; Spolansky 1951; *New York Times*, 23 August 1922; on the Bridgman Convention, see Mears 2010; on the 1922 strike, see Davis 1997.

Unions, and József Pogány, a Hungarian exile who was supposed to work with the Hungarian federation but soon played a more important role in the party. Valetski had experienced internecine factionalism in the Polish movement, and the Bolsheviks no doubt expected him to cut through the problems in the American Party, with the assistance of Reinstein.

The representatives of the Comintern represented the distance and relative insignificance of American Communism in the Comintern's universe. All three had become Communists *after* the Bolshevik Revolution; as it turned out, all three would also be distinguished in the coming decades for their ability to adapt themselves to the political winds in Moscow. Valetski and Reinstein had been imprisoned for revolutionary activity in the Russian empire, and Reinstein's wife had been arrested during the Red Scare; Pogány was in exile from the defeated Hungarian Revolution of 1919. As a result, all had credentials of illegal work, and perhaps could be expected to bring a sense of proportion to the American Communists.[41]

The main accomplishment of the Bridgman Convention was to unify all the competing tendencies into one party. The leaders of the 'left opposition', Ballam, Dirba and Ashkenudzie, resigned from the CEC. Robert Minor, Alfred Wagenknecht and Earl Browder were elected to that body; both Foster and Pogány were elected to the CEC as well, ironically as 'non-factional' members. But the convention faced a new battle over legality, between the 'Geese' and 'Liquidator' factions.[42]

The Geese, centred on the foreign-language federations, advocated keeping the illegal organisation ('Number 1') dominant over the legal party ('Number 2'). The Liquidators, supported by most of the native-born or Americanised cadres (including Cannon, Foster, Lovestone and Ruthenberg), sought to abolish

---

41 For the Comintern delegation, see Draper 1985, pp. 363–5; on Horwitz, see Zimmerman 2010. Pogány is dealt with in the following chapters, but for his role in the Bridgman Convention, see Sakmyster 2012, pp. 78–81; on Boris Reinstein's arrest in France for allegedly being part of a conspiracy to assassinate the tsar, see Falkowski 1994 and Lesure 1965, pp. 283, 286; on Anna Reinstein being charged with 'criminal anarchy', see *New York Times*, 1 January 1920. In a letter to Theodore Draper of 18 August 1954, Cannon emphasised that Valetski's factional experience in Poland was seen as a plus. On the future role of Valetski after the rise of Stalin, see Trotsky 1974a, pp. 242–3: 'People of the calibre of Valetski will never conquer anything. But they are perfectly capable of losing that which has been conquered'.

42 Sakmyster 2012, p. 79; Earl Browder, 'No Man's Land: A Political Autobiography', undated, in Earl Browder papers, p. 167; According to Gitlow's later anti-Communist book of 1939, *I Confess*, Ashkenudzie eventually transferred to the Russian Party, and by the late 1920s was working within the Comintern; Gitlow 1939, p. 425.

the underground work and create an above-ground party. These American leaders believed that in order to be of influence within the labour movement in the US, Communists would need to transcend a subterranean existence and branch out beyond immigrants into the English-speaking proletariat.[43]

At the conference, the Geese submitted their 'Thesis on Relations of One and Two', which argued the 'legal political party ... can not replace the Communist party'. The 'underground machinery of the Communist party' should be 'not merely a temporary device' but 'for permanent use ... It is for constant use'. The illegal party must retain 'full control' of the legal party, and the 'personnel of committees of Number Two' should have majorities of 'personnel of the corresponding committees of Number One'. That is, the illegal party should be a parallel and dominant organisation.[44]

Against this, the Liquidators argued that 'not only had the No. 2 absorbed almost all the ordinary tasks carried out through the C.P. in the workers' everyday struggle but [that] these tasks are performed more efficiently by the No. 2', instead of the illegal party. It was difficult to recruit workers to an underground party, and a dual-party structure was chaotic. The document by Joseph Zack ended by urging the party to 'get away from this hocus-pocus and on to the task of developing an open Communist Party'. Zack did not advocate creating a completely legal party immediately. Rather, the illegal party should still 'carry out the many tasks that will develop during the struggle which cannot and should not be done in the open', but he emphasised that 'No. 1 cannot remain the kind of organization it is now'.[45]

Luckily for the historian, Valetski wrote a detailed report to the Comintern. He began by noting that at the time of his arrival, the 'meetings of the family council were spent wholly on personal matters, [while] the big struggles which were going on outside never came up for discussion'. Even though there was only a 'slight difference of views' between the factions on any serious matter,

> they have conducted their fight in such a way that the interests of the Party as a whole disappeared behind those of the factions, and because without the timely intervention of your representative and his two

43 The curious names came from each faction's insult about the other. Lovestone had once remarked that the undergrounders-on-principle cackled like geese about saving the underground party. The 'Geese' in turn sought to associate their opponents with a faction within the pre-revolutionary Bolshevik Party that had wanted to abolish underground activity after the defeated 1905 Revolution; Whitney 1924, p. 158.

44 *Communist* (majority), July 1922; see also Whitney 1924, pp. 225–30.

45 Whitney 1924, pp. 14–16.

> friends a new split might have taken place, the most senseless of all splits that ever took place in the American movement.

The factions, he continued, 'represented more different frames of mind than different tendencies'. Valetski created an eight-person committee to reach agreement between the factions. He played a prominent role: 'I adopted no conciliatory attitude, did not pose as arbitrator; rather I fought openly every heresy, every false judgement of the political solutions in the published theses'. The most important goal of his intervention into the American Communist movement was to flex Comintern muscle to safeguard the party's unity and prevent unnecessary splits.[46]

Presumably with the Comintern delegation's blessing, Robert Minor developed a 'compromise' resolution. It recognised 'open work' as 'the main task of the party', while asserting that 'the illegal Communist party must continue to exist' and 'direct the whole Communist work'. The resolution stated: 'A legal Communist party is now impossible'. To justify this, the resolution claimed that 'in spite of all the differences, America belongs in the category of countries, like Finland, Poland, Roumania, Jugoslavia, where the Communist party must be illegal'. As Draper put it, although Minor's resolution 'came down heavily on all sides of the question', the result 'on balance ... represented a victory of the Geese over the Liquidators'.[47]

Valetski also met with the Workers' Council. Although he found some of its leaders, particularly Salutsky, more right wing than others, he saw them as generally being pulled to the left. In addition, he addressed a meeting of the 'left opposition', representing some 2,500 people, and convinced them to return to the official party. This required their backing down from more extreme positions, including labelling the WP a 'palpable fraud' and a 'centrist sect', as well as their demand that reunification be based on the expulsion of Bedacht, Cannon, Lovestone and Ruthenberg—that is, the leadership of the party. After the Bridgman Convention, the party faced a crossroads. While officially accepting the Comintern's insistence on legal work, in practice many members, particularly foreign-language comrades, emphasised illegal work. Such a balancing act was not tenable and it kept the party isolated from American society.[48]

46 Walesky to Kuusinen, 8 October 1922, Comintern archives, 515:1:128. The report begins cryptically and becomes clearer, perhaps because the author could not keep up the subterfuge or did not expect the police to read more than a passage or so.

47 Ibid., pp. 24–5; Draper 1985, p. 361.

48 For details on this convention, see the 'Continuation of Report', appended to Walesky's 8 October 1922 letter to Kuusinen; see also the 'Manifesto of the Communist Party of

Convincing the Comintern

In late 1922, leaders of both factions were in Moscow for the Fourth Congress of the Communist International. Katterfeld attended for the Geese. Among the Liquidators present in Moscow were Bedacht, Bittelman (whose official remit was to present a report on the Jewish movement in the US and make contact with Jewish Communists in Russia), and Cannon, chairman of the WP, who had been in Moscow since spring.

On the eve of the Congress, Trotsky argued that 'a revolution in the United States would be most advantageous', since it was 'the most independent' and 'the richest country in the world'. He criticised the Communists in the US: 'in this strongest, largest, and most decisive leading capitalist country, the political premises, i.e., premises on the plane of the creation of a systematic party and class organization, are the least prepared'. The Congress's American Commission reflected such concern, comprising Bolshevik heavyweights such as Bukharin, Radek and Zinoviev.[49]

Cannon and Bittelman lobbied the Comintern leadership on the importance of legal work. Bittelman, a Russian-speaker, helped arrange meetings with leading Bolsheviks, including Bukharin, Radek and Zinoviev, as well as the ECCI secretary Kuusinen. These leaders were 'extremely friendly and patient', Cannon recalled, but 'as though by a prior decision on their part, remained noncommittal'. At the same time, he got 'the impression at the time' that leading Bolsheviks thought he was an opportunist—an impression reinforced by the delegation's approval of Minor's resolution. Cannon took pains to dissociate himself from the earlier 'Liquidator' faction in Russia, stressing that while he supported Lenin in that historic struggle, he 'thought there was a difference between Czarist Russia and Harding's America'.[50]

This was the crux of the issue. The Liquidators wanted to anchor Communism in the United States in American society and the labour movement. They believed that this could not happen through a small underground organisation composed of foreign-language groups. The Geese, on the other

America on the Workers' Party' for the positions of the 'Left Opposition', attached to the Report. All are in Comintern archives, 515:1:128. Adding to the irony of the Bridgman Convention was the fact that the decisive vote in favour of maintaining the illegal apparatus was cast by one Fred Morrow, a government agent; see Browder, 'No Man's Land', p. 179; Draper 1985, pp. 366–9.

49 Trotsky 1973a, I, p. 186; Cannon 1962, p. 70.

50 Cannon 1962, pp. 65–6; Bittelman, 'Things I Have Learned', folder 13, p. 363; folder 14, pp. 365–76.

hand, believed that America was similar to tsarist Russia, and that Cannon and other American leaders were opportunists.

Cannon and Bittelman remained frustrated until they met Max Eastman. The socialist writer, who was in Moscow working on a biography of Trotsky, had already complained to Trotsky about the domination of the American party by Russian immigrants; he arranged an audience with his subject, the second-in-command of the Comintern. When calling upon Trotsky, Cannon emphasised the political backwardness of the American working class and the possibility of a legal party. He stressed 'the necessity of Americanizing the party, of breaking the control of the foreign-language federations and assuring an indigenous national leadership'. Cannon later recalled that this discussion with Trotsky 'changed everything overnight'.[51]

Trotsky came out in support of the Liquidators. He ordered Cannon to write his position on 'one sheet of paper—no more', to facilitate making his case to the ECCI. In the two-page document, 'The American Question', Bedacht, Cannon, Arne Swabeck and others argued as follows: 'The objective conditions in America are not revolutionary, and the American workers are not class-conscious, even to the point of independent political action'. Nonetheless, there was a deepening 'revolt in the trades union movement against the official bureaucracy' and a sentiment for a labour party. 'The illegality of the C.P.A. is a great hindrance in its work'. This was especially the case since 'American workers are still under democratic illusions and do not understand why we have an illegal, conspirative organization'.

The document urged an attempt to form a legal party. If successful, this would allow the party to enjoy the benefits of legality. If a failure, such an attempt would demonstrate to workers why an illegal party was necessary. A key obstacle, however, was that 'a majority of the party membership are foreign born comrades, chiefly of Russia origin', many of whom do not base their opinions on the 'objective conditions in America', but on their subjective view of Europe. The document ended by urging the Comintern, should a split occur over the question of legality, to 'not insist upon a mechanical formula of unity'.[52]

51 Eastman 1964, pp. 332–3; Cannon 1962, pp. 68–9. According to Eastman, when he complained to Trotsky about the prominence of Russian émigrés in the American party, Trotsky responded: 'we are ready to burn up a few thousand Russians in order to create a real American revolutionary movement'; Eastman 1964, p. 333.

52 'The American Question', signed by Marshall [Bedacht], Cook [Cannon], Lansing [Swabeck], *et al.*, in Comintern archives, 515:1:60. A slightly different translation (from the German copy presented to the ECCI, which is also in the Comintern archives) can be found in Cannon 1992, pp. 95–7. There were a total of nine signatories, including two

The American Commission opened soon afterward. Katterfeld, for the Geese, argued that the 'objective as well as the subjective conditions within our party make it essential to have an illegal Communist Party and to develop as an instrument of that party a legal political party'. This legal party should 'not take ... the place of the old existing Communist Party, but ... serve as an instrument of the Communist Party for its work'. For the 'Left Opposition', Sullivan, a Latvian from Boston, argued that the party 'must continue its underground existence, conduct communist propaganda as far as it cannot be done legally, organize, direct and supervise the Communist nuclei, legal work and organizations, the party press, and all forms of party activity'. Several Americans opposed legalisation, including the only black delegate, Otto Huiswoud. Both Reinstein and Sen Katayama, two Comintern functionaries with experience in the US, intervened against 'liquidating' the underground party.

Cannon, by contrast, argued that the American working class was politically backward, and that Communists must carry out painstaking work to win workers. He advocated the party fight for a labour party similar to the British Labour Party. He advocated that the party fight for legality, in the tradition of the IWW's struggles against repression. American workers would not join a party that did not fight for its own legal existence. 'The illegality of our party is a tremendous handicap', he argued. 'The working class in America have democratic illusions', he continued, and 'do not understand why we are underground as a party'. 'Our underground party', he added, 'instead of having the sympathy and attraction of the workers is regarded by the masses as a good deal of a joke. They think it is illegal because we want to be illegal, and I must say that is true of a large majority of the illegal party'.[53]

Cannon recalled that after the presentations, 'the big guns began to boom'. The commission attacked the notion that Communist parties must be illegal as a matter of principle. It ordered the party to become legal, work for a labour party, and tell the 'left opposition', once again, to rejoin the party (and, again, assure them full rights). This highlights the complexity and importance of

delegates to the Young Communist International, three delegates to the Profintern, and the party's agrarian organiser.

53 American Commission, 27 November 1922, in Comintern archives, 495:37:1; American Commission, 30 November 1922, in Comintern archives, 491:1:332. For a printed version of Cannon's speech, see Cannon 2007. Claude McKay, a Jamaican-born member of the Workers' Party, was also at the Congress, as will be examined in the chapters on the development of the 'Negro Question'. There was opposition to his speaking, in part because of his support of legalisation. McKay's appeals to the Mandate Commission for the right to attend and speak can be found in Comintern archives, 491:1:353 and 491:1:354.

the relationship of the Comintern to the early American Communist movement. While Comintern intervention was decisive, the Bolsheviks leading the International did not attempt to merely force their American comrades to duplicate Russian conditions. Instead, American leaders like the Liquidators were able to convince them of the crucial differences between the two countries. And when the Comintern finally did intervene forcefully, they tried to win over their Communist opponents, not smash them to oblivion. In the final balance, the intervention of the Bolshevik-led Comintern was crucial to make the leaders of the American Communists 'Americanise' their party.[54]

One of the first attempts to legalise the party was the struggle to defend Communists' rights in the face of prosecution stemming from the Bridgman raid. As a 1923 report to the ECCI put it, 'The party took advantage of this persecution to strengthen its support among the masses'. The party organised the Labor Defense Council (LDC) with Foster (a defendant but not yet an open Communist) as its head. While Communists were prominent in the organisation, its National Committee included prominent non-Communist liberals and radicals such as Debs, Flynn and Roger Baldwin of the American Civil Liberties Union. Frank Walsh was the chief counsel. The LDC reportedly raised $100,000. The legal team secured a mistrial for Foster (the first defendant to go on trial), but Ruthenberg was found guilty of one count of violating Michigan's criminal syndicalism laws. Over the next decade, the LDC posted some $90,000 in bail for Ruthenberg and the other defendants while Ruthenberg's case was on appeal. (The prosecution held off against the other defendants until Ruthenberg's case was decided; the Communist leader died while an appeal to the US Supreme Court was pending. As late as 1933, eighteen defendants, including Foster, faced prosecution and the original bail money had not been returned). If its success on the legal field was uneven, the LDC did show that the party was serious about protecting its rights and allowed it to make alliances with the broader left and labour movement.[55]

54 Cannon 1962, pp. 70–1. For a detailed description of the Commission, see Palmer 2007, pp. 158–63.

55 Ruthenberg, Pogány and Jakira, 'The General Party Situation', 11 April 1923, in Comintern archives, 515:1:201. Uhlman 2007, pp. 67–73; *New York Times*, 4 January 1933. On the legal travails of Ruthenberg and other Bridgman defendants, see Collins and Skover 2005; Mears 2010. Making alliances with the left and liberals was not smooth. See the correspondence between the LDC and the Garland Fund (American Fund for Public Service papers, reel 15), and the ongoing dispute between the party and Frank Walsh over payment of legal fees in 1923, in Comintern archives, 515:1:202; see also Jenkins 1978.

In February 1923, in a letter to Zinoviev, Foster complained that the 'transition from an underground party to an open party must be proceeded with care ... because there is a deeprooted conviction on the part of a large number of the comrades that a Communist Party must of necessity and at all times be a conspiratorial organisation'. However, in early April, the party held its Third National Convention, which despite some grumbling by Katterfeld, unanimously passed a motion 'that the Workers' Party of America become immediately the open Communist party', while keeing 'an apparatus within the Workers' party to safeguard the organization and to carry on confidential work'. According to a report by Ruthenberg, while a right-wing grouping still opposed all illegal work, and a left-wing grouping demanded an underground party, the former Geese and Liquidators had dissolved and the majority of the members, and three-fourths of the CEC, 'support[ed] the open party' and were 'more and more being thrown into active work among the masses'.[56] The party never stopped facing repression, but the leadership remained determined to defend its right to organise.

In an article published after the Comintern Congress, Cannon credited a 'long argument and a push from Moscow' for this change in policy. The Comintern's shove was necessary to get the American party to seize the opportunities to do legal work. But equally important was the argument. Trotsky and the rest of the Comintern leadership did not make Communist pronouncements from Mount Olympus, but pursued a policy only after intense discussion with the leadership of the American party. The fight over legalisation illustrates the dialectical relationship between the American Communists and the Comintern at this time. In a letter to Draper decades later, Cannon argued that 'a great problem of American communism, which it had not been able to solve by itself, was settled conclusively and definitely for the good of the movement'. Two years after this commission, Israel Amter noted that legalisation 'widened the vista of the Communist movement in the United States to a degree hardly conceived by the American Communists'. Legalisation illustrates the beneficial relationship between the Communist International and its American section in the attempt to root Communism in the reality of American society.[57]

56 Wm. Z. Foster to Zinoviev, 17 February 1923; Ruthenberg, Pogány and Akira, 'The General Party Situation'. 11 April 1923, both in Comintern archives, 515:1:201.

57 Cannon 1992, pp. 117–23; Cannon 1962, p. 71; Amter 1924.

CHAPTER 3

Communists and the Labour Movement

The Communist movement in the United States saw itself as part of the broader labour movement, as witnessed by such names as the Communist Labor Party, the Workers' Council, or the Workers' Party. Many early Communists, including Browder, Cannon and Larkin, had considerable trade-union experience. However, the young Communist Party is often depicted as isolated from the labour movement. Most historians who study the influence of Communists in the trade-union movement usually begin in the 1930s, skipping the party's first decade to move on to the era of the CIO. One such study simply called the 1920s a 'decade of failure'.[1]

Objectively, this is true. However, it misses two key aspects of Communist labour work in this period. First, despite the ultimate fiasco and isolation the party faced at the end of the decade, in the mid-1920s, the vista for Communist work appeared wide. Second, if Communist work in the labour movement did not pay immediate dividends, many of the cadres in the Communist movement in the 1920s went on to play important roles in the 1930s (both inside and outside the Communist Party). Furthermore, the relationship between Communists and important labour leaders in the 1930s—especially John L. Lewis—were conditioned by the party's activities in the 1920s. Understanding the Communists' activities in the labour movement in the 1920s is essential to evaluating their much larger role during the Depression.

In 1919, the American working class seemed increasingly militant. Workers were on strike for more man hours than in the next six years combined. This militancy soon collided with an anti-union offensive by business coupled with anti-radical 'Red Scare' repression by the government. The 'roaring twenties' saw the rise of mass consumer culture and increasing business profits, but a declining share for workers. Productivity rose 72 percent between 1919 and 1929, but real wages grew only 9.1 percent between 1923 and 1928. At the start of the decade, the American Federation of Labor (AFL) had 5 million members and some twenty percent of non-agricultural workers were unionised. Ten years later, the AFL had 3.5 million members and barely ten percent of non-agricultural workers belonged to unions. Irving Bernstein conveyed this in the

1 Cochran 1977, p. 20.

title of one of the chapters in his history of the working class in the 1920s: 'the paralysis of the labor movement'.[2]

This chapter examines the Comintern's intervention into the American party's perspectives on the labour movement: while opposing 'dual unionist' refusal to work within the AFL, the Comintern strove to recruit members of the IWW.

The AFL, the IWW and the Birth of American Communism

By the 1920s, most American workers were not organised and many lacked basic class consciousness. The United States lacked a mass social-democratic movement party that even in a distorted way reflected class divisions in society. Most workers in the country—divided by ethnicity, race, religion, region, skill and language—did not think of themselves as members of a unified and permanent proletariat. Workers in the US were among the most economically militant in the capitalist world, but most did not see the goal of their struggles as the elimination of capitalist class society.

The leadership of the largest trade-union federation in the country, the AFL led by Gompers, eschewed even rhetorical radicalism in favour of working from within the capitalist system. Gompers was not hegemonic within the trade-union movement. In addition to the radical IWW, many important unions were outside the AFL, and even among AFL unions, there was significant dissent with Gompers. James Fitzpatrick of the Chicago Federation of Labor (CFL), and James Duncan from the Seattle Central Labor Council, often opposed Gompers from the left. In 1921, John L. Lewis, head of the largest AFL union, the industrial-based United Mineworkers of America (UMWA), challenged Gompers for leadership of the AFL (although, for radicals, the Republican Lewis was no better than the 'nonpartisan' Gompers).[3]

The left had developed two ways of dealing with the political backwardness of the American working class and the reactionary AFL leadership. The first was 'boring from within', that is, working within AFL unions, often by challenging their leadership. The second was 'dual unionism', that is, organising radical unions (such as the IWW) that proclaimed their militant opposition to

2 Bernstein 1960.

3 On the dangers of confounding the AFL leadership with its membership, see Strouthous 2000, p. 2. On the CFL, see Keiser 1965. On dissent within the AFL, see Dubofsky and Van Tine 1986, pp. 57–8; Montgomery 1987, pp. 404–6; Shapiro 1967, pp. 76–7.

capitalism. Since 1910, support for the IWW had been central to the left-wing Socialists.[4]

This was second nature to many early Communists. 'Both American communist parties were officially under the influence of the IWW idea of smashing the old unions and building revolutionary new unions', Louis Fraina recalled. 'AFL unions were viewed as corrupted by imperialism and not to be built up, but blown up', according to Arne Swabeck. The June 1919 conference of the left wing declared: 'The American Federation of Labor, in its present organization and under its present leadership, is *entirely reactionary*, and *cannot be of any value* in the workers' struggle for emancipation'. Still, some early Communists opposed dual unionism. Bittelman recalled that Jewish Communists advocated work in the AFL, because many Jewish workers belonged to AFL unions while few belonged to the IWW. Similarly, James Larkin, reflecting his experience in Britain and Ireland, as well as the fact that many Irish Americans were AFL members, advocated that Communists 'go into labor unions and try to revolutionize them'. (Of course, Larkin's influence on American Communism was shortlived given his legal problems).[5]

In the first years of the movement, the question of tactics towards the trade unions appeared irrelevant to many Communists. The major strikes of the period, combined with the Russian Revolution and struggles in Europe, Bittelman later recalled, indicated 'that the socialist revolution was maturing also in the United States and that we must get busy preparing ourselves to lead it'. The 1919 general strikes in Seattle in February and Winnipeg in May–June were 'eloquent indications that things were coming to a showdown of some kind'. Or as Max Shachtman put it, 'all these events were interpreted by us through Russian glasses'. Thus the long, hard task of winning influence among organised workers appeared a diversion. One result of this were trade-union leaflets such as during the 1920 transport workers' strike in Brooklyn, which urged workers to 'stop asking for merely a little more wages' and 'get

4 See Bell 1967, p. 65; Foner 1964, pp. 368–9; Saposs 1926.

5 Lewis Corey (Fraina) to Granville Hicks, 30 December 1935, in Corey papers, box 1; Arne Swabeck, 'From Debs to Mao' (1975), memoirs, in Prometheus Research Library. 'Left Wing Section of the Socialist Party: Report of the Labor Organization Committee', 21 June 1919, in John S. Reed Papers, Houghton Library, Harvard University, bms Am 1901:1449, emphasis added; Bittelman, 'Things I Have Learned', folder 13, p. 343; this opposition to dual unionism perhaps explains why Bittelman became a firm ally of William Z. Foster in the 1920s factionalism: see Holmes 2007, p. 179; Larkin 1990, pp. 234–43; O'Connor 2002. Larkin's voice was muted by his arrest and imprisonment in 1919 for his politics; he played no role in American left-wing politics afterwards, and was pardoned in 1923 before returning to Ireland.

ready for armed revolution to overthrow the Capitalist Government and create a Workers Government'. Such an approach was not fruitful. According to Melech Epstein, almost forty years later, fellow former Communist 'Charles S. Zimmerman remember[ed] how fast he had to run across the street to save himself from the strikers'.[6]

When the Communists emerged from the underground, about three-quarters of them were working class, including metal and machine workers, construction workers, miners and needle trades workers. However, barely one-third of Communists were union members. This was not surprising given the weakness of unions and the immigrant composition of the CP. The Communists' paucity of English-speakers, and their trouble in recruiting English-speaking workers, compounded their isolation from the organised labour movement. In the car industry, the party recruited from the third of the workforce comprising immigrants, but had trouble among the other (American) two-thirds.[7]

Some early CP leaders, like Browder or Cannon (a former protégé of Vincent St. John), had experience in the IWW. William F. Dunne, along with his brothers, had been active among unions in Montana; Swabeck, a charter Communist, had been a leader in the Seattle general strike. Ella Reeve Bloor, a former member of both the SLP and the SP, had been an organiser among women textile workers and had collaborated with Elizabeth Gurley Flynn in the Workers Defense Union. Rose Pastor Stokes, an SP leader who joined the left wing, had been active in strikes by garment, hotel and other workers, as well as being a socialist journalist and advocate of birth control. Such cadres would prove crucial to intervene in the labour movement.[8]

Early Communists and the IWW

The first union from which the early Communists sought recruits was the IWW. Surprisingly, historians have not dealt much with this campaign. Melvyn Dubofsky's authoritative study of the union, 1969's *We Shall Be All*, devotes just

6 Bittelman, 'Things I Have Learned', folder 12, p. 311; folder 13, p. 330; Shachtman Reminiscences, Columbia University Oral History Collection, p. 55; 'BRT Strikers!', Comintern archives, 515:1:30; Epstein 1959, pp. 41–2. Epstein mistakenly dates the strike as taking place in 1921.

7 Palmer 2007, pp. 167, 53; Keeran 1979, pp. 190, 205–7.

8 Cannon 1962, p. 111. On Cannon's IWW experience, see Palmer 2007, Chapter 3; on Dunne, see Barrett 2002, p. 113; Wetzel 1970. On Bloor see Brown 1987, pp. 221–2, 280–6; on the Workers Defense Union, see Camp 1995, Chapter 4. On Stokes and the labour movement, see Sharp 1979, Chapter 3.

two of almost 500 pages to this.[9] Communist interest in the IWW reflected the Comintern's approach to left-wing syndicalists internationally. Communists in Latin America and Europe had more initial success in recruiting syndicalists than in the US. American Communists did not lack appetite. The founding convention of the CLP invited IWW-leader William D. Haywood to address the meeting, evidently at Benjamin Gitlow's suggestion. (Haywood politely declined). John Reed declared in the *Communist International* in 1920:

> If these men can be reached, if the position of the Communist can be explained to them in their own language, their native common sense will show them that we are right. And this must be done, for the I.W.W. is the advance guard of the American proletariat, and it is they who must lead the assault on capitalism in America.

When Reed wrote those lines, they did not appear fanciful. After the October Revolution, many Wobblies sympathised with the Bolsheviks.[10]

In late 1917, the IWW wrote to Lenin as 'colleagues in the struggle for social revolution', and hailed the Bolsheviks for 'inspiring and accelerating a revolutionary movement, the like of which has never been seen before'. *Industrial Worker* in this period described the Bolshevik Revolution as achieving the IWW's goals. In 1918, the union published a pro-Bolshevik pamphlet, *Red Dawn*, by Harrison George, an imprisoned Wobbly. He declared the Soviet government 'pure and simple working-class rule' and saluted the Bolsheviks as 'entitled to first place among the tacticians of the Modern Working Class'. In this period, pro-Bolshevik Wobblies depicted the Revolution as a reflection of their own syndicalism.[11]

The Comintern wanted to recruit the IWW. J.T. Murphy, a former syndicalist who became a British Communist, remembered Lenin's 'admiration' for the IWW 'as fine courageous fighters'. When George Hardy met Lenin in 1921, the Bolshevik leader was eager to meet a member of the IWW. A 1919 note by the ECCI to American supporters foresaw support for the dictatorship of the proletariat and revolutionary mass action as being able to 'unite the left elements of the disintegrating Socialist Party and the I.W.W.' While recognising that the IWW were opposed to 'political action', the Comintern argued that this

9 Dubofsky 1969, pp. 462–5.

10 On the difficulties of the American CP's recruiting syndicalists, see Peterson 1984, p. 128; Baev and Grozev 2008, Part 1, p. 52; Reed 1920.

11 'Letter from American Workers', pp. 27–8; McEnroe 1960, pp. 340–4; George 1918, pp. 12, 15–17.

opposition was aimed at social-democratic parliamentarism and that IWW members could be recruited to Communist politics.[12]

The IWW was ambivalent towards the Communists. Wobbly leader Ralph Chaplin described the Russian Revolution as dividing the IWW 'into antagonistic camps'. Many Wobblies—especially those in prison—rallied to the Bolshevik Revolution, which George described as an 'inspiring light that penetrates even the prison windows and floods my cell with the glory of the Red Dawn'. Charles Ashleigh became a Communist in prison, along with other fellow Wobbly prisoners, and Haywood become a supporter of the Bolsheviks as well. At the founding of the Comintern, *New Solidarity* was enthusiastic towards the Bolsheviks. In December 1918, it reprinted an article by Reed from the *Liberator* under the headline, 'Composition of the Soviets: Working Class Democracy'. In January 1919, an editorial titled 'The Star of Hope' declared: 'It is to Russia that the workers of all lands are now looking for inspiration'. The support for the Bolsheviks came from a syndicalist vantage. Unlike traditional Social Democrats, Lenin and his followers had eschewed parliamentary opportunism. Thus in early 1919, they reprinted a self-critical piece by Otto Kuusinen—described as the Finnish Kautsky—which described the failure of revolution in Finland as a result of social-democratic opportunism.[13]

The IWW's *New Solidarity* in the spring of 1919 exhorted its comrades that 'Russia has blazed the way, let us broaden the trail to make Freedom a fact and Industrial Democracy a reality thout [sic] the world'. *Rebel Worker*, another IWW paper, declared in July 1919: 'The Soviet is One Big Union and nothing else', while urging its readers to 'Line up with the Soviet both in theory and fact'.[14]

Although Lenin had forged his party in opposition to what he saw as social-democratic betrayals, he was not a syndicalist. The Bolsheviks advocated revolutionary political action. The paper printed the manifesto of the Communist International, but while critical of its emphasis on political action, it explained that 'in many European countries the state, the government, is the largest capitalist employer within its borders'. Underlying the difference on this issue was the proposition that the paper put to Communist sympathisers in the US: 'If you are really interested in establishing an American soviet, then you [should]

12 Murphy 1941, p. 129; *Industrial Pioneer*, June 1921; N. Bucharin and J. Bersin (Winter) for the Bureau of the Communist International, 'Parliamentarism, Soviet Power and the Creation of a Communist Party of America: Thesis of the Executive Committee of the Third International', undated [1919?], in Comintern archives, 515:1:1.

13 Charles Ashleigh, interviewed by Patrick Renshaw, 19 November 1965; *New Solidarity*, 28 December 1918; 11 January 1919; 18 January 1919.

14 *New Solidarity*, 1 March 1919; *Rebel Worker*, 15 July 1919, quoted in Anderson 1942, p. 53.

join the I.W.W.' While these differences could have been resolved through common work and discussion, in fact they exploded into hostility over the subsequent years. The only anticipation of this was in the writings of John Sandgren, editor of the IWW's Swedish-language newspaper; he denounced the Bolsheviks as 'very likely *radical political socialists*'.[15]

In August 1919, the General Executive Board (GEB) voted unanimously to organise 'a committee on international relations' to liaise with the Comintern because 'it was time for the I.W.W. to assume its proper place as the American unit of the Workers' Red International'. The motion also directed a barb against the newly formed Communist parties: it declared 'the I.W.W. the only revolutionary organization in the United States whose program is absolutely scientific and uncompromising' and 'the logical American unit of the Third International'. This motion seems to have gone nowhere.[16]

In January 1920, Zinoviev wrote to the IWW, urging them 'to rally to the Communist International, born in the dawn of the World Socialist Revolution', and 'to take the place to which your courage and revolutionary experience entitles you to in the front ranks of the proletarian Red Army fighting under the banner of Communism'. The letter appealed to the IWW as fellow revolutionaries 'to join the Communist International' and discard anarchist and syndicalist positions. Parliamentary cretinism was a hallmark of opportunist social democracy, but revolutionaries could not ignore politics. Zinoviev emphasised the need for a post-revolutionary state, the dictatorship of the proletariat, instead of abolishing the state at once. The letter was polemical, but friendly and comradely. It ended with the words: 'The Communist International extends a brotherly hand to the IWW'.[17]

It is important to take into account two characteristics of the IWW in this period. First, it was reeling from massive state repression, which left most of its historic leaders in jail. Second, as Ralph Darlington has stressed, the organisation was beset by internal divisions, which were deepened and extended by questions of how to deal with the Bolsheviks. The IWW did not receive Zinoviev's letter for several months. When Haywood read it, he declared: 'Here is what we have been dreaming about; here is the IWW all feathered out'. The February 1920 *One Big Union Monthly* reprinted an article by Trotsky, noting it had been sent to Haywood. The same issue contained an appeal by A. Lozovsky

15 *New Solidarity*, 1 February 1919; June 1919; August 1919.

16 *New Solidarity*, 27 September 1919.

17 *Communist* (UCP), 17 July 1920; *Solidarity*, 14 August 1920; *One Big Union Monthly*, September 1920. See also Degras 1956, I, pp. 71–4. George Hardy claimed that Zinoviev confirmed that the letter had been drafted by John Reed; see *Industrial Pioneer*, June 1921.

and other Russian Communists urging an international labour conference of socialist unions, with the following note by George Andreytchine: 'We are sure our organization will be there'.[18]

Support for the Bolsheviks did not always translate into IWW members' jettisoning their long-held syndicalist opposition to 'politics'. 'The Third International is one thing', the *One Big Union Monthly* wrote, 'and the Russian Revolution another'. Moreover, the IWW supported Lenin because he had made a revolution; they were often more hostile to his followers in the US, who could claim no such accomplishment. One article supported the Comintern's call for an International of unions; it granted that the *political* rule of the Bolsheviks was justified since the writer claimed that the Bolsheviks understood 'the dictatorship of the Communist Party in Russia is to be superseded as soon as possible by an industrial union administration'. However, the author emphasised: 'we do not fancy having a dictatorship exercised over us in the name of the proletariat by the leaders of American bolshevism, such as Fraina, Reed, Fergusson, Carney, Ruthenberg, Stoklitsky and others'.[19]

Indicating the pro-Bolshevik sentiments in the organisation, in August 1920 the GEB expelled with 'horror and disgust' their Philadelphia dockers' union upon discovering that some IWW stevedores there had loaded war materiel destined to Russian to be used against the Bolsheviks, 'our brave fellows in Russia who have established the first working class government in the world'. While *Solidarity* noted the expulsion, 'hold[ing] out the clean hand of brotherhood to the revolutionary workers of the world', the GEB rebuffed appeals by the UCP for joint work.[20]

George Hardy, an IWW leader who would later join the Communists, recalled that many Wobblies disagreed with anti-IWW polemics in the

18 On state repression against the IWW, see Renshaw 1968; Chaplin 1948, p. 288; George 1919, p. 2; *Solidarity*, 14 August 1921 and 21 August 1921; *One Big Union Monthly*, February 1920. Darlington 2008, p. 167; Haywood 1929, pp. 360–1. On the impact of the Zinoviev letter, see McEnroe 1960, pp. 347–63. On the reaction to the Bolsheviks among IWW prisoners, see Hardy 1956, pp. 82–3. George Iliev Andreytchine emigrated to the US in late 1913 and became a leading member of the IWW. In 1916, he was a leader of the Mesabi Iron Range strike in Minnesota, and was arrested and subjected to a lengthy attempt to deport him. For the first several months of 1920, he was an editor of *One Big Union Monthly*, *Solidarity*, and the Bulgarian-language *Workers' Thought*. Information on Andreytchine is taken from Baev and Grozev 2008. I am grateful to Professor Baev for providing an unpublished English translation.

19 *One Big Union Monthly*, April 1920; September 1920.

20 *Solidarity*, 14 August 1920. The local in question was atypical because of its largely black membership, as well as its less political posture; see Kimmeldorf 1999, pp. 61–4.

Communist press. In the words of the *One Big Union Monthly*: 'Like the Huns of old with Attila at their head these "massactionists" tried to overrun everything and throw themselves at the head of the labor movement, both in the world of thought and on the field of action'. Vladimir Lossieff, a former editor of the IWW Russian-language paper who had been convicted with Haywood in 1918 for anti-war activity, noted in the *Communist International* that 'all the distrust that the I.W.W. felt towards the Socialist parties, is transmitted to the Communist parties of America'. Reed also recalled being told: 'I am a Bolshevik, but not a Communist. A Communist is a member of a political party'.[21]

In May 1920, the IWW held a General Convention. According to Hardy—the meeting's chairman and soon to be voted General Secretary—the meeting unanimously approved affiliation with the Comintern, but with very little discussion. This allowed the divisions over Communism to fester. A combination of overenthusiastic and maladroit Communist polemics against the IWW, and a vehement anti-Communist campaign by Sandgren (then editor of the *One Big Union Monthly*), dampened pro-Communist sympathies. An internal Communist report a year later described this referendum as 'premature' and criticised 'the executives of the two communist parties in America, knowing little of the peculiar conditions in the ranks of the I.W.W.' who 'attempted to influence the membership by ill-advised publication of manifestos and articles of a dictatorial and antagonistic nature', which 'considerably impeded' the efforts of pro-Bolshevik Wobblies.[22]

In a debate over the course of some months, Sandgren, H.F. Kane (editor of the Seattle-based *Industrial Worker*) and the newly-elected General Executive Board all opposed affiliation. *One Big Union Monthly* ran a stream of anti-Bolshevik and anti-Communist articles, describing American Communism as 'largely a provocateur movement manipulated by the United States Department of Justice' and retailing stories of 'bolshevik atrocities' towards workers. Sandgren's hostility was so intense that when Hardy visited Europe in 1921, he reported being asked about it.[23]

On the other hand, *Solidarity* supported affiliation so fervently that, to one historian at least, it 'seemed during this period to belong to a different organization'. In late August 1920, the GEB defeated a motion to endorse the

21 On the UCP's approach to the IWW, see McEnroe 1960, pp. 364–5; *One Big Union Monthly*, May 1920; Lossieff 1921; Reed 1920.

22 Hardy 1956, pp. 129–31. Hammer, Stanton and Evans, with the cooperation of Dixon [Browder], 'Confidential Report on the IWW' [1921], Comintern archives, 515:1:81. Sandgren's anti-Communism can be seen in *New Solidarity*, 1 February 1919.

23 On the difference between the new and old GEB, see McEnroe 1960, pp. 356–7; *One Big Union Monthly*, July 1920, December 1920; *Industrial Pioneer*, June 1921.

Comintern, instead moving to 'not endorse the Third International officially', underlining that their anti-political 'position makes it impossible' to support the view as 'outlined in the Zinovieff appeal'. The GEB endorsed the Third International 'with reservations' because they would 'take no part in parliamentary action whatsoever and that we reserve the right to develop our own tactics according to conditions prevailing'. The GEB unanimously decided to submit the resolutions to the general membership. Unconditional affiliation to the Comintern failed, 602 votes to 1658, but conditional affiliation passed. Ironically, the IWW had taken a position similar to that of the SP, although for different reasons.[24]

Fights Over 'Dual Unionism'

As Communists were trying to recruit members of the IWW, the Comintern was waging a fight with their American comrades over their aversion to work within 'reactionary' unions like the AFL. In 1919, the Bolsheviks had not taken a position during the debate over this issue at the founding congress of the Comintern. Boris Reinstein argued against leaving established unions, stressing that despite the betrayals of Gompers and his ilk, the 'problem is to free the union movement from the disastrous influence of these capitalist flunkies'. A year later, however, in preparation for the Second Comintern Congress, Lenin wrote his pamphlet, *'Left Wing' Communism, An Infantile Disorder*; this was originally published in the US under the title: *Should Communists Participate in Reactionary Trade Unions?*. To win the mass of workers to Communism, Lenin stressed, revolutionaries 'must absolutely *work wherever the masses are to be found*'. Lenin did not dispute the anti-Communist, class-collaborationist nature of the trade-union bureaucracy, even quoting favourably Daniel De Leon's 'profoundly true' description of the AFL leaders as 'labour lieutenants of the capitalist class'. Nonetheless, Lenin argued that the best place to defeat such leaders was *inside* the unions they led, because they counted large numbers of workers as members.[25]

Zinoviev and Radek, in the call for the Second Congress, invited the IWW and other revolutionary syndicalists. There was no delegate from the American

24 Gambs 1932, p. 80; *Solidarity*, 28 August 1920; *One Big Union Monthly*, September 1920; October 1920.

25 For Reinstein's report, see Riddell 1987, pp. 139–41; Reis 1964, pp. 14–15. Lenin 1922; Lenin 1966d, p. 53. In fact, De Leon did not invent the phrase, but borrowed it from a leading Republican operative, Mark Hanna.

IWW, although Wobblies from other countries did attend.[26] Several times in his report, Zinoviev criticised the IWW for their position that revolutionary unions, and not a revolutionary political party, were necessary to make a workers' revolution. The 'Theses on Parliamentarism' also contained a polemic on the need for Communists to engage in political work, even standing for elections, so long as this were done in a revolutionary and not opportunistic manner. American and British delegates objected to Lenin's suggestions in *'Left Wing' Communism* that Communists work in reactionary-led unions and affiliate with the British Labour Party. During the Congress, Reed repeatedly tried to have English replace French as an official language to facilitate the discussion, and tried to avoid giving a presentation on the oppression of black people in the US to focus on the trade-union issue. When the trade-union question came up for discussion, English was adopted as an official language.[27]

The resolution on the trade-union question under discussion stated:

> Bearing in mind the rush of the enormous working masses into the trades unions, and also the objective revolutionary character of the economic struggle which those masses are carrying on in spite of the trade union bureaucracy, the Communists must join such unions in all countries, in order to make of them efficient organs of the struggle for the suppression of capitalism. They must initiate the forming of trades unions where these do not exist. All voluntary withdrawals from the industrial movement, every artificial attempt to organize special unions ... represents a great danger to the Communist movement.[28]

Radek gave a report in defence of the theses, after a frustrating discussion with the Americans, particularly Reed. Radek noted that since the end of the war, the trade unions had grown, but that workers were joining 'the big trades unions', not revolutionary unions like the IWW. He underlined the importance of the struggle for higher wages, even if it was not revolutionary. He allowed that since most workers in the US were unorganised and the AFL was hostile to organising unskilled workers, it was necessary to form new unions.

26 Riddell 1991, I, p. 69. IWW members from Australia, Britain and Ireland attended; see Ridell 1991, II, pp. 839–43. According to *One Big Union Monthly* (December 1920), 'The I.W.W. had no accredited representative ... and if anyone appeared as our accredited representative for this particular occasion, he was an imposter'.

27 *Second Congress* 1977, II, pp. 2, 46, 50, 82; II, pp. 2, 51. Reed's note to Lenin, with Lenin's handwritten reply, fms AM 1091:533, John S. Reed papers, Houghton Library, Harvard University.

28 *Second Congress* 1977, II, p. 279.

His report recognised that there was 'in the IWW an organization which is setting to work on this task'. Yet he returned to the theme of the AFL: 'we must not only attack capitalism through the new organizations, we must also go into the [American] Federation of Labor'. He declared 'the AF of L is itself in a process of change' and 'no longer a uniform block'. He concluded the section on the US by emphasising, 'there is no tactical interest that requires us to be obstinate and refuse to go into the AF of L'.[29]

Reed opposed Radek's report. He agreed that the IWW would not soon supplant the AFL, and granted that 'as an organisation, the I.W.W. will never be able to gain the majority of the workers'. But this was not decisive. As he argued in his article in the *Communist International*:

> But as a propaganda centre, as a destructive and revolutionary force, it is one of the chief agents in wrecking the great American Federation of Labour, in reaching and making class conscious vast proletarian masses, and for fifteen years it has held aloft with unflinching heroism the ideal of the overthrow of capitalism, an example to the workers everywhere.

Reed argued that since the AFL had not organised the majority of American workers either, there should be a combination of independent unions and work within the AFL. He regarded Radek's position as contradicting the Bolsheviks' earlier overtures to the IWW.[30]

Fraina was also a delegate at the Congress. In the 1930s, after he had left the Communist Party, Fraina claimed that he had broken from a dual-unionist position upon reading Lenin's *Left-Wing Communism*. At the Congress, he staked out a middle ground between Radek and Reed. He argued that the value of the IWW was not that the union actually organised any workers, but that the Wobblies 'expressed the awakening of consciousness and action of the great masses of unorganized and unskilled workers excluded from the American Federation of Labor'. He agreed that Communists should work within the AFL, but argued that since 80 percent of American workers were in no unions, and the AFL refused to organise them, Communists should try to organise the unorganised into new unions. In his report on the conference, Fraina claimed that he helped amend Radek's theses, along with J.T. Murphy, to reflect this.[31]

29 Radek's report, during the Ninth Session, is found in *Second Congress*, II, pp. 61–76.

30 Reed 1920; Reis 1964, pp. 54–5.

31 For Fraina's subsequent recollection, see Lewis Corey (Fraina) to Granville Hicks, 30 December 1935, Corey papers, box 1; for Fraina's speech at the Congress, and his report on it, see *Communist* (CPA), April 1921.

Further underscoring the openness to debate in the early Comintern, Reed passed a note to Lenin during the conference:

> I object to Radek's assertion that we have tried to sabotage the work of the Commission on Trade Unionism. That sort of remark takes the place of argument with Comrade Radek, because, knowing very little about Trade Unionism, he naturally has no attitude on the question. This is the real explanation.

Reed told Alfred Rosmer, a former French syndicalist on the ECCI and a leader in the campaign to recruit syndicalists: 'We cannot go back to America with a decision like that. In the trade unions [in the United States] the Communist International has supporters and sympathy only among the Industrial Workers of the World, and you're sending us to the American Federation of Labour where it has nothing but implacable enemies'. In the end, even though Radek conceded that building independent unions might be possible if the existing trade-union leadership refused to organise certain workers or expelled Communists, Reed lost the battle: the trade-union commission endorsed Radek, 57 to 8.[32]

Opposing Radek meant opposing Zinoviev and Lenin. But rather than punish Reed for his dissent, the Comintern's leadership nominated him for the ECCI. At this point, the Comintern valued political debate, not rigid centralisation. Lenin's notes make it clear that he wanted to bend over backward to ensure that British and American syndicalists 'should remain affiliated to the Third International', despite his differences with them.[33]

The Third Congress and the Profintern

The importance of the trade unions for Communist strategy increased by the Third Congress in 1921, since revolution in the West was not immediately posed and there was a greater need to methodically win over the working class. In a letter to Zinoviev in the lead-up to the Congress, Lenin asserted: 'The tactics of the Communist International should be based on a steady and systematic drive to win the *majority of the working class*, first and foremost *within the old trade unions*'. One aspect of this was the Red International of Labour Unions (RILU) or Profintern. The Profintern was organised, under the leadership of

32 Note from John Reed to Lenin during meeting of executive committee, in John S. Reed papers, fms AM 1091:557; Rosmer 1971, p. 74; Rosenstone 1975, pp. 373–6; Reis, pp. 56–9.

33 Lenin 1969a, p. 202.

veteran Bolshevik A. Lozovsky, to realise the call from the Second Congress for 'an international centre for the trade union movement which, together with the Communist International, will make one whole, single block'. In July 1921, 380 delegates from 41 countries attended the first Profintern Congress.[34]

One resolution at the first Profintern Congress, put forward by Lozovsky, described the leadership of the AFL as 'direct agents of capital' and 'a classic example' of the 'fusion of working-class leaders with the bourgeois state'. At the same time, the IWW was 'still too weak to replace the old unions' and imbued with 'purely anarchist prejudices against politics and political struggle'. Communists in the US needed 'to form revolutionary groups and cells in the heart of the AFL and independent unions' with the goal of 'conquering the working masses in America' through 'systematic struggle in the heart of these unions'. Lozovsky added that 'the more the IWW is isolated from the masses, the more aloof their organisations will be, the longer and slower the development of class consciousness among the American proletariat'. Thus, the 'coordination and unity of action within AFL locals affiliated' to the Profintern was obligatory for the IWW. The IWW representatives at the Congress resented this, decrying what they saw as the Comintern's plan to 'liquidate the revolutionary labor organizations in the conservative labor bodies of various countries'.[35]

Much of the efforts to build the Profintern were directed towards syndicalists. Many former syndicalists, such as Alfred Rosmer, Tom Mann, J.T. Murphy, Andreu Nin and Joaquín Maurín, were active in it. The Profintern and Comintern sought to recruit prominent Wobblies. In January 1921, in the run up to both the Third Comintern Congress and the First Profintern Congress, the ECCI addressed a letter to the 'comrades and fellow workers' of the IWW. It asserted that 'our greetings to you [are] a recognition that your historic position entitles you to a place in the front ranks of the revolutionary army of labor'. The letter again spelled out the central disagreements between the Comintern and the IWW: the question of political action and the need for

34 Lenin to Zinoviev in 1969a, pp. 320–1; the call for the Profintern in August 1920 is in Degras 1956, I, p. 187. On the first Profintern conference, see Chambelland 1964. On the early years of the Profintern, see Murphy 1941, pp. 157–8; E.H. Carr 1966, pp. 395–8; Degras 1956, I, p. 274. On Lozovsky, see Ro'i 2010. Lozovsky (rendered in the 1920s 'Losovsky') was a pseudonym for Solomon Abramovich Dridzo.

35 Lozovsky, 'Les taches et la tactique des syndicats' and 'La question d'organisation', in *Résolutions et Décisions* 1921, pp. 24–5, 50. The *Voice of Labor* carried regular coverage of the discussion at the Profintern Congress in its summer 1921 issues; Morray 1983, pp. 76–7; Cascaden 1922, p. 34.

a proletarian state. The letter concluded: 'You must dethrone the Gompers machine and drive them into oblivion'.[36]

In an interview in the 1960s, Charles Ashleigh bemoaned that 'there were so few people with the ability to the make the R.I.L.U. demands known' to rank-and-file Wobblies. Still, the American Communists attempted to convince the IWW to affiliate with the Profintern and ally with the Bolsheviks. In 1921, a 'Confidential Report on the IWW' proposed the 'Formation of communist nuclei' and 'the carrying on of communist propaganda' inside the IWW, as well as advocating 'Affiliation with the Red Labor International'. The report also proposed 'the placing of communists in important appointive and elective positions in the I.W.W.' This included the central IWW headquarters, as well as the editorship of the *Industrial Unionist*, the New York IWW paper.[37]

One noticeable change was the Chicago-based *One Big Union Monthly*. Under Sandgren, it had become increasingly anti-Communist. In January 1921, the GEB removed him from the editorship because of 'so many complaints coming into the General Office' about articles 'severely criticising and condemning in rash language and on objectionable evidence certain activities and tactics of the Russian Bolsheviki and other revolutionary organizations'. The next month, the paper's name was changed to *Industrial Pioneer*. Its columns became pro-Communist. The first issue of the new paper, for example, reprinted Lozovsky's call for the Profintern with a positive note by Andreytchine. The March issue contained a commemoration by Andreytchine of the Paris Commune that commented that the Communards, 'just like their Russian comrades', had needed to create a workers' state. The article criticised the Communards for lacking a 'directing dominant party'.[38] The April issue even advocated that Wobblies not ignore rank-and-file members of the AFL and 'get into other labor organizations and try to win them over to the I.W.W. bodily'. The May issue contained a letter by Hardy that labelled the IWW 'mainly a Marxian organization'. The June issue contained Hardy's report to the IWW's Thirteenth Convention that told of his meetings with Lenin and

36 ECCI letter to 'Comrades and Fellow Workers', 25 January 1921, in Comintern archives, 515:1:38.

37 Ashleigh interview with Renshaw, p. 16; Stanton *et al.*, 'Confidential Report on the IWW', Comintern archives, 515:1:81. One of the indicated supporters, 'Hammer', was instructed to 'continuously write for Bulgarian and English I.W.W. press'. This was likely Andreytchine, who a year earlier had resigned as editor of *Solidarity* to edit the Bulgarian IWW paper (according to *Solidarity*, 24 April 1920).

38 These attributes are even more pronounced when compared to a previous article on the Commune by Andreytchine in the March 1920 *New Solidarity*.

Zinoviev. By this time, the journal looked like a Communist paper, reprinting articles by leading Bolsheviks (such as Radek) and using graphics similar to those in Comintern papers.

In early 1921, Haywood, Andreytchine and anarchist-turned-Communist Robert Minor spoke at an IWW meeting in New York City on the IWW and the Russian Revolution. Haywood advocated sending representatives to the upcoming Profintern gathering, arguing that American workers should 'stop signing contracts with your bosses and make a contract with the workers of Russia who have done and are doing everything possible to accomplish their freedom and our own'. Andreytchine stressed that Wobblies 'must not allow our name to be linked with the enemies of the workers of Russia'. Neither saw a contradiction between the syndicalism of the IWW and the Communism of the Bolsheviks.[39]

Shortly after this meeting, the Supreme Court refused to review the conviction of scores of IWW members in the 1918 Espionage Act trial. Haywood, Andreytchine and Lossieff, each facing 20 years' imprisonment, fled the US with seven other convicted IWW members. Haywood and Andreytchine, at least, attended the Profintern Congress. While Haywood's support lent prestige to the Bolsheviks, in the short-term, his leaving damaged IWW-Communist relations. He and those who escaped with him forfeited tens of thousands of dollars in bonds, and anti-Communist IWW leaders seized on this. 'Haywood has committed hari-kari so far as the labor movement is concerned if he really has run away', Haywood's attorney told the *New York Times*, adding: 'He will be disowned by the I.W.W. and all sympathizers'. A year later, the IWW complained that it held 'the Communist Party and the Soviet government responsible for the payment of the money which has been forfeited by William D. Haywood'.[40]

39 The meeting is described in *Industrial Unionist*, 1 April 1921, a copy of which (inscribed by Haywood) is in the Comintern archives, 515:1:83. Baev and Grozev 2008, Part 1, p. 49, cite an FBI report that Andreytchine, Minor, Haywood and Charles Ashleigh spoke at a mass meeting in New York on 28 March 1921.

40 *New York Times*, 12 April 1921, 22 April 1921; see also articles in the 21 April 1921 editions of the *New York Call*, *New York Journal*, and *New York Evening Post*, all in David Karsner papers, box 1, folder 5; Darlington 2008, p. 169; Renshaw 1968, p. 70. John Grady to Mont Schuyler, 11 August 1921 and John Grady to William D. Haywood, 31 August 1922, both in Comintern archives, 515:1:158. The *New York Times* states Haywood's bonds were worth $15,000. Grady, the IWW's General Secretary-Treasurer, lists a higher amount, although this is presumably for both Haywood and Andreytchine. The *One Big Union Monthly* (March 1920) described Haywood as free on $15,000 bond, and Andreytchine and Lossieff free on bonds of $10,000 each. *Industrial Pioneer* (June 1921) claimed that nine IWW members had forfeited their bonds, worth a total of $65,000, of which $20,000 was held by the IWW itself.

In May 1921, after Haywood left the US, the Thirteenth Convention of the IWW rejected affiliation with the Profintern. However, over the objections of more anti-Communist Wobblies, the union did send an official delegate to the Congress, George Williams. He did not represent the previous, pro-Bolshevik leadership, but the new, anti-Communist leaders. Williams was 'instructed to stand firm on all issues dividing syndicalists from Bolsheviks', according to historian Ralph Darlington.[41]

Another American with IWW experience was Reinstein, who worked with Karl Radek in the Foreign Ministry's bureau for revolutionary propaganda abroad. Reinstein was not the most effective instrument to recruit Wobblies. By 1922, Reinstein had not lived in the US for almost five years. He had been a member of the Workers' International Industrial Union—the so-called 'Detroit IWW'—a split from the IWW led by Daniel De Leon over political action. Thus his opposition to dual unionism and his support to political parties clashed with most IWW members' views. Furthermore, his role in the 1912 Passaic, New Jersey, textile strike—when he clashed with the official IWW leaders—made him anathema to Wobblies. Haywood and Andreytchine, along with other members of the 'Communist Caucus', including Browder, Hourwich and Minor, signed a letter to Lozovsky protesting against Reinstein's appointment as manager of the American section of the Profintern after the Congress.[42]

See also Dubofsky 1969, pp. 459–60. On the IWW Convention, see the *Industrial Pioneer*, June 1921, reprinted in Kornbluth, p. 324. Haywood's situation was unenviable. Suffering from diabetes, the serving of his sentence may have meant dying in prison. His life in Russia, while preferable to prison, was marked by alcoholism and alienation in a country where he did not speak the language. While he was treated well by the Bolsheviks, he apparently was not particularly productive (with the exception of conceiving of the ILD, which is dealt with below). Haywood died in 1928 in poor health. See Darcy's memoirs for a description of Haywood's time in Moscow. There is no evidence that the Soviet government induced Haywood to flee, although they did not stop it. Charles Ashleigh, in 1965, noted that he thought 'it was a mistake for him to go, but I did not think so at the time and I was once consulted and I said, "Yes let him go"'; Ashleigh interview by Renshaw, p. 15. Andreytchine and Lossieff, being Bulgarian and Russian, respectively, and in better health, were better able to integrate into Soviet society.

41 Darlington 2008, p. 192. Boris Souvarine, who sided with the Communists, described Williams as 'particulièrement incompétent, et faisant pauvre figure à côte d'un Haywood, d'un Andreytchine (qui n'avient pas le mandat)'; Souvarine to Pierre Monatte, 9 August 1921, in Chambelland 1964, p. 41.

42 Baev and Grosev 2008, Section 2, p. 2; letter from the Communist Caucus of the American RILU delegation to Lozovsky, 7 August 1921, in Comintern archives, 515:1:80. On Reinstein and the IWW, see Ebner 1970.

At the Profintern Congress, the Bolsheviks put forward two perspectives that alienated syndicalists. First, they argued that the RILU be connected with the Comintern, offending the 'non-political' views of many syndicalists. Second, they continued to stress Communist work within non-communist unions and emphasised the differences between trade unions and revolutionary parties. This caused a split in the delegates between the majority of delegates who supported the Profintern, and anti-Communist syndicalists. A minority, centred on delegates from Argentina, France, Germany, the Netherlands and the US (which included the IWW's Williams), met in Berlin after the Profintern Congress to organise an anti-Profintern syndicalist bureau.[43]

Many American delegates, even in the 'Communist Caucus', still opposed 'boring from within'. Haywood argued that it was 'absolutely impossible to carry on any work inside the Federation [AFL], so reactionary is it'. He went so far as to blame the 'institutional paralysis which exists in Russia' on the absence of an IWW-type group in tsarist Russia that could have trained workers 'in the technical and industrial control of industry'. For Haywood, the AFL was 'the buffer organisation of capitalism' that had 'never during ... nearly forty years of existence ... done a single thing in the interests of the Working Class'. Haywood was vehement in his private criticism of the Profintern position. He denounced the 'majority of the American Delegation' as an anti-IWW 'reactionary outpost' that planned to 'return to the U.S. against I.W.W.' Until his death in exile in 1928, Haywood opposed this position.[44]

Against Haywood, Bedacht—whose origins were in the Socialist Party and not the trade unions—argued that 'Gompers, as well as the Industrial Workers of the World, wished and still wish one thing: that the revolutionary workers should leave the trade unions, i.e., they pursue the one and the same reactionary project'. In a letter to Communists in the United States, Bukharin, Radek and Kuusinen stressed:

> It is unthinkable ... that a colossal trade union organisation such as the American Federation of Labor could be composed entirely of enemies of the working class, as are such organisations like the Ku Klux Klan or the various professional strike-breaking bodies. Here a strict distinction must

43 Williams 1922; Cascaden 1922; Tosstorff 2000a; Thorpe 1989; McEnroe 1960, pp. 375–8.

44 *Third Congress*, pp. 141–2; Haywood 1921; W.D.H. [Haywood] to Chas E. Scott, 10 August 1921, in Lovestone papers, box 195, folder 12; Johanningsmeier 2001, pp. 164–6. A description of his last years in Moscow is provided in the unpublished memoirs of Sam Darcy, an American representative to the Comintern in 1927–28: see 'The Storm Must Be Ridden' (1945?), in Sam A. Darcy papers, box 3, folder 16.

> always be made between the reactionary traitorous leadership and the unconscious petty-bourgeois-minded mass which we have to win.

The letter described recruiting 'the best elements of the I.W.W.' as the Communists' 'special duty'. However, it also underlined the importance of Communists intersecting the working class, via such means as pursuing electoral activity, publishing a daily English-language paper and emerging from illegality. The party's chief task in the labour movement was to 'immediately advanc[e] the slogan of a united front for Labour, as for instance, for the protection of the unemployed'. Such an approach, like the united-front tactic developed at the Third Congress, was designed to either effect class struggle to benefit the workers, or to undermine the authority of Gompers and other labour leaders if they refused.[45]

The party continued to try to recruit Wobblies. In August 1921, after the Profintern Congress, the party's representative to the ECCI claimed that due to a 'special drive', Communists had 'succeeded in winning to the Party ranks almost all of the best known leaders' of the IWW. He bragged that 'Communist nuclei are so strong in the I.W.W. that the capture of the organization is likely to come at an early date'. In November, the minutes of the CEC note that some 25,000 copies of the Profintern's resolutions and appeals had been distributed amongst the IWW, and that 'things [were] coming to head in the I.W.W.'[46]

In fact, the union's hostility towards the Communists hardened. This reflected political differences over political action and work within the AFL, and fears among IWW leaders that affiliation with the Bolsheviks would destroy their autonomy. In Moscow, Williams, the official IWW delegate, was hostile to the Bolsheviks. He asserted that 'the trade unions are not merely tools in the hands of the government for the capture of power; their purpose is the realization of immediate control over production in the factories and the workshops'. When he returned from Europe, Williams wrote a pamphlet against the Bolsheviks and the RILU.[47]

In December 1921, the GEB refused to affiliate with either the Comintern or the Profintern, and denounced working within the AFL or political action.

45 *Voice of Labor*, 19 August 1921; Bukharin, Radek and Kuusinen, 'Concerning the Next Tasks of the CP of A' 1921, in Comintern archives, 515:1:138; 'Theses on the United Front For Labour', *Bulletin of the Executive Committee of the Communist International*, 7 July 1922.

46 Murphy 1921; George Baldwin, 'Statement of the Communist Party of America to ECCI', August 1921, in Comintern archives, 515:1:39; CEC minutes, 3/9 November 1921, in Comintern archives, 515:1:51.

47 *Voice of Labor*, 28 October 1921; Williams 1922.

Noting that since the Communists advocated 'liquidating' dual unionists, 'the G.E.B. does not expect the I.W.W. will care to be a party to a carefully conceived plot for its own destruction', the GEB declared it 'impossible to cooperate with the Communist Party of America'. Several months later (in a letter to the Berlin syndicalists), the GEB declared that the Profintern that had 'at first promised a glorious future to the international proletariat, has proven abortive and has dwindled to insignificance and is now in a state of rapid disintegration'. It called the RILU a tool of the Russian Communists, and the majority of American delegates to its founding conference 'dummies who represented no labor organization ... with no other intention than to control the Congress' for the Communists.[48]

In the end, the IWW did not affiliate with the Berlin syndicalists. However, the defeat of the proposal to affiliate with the Bolsheviks blocked the systematic recruitment of Wobblies. This bitter divorce harmed both sides. In the *Voice of Labor* (a legal paper run by the underground Communist Party), Andreytchine denounced the IWW leadership and called Williams an 'informer'. 'We feel confident that the honest revolutionists in the I.W.W.', he wrote, 'will wipe out the blot on its name by the present Executive Board and lead the organization to the road of Social Revolution'. *Voice of Labor* published a letter by Lozovsky to the IWW, which denounced Williams's book as 'so full of lies, that a complete reply to it would be useless'. It reiterated the standard Communist criticism of the IWW leadership, and appealed for Wobblies to attend the second Profintern congress. The paper's introduction stated that 'the I.W.W. has degenerated into a burlesque' with an incompetent and anti-communist leadership.[49]

The IWW in 1921 was a shadow of its former self, having been devastated by repression and led by different leaders than in 1914 or 1905. Many IWW prisoners—representing these earlier leaders—supported the Bolsheviks. As Andreytchine noted in spring 1921, 'many of our members have left the organization, many of those who had spent years working for the I.W.W. have dropped out discouraged'. The remaining IWW membership was more anti-Communist and anti-political than those who had left. After the Profintern Congress, Andreytchine described the IWW as 'passing through a crisis;

48 Letter from GEB to Delegates of the International Syndicalist Congress, 1 June 1922, appended to IWW *General Office Bulletin* [1922] in Comintern archives, 515:1:158; see also Darlington 2008, pp. 192–3.

49 On the IWW's decision not to affiliate with the Berlin syndicalists, see *Agricultural Workers Industrial Union No. 110 of the I.W.W. Bulletin*, 22 November 1922, in Comintern archives, 515:1:158; *Voice of Labor*, 7 April 1922, 13 October 1922.

a process of dissolution, a profound crisis in its very existence as a revolutionary organization'.[50]

In 1928, Cannon recalled that it was tragic that the party had 'allowed so many good proletarian fighters in the west to fall into the hands of syndicalists and anarcho-syndicalists' because it 'had not learned to combine the ideological fight against syndicalism with the task of fighting side by side with the syndicalistic workers and winning them to the Party'. In his history of American Communism decades later, Cannon described the 'failure of the main [IWW] cadres to become integrated in the new movement for the Communist Party in this country' as 'a historical miscarriage which could have been prevented', since 'in their practice, and partly also in their theory, the Wobblies were closer to Lenin's Bolsheviks than any other group in this country'.[51]

Continued Communist Attempts to Recruit Wobblies

Communists did not stop trying to recruit IWW members. From Moscow, Haywood sent letters to his former comrades urging support for the Profintern. Hardy, who had visited Moscow and met Lenin, returned to the US via London and organised a tour with Jack Tanner, a former British syndicalist who became a Communist, to win Wobblies. After the GEB forbade him from speaking, he continued to help organise a pro-Communist 'minority movement within the I.W.W.' and published *Unity Bulletin* to advance this view. He recalled that anti-Communist forces responded with violence and gangsterism. In January 1922, the GEB threatened to withdraw bail money it had provided when he and other Wobblies had been arrested; this would have subjected Hardy (who was English) to immediate arrest and deportation. Finally, in early 1922, the IWW expelled Hardy, the union's former General Secretary, making it (according to Hardy) the first North American union to expel Communists.[52]

The repeated votes within the IWW indicate significant pro-Communist sympathies, despite the leadership's hostility. In 1922, Cannon wrote to all editors of party publications about a campaign to refute anti-Bolshevik attacks by the IWW and Emma Goldman. In February 1923, Cannon advocated a united-front approach to the IWW. He described a presentation he gave in Chicago

50 *Industrial Unionist*, 1 April 1921, in the Comintern archives, 515:1:83; *Voice of Labor*, 21 October 1921.

51 Cannon at Ninth W(C)P Plenum, 5 February 1928, in Lovestone Papers, box 213, folder 7; Cannon 1962, p. 302.

52 Chaplin 1948, p. 333; Hardy 1956, pp. 131, 141, 145–7.

to an audience containing many Wobblies. He polemicised against their 'syndicalist nonsense' while 'demanding of them a united front in the struggle in *spite* of these differences'. The IWW contained 'real militant workers' who had become 'prejudiced and embittered against Communists'. Minutes exist from a meeting in April 1923 between the Trade Union Educational League (TUEL, dealt with in the next chapter) and a Communist fraction in the IWW, attesting to continued efforts to recruit Wobblies (and the difficulties in doing so).[53]

The Comintern continued to pressure the CP to recruit Wobblies. In May 1923, Ruthenberg described the leadership of the IWW, 'which now has the support of a great majority of that organization', as 'hostile to Soviet Russia, to the Red International and to the Communist International'. He urged the Comintern to refrain from giving them 'ammunition to be used against us'. In November, Foster claimed that the party had 'very few connections in the I.W.W., almost none in fact', because 'practically all comrades with Communist leanings quit the I.W.W.' Foster (by then in charge of the party's industrial work) described trying to 'colonize the organization with our militants' by sending 30 members 'to go back into the I.W.W. and try to win control there'.[54]

This orientation continued for several years. Thus Cannon sent a form letter in April 1924 to Communists in the IWW soliciting information on the attitudes of Wobblies and stressing the importance of winning over its ranks to Communism. In 1924–6, Foster's TUEL members worked in the IWW's agricultural workers' and sailors' unions. In early 1926, for example, Harrison George, in the context of a Pan-American seamen's conference called by the IWW, recalled 'working within it to bring it closer to the Red International'. That September, the minutes of the national committee of the TUEL detailed the organisational disarray of the IWW and the planned Communist intervention into the union. By early 1927, the minutes indicated that the 'I.W.W. is so dead that it cannot stir up an effective faction fight'. Nonetheless, through to at least 1928, the party maintained nuclei in the IWW.[55]

53 James P. Cannon to Charles Johnson, 14 February 1923, Comintern archives, 534:7:464; James P. Cannon, 'To All Party Editors', 27 May 1922, in Comintern archives, 515:1:146; 'Joint Meeting of T.C. [Temporary Committee] for W.U. [Working-Class Unity] and T.U.E.L. for Reorganizing the Minority for Work in the I.W.W.', in Comintern archives, 515:1:246.

54 C.E. Ruthenberg to W. Kolaroff, 16 May 1923, in Comintern archives, 515:1:201; Foster to Lozovsky, 1 November 1923, in Comintern archives, 515:1:245.

55 The form letter, dated 1 April 1924, is in Comintern archives, 515:1:285. On pro-Bolshevik support, see Cannon, 'The IWW and the Red International of Labor', *The Worker*, 1 December 1922, and 'The IWW Convention', *Labor Herald*, January 1924, in Cannon 1992, pp. 183–95. For TUEL work in the agricultural workers' and seamen's unions, see H. George to Lozovsky, 22 October 1925; 1 December 1925, and 25 December 1925, in Comintern

The Communist Party recruited a significant number of ex-Wobblies. By 1932, one historian estimated that as many as 2,000 IWW members had joined the CP, some ten to twenty percent of party membership. Many of these were IWW cadres or leaders, not rank-and-file members. In addition to Cannon, a former IWW organiser, Hardy, the former General Secretary, and one-time IWW member Foster, the list includes Ashleigh, Roy Brown, Harrison George, Harold Harvey, George Mink and Vernon Smith. Elizabeth Gurley Flynn worked closely with the party in the mid-1920s, finally joining it a decade later. Flynn—probably like other former Wobblies—came closer to the party through the International Labor Defense (ILD), organised by Cannon to defend 'class-war prisoners', including many Wobblies.[56]

Many East European Wobblies joined the Communists and a significant number returned to Europe. Andreytchine remained in Moscow with Haywood and Lossieff, and was selected to the Profintern's six-member Executive Bureau (headed by Lozovsky). Andreytchine was a Soviet diplomat in the interwar period, and returned to Bulgaria after World War II. Bill Shatoff, a Russian anarchist who was active in the IWW, returned to Russia and helped in the construction of railroads in Siberia. A.M. Krasnoschekov, a high Bolshevik functionary in Siberia shortly after the Revolution, had also been an IWW member. Finnish IWW leaders, such as Leo Lauki and William Tanner, joined the CP along with between 'a few hundred' and a thousand Finnish American Wobblies. According to Ashleigh, 'some of those Finnish newspapers and so on later moved on bodily into the Communist Party'. Ashleigh himself, the English socialist-turned-Wobbly, had joined the Communists while in Leavenworth with other IWW prisoners. Upon his release in early 1922, he was deported, and was active in the Profintern in Moscow and Germany, and remained in the British Communist Party until his death.[57]

These recruits indicate the calibre of many Wobblies. Those syndicalists who did join, although few in number, contributed to the richness and

archives, 515:1:246; Harrison George to James N. Soger, 2 January 1926, in Bertram D. Wolfe Papers, box 4; see also Saposs 1926, pp. 177–8; TUEL National Committee Minutes, 21 September 1926 and 17 January 1927, in Earl Browder Papers, series 2–150; Cannon, speech at Ninth W(C)P Plenum, Lovestone papers, box 213, folder 7.

56 Gambs 1932, pp. 88–9; Gambs's estimate is derived from 'guesses, based on conversations of both organizations'; Kostiainen 1978, pp. 64, 128–37; Camp 1995, p. 122; Tosstorff 2000b.

57 On Shatoff, see *New York Times*, 9 March 1930; on Andreytchine, see Baev and Grozev 2008 as well as *Voice of Labor*, 27 January and 17 February 1922 on his deportation; on Krasnoschekov, see Liu 2000, p. 171; Ashleigh's history, including his work with the Comintern, is described in his interviews deposited in the Nuffield College Library, Oxford, and Wayne State University Library. Ashleigh interview by Renshaw, p. 8.

strength of the early Communist movement, complementing former Socialists and foreign-language militants. This cross-fertilisation made the movement more vital.

Yet they also indicate the *individual* nature of this recruitment. There were also failures. Cannon recalled spending hours arguing with Vincent St. John about Communism, and while coming close to recruiting him, he ultimately failed. Cannon speculated that had the Communists been able to recruit St. John and his followers, it 'could have made a big difference in everything that went on in the CP in the Twenties'. According to Cannon, 'a fast-moving situation, a number of untoward circumstances, combined with the inadequacy of the American communist leadership, barred the way' for the mass of IWW cadres to fuse with the Communists.[58]

This is explained in part by the massive repression against the IWW that had destroyed much of the union and left it in disarray. The inexperience and mistakes of the young Communist movement militated against Communist efforts. What is clear, however, is that this failure to 'Americanise' the party cannot be blamed on the Bolsheviks or the Communist International. Perhaps, as Ralph Darlington has argued, Zinoviev and Radek were 'patronising' and engaged in 'sectarian bullying' towards syndicalists, especially when compared to Lenin's patience.[59] Still, the Comintern repeatedly reached out to the syndicalists, including the IWW, respectful of their experience and authority while underlining political differences. But neither the American Communists nor the IWW was able to consummate a fusion.

58 Cannon 1962, pp. 303, 305–7. On the importance of the early syndicalist recruits to the CP, see the Prometheus Research Library's introduction to Cannon 1992.

59 Darlington 2008, pp. 195–6.

CHAPTER 4

William Z. Foster and the Turn Towards the Labour Movement

In the lead-up to the Profintern's founding, Cannon suggested that Browder be enlisted to find suitable American delegates. In May, Browder bragged in a letter to Trotsky that 'it was within the realm of possibility in the immediate future for the Communists of America to take over the direction of the labor movement'. In retrospect, this appears outlandish, but at the time, it had a ring of truth. Although attempts to recruit the IWW were frustrated, Browder did convince other important labour figures to attend. One delegate was Ella Reeve 'Mother' Bloor, one of the party's experienced labour organisers. But Browder's most important catch was William Z. Foster, with whom Browder had worked before the war. Not then a Communist, Foster—at times a Socialist, dissident Wobbly, and AFL organiser—was a hero of radical labour militants, and arguably the period's greatest labour leader. Foster soon joined the Communist Party, and with Browder, Cannon and Cannon's associate William F. Dunne, was instrumental in 'Americanising' Communism and rooting it in the labour movement.[1]

Foster, who would head the Communist Party during much of the Cold War, has received much attention from scholars, including two full-length biographies published after the opening of the archives in the former Soviet Union. Part of this attention is due to his varied history in the American labour movement, perhaps best encapsulated in the title of his 1937 autobiography, *From Bryan to Stalin.* He joined the Socialist Party in 1901, after becoming interested in politics by a SLP soapboxer the year before. In 1909, in Seattle, Foster split from the SP with a local leftist, Herman Franklin Titus; later that year, he joined the IWW and played an important role in the Wobblies' fight for free speech in Spokane. Soon IWW leader Vincent St. John commissioned Foster to travel to Europe as a reporter for the *Industrial Worker*. There he was influenced by British and French syndicalism. From British syndicalist Tom Mann, he developed his lifelong union philosophy. Unlike the IWW's insistence of forming new revolutionary unions, Foster believed that radical workers should 'bore

1 Earl Browder to Leon Trotsky, 9 May 1921, in Comintern archives, 515:1:39; on Bloor, see Brown 1996.

from within' conservative-led unions. In this way, radicals could influence the rank and file, instead of perpetuating their own isolation.[2]

Upon returning from Europe, Foster struggled within the IWW to 'give up the attempt to create a new labor movement' and instead 'turn itself into a propaganda league, get into the organized-labor movement, and by building up better fighting machines within the old unions than those possessed by our reactionary enemies, revolutionize these unions'. He lost the battle, which is not surprising since it would have meant renouncing the IWW's reason for existence. Foster then organised the Syndicalist League of North America, which by 1915 had become the International Trade Union Educational League.[3]

Foster spelled out his views at the time in a 1913 pamphlet titled *Syndicalism*. Many of his views were similar to the standard Wobbly perspective. He advocated a general strike to place society in the hands of the working class. After this, he theorised, 'there will be no state', since 'the workers in each industry shall manage the affairs of their particular industry' with 'no need for any general supervisory body'. Like most syndicalists, he advocated industrial struggle instead of political action. He wrote that only 'one working class organization—the labor union—is necessary' to overthrow capitalism and denounced 'working class political action' as 'even worse than useless'.[4]

Foster believed that the masses of workers could not be won to socialism, but that a 'militant minority' would lead the workers. Thus he dedicated his book to that rare 'American worker who arouses himself from the customary state of indifference characterizing workingmen'. Since sabotage—'all those tactics, save the boycott and the strike proper, which are used by the workers to wring concessions from their employers'—did not depend upon organising a majority of the working class, it fitted in with Foster's perspective. It was, he wrote, 'peculiarly a weapon of the rebel minority'.[5]

None of this differed greatly from the IWW's disdain for 'Scissor Bill' and 'Mr. Block', characters in songs by Joe Hill who came to represent docile, pro-capitalist workers. What made Foster different from the standard Wobbly

2 The two biographies are Barrett 1999 and Johanningsmeier 1994. For Foster's early years, see his own autobiography, Foster 1937, and Johanningsmeier 1993. On his political evolution, see Foster 1937, pp. 19–24, 30, and Johanningsmeier 1994, pp. 37–47. For Titus, see Schwantes 1994, pp. 95–6. In the early 1930s, Foster wrote a short autobiographical statement that is in the Comintern archives, 615:1:1.

3 Quote from *Industrial Worker*, 2 November 1911, reprinted in 'Boring From Within' 2001, p. 16; Johanningsmeier 1994, pp. 48, 79; Brody 1987, p. 140.

4 Ford and Foster 1913, pp. 3, 5, 19, 23.

5 Ford and Foster 1913, pp. 9, 12, 17.

was his argument that this militant minority should build the broader labour movement and manoeuvre to control it. The greatest sin, according to Foster, was to leave the labour movement in the hands of the pro-capitalist bureaucrats, as had De Leon and the IWW.

There was a certain symbiosis between Foster's 'boring from within' radicalism and Gompers' 'pure and simple' trade unionism. Gompers, of course, eschewed politics and any talk of socialism. The goal of the AFL was to advance the interests of its members, not change society. Foster believed that the labour movement, regardless of who led it, was inherently leading towards workers' power and should be built. Thus, while differing on the ultimate goal, Gompers and Foster agreed that it was necessary above all to strengthen the existing labour movement and avoid debilitating splits.

The First World War highlighted both the strengths and weaknesses of Foster's approach. Gompers and the AFL officialdom supported the war and sought to rally labour support. In *Syndicalism*, Foster had denounced militarism. Yet once war broke out, he sold Liberty Bonds. It is unlikely that Foster supported the war aims of the government. Those labour radicals who continued their class-struggle tactics during the war were crushed. The IWW, which, under Haywood's lead, officially took no position on the war, was still repressed. Bending and supporting the war and exploiting the government's desire for labour peace, instead of taking the principled yet suicidal approach of opposing the war, must have seemed logical to Foster. Those radicals who braved jail for opposing the war must have seen his attitude as at best opportunist and at worst traitorous.[6]

From this vantage point, Foster was successful, since in the post-war period, while the IWW was reeling from repression, Foster became an important national labour organiser. Foster's strategy first found resonance in the Chicago Federation of Labor (CFL). The CFL, led by John Fitzpatrick, had a reputation for being more to the left than the AFL in other cities. Foster became the business manager of the CFL's *New Majority* and the official CFL delegate to the 1918 AFL convention. Along with Edward Nockels and Robert Buck, Foster played an important role in the CFL leadership in this period, even though the *New Majority* focused on organising a CFL-supported Labor Party.[7]

6 Johanningsmeier 1994, pp. 80–3, 88–90; Cannon 1962, pp. 105–8; on the IWW and the war, see Dubofsky 1969, pp. 354–5.

7 On Fitzpatrick and the CFL, see Strouthous 1996, pp. 23–4, 31–8, 52–3; see also Keiser 1965; on Fitzpatrick himself, see O'Donnell 1997, Chapter 6. On the *New Majority*, see Bekken 1992, Chapter 9.

In 1919, Foster sprung to national prominence amid one of the largest strike waves in North America. Under the auspices of the AFL, and with the close support of Fitzpatrick and the CFL, he led strikes by slaughterhouse workers in Chicago, and then steel workers throughout the country. These strikes captured the restlessness (and power) of labour in the post-war period. They were both defeated, but they marked Foster's debut in the national imagination as a dynamic trade-union organiser. These strikes also seemed to confirm Foster's strategy of working within the AFL and giving wide berth to radical politics. In 1922, Foster extolled how 'the work of a mere handful of rebels', with 'no backing from the thousands of militants' outside the AFL, was able to display 'the power of the militants among the organized masses'.[8]

The Steel Strike also confirmed Foster's belief in the inherently revolutionary nature of labour unions. His *Great Steel Strike and Its Lessons* of 1920 criticised radical opponents of the existing labour movement, and asserted that trade unions were 'directly anti-capitalistic'. Conservative slogans used by AFL leaders, whether believed by the leaders themselves or not, were nothing but 'a sort of camouflage layer or protective covering'. He continued:

> The trade unions will not become anti-capitalistic through the conversion of their members to a certain point of view or the adoption of certain preambles, they are that by their very make up and methods. The most that can be done is to clarify the aims and intensify their efforts toward freedom.

One of the strike's lessons was that dual unionism was a 'devitalizing drain' that 'must be stopped, and the great body of progressives and radicals won over to a whole-hearted support of the trade unions'. In an article published in 1921, Foster asserted that 'dual industrial unionism' was 'the principle ailment of American radicalism'. He added: 'If the trade union movement in this country is weak and conservative, the radicals are chiefly to blame'.[9]

Boiled down to its essentials, Foster's perspective in the early 1920s was to build the labour movement through strengthening the existing unions in cooperation with their leaderships, if possible. In November 1920, he and a small number of followers organised the Trade Union Educational League (TUEL). This group quickly became a vessel for Foster to fill. One contemporary remarked that 'not often does one find an organization so completely

8 Johanningsmeir 1994, pp. 88–149; on the steel strike, see Brody 1987 and Foster 1920; Foster 1922a.

9 Foster 1921a.

dominated by the philosophy and personality of one man as is found in the case of the Trade Union Educational League'. Foster stamped the TUEL with his trade-union philosophy. The early TUEL was peopled with his supporters such as Browder and Jack Johnstone, a Scots veteran of the Boer War who had been with Foster since the Syndicalist League of North America.[10]

The *New York Times* during the Steel Strike denounced Foster as an 'extreme radical' and rehashed his radical history, including *Syndicalism*. While Foster's address at the 1920 Socialist Party convention received an ovation second only to that of Debs, he was not universally popular among radicals in this period. In part this is because he claimed to have changed his opinion since the publication of *Syndicalism*, and he counted on the backing of the AFL. One historian has claimed that 'without a scorecard it would have been hard to distinguish Foster's followers from other AFL trade unionists' in this period; many early Communists distrusted him. Not surprisingly, Haywood called the Steel Strike a 'dismal failure' because Foster had squandered an 'opportunity for revolutionary propaganda', instead wrapping the organising campaign in patriotic colours. Black radicals also distrusted Foster, since the IWW recruited black workers (and supported racial equality) unlike many AFL unions.[11]

Foster attended the Profintern Congresses in 1921 as an observer and reporter for the left-wing Federated Press. His more than three months in Moscow impressed him. One of his dispatches, about a Communist parade in Moscow, began: 'Once in a while one has an experience that can never be forgotten so long as life lasts'. In a booklet written in 1921 after his return, *The Russian Revolution*, he described the fledging Soviet Republic as realising his own political perspectives, predicting that 'the Russian revolution will live and accomplish its great task of setting up the world's first free commonwealth'. Upon his return he decided to join the Communist Party, although he would keep his membership secret for several years.[12]

10 Barrett 1998, p. 311; Beckner 1925, p. 410; on Johnstone, see *New York Times* obituary, 19 April 1942.

11 On the attacks on Foster's radical history, and Gompers's defence of him, see *New York Times*, 27 September 1919, 29 September 1919, 22 October 1919; Devinatz 1996, p. 11. On the 1920 SP Convention, see Ottini 1948, pp. 36–7. On Haywood's criticisms, see W.D. Haywood 1921; on criticisms of Foster on the racist nature of the AFL leadership, see McKay 1979, pp. 31–3.

12 Barrett 1999, pp. 105–7; *Voice of Labor*, 26 July 1921; Foster 1921b, p. 7. In his later autobiographical statement, Foster claimed to have joined the Communist Party in August 1921 (in Comintern archives, 615:1:1). An announcement that Foster had decided to ally himself with the Comintern is found in Ballister to Lozovsky, Radek, Zinoviev, marked 'urgent and private', 26 September 1921, Comintern archives, 515:1:39.

At the time, Foster was the only radical in the labour movement who could be seen as a counterweight to Samuel Gompers—especially since Haywood was out of the picture. What compelled him to join the fledging Communist movement, comprising infighting immigrants so distant from the organised labour movement? He claimed that it was 'Lenin's stand on the trade union question' that attracted him. 'After more than twenty years of intellectual groping about', he added, 'I was at last, thanks to Lenin, getting my feet on firm revolutionary ground'. Alfred Rosmer, a French syndicalist who became a Communist, observed that Foster was 'very excited about the Third International' because its position on the need to fight within the existing trade unions. The fights in Moscow, where the Bolshevik leadership forcefully if comradely fought American Communists (including Haywood, the former head of the IWW) over this issue, impressed him (especially since, according to Rosmer, 'it was difficult to get him to talk about anything else'). But the 'firm revolutionary ground' must have included not only the position on trade unions, but the building of a workers' state on Soviet soil itself.[13]

Foster's attraction to Communism lay beyond its American followers—to whom Foster likely felt superior—and instead came from the Bolshevik Revolution and the Comintern. As Rosmer's letter indicates, Foster was in his element among the various syndicalists at the Profintern Congress who supported the Bolsheviks. One of Foster's biographers explains his conversion to Communism: 'The fact that the Russians seemed to have created an effective, exportable workers' system was what attracted Foster, not Marxist-Leninist theory'. Cannon, Foster's former factional ally turned Trotskyist, suggested that his trajectory was based on adapting to powers stronger than himself within the labour movement to use them for his own purposes. After 'Gompers insisted on using the adaption for his purpose' in 1919–20, 'Foster could find an alternative field of operations, still within the labor movement, by adapting himself to Moscow'.[14]

Today, after the Cold War and the stagnation of the American labour movement, and the general rightward drift of the left since the collapse of the Soviet Union, it may appear quixotic for a labour leader of such stature to have allied himself with the Bolsheviks. However, in 1921 this was not the case.

13 Foster 1939, p. 295; According to Rosmer: 'Il est très emballé pour la IIIe. Intle. parce que les thèses lui donnent pleine satisfaction en ce qui concerne à present sa préoccupation dominante: la lutte dans les vieilles *trade unions*. Il est plein de son sujet et il est assez difficile de le faire parler d'autre chose'; Rosmer to Pierre Monatte, 14 July 1921, in Chambelland 1964, pp. 35–6.

14 Barrett 2002, p. 469.

If Foster perhaps did not share the belief of some American Communists that revolution was around the corner, it was not too hard to imagine an increasing radicalisation and class struggle in the US.

Foster was not the only labour leader affected. Sidney Hillman, a Lithuanian-born exile from tsarist repression and the leftist leader of the independent Amalgamated Clothing Workers (ACWA) union, travelled to Soviet Russia at the same time as Foster, and met with Lenin and other Bolshevik leaders. Hillman, according to his biographer, was drawn to the Soviet Communists 'less out of admiration for their tangible accomplishments than for his own magnetic attraction to power'. Hillman did not become a Communist, but helped organise famine relief for the Soviet Union and general assistance to reconstruct Russian industry. (In October 1921, Lenin wrote to 'Comrade Hillman' to 'thank you with all my heart for your help'). Hillman allied himself with Foster and the Communists in the garment industry for a time. Whatever other political considerations informed this, it is also important that Hillman, unlike Foster, had an organisational base of support, namely, the ACWA.[15]

It is possible that John Keiser was correct that Foster would not have become a Communist if the Steel Strike had won 'and if the legitimate trade-union movement had offered a better outlet for his talents'. Be that as it may, the Communist movement offered Foster something: the power and prestige of the Bolshevik Revolution, as well as an organisational apparatus to support his trade-union goals. In return, Foster gave the party his knowledge and connections in the labour movement, the TUEL and its supporters, and the opportunity to build a base in the organised working class. In a 1923 report to the Comintern, Amter spelled out the early relationship between the party leadership and Foster: 'The CEC, of which Foster is a member, lays down the general policy for the trade union work, which Foster is then free to carry out according to the methods best suited, in his judgement'. The recruitment of Foster is an illustration of the crucial role of the Communist International in helping American comrades break out of their isolation and establish roots in the working class. And in turn, Foster would play a crucial role in 'Americanising' Communism in the 1920s.[16]

15 Hillman 1922; S. Fraser 1991, p. 184.; Lenin 1966d, pp. 526–7.

16 Keiser 1965, p. 15; I. Amter, report to Comintern, 7 March 1923, Comintern archives, 515:1:174.

Early TUEL Activity

Foster participated in the August 1922 underground convention in Bridgman, Michigan. Still not publicly a Communist, he outlined his conception of how the party should approach trade-union work. 'The fate of the party', he stressed, 'depends upon its control of the masses ... When we lay stress on the importance of this work, we realize we must capture the trade unions if we want to get anywhere'. He asserted that 'it is absolutely impossible to have a revolution in this country unless we control the mass trade unions'.[17]

The TUEL was the instrument that the Communist Party intended to use to realise this. An advertisement in Foster's 1921 *Russian Revolution* described this as 'an organization to carry on educational work in the trade union movement', aiming to 'infuse the mass with revolutionary understanding and spirit'. As James Barrett emphasises, the early TUEL built upon both Foster's pre-Communist experiences and his tremendous organising skills. The TUEL opposed dual unions, instead advocating 'the closer affiliation and solidification of our existing unions until they have been developed into industrial unions'. The ultimate goal of the TUEL was 'to bring the policies and the structures of the labor movement into harmony with present-day economic conditions'. At the 1922 TUEL convention, according to the *New York Times*, 'Foster declared that it was formed to supplant the Industrial Workers of the World' and its 'membership was composed of syndicalists, anarchists and other radicals'.[18]

The TUEL's early perspectives are put forth in the *Labor Herald*, which Foster edited. In its first issue, Foster described the US as home to a 'very elaborate industrial system and the world's most militant and powerful capitalist class', as well as 'a trade union movement which, for general weakness and backwardness, has few if any equals in the predominately industrial countries'. Unions in the United States were 'at about the point of development that European unions were 15 years ago', unique in their 'unequaled lack of idealism and social vision' and 'the laughing stock of the international labor world, revolutionary and reformist alike'. Capitalists in the US attacked the labour movement more ferociously than in other industrialised capitalist countries. Dismissing explanations rooted in the diversity of the working class or the strong capitalist economy, Foster located the 'prime cause of the stagnation of the American movement' in radicals' 'chronic secessionism'. Thus

17 Whitney 1924, pp. 24–6.

18 Barrett 1999, p. 119; Foster 1921b, inside front cover; *New York Times*, 27 August 1922.

'progressive and revolutionary unionists ... systematically deserted and neglected the trade unions' through dual unionism.[19]

Two of the most important demands of the early TUEL were the amalgamation of the trade unions into industrial unions, and recognition of Soviet Union. Within the unions themselves, TUEL activists sought to vanquish dual unionism and organise a bloc of leftists and 'progressives'. *Labor Herald* stressed that the TUEL was 'an informal grouping of progressive and revolutionary elements throughout the entire trade union movement', not a dual union. In practice, 'progressives' was an elastic term that encompassed everything from militant rank-and-file oppositionists to left-talking labour bureaucrats (such as in the needle trades unions), and, as we will see, the Farmer-Labor movement. To further complicate the issue, the Communists did not always distinguish between united fronts focused on particular actions and longer-term political blocs. The TUEL was 'an auxiliary of the labor movement, not a substitute for it'. In his Bridgman speech, Foster explained that to avoid charges of dual unionism, the TUEL did not set up a parallel structure to the established unions.[20]

In the lead-up to the Bridgman Convention in 1922, the party established a national industrial organiser, and instructed its membership to 'take active part in the trade union movement'. All members were urged to 'become active at once' within the TUEL. At this time, the TUEL's programme stressed amalgamation, attacked Gompers, and criticised dual unionism. It supported affiliation to the Profintern, but downplayed other aspects of the Communists' programme. At Bridgman, Foster explained: 'We did not dare say it was a Communist organization. It was necessary to camouflage to a certain extent, and for that reason it had to start differently'. To do otherwise would have invited repression by the AFL bureaucracy. At the Bridgman Convention, Foster explained that the TUEL had begun to gain respect in the unions, so it could 'adopt a clear-cut revolutionary program'.[21]

(From Moscow, Haywoood criticised much of Foster's perspective. In a review of Foster's *Bankruptcy of the American Labor Movement* of 1922, Haywood argued that the labour movement in the US was not bankrupt, but

19 *Labor Herald*, March 1922.

20 Arne Swabeck, 'From Debs to Mao' memoir (1975), copy in Prometheus Research Library, Chapter 8, p. 5; *Labor Herald*, March 1922; Whitney 1924, p. 27.

21 See 25 April 1922 report on the 21 April 1922 WP Administrative Council meeting and C.E. Ruthenberg, memo to all party branches, 13 June 1922, both in Comintern archives, 515:1:146. A similar resolution was passed at the Second National Convention of the WP, 24–6 December 1922, in Comintern archives, 515:1:141. On the directive to join the TUEL, see James P. Cannon to all branch and local secretaries, 21 April 1922, in Comintern archives, 515:1:146. On the TUEL programme, see Whitney 1924, pp. 27–8; on affiliation, see *Labor Herald*, April 1922.

that the unions had been 'fostered by and nurtured the spirit of Americanism, which is arrogance, selfishness and spleen, responsible for the existing arbitrary hide-bound labor movement in the greatest industrial country of the world'. Haywood—perhaps the only Communist with enough stature to argue against Foster's labour perspective—defended the IWW's 'industrial unionism, young and virile', and savaged the AFL for its anti-black, anti-immigrant and anti-Asian exclusionary practices. He labelled 'without merit' Foster's assertion that dual unionism was the cause of the weakness of American labour, pointing out that many strong unions like the ACWA were competitors to the AFL. The IWW 'certainly cannot be referred to as dual unionism, it is the chief revolutionary expression of the working class in America', he added. However, his document was without much practical advice, except that the TUEL members should work with the IWW. While Haywood's document seems to have been circulated at least to the Comintern leadership—the copy in the Comintern archives seems to have belonged to Trotsky—his criticisms from Moscow did not resonate in the US at the time).[22]

The TUEL faced immediate hostility by Gompers. (During the Steel Strike, the head of the AFL defended Foster from charges of radicalism). On 1 May 1922, Gompers asserted that 'under Foster's direction a political machine was being built with Bolshevist funds to undermine American labor', in the words of the *New York Times*. Foster defended the TUEL as 'purely an educational organization, designed to strengthen the trade unions and give them a more militant philosophy', and blamed Gompers's hostility on 'an anti-Russian complex'.[23]

The government also saw the organisation as a threat. In August 1922, police raided the League's headquarters in Chicago. Foster was accused of involvement with the supposed sabotage of a train in Gary, Indiana, during a railroad strike. Foster himself was arrested for his role in the Bridgman Convention; federal agents raided the second TUEL convention in late August 1922, arresting two people for supposedly attending the Bridgman Convention, and holding nine others 'for deportation as undesirables', as the *New York Times* put it.[24]

22 W.D. Haywood, Review of *Bankruptcy of the American Labor Movement* [1922] by W.Z. Foster, undated, in Comintern archives, 515:1:251. The document is stamped (in German, English and French) that it must be returned to the Secretariat in two days and (in Russian) 'Secret'. For Foster's book, see Foster 1922b.

23 *New York Times*, 2 May 1922.

24 On the raid on the TUEL headquarters, see *New York Times*, 21 August 1922 (the same issue has an article on the Gary train wreck, in which two scabs died); on the raid on the TUEL convention, see *New York Times*, 27 August 1922; on Foster and the Bridgman Convention, see *New York Times*, 13 September 1922.

In 1921–3, despite this repression, the TUEL seemed to make headway. Foster was still close to Fitzpatrick, which gave the early TUEL some protection in the unions. The needle trades, a longtime stronghold of Jewish Socialists, appeared to be fertile ground. Hillman travelled with Foster to Moscow to observe the Profintern. Afterwards, he decided (as Robert Minor put it) to 'not formally affiliate with the International but to work out with the International a system of relationship by which the International could direct the crystalization of a left bloc in the American trade union movement'. The formation of the Workers' Party also helped in the industry, by providing cadres and a literary apparatus in Yiddish. Jacob Salutsky (Hardman), a high ACWA official, had become a member of the Workers' Party CEC through the fusion with the Workers' Council group in 1921. Thus by 1922, the party could report to the Comintern that it had 'a very able leadership which [was] moving quite readily towards the Left Position', and that the party had 'a working agreement with the administration of the union against the reactionary elements' in the Socialist Party and Abraham Cahan's Yiddish daily *Forward*. The party hoped to use its relationship with Hillman as a springboard to influence the needle trades, whose workers were often Jewish socialists or Italian syndicalists. In November 1922, the TUEL formed a needle trades section, with significant support among the ACWA, women's garment workers (ILGWU), and furrier (IFWU) unions. Benjamin Gitlow, the head of this work, later claimed that the party had 2,000 members in the New York City needle trades, while a more recent study put the numbers even higher, at 3,000 members.[25]

The TUEL also had supporters in other unions and industries. In early 1922, Fitzpatrick's CFL 'endorsed the prominent features of the League's program' such as amalgamation. This was the first federation to do so, angering Gompers, who in retaliation cut off the CFL's subsidy from the AFL. By its National Convention in August 1922, the TUEL claimed to have local organisations in 300 cities, divided into 13 industrial groups. To avoid criticism of dual unionism, members affiliated individually, not through their local unions, and did not pay dues or fees. Substantial numbers of members were in the clothing trades (90,000 members), the railroads (80,000), mining (60,000), metal trades (48,000), and general transport and printing trades (35,000 each). In total, the TUEL claimed 422,800 members. Active members were certainly a

25 Ballister [Minor] to Lozovsky, Radek and Zinoviev, 26 September 1921; unsigned 'Report on the United States of America' [1922?], both in Comintern archives, 515:1:39. Gurowsky 1978, p. 103; PS Foner 1950, pp. 124–6; Gitlow 1939, p. 337; Prudson 1984, p. xvi. (The bulk of this study is in Hebrew; references are to the English summary). On Communist work in the needle trades, see Barrett 1999, pp. 126–8; Holmes 2007; Seidman 1942, Chapter 9.

fraction of this, since the September 1922 circulation of the *Labor Herald* was 20,000 and James Barrett estimates that the League 'had about 500 hard-core activists' at its height. There were 59 cities described as having 'the most active groups', mainly in the Northeast and Midwest, but ranging from New Orleans to Seattle, and from Los Angeles to Boston. Without the Comintern's fight on work within the AFL, the party would never have won Foster and could never have begun such work.[26]

Early Work of the TUEL: The Building Trades

In a semi-autobiographical account, Morris Rosen, a TUEL activist in the building trades in New York City, described his involvement with the TUEL. While the industry is not usually seen as a Communist focus, Rosen's detailed account provides the historian with a better sense of how the TUEL worked in this period. In the early 1920s, construction workers, unlike many other workers, were experiencing a boom, and wages were relatively high. However, they faced speed-up, long hours and horrendous conditions. The more than two million construction workers in the country were divided among some 18 craft unions. The carpenters union (UBCJA) was the largest such union, and, after the UMWA, formed the second-largest union in the country with 400,000 members in 1920. It also had a right-wing and corrupt leadership under William Hutcheson, who opposed any move towards industrial unions and frequently raided other craft unions for members.[27]

In 1922, Rosen, a member of UBCJA Local 376 in Manhattan, received a letter from Foster inviting him to join the TUEL. He recalled meeting in the Lower East Side with four other construction workers. 'We will organize a system of informal committees in all the building trades, educate the rank and file and infuse them with understanding and spirit', the character based on Rosen explained. According to the August 1922 report cited above, the TUEL had 25,000

26 Becker 1925, p. 426; Johnstone and Knudsen, report on TUEL to Profintern, August 1922, in Comintern archives, 515:1:157; Barrett 1999, pp. 122, 126. Barrett's membership estimate (for 1923–4) is based on an 1955 interview with Browder.

27 Mike Ross [Morris Rosen], 'Man Made Cliffs', in Morris Rosen Papers, folder 2, p. 25; Johnstone 1924, p. 38 (copy in Rosen papers). The memoir is written under the name Mike Ross, which was the name Rosen used to write articles in the CP and TUEL press, but is explicitly about Morris Rosen. Membership figures taken from the history section of the UBCJA website: <www.carpenters.org/WhoWeAre/History/1900-1930.aspx>. Hutchenson would later be famous for getting in a fistfight with UMWA leader Lewis at the 1934 AFL convention over the formation of industrial unions.

members in the building trades unions at that time, making it the League's seventh-largest concentration of members (out of 13 different industries).[28]

Rosen and his comrades were careful to avoid becoming known as reds to the local leadership (by using pseudonyms, for example). Rosen recalled the 'tremendous preliminary organization' required to deal with 'the trickery of crooked lawyers, with the political scheming and vote juggling of a Tammany Hall, and with the intimidation, threats and methods of gangsterism'. Through a variety of tactics, Rosen and his supporters gained strength and pressured the local leadership to give financial reports at meetings as a way of 'awakening and organizing the divergent elements into a unified struggle' for internal union democracy. In January 1923, they advocated sending a delegate to a labour defence conference to defend the Bridgman defendants. Even this was not an openly Communist endeavour; while the Legal Defense Council was led by the Communist Party, it counted various radicals and liberals on its National Committee.

By 1924, Rosen had outmanoeuvred the UCBJA leadership to gain control of the local (including forming a 10–15 member 'sort of flying squad' to protect themselves against the leadership's thugs and using some of the bureaucracy's own methods, such as bribing local cops). By the time of the September 1924 UCBJA conference in Indianapolis, Rosen indicated that 'the progressives had won control over several locals throughout the country and in a substantial number of locals they had elected officers in a minority'.[29]

Rosen detailed the dirty tactics of the national bureaucracy, headed by William Hutcheson, to maintain control of the union against an alliance that pro-TUEL militants made with other 'progressive' unionists. The TUEL demanded organising the unorganised, 'job control' (that is, the ability of the union to shut down unsafe worksites), amalgamation of the building trades unions, 'independent working class political action', 'recognition of, and trade relations with, Soviet Russia', as well as greater rank-and-file control over the union. In 1925–6, the UCBJA bureaucracy under Hutcheson expelled TUEL militants nationally, including Rosen, and eventually suspended Local 376. While Rosen does not address it, the tactic of supporting a group of out-bureaucrats in the union underlines some of the weaknesses of the TUEL's 'progressive'

28 Ross, 'Man Made Cliffs', in Rosen Papers, folder 4, pp. 47–8; Johnstone and Knudsen, report on TUEL to Profintern, August 1922, in Comintern archives, 515:1:157.

29 Ross, 'Man Made Cliffs', Rosen papers, folder 4, pp. 68–9; folder 5, p. 86.

alliance, something that bore a certain similarity to Foster's own history of manoeuvres.[30]

In 1923, this was in the future. In the building trades, as in other industries, the TUEL seemed to face great opportunities. In early 1923, Debs hailed the TUEL as 'the one rightly directed movement for the industrial unification of the American workers'. In the early 1930s, after he had broken with the Workers' Party, J.B.S. Hardman labelled this period 'the heyday of American Communism' because of the party's influence in the unions. In a few years, American Communists had gone from having little intersection with the organised working class to being seen as stalwart fighters for workers' interests by militants. The recruitment of Foster was an important part of this. And his recruitment highlights the relationship between the 'American' and the 'foreign' in the rooting of Communism in the reality of the labour movement in the US. Left to their own devices, it is unlikely that the original Communists would have been able either to recruit Foster or to establish the TUEL. Once recruited, Foster opened up possible avenues for Communist development, which would have been unimaginable otherwise. In 1923, a shadow appeared on the horizon, which threatened all the gains the Communists had made in the unions so far.[31]

30 On anti-Communist repression, see Johnstone 1925 and *What's Wrong* 1925. The TUEL demands are taken from Ross, 'Points for Carpenters', *Progressive Building Trade Worker*, January 1924 (clip in Rosen papers) and *What's Wrong* 1925, pp. 53–4.

31 *Labor Herald*, April 1923; Hardman, 'Communism in America', Hardman papers, box 14, folder 10, p. 16. The manuscript is not dated, but it is before the rise of the CIO.

CHAPTER 5

The Farmer-Labor Party

The combination of an anti-Communist labour bureaucracy, and the decline in union strength, limited the Communists' opportunities in the labour movement, whatever strategy they chose.[1] Still, after the promise of the early TUEL years, the party's manoeuvres increased their isolation in the labour movement for much of the decade. Central to this failure were the disastrous efforts at forming a 'farmer-labour' party, which left the party with few allies in the broader labour movement and damaged its internal health. In the end, the Comintern leadership, particularly Trotsky, helped the party navigate these dangers. However, by 1923–5, the Comintern itself was changing, reflecting the bureaucratic degeneration of Soviet Russia. As a result, the party's labour work in this period cut to the core of the US and international Communist movement.

This chapter analyses the role that the Communist Party played in the labour movement in the mid-1920s, as well as the Comintern's intervention in the party's labour activity. By this time, the party was becoming increasingly isolated, with TUEL militants being driven out of the trade unions. The leadership of the party sought to escape this isolation. 'Progressive' radicalism—first the farmer-labour movement and then the 'third-party alliance' around Republican Senator Robert La Follette—appeared to be answers. However, instead of polarising these movements on class lines, the Communists' actual work in these milieus threatened to jettison the Marxist principle of proletarian independence. This would have meant retreating from the left wing's fight for revolutionary politics in favour of trying to pressure the capitalist parties, namely, returning to social-democratic reformism. In 1924, the Comintern intervened forcefully, if clumsily and belatedly, to prevent the party from liquidating itself politically. The *deus ex machina* nature of this intervention compounded the party's isolation.

Campaign for a Labour Party

After the World War, amid an upsurge in working-class militancy, the creation of a labour party seemed possible, just as the British Labour Party had recently

1 Cochran 1977, pp. 45–6.

emerged from the Liberal movement. Important sectors of the labour leadership sought a larger role in politics, while many Progressives, disillusioned with the two established parties, saw the working class as a progressive social force for post-war 'reconstruction'. Had even a reformist mass labour party—like the British one—been formed, it would have been a defeat for the AFL's long-standing 'non-partisan' hostility towards a workers' party and a political reflection of the social division between workers and capitalists, albeit in a distorted way.[2]

According to Andrew Strouthous's study of the labour party movement, in the early 1920s 'the AFL was riven by civil war to determine its political policy'. John Fitzpatrick's Chicago Federation of Labor (CFL) was a major advocate for a labour party. Fitzpatrick, an Irish American blacksmith who had been head of the CFL for some two decades, had worked with radicals including William Z. Foster. In November 1919, the CFL's *New Majority* published the entire Soviet Constitution; that month Fitzpatrick helped organise the Cook County Labor Party (CCLP). This advocated 'democratic control of industry and commerce for the general good by those who work with hand or brain, and the elimination of autocratic domination of the forces of production and distribution either by selfish private interests or bureaucratic agents of government'.[3]

Fitzpatrick, the CCLP's candidate for mayor of Chicago, received about 60,000 votes in 1919 (8 percent). Seeking allies, the next year the Labor Party added 'Farmer' to its name, forming the Farmer Labor Party (FLP). This search for rural support reflected the fact that, as German Socialist Karl Kautsky had observed two decades earlier, 'the United States, in spite of their highly developed industrial capitalism, are a strongly agrarian country'. At this time, more Americans still lived in rural areas than in urban ones, and there was a history of rural radicalism. Although the farmer-labour movement attracted more support among farmers than the trade-union movement, the new Farmer Labor Party diluted the proletarian focus of the labour party movement by trying to create a two-class party. When they attempted to unite forces with progressive Republican Senator Robert La Follette from Wisconsin, they ignored the class line altogether. La Follette refused, claiming he was searching for a party with an 'advanced but not socialist' programme. In 1920, farmer-labour presidential candidate Parley P. Parker received only 265,000 votes (compared to more than 900,000 for Debs and 16 million for Harding). However, farmer-labour

2 Shapiro 1967, pp. 29–31; Dubofsky and Van Time 1986, p. 83.

3 Strouthous 2000, p. 2; Shapiro 1967, pp. 29–31; Bekken 1997; Fine 1928, pp. 382–6; Shideler 1945, pp. 20–41.

gubernatorial candidates received between 23 and 35 percent of the vote in Minnesota, Washington, South Dakota and Nebraska.[4]

At the same time, labour leaders remained dissatisfied with the two main capitalist parties. In February 1922, the railway unions' traditionally conservative leadership supported an independent, vaguely radical, party at the founding meeting of the Conference for Progressive Political Action (CPPA). The CPPA was formed amid anger over the defeat of the union-supported 'Plumb Plan' to nationalise the railways. Railway unions had grown almost six-and-a-half times between 1914–20, compared to the 30 percent decline suffered by the AFL as a whole. After a draconian government response to the 1922 railway strike, the unions' leadership was feeling pressure from the ranks for more militancy and trying to pressure the government for more favourable policies.[5]

The Socialist Party formed the left wing of the CPPA, while a liberal 'Committee of Forty Eight' comprised the right wing. Between these were some 50 unions, labour leaders (including Fitzpatrick), and various liberals. When Hillquit proposed supporting a third party, he was defeated in favour of working within the Democratic and Republican parties. The CPPA endorsed candidates such as Alfred Smith of New York, a Democrat, and La Follette, a Republican. The CPPA and the CCLP were the last echo of post-war labour radicalism; rather than a movement towards a labour party, they were a waystation for those leftists and bureaucrats who had flirted with a labour party, but were on the way back to the two-party fold.[6]

The Communists and the Labour Party Movement

In reaction to Socialist Party electoral reformism, by the 1920s left-wing socialists had long dismissed all electoral politics. Louis Fraina's left-wing *Revolutionary Age* denounced the movement for a labour party as an expression of 'the reactionary tendency and purposes of the A.F. of L.'. This attitude was carried into the early Communist movement. For the 1920 election, the United Communist Party issued a leaflet, 'Boycott the Election', that denounced the capitalist parties, urged workers not to vote, but to 'Hail ... the Workers'

4 Shapiro 1967, p. 113; Shapiro 1985, pp. 415–20; Draper 1985, pp. 197–8; Kautsky 1902; Dyson 1982, p. 6. See also Palmer 2007, pp. 178, 182. 1920 presidential election results taken from *New York Times* 2000.

5 Chester 2004, Chapter 4; Fine 1928, p. 398; Waterhouse 1991, pp. 17–20. See also Leuchtenburg 1958, pp. 40, 70; Strouthous 2000, pp. 7–8. On the strike, see Davis 1997; Bernstein 1960, p. 212.

6 *New York Times*, 22 February 1922.

Councils and the Dictatorship of the Proletariat!' An August 1921 report to the Comintern denounced the Farmer-Labor Party as 'practically an expression of the mildest section of the opposition to Gompers in the American Federation of Labor'. Just as early Communists opposed work within the AFL, they saw labour party politics as a diversion from the approaching revolution instead of an opportunity to break workers from capitalist parties. They had no perspective of intervening in the movement, much less of polarising it to break left-wing workers from the trade-union and liberal leaders.[7]

American Communists' disdain towards any electoral politics or tactics was shared with the early British Communists who opposed affiliating with the Labour Party. In his 1920 *'Left Wing' Communism*, Lenin advocated critical support for the Labour Party. Communists, he wrote, should 'take part in the election campaign, distribute leaflets in favour of Communism, and, in all constituencies where we have no candidates ... urge the electors to vote for the Labour candidate and against the bourgeois candidate'. Working-class political independence and awareness of Communism was the goal; the Communists should expose the betrayal and pro-capitalist loyalty of Labour leaders like Arthur Henderson through such tactics as supporting 'Henderson in the same way the rope supports a hanged man'.[8]

In the aftermath of this fight against 'left' errors (connected with the struggle to work within the AFL unions and for a legal party), American Communists re-examined the movement for a labour party. The Fourth Comintern Congress was crucial in resolving these issues. For example, in November 1922, Cannon's presentation to the American Commission not only advocated 'an open Communist Party', but also endorsed 'the idea of a labor party, something after the nature of the English Labour Party'. The ECCI in response advised the Workers' Party to enter the labour party movement, which it credited with 'enormous political importance'. 'The basis of our activity', the ECCI emphasised, 'must be the Left Wing of the Trade Union Movement'. Cannon later recalled that 'the initiative for a positive attitude toward a prospective Labor party in the United States came from Moscow'.[9]

Unfortunately, while the Communists had ignored the question in 1919, when the possibility of a labour party was palpable, the movement had largely receded by the time they started to intervene. In early 1922, after the

7 *Revolutionary Age*, 18 December 1918; 'Boycott the Election', UCP leaflet, no date [1920], in Cannon papers, reel 47, frame 20; George Baldwin, 'Statement of the Communist Party of America to the ECCI', August 1921, in Comintern archives, 515:1:39.

8 Lenin 1966c, pp. 90–1.

9 Cannon 2007, p. 45; ECCI 1987.

announcement that the CPPA was going to meet in Chicago, the CEC passed a motion to 'make every effort to participate in the Chicago conference thru [sic] regular delegates'. In February, on the eve of the meeting, the WP issued an open letter to the CPPA. After denouncing the union leadership's conservatism, the letter urged them to 'form a united industrial front' and create the movement's 'own representatives, responsible to Labor alone'. The appeal ended with the call for the conference 'to move for a general Labor Congress to be elected by the rank and file'. Foster attended the meeting—along with assorted liberals and radicals such as Hillquit, Berger, A.C. Townley of the Non-Partisan League, and Frederic C. Howe, ex-Commissioner of Immigration in New York.[10]

The party reported to the Comintern, however, that the actual 'results ... are of little importance' compared to the fact that the party 'took a very serious view' of the CPPA. The main 'result' of the CPPA conference was an 'Address to the American People', modelled on the Declaration of Independence, that stressed restoring 'the government of the United States to the noble ends and high purposes for which it was conceived'. While praising the 'splendid structure of the visible American government', the statement protested against the people's interest being 'sacrificed on the altar of greed', and denounced the Federal Reserve System, farmers' poverty, war profiteering, railway speculation and 'a campaign of ruthless imperialism' in the Caribbean. In the upshot, the CPPA promised 'united political action suited to the peculiar conditions and needs of each section and state', while pledging 'to organize for the coming campaign in every state and congressional district, so that this may become once more in very truth a government of the people, for the people, and by the people'. The February meeting chose working within the two established capitalist parties instead of organising a third party.[11]

Soon afterwards, the Communists reassessed their labour party policy. The spring 'Theses on the United Front of Labor' declared that 'to oppose this tendency toward the formation of a labor party would be folly'. Communists were directed to be active in the labour party campaign and 'fight to make the labor party a real instrument in the class struggle'. In November, the party argued that Communists needed to play an active role in the struggle for a labour party and fight for 'a class program'.[12]

10 James P. Cannon and Caleb Harrison, 'To the Conference', 20 February 1922, in Comintern archives, 515:1:146; *New York Times*, 22 February 1922.

11 'Address to the American People Adopted by the Conference for Progressive Political Action', 20–1 February 1922, in Hillquit papers, document no. 982.

12 'Theses on the United Front of Labor' [May 1922?], in Comintern archives, 515:1:146; 'The Workers' Party and the Labor Party', 2 November 1922, in Comintern archives, 515:1:147.

In December 1922, the CPPA held a conference in Cleveland. The party sent four delegates to demand that the CPPA 'create a labor party'. This attempt to 'affiliate' (as Foster described it a year later) with this lash-up of SP leaders and disgruntled trade-union bureaucrats was rebuffed. Neither Ruthenberg (a fixture in Cleveland politics) nor Foster (one of the more popular radical labour leaders) was allowed to sit as a delegate. The Workers' Party was denounced for being 'un-American', 'disrupt[ing] legitimate labor organizatons', and 'officered and managed by representatives of the private detectives' agencies controlled by Burns, Thiel, and Pinkerton'. When Fitzpatrick withdrew from the convention in response to opposition to a new party, the Communists followed.[13]

At this point, Fitzpatrick and Foster had a positive relationship. For Fitzpatrick, the Workers' Party and the TUEL were valuable junior partners in the farmer-labour party project. The Communists saw Fitzpatrick as a protector against anti-Communist attacks and his support as essential for a labour party. Their view of a labour party seemed to be of a bloc with Fitzpatrick, with the end to increase Communist influence in the labour movement. The *Labor Herald* (December 1922) ran a long article by Foster about the CFL, calling the federation 'one of the bright spots' in the labour movement because of the 'progressiveness of its politics'. Its leaders were 'real fighting trade unionists' and Fitzpatrick, 'one of the strong oaks of the labor movement'.[14]

The party hailed Fitzpatrick's withdrawal from the Cleveland Conference, arguing that 'The Workers' Party, although barred from the Conference, came out of it a victory' because it had 'made its appearance in the life of the American workers and farmers as a definite political force'. They predicted that this 'was only the first skirmish in the battle for the Labour Party'. After the Cleveland convention, *Labor Herald* called for 'a general labor party' and criticised the CPPA for not organising one. The Workers' Party second national convention, held in December 1922, 'greet[ed] with joy' the movement towards a labour party, and called on the party to 'actively participat[e] in the campaign'. The convention also condemned the CPPA and called for a labour party based on the unions.[15]

---

13 *New York Times*, 13 December 1922; Cannon 1962, p. 62; *Report of the Proceedings*, p. 11; Draper 1986, pp. 29–37. Foster's description is from his speech to the American Commission of the Comintern, 29 April 1924.

14 Foster 1922c.

15 Ruthenberg 1923; C.E. Ruthenberg, 'Manifesto on the Cleveland Conference by the Central Committee of the Workers Party', undated, in Comintern archives, 515:1:196; *Labor Herald*, December 1922, January 1923. See also, William F. Dunne, 'Workers' Party Demands Admission to Gathering of Conference for Progressive Political Action', Workers' Party

The TUEL emphasised that it 'must be definitely rooted in the economic needs of the workers, it must be a party of the working class, yet it must be broad and inclusive enough to take in all the various political parties of Labor'. Above all, it must be a 'political United Front of Labor against the capitalists'. According to the *Labor Herald*, 'it is a *desirable* thing that the Labor Party shall not be a homogenous mass'. Thus, all tendencies among the labour movement should operate within it, while the new party's programme 'should challenge capitalism and hold up the ideal of a workers' society' while being 'essentially, a party of battle'. This required two things. First, the labour party needed to 'fight and defeat' Gompers' bureaucracy in the AFL, which opposed class-based politics. Second, although the party should support 'exploited small farmers', it was crucial that 'actual workers ... must dominate the party' and 'fight for class independence and be a Labor Party in fact as well as name'.[16]

Meanwhile, the farmer-labour movement was breaking apart. Many of Fitzpatrick's fellow labour leaders opposed any independent party, especially if Communists were to play a role. Under pressure from Gompers's AFL bureaucracy, Fitzpatrick became ambivalent about a labour party. Foster later described Fitzpatrick and his supporters as 'very timid'. They wanted to keep a foot in both camps, without antagonising Gompers (whose neutrality, at least, was needed to keep the CFL functional), or breaking with the Workers' Party (whose organisers he respected and whose support helped him retain radical credentials). As Fitzpatrick's interest waned, many farmers were more open to breaking with the two main parties, further undercutting the working-class nature of the movement.[17]

The FLP made plans to hold a convention on 3 July 1923 and invited the Workers' Party. The invitation said nothing about organising a political party, but called for 'devising means for knitting together the many organizations in the country in such a manner that will enable the workers to really function

press release, 12 December 1922; Dunne, 'Cleveland Conference Fails to Launch Labor Party'; and Dunne, 'Refuses Seat to Communists. Independent Political Action Defeated by Vote of 62 to 52', Workers' Party press releases, 15 December 1922, in Comintern archives, 515:1:148. On the conception of the Farmer Labor Party as a united front, see Bittelman, 'Things I Have Learned', folder 14, p. 374; Swabeck, 'From Debs to Mao', section VIII, p. 6; the resolutions from the Second National Convention of the Workers' Party can be found in the Comintern archives, 515:1:141.

16 *Labor Herald*, December 1922.

17 Foster to Lozovsky, 19 September 1923, in Comintern archives, 515:1:245 (the conclusion to the letter is missing, but by content and context, the letter appears to be written by Foster); Dyson 1982, p. 9.

politically'. The party was divided over how to react to Fitzpatrick's equivocation. Fitzpatrick told the three-man team (comprising Earl Browder, Charles Krumbein and Arne Swabeck) assigned by the Workers' Party to arrange the July convention: 'Let's get the record straight—we are willing to go along, but we think you communists should be occupying a back seat in this affair'. To compound this, John Pepper (discussed below) outed Foster as a Communist in the *Worker* in the run up to the conference; this undercut Foster's position and raised the prominence of the Workers' Party in the Farmer-Labor movement—exactly what Fitzpatrick did not want.[18]

The party's goal was not to wage a fight within the FLP and polarise it over whether to have an unambiguous working-class party shorn of pro-capitalist progressive reformers. Nor was there any recognition that the farmer-labour movement, far from serving to create a working-class party, was based on two *different* classes, petty-bourgeois farmers and workers. Instead the party sought a broader organisation in which Communists could work. Union support was crucial in this view, since 'a Labor Party without the big unions in it will be a miscarriage', as Israel Amter wrote to the Comintern in April 1923. 'My perception of the situation', Foster wrote to Lozovsky later, was 'that it was totally impossible for the Workers' Party to, of itself, lead the rank and file revolt to establish the Labor Party, but what was necessary was an alliance between it and the Farmer-Labor Party [Fitzpatrick], together with as many progressive unions as possible'.[19]

Five decades later, Swabeck recalled: 'This alliance, opening a direct entry for our participation in the labor party movement, we interpreted as a correct application of the united front policy'. A labour party would be militant, but not Communist. It would be a 'reformist party with different and even conflicting ideologies' because it would be 'absurd for the communists to attempt to lead it'. Keeping with this conception, the Chicago leadership, especially Browder and Swabeck, did not want to antagonise Fitzpatrick. They believed that he was indispensable for a labour party and in a stronger position than they were. Foster went along with the move, despite his misgivings. He later explained to Cannon: 'When people who all want to see the same thing, get together in a closed room, they tend to see what they want to see and they can

18 J.G. Brown for the Farmer Labor Party to Workers' Party, 9 May 1923, in Comintern archives, 515:1:141; Swabeck, 'From Debs to Mao,' section VII, p. 7; Palmer 2007, p. 180; Sakmyster 2011, Chapter 5.

19 I. Amter to Comintern, 7 April 1923, in Comintern archives, 515:1:174; Foster to Lozovsky, 19 September 1923, in Comintern archives, 515:1:245.

talk themselves into almost anything'. For his part, Cannon was not involved in the decision, having been on a national tour after returning from Moscow.[20]

So Far from Moscow, So Close to Pepper

By this time, however, a new element had been introduced into the party leadership: John Pepper. Recalling the internal life of the Workers' Party in 1923–4, Cannon noted that it 'revolved mainly around Pepper' and labelled it 'the Pepper era'. Not without reason did Bryan Palmer title his chapter on this period, 'Pepper Spray'. Pepper (whose original name was József Schwartz but who had changed it to József Pogány to avoid anti-Semitism) was a Jewish Hungarian in exile after the defeated Hungarian Revolution of 1919. In 1921, the Comintern sent him, along with fellow Hungarian revolutionary Béla Kun, to Germany where he helped organise the disastrous 'March Action'. As Palmer emphasised, 'Over the years 1921 to 1929, Pepper was the kind of communist functionary who destroyed Bolshevism, internationally as well as in its home base of Soviet Russia'. A recent biography of Pepper, based on Hungarian as well as Soviet and American sources, underlines that opportunism, adventurism and a lack of political principles guided Pepper's career from Hungary to his death in the Stalinist purges of the 1930s. His new comrades in America were of course unaware of this, and he passed himself off as an experienced revolutionary.[21]

Pepper had arrived in 1922 with Valetski and Reinstein at the time of the Bridgman Convention. His original mandate was apparently to work with the Hungarian Federation. In April 1922, the federation had begun a new paper. By the end of the year, the federation had some 600 members in 30 branches, and its daily paper—the only Hungarian-language Communist daily in the world—had a declared circulation of 8,500. This made it a middling-sized federation.[22]

20 Swabeck, 'From Debs to Mao', section VII, p. 6; Foster to Lozovsky, 19 September 1923, in Comintern archives, 515:1:245; Foster, quoted in Cannon 1962, p. 87.

21 Material from the previous two paragraphs is taken from Palmer 2007, pp. 175–7. See Sylvers 1987 for an overview of Pepper's career in the American Communist movement. For a complete biography of Pepper/Pogány, see Sakymyster 2012. *New York Times* 24 March, 5 May, 9 June and 29 November 1919 mention Joseph Pogány in his role as Minister of War for the revolutionary regime; the last two blame various Communist 'atrocities' on him. The Trotskyist *Militant* (1 March 1929) published an article on Pepper's activity in Hungary; Kun and Pogány's role in Germany is described in E.H. Carr 1966, pp. 334–5.

22 Cannon 1962, pp. 51, 78. On the launching of the Hungarian paper, see James P. Cannon to All Party Editors, 20 April 1922, in Comintern archives, 515:1:146; on language federation

According to Thomas Sakmyster, Pepper's biographer, the real purpose of his transfer was to get him out of Moscow and break up what Sam Darcy, American representative to the Comintern later in the decade, described as the 'endless factionalism among the Hungarian emigration'. His danger to world revolution was much less in Chicago than Berlin. He soon threw himself into the central leadership of the party. Salutsky, a member of the CEC at this time, recalled that 'Pepper spoke no English, but his words counted'. At the Bridgman Convention in the summer of 1922, he was elected to the CEC. In April 1923, Ruthenberg again wrote to the Comintern, asking for another Hungarian to be sent to edit the paper (which he claimed had a circulation of up to 12,000), in part because 'comrade Joseph has no time at all for the Hungarian Section because all of his time is taken up in the General movement—the American Party'.[23]

Upon arrival in America, Pepper passed himself off as the voice of the Comintern, and set about to construct an apparatus of supporters. Darcy, a friend of Foster, recalled in his memoirs that Pepper was 'an extremely self-centered egoist' who was 'respectful only towards Ruthenberg. Others he either patronized, frankly insulted, or disdained. No one liked him'. Yet Darcy added: 'Among the men of limited experience who led our young Communist movement, Pepper towered like a giant'. Swabeck recalled that Pepper was viewed as 'a sophisticated European intellectual'. Cannon remembered him as 'a manipulator deluxe' whose method was to parlay his European sophistication and experience, as well as his organisational and literary skills, to pass himself off as an envoy from the Comintern, despite having no such mandate. 'Comrade Pepper has posed as a representative of the Comintern, thereby gaining great prestige', Foster complained to Zinoviev in 1924. 'His active supporters have circulated statements of this kind until the entire membership come to

sizes, see 'Report of CEC to Second National Convention, 24–26 December 1922', Comintern archives, 515:1:148. On the Hungarian federation and its paper, see Sakmyster 2005a, which cites lower membership figures. By comparison, according to the report cited, in 1922 the Finnish federation claimed 6,500 members and three daily papers with a combined circulation of 22,500, while the Lettish federation claimed 200 members and no paper.

23 Sakmyster 2005b, p. 60; Sam Darcy, 'The Storm Must Be Ridden', unpublished memoir [1945?], in Sam A. Darcy papers, box 3, folder 16, p. 13; Hardman, 'Communism in America', undated manuscript [early 1930s], in J.B.S. Hardman papers, box 14, folder 10, pp. 17–18; on Pepper's becoming a member of CEC, see Swabeck, 'From Debs to Mao', section VI, p. 3; on Ruthenberg's asking for another Hungarian, see C.E. Ruthenberg to Comrade Kolaroff, 29 May 1923, in Comintern archives, 515:1:201. According to his biographer, 'from 1922 to 1924 items by or about [Pepper] appeared in nearly every issue' of the Hungarian paper, despite Ruthenberg's complaint; see Sakmyster 2012, Chapter 5.

look upon him as such a representative'. Writing to Draper in 1954, Cannon still did not know what Pepper's official role, if any, had been.[24]

On the eve of the 3 July 1923 conference, Pepper worried less about alienating Fitzpatrick than did Communists with roots in the labour movement. Pepper, his ally Ruthenberg, and especially Ruthenberg's lieutenant Jay Lovestone, did not see the labour party as a way to gain influence among labour militants. Instead, it was a get-rich-quick scheme—and hence something to be pursued as soon as possible, whatever the damage done to the party's relationship with Fitzpatrick and the Chicago trade-union leadership. Bittelman described Pepper as interested above all in 'short cuts to Communist mass influence' and 'clever maneuvres'. After the fact, Foster indicated that Ruthenberg had been sympathetic to Cannon and his desire to avoid antagonising Fitzpatrick, but 'the overwhelming majority' of the CEC 'was against it and took a very belligerent attitude toward the Farmer-Labor Party'.[25]

One manoeuvre was to stack the 3 July meeting with party sympathisers and supporters. The WP Executive Council voted to 'send as many delegates—party members whenever possible—from the Trade Unions and fraternal organizations'. Various reports after the fact indicate that the party's leaders themselves were not sure how many Communists attended the meeting.[26]

The *New York Times* reported that more than a thousand people attended the conference, including veteran labour organiser 'Mother Jones', then 94 years old. Under Ruthenberg's leadership, the Communist delegates gained control of the convention, prompting the ACWA delegation to walk out during the second day. The Communist delegates succeeded in getting their platform approved. Far from advocating socialist revolution, this called for nationalising public utilities; workers' and farmers' control of industry and agriculture;

24 Sam Darcy, 'The Storm Must Be Ridden', box 3, folder 16, p. 3; Swabeck, 'From Debs to Mao', section VIII, p. 4; Foster to Zinoviev, 9 May 1924, in Comintern archives, 515:1:297; Cannon 1962, p. 76.

25 Bittelman, 'Things I Have Learned', folders 14 and 15, pp. 390–408; Foster to Lozovsky, 19 September 1923, in Comintern archives, 515:1:245. On Ruthenberg, see Sakmyster 2012, Chapter 5.

26 In a report, Amter claimed 10 official Workers' Party delegates and 160 Communist delegates attending in other capacities; Pepper claimed 170 other delegates, while Ruthenberg recalled 180. For discussion on the convention, see the minutes of the WP Executive Committee in May and June 1923, in Comintern archives, 515:1:190. Amter's estimate is from a report of 7 April 1923 (Comintern archives, 515:1:174); Ruthenberg's report is in the Comintern archives, 515:1:196; Pepper, 'The First Mass Party of the American Workers and Farmers', 12 July 1923, Comintern archives, 515:1:212; Motion of WP Executive Council, 31 May 1923, in Comintern archives, 515:1:190.

'making the Federal Reserve Board serve the farmers and workers'; child labour laws; a soldier bonus; social and maternity insurance; and a living minimum wage. Despite the platform's emphasis on reforms, Fitzpatrick denounced this as 'too Red, Communistic, and Bolshevik'.[27]

Outmanoeuvred at his own meeting, Fitzpatrick walked out; this left two farmer-labour parties. Pepper glowed that 'like Zeus the son of Cronos', the party had defeated Fitzpatrick, who 'had entered the Ashland Auditorium as the future leader of the American working class, and left a politically isolated man'. The Communist-controlled rump convention called itself the 'Federated Farmer-Labor Party' (FFLP), signifying that membership was based on the trade unions, unlike Fitzpatrick's FLP. The political platforms of the two parties were almost identical; both blunted the working-class nature of the new parties in favour of alliances with farmers.[28]

Pepper hailed the FFLP as 'the first mass party of American workers and farmers'. This typical hyperbole emphasised that Pepper's genius lay not only in his opportunism and impressionism, but his facile ability to create grand theoretical justifications that wrapped such opportunism in Marxist phrases. Pepper's biographer notes 'his propensity for applying the basics of Marxism in new and unexpected ways'. Gitlow (a former Ruthenberg supporter who became an anti-Communist) later called him the 'Hungarian political Christopher Columbus', because he 'rediscovered America for the American communists'. By himself, Pepper was not responsible for the farmer-labour opportunism. It is likely that a switch from abstentionism to intervention would have resulted in problems. Rather, like a chemical catalyst, Pepper made the explosion more spectacular.[29]

The party bragged to the Comintern that the FFLP Executive Committee 'contains a majority of Party members representing various organizations'. Of seven members, three were WP members and one a sympathiser. Joseph Manley, the executive secretary, was a Workers' Party member (and Foster's son-in-law). The party claimed that it had 'obtained the contact and direction of a mass organization of workers and farmers'. Pepper and Ruthenberg described the FFLP as 'a real mass party' under Communist leadership. Another report to the Comintern by Amter declared: 'The Federated Farmer-Labor Party is

27 *New York Times*, 4 July 1923, 5 July 1923; 6 July 1923.

28 *New York Times*, 7 July 1923; Pepper, 'The First Mass Party', 12 July 1923, Comintern archives, 515:1:212; introduction to Cannon 1992, pp. 23–4; Draper 1986, p. 48; for a description of the convention and its aftermath, see also MacKay 1947, pp. 81–4.

29 Pepper, 'The First Mass Party', 12 July 1923, in Comintern archives, 515:1:212; Saknyster 2012, Chapter 5; Gitlow 1965, pp. 109–10; for less grandiose language but with the recognition of Pepper's role, see Bittelman, 'Things I Have Learned', folder 14, p. 400.

a *real* entity'. The party claimed credit for this momentous advance, describing how 'The Workers' Party was obliged to take the leadership in the formation of the party, otherwise there would have been no party'. In response, the Communist International congratulated the party for their 'achievement of primary importance'.[30]

After the Hangover, Loneliness

Lost in the jubilation was any understanding that the FFLP was an almost entirely Communist-controlled affair. The party started seeking support among left-wing union leaders. The leadership asked Radek and Zinoviev to draft a letter to Sidney Hillman, urging the ACWA to affiliate. This underlines the unrealistic FFLP perspective: the ACWA had walked out of the 3 July meeting, and the very same meeting requesting the letter to Hillman also expelled Salutsky, by then ensconced in the ACWA bureaucracy, for having refused to defend the party at the CPPA meeting in Cleveland (where he was a delegate for the ACWA).[31]

The split with Fitzpatrick, and to a lesser degree Hillman, cut the party off from the labour movement. 'Where the Communists had once been at the very heart of a powerful progressive movement, they were now clearly on the margins, discredited and distrusted', according to James Barrett. Non-communist 'progressives' in the trade-union leadership, who did not like Gompers and had supported a working-class party, withdrew from the FFLP and returned to the AFL fold.[32]

30 I. Amter, report to the Comintern, 7 August 1923, Comintern archives, 515:1:174; Pepper and Ruthenberg, 'Report on the Creation of the Federated Farmer-Labor Party', for Presidium of Comintern, Comintern archives, 515:1:199; W. Kolarow for the ECCI to the WPA, 7 December 1923, in Comintern archives, 515:1:164.

31 Minutes of Political and Organizational Committee, 14 July 1923, in Comintern archives, 515:1:197; on Salutsky, see C.E. Ruthenberg, 'J.B. Salutsky—A Communist?', Workers' Party press release, 13 December 1922, in Comintern archives, 515:1:148. The minutes from the spring and summer of 1923, in the Comintern archives, 515:1:197, contain extensive discussion about the case; see also the correspondence between Salutsky and Ruthenberg in the Hardman papers, box 38, folder 3. Salutsky by 1923 had already grown tired of the Workers' Party, and preferred his role as an editor in the ACWA and did not want to follow Communist discipline. When he refused to place the journal he edited, *American Labor Monthly*, under party control, he was expelled.

32 Barrett 1999, p. 140.

Other than the fiat of the Workers' Party, the FFLP was indistinguishable from its predecessor. Not only did this carry over the weakness of the farmer-labour movement from the outset—a dilution of the proletarian centrality of the new movement—but it also placed the split on organisational ground. Enraged by what he saw as Communist perfidy, Fitzpatrick red-baited the Workers' Party as being interested only in its own power. He refused to collaborate with groups that he labelled committed to illegal or unconstitutional change or affiliated to foreign organisations like the Comintern. This left TUEL and FFLP supporters vulnerable to anti-Communist repression within the unions. Soon the needle trades unions and the mineworkers expelled TUEL supporters. In August, somebody shot at (and missed) Foster while he spoke at an ILGWU meeting in Chicago.[33]

According to David Saposs, 'Never before in the history of the labor movement has there been such a wholesale expulsion of members'. The anti-Communist campaign reached a crescendo at the October 1923 AFL Convention in Portland, Oregon. William F. Dunne, an official delegate representing the Montana Silver Bowl Trades and Labor Council, was expelled because he was a Communist—the first time a delegate was purged for his politics. The AFL leaders denounced him as anti-labour, and amid what one historian called a 'lynch mob atmosphere', Dunne was expelled by a vote of 27,837 to 108. UMWA leader Phil Murray, according to the *Butte Daily Post*, 'called upon the convention to eliminate a "traitor"', while William Green, another UMWA leader and future head of the AFL, declared that 'we should purge ourselves of this outspoken agent of the workers' party and the communists'. The delegates also voted down resolutions for industrial unionism and independent labour politics.[34]

Writing in the *American Federationist*, Gompers called to 'rid the trade union movement of the last remnants of destructive and revolutionary effort', complained that the AFL had 'been too tolerant' of Communists, and accused

33 *Labor Herald*, August 1923. On anti-Communist propaganda among the UMWA, see *Attempts by Communists* 1923; Foster *et al.* 1925, pp. 18–31; Barrett 1999, p. 141.

34 Saposs 1926, p. 56; *New York Times*, 9 October 1923. The votes represented bloc votes, not individual votes; of the 378 delegates, 52 were absent or not voting, six voted for Dunne, and the rest voted for his expulsion. I am grateful to Tim Davenport for pointing out that there was no building in Portland in 1923 capable of holding 30,000 delegates; Montgomery 1987, pp. 433–4; *Butte Daily Post*, 8 October 1923, in William F. Dunne papers, box 1, folder 1; Barrett 1998, p. 323; for Dunne's speech, which included an attack on the UMWA leadership, see Dunne 1923. On Communist work in the UMWA, and Lewis's response, see Howard 2004, Chapter 2; Howard 2004, Chapters 2 and 3.

Dunne of having bought delegate status. John L. Lewis, the powerful head of the UMWA, attacked the TUEL while the ILGWU waged war on party supporters.[35]

(Befitting their role as the brain-trust behind a farmer-labour party, Communists attempted to organise farmers. W.H. Green, the vice-president of the FFLP, travelled to Moscow for the founding of the 'Red Peasant International' (or Krestintern) in October 1923 where he was elected to its 12-man presidium. In the autumn of 1923, Communists organised the United Farmers Educational League (UFEL). This group published the *United Farmer* and was 'to perform functions similar to the TUEL among the farm organizations in the United States', Ruthenberg wrote to the Comintern. Unlike workers, the Communists had few farmers: Ruthenberg claimed that there were about 150 farmer-Communists, and another 50 members of the UFEL. Ruthenberg outlined a plan to recruit one thousand farmers to the Workers' Party, using them to build the FFLP, particularly in North and South Dakota, Nebraska and Kansas, but also in Oklahoma and Texas. While the Communist Party in the 1920s remained an urban, working-class organisation, it did recruit some farmers, both as a result of efforts to address farmer issues and because much of the party's Finnish membership were farmers. In some places, such as Montana and Wisconsin, the party found surprising support among farmers).[36]

The split with Fitzpatrick, and the subsequent isolation from the labour movement, set off a new factional battle in the party. This factionalism would hobble the party for the rest of the decade, even after the immediate issues had been resolved. Pepper, supported by Ruthenberg and Lovestone, heralded the FFLP as a great success that could form the basis for a mass Communist Party. Pepper described Dunne's expulsion from the AFL convention as 'a Communist Bunker Hill' and the 'greatest victory for the cause of Communism'.[37]

35 *American Federationist*, November 1923. See the 3 November 1923 letter from Bonanza Lodge of the Brotherhood of Locomotive Firemen and Engineers in Missoula, Montana, attesting to Dunne's legitimate delegate status, in Dunne papers, box 1, folder 18.

36 Dyson 1972, p. 960; C.E. Ruthenberg to W. Kolaroff, 14 September 1923, in Comintern archives, 515:1:201; on Communist recruitment of farmers in Montana see McDonald 2010, especially Chapter 7; The best overview of the Communist effort to recruit farmers is Dyson 1982; see especially the first three chapters, which detail the farmer-labour movement, the UFEL, and Finnish-American cooperatives. In the 1930s, Communists did make some inroads among farmers in the Midwest. On this, see the later portions of Dyson 1982 and W.C. Pratt 1988. Dyson claims that the UFEL was organised in 1926, but Ruthenberg's letter indicates that, in some form at least, it existed earlier; Dyson 1972, pp. 962–3.

37 Pepper, 'Portland—A Communist Bunker Hill!', Comintern archives, 515:1:213. The relationship between Foster's supporters (primarily Bittelman, Browder and Johnstone) and Cannon's (Dunne and Swabeck) is described by Bittelman in his memoirs.

Cannon and Foster moved closer because they sensed the negative effects of the FFLP fiasco. 'Sobering thoughts about the July 3 convention split were confined to what from then on became known as the Foster-Cannon group', recalled Swabeck in his memoirs. Foster was affected most by the split, since it cut him off from his pre-Communist contacts in the labour movement. As he told the Comintern later, after the split, 'we lost contact with the trade unionists'.[38] Cannon and his allies, such as Dunne and Swabeck, with roots in the trade-union movement, had few illusions about the FFLP. Jewish militants in the garment trades, such as Rose Wortis, were less enthusiastic about the manoeuvre since it set them up for victimisation. Ludwig Lore, in the German federation, grumbled about the move.

In a private letter in 1923, Cannon commented on this 'pessimism and skepticism' and noted that Pepper had become more belligerent against his opponents, even accusing the Chicago comrades of sabotage. He observed that the FFLP 'has met a united front of savage opposition from our enemies and has not, so far, been able to gain the affiliations which were hoped for by those who were enthusiastic ... We are facing a bitter fight all along the line'. He noted the UMWA and needle trade unions' 'open war against the T.U.E.L.' and bemoaned that 'even the Amalgamated has demanded the dissolution of the T.U.E.L.'[39]

This division developed *after* the split with Fitzpatrick. In his memoirs, Bittelman, a key ally of Foster, emphasised that 'At the July 3rd Conference itself we had no realization of all these consequences' of forming the FFLP without Fitzpatrick. Although the manoeuvre had been developed by Pepper, 'we all went along' except for Ludwig Lore in the German federation and M.J. Olgin in the Yiddish federation. 'We had no difference that we knew of with Pepper's labor party theory and strategy that we knew at that time and, therefore, went into their application with energy and enthusiasm'.[40]

The difference between the two sides was that for Foster and Cannon, this energy and enthusiasm faded when they realised the disastrous effects of the FFLP. In a November 1923 'Statement on Our Labor Party Policy', they argued that 'the apparent break of the Communists with the progressive wing of the labor movement emboldened the reactionaries for a great counter-offensive against the Communists, which continues to be one of the most pronounced features of the current labor situation'. Communists in the unions 'were almost completely isolated'. The FFLP, far from gaining a mass audience

38 Swabeck, 'From Debs to Mao', section VII, p. 11; Dorsey [Foster] to American Commission, 6 May 1924, in Comintern archives, 515:1:257.

39 Jim Cannon to Charley [Johnson], late 1923, in Comintern archives, 534:7:458.

40 Bittelman, 'Things I Have Learned', folder 14, pp. 400–2.

for Communist politics, comprised 'ourselves and our closest sympathizers', as Bittelman put it in his memoirs.[41]

Cannon and Foster saw the FFLP as an albatross that had 'proved itself a failure'. Anti-Communists 'brand[ed] it before the labor movement as merely another name for the Workers' Party'. Even in unions where Communist supporters were active, such as the garment trades, the FFLP could not gain affiliates. They attacked Pepper and Ruthenberg's falling ill to the 'old sickness ... to get unduly excited, to overestimate the radical development, and plunge into premature actions which bring disastrous defeats and paralysing reactions in our own ranks'. They described what they called a trend of 'progressivism' in the unions, 'a revolt against Gomperism that has not yet developed a systematic outlook'. The creation of the FFLP blunted the ability of the Workers' Party to win such 'progressives' to Communism, Foster and Cannon complained. They insisted that the party discard the illusion that the FFLP was a mass party, and instead begin to organise for a *real* mass labour party.[42]

In retrospect, these criticisms seem essentially correct. There is another dimension to the FFLP adventure. Pepper's plan had set up the party for red-baiting in the unions. But at the same time it saddled them with a non-Communist organisation to defend. The FFLP's emphasis on social reforms and farmers' demands was not even an open Communist programme. Swabeck, decades later, described how 'Communists had come into leadership of a reformist and artificially constructed political party, the contradiction we should have avoided'. Pepper's get-rich-quick scheme threatened the party with bankruptcy.[43]

Pepper and Ruthenberg saw things differently, of course. Their 'August Theses' hailed the split with Fitzpatrick and the formation of the FFLP as a 'great victory' and 'the greatest political advance which our party has been able to make so far'. They predicted that by the end of 1923, some 250,000 workers and between 50,000 and 80,000 farmers would join the new party. Its creation had 'put the [Workers'] Party in a most favorable position' and made it 'a political factor'. Communists needed to organise the FFLP 'as a real party' and to 'transform the Federated [Farmer-Labor Party] to a Communist mass party'. They attacked the 'party comrades who chiefly concern themselves with trade union problems' for complaining that the aftermath of the 3 July split would

41 Cannon 1992, pp. 159–60; Bittelman, 'Things I Have Learned', folder 15, p. 411;
42 Cannon 1992, pp. 127–49, 153–78.
43 Swabeck, 'From Debs to Mao', section VII, p. 9.

cause the party to 'lose the support of these progressive [labour] leaders who until now supported the amalgamation campaign'.[44]

The Farmer-Labor adventure had accentuated the isolation of the party within the labour movement and initiated a new round of factionalism. It had also left the party politically weakened, open to ways to increase its influence through compromising the Marxist principles of working-class centrality and independence in the struggle to transform society. These problems would become more acute in the run up to the 1924 presidential election.

---

44 John Pepper and C.E. Ruthenberg, 'Thesis on Labor Party Policy', 24 August 1923, Prometheus Research Library collection.

CHAPTER 6

The La Follette Fiasco, 1923–4

By the 1920s, Progressivism in American politics had peaked. Large corporations dominated politics, as capitalists seemed to have attained the nirvana of never-ending prosperity and an ever-weakening labour movement. Ferdinand Lundberg observed that in the 1924 presidential election between Calvin Coolidge and John W. Davis, 'J.P. Morgan and Company had the unprecedented distinction of controlling both candidates'.[1] Resentment towards traditional capitalist politics arose from anger from the trade-union bureaucracy (especially the railroad brotherhoods) over anti-labour laws and court rulings, and from disgust with the corruption epitomised by the Teapot Dome scandal. In a last gasp of Progressivism, liberal and radicals—including Farmer-Laborites, trade unionists, and other restive reformers—looked towards discontented politicians to oppose mainstream Democrats and Republicans. They accepted the framework of bourgeois politics, and many wanted to reform the Democrats or Republicans. Others saw La Follette, a maverick Republican Senator from Wisconsin, and investigator of the scandal, as a leader of a third-party—a role he opposed.[2]

By this time, the Farmer-Labor Party (those who did not go with the Workers' Party) liquidated into the wider bourgeois Progressive movement, losing what specifically working-class character it had in favour of dissident capitalist politics. The FFLP's few non-Communist supporters soon deserted it, many to the third-party movement developing in anticipation of the 1924 presidential election. Given the political mood of the time, it is unlikely that anything the Communists could have done would have resulted in mass influence, despite Pepper's grandiose visions.

The FFLP episode demonstrates how far down the opportunist road the Communists had gone under Pepper's tutelage. It meant disregarding the guiding Marxist principle that support for capitalist politicians (who, by definition, seek to maintain the capitalist system) was a betrayal. It also meant discarding a long left-wing socialist tradition in the US of denouncing Progressivism for merely trying to make capitalism better. (In 1906, even Victor Berger denounced La Follette, his fellow Wisconsinite, for 'steal[ing] our thunder' and fighting to *'preserve the system'*). The desertion of right-wing Socialists

1 Lundberg 1946, p. 171.

2 La Follette and La Follette 1953, II, p. 1111.

during the war, and the electoralism of sewer socialists like Berger, had consolidated left-wing disdain for reform-minded capitalist politicians.[3]

For Pepper, this did not matter. Having already supported the FFLP, with its reformist programme and two-class nature, he predicted opportunities in the La Follette movement. Pepper hailed what he called the 'La Follette revolution', comprising 'elements of the great French Revolution, and the Russian Kerensky Revolution'. He expanded: 'In its ideology it will have elements of Jeffersonianism, Danish cooperatives, Ku Klux Klan and Bolshevism' although 'the proletariat *as a class* will not play an independent role in this revolution'. He advocated that Communists 'support the La Follette revolution at the same time criticizing and fighting for a Communist mass party'. Here his creativity in wrapping any policy, no matter how opportunist, in Marxist garb came in handy: he concocted a 'theory of two splits': first, the nascent third-party movement would split the petty-bourgeoisie from the big capitalists, and then the Communists would split the proletariat from the petty-bourgeoisie.[4]

La Follette and the 'Third-Party Alliance'

In December 1923, Pepper put forward a motion at a CEC meeting that committed the FFLP to 'initiate a campaign to bring about a split of the La Follette forces from the Republican Party', implying that it would be principled for Marxists to support this capitalist politician if he were not a Republican. A pamphlet by Ruthenberg, *The Farmer-Labor United Front*, described the farmer-labour movement as an opportunity to build 'for the first time ... a class party on a mass scale fighting against the parties of the capitalist class'. The pamphlet, written in the lead-up to the Minnesota convention in June, asserted that Communists should be politically open. It denounced the third-party movement as representing 'the class interests of the petty bourgeoisie'. Still, the bottom line was support to the La Follette movement, however couched in Marxist rhetoric.[5]

3 Berger 1913, p. 3. Lovestone's anti-La Follette pamphlet of 1924 also contains a section on Berger's attacks on La Follette to attack the SP's support of his campaign that year.

4 Draper 1986, p. 83; Political and Organizational Committee Minutes, 19 September 1923, in Comintern archives, 515:1:197.

5 Ruthenberg 1924, pp. 2, 18. The pamphlet is undated, but refers to the July 1923 formation of the FFLP as 'last year' (p. 19) and was clearly written before the June 1924 Minnesota FFLP convention.

Coupled with this was an overblown sense of the campaign's importance: 'There is probably not a Communist Party in the International except for those that are face to face with the proletarian revolution which has the responsibilities and the opportunities of our Party at the present time'. Ruthenberg argued that 'victory will be over the dead body (politically) of La Follette'. He asserted that there must be no unity between the farmer-labour movement and the La Follette movement, even though both supported La Follette. 'We are opposed to La Follette', Ruthenberg asserted, but then added that if a majority of farmer-labourites supported him, Communists 'will vote for La Follette in the elections'. To do otherwise, Ruthenberg claimed, 'would mean that we would turn over the class Farmer-Labor Party movement to the Third Party movement'. In the pamphlet, Ruthenberg denounced Communists in Washington State and Minnesota who advocated openly supporting La Follette, but the logic of the party's position was to tail this bourgeois movement. That it could be possible to support the La Follette 'movement' without supporting La Follette could be defended only through obfuscation.[6]

Although Pepper and his supporters were the most vociferous and creative in touting this position, it was shared by almost all the leaders, including Foster and Cannon, despite tactical differences. In a report on the discussion, Amter, the party's representative to the Comintern, described how a majority of the CEC would support 'a third bourgeois party ... being formed' under 'certain conditions'. According to Bittelman, Pepper and Ruthenberg wanted to take over leadership of the third-party movement as a 'prelude or introduction to the socialist revolution in its opening phase'. Foster and Cannon saw the third-party movement as an opening for 'independent political action and expanding the influence of the party'. Swabeck noted in his memoirs that 'we all accepted the idea of the "third party alliance" and were ready to support the La Follette candidacy'. In other words, most of the party's leadership was ready to renounce the Marxist principle of working-class political independence.[7]

The only opposition came from Olgin and Lore, leaders in the Jewish and German federations, respectively, and among the large Finnish federation. Lore and Olgin argued: 'It is absurd to assume that we can have common campaigns with the third bourgeois party for its bourgeois candidates and at the same time conduct an independent campaign for our program'. Cannon's, Foster's

6 Minutes, Executive Council of WP, 14 December 1923, in Comintern archives, 515:1:190; Ruthenberg 1924, pp. 2, 22–6.

7 Bittelman, 'Things I Have Learned', folder 15, p. 414; I. Amter, 'Further Report on Workers' Party Convention', 7 February 1924, in Comintern archives, 515:1:271; Swabeck, 'From Debs to Mao', section VII, p. 12.

and Pepper's groupings all opposed Lore and Olgin. A CEC resolution stated: 'The third party movement accelerates the development of the class struggle, produces a clearer crystallization of political groupings on the basis of real economic interests, and weakens the united capitalist front against the working class'. In other words, support for a capitalist reform politician could lead to the political independence of the working class from capitalist politicians.

In a polemic of April 1924, Cannon and Bittelman criticised Lore and Olgin for attempting 'to dump all non-proletarian groupings into one reactionary heap'. They denounced Lore and Olgin for their 'propos[al] to treat this movement, which is a revolt against big capital, precisely as we treat the Republican and Democratic Parties, which are parties of big capital'. Pepper, Foster and Cannon thus agreed on the need to support capitalist politicians under certain circumstances.[8]

From Moscow in May

Despite this broad agreement, Cannon and Foster were in a bloc with Lore and Olgin against Ruthenberg. In this time, Bittelman recalled: 'The rival groups were becoming tightly organized and operating in fact as two separate political organisms within the party'. These divisions to an extent reflected personal antagonisms, especially revolving around Pepper. Those who felt his wrath hated him, while those in his grace—such as many former Geese leaders—were grateful. Meanwhile, Lovestone was emerging as a brass-knuckle intriguer whom even his co-factionalists distrusted. The divisions also reflected the social backgrounds of the factional leaders. Cannon, Foster and Dunne were not only from a working-class background, but their formative years were in the radical trade-union movement; even Bittelman, their main theoretician, had graduated from the underground trade-union movement in Russia and not university. Foster criticised his opponents for having 'never had anything to do with the unions in their lives', adding that 'it has been said that they would not know a trade union if they saw it coming along the street'. Ruthenberg's

8 Material in preceding three paragraphs is taken from: C.E. Ruthenberg, 'Our Party—Three Tendencies', typescript in Ruthenberg papers, box 7, folder 2; later printed in *Daily Worker* magazine supplement, 19 January 1924; Cannon and Bittelman, 'Reply to Thesis of Comrades Lore and Olgin', *Daily Worker* magazine supplement, 12 April 1924, in Cannon 1992. On Finnish support for Lore and Olgin, see Amter, 'Further Report on the Workers' Party Convention', 7 February 1924, in Comintern archives, 515:1:271.

supporters included more university-educated members and people with experience in the social-democratic left-wing movement.[9]

An upcoming Farmer-Labor conference in Minnesota posed the immediate question. Communists and Minnesota farmer-labourites, led by William Mahoney, organised a conference for late May 1924 to nominate candidates for the upcoming election. The Minnesota FLP complained that under both Democrats and Republicans, 'the condition of the masses of producers, the farmers and industrial workers, has not been benefitted, but in fact has grown steadily worse'. The FLP in the state declared that its goal was 'disrupting private monopoly in the United States'. One historian noted that 'there was very little that had not been in the previous political platforms of the past twenty years'.[10]

Meanwhile, the CPPA had called a convention in Cleveland on 4 July as part of a campaign to stand La Follette for president. Even though the Communists were in charge of the rump FFLP, they were dwarfed by the La Follette 'movement'—especially since they had split on organisational and not programmatic issues, and a majority of even the FFLP supported La Follette (even though the Senator wanted nothing to do with the farmer-labourites). The Communists were left with the task of supporting the movement while trying to appear independent. After internal debate, the Communists moved the Minnesota

9 Browder, 'No Man's Land', Browder papers, p. 207; Bittelman, 'Things I Have Learned', pp. 429–33; Foster at American Commission meeting, 27 November 1925; the next day Pepper responded, 'I am no so-called "trade unionist"; but if I met a trade union on the street I would immediately see that it was a trade union and not a pretty girl'; both in Comintern archives, 495:37:5. It is clear from French syndicalists-cum-Communists Boris Rosmer's and Boris Souvarine's letters to Pierre Monatte at the time of the First Profintern Congress (reprinted in Chambelland 1964) that they regarded Foster as part of the left-wing syndicalist movement. In contrast, Ruthenberg 'had never belonged to a union', according to his sympathetic biographer, except for a brief period when he helped organise the Retail Clerks' Fraternal Association in Cleveland; see Johnson 1957, pp. 98–9. Such sociological generalisations are indistinct, of course. Thus, while Ruthenberg had trained as a bookkeeper at junior college, both Browder and Cannon had done office work as well; Wolfe, Lovestone and Cannon had briefly attended law school as well; see Draper 1985, p. 306; Morgan 1999, p. 13. Gitlow was the leading Ruthenberg factionalist with the most trade-union experience, having been a leader in the retail clerks' union in New York City; see Lendler 2012, pp. 8–9; see Gitlow's 1912 testimony to the Senate Commission on Industrial Relations 1914, III, p. 2334–44. On the anti-Pepper dynamic of the Cannon-Foster group, see Sakmyster 2012, Chapter 6.

10 St. Paul *Farmer-Labor Advocate*, 9 February 1923; 12 June 1923. Jansen 1985, pp. 55–86.

convention to 17 June, despite it being clear that most of the FFLP supporters would jump ship if La Follette ran.[11]

In early May, Ruthenberg announced how the Communists would try to deal with this situation: if enough industrial workers and poor farmers were represented at the Minnesota FFLP meeting, the party would advocate a National Farmer-Labor Party based on the FFLP programme. If there was not enough support, 'then we should not make a fight for the organization of a party, but accept a loose coalition for the election campaign' and struggle for a 'clear-cut class program' at the convention. In other words, in the expected face of immense support for La Follette, Communists should support La Follette, 'but stating our Communist attitude toward La Follette'. The CEC unanimously supported this policy—even though it would become clear that there was much confusion about what was the 'Communist attitude'.[12]

Ruthenberg advocated an additional policy, which failed on a factional vote:

> We must, however, be careful to see to it that manouver does not defeat La Follette, for to nominate another candidate and to permit La Follette to become the candidate for the July 4th [CPPA] Convention in opposition to our nominee would be to destroy the mass Farmer-Labor Party as a mass organization.

This exposed the opportunist basis of the FFLP. Since the FFLP was not based on a proletarian perspective, there was no reason for its followers to not support La Follette, a bourgeois politician who could gain more votes than the FFLP. Charles Taylor—a Republican State Senator in Montana, long-time farmer activist, and secret Communist active in the FFLP—made clear the opportunist basis of the Communist perspective in an oral history: 'we had hoped that La Follette and [running-mate] Wheeler would run Farmer Labor, and that would give the [Federated Farmer-Labor] party a real proper launching'. The hope was that this 'would have brought a lot of those populistic farmers into the party'. While it was reasonable to imagine a radical populist movement among disaffected farmers, this would have entailed jettisoning the perspective of building a *revolutionary, working-class*, that is, Communist, party.[13]

---

11 MacKay 1947, p. 58; *Where La Follette Stands* 1924, pp. 7–8; for continued FLP support for La Follette, see Shideler 1945, pp. 223–35; *Farmer-Labor Advocate*, 6 June 1923.

12 CEC minutes, 2 May 1924, in Comintern archives, 515:1:270.

13 CEC minutes, 2 May 1924, in Comintern archives, 515:1:270; Charles E. Taylor Reminiscences, Columbia University Oral History archives, pp. 64, 69; Dyson 1982, Chapter 1. Taylor had joined the Socialist Party in Minnesota in 1907, passed through the Non-Partisan League

The Fifth Comintern Congress: Bolshevisation and Anti-Trotskyism

All sides travelled to Moscow in the spring to argue their case at the Fifth Comintern Congress (June through July 1924). Both factions appealed to the Comintern to again orient the party's tactics and resolve organisational disputes. What most American Communists did not know was that by 1924 the Bolshevik Party was engaged in a fierce struggle over the future of the Russian Revolution and the Comintern. While La Follette's campaign was not the cause, issues raised by the third-party alliance, especially the relation of Communists to non-working-class organisations, formed a key part of this dispute. Factionalism in the American party became intertwined with developments in the Bolshevik Party.

This Congress took place in the shadow of Lenin's recent death and the defeat of the October 1923 Revolution in Germany. At the time of the German events, Trotsky launched a struggle over what he saw as the degeneration of Soviet Russia and the Bolshevik Revolution, forming the Left Opposition. By Lenin's death in January 1924, a 'troika' (or 'triumvirate') of Zinoviev, Kamenev and Stalin (in that order) had formed a bloc in the leadership of the Russian party against Trotsky, who many had assumed would succeed Lenin. By the Congress, the founder of the Red Army maintained support among the urban working class and rank and file of the army, but the troika worked to lessen his influence, for example, by rigging the voting for the Thirteenth Conference of the Russian Party in January 1924 (the last time there was open debate in the party).[14]

From afar, the political issues were not clear in 1923–4. Zinoviev, the head of the Comintern and better known and respected than Stalin, was seen as a leftist. He drew support from the working class in Leningrad, and Kamenev's base was in the Moscow working class. Stalin was much less known by Communists abroad, and was far from the obvious Soviet leader. His political base was the growing Soviet bureaucracy and party apparatus. He was increasingly responsive to the mood within these milieus of wanting to slow down the revolutionary process after the Civil War and to emphasise constructing socialism at home instead of revolution abroad—pressures fed by the dashing of revolutionary hopes in Germany.

a decade later, and ended up in Sheridan County, Montana, where he became a secret Communist Party member, local newspaper editor and State Senator. See McDonald 2010.

14 The formative documents of the Left Opposition are in Trotsky 1975; a broader collection of documents can be found in Vilkova 1996. For a recent analysis of the failed German revolution of 1923 on Soviet politics, see Albert 2011.

Writing more than a decade after this process, Trotsky recalled: 'The leaders of the bureaucracy promoted the proletarian defeats; the defeats promoted the rise of the bureaucracy'.[15] A few months after the Comintern Congress, in December, Stalin would crystallise this with his concept of 'socialism in one country', which he counterposed to Trotsky's orthodox Marxist stress on international revolution. Stalin's idea that a socialist society of abundance without human exploitation could be realised in a backward, isolated country like Russia in the context of imperialist hostility was at first a blind alley of impossible economic autarky and isolation. It soon became the ideological justification for transforming Communist parties abroad into bargaining chips in the search for what became known as 'peaceful coexistence' with international capitalism. This was a complex process and spread throughout the Comintern's sections at different rates, and foreign Communists were not always aware of the full dynamic.[16]

Although few Communists had worked with Trotsky during his months in New York before the Revolution, many viewed him as one of the most talented and important Bolshevik leaders. Alexander Bittelman recalled that when he visited Moscow in 1922, Trotsky's prestige was 'sky-high' while Stalin's name 'meant very little to me at that time'. Certain ideas that were later considered 'Trotskyist'—such as the need for international revolution—were accepted by all leading Communists.[17]

In 1924, the exception to this admiration of Trotsky was Pepper, who recalled the polemics directed against him at the Third Comintern Congress in 1921. In

15 Trotsky 1937, p. 90.

16 E.H. Carr captured the confusing nature of this in his observation that the 'Bolsheviks knew that the French revolution had ended in a Napoleon, and feared that their own revolution might end in the same way. They therefore mistrusted Trotsky, who among their leaders looked most like a Napoleon, and trusted Stalin, who looked least like a Napoleon'; Carr 1967, p. 90.

17 Bittelman, 'Things I Have Learned', folder 14, pp. 380–1; in 1918, M.J. Olgin had edited a collection of Trotsky's writings. John Reed's *Ten Days That Shook the World* of 1919 highlighted Trotsky's role in the Revolution—while Stalin was barely mentioned. In 1921, Foster described him as 'next to Lenin, the biggest figure of the Revolution'; see Trotsky 1918; Reed 1967; Foster 1921b, p. 90. In the same pamphlet, Foster noted: 'When they carried out their uprising in 1917 the Russian Communists had been long convinced that for a proletarian revolution to be successful it would almost necessarily have to extend over several big countries simultaneously'. In words that would be heresy less than a decade later, Foster stressed that 'the possibility of a working class republic maintaining itself in one country, while the rest remained capitalist, was almost negligible'; Foster 1921b, p. 108. Foster was not unique; rather, this was the standard Communist view in the formative years of the Comintern.

May 1924, Pepper submitted a motion to the CEC to 'endorse the position taken in the Russian Communist Party Congress on the controversy in the Russian Party'. Bittelman recalled that 'Pepper raised the issue in our party, calling for condemnation of Trotzky and his views, and using this issue in his fight against our group'. In response, Foster temporised. He asserted that since the dispute in Russia had been settled, 'it is not called upon at this time to take a position on the merits of the controversy'. Instead, the party should reprint relevant documents to inform the membership. 'The CEC will condemn any attempt to make a factional issue of the matter in the American Party'. The motions were voted along factional lines, with Foster's motion winning.[18]

'Trotskyism', like other issues, was subsumed by the ongoing factionalism, and became a cudgel that the factions used against one another. Nobody in the party leadership had any real sense about what was happening in Moscow. As Browder recalled, to probe further 'threatened to unleash a veritable Pandora's box of issues quite beyond our comprehension or control'. Despite having the vote at the CEC in May, Ruthenberg soon cabled the Comintern in support of the 'Old Bolsheviks' against Trotsky. Ruthenberg admitted he had no authority from the CEC to do this, but the CEC fell in line. Foster proposed a motion to 'endorse the position of the [Russian party] majority and support the leadership of the old guard Bolsheviks and instruct the secretary to immediately convey this decision by cable' to Moscow. The only vote against this was by Lore.[19]

The Farmer-Labour Debate in Moscow

Prior to the trip, Pepper's role in the party became a factional issue. The Foster-Cannon majority of the CEC wrote to the ECCI in late March, noting that 'The status of Comrade John Pepper in America has not been clearly established' although 'an impression has been prevailing in the Party that he is here by the authorization, direction, or commission of the E.C.C.I.' 'If this is the case', the letter continued, the majority petitioned to 'recall Comrade Pepper' because 'the welfare of the American Party imperatively demands that it be granted'. Noting that the Foster-Cannon majority and the Ruthenberg minority

18 On Trotsky's attacks on Pepper, see Trotsky 1945a, I, pp. 230–2; CEC minutes, 18 May 1924, in Comintern archives, 515:1:270; Bittelman, 'Things I Have Learned', folder 15, p. 421.

19 CEC minutes, 7 June 1924, in Comintern archives, 515:1:270. Both Cannon and Abern, future Trotskyists, voted for Foster's motion; Browder, 'No Man's Land', p. 211.

on the CEC tended to agree, in a longer letter to Zinoviev, Foster accused Pepper of endangering the party:

> In this reckless struggle for power he is gambling with the life and health of the Party. In his search for 'issues' he takes the slightest differences of opinion among the centre group, which ordinarily could be adjusted without any real difficulty, and makes them into matters of life and death struggle.

'His program is one of rule or ruin', Foster concluded. In Moscow, Foster acknowledged that factionalism would continue without Pepper, but not at the same intensity. 'Pepper has done one service', he quipped, 'that is, to teach all the American comrades the most up-to-date methods of factional fighting'.[20]

In response to this anti-Pepper offensive, a legion of minority supporters—including Gitlow, Joseph Manley, John Ballam, Henry Askeli and Robert Minor—wrote letters defending Pepper and the party's trajectory. Pepper, according to Manley (Foster's son-in-law and long-time comrade) was responsible for the party's work among farmers. 'Never', he gushed, 'until I heard Comrade Pepper discourse in the C.E.C. meetings, had I been able to get the realistic Communist interpretation as applied to the American condition'. Gitlow also gave credit for the Farmer-Labor policy to Pepper, and added that 'not a single policy of the party has been carried out without John Pepper in one way or another taking an active part'.[21]

In Moscow, Olgin argued against the third-party alliance; Pepper defended the original split with Fitzpatrick, and argued for an orientation towards La Follette. His 'Thesis on the American Situation' stressed that 'America is the most developed industrial country in the world, but at the same time she is one of the greatest agricultural countries' and hence, in some ways, 'bears more resemblance to pre-revolutionary Russia than to England'. This was by way of explaining that since finance capital exploited farmers, and since agriculture was in crisis, there was 'a remarkable new psychology in the American farmer:

20 Petition to ECCI, signed by William Z. Foster, James P. Cannon, Fahle Burman, Earl Browder, William F. Dunne, Alex Bittelman and Martin Abern, 27 March 1924; Foster to Zinoviev, 9 May 1924, both in Comintern archives, 515:1:297; Foster at American Commission meeting, 17 May 1924, in Comintern archives, 495:37:4.

21 The various letters are in the Comintern archives, 515:1:297; those quoted are Joseph Manley to Zinoviev, 2 April 1924; Benjamin Gitlow to Zinoviev, 2 April 1924. On this pro- and anti-Pepper campaign, see Sakmyster 2012, Chapter 8.

a kind of solidarity with the industrial workers, which does not manifest itself in any other country'.[22]

Foster asserted that La Follette was not the main issue, and argued that the Workers' Party had the strength to carry out a complicated manoeuvre. He lashed out at Ruthenberg and Pepper for 'neglect[ing] the trade union work and ... even sabotaging it', and for 'spending too much energy in trying to organise the farmers, and too little energy in trying to organise the workers'. He labelled this 'madness' and 'opportunism pure and simple'. Sensing a lack of support for the party at the upcoming Minnesota convention, Foster predicted that the FFLP would soon degenerate into 'just a small group of communists and communist sympathisers'.

Foster warned that this would 'isolate our movement, not only politically but industrially as well', causing Communists to 'be discredited throughout the trade union movement of the United States'. Foster's solution, however, was not to break with the opportunist farmer-labour campaign and third-party alliance, but to hitch the party to the non-working-class La Follette movement in the hopes of being towed to safety. Foster stressed the need to orient towards La Follette, asserting that the campaign was 'much stronger than La Follette' because 'La Follette is not leading it, but being driven by the movement'.[23]

It was necessary to 'carry on this propaganda [critical of La Follette] and still remain part of the [third-party] movement'. Foster added: 'We cannot divide this big movement at this particular juncture. We must, provided it is not a big capitalist party, go along with it to the extent of a common candidate for president'. He warned that if the Communists split the movement, the party 'is going to be thrown back, is going to be detached from the masses, and its work is going to be greatly hampered, not for a few months, as Olgin says, but for a long time to come'.[24]

The La Follette debate intersected a major struggle in the Bolshevik Party. Stalin, then allied with Zinoviev, sought to solidify his power within the post-Lenin Russian party, based on the growing Soviet bureaucracy. Part of this was 'socialism in one country'. A corollary was the resurrection of the Menshevik idea that socialists should systematically collaborate with non-working-class forces. In the 1930s, this would fully blossom as the Popular Front.

22 John Peper [sic], 'Thesis on the American Situation' [1924], in Comintern archives, 515:1:253.

23 Dorsey [Foster], presentation to American Commission of ECCI, 6 May 1924, in Comintern archives, 515:1:257. The entire debate can be found in ibid., 515:1:257; 515:1:258; and 495:37:4.

24 Dorsey [Foster] at American Commission meeting, 29 April 1924 and 6 May 1924, in Comintern archives, 495:37:4.

Trotsky, by 1924 in opposition to much of the leadership of the Russian party, denounced the manoeuvre as a betrayal of principle that crossed the class line separating working-class politics and the bourgeoisie. In a preface to a collection of his writings, dated 20 May 1924, the same day as the Comintern's decision, he warned: 'For a young and weak Communist Party, lacking in revolutionary temper, to play the role of solicitor and gatherer of "progressive" votes for the Republican Senator La Follette is to head toward the political dissolution of the party in the petty bourgeoisie'. Although the 'triumvirate' of Zinoviev, Kamenev and Stalin was in a position of strength, they still felt compelled to concede to Trotsky.[25]

The Political Bureau of the Russian Communist Party appointed a commission of Zinoviev, Radek, Lozovsky, Trotsky and Kamenev to discuss the matter. According to Amter, Trotsky was the most adamant opponent of the third-party manoeuvre; Radek also opposed it, but alternated between principled and tactical explanations. Zinoviev, Bukharin and Stalin seemed more ambivalent. Amter's reports to the CEC in the US indicate the tension on the commission and the seriousness afforded the issue by the upper layers of the Soviet government.[26]

During the commission's meetings, the Bolshevik delegation on the American Commission was sceptical of the third-party alliance—not only Pepper's wild 'revolutionary' justifications, but also Cannon and Foster's more reality-based opportunism. Radek criticised Pepper's inclination to confound American farmers with Russian peasants, and speculated that the split with Fitzpatrick had been ill conceived. Zinoviev stressed that 'we cannot support La Follette', and suggested that the party advocate an independent labour party. Lozovsky warned that the party's 'clever tactics which would make our Party a left wing of the bourgeoisie are leading to a disintegration of our Communist movement', and argued that the party must oppose La Follette. He claimed it was better 'to receive three thousand or a hundred thousand' votes while running as Communists 'instead of getting 2,000,000 for La Follette'.[27]

The Comintern instructed the party 'to strive by all means to enter the broad current of the masses in order to assist the masses of petty-bourgeoisie in detaching themselves from the capitalist class'. The Comintern also criticised the party, asserting that it 'has not only drawn insufficiently the line between

25 Trotsky 1945a, I, p. 13. See also Trotsky 1974a, pp. 91–2.

26 Amter's reports to the CEC in April and May (written under the name Grove) are in the Comintern archives, 515:1:274. For Trotsky's recollection of the controversy at the American Commission, as recalled by Max Shachtman, see Trotsky 1979.

27 Report of the American Commission in the Presidium of the ECCI, 20 May 1924, in Lovestone papers, box 210, folder 1.

itself and the petty-bourgeois elements which endeavour to establish a petty-bourgeois Third Party, but the Workers' Party has to a certain degree itself fallen under the influence of petty-bourgeois elements'.

At the upcoming FFLP convention in St. Paul, the Comintern instructed the party to come out against La Follette and to stand candidates. The Communists were to tell farmer-labourites who supported La Follette:

> You have confidence in La Follette or other similar politicians; we have no such confidence in them. But we are ready to support such candidates if, 1) they will immediately break with the Republican Party after having a specific clear declaration; 2) if they will accept a properly worked-out programme of the farmer-labour bloc; 3) if they will come to this conference ready to assume specific obligations to work under the full control of the Farmer-Labour Party, and especially if they will accept the control over their campaign funds.[28]

Much stress was put on the danger that the party, riven by factionalism and divided between language federations, would (in Amter's words) 'slap La Follette on the wrist, call on the workers and farmers to vote for him, and then our own party will disintegrate'. At the same time, the majority of the Comintern leadership, unlike Trotsky, did not rule out such class-collaborationism on principle. Amter noted that he had asked Bukharin in private 'to put in a clause as to the principle of the tactic, but he said that they were occupied only with the tactical question'. Ruthenberg reported: 'The decision of the Communist International was not based on opposition to such a maneuver in principle. In fact, the decision of the Communist International was made on the basis of the situation of our Party … but not because the maneuver was incorrect in principle'.[29]

Pepper, an astute observer of factional divisions, picked up on this. Amter reported during the commission that while Olgin's opposition to La Follette resonated most with Trotsky, Pepper had hoped to convince Stalin. Having clashed earlier, a strong animosity between Trotsky and Pepper developed in this period, and Pepper championed attacks on Trotsky. According to Bittelman, 'Pepper raised the issue [of Trotsky] in our party, calling for condemnation of Trotzky and his views, and using this issue in his fight against our group'. Lore, who had been friendly with Trotsky, would henceforth be tarred as a supporter of Trotsky for their common opposition to the farmer-labour party;

28 ECCI to WPA, no date [20 May 1924?], in Comintern archives, 515:1:164.

29 Grove [Amter] to CEC, 6 May 1924 and 18 May 1924, in Comintern archives, 515:1:274; Ruthenberg 1925.

Lore's allies in the American party would also be seen as soft on Trotsky (even though Trotsky's Left Opposition had no supporters in the American party at this time).[30]

Pepper, for his part, remained in Moscow after the commission's decision. He worked in the Comintern apparatus, including the Anglo-American Commission. It seems that Foster and Cannon convinced Zinoviev that it would be better for the American party if Pepper stayed in Moscow. Seeing the writing on the wall, Pepper petitioned to be allowed to stay in Moscow. Amter claimed Pepper 'presented a letter in which he asked the [ECCI] Presidium' to be allowed to stay in Moscow because he did not 'wish to be the center of a continued fractional fight since such a struggle can only harm the party'. By this time, according to Amter, Foster claimed 'that the majority of the CEC had officially asked the Presidium to recall Pepper'. Even from a distance, Pepper continued to agitate the factionalism of the American party—as the stream of correspondence between him and Lovestone, Amter, Minor and Bedacht in the Comintern archives attests. According to his biographer, in this way Pepper 'could continue to guide his flock, much as the early Christian apostles had kept in touch with their far-flung congregations'.[31]

The Comintern decision was a surprise to most American Communists. Amter denounced the decision as a 'black eye' based on an 'absolutely wrong' premise. Bittelman recalled that 'both main groups in the party were somewhat disappointed'. Browder later claimed: 'The decision was a heavy shock to me politically, as it was for the whole movement…I demanded explanation of this unavoidable contradiction. There was none'. Lovestone, writing to Pepper, described the shift as having 'made the Party membership somewhat dizzy', adding that 'there is no organized mass opposition' within the party to the decision, 'but there is a total lack of that organized and spontaneous sympathy' that had marked the previous work.[32]

30 Grove [Amter] to CEC, 6 May 1924, in Comintern archives, 515:1:274; [John Pepper] to 'Dear Comrade', undated [May 1924?], Lovestone papers, box 196, folder 3; Bittelman, 'Things I Have Learned', folder 15, p. 421. For example, see an undated memorandum castigating Lore's New York *Volkszeitung* for serialising a book by Trotsky as being 'positively harmful to a correct understanding of Bolshevism and Leninism' (in Comintern archives, 515:1:261). On Pepper and Trotsky at the time of the American Commission, see Trotsky 1979; Sakmyster 2012, Chapter 8.

31 Grove [Amter] to CEC, 18 May 1924, in Comintern archives, 515:1:274; Pepper's correspondence is in the Comintern archives, 515:1:272. On the struggle over Pepper's return to the US, and his continued contact with his allies from Moscow, see Sakmyster 2012, Chapter 7.

32 Grove [Amter] to CEC, 18 May 1924, in Comintern archives, 515:1:274; Bittelman, 'Things I Have Learned', folder 15, p. 415; Browder, 'No Man's Land'; Lovestone to 'Dear John [Pepper]', 24 August 1924, in Comintern archives, 515:1:273.

The decision came with an addendum, 'As to the Situation in the American Workers' Party', in which the ECCI declared 'the necessity for harmonious work between the group of Comrade Foster and that of comrade Ruthenberg'. It criticised Pepper and Ruthenberg for 'not realising sufficiently the dangers besetting the party on the long path to securing the co-operation of petty-bourgeois masses'. It then criticised 'the comrades gathered around the other group, such as comrade[s] Hathaway and Cannon' for having 'made a number of declarations which show that in their efforts to secure influence on the petty-bourgeoisie they failed to maintain the Communist position'. It denounced Lore for his 'dangerous tendencies' to 'manifest ... remnants of views of the Two and a Half International' regarding issues before the Comintern.[33]

The party put the decision into practice, despite the leaders' misgivings. Foster, writing under the name John Dorsey in the *Labor Herald*, denounced 'the La Follette effort to destroy the Farmer-Labor movement'. He insisted that the Republican Senator was 'against the movement of the workers and farmers' and 'acting today as the protector of the capitalist parties'. But the way to 'break with the capitalist parties' was to build a genuine Farmer-Labor Party—that is, to maintain the two-class party perspective, just without an open Republican at its head.[34]

To Minnesota in June

Prior to the convention, the CEC decided that, based on the Comintern's instructions, the party would stand candidates 'as a demonstration'. If, as expected, support for La Follette was strong, the party would offer to support La Follette on the conditions proposed by the Comintern. This offer was to be made only if 'there is a danger of a serious split and [as] a concession to safeguard the unity of the movement'. Should the party's offer be rejected, 'we shall split'.[35]

In the lead-up to the Minnesota convention, La Follette denounced the Workers' Party as 'mortal enemies of the Progressive movement and democratic ideals'. Gompers called upon workers to avoid the convention. In defiance of this red-baiting, some 700 people attended. A year later, when the whole Farmer-Labor campaign was a subject of intense factionalism, Foster and Cannon described the convention as having 'consisted merely of Communists,

33 ECCI statement, 'As to the Situation in the American Workers' Party' [May 1924?], in Comintern archives, 515:1:254.

34 *Labor Herald*, July 1924.

35 CEC minutes, 8 June 1924, Comintern archives, 515:1:270.

their close sympathizers, and a scattering of lukewarm trade unionists and farmers'. While leading Communists, such as Foster and Ruthenberg, did not hide their affiliation, they also did not fight for Communist politics. According to the minutes, Foster stressed that the goal was a 'mass Farmer-Labor Party' and not a Communist party, while his son-in-law Joseph Manley, a member of the platform committee, stated that 'it was necessary for him to forgo some of his ideals' in the party's platform. A grotesque example of the party's opportunistic course was when Communists capitulated to racism at the gathering. A delegate from Texas demanded that the draft platform's support for 'the political and economic emancipation of the Negro workers and farmers' be excised because this 'would hinder the organizing of the party in the Southern states'. Communists went along with this. The only exception was Otto Huiswoud, one of the few black Communists and a delegate. He publicly opposed this, and, as a consequence, was suspended from the party for one year for breaking discipline.[36]

The convention chose Duncan MacDonald as candidate for president and William Bouck for vice-president. MacDonald was an UMWA official, ex-Socialist, head of the Illinois Federation of Labor and Communist sympathiser. Bouck was a former Populist and Non-Partisan League leader and current Washington state FFLP member.[37]

Decades later, in an oral history, Taylor (who had been the chairman of the convention) explained why the convention delegates did not nominate La Follette outright: they were afraid he would repudiate them for being allied with Communists. But while willing to work with the Communists, and defy red-baiting, the non-Communist delegates wanted La Follette to run, preferably on a farmer-labour ticket. The Communists opposed nominating La Follette, but put forward a motion allowing his nomination so long as he agreed

36 *New York Times*, 29 May 1924, 30 May 1924; 'Report of the Organization Committee of the National Farmer-Labor Party' and 'Report of the National Farmer-Labor-Progressive Convention, St. Paul, Minn., 17 June 1924'; Wm. Z. Foster and James P. Cannon, 'Outline of the American Situation and Controversial Questions' [1925], all in Cannon papers, reel 47. On Huiswoud, see Enckevort 2001, p. 35.

37 Taylor reminiscences, p. 74; the CEC noted that MacDonald 'had considered joining the Party' earlier in February, which the CEC agreed to with certain provisions, but there is no evidence that he did. See minutes, 15/16 February 1924, Comintern archives, 515:1:270; in his 1965 interview, Taylor states that MacDonald was probably never a Communist but only a 'fellow traveler', while Bouck was definitely only a sympathiser; Taylor reminiscences, pp. 56, 72; On Bouck, see Dyson 1972, p. 964. He eventually became a member of the UFEL National Committee. For coverage of the convention itself, see *New York Times*, 20 June 1924.

to Farmer-Labor control. In covering the convention, the St. Paul *Farmer-Labor Advocate* described how 'it was conceded apparently by all—in fact it was specifically conceded in the adoption of the plan of organization—that any candidates the St. Paul convention might name would be subject to withdrawal if La Follette should become a candidate'. Taylor, four decades later, recalled that there was a 'definite understanding' that if La Follette 'accepted our support, also the support of the Farmer Labor Party, then these candidates would be withdrawn'. Even Taylor, an important Communist in farmer-labour circles, claimed to have been unaware of the Comintern decision against supporting La Follette.[38]

The 4 July CPPA convention banned Communist sympathisers, supporters of the FFLP, or representatives of the St. Paul convention. Mahoney was refused a seat. The CPPA *endorsed* La Follette and Burton K. Wheeler, a Democratic senator from Montana. La Follette declined to be *nominated* because he was adamant in refusing to break with the two major parties and form a new one. The AFL, Socialist Party and many labour and agrarian radicals supported La Follette and Wheeler's campaign, although many saw it as a mechanism to pressure the established parties, not form a new one.[39]

This finalised the split between the Communists and the farmer-labourites. Four days after the CPPA convention, the Workers' Party withdrew support from MacDonald and Bouck, and stood Foster and Gitlow on its own ticket. The Communist-controlled National Committee of the FFLP withdrew its candidates, while Mahoney's Minnesota Farmer Labor Party endorsed La Follette. The *Advocate* urged 'complete, vigorous support of La Follette' and denounced the Communists. Cannon, writing in the *Daily Worker*, justified the Communist ticket on the basis that since many farmer-labourites were joining La Follette's movement, 'the Farmer-Labor Party represents in reality nothing but the Communists and a circle of close sympathizers'. Communists were 'duty bound to raise our own revolutionary standard and fight in our own name in order that we may not be hampered in making the most out of the campaign for the Communist Party and the Communist principles'. Insisting on a Farmer-Labor ticket in this situation meant 'there would have been no one

38 *Farmer-Labor Advocate*, 30 June 1924; Taylor reminiscences, pp. 72–5.

39 La Follette and La Follette 1953, pp. 1111, 1124; Waterhouse 1991, pp. 12, 22–5, 39, 66–8; for the AFL endorsement, see Fine 1928, p. 411 and *A.F. of L. News Budget*, October 1923 (copy in Widener Library, Harvard University, US7124.7000); on SP support, see Shideler 1945, pp. 236–53; Karsner 1964.

to help us, no united front, no mass movement'. There was no opposition to a two-class party on principle, only the recognition that the FFLP was doomed.[40]

During the campaign, the party denounced La Follette and his Socialist Party and AFL backers. Lovestone wrote a pamphlet, *The La Follette Illusion*, which denounced him as:

> the spokesman of the less developed owning interests which have been smarting under the whip of highly developed, monopolized, trustified industry [who] is now attempting to lead and control the slowly crystalizing class resentment of the working and poor farming masses against the biggest exploiters through a loose political alliance of the discontented working class and poor farmers with the middle class.

A shorter pamphlet by Bittelman attacked La Follette's movement as representing small capitalists, the liberal petty bourgeoisie, 'and the labor aristocracy and labor bureaucracy who have submitted to a bourgeois point of view'. At the Fourth National Convention of the Workers' Party, Ruthenberg claimed that despite the low turnout, this open campaign put the Communist cause before the whole country.[41]

Calvin Coolidge, the Republican candidate, won re-election with 15.7 million votes; Democrat John W. Davis received 8.3 million votes, and La Follette received 4.8 million votes. Foster and Gitlow's Communist ticket received some 33,000 votes. Despite La Follette's respectable showing, by the end of 1925, his movement foundered. Its focus on La Follette, who eschewed independent political action, did not leave much of a basis to build a movement. By the following summer, La Follette would be dead and the CPPA would disintegrate.[42]

The ECCI sent a telegram to the party acknowledging: 'It cannot be expected that the politically backward and unawakened majority of the working class of the United States can be aroused and won over by your party already

40 *New York Times*, 11 July 1924; 18 August 1924; Cannon 1992, pp. 226–7; *Farmer Labor Advocate*, 12 August 1924; La Follette and La Follette 1953, p. 1148. For the Communist rationale for standing their own candidates, see also the Communist document, 'Our Election Campaign and the Farmer-Labor Party', undated [8 July 1924?], in Cannon papers, reel 47, frame 103. For his part, Taylor was so unhappy with the shift that he refused to vote for Foster and instead voted for the local farmer-labour ticket, which received 46 percent of the votes in Sheridan County, Montana. (Taylor later returned to the CP, which remained popular in northeastern Montana, until he became a supporter of the Trotskyists in the 1930s); see McDonald 2010, p. 108; Taylor reminiscences, p. 82.

41 Lovestone 1924a, pp. 6–7; Bittelman 1924, p. 5; *Fourth National Convention* 1925, pp. 9–10.

42 Bornet 1964, p. 48; Chester 2004, pp. 138–45; Waterhouse 1991, p. 1.

during this year's election campaign'. By standing candidates, 'the Workers' Party will do its utmost to herald the truth about the proletarian revolutionary class struggle' and 'for the first time in the history of the United States a party of the revolutionary proletariat has put forward its own candidate in the presidential elections'.[43]

Isolation

The farmer-labour diversion had several negative effects on the Communist movement. Creating a two-class party threatened the working-class centrality of the Workers' Party. It inflamed factionalism, laying the basis for a debilitating struggle that would last until the end of the decade.[44]

The immediate effect of the split with the farmer-labour movement was to worsen the party's isolation in the labour movement. This was especially true in the garment trades. What one historian called the 'civil war in the needle trades' were multifaceted, intersecting factional divisions within the Communist movement, divisions between the different unions, and a pre-existing left-right division within the unions. But the fallout from the splits with Fitzpatrick, La Follette and the farmer-labour movement compounded the situation.[45]

Sidney Hillman, head of the ACWA, for a time remained a valued Communist ally. In December 1923, Foster described the anti-TUEL repression in the ILGWU: 'The Forward crowd tried desperately to line up Hillman in the drive against the left wing, but did not succeed. On the contrary, the Amalgamated

43 Undated telegram from G. Zinoviev for the ECCI to the Workers' Party [1924], in Comintern archives, 515:1:255.

44 Ironically, the party maintained friends in the farmer movement while losing allies in the labour movement. Within two years, the UFEL, with Bouck on its national committee, grew to some five to six thousand members. For example, the local farmer-labour ticket in northeastern Montana, with Taylor's support, received 46 percent of the votes in Sheridan County, Montana. Dyson 1972, pp. 962–4; McDonald 2010, p. 108; Taylor reminiscences, p. 82.

45 See, for example: J.B.S. Hardman, 'Communism in America' [1930?], in J.B.S. Hardman papers, box 14, folder 10. Of course, Hardman conveniently dates the decline of the Communist Party after his leaving. On the factionalism in the needle trades, see Holmes 2007 and Seidman 1942, Chapter 9.

administration are pursuing a policy of collaboration with the left-wing'. This 'collaboration' did not last.[46]

In 1924, Hillman supported La Follette. He took the offensive against the TUEL in the ACWA. Salutsky, a key Communist in the union leadership, had chosen to remain close to Hillman and the ACWA bureaucracy and split from the party a year earlier. Benjamin Gitlow, a member of the cutters local, director of the Communist needle trades work, and its vice-presidential candidate, was expelled. Steven Fraser, Hillman's biographer, described the Communists as 'ever more isolated' within the union. 'Internally divided and politically excommunicated, the status of the party in the ACW was soon reduced to that of a sectarian clique'. Anthony Bimba, a Communist who had edited the union's Lithuanian paper, recalled that 'by 1925 the persecution of militants was at its highest point' in the ACWA. For Foster, with no independent organisation behind him, the events of 1923–4 formed a point beyond which there was no return; for Hillman, head of a massive union, they were a frontier beyond which he would not travel. Hillman purged the TUEL because the Communists hindered his goal, in Fraser's words, of 'transforming the "new unionism" from a set of imaginative possibilities into an organization of more businesslike regularity'. With the rightward shift in US politics under Coolidge, union bureaucrats like Hillman probably would have broken from the Communists regardless of party strategy. The party's unprincipled manoeuvring combined with tactical ineptness ensured this.[47]

In the mid-1920s, the party, as part of a broader left wing, still had significant supporters and influence in the ladies' garment workers' union. The ILGWU's leadership staunchly supported the Socialist Party. (Until 1924, a member could not stand for political office except as a socialist). Both the Bolsheviks in Russia and the TUEL (led by Charles Zimmerman) were popular among the rank and file.

By 1924, the ILGWU was already wracked by fights between the Socialist leadership and TUEL supporters. In Spring 1923, several TUEL members were deposed from leadership positions in the union and dissident locals suspended or expelled. The 1924 convention 'refused to seat a number of leftist delegates because of membership in the T.U.E.L., in violation of the rules of the union', according to Joel Seidman. In late 1924 and early 1925, candidates in several

46 William Z. Foster to 'Dear Friend Charlie', 11 December 1923, in Comintern archives, 515:1:245.

47 Fraser 1991, pp. 182, 194, 201–5; Gitlow 1939, p. 337; Bimba 1936, p. 341. In April 1924, Gitlow stated he had been a member of the ACWA since 1918; Gitlow to ECCI, 2 April 1924, in Comintern archives, 515:1:297.

locals were required to take anti-Communist pledges. The eighteen-day 1925 convention of the union 'was one long battle between the right and left wings', according to Seidman.[48]

The Importance of the Comintern Decision

The Comintern decision was belated and incomplete, but essential. It steered the party away from liquidation into capitalist politics. This is seen in the experience of the Socialist Party, which for the first time in its existence did not run a candidate, instead endorsing La Follette. The La Follette campaign, wrote Eric Thomas Chester, pulled the SP 'away from its previous commitment to independent political action and toward a pragmatic acceptance of the lesser evil'. The Socialists, under similar pressures as the Communists, had sought to be part of a broader reform movement, the logical outcome of their leadership's fight against the left wing earlier in 1919. Were it not for the Comintern decision, the Communists would have followed suit, liquidating themselves into capitalist reform politics, and (politically) undone the 1919 split, rejoining Hillquit and Berger—a point not lost on astute radical observers, such as Louis Boudin.[49]

There is little that the Communists could have done amid the conservative 1920s to gain mass influence among a rightward moving trade-union bureaucracy. However, the farmer-labour and La Follette manoeuvres—originally seen as a get-rich-quick scheme—exploded in the Communists' faces and made them even more isolated. By emphasising organisational lines while blurring the political issues, the fiasco left the party less able to intervene and fight for its programme inside the labour movement. As Barrett emphasised, for Communists, this 'destroyed their credibility and cut them off from their most valued allies'. Palmer criticised the Comintern's decision because 'the mechanical reversal of communist policy spoke to the ways in which the WP was now subject to a Communist International bureaucratism that had no sensitivity to international realities and little flexibility in its local renegotiation

48 Seidman 1942, pp. 160–3.

49 Chester 2004, p. 137. In addition to being an academic, Chester was the SP's vice-presidential candidate in 1996. On the Socialists and the 1924 elections, see Chester 2004, Chapter 5; Johnston 1953. In 1924, before the Comintern decision, Boudin wrote a scathing critique, arguing that the Communists had united in practice with Berger and in theory with right-wing Socialists; see 'United Front and the Third Party Movement', in Boudin papers, box 5.

of programmatic error'. It is hard to understand what 'flexibility' would have accomplished: at this late date, deep incisions were necessary, whatever scar tissue was left behind.[50]

All factions shared the opportunism of the period, even if Pepper dressed up the opportunism in flashier clothes. The leadership of the Foster faction, who headed the party in the 1930s popular-front period, remained confused by or opposed to the decision. Bittelman, writing to Theodore Draper in 1970, criticised the historian's use of 'fiasco' to describe the farmer-labour chapter of party history. He insisted: 'the Comintern advised us to [break with La Follette] against our better judgement, [and] brought about a split between the TUEL and many influential trade union people'. In his memoirs, Bittelman criticised the decision to seek the Comintern's advice in the first place and defended the third-party alliance as the predecessor to the party's support for Roosevelt in the 1930s.[51]

Browder also saw the aborted La Follette campaign as a precursor to the pro-Roosevelt popular front of the 1930s. In an essay explaining the party's influence a decade later, he decried the isolation of the party after splitting with La Follette. His description of the party's perspective towards Roosevelt in the 1936 elections sounds like Ruthenberg's backhanded support to La Follette in 1924. Rather than openly supporting Roosevelt, the Communists ran an 'ambiguous campaign in favor of "my rival", Roosevelt'. The party 'put up our own candidates but conduct[ed] such a campaign that would assure Roosevelt all votes under our influence except the diehard opponents of all "capitalist" candidates'. In fact, supporting a bourgeois 'movement' while claiming to oppose the bourgeois figures leading it became a feature of Stalinist politics ever since. The Comintern intervention saved the party from this class collaboration—in the short term at least.[52]

This demonstrates that while the Comintern played a role in the danger of opportunism in its American section, the party's leaders were acting on their own opportunist impulses. The isolation in 1924 increased pressures towards opportunism. In the next five years, the fundamental difference is that the Comintern no longer would pull the party back.

50 Barrett 1999, p. 146; Palmer 2007, p. 231.

51 Alexander Bittelman to Theodore Draper, 19 October 1970, in Bittelman papers, box 3, folder 30; Bittelman, 'Things I Have Learned', folder 15, pp. 415–18.

52 Browder 1967, pp. 218, 234.

CHAPTER 7

The Double-Edged Sword of 'Bolshevisation', 1924–6

The Fifth Congress of the Comintern (June and July 1924), in the aftermath of the defeat of revolution in Germany, adopted the 'Theses on Tactics' that made 'the bolshevisation of its sections' the 'most important task'. After Lenin's death, the definition of 'Bolshevisation', like Bolshevism itself, was contested. For Zinoviev, it meant 'utilizing the experience of the bolshevik party in the three Russian revolutions (and the experience of the best Comintern sections) in its applications to the concrete situation of the given country'. However, at a meeting of the Comintern's Bolshevisation Commission, he complained, 'in few questions has so much stupidity been uttered as about the question of the Bolshevisation of our Parties'. *Communist International* admitted that 'Any attempts to give Bolshevisation a kind of inclusive formula, embracing all the tasks of our brother parties of the West, has been of schematic nature'.[1]

Historians often describe Bolshevisation as 'Stalinisation'—the domination of national parties by the ECCI central apparatus, itself coming under the power of Stalin. In their history of the Comintern, Kevin McDermott and Jeremy Agnew describe Bolshevisation as 'a trend towards Russian dominance of the Comintern and its member sections', both ideologically and organisationally. They also label it 'Russification in an embryonic Stalinist form'. A history of the Comintern by British leftist Duncan Hallas in the 1980s defined it bluntly: 'unqualified submission to the Troika as the supposed guardians of Leninist orthodoxy and hostility to all critical voices, above all to Trotsky'. A more recent study of the Spanish Communist Party emphasised 'ideological and organizational conformity' and the 'centralized suppression of dissent and enforcement of conformity' in this process.[2]

With hindsight, these descriptions are apt. But in 1924, the rise of Stalin was in the future and not inevitable. The period was key in the degeneration of the Soviet workers' state—'Stalinisation'—that was reflected in the Russian Communist Party and throughout the Comintern. 'The year 1924', Trotsky wrote, 'that was the beginning of the Soviet Thermidor'.[3] But he wrote those lines more than a decade later. The bureaucratisation of a workers' state was

1 'Theses on Tactics' in Degras 1956, II, pp. 153, 188; Zinoviev at Meeting of Bolshevisation Commission, 6 February 1925, in Shachtman papers, box 1, folder 1b; Manuilsky 1925, p. 52.

2 McDermott and Agnew 1996, pp. 42–5; Hallas 2008, p. 108; Rees 2009, pp. 131–2.

3 Trotsky 1974b, p. 174.

new, and Trotsky's opposition in this period emphasised the internal party regime and rapid industrialisation. Zinoviev's 'Bolshevisation' campaign amounted to eliminating political opposition throughout the Comintern, particularly factionalism, and thus laid the basis for further degeneration. Since Zinoviev himself did not see his goal as 'Stalinisation', foreign Communists could be forgiven for accepting 'Bolshevisation' as good coin, given the ravages of factionalism that many sections suffered.

This process was even murkier for American Communists (many of whom would have had trouble identifying a picture of Stalin). Having been helped by the Comintern's intervention in the past, American Communists looked forward to continued Comintern assistance in overcoming the severe problems the party faced: ending the interminable factionalism, unifying a membership divided among more than a dozen language groups, and raising the ideological level of the party. Most American Communist leaders, including Cannon, the future leader of American Trotskyism, supported Bolshevisation as a solution to the party's problems.[4]

However, Bolshevisation had two edges: it promised a strong party, transcending the weakness that had plagued the American Communists for five years. At the same time, it undermined the party, bringing it more and more into line with the international campaign against the Left Opposition and sapping much of the revolutionary strength of the Comintern and its sections. Although James Ryan has argued that 'Bolshevisation helped rid the party of internecine warfare', its immediate effect was to *increase* such divisions.[5]

According to the Fifth Congress, Bolshevisation consisted of five interrelated tasks. Sections needed to become 'real mass part[ies]' with 'the closest and strongest contacts with the working masses'. They needed to be 'capable of manoeuvre' instead of 'sectarian or dogmatic'. They should be 'revolutionary, Marxist, in nature', as well as 'centralized ... permitting no factions, tendencies, or groups', but 'based in one mould'. Finally, Bolshevik sections must work in the military.[6]

The main motion at the Russian party's Thirteenth Congress concluded with a call for 'a firm and monolithic' organisation, 'based on the unwavering principles of leninism'. The connection to the ongoing fight against Trotsky

4 See Cannon 1924. Walter Kendall and Paul Kellogg polemicise against Cannon for this; Kendall 1994, pp. 226–7; Kellogg 2009, pp. 42, 59. They ignore the real problems that the party faced at this time and their assumption that Cannon should have grasped the broader implications of Bolshevisation at the time seems ahistorical and unfair.

5 Ryan 2004, p. 206.

6 'Theses on Tactics', in Degras 1956, II, pp. 153–4.

was spelled out in the ECCI theses on Bolshevisation, passed a year later, which posed 'the final liquidation of Trotskyism within the party' as the primary task for the 'Bolshevisation' of the Bolshevik Party itself.[7]

The Fight Against Lore

The first American target in the 'final liquidation' of 'Trotskyism' in America was Ludwig Lore, then in an alliance with Foster and Cannon. His role captures both sides of the 'Bolshevisation' campaign. Although he was not a supporter of the Left Opposition, Lore was sympathetic to Trotsky, both personally (having met him in 1917) and as a symbol of resistance to centralisation. He was openly contemptuous of Pepper, Zinoviev and the Comintern leadership.

A graduate from Berlin University (where he had studied under Werner Sombart), he emigrated early in the century. Since 1905, he had edited the *New Yorker Volkszeitung*, the oldest left-wing newspaper in the US. Founded in 1878, the paper had become an institution on the American left, and in the mid-1920s Louis Boudin called it 'the most important if not the most read communist paper in the country'. At bottom, Lore was a left-wing social democrat: his politics had been forged in the German Social Democracy, and in the US he had been a maverick within the socialist movement. He had been an editor of *Class Struggle* with Boudin and Fraina, and the *Volkszeitung* helped finance the journal. In 1919, he initially opposed the formation of left-wing groupings within the Socialist Party, but helped to found the Communist movement.[8]

Even outside of the Left Opposition, Lore posed problems for the Stalinising Comintern. Lore was respected on the left, and the possibility of a German-language daily newspaper sympathetic to Trotsky was a threat, especially as another long-time American left-winger, Max Eastman, became a key opponent of Stalin in the mid-1920s. Within the party, Lore (along with Olgin) offered the only resistance to the La Follette fiasco. He also resisted party control of the *Volkszeitung*—which echoed a fight between the paper's editors and Daniel De Leon twenty years earlier. (As a result of that fight, the *Volkszeitung* was

7 'On the Central Committee Report', in McNeal and Gregor 1974, p. 227; 'Theses on Bolshevization', in Degras 1956, II, p. 195.

8 See Lore to Eugene V. Debs, 3 March 1919, in Debs Collection, Indiana State University, reprinted in Eugene V. Debs papers, microfilm edition, reel 2; Louis Boudin, 'History a la Mode', unpublished essay in Boudin papers, box 5, folder 3. On the funding of *Class Struggle*, see 'FBI Interrogation of Lewis Corey [Louis Fraina], 1949–1950', Corey papers, box 2, folder 5, p. 100; *New York Times*, 6 December 1931; 9 July 1942.

owned by the Socialist Cooperative Publishing Association, which was separate from the Communist Party). In 1924, several controversies broke out in the CEC over the paper, including when it criticised Zinoviev, ran advertisements for bonds for the counterrevolutionary Miklós Horthy regime in Hungary, and excerpted Trotsky's writings. Much of Lore's support came from the foreign-language federations, who also chaffed at central party control.[9]

Lore and Olgin, although they opposed both major factions on the third-party question, were allied with Foster and Cannon's tendency. In part, this stemmed from the key role of Ruthenberg's faction in the FFLP and La Follette adventure. Bittelman, a Foster supporter, recalled in his memoirs that both factions had courted Lore, because his vote made a difference in the divided CEC. In 1923, the Jewish federation had been racked by a dispute between Olgin and Bittelman. Cannon had helped resolve the dispute, Bittelman recalled, bringing him and Lore closer to Foster and Cannon. Cannon recalled that Lore 'was decidedly anti-Pepper'. 'Lore', Cannon wrote to Draper in 1955, 'had been with us, so to speak, but not of us; we did not feel responsible for him as an all-out member of our fraction'. Whatever the exact relationship, Foster and Cannon's alliance with Lore left them open to charges of disloyalty and 'Trotskyism'.[10]

9 On the *Volkszeitung*, see Conolly-Smith 2004, pp. 63–73. See the CEC minutes, 17 May 1924 for the censure of Lore for criticising Zinoviev, in Comintern archives, 515:1:270. On the Horty bonds, see the CEC minutes, 11 August, 18 August, 25 August 1924. (Lore claimed that the managing editor accepted the advertisement without having read it and printed a denunciation of the regime: one wonders if this was aimed at Pepper). For the excerpts, see the CEC minutes 7 December and 16 December 1924. All in Comintern archives, 515:1:299. See also undated [December 1924] CEC statement in Comintern archives, 515:1:261. See also the dossier, 'Die Linke Sozialdemokratische Tendenz in der Workers' Party of America, Dargestellt Durch Artikel des Gen. Lore', containing excerpts from 20 *New Yorker Volkszeitung* articles from 1924, in Comintern archives, 495:37:8. On the difficulties of assuming political control of the *Volkszeitung* without ownership, see Max Bedacht, 'To the Secretariat of the CEC of the WP', 26 May 1925, in Comintern archives, 515.1.511.

10 Bittelman, 'Things I Have Learned', folder 14, pp. 393–5; Cannon 1962, pp. 188–90; Cannon 1956, p. 27. Although Cannon became the leading American spokesman for Trotsky in the late 1920s, it would be too facile to read this support retrospectively so as to explain his alliance with Lore. After all, Bittelman, Foster and Olgin became supporters of Stalin. A undated Comintern memorandum, 'Party Fractions [sic] and Party Differences in the Workers' Party: Report Varga's Office on American Situation', most likely written before the 1925 Convention, criticised both factions for only 'dr[awing] a line of distinction between themselves and this group [Lore] for fractional reasons; and that they exploited this group, especially Lore himself, in the fractional struggle and thus strengthened it'; Comintern archives, 495:37:8.

Factionalism was also discussed during the Comintern's American Commission debate about the La Follette campaign in late April and May 1924. Although the Comintern concurred with Lore and Olgin's opposition to the 'third party' manoeuvre, it nonetheless attacked Lore as a surrogate for Trotsky. Radek declared that Lore's 'centrist tendency' represented German social democracy within the American party and told the party it 'must oppose Lore in the press' and 'must attack him'. Zinoviev asserted that 'Lore proves that he is in no case a Communist', and advocated that the party remove Lore from the CEC and publicly denounce him.[11]

Meanwhile, the party increased its support for the Russian anti-Trotsky campaign. In December 1924, Foster and Ruthenberg co-signed a telegram to Moscow against Trotsky. This concluded: 'We again express our complete solidarity with the CEC of the RCP and expect the entire Comintern to stand behind the Old Bolshevist guard'. Pepper and Lovestone may have introduced anti-Trotskyism into the American party's factionalism, but they did not have a monopoly on it. Abern, Browder, Bittelman, Cannon, Dunne and Foster signed a *Daily Worker* article in December that hailed 'the powerful speeches by comrades Kamenev and Stalin against Trotskyism'. When these speeches were reprinted in a pamphlet, *Bolshevism or Trotskyism?*, Bittelman wrote the introduction. It argued that 'the controversy between Trotskyism and Leninism is not a new thing in the Russian Communist movement', adding that 'Comrade Trotsky's struggles in the Russian party are a constant danger to the integrity of the Communist movement'.[12]

Each faction depended upon a Russian 'expert' who scoured the latest papers from Moscow. Bertram Wolfe fulfilled this role for Ruthenberg, and was helped by Pepper's connections in the Comintern. Bittelman played this role for Foster and Cannon's group. Yet the initial anti-Trotsky campaign in the American party was partial and tentative. It attacked Trotsky for supposedly being a newcomer to Bolshevik politics, emphasising 'permanent revolution' and underestimating the peasantry. The concept of 'socialism in one country' had not yet become central to attacks on the founder of the Red Army.[13]

11 Minutes of the American Commission, 30 April 1924; 'Excerpt from the Report of the American Commission in the Presidium of the ECCI', 20 May 1924, both in Comintern archives, 515:1:257

12 Telegram from Foster and Ruthenberg to Moscow, 12 December 1924, in Comintern archives, 515:1:297; Draper 1985, pp. 107–13; Cannon 1992, p. 285; Bittelman in Zinoviev, Stalin and Kamenev 1925, pp. 1–2.

13 Cannon 1962, p. 128.

Wolfe, a leader in the Mexican Communist Party, continued to write pro-Trotsky articles in Mexico. Although Lore was criticised for excerpting Trotsky's writing in the *New Yorker Volkszeitung*, the *Daily Worker* published several articles by Trotsky in 1924, especially on the Red Army. Various Communist writers praised Trotsky, and party-affiliated publishers printed some of his books. Even an anti-Trotsky editorial by Ruthenberg in the *Daily Worker* in late 1924 admitted that 'Comrade Trotsky approaches genius in many ways'.[14]

Bittelman recalled that he found the fight against Trotsky in Russia 'very complicated and also confusing' and claimed that at the time he did not know 'enough to be able to form an independent judgement'. While he would have preferred Trotsky to unite with the rest of the Soviet leaders, when forced to choose, Bittelman supported the leadership of the Comintern against the Left Opposition. In part this was because the 'troika' were long-time Bolsheviks, while Trotsky was a newcomer to Bolshevism. Most of the Communist leaders made a similar choice.[15]

Meanwhile, the anti-Lore campaign continued. In 1924, after labelling Lore's supposed support for European centrists as 'dangerous', the ECCI declared that 'The C.E.C. must carry on an ideological campaign against such a tendency'. A longer 'Resolution on Lore' detailed the *Volkszeitung* editor's supposed opportunism and social-democratic views. Furthermore, the WP 'must clearly state and recognise its error of not having issued an official statement ... against the opportunist deviations ... of comrade Lore'. Throughout 1925, the Comintern demanded that Lore be removed from the CEC.[16]

In August 1925, the Fourth National Convention of the party expelled Lore altogether for having 'embarked upon a course of open opposition and hostility to the party and to the Communist International'. The 'Resolution on Loreism' stated that 'Loreism is opportunism' that 'must be relentlessly combated'. For the Ruthenberg-Lovestone minority, Lore was a perfect scapegoat.

14 In February 1925, the party-affiliated Jimmie Higgins Bookshop published a book by Trotsky. That same year, International Publishers, the official Communist publisher in the US, issued Trotsky's *Literature and Revolution*. Reviewing this work in the *Workers Monthly* in 1926, Olgin called its author 'a rare master' who was 'intense with thought and astir with theoretical passion'. For Wolfe, see Spenser 1999, p. 118; see also Wolfe 1981, pp. 307, 323; *Daily Worker*, 18 October and 15 November 1924 (articles); 8 December 1924 (Ruthenberg editorial); Elmer T. Alison to 'Comrade Editor', 25 February 1925, in Jay Lovestone papers, box 196, folder 6; 1925; Olgin 1926.

15 Bittelman, 'Things I Have Learned', folder 15, pp. 421–8.

16 ECCI statement, 'As to the Situation in the American Workers' Party', [May 1924?], in Comintern archives, 515:1:254; 'Resolution sur Lore', [1924], in Comintern archives, 515:1:253. In French, the resolution is five pages long.

Going after him increased their anti-Trotsky credentials and called into question the Foster-Cannon group's loyalty. It also eliminated one of the majority's key allies. Finally, it highlighted the importance of taming the foreign-language groups, as well as the difficulty of such a task. When Lore was expelled, the *Volkszeitung* ceased to be a Communist paper, and became critical of the party's positions. The fight with Lore, intersecting Zinoviev and Stalin's fight against Trotsky, muddied the issues instead of clarifying the political differences between a Communist party and a left-wing social-democratic one.[17]

At the 1925 Convention, Ruthenberg's minority put forward a motion that 'the hesitancy and vacillation which the C.E.C. majority [i.e. Foster] showed on the question of Trotskyism was an expression of its relation with the chief defender of Trotskyism, Comrade Lore'. Max Bedacht, a Ruthenberg supporter, tied fighting 'Loreism' to 'Bolshevisation' in his pamphlet published the next year, *The Menace of Opportunism: A Contribution to the Bolshevisation of the Workers' (Communist) Party*. Swabeck—a Cannon supporter who later became a Trotskyist—speculated that Foster and Cannon's group was 'suspected of Trotskyist leanings' starting in 1925.[18]

Factional Gang Warfare

In late 1924 and early 1925, Cannon and Foster's group opposed Ruthenberg and Lovestone's faction (which Pepper supported from Moscow). Factionalism had originated in the dispute over the Farmer-Labor Party and the La Follette movement, but the struggle for party control displaced these differences by 1925. Leading bodies often passed important political motions unanimously, yet factionalism hardened. In their subsequent writings, almost all leaders of this period note the futility of factionalism. When Bertram Wolfe returned from Mexico, he asked each faction's leader to explain the division. He recalled that 'each explanation, filled with factional bitterness, left me more bewildered than before'—although he still resumed his place in the Ruthenberg faction.[19]

17 *Daily Worker*, 19 May 1925; *Fourth National Convention* 1925, pp. 66, 93, 96–8; Foster at Meeting of American Organisational Commission, Moscow, 1 December 1925, Comintern archives, 495:37:6; *New York Times*, 6 December 1931.

18 *Fourth National Convention* 1925, pp. 96–8; Bedacht 1926; Swabeck, 'From Debs to Mao,' section VIII, p. 13.

19 Wolfe 1981, p. 378; see also Cannon 1962, p. 134; Browder, 'No Man's Land', p. 228.

In late March and early April 1925, the ECCI held its Fifth Enlarged Plenum. Americans attending included Cannon and Foster for the majority, and Ruthenberg, Lovestone and Pepper (who was working in the Comintern's information department) for the minority. The Plenum overall was marked by Zinoviev's concept of 'partial stabilisation' and Bukharin's ascent. The ECCI passed the 'Theses on the Bolshevisation of Communist Parties', as well as a resolution on 'the discussion in the Russian Communist Party' that denounced Trotsky's 'attempt to revise Leninism and to change the leadership' in the Russian Communist Party.[20]

As had become common, there was an American Commission, organised by Otto Kuusinen (from Finland) and Jules Humbert-Droz (from Switzerland). The Commission opened with a dispute over Pepper: since he was in Moscow, the Minority wanted him to speak because he was a member of the CEC, while the Majority labelled him 'a constant menace to the work of the Party' and claimed his CEC membership had ended upon transfer to Russia.[21]

Each faction warned of possible destruction of the party at the hands of its opponents. Ruthenberg, Lovestone and Pepper complained to the Commission of a 'growing danger of a split in the American Party' and of Foster and Cannon's supposed 'carrying on a relentless policy of suspensions, disciplinary [actions] and expulsion of the opposition'. Foster and Cannon in turn asserted that 'the Minority is encouraging gross violations of discipline and in propagating the idea of a split in the Party'. They diagnosed a 'disease' of 'Pepperism' in the party, marked by 'a desperate grasping of power to detriment and sabotage the Party as a whole'. Both factions urged Comintern intervention. In fact, Ruthenberg, Pepper and Lovestone urged 'that the CI shall instruct the CEC to organise a Political Committee consisting of an equal number of representatives of the Foster and Ruthenberg group (to be chosen by each group) and to send a representative of the CI to preside over this committee'. This Committee would be in charge of both general party work and preparations for an upcoming conference. Comintern intervention had become a way to obtain power within the party, not a way to resolve political issues.[22]

20 On the Fifth Enlarged Plenum, see Degras 1956, II, pp. 183–208; Draper 1986, pp. 133–5.

21 See the American Commission, 13 February 1925, in Comintern archives, 495:163:339. The quote comes from Cannon's intervention. The question was resolved by allowing Pepper to speak but not increasing the total speaking time of the Minority. Shortly after the start of the session, Foster accused Pepper of embellishing translations into German.

22 Letter to American Commission by C.E. Ruthenberg, Jay Lovestone and John Pepper, 24 March 1925; Letter to American Commission by William Z. Foster and James P. Cannon, 28 March 1925; both are reprinted in C.E. Ruthenberg to All Party Branches, 26 May 1925,

The factions clashed over the demand for a labour party. After gaining the right to speak, Pepper denounced Cannon and Foster as 'trade union officials, who have done no manual labor for twenty years', and defended the slogan calling for a 'Labor Party'. Comparing changes in American society to the 'new unionism' in Britain that gave birth to the Labour Party, Pepper offered this future labour party in the US as an example of 'non-partisan organizations... which are not Communist organizations, but which can assist us to link up the masses of workers with the party'. He even likened this non-existent labour party to workers' councils in Germany, unemployed councils, and Russian Soviets—that is, instruments of revolutionary struggle. The bottom line, Pepper argued, was that Foster and Cannon wished to preserve 'Communist chastity' in favour of 'Communist propaganda only, *abstract*, not connected with the actual stage of class-consciousness of the working class'. The labour party slogan would help break the working class from pro-capitalist to revolutionary consciousness.[23]

In a lengthy document, Ruthenberg reiterated his belief that a labour party was necessary 'to break the workers away from the outspoken parties of capital—the Republican and Democratic Parties'. While not directly criticising the May 1924 decision on La Follette, Ruthenberg argued that the labour party movement was still vital, that Foster's group had prematurely pronounced it dead and that this movement should be the focus of Communist activity.[24]

Foster's presentation to the commission gave a bleak history of farmer-labour work. He claimed that the party 'had over estimated the degree of consciousness of the American workers' and that 'there is no substantial support to the class Farmer-Labor Party'. The so-called Farmer-Labor Party was 'merely the Workers' Party under another name and form', and after the St. Paul Convention, Communists 'were left almost completely isolated, with the dead National Farmer Labor Party on our hands'. He opposed the slogan for a farmer-labour party without 'mass sentiment behind it'. He attacked the Ruthenberg faction for having 'hypnotised themselves into believing that we are on the eve of a big revolution in America'. Furthermore, the nastiness of the dispute had a personal source: 'Much of the internal bitterness comes from the interference of Comrade Pepper'. He complained that Pepper, in

in Shachtman papers, box 1, folder 19; C.E. Ruthenberg, Jay Lovestone and John Pepper, 'To the American Commission', 20 March 1925, in Comintern archives, 495:37:9.

23 'Speech of Comrade John Pepper at the Session of the American Commission', 4 March 1925, in Cannon papers, reel 47, frame 131.

24 C.E. Ruthenberg, 'The Issues in the American Party', no date [Spring 1925?], in Comintern archives, 495:37:86.

Moscow, was trying to manipulate the factionalism in the US, including by sending cables in favour of Ruthenberg in the name of the ECCI.[25]

The 1925 Comintern Resolution

In keeping with Zinoviev's perspective that world capitalism had stabilised, the resolution of the commission began by announcing that 'American capitalism has temporarily overcome its crisis'. It added that 'on the whole the situation of the American working class is at present far from being pregnant with revolution; it is different, however, from what it was ten years ago'.

The resolution in essence revised the previous year's decision on La Follette, and echoed Ruthenberg's arguments. While the Workers' Party volte-face was necessary, it had been 'without the prospects of much success'. The Wisconsin Senator—who would die within two months of the resolution—had 'gained an important victory' in the elections while 'our Party only met with a defeat which was not to be avoided under the given circumstances'. The resolution recognised 'a certain confusion … in the ranks of the Workers' Party'.

The decision criticised Foster and Cannon's position that the demand for a Farmer-Labor Party 'had to be abandoned as useless'; La Follette's 'victory' demonstrated the basis for this demand. While granting that the party should fight for a *labour* party since there was no reason to expect a radical *farmer* movement, the resolution credited Ruthenberg's faction for agitating for a labour party. The decision instructed the party to 'induce the working masses to present these ['urgent everyday'] demands to the reformists and to the leaders of the LaFollette organisations and to call upon them for joint action with the Workers' Party'. While calling on Communists to 'drive an ever deeper wedge into the LaFollette movement', the decision agreed with the majority that there was no immediate basis for a labour party. The resolution stated 'that it is not advisable to endeavour to split off a Left Wing from the L.[abor] P.[arty] as soon as possible in order to transform this split off section into a mass Communist Party'. Instead, the TUEL should be built up and developed 'into a great, opposition of the Left block' [sic] in the labour movement.

The resolution underscored that 'Lore represents a non-Communist tendency' within the party, and called for an 'ideological struggle' against him. The next conference would have to resolve the question, the resolution ordered, while underlining that the 'opportunist' Lore should not remain on the CEC. At the same time, the factionalism in the party 'must now absolutely cease'.

25 Foster at American Commission, 4 March 1925, in Lovestone papers, box 201, folder 3.

The resolution opposed the Foster and Cannon group's 'campaign conducted against Comrade Pepper' and praised his 'services' to the Workers' Party. At the same time, it added that Pepper was not planning to return to the US since the ECCI desired 'to use his energies for other important tasks'.

Finally, to deal with factionalism, the resolution essentially adopted Ruthenberg's earlier proposal. Noting that the Workers' Party would hold a convention soon, the resolution stated that any factional disputes were 'to be settled in a Party commission under the chairmanship of a neutral comrade (the representative of the ECCI)' and that this commission 'shall also control the actual conduct of the Party discussion'. (Later published versions of the decision refer to this as the 'parity' commission and omit reference to the ECCI representative).[26]

Ruthenberg voiced his 'full approval' for the decision, and Foster declared that he 'fully accept[ed] the resolution of American Committee'. This decision was a perfect setup for increased factionalism. As Draper noted, 'It placed Foster's majority in the equivocal position of being politically weaker but organizationally stronger than its rivals'. In motivating the decision, Zinoviev stated that he had originally proposed mandating a Foster majority on the CEC (while safeguarding a strong minority), but he had discarded this as 'inexpedient': 'We are of the opinion that after having formulated a unified political platform, we may leave it to the Party itself to elect its Central Committee at the next Party Convention as it sees fit'. Both Foster and Ruthenberg's factions deserved to be part of the leadership, although 'it is not easy for both wings to obtain a majority ... the future will tell which of the two has deceived itself. We can only wish both wings the best of luck'. The Comintern only insisted that Lore not be a part of the new CEC. While apparently evenhanded, Zinoviev's statement underlined the cynical nature of factional struggle at the time, as well as the disconnect between factional power and political programme.[27]

At first glance, a 'parity commission' made sense: since the factions had brought the party to a dead-end, an external, neutral comrade could help the factions work out their differences instead of driving the party to the ground. As noted above, this was originally suggested by Ruthenberg's faction. Sending a Comintern representative to hash out the factional differences had also been

26 'Resolution of the American Question', in Cannon papers, reel 47, frame 226. The *Daily Worker* (27 May 1925) and *International Press Correspondence* (4 June 1925) also reprinted the resolution.

27 Statements of Sanborn [Ruthenberg], Dorsey [Foster], Kuusinen and Zinoviev at the 14th Evening Session of the American Session, 6 April 1925 in Cannon papers, reel 47; Draper 1986, pp. 138–9.

discussed. According to Foster, in late 1924 Zinoviev had been 'of a mind to send a representative of the Comintern to the United States to bring about more unity to the Party'. Foster's allies had opposed the idea at the time, but by March 1925, Foster wrote to Zinoviev 'to specifically request that the Comintern delegate a comrade of standing to come to America to assist in liquidating the existing factional situation'. Foster's preferred 'comrade of standing' was Kuusinen, but he indicated that Manuilsky or Humbert-Droz would also be acceptable.[28]

In the upshot, the delegate was Sergei Ivanovich Gusev. Unlike the Comintern delegation to the Bridgman Convention, Gusev was a long-time Bolshevik. Born Yakov Davidovich Drabkin, Gusev had been active in the Russian socialist movement since the 1890s, and had voted with Lenin as a delegate to the 1903 Russian Social Democratic Congress in London that split the movement between Mensheviks and Bolsheviks. He had played an important role in the Russian Civil War; he was also a staunch ally of Stalin in the fight with Trotsky and the Opposition within the Bolshevik Party.[29]

Gusev Sings Lovestone's Love Songs

Between 22–30 August 1925, the party held its Fourth National Convention. The run-up to this convention was marked by inflamed factionalism. The parity commission under Gusev (who used the name Green during his sojourn in the US) achieved its purpose of fashioning unanimous motions between the factions, but did not eliminate factionalism. According to Gusev, it took three days to work out key political issues, but almost four weeks to hash out factional disputes. Meetings lasted as long as twelve hours daily, and members were not supposed to discuss the meetings. Browder recalled: 'Although the commission produced a completely "unanimous" resolution, the Party membership was completely divided into hostile factions in preparation for a split—with not a single issue defined'. Foster later complained to the American Commission in Moscow:

> If it is a question of personal polemics, I do not know where can be found a group as bitter as the Lovestone group.... Their campaign against all our leading comrades was bitter and unscrupulous. My own character

28 [Foster] to Comrade Zinoviev, 22 March 1925, in Cannon papers, reel 20, frame 4.

29 Information on Gusev taken from Lazitch and Drachkovitch 1986, pp. 160–1.

> has been assassinated in every conceivable form, even to that of my being called a thief.

Referring to the nastiness of the polemics, he added: 'both our groups are guilty of this'.[30]

Foster and Cannon's group received almost twice as many delegates as Ruthenberg and Lovestone's faction. Because of this, with Gusev's backing, the parity commission gave Foster and Cannon's group two-thirds of the new central committee—essentially Zinoviev's proposal in April. Lacking any serious political differences, and with the help of Gusev, the delegates unanimously approved a document, 'The Present Situation and Immediate Tasks of the Party', as well as motions dealing with trade-union work, and party activities among blacks and women. Still, factional strife continued at a fever pitch. 'Pro forma resolutions aside', Bryan Palmer wrote, 'the end-of-August meeting was taking on the character of a Wild West show'. The Cleveland and Philadelphia locals had effectively spilt into two different organisations. Max Shachtman, William F. Dunne and other supporters of Foster and Cannon had barricaded themselves in the *Daily Worker* editorial offices, refusing entry to Ruthenberg supporters, including J. Louis Engdahl, the paper's co-editor. It was for this reason that, according to Bedacht, Gusev described the majority's 'victory [as] the equivalent of a split' and 'therefore … a bad victory'. Gusev, again according to Bedacht, had told the minority that he believed that the key to preventing a split was to get both factions working together against Lore and that in two months' time, district elections could be held in a calmer atmosphere.[31]

---

30 Green [Gusev], speech at American Commission, [fall 1925], in Lovestone papers, box 209, folder 31; [Lovestone] to 'Dear Will' [Weinstone], 11 July [1925], in Lovestone papers, box 219, folder 1; Browder, 'No Man's Land,' Browder papers, box 10, p. 134; Foster to American Commission, 27 November 1925, in Comintern archives, 495:37:5. For the resolutions adopted for the Parity Commission to be proposed at the convention, see the dossier, *Report of the Central Executive Committee and Resolutions of the Parity Commission to the Fourth National Convention of the Workers' (Communist) Party of America* (1925), in Zimmerman papers, box 1.

31 *The Fourth National Convention* 1925, pp. 72–86; Draper 1986, p. 143; Palmer 2007, p. 245. While the pamphlet published after the convention gives a sense of the divisions, the transcripts of the convention itself express the abusive atmosphere. See, for example, Comintern archives, 515:1:449. For Gusev's analysis, see Bedacht's translations of his remarks at a minority caucus, 20 August 1925, in Lovestone papers, box 203. The move towards a split in general, and the situation in the Cleveland district in particular, is described in 'Declaration of the Parity Commission' [1925], Lovestone papers, box 203; see also 'Resolution on Cleveland' [1925], Lovestone papers, box 207.

At the start of the Convention, Foster and Cannon's majority status was clear. 'There is no contest on that question', Ruthenberg conceded for the minority in his report to the Credentials Committee on 22 August (although the minority claimed that the Foster-Cannon group had manipulated the votes to give itself a larger majority). Gusev later reported that during the convention he had sent some 15 letters to the Comintern as his frustration with factionalism increased. Then, on 27 August, the Comintern sent a cable that blew apart the convention. The cable declared that 'it has finally become clear that the Ruthenberg group is more loyal to the decisions of the Communist International and stands closer to its views'. It continued that the 'Foster group employs excessively mechanical and ultrafactional methods'. The cable demanded that Ruthenberg and Lovestone supporters comprise no less than 40 percent of the incoming CEC; that Ruthenberg remain party secretary; Lovestone become a member of the CEC; that the Foster-Cannon group not target the minority for 'removals, replacements, dispersions'; Ruthenberg's faction retain co-editorship of the *Daily Worker*; and the 'maximum application of parity on all executive organs of the Party'. The cable ended:

> If majority does not accept these demands then declare that, in view of circumstances of elections, unclear who has real majority and that methods of majority raise danger of split and therefore Communist International proposes that now only a temporary Parity Central Executive Committee be elected with neutral chairman to call new convention after passions have died down. Those who refuse to submit will be expelled.

In other words, the Comintern wanted Foster to assume leadership of the party in the shadow of being 'disloyal'. In his autobiography, Wolfe recalled that after Gusev showed the party the cable, he 'sat at the front of the table among [the Ruthenberg] caucus leaders as if he were one of them and a member of our group'.[32]

Draper and other historians have assumed that the Comintern cable to Gusev was based on Gusev's instructions to the Comintern; Thomas Sakmyster (in a biography of Pepper) has indicated that Pepper, in Moscow, played a key role in the cable. Foster's faction later exerted quite a bit of effort to sort out

32 Report of Minority to the Credentials Committee by Comrade Ruthenberg, 22 August 1925, in Comintern archives, 515:1:449; telegram from Comintern in Lovestone papers, box 196, folder 11; see also Ruthenberg 1925; Wolfe 1981, p. 384; Sakmyster 2012, Chapter 6; A.B. [Bittelman], to 'Dear Comrade', 15 November [1925], in Cannon papers, reel 20, frame 8; Bittelman, 'Lessons I Have Learned', folder 16, p. 439.

the cable's origins. In November, one Foster supporter (probably Bittelman) reported on meetings with Kuusinen, Lozovsky and others: 'We still do not know what information the telegram was based on. Practically everybody we have interviewed was absent from the session at which it was adopted, and those who were present do not seem to know what it was based on'. Bittelman, reporting on his interview with Zinoviev in late 1925, recalled that the leader of the Comintern 'got elaborate reports from Green' during the Convention, but 'did not state however the exact circumstances under which the decision was taken'. Even later, in his memoirs, Bittelman recalled that Stalin claimed not to know who sent the Gusev telegram. Finally, the Foster representative in Moscow reported that 'Green says cablegram based on personal polemics [by] Lovestone [and] Ruthenberg'. In the end, whether Pepper or Gusev prepared the cable is less important than the fact that the two were acting in factional harmony.[33]

The End of the Cannon-Foster Group

The Gusev cable destroyed the alliance between Foster and Cannon. While Cannon counselled acceptance of the cable's terms, 'Foster exploded in a belligerent outburst', according to Swabeck. Foster no doubt sensed that the cable offered him no good option. If he accepted the cable and took leadership of the party, he would be agreeing that he was less loyal than Lovestone; if he refused the cable's terms, he would *prove* that he was less loyal. Foster argued that the group should refuse to accept the cable, and hand Ruthenberg's group control of the CEC and refuse to participate while appealing directly to the Comintern. In Moscow, Foster explained that 'the decision ... is in conflict with itself' and 'the political phase is in conflict with the organisational phase'. Thus he believed that 'if the Ruthenberg group is more loyal to the decisions of the Comintern we feel we can not take the majority of the CEC'.[34]

33 Sakmyster 2012, Chapter 6. Foster circular to 'Dear Comrades', 1 December 1925 in Cannon papers, reel 47, frame 291; A.B. [Bittelman], to 'Dear Comrade', 15 November [1925], in Cannon papers, reel 20, frame 8; Bittelman, 'Lessons I Have Learned', folder 16, p. 439.

34 Cannon 1962, p. 136; Swabeck, 'From Debs to Mao', section VIII, p. 14; Foster at American Commission meeting, 27 November 1925; in Comintern archives, 495:37:5. In a speech before the American Commission, Gusev attacked Foster, saying he 'tried to show that he was "100% loyal", and in order to do this he committed a new disloyalty toward the Comintern'; Green [Gusev], speech at American Commission [1925], in Lovestone papers, box 209, folder 31.

The destruction of the Cannon-Foster alliance was likely the whole point of the cable. Gusev's speech to the Ruthenberg caucus before the convention highlighted 'a difference … between Foster and Cannon' over the issue of factionalism. In Moscow after the convention, Foster speculated that Gusev had tried 'to get the Cannon group away from us'. Zinoviev reportedly told Bittelman after the fact that Gusev 'had been given instructions to pursue a policy to amalgamate the two groups'.[35]

Since Foster had refused to assume leadership of the party under such conditions, and since this refusal had undone his majority in the CEC in any case, the parity commission ordered 'that the Central Executive Committee be constructed on the basis of an equal number from each group, with a neutral chairman'. The Comintern put the party in receivership: 'The representative of the C.I. shall be given power by a resolution of the convention to participate in the C.E.C. meeting and cast a deciding vote and act as chairman'. Since Gusev supported Ruthenberg, a decisive Foster-Cannon majority had been transformed into a Ruthenberg leadership. At a meeting of the reconstituted CEC, Gusev explained his support to Ruthenberg:

> Of course we now have a parity C.E.C. but it is not exactly a parity C.E.C. With the decision of the Communist International on the question of the groups in the American Party, there goes parallel instructions to the C.I. representatives to support that group which was the former minority. If the C.I. continues this policy, that will always be the case, that is, the C.I. will be supporting that group and therefore altho [sic] we have nearly parity C.E.C. we have a majority and a minority in the C.E.C.

The factionalism that wracked the party cannot be blamed on the Comintern. But the Comintern encouraged factional power and not political programme to be at the centre of the dispute, made factional power dependent on Comintern support, and doled out support based on Moscow realpolitik, not Communist programme. Pepper added heat to this process, schooling co-factionalists like

35 Bedacht's translation of a speech by Green [Gusev] to minority caucus, 20 August 1925, in Lovestone papers, box 203; Foster at American Commission meeting, 27 November 1925; in Comintern archives, 495:37:5; A.B. [Bittelman] to 'Dear Comrade', 15 November [1925], in Cannon papers, reel 20, frame 8; see also Bittelman, 'Things I Have Learned', Bittelman papers, folder 16, p. 439.

Lovestone and Gitlow in cynicism and nastiness. This accelerated the political degeneration of the American party.[36]

The Brooklyn Bridge School of Party Building

A joke among the leadership captured the situation and the cynicism necessary to prosper in it: *why is the Communist Party like the Brooklyn Bridge? It is suspended by cables.* Cables, like the Brooklyn Bridge, went both ways. Although Lovestone would prove more adroit—at least temporarily—both factions courted Comintern intervention to bolster their positions. The March 1925 factional letters to the American Commission illustrate this. Ruthenberg's letter ended: 'we are compelled to communicate these facts and to request the intervention of the American Commission'. Foster and Cannon's letter ended: 'we earnestly request the sending of a cablegram to America detailing the following', with a list of factional demands. And a letter from Browder, temporarily in charge of the party during the plenum, informed the Comintern of the section's new equipment facilitating easier cable communication. Gusev's cable was the *deus ex machina*, but both factions comprised the Greek chorus.[37]

If the Gusev cable was designed to force factional peace, it had the opposite effect. 'Instead of uniting the party', Bittelman recalled, 'it tended to aggravate all divisions and differences', making the factionalism 'worse than before the convention'. Shortly after the convention, Bittelman and Foster travelled to Moscow to appeal the decision. Stung by the accusation of disloyalty,

---

36 Gitlow 1939, p. 187; Wolfe 1981, p. 374. See also Ruthenberg's speech at the American Commission in Moscow, 16 February 1926, for his description of this period. In Comintern archives, 495:164:373.

37 Ruthenberg, Lovestone and Pepper letter, 24 March 1925, and Foster and Cannon letter, 28 March 1925, in Ruthenberg to All Party Branches, 26 May 1925, in Shachtman papers, box 1, folder 19. On 28 March 1925, Earl Browder, in his capacity as acting secretary of the party, sent a letter to the Comintern complaining that 'all communications from the ECCI and its various departments arrive here from two weeks to six weeks later than they should ... We request that special pains be taken to give prompt dispatch to all communications intended for us, especially in view of the tremendous distance that has to be covered. We are establishing a new set of mail connections by cable, which we trust will assist in expediting receipt of communications in the future'; in Comintern archives, 495:37:9. In dealing with its own section, the American leadership assimilated the Comintern model. In 1925, a large portion of cables in the Comintern archives (515:1:511 and 515:1:516) are *within* the American party, not with the Comintern.

they issued a statement to the American Commission 'repudiat[ing] and condemn[ing] most emphatically the rumours and insinuations' that they were preparing to split from the Communist Party or were 'either directly or indirectly in conflict with the C.I.' Pepper, still in Moscow, represented the Ruthenberg faction before the Commission, along with William F. Kruse, a student at the Lenin School.[38]

Bittelman recalled that Stalin was non-committal. Zinoviev, who saw Bittelman from his private Kremlin apartment in the Kremlin while ill in bed, 'was very friendly'. After an hour and half, he told Bittelman to 'be cheerful'. Bukharin agreed that Bittelman should remain on the party's Political Committee. But he also proposed that Ruthenberg retain the party leadership while Foster run the party's trade-union work. This appeared a recipe for disaster, and Bittelman wrote in his memoirs: 'I can't say that we felt satisfied with the outcome of our trip'.[39]

Cannon's Anti-Faction Faction

Against Foster and Bittelman, Cannon and his supporters, particularly Martin Abern, Dunne, Shachtman and Swabeck, urged acceptance of the Comintern cable. In November 1925, Cannon and Dunne, along with Ruthenberg, Lovestone and Bedacht issued an appeal, 'Unite the Party!', which urged 'a unification of all those who follow and fight for the political line of the Communist International'. Ruthenberg lieutenant Jack Stachel labelled Cannon 'the most effective opponent of Fosterism'. Ruthenberg's faction believed that Cannon's submission to the Comintern cable spelled the end of his faction. Cannon and Dunne 'have definitely broke from the Foster group and have united with the Ruthenberg group', Lovestone bragged to the Comintern. 'The Cannon group is in dissolution like every middle group' in the Comintern, Pepper told the

38 Wm. Z. Foster and Alexander Bittelman, 'Statement to the American Commission', no date [late 1925?], in Comintern archives, 495:164:390. According to the 'Protocol' of the meeting, the Commission comprised Humbert-Droz as chair; the Finns Mauno Heimo, Otto Kuusinen, and [Atos?] Wirtanen; Béla Kun; Green (presumably Gusev); the Germans Ruth Fischer, [Hugo?] Gerisch, and Richard Gyptner; and Boris Reinstein; see Protocol of the Second Meeting of the American Commission, 1 December 1925, in Comintern archives, 495:37:6.

39 Bittelman, 'Things I Have Learned', folder 16, pp. 438–42. Report on meeting with Zinoviev taken from A.B. [Bittelman], to 'Dear Comrade', 15 November [1925] in Cannon papers, reel 20, frame 8.

American Commission in December 1925, and predicted that the 'Cannon group will not live long, that they must go over completely to the Ruthenberg group'. Pepper urged the Comintern to 'facilitate the assimilation of the Cannon group by the Ruthenberg group' to end factionalism. In late January, in the lead-up to the American Commission in Moscow, Cannon even signed, along with Pepper and Bedacht, a statement attacking the Foster faction as anti-Comintern.[40]

In internal factional correspondence, Lovestone sneered at Cannon: 'The rank and file of our new roommates is far above in intelligence than that of some of their corporals, colonels, generals and field rats', he wrote. In another letter, he wrote of his desire to marginalise the leadership of Cannon's group and annex its members: 'I am working overtime to make it impossible for the development of a sort of puppet-republic called Abernia or Cannonia'.[41]

Ruthenberg's faction saw Cannon's break with Foster as an opportunity; Foster saw it as a betrayal. Cannon's path was not based on factional calculus. As what he later described to Draper as a 'convinced "Cominternist"', Cannon trusted the Comintern, even if he did not understand its logic. Cannon later summarised his reasoning: the cable 'was sent by the CI, we could not alter a decision of the CI, and could we refuse the responsibility of the Party?' According to Swabeck, the Cannon group advocated 'loyalty to the Communist International, readiness to accept its decision and carry it out responsibly'. Cannon saw the Comintern's intervention as a path out of factionalism, and wanted to unite on that basis. As he argued in Moscow: 'we must have peace in the Party; we must have unity in the Party—at all cost, we must have unity in the Party and have an end to factionalism'.[42]

By early 1926, Cannon and his supporters remained separate from both of the main factions. They voted with whichever faction they agreed with on a

40 Cannon 1992, pp. 363–4; Jack Stachel to 'Dear Comrades', undated [1925], in Lovestone papers, box 288, folder 5; Jay Lovestone to 'Dear Comrade', 16 November 1925, in Comintern archives, 515:1:518; Pepper's speech to American Commission, 1 December 1925, in Comintern archives, 495:37:6; Max Bedacht, J.P. Cannon and Pepper, 'To the Members of the American Commission', 30 January 1926, in Comintern archives, 495:164:390.

41 [Jay Lovestone] to 'Dear Boys', 12 February 1926, in Lovestone papers, box 197, folder 4; J. [Lovestone] to 'Dear Comrades', 22 March 1926, in Lovestone papers, box 197, folder 5. See also Cannon's speech at the American Commission, 19 June 1927, for Cannon's description of Lovestone's duplicity; in Comintern archives, 495:37:12.

42 Cannon explained his decision at a meeting of the American Commission at the Enlarged Sixth ECCI Plenum in February 1926: minutes of American Commission of the Communist International, 16 February and 18 February 1926, in Prometheus Research Library collection and Comintern archives, 495:164:375.

particular issue. Cannon began to construct a 'faction to end factions'. This perspective found some resonance: William W. Weinstone, a leading Ruthenberg supporter in New York, wrote to Cannon stating that 'the Party needs unity of the leaders and leadership' and that 'the differences and opportunities facing the Party undoubtedly requires [sic] a unified leadership'. Still, Cannon became disaffected by the attitude of the Ruthenberg group as a whole, and its continuation of factional manoeuvres in the CEC. By September, Lovestone, instead of courting Cannon and Dunne, was denouncing their 'policy of destructive factionalism' for remaining independent.[43]

43 See anonymous 25 June 1926 letter which contains minutes of meeting between Cannon and Dunne and Ruthenberg and Lovestone, held the previous day, in Lovestone papers, box 197, folder 7; Will W. [Weinstone] to Jim [Cannon], 14 September 1926, in Cannon papers, reel 3, frame 38; [Jay Lovestone?] to Dear John [Pepper], 8 September 1926, in Lovestone papers, box 197, folder 9.

CHAPTER 8

The Foreign-Language Federations and 'Bolshevisation'

Much of the 'Bolshevisation' campaign in the United States focused on trying to reduce the independence of the foreign-language federations and subordinate them, politically and organisationally, to the central party. These federations posed the question of 'Americanising' the party. On a *sociological* level, the federations' strength and persistence, in reflecting the immigrant roots of the working class, were quite American. Yet these federations hindered the *political* Americanisation of the party.

The seeds of American Bolshevism were sown by organisations that were neither 'American' in their composition, nor Bolshevik in their organisational methods. While based on programmatic agreement with the Bolsheviks, the marriage of convenience between left-wing 'American' Socialists—like Cannon, Fraina, Reed and Ruthenberg—and radical Eastern Europeans—like Nicholas Hourwich—was uneasy. The foreign-language federations wanted what the Jewish Bund had demanded from the Russian Social Democracy decades earlier: a monopoly over work among their particular ethnic or language group. Given the Communist emphasis on a common political programme and organisational unity, the foreign-language federations were less compatible with the Communist movement than with the heterogeneous, decentralised Socialist Party. By the mid-1920s, the Communist Party faced the same problem that the SP had faced on the relationship of the federations to the national party.[1]

The merger of the UCP and the CPA further institutionalised the language federations. In 1922, only 10 percent of the organisation was in English-language branches. 'This is the most serious problem which we face', the CEC reported at the Second Workers' Party Convention. 'It affects all our work'.[2] Some of the

1 On the Bund, see Tobias 1961. Many former Bund militants were active in the left wing of the American labour movement in the late 1910s and 1920s; see Orenstein 1978. On the political and organisational influence of the Bund in the US, see Wolff 2012. Since the US is a society of immigrants, 'American' is a relative term. It is used here to refer to whether militants saw themselves as part of American society and desired to effect radical change in the US, or whether they saw themselves as merely exiles. Thus Nicholas Hourwich, a leader of the Russian Federation, was less American than his father, Isaac Hourwich.

2 'Report of the CEC to the Second National Convention', December 1922, in Comintern archives, 515:1:141.

federations were wealthier or stronger than the party as a whole. The party was often dependent on the dues paid by these federations, but the federations themselves often ignored Comintern or party instructions.

Furthermore, the federations saw themselves as belonging to a radical tradition that extended beyond the Communist movement, and, indeed, the federations were more important in their ethnic circles than the party was in American society at large. From the beginning, the Comintern and more far-sighted American leaders recognised the danger in this situation. In 1921, Kuusinen, Radek and Bukharin wrote to the party, noting that 'As long as the Party does not possess at least one or two legal dailies in the English language, it is still crawling around on all fours'.[3]

Beyond language, the lack of a newspaper reflected the non-Bolshevik origins of American Bolshevism. While Lenin argued (in 1901's *Where to Begin?* and 1902's *What is to be Done?*) that a party's newspaper should be its 'scaffolding' and 'collective organiser', the American Socialist Party opposed having a centralised newspaper, leaving its press in the hands of private companies (like Charles H. Kerr & Company, the Social Democratic Publishing Company, or the Appeal to Reason Publishing Company) and ethnic groups. Thus some papers—like the *Volkszeitung* or *Class Struggle*—were on the left and others on the right—like Berger's *Milwaukee Leader*. This decentralisation gave the nascent left wing space to develop, but it was an obstacle to a unified Communist Party.[4]

In 1922, Cannon complained that the party's central office did not even 'have a complete list of all the foreign language papers' owned or controlled by the party. The Lithuanian, Polish and Ukrainian newspapers each had a circulation as large as or larger than the official English-language Communist paper. The Finnish Federation published *three* daily newspapers. Thirty Hungarian branches, with 600 members, published a daily and a weekly paper with a combined circulation of 13,500. The similar-sized Italian federation published 9,000 weekly copies of its paper, while the Greek federation, with fewer than 300 members, circulated 2,000 issues of its paper. The 1,100 members of the Jewish federation, organised in 66 branches, distributed 30,000 issues of the daily *Freiheit*— a readership amounting to 150 percent of the total party membership. Edited by Olgin, the paper was a counterweight to Abraham Cahan's anti-Communist *Forward*, and, according to historian Tony

3 ECCI letter 'Concerning the Next Tasks of the CP of A', nd [1921?], in Comintern archives, 515:1:38; also printed in CEC's, 'Special Bulletin on the Party Situation', in Comintern archives, 515:1:28.

4 Martinek 2012.

Michels, 'attracted the most impressive array of poets and fiction writers of any Yiddish newspaper'. Not until 1924 did the party turn the weekly English-language *Worker* into the *Daily Worker*; the same year, the *Liberator*, the TUEL's *Labor Monthly* and *Soviet Russia Pictorial* were merged to create a regular English-language theoretical journal, *Workers Monthly*.[5]

The German federation (Lore's stronghold) was another example. Not only was the *New Yorker Volkszeitung* one of the oldest Marxist papers in the US, having passed through the SLP and SP, but it was also effectively outside of party control. In 1920, a party organiser complained that a German branch in Akron, Ohio, wanted 'to act for a while as a legal, neutral organization outside of all party activities' while the party was underground. A motion in the CEC in 1924 congratulating the Lawrence, Massachusetts, German branch captured the semi-autonomy of the federations by noting that the local 'has been in existence as a branch for the past fifty years and functioning as part of the revolutionary movement of this country in its various manifestations in the SLP, SP and Communist Party'. Even when the relationship between a federation and the party was warm, many federation members focused on their homelands instead of the work of the American party. Paul Buhle termed this 'fraternal style activity at the fringes of the party'.[6]

These numbers highlight the strength and weakness of the federation system. Since many immigrant Communists could not read English well, propaganda in different languages was necessary. The federations allowed the party to become rooted among many immigrant groups—who, after all, comprised a large part of the urban working class. These socialists also created a rich, ethnic radical culture among immigrants—most seen in the case of the Jews. According to David Prusdon, 'the Jewish Communist periphery of the Party was comprised of some 100,000 members of choirs, orchestras, theaters, workers clubs, workers universities, schools and cooperative movements'. In some industries (particularly the needle trades), such a cultural and ethnic apparatus could be useful for recruiting workers, but in general, from the perspective of

5 James P. Cannon, 'To All Federation Secretaries', 23 May 1922, in Comintern archives, 515:1:46; George Baldwin, 'Statement of the Communist Party of America to the ECCI,' August 1921, in Comintern archives, 515:1:39; C.E. Ruthenberg, 'Report of Secretary to CEC', autumn 1922, in Comintern archives, 515:1:143; 'Report on the CEC to the Second National Convention', December 1922, in Comintern archives, 515:1:141; Michels 2005, p. 241; On *Daily Worker*, see Draper 1985, p. 443, n. 7; information on *Workers Monthly* taken from entry in New York Public Library's Catalogue: <www.catalog.nypl.org>.

6 J.E. Wood to 'Dear Comrade', 1 April 1920, in Jay Lovestone papers, box 195, folder 10; CEC Minutes, 2 May 1924, in Comintern archives, 515:1:270; Buhle 1987, pp. 129–30.

building a revolutionary workers' party in the US, it was a diversion—whatever its cultural value.[7]

Tony Michels has criticised the Communist Party, writing that 'insofar as Communists viewed ethnicity as a problem to be overcome, they fitted comfortably with the prevailing climate of "100 percent Americanism"', because although opposed to anti-immigrant bigotry, Communists 'nonetheless favored cultural assimilation'. This cuts to the quick of the question: what was the point of the Communist Party, and how did federations fit into this? In political terms, the Bolsheviks defended the rights of immigrants, as well as ethnic and linguistic minorities; however, ethnicity *per se* did not concern them. The purpose of the Communist Party was not to create a cultural movement, in whatever language, but to win workers to the need to struggle against capitalism and fight for socialism.[8]

In the US, the Communists focused on fighting for working-class unity. According to a 1923 pamphlet, the Workers' Party 'denounce[d] laws directed against the foreign-born' and called 'upon the workers everywhere to organize local councils for the protection of foreign-born workers'. It called upon workers, both native- and foreign-born, to 'wage an active campaign to uproot the prejudices fostered by the capitalist class against the foreign born', and urged unions to 'wage a strong campaign of unionization amongst all unorganized workers, especially amongst the unorganized foreign-born workers in the basic industries'. In 1926, at the height of the Bolshevisation campaign, the party issued a leaflet, 'Fight Registration of Foreign-Born Workers!', and was active in the campaign to defend the foreign-born.[9]

While Communists defended immigrants, strengthening ethnic identity was not a Communist goal. Some federations' cultural importance, propaganda and real estate resources, roots in European socialism and the American SP, and decentralisation, served as a social-democratic pressure on the party. They remained social and cultural clubs more than programmatically-based organisations. Not all of their members had been recruited to the need for a Communist cadre organisation, and many of the groups had come over to the CP based on the leaders' decisions. In fact, the two largest federations, the Jewish and Finnish, had remained aloof from (or hostile to) the left

7 Prusdon 1984, p. xii.

8 Michels 2011, p. 28. It is striking that in its focus on ethnicity, Michel's biography of Olgin does not mention his role in the party as a whole in the 1920s, for example, the La Follette issue.

9 Ware 2005, p. 19; 'Fight Registration of Foreign-Born Workers!', Workers' Party pamphlet, no date [1926], signed by C.E. Ruthenberg, in Comintern archives, 515:1:918. For the party's activities in defence of immigrants, see Comintern archives, 515:1:918 and 515:1:919.

wing in 1919. Arne Halonen, a leader of the Finnish federation who opposed Bolshevisation, stressed later that 'as a rule, the Finnish members scorned the ridiculous ultra-revolutionary doctrine of the Comintern'. The transformation of the federations, and their members, into Communists would have been difficult in any circumstance.[10]

The 1922 conference resolved that the party needed 'a greater centralization of the language sections'. In May 1923, the ECCI wrote to the party, criticising its federal composition and calling for an English-language paper by November. Another letter from the same period demanded the party 'supersede the language structure and … draw immigrants into the general American work'. The federations should focus only on 'agitation and propaganda'. The ECCI sent a similar directive in late July. A 'Bolshevised' party, with neither political factions nor language federations, would have appealed to frustrated Communist leaders.[11]

By the mid-1920s, the once dominant Russian federation was much weaker because many members and leaders had returned to Russia. Stoklitsky stayed in Russia after the Second Congress of the Comintern in 1920, and worked for the ECCI for several years before becoming a journalist in the Soviet Union. (He was expelled from the Communist Party in 1939 for being an 'enemy of the people' and presumably executed). Hourwich remained in Russia after the Third Congress, where he taught politics at the university level until his death in 1934.[12]

Many rank-and-file Communist émigrés also wanted to return to Russia to build socialism. 'At the present moment a whole million of former Russians would like to come back to Russia', an American delegate to the Comintern's Second Congress told *Petrograd Pravda*, 'of every 100 Russian workmen in America, 99 wish to return to Russia'. By the end of the 1920s, Russian-Americans comprised a large portion of the 22,000 'foreigners' officially living in Soviet Russia. (A milieu of these former immigrants in America, such as Max Goldfarb [known as Petrovksy and A.J. Bennet], Boris Reinstein and Bill

10 Halonen 1945, p. 99. Of course, there was not an exact correlation, since the Russian federation had been the most ultra-left of the early Communists.

11 ECCI letter to 'WPA and All Its Language Federations', 19 May 1923, in Comintern archives, 515:1:164; ECCI letter, 'Only for Use of CEC, Not To Be Published', early 1923; ECCI letter to CEC of WPA, 23 July 1923, all in Comintern archives, 515:1:64.

12 Klehr 1978, p. 24; State Department 1920, p. 145; information on Hourwich from correspondence with Mark Donnelly, 23 June 2011; Hourwich stayed in Ukraine for two years before settling in Russia; information on Stoklistky from Comintern archives, 495:261:1085; research assistance by Andrei Nesterov.

Shatov; Americans resident in Moscow; as well as foreign Communists with American experience, such as Andreytchtine, Katayama and Pepper, helped the Comintern navigate American politics). So great was the desire for emigration among Russian-American Communists that the party repeatedly passed motions condemning unauthorised return, although immigrants with skills useful to the Soviet state were encouraged. Some Finnish and Jewish Communists moved to the Karelian and Birobidzhanian Soviet regions in the late 1920s and early 1930s, but the Finnish and Jewish language federations remained the largest in the party in the mid-1920s.[13]

The Strange History of Finnish American Communism

In 1925, out of a total party membership of 16,300 comrades, 6,500 were Finnish. The Finnish Federation had its own journals, leaders and political culture. There was even a term, 'hall socialism', to describe the loyalty of Finnish American Communists to their federation. In Superior, Wisconsin, according to one official party report, 'the local Finnish branch with 150 members is the largest single branch in the local, they maintain headquarters and have an orchestra, dramatic club, male choir, brass band and athletic club', along with a daily newspaper. This was five times the size of the English-language branch. The Finnish federation's buildings, papers and agricultural cooperatives were worth millions of dollars.[14]

The influence of Communism among Finnish Americans in the early twentieth-century was disproportionate to the influence of Finns or Communists in American society. While the number of migrants was substantial compared to the total population of Finland, this was not the case compared to the

13 Graziosi 1988, p. 39; on Karelia, see Ahola 1981, pp. 175–80; on the fate of the Karelian Finns in the Stalinist purges, see Klehr, Haynes, Andersen 1998, pp. 227–43; on Birobidzhan, see Srebrnik 1999, pp. 129–47, and Srebrnik 2010. In his interview (as Lewis Corey) with the FBI in 1949–50, Fraina claimed that Stoklitsky and Hourwich, leaders of the Russian federation, recruited large numbers of people with 'the sales talk that if they became members of the Federation and wanted to go to Russia, they would get special privileges. When this did not materialize, they just fell off'; 'FBI Interrogation of Lewis Corey, 1949–1950', Corey papers, box 2, folder 5, p. 58.

14 Glazer 1961, pp. 39–41; Kostianen 1989, p. 34; 'Report on Administrative Council Meeting [of WPA] of 21 April', 25 April 1922, in Comintern archives, 515:1:146; Dyson 1972, Chapter 3. For a description of the New York City Finnish labour hall, built at a cost of $300,000, see Halonen 1945, pp. 103–5; for a description of the cultural and social apparatus of the Finnish clubs, see ibid., pp. 118–28.

US population. In 1920, only 250,000 people born in Finland or claiming one Finnish parent lived in the Continental US, out of 106 million people. In contrast, 1.7 million Americans were born in Germany and 1.6 million were born in Italy. Further, in 1923, more than five percent of Finns in the US were members of the Workers' Party, and an equal number could be counted as Communist sympathisers. Further, some twenty-five to thirty percent of Finnish immigrants could be considered radical during this period, active in the Socialist, IWW, Communist or co-operative movements. If these same rates had been the same for all Americans, there would have been more than a million Communists or sympathisers and some thirty million radicals in the US. Finns were active on the left at levels much higher than American society as a whole.[15]

For Finns, political radicalism was connected to ethnic identity. Because of their unique language, culture and rural lives, Finnish immigrants tended to stick together and isolate themselves from broader American society, and (like many immigrant groups) were often labelled 'clannish'. Consequently, Finnish institutions, from the church to the co-operative, were central to Finnish American identity. While right-wing Finns looked to the church, left-wing Finns looked to radical institutions including the Finnish Socialist Federation. The Finnish Civil War, which exacerbated divisions between 'red' and 'white' Finns, made politics more important for Finnish American identity.[16]

While Jewish Communists' ethnic identity was linked to politics, Jewish radicals (especially the second generation) saw politics as a means to assimilate into the American labour movement and American society. Many radical Finns saw radicalism as a way to preserve a distinctive ethnic culture. More assimilated Jewish Americans than assimilated Finnish Americans were active on the left.[17]

15 United States Census Bureau 1921, I, p. 13; II, pp. 690–1; Kostiainen 1978, pp. 142–5; Karni 1975, p. 19. Two sociologists have argued that there is a direct correlation between the presence of Finns and the strength of the left in a particular area during the 1920s; see Stark and Christiano 1992. In 2003, the director of the Institute of Migration at the University of Turku estimated that if the emigrants to Sweden and the US had stayed in Finland the total population of the country would have been around 30 percent higher; see Koivukangas 2003, p. 8.

16 Gedicks 1976, pp. 28–9; Hudelson 1993; Hudelson 2002; Hummasti 1996; Kero 1973; Kero 1975. On descriptions of Finns as 'clannish', see Holmio 2001, p. 149; Minnesota Federal Writers Project 1938, p. 292.

17 On politics and ethnicity among Jewish Communists, see Buhle 1980; Michels 2011; Prusdon 1984; Zucker 1991. For a comparison of Finns and Jews in the Communist movement, see Mishler 1995, pp. 147–9.

The party leadership was frustrated that the Finnish Communists tended to have little intersection with the American working class as a whole. As John Wiita (known as Henry Puro), a leader of the Finnish federation, later recalled, 'It seemed an impossible task to convince Finnish communists to leave their Finnish halls in convenient meeting places and go to meet in inconvenient meeting places [for] other nationals and use English [that] they did not fully understand [and] in which they were unable to express themselves'. In the summer of 1923, Comintern official and Finnish Communist Otto Kuusinen admonished the Finnish Federation 'that your membership from an agitational standpoint does not amount to much' for the struggle for socialism in the US because, despite their great numbers, Finnish Communists were insular and did not speak English. He urged them to use their resources, particularly their cooperatives and printing presses, for the Communist Party as a whole.[18]

The Finnish federation was the most extreme example of the danger of the party's federal structure. While some workforces were dominated by one ethnic group (like the needle trades), in others language groups hindered the trade-union work of the party by preventing common activity among workers from different federations. In a meeting in Moscow in 1925, Foster explained that 'when we come to organise our nuclei, we will probably get a nucleus, for example, consisting of a Pole, a Finn, a Jew and a Spaniard—different types of people who are not accustomed to work together'. Sure enough, a year later, Lovestone described to the American Commission a shop nucleus in New York with 13 members who spoke 11 different languages. At the same meeting, Bittelman recalled that in such situations, an attempt had been made to require nuclei members to carry out party work in English, but since many had at best a passive knowledge of the language, 'they could not participate in any activity of the Party'. The loyalty that immigrant workers felt to their federation was not always transferred to the party as a whole. And in 1924, a report noted that even though some 50 percent of the membership spoke English, many joined language groups anyway. Still, with such a high non-English-speaking membership, the language groups could not be abolished altogether. Many Communists would have sympathised with the ECCI's statement that the 'Language federations constituting the Party are a necessity and yet a hindrance to unification of the membership'.[19]

18 John Wiita [Henry Puro], 'The Crisis in the Finnish American Left, 1925–1930', box 1, folder 2, p. 7, in John Wiita papers; O.W. Kuusinen to Finnish Federation of WPA, 3 August 1923, in Comintern archives, 515:1:164.

19 *Second Year of the Workers' Party of America*, pp. 29–30, 58; Foster to Meeting of American Organisational Commission, 1 December 1925, in Comintern archives, 495:37:6. Unlike the

In the summer of 1925, the ECCI wrote another letter to the American party's leadership. The party's weakness 'lies in the defects of the organisational structure of the Workers' Party, which are greater than in any other party'. The party had 'no single guiding Party centre', decisions were made on a federal basis, and 'each of its 17 national sections represents almost a separate and independent Party within the Workers' Party, enjoying a large degree of independence and isolation to the leading organ, the Central Committee'. This situation had to be turned around, but not, the letter stressed, by administrative fiat. The ECCI suggested several practical measures. Instead of each group having its own leadership, the party should organise pan-federation local and district councils not based on proportional representation. Dues should be collected by the party and then distributed to the federations. The party should centralise control of the federations' press. Finally, membership should be based on factory nuclei and neighbourhood groups, instead of language federations. The goal was to integrate the federations and their membership into the common movement, not to purge them. The letter stressed, 'To break ... one organisation without creating something in its place would be *extremely dangerous*'.[20]

A motion voted by the CEC echoed this, warning that the creation of shop-nuclei organisation needed to be done with care 'in order not to break up prematurely or endanger the existing Party structure to such an extent as to make it incapable to carry out the necessary work of the Party'. The plan was to reorganise the membership based on where they worked: if three or more comrades worked in the same shop, they would be in the same nucleus, regardless of their membership in a federation. This made sense in the abstract, but not all workers in the same workplace spoke the same language. Members in such nuclei would retain the right to participate in the internal life of the federations, but would vote within their nuclei on all broader party issues. ('Street nuclei'—based on neighbourhood—were also created, although factory nuclei were preferred).[21]

Lovestone spelled out in detail what this process was to entail. 'With the reorganization of the Party', he wrote, 'the Federations will cease to exist as

other groups mentioned, there was no Spanish federation; Presentations of Lovestone and Bittelman to American Commission, 27 December 1926, in Lovestone papers, box 210, folder 13; I. Amter, 'Report to Comintern', 7 March 1923, in Comintern archives, 515:1:174.

20 Letter from ECCI to Central Executive Committee of the Workers' Party, stamped 20 June 1925, in Lovestone papers, box 208, folder 18.

21 'Thesis on Reorganization of the Party on Basis of Shop Nuclei', adopted unanimously by CEC; no date, in Comintern archives, 515:1:285; on shop nuclei, see also Draper 1986, pp. 192–3.

independent propaganda units of the Party'. Instead, the federations were to become 'auxiliary organizations for the Party for Communist work amongst the proletariat of a particular language group'. There was to be a central 'Agitprop' (agitation and propaganda) department to unify and coordinate the party's press. 'The Property, as well as the press, of every language section is to be owned by the Party as a whole', Lovestone added. Or as Foster told the Comintern in Moscow, 'The Finns have a large amount of property in all kinds of organisations; they have halls, institutes, and various other kinds of other Party branches and sections have property as well ... The question is how shall the Party get control of this property'.[22]

The desire to control these assets was not just based on centralising the party, but also on the financial strains of a daily paper. In 1924, to finance the *Daily Worker*, the party had taken out a $10,000 loan from the Amalgamated Bank (formed the year before by the ACWA), which was then transferred to the radical American Fund for Public Service (the so-called Garland Fund) administered by Roger Baldwin. Over time, the party took out more loans to cover an array of publishing efforts. The paper's building was collateral for the loans, and the party had trouble making payments. An audit by Stuart Chase, the Fund's accountant, in September 1924 declared: 'It looks as if this paper would be a money loser and a large one for some time to come'. (He labelled the loan 'a wild gamble', which proved to be true: in 1928, the party defaulted on the then more than $30,000 in loans from the Fund. Even after the building was taken into account, the Fund lost $14,000).[23]

According to a later Comintern report, 'three months after the 4th Convention [in August 1925], the reorganisation was declared to be 70 percent complete', with the creation of 207 shop nuclei and 46 street nuclei in New York City alone. Despite this, reorganisation did not proceed smoothly. Lovestone admitted: 'We had reorganised the Party with too great rapidity'. The federations resisted losing their control, and their assets. The messiness of reorganisation reflected the fact that it targeted not only federations but also political

22 Jay Lovestone, 'Eight Questions Answered', nd [1924/1925], in Comintern archives, 515:1:294; Foster at Meeting American Organisational Commission, 1 December 1925, in Comintern archives, 495:37:6.

23 The saga of the loans is found in the *Daily Worker* correspondence file in the papers of the American Fund for Public Service, reel 15; material above taken from Moritz Loeb to AFPS, 12 August 1924; Roger Baldwin to Moritz J. Loeb, 10 September 1924; Stuart Chase, CPA, to AFPS, 13 September 1924; 'Statement of Accounts by the American Fund for Public Service, Inc., to the Daily Worker Publishing Co.', 25 October 1928; Roger Baldwin to Jay Lovesone, 5 November 1928.

dissent and opposition. While representing an attempt to focus the party's efforts on the working class, this reorganisation atomised and dispersed the membership, undercutting possible political opposition.[24]

That Lore found support in the German-language federation and among Finns was not lost on the party's leaders. In the mid-1920s, Wiita recalled, both factions courted the Finnish federation as they had courted Lore, to gain power in the party. In February 1925, leaders of the Ruthenberg faction complained to the Comintern that Foster's supporters in the Russian federation were manoeuvring against them. The next month, Pepper made the same charge, in a speech to the American Commission, against the Finnish federation's 'through and through social-democratic and opportunist' leadership. The resolution on Bolshevisation passed by the Fourth National Convention highlighted that 'the Federation form of organization is a most fertile soil for factionalism'.[25]

Ruthenberg reported to the American Commission, stating that 'naturally, this reorganization was a great shock to the language federations and particularly to the Finnish section'. Gitlow, given the task of Bolshevising the party in New York City, recounted that since this involved destroying then rebuilding entire branches, 'By securing the Bolshevization task, our faction had the opportunity to build its support among the membership anew from the ground up'. What had been justified to unify the party 'became a factional football', in Gitlow's words. This was underscored by a Ruthenberg faction letter of 1925, which surveyed the effects of Bolshevisation on the party's seventeen language federations. The letter predicted that reorganisation would hit Foster's allies hardest. In the Finnish section, there was 'a decisive majority against us', so the federation 'will lose almost 50% thru reorg'. However, the Hungarian faction (in which Pepper was influential) was 'solidly for us', and as a result 'will not lose many thru reorganization'. Similarly, the Czechoslovakian and Slovakian federations, who had sided with Foster, faced the loss of many members, while the pro-Ruthenberg Lithuanian and South Slav federations would be less damaged.[26]

---

24 Communist International 1928a, p. 347; Lovestone at American Commission meeting, 27 December 1926, in Lovestone papers, box 210, folder 13.

25 *Fourth National Convention of the Workers' (Communist) Party* 1925, p. 87; John Wiita [Henry Puro], 'The Crisis in the Finnish American Left, 1925–1930', box 1, folder 2, p. 6, Wiita papers; Max Bedacht, Benjamin Gitlow and J. Louis Engdahl to ECCI, 23 February 1925, in Lovestone papers, box 209, folder 1; John Pepper, speech to American Commission, 4 March 1925, in Comintern archives, 495:37:5.

26 C.E. Ruthenberg, American Commission of the ECCI, 16 February 1926, in Prometheus Research Library collection; Gitlow 1939, pp. 229–30; [Jay Lovestone?] to John [Pepper], 8 October 1925, in Lovestone papers, box 197, folder 1.

The dismantling of the language federations met with mixed success. One result was the loss of almost half the members: the 14,037 members in September 1925 were reduced to 7,215 in October. While a report by the ECCI blamed this on inaccurate membership figures in the US party, it noted that throughout the Comintern as a whole, 'The first external result of the reorganisation in all countries (with the exception of Germany) was a loss in members and in some cases this loss was quite considerable'. Some of this loss was related to the elimination of dual-stamp dues (in which husband and wives could buy one monthly dues stamp instead of two), itself part of Bolshevisation. But several language federations, such as the Italians and Germans, were decimated. Of the 6,000 members in the Finnish federation, only 1,500 re-enrolled in the party, and many leading Finnish cadres quit or were purged.[27]

The reorganisation process involved reforming the party's financial structure. By the summer of 1925, the central party was playing a larger role in financing the language federations, instead of the other way around. For example, in May, the Jewish Federation asked for 'at least $30,000' to keep the *Freiheit* afloat. The CEC refused this request, claiming it had 'no financial resources which it will be able to use for the assistance of the Freiheit'. In the fall, in addition to ending the dual-stamp system, the CEC eliminated the control of the federations over dues. 'Beginning October First', Lovestone and Ruthenberg wrote in a memo, 'all Party dues will be paid directly through the District Office'. This had its desired effect. The next month, the Scandinavian Federation wrote to Lovestone: 'Due to the new arrangements in the Party structure our federation income has now disappeared and our funds are therefore depleted leaving us nothing on hand for further work'. This did not make the party wealthy, but it meant that the central party apparatus—not the federations—controlled the finances.[28]

27 Ahola 1981, pp. 34, 81; Buhle 1987, p. 135; Draper 1986, p. 187; Klehr 1978, p. 22; Kostianen 1989, pp. 32–3; Morray 1983, p. 39; Communist International 1928a, pp. 17, 351. The elimination of dual-stamp dues was also part of the Bolshevisation campaign; Bittelman told the American Organisation Commission in Moscow that 'the family question is the biggest problem in our Party reorganisation'; Comintern archives, 495:37:6.

28 See Morris Holtman, R. Salzman and Ben Lifshitz to Executive Committee, WPA, 7 May 1925; C.E. Ruthenberg to R. Salzman, 18 May 1925; C.E. Ruthenberg to R. Salzman, 3 June 1925, all in Comintern archives, 515:1:500. Jay Lovestone and C.E. Ruthenberg, 'To All District Organizers and Federation Secretaries', 12 September 1925, in Comintern archives, 515:1:520. Party dues were 50 cents per month, and then, for members earning more than $100 per month, an additional 1 percent of this additional income; there were also periodic special assessments. Members who were ill, unemployed or on strike were exempt from dues. N. Jane Christiansen [?] to Jay Lovestone, 21 October 1925, in Comintern archives, 515:1:524.

Bolshevisation precipitated years of internecine fighting within the Finnish American community over control of the federation's resources. The fight within the Central Cooperative Exchange (CCE), a largely Finnish group in Superior, Wisconsin, was one example of this. Much of the once pro-Communist membership of the CCE deserted the party when the Communist leadership insisted that the CCE make available its substantial financial assets to the party. When the CCE leadership (including many party members) refused, the party and the CCE began attacking one another. The split was bitter, and while the CCE continued until the early 1960s, it was not part of an organised political movement. The Finnish question in North America was so important that the Comintern dispatched Aino Kuusinen—Otto Kuusinen's wife—to sort out the wreckage; in 1930, the ECCI sent Aino Kuusinen and the former head of the Finnish Communist Party, Kullervo Manner, to Canada to deal with a similar problem there.[29]

Many ethnic Communists who left the party during Bolshevisation remained sympathetic to Communism and stayed in the party's periphery, most prominently in the International Workers Order (IWO). The precursor to the IWO, the Jewish People's Fraternal Organization, was a left-wing split from the social-democratic Arbeter Ring (Workmen's Circle) Jewish fraternal society. The IWO was led by Communists—most notably Max Bedacht—and provided low cost insurance and benefit schemes to workers, including black workers. Like the pre-Bolshevisation CP, the IWO was organised into ethnic federations. One later Communist leader described the IWO's members as 'those sympathizers who still clung to ethnic allegiances'. Until New York State revoked its charter to sell insurance during the McCarthy era, the IWO was successful, with its membership growing from 3,300 in 1933 to some 50,000 in 1950. The IWO helped finance the *Daily Worker* and the *Freiheit*. In a broad sense, then, the IWO was the successful face of Bolshevisation: its members had the ethnic-based organisation they wanted, the Communists were rid of the language federations while drawing on their resources.[30]

The party set up 'Workers Clubs', comprising party members and non-party members, designed to 'carry on all the social and cultural work formerly done by the old federation branches'. At an American Commission meeting in late

29 On the Communist/Cooperative split, see Wiita, 'Crisis in the Finnish-American Left', Wiita papers; Dyson 1982, Chapter 3; Halonen 1945, pp. 111–18. On Aino Kuusinen, see Kuusinen 1974, pp. 82–102; Klehr, Haynes and Andersen 1998, pp. 176–80; on Canada, see: Angus 1981, p. 309; Avakumovic 1975, p. 35; Markotich 1992, pp. 63, 72, 75.

30 Mishler 1995, p. 65; Keeran 1995, pp. 23–5; Liebman 1997, pp. 331–2; Prusdon 1984, p. xii; Walker 1982, pp. 16–27; Zucker 1991. Quote from Starobin 1972, p. 25.

1926, Lovestone defended reorganisation despite the drop in membership, and claimed that 'many of the former Party members are in the Workers' Clubs doing actually as much Party work as they did before'. Even many of the ex-Communist Finns did not leave the party's orbit. In 1925, to safeguard federation property from party control, dissident Finns established the Finnish Workers Federation (FWF) as a separate entity. Wiita convinced party leaders that since less than a third of members of the former Finnish foreign-language federation joined the party, the FWF would offer a home for 'the others [who] are still close to the Party and could be kept as Party sympathizers, given leadership by their own central organization'. In late 1925, Israel Amter, in charge of the party's work in Ohio, reported that many of the Finnish members there 'will remain dead timber' inside the party, but 'in the clubs, on the contrary, they will be good supporters of the actions and campaigns of the Party'. As one author has argued, the FWF was 'a mass organization of the Communist Party in the truest sense', since it combined Communist and non-Communists under the political direction of the party. In 1941, the FWF affiliated with the IWO.[31]

When the party needed money for the *Daily Worker* in March 1927, it looked to the language federations. However, the relationship between the central party and the language groups was still uneasy; an article in August complained that 'the Language Fractions are still playing a too important role', while the central party's 'Language Bureaus however has [sic] not yet started to function as they should'. Nor could Bolshevisation eliminate the objective conditions that had given rise to the federations. Jack Stachel admitted in the *Daily Worker* in February 1927 that 'the great bulk of them [immigrant workers] must still be reached thru the propaganda in their own language, and since there is lacking trade union organization in most of these industries', many immigrant sympathisers 'are to be found in the different fraternal organizations'. He complained that, despite this reality, these organisations 'must pay more attention to America' and less to the 'home country'.[32]

31 Lovestone speech at American Commission, Lovestone papers, box 210, folder 13; Communist International 1928a, p. 350; Jay Lovestone, 'The Question of Workers' Clubs', 15 June 1925, in Comintern archives, 515:1:520; Karni 1975, p. 239; Kostiainen 1989, p. 33; Halonen 1945, p. 101; Wiita, 'Crisis in the Finnish-American Left', p. 10; IA [Israel Amter] to 'Dear Comrade' [Jay Lovestone?], no date [late 1925] in Lovestone papers, box 350, folder 27; Ahola 1981, pp. 230–2. Of course, not all Finns left the party to begin with. As late as 2000, the party was led by a Finnish American, Arvo Holberg (better known as Gus Hall).

32 Peterson 1927; Stachel 1927. According to Michael Brook, Peterson was really Allan Wallenius, a Swedish-Finnish man who lived in the US intermittently in the first decades of the twentieth century, as well as being an official in the Comintern; Bengston 1999, p. 207.

In the spring of 1928, the *Party Organizer* outlined a campaign to increase readership of the *Daily Worker* among party members because 'the greatest majority of our Party members are still filled with the Federation ideology and are supporters of their language papers, while reading the *Daily Worker* is only a secondary matter'. In one sub-district in New York City, according to the article, only 35 percent of party members read the *Daily Worker*, but 70 percent read the *Freiheit*. The next month, *Party Organizer* complained: 'there still are Language Federations in our Party,' but now 'they only carry other names'. In March 1930, the *Party Organizer* returned to the theme, noting that 'in reality most of our language comrades work isolated—more or less—from the general Party work'. The author continued: 'Their main activity is concentrated in the language field'. In response, the party held English-language classes for its members at 'every party school', which drew 'record-breaking attendance', according to a report in 1928. However, since as late as 1936 more than half of all members were foreign-born, foreign-language propaganda was necessary.[33]

'Bolshevisation', then, carried out necessary changes in the party organisation, especially in taming the language federations. However, this reorganisation at once weakened the party while strengthening it. The party was half the size, but comprised a more committed membership. Not only did 'Bolshevisation' emphasise anti-Trotskyism and fealty to the 'troika' in Russia, but it was realised in a factional manner.

33 *Party Organizer*, March/April 1928; May/June 1928; March 1930. Communist International 1928a, p. 351; see *Daily Worker*, 21 January 1929, for an example of a description of these classes. On foreign membership, see Alperin 1959, p. 64.

CHAPTER 9

Factionalism and Mass Work, 1925–7

In the mid-1920s, the party began to emerge from the isolation caused by the rightward shift in national politics, compounded by the farmer-labour and La Follette disasters. To be sure, socialist revolution appeared more distant than at the party's founding, and the party, with 12,000 members in 1928, was a fraction of the total left-wing support following the Bolshevik Revolution. Still, the party's influence was growing. The combined circulation of daily, weekly or monthly Communist periodicals in all languages was 170,000. For each Communist Party member, there were almost one thousand readers of the party's daily newspapers.[1]

The party formed several organisations at this time, including the All-American Anti-Imperialist League in late 1924, led by Cannon supporter Manuel Gomez, and the American Negro Labor Congress in 1925, led by Ruthenberg supporter Lovett Fort-Whiteman. Communists earned respect in the labour movement through the Passaic strike of 1926–7 and the fight led by the International Labor Defense (ILD) to save anarchist militants Nicola Sacco and Bartolomeo Vanzetti from execution. While both these defensive struggles were defeated, they demonstrated that Communists could lead mass struggle, and highlighted the potential of the party.[2]

The persistent factionalism was an obstacle to realising this potential and corroded the internal life of the party; it both reflected and magnified the pressures of the period. The mid-to-late 1920s, Cannon later wrote to Draper, 'must present far more difficulties for the inquiring student than all the preceding years put together'. In this period, he continued, acute factional struggle 'became bankrupt for lack of real political justification for the existence of factions'. The party needed to transcend these factions through common work that would unify the party and bring new political issues to the fore. Given the rancour between the factions, forged in half a decade of bitter animosity, this unity could have been achieved only through Comintern intervention.

In the period 1925–7, the intervention of the Comintern qualitatively shifted. Just as with Bolshevisation, the intervention of the Comintern, while promising an end to factional warfare, manipulated factionalism for the

1 Communist International 1928a, pp. 20, 345.

2 On the Anti-Imperialist League, see Shipman 1993 and Kerssfeld 2007. The ANLC is dealt with in the chapters below on the party's work among black Americans.

benefit of its own increasingly Stalinist leadership. The ECCI played factions off against one another, and kept the factional cauldron boiling. Combined with the apparent strength of American capitalism amid the prosperous 1920s, factionalism created a cynicism among many leading cadres. In the pursuit of power within the party, subservience to the Comintern apparatus and Stalinist dogma became paramount, instead of the revolutionary programme that had animated the early Comintern. At the same time, this degeneration cannot be blamed entirely on the Comintern, since it was a result of the interaction of both internal and external processes, even if the political actors in this drama were not entirely aware of their roles at the time.

Factionalism and Trade-Union Work

Factional ire seeped into every nook and cranny of party activity, especially its work in the trade unions (which was Foster's claim to leadership). The needle trades unions—with their strength in New York City and Chicago, their historically Socialist leadership, and radical Jewish membership—were the focus of much of this factionalism.

Charles Zimmerman and Rose Wortis, leading Communists in the ILGWU, along with Gitlow, a leader in the party's Textile Committee and former member of the ACWA, supported Ruthenberg. In 1925, there was a dispute over how to approach the upcoming ILGWU conference. Jack Johnstone, who was in charge of the TUEL while Foster was in Moscow appealing the Gusev letter, advocated playing elements of the social-democratic Morris Sigman leadership against each other. His goal for the TUEL was to 'negotiate for organizational guarantees, which will completely protect it in the control of its present conditions'. Cannon and Dunne opposed this perspective, which they saw as emphasising organisational manoeuvres over political struggle. The CEC issued a 'statement on the needle trades situation' that attacked the TUEL for downplaying the party's programme so that it retained only a 'secondary importance and is fast becoming a memory'. This underscored a key difference over the role of the TUEL.[3]

Ruthenberg's faction had been critical of the TUEL. In Moscow in April 1925, Pepper had declared that 'the *organisational form* and even the *name* of the Trade Union Educational League is often a hindrance to the progress of this Left movement' in the unions. 'If we do not understand how to *put the TUEL*

3 Johnstone quoted in Cannon 1992, pp. 359–60; CEC statement quoted in Gurowsky 1978, pp. 176–7.

upon a broader basis it cannot live despite the progress of the Left Wing movement'. The TUEL, he added, 'should have a broader conception of its tasks and not repulse the masses through a name-fetishism'. Since 'millions of real proletarian elements have left the American Federation of Labour', and attacks on the UMW might 'shatter' the miners' union, 'I fear that this result in this situation will seriously hinder Communist politics in America if we do not understand how to make the slogan, organise the unorganised, into a real mass movement'. Again citing the development of the Labour Party in Britain as a precedent, Pepper claimed that a new labour upsurge could spur the creation of a working-class party. Against this, Bittelman argued that 'the Ruthenberg group have been showing for a long and considerable time opposition' to the league and 'has been sabotaging the TUEL for a long while'. In fact, the TUEL was 'functioning now under many names' and had proven itself to be more dynamic than Pepper allowed. Foster and Bittelman submitted a document to the American Commission, 'Liquidating the Party Trade Union Work in America', which contained more than twenty examples of what they labelled hostility to the TUEL, from 'removal of our best trade union comrades from party activity for purely factional reasons' to a 'constant display of dual union tendencies on the question of organizing the unorganized'.[4]

Hell in New Jersey

Foster's fear of dual unions grew in January, with the start of the year-long textile workers strike in Passaic, New Jersey. The strike captured the imagination of liberals and the labour movement, and placed Communists in the centre of the struggle to re-energise the trade-union movement amid the anti-labour 1920s. The Passaic workers came to symbolise the entire working class in the 1920s, as they faced poor conditions and declining pay with no union protection. Foster must have seen the strike as a Ruthenberg affair, given the lack of involvement of the TUEL or Foster himself, and the influence of Albert Weisbord, a Ruthenberg supporter.

Passaic—about eight kilometres south of Paterson, New Jersey, and 22 kilometres west of Union Square in Lower Manhattan—had long been a centre of the textile industry. Workers, largely East European immigrants and their

4 Second Session of American Commission; 1 December 1925 (Pepper) and 2 December 1925 (Bittelman), in Comintern archives, 495:37:6; Wm. Z. Foster and Alexander Bittelman, 'Liquidating the Party Trade Union Work in America', 14 December 1925, in Comintern archives, 495:37:9.

children, faced horrible conditions and low wages. In 1912, the IWW had led a silk workers' strike in Paterson, which spread to Passaic. In 1919, there had been another strike. By 1926, the AFL textile workers' union, the United Textile Workers (UTW), had dwindled and did not count any members in Passaic. A historian of Passaic described the 1926 strike as 'the final, most tragic act in a fourteen-year saga of industrial disruption in this North Jersey city'.[5]

The cause of the strike was a 10 percent wage cut at one mill. Gustave Deak, a mill worker, approached the UTW to help fight the cut, but its leadership refused. It then fell to the Communists to organise workers to fight the attack. Albert Weisbord, a recent graduate from Harvard Law School[6] and recent recruit from the Socialist Party, played a key role in organising the strike. He had recently moved to Paterson and was employed as a silk worker. Ironically, in the midst of Bolshevisation's anti-foreign-language-federation campaign, the groundwork for the most important strike in the party's history so far was prepared by language groups. (Almost two-thirds of Passaic's residents were foreign-born, and they spoke more than thirty languages). There had been a Polish branch at least since 1923, and it appears that there were already German, Jewish, Russian and Ukrainian branches before the strike as well; with the aid of Hungarian comrades (particularly Deak), Weisbord organised the United Front Committee (UFC) against the wage cut.[7]

The UFC elected a committee to protest against a supporter's firing. In response, the mills fired the committee's members. The strike began on 22 January 1926, and by spring included 16,000 workers from several mills. They

5 Ebner 1970, p. 453. The 1912 strike, led by a disident IWW faction sympathetic to Daniel De Leon, should not be confused with the more famous Paterson strike of 1913; see Dubofsky 1987, chapter 11.

6 There are discrepancies among historians as to whether Weisbord finished law school or dropped out. According to the registrar's office of Harvard Law School, he was awarded a law degree on 19 June 1924: Samatha Fitzgerald, Harvard Law School Registrar's Office, to author, 22 June 2011.

7 C.E. Ruthenberg to Charles Krumbein, 25 June 1923, in Comintern archives, 515:1:201. On the importance of the foreign-language groups, see Weisbord 1977, pp. 101, 135. On the Hungarian federation and Passaic, see Sakmyster 2005a, pp. 47–8. Evidence on the existence of other branches comes from the Ruthenberg factional memorandum, 'Sections in District Two', undated but apparently from the summer of 1925, in Lovestone papers, box 220, folder 1. On the foreign population—and the general state of Passaic at the time of the strike, see McMullen 2005, pp. 152, 155.

demanded higher wages, time-and-a-half overtime pay, better conditions, union recognition and no reprisals against union members.[8]

The relationship of the Communist leadership to the strike is still contentious. In November 1924, Foster had written to Charles Zimmerman, in reference to Paterson, of 'the plan to reach out to other centers to organize the silk workers there'. Reports by Bert Miller (Benjamin Mandel), the party's organisational secretary for New York, indicate that Communists had been paying attention to the Paterson-Passaic textile industry since at least the autumn of 1925.[9]

During the strike, Ruthenberg stated: 'It is no secret that our Party initiated the movement among the Passaic workers'. Martha Stone Asher, a high school student from Brooklyn and a member of the Communist youth group, recalled decades later: 'The party assigned people to go to Passaic and encourage the workers, whose concerns were primarily economic and not political, to take strike action in their own defense'. Predictably, the mill owners and the AFL sought to depict the strike as an illegitimate publicity stunt by Communists. After he had been expelled from the party, Weisbord later bitterly argued that 'Even though I was a member of the party at the time, I received no help from them at the time', and that the faction-ridden Communist leadership had to be 'dragged by the hair' into the strike.[10]

According to Weisbord, after joining the Boston Communists, he had worked as a textile worker outside of the city, where he developed the perspective of organising workers outside of major cities. Upon returning to New

8 The strikers' position is spelled out in two pamphlets issued by the General Relief Committee, *Hell in New Jersey* and *The Textile Strike of 1926*; Weisbord also wrote two pamphlets on the strike. The first, *Passaic* (1926), was published by the Communist Party while the second, *Passaic Revisited*, although undated was written some time after his expulsion from the CP and is hostile towards the party. The most comprehensive historical treatment of the strike is Siegel 1953, although see also McMullen 2005, Chapter 5, and McMullen 2010, Chapters 9 and 10.

9 Bert Miller, 'Report of the District Industrial Organizer, District 2, from September 1 1925 to January 15 1926'; Miller, 'Report of the Industrial Organizer, District 2', 28 September 1926; Miller, 'Industrial Activity, District 2', 25 October 1925, all in Lovestone papers, box 220, folder 3; W.Z. Foster to 'Comrade Zimmerman', 11 November 1924, original in Zimmerman papers, Cornell University; copy in Prometheus Research Library collection.

10 C.E. Ruthenberg, 'The Achievements of Our Party', no date [November 1926], in Comintern archives, 515:1:923; the mill owners' anti-Communism will be dealt with below; Asher 1990, p. 8; the first Weisbord quote is from *Passaic Herald News*, 18 October 1976, in Passaic Strike Vertical File; the second is in Weisbord 1976, p. 1. Weisbord was suspended from the Communist Party in 1929; see *New York Times*, 17 December 1929.

York—he had been born in Brooklyn and graduated from City College—he obtained the permission of Ruthenberg supporter Miller to work in Paterson. Although his later loyalties were to himself, at the time of the strike Weisbord supported Ruthenberg's faction, and the faction claimed credit, although it is not clear how closely the faction supervised his work. Weisbord's background, including studying at City College, was similar to many members of the faction. Another Ruthenberg supporter, Gitlow, the head of the party's textile committee, supervised Weisbord, and Pepper had a strong influence among Hungarian American Communists, including in Passaic. In mid-1927, J. Louis Engdahl included Weisbord, Deak and five other Passaic strike leaders on a list of trade-union Lovestone supporters presented to the American Commission. That summer, in the lead-up to the National Convention, Kruse wrote to Engdahl, calling Weisbord 'our best mass leader, a potential foil to Foster' on the Central Committee.[11]

The strike, under Weisbord's guidance, surprised the top leadership, which was in Moscow. Foster, the traditional trade-union expert, was conspicuously uninvolved in this, the party's most important labour battle. Weisbord's involvement with Ruthenberg's faction, and his not involving the TUEL, were bad enough, but what upset Foster most was the fact that the Passaic strike underscored the limitations of working within the AFL.[12]

The AFL unions had ignored the Passaic workers for more than a decade, without any serious attempt to organise workers since the 1910s. Fifty years after the strike, a former leader of the silk workers' union in Paterson blamed

11 See Weisbord 1976, pp. 1–21; Engdahl at American Commission, 17 June 1927, in Comintern archives, 495:37:12; 'K' [William Kruse?] to 'Dear J' [Engdahl?], 8 August 1927, in Comintern archives, 515:1:946. In 1928, Weisbord was evidently put in a post of responsibility in Detroit. After members complained, he earned the dubious honour of being attacked by Lovestone as too factional, being described as having 'acted too often as a faction rather than Party leader and ... not taken the comrades sufficiently into consideration, especially comrades of the former majority'; minutes of Political Committee meeting number 33, 2 May 1928, in Lovestone papers, box 225, folder 11. Sixty years after the strike, Deak recalled Weisbord as 'an egomaniac'; interviewed by Joe Doyle, 13 January 1986, in Passaic Strike Oral History Project. In his later writing, Weisbord's hostility to the entire Communist leadership seems almost pathological, especially his insinuation that most of the leadership was in the service of both the US and Soviet intelligence services. The correspondence between Weisbord and Draper in 1958 gives a sense of this too; see <www.weisbord.org/Draper.htm>.

12 For Lovestone's attempt to take credit for the strike, see 'Dear Comrades' Lovestone circular, 11 June 1927, in archives of Prometheus Research Library. On Foster, see Siegel 1953, p. 151.

the workers themselves for their lack of organisation, claiming that after the 1919 strike was defeated, 'the people [in Passaic] refused to organize'. The UFC advocated amalgamation of the 16 existing unions in the industry, and the organisation of the mainly immigrant and women workers ignored by the AFL. Some 10,000 people joined the UFC during the strike. It claimed that 'the strike is thus not merely a rebellion against the intolerable conditions but a determined struggle for *organization*' and 'the beginning of a determined effort to organize one union for the whole textile industry'. The UFC tried to get AFL leader William Green to 'call a conference of all textile workers' organizations in order to unite them in one textile union under the banner of the A.F. of L.'[13]

In practice, the UFC acted as its own union, issuing membership books and dues stamps. It organised solidarity with the strike, raised relief funds and, with the ILD, defended strikers from repression. Deak, the UFC's secretary, recalled that $30,000 was spent weekly in relief. For Foster, this was dangerously close to organising a new union outside of the AFL. (The situation in Passaic, where the AFL unions did not exist, was different from that in the Chicago stockyards a decade earlier, where Foster had fought to amalgamate the existing AFL unions and have them organise unskilled workers).[14]

In January 1926, shortly after the strike began, the party decided that workers should try to join the AFL's UTW. The AFL wanted nothing to do with the strike. In early July, the AFL denounced the strike as 'communistic' and withheld contributions to the UFC's relief effort. According to Green, 'The membership of organized labor should not contribute funds'. This was echoed by the anti-strike 'Citizens' Committee', which placed advertisements in the local papers urging workers 'to reject these communist leaders'. The advertisement cited the 'sober judgment' of the AFL that the UFC was 'not a legitimate labor organization', and that the strike leaders were 'communists who are using the honest deceived employees of the woollen mills as dupes for their own political glory and the spread of their political beliefs'.[15] Even as the AFL wanted nothing to do with the strike, Foster still resented Weisbord for doing an end-run around the TUEL.

13 *Passaic Herald News*, 18 October 1976, in Passaic Strike Vertical File; Liberman 1963, p. 26; *Hell in New Jersey*, pp. 17–18.

14 Minutes of District Industrial Committee, 8 January 1926, in Lovestone papers, box 197, folder 2; *Passaic Herald News*, 7 October 1972, in Passaic Strike Vertical File. Seigel 1953, p. 163; Draper 1986, pp. 223–6; V.B. Weisbord 1977, p. 121.

15 *Passaic Daily Herald*, 2 July; 8 July 1926.

The Comintern and the TUEL

At the same time, Ruthenberg and Lovestone stepped up their attacks on the TUEL as too narrow. In mid-January 1926, the ECCI sent a cable to the CEC 'demand[ing] cessation [of] factional struggle', and told the party to 'strengthen [the] TUEL and its development into [a] mass movement of [the] left wing in [the] trade unions'. The ECCI explicitly denied rumours that it was critical of the TUEL. (The draft cable was even stronger, and had defended Foster by name, but Pepper and Gusev had insisted it be softened).[16]

Ruthenberg opposed the cable, claiming it would 'encourage [the] Foster caucus to intensify destructive factional fight'. He advocated dissolving the TUEL, which he called a sectarian group 'made up of our Party members with only a few additional members'. The League, he reasoned, shared much of its programme, leadership, journal and office with the Communist Party, and lacked an independent existence. The TUEL had served its purpose and needed to be replaced by a 'new broad left-wing organisation' with 'the right programme and the right tactics' that would absorb the remnants of the TUEL and win new allies in the labour movement. If Ruthenberg attacked the TUEL for being too Communist, he criticised Foster for not being Communist enough: 'Comrade Foster is not yet a Communist and has not basic Marxian conceptions to guide his policies', but 'later is able to swing completely about to a sectarian viewpoint'.[17]

For his part, Cannon agreed that the 'TUEL is not in any sense of the word a broad Left-Wing movement', and that 'the National Committee of the TUEL is nothing but a sub-committee of the CEC'. To avoid repression at the hands of the anti-Communist trade-union bureaucracy, he advocated that the party 'legalise' the TUEL by changing its name and programme. 'The program of the TUEL should not be a political program', he argued, 'it should bear no party characteristics' because 'the TUEL is a united front organ; its program must therefore be broad enough for all the left wing elements'. This meant emphasising class struggle, organising the unorganised, and democracy in the unions.[18]

16 Cable from Presidium of ECCI to CEC of Workers' Party, 15 January 1926, in Lovestone papers, box 197, folder 3. 'On Point 4 of the Agenda', in Comintern archives, 495:37:10; [Jay Lovestone?] to 'Dear John [Pepper], 17 January 1926; 'Deferred Cablegram' from Ruthenberg to Pepper, 18 January 1926; both in Lovestone papes, box 197, folder 3.

17 Ruthenberg speech at American Commission of Comintern, 16 February 1926, in Prometheus Research Library; Ruthenberg at American Commission meeting of Comintern, 3 March 1926, in Comintern archives, 495:164:381.

18 Cannon 1992, p. 367.

Foster insisted that the TUEL had a mass base, and he highlighted the trade-union inexperience of Ruthenberg's followers. In the middle of the Passaic strike, he stressed what he called 'the inability of the present Central Executive to conduct any kind of mass struggle. They have no experience with the masses. They do not understand the first thing about mass work'. Foster highlighted the factional basis for attacks against the TUEL, since 'to destroy us, they had to destroy the Trade Union Educational League'. He argued that 'the policy of the Central Executive Committee has been to liquidate the TUEL'. He advocated that the party 'stick to the basic policy of the Trade Union Educational League'.[19]

At first glance, the Comintern decision on Foster's appeal makes no sense. It solidified the organisational position of Ruthenberg's faction, but endorsed Foster on the trade-union question. The only possible result of this was to make the factionalism permanent and destabilise the party. It would have, however, allowed the Comintern to play one faction off against the other, giving the Comintern itself decisive power in the American party. The ECCI refused to give Foster's supporters a majority of the CEC, and declared 'there can be no question of a change in the composition of the C.C. at its party conference'. Nonetheless, the Comintern kept Foster in the leadership of the TUEL, and endorsed his trade-union policy. It declared that 'secessional movements and formation of parallel trade unions should not be instigated or encouraged in any form'.[20]

The End of the Passaic Strike

By this time, the Passaic strike had become a national issue. Cannon recalled that it 'really put the party on the labor map' and 'revealed the Communists as the dynamic force in the radical labor movement and the organizing center of the unorganized workers disregarded by the AFL unions'. The strikers braved police brutality and economic privation for almost a year. The strike seemed to portend the end of the party's isolation in the labour movement since the break with Fitzpatrick. Radicals like Elizabeth Gurley Flynn helped legitimise Communist activity in the labour movement.[21]

19 Foster, speech at first session of the American Commission of the Comintern, 16 February 1926, in Prometheus Research Library collection.

20 Quoted in Draper 1986, pp. 228–9.

21 Cannon 1962, p. 142; Siegel 1953, Chapter 10. Thus David Lee McMullen's comment that 'one of the biggest ironies associated with the strike is that the communists were only given an opportunity to represent the Passaic workers because American Federation of

If, with hindsight, the strike anticipated union struggles of the next decade, at the time, the Comintern policy of avoiding any semblance of 'dual unionism' led to disaster. Weisbord and the Communists had become the central rallying cry against the strike by the employers, the AFL and the Citizens' Committee. 'Who are the leaders of the Passaic strike?', the latter group asked in a July advertisement in both of Passaic's daily newspapers, which highlighted the radical credentials of supporters of the strike. Two weeks later, the Citizens' Committee produced documents, supposedly seized by the police, which purported to show that the Communist leadership in Chicago was directing the strike.[22]

The Comintern's anti-dual-union policy led the UFC to sue for unity with the UTW. The AFL, always hostile to the strike, had rejected UFC attempts over several months to affiliate with the UTW. They made it clear that the condition for its assuming leadership was that Weisbord leave. Over Weisbord's objections, the party agreed and forced him to quit. In mid-August, the UTW admitted the UFC on the condition that Weisbord and more than twenty other supposed Communists be purged. A spokesman for the UTW stated: 'We will never allow any communist or those thought to be communists into the United Textile Workers of America'. The party labelled the absorption of the UFC into the AFL a 'great victory'. Publicly, Weisbord claimed:

> The union had become so strong that, once it secured settlement or affiliation it could carry on without [Weisbord]. So the United Front Committee declared it was ready to accept even the humiliating conditions laid down to affiliate. This forced the hand of the A.F. of L. bureaucracy. They were compelled to take in the strikers.[23]

Winning the strike would have been difficult, and perhaps beyond the capacity of the party and its leaders. However, punting the strike to the AFL while claiming victory was disastrous. Over several months, the UTW settled the strike that

---

Labor's textile union, the union that ultimately represented the workers, initially declined to get involved': McMullen 2005, pp. 181–2. While true, this comment misses the true significance of the strike: the AFL leadership was bankrupt, and Communists understood the need to organise the unorganised.

22 *Passaic Daily Herald*, 14 July 1926; *Passaic Daily News*, 14 July 1926. *Passaic Daily Herald*, 29 July 1926; *Passaic Daily News*, 29 July 1926; see also *New York Times*, 30 July 1926.

23 *Passaic Daily Herald*, 2 July 1926; *Passaic Daily News*, 13 August 1926; Siegel 1953, p. 250; Weisbord 1926, p. 58; Draper 1986, p. 231. Joseph Zack also opposed this policy; see his statement attached to 8 May 1927 PC minutes, in Prometheus Research Library collection. See Siegel 1953, Chapter 9; on the expulsion of the Passaic local, see ibid., p. 343.

it had always opposed. One settlement was reached in November, another in mid-December, and the final one in late February 1927. The piecemeal settlements rescinded the wage cuts, and guaranteed the right to organise, but were otherwise a disaster. Despite the promise of no discrimination against union members, militants were fired and blacklisted. In February 1927, Deak, then the president of the Passaic UTW local, called the settlement a 'defeat'. In 1928, the UTW expelled the local because its leaders participated in the Communist-led New Bedford, Massachusetts, textile strike. In 1928, the Comintern report, *The Communist International between the Fifth and Sixth World Congresses*, nonetheless claimed that the strike 'was settled by the winning of the main demands'. The UTW's official history, published in 1950, did not even mention the strike—at its time the most important textile strike in the US. Meanwhile, workers in the city would remain unorganised for more than a decade.[24]

The International Labor Defense

Despite its defeat, the Passaic strike re-established the party's connections with the radical labour movement, and showcased the party's organising skills. In a period marked by declining union membership, and conservative bureaucrats who seemed only interested in skilled workers, Communists fought for immigrant, unskilled, low-paid and marginalised workers. This militancy would, a decade later, contribute to the rise of the CIO.

The International Labor Defense was important for reinvigorating the party's ties with the labour movement. According to Bryan Palmer, the ILD offered the party a 'bridge back to a politics of mass activity'. Under Cannon's leadership, the ILD defended 'class-war prisoners'—workers and radicals who had been targeted by the capitalist state, including scores of former Wobblies and militants behind bars from the Red Scare. Combining Communist experience in the militant labour movement (especially Cannon's roots in the IWW) and Comintern defence efforts internationally, the ILD helped root the party

24 *Passaic Daily News*, 1 March 1927; *Dateline Clifton*, 20 January 1982, in Passaic Strike Vertical File. On the humiliating end of the strike at the hands of the UTW, see Siegel 1953, Chapter 9; Brooks 1935, pp. 260–5; Communist International 1928a, p. 342. For the official UTW history, see *AFL Textile Workers* 1950, p. 18. In 1986, Deak recalled that 'there was no settlement, really' that the workers had returned with 'no terms', and that around twenty workers (including himself) were blacklisted from the mills; Gustave Deak, interviewed by Joe Doyle, 13 January 1986, in Passaic Textile Strike Oral History Project, pp. 12, 33.

in American reality by forging a 'combination of Comintern inspiration and homegrown adaptations', in Palmer's words.[25]

There were several Comintern-affiliated organisations in the early 1920s that helped lay the basis for the ILD. In response to the famine in Russia in 1921–2, Communists set up an American section, the Friends of Soviet Russia (FSR), drawing together elements from the American Labor Alliance (a legal front of the underground party), the Society for Technical Aid for Russia and the Medical Relief Committee for Soviet Russia. The FSR raised money to aid Russia as a working-class counterbalance to the bourgeois efforts spearheaded by Herbert Hoover. By early February 1922, the FSR had raised more than $300,000 and had branches in 130 US cities. Communists, including Caleb Harrison and Alfred Wagenknecht, played a prominent role in the FSR; it drew on support from local unions, ethnic and left-wing organisations, and reflected broad working-class horror at the famine and pro-Bolshevik sympathies. Wagenknecht, a former Socialist leader from Ohio, earned a reputation for fundraising; in Chicago, the FSR efforts were headed by Rose Karsner, Cannon's romantic partner and future ILD assistant. International Workers Aid was established after the Third Comintern Congress and organised by German Communist Willy Münzenberg. By 1926, the FSR had become International Workers Aid.[26]

In the summer of 1922, anti-Communist radicals and liberals, especially Abraham Cahan of the *Daily Forward*, accused the FSR of misusing money (including by subsidising the Communist Party). Based on an audit by radical accountant Stuart Chase, a committee comprising liberals cleared the FSR of financial improprieties.[27]

A more immediate Comintern root was International Red Aid (IRA; also known by the Russian acronym MOPR), founded in 1922 to aid victims of counterrevolution and 'white terror' internationally, especially after the defeat of the revolutionary wave in East and Central Europe and the rise of fascism in Italy.[28] The ILD was the American section of the IRA, but it was also more than

25 Palmer 2007, pp. 261, 271.

26 Davenport 2007; Draper 1986, pp. 176–8; McMeekin 2003, pp. 113–15; *New York Times*, 11 February 1922. Cannon and Karsner married in 1955, after being together for 31 years, to obtain Social Security benefits. See Harry Ring interview with Cannon, 12 September 1973, in Cannon papers, reel 1. Karsner (*née* Greenberg) had been married to socialist journalist David Karsner before meeting Cannon.

27 *New York Times*, 18 October 1922. The members of the committee were Roger Baldwin (American Civil Liberties Union), Timothy Healy (Stationary Firemen's Union), Robert Morss Lovett (*New Republic*) and Norman Thomas (League for Industrial Democracy).

28 On IRA/MOPR, see Ryle 1970.

this, since Cannon drew upon his own and the party's experiences in legal and social defence.

Even before the party's founding, left-wing Socialists and IWW syndicalists experienced state repression during the War. By the start of the ILD, almost every leading Communist had been imprisoned, and many had legal charges hanging over them from the underground period. Although the end of the Red Scare made legal Communist work possible, it did not stop the regular persecution of strikers, as shown by the Passaic Strike. Communists continued to face prosecution as well; in February 1926, Lithuanian American Communist Anthony Bimba was convicted of sedition (and acquitted of blasphemy) for a speech in Brockton, Massachusetts.[29]

Communists drew upon previous defence work in the left. Elizabeth Gurley Flynn, a former Wobbly and future ILD leader who would join the CP in the 1930s, was active in several pre-Communist defence campaigns. In 1918, Flynn organised the Workers Defense Union (WDU) to build support in the labour movement for victims of the Red Scare, to 'work for an amnesty for all industrial and political prisoners convicted during the war' by 'emphasizing the class struggle as the cause of this oppression, and recognizing that, if other means fail, it will be necessary for the workers to use their organized power in industry to bring about the release of their comrades and fellow workers'. Fred Biedenkapp and Ella Reeve Bloor, two early Communists, were active in the WDU.[30]

Early Communist efforts such as the CPA's National Defense Committee and the CLP's Workers Defense Committee—both organised around 1920—defended party members during the Red Scare. After the raids on the Bridgman Convention, Communists organised the Labor Defense Council (LDC) in September 1922. The LDC fought 'against all infringements upon the right of free speech, free press, and freedom of assemblage and all measures restricting the rights of the workers'. Under the leadership of Communist George Mauer, the LDC's National Committee included Roger Baldwin, Debs, Flynn and the Rev. John Haynes Holmes. Frank J. Walsh was the defence attorney. Although

29 On Bimba, see: *New York Times*, 27 February; 28 February; 3 March 1926.

30 See the 1919 pamphlet *Workers Defense Union*, in Ella Reeve Bloor papers, box 10, folder 19; Uhlmann 2007, p. 41. Not all defence experience was positive. Cannon recalled that in Sacramento, California, during World War I, Wobblies practised the 'silent defence' by not saying anything. For Cannon, the failure of this tactic seemed to have drawn home the need to mount a defence campaign; see Ring interview with Cannon, 30 May 1973, in Cannon papers, reel 1.

most of the LDC leadership were Communists, there had been tensions with Baldwin and Walsh over money and the political direction of the defence.[31]

The fusion of these American and foreign experiences began in Moscow under the influence of exiled IWW leader Haywood. In April 1922, Haywood gave a report to the ECCI's Anglo-American-Colonial Group on the 'several hundred men in prison in the US, some of the best men in that country'. These included Tom Mooney, IWW militants in Leavenworth prison, Communists such as Larkin, Gitlow and Ruthenberg, and coal miners in West Virginia and Kentucky.[32]

In late 1923, the Berlin Bureau of the IRA urged the American Communists to organise 'a Bureau for International Red Aid, on which will sit representatives not only from the Workers Party, but from all the left-Socialist and radical organizations that are willing to form a united front on the question of International Relief to Class War Prisoners, and whose combined actions may reach a wider public and larger funds than a purely party organization could achieve'.[33]

In April 1924, Cannon described plans 'that the FSR should and will be transformed into a section of the International Red Aid (for Victims of the White Terror) and the Labor Defense Council, National Defense Committee and the various local Defense Committees amalgamated with it into an organization, local and national'. This organisation, tentatively called the 'International Workers Defense Committee', would raise money and 'conduct special campaigns' for European and American prisoners.[34]

The planned organisation was still modest, and focused on European prisoners. According to Cannon, it was Haywood's idea to 'Americanise' defence work and broaden it beyond Communist prisoners. In 1925, most likely at the time of the ECCI's Fifth Plenum in the spring, Cannon and Haywood, both ex-Wobblies, came up with what would become the ILD. Upon returning to

31 William Z. Foster to Elizabeth Gurley Flynn, 18 September 1922; John Hayne Holmes to Elizabeth Gurley Flynn [27 November 1922]; William Z. Foster to Elizabeth Gurley Flynn, 4 December 1922, in Flynn papers; Jenkins 1976; Jenkins 1978; Uhlmann 2007, pp. 40–3; 67. According to Jenkins 1978, Walsh required a $25,000 retainer plus a promise to pay $20,000 later.

32 Minutes of Anglo-American-Colonial Group, 10 April 1922; William Haywood to Presidium, 'Political Prisoners in the United States', attached to Minutes of Anglo-American Colonial Group, 13 April 1922, both in Comintern archives, 495:72:2.

33 L. Wilhelm to Executive Committee of WPA, 4 November 1923, in Comintern archives, 515:1:164.

34 [James P. Cannon] to 'Comrade [Noah] London', 29 April 1924, in Cannon papers, reel 3, frames 7 and 8.

the US, Cannon found the already-organised IRA affilliate 'a very quiet, inoffensive organization'. Cannon had a different vision. According to Cannon, the ILD was 'a non-partisan body which could defend any member of the working class movement, regardless of his opinion or affiliation, if he came under persecution by capitalist law'. [35]

The ILD was founded in late June 1925, shortly before the Fourth National Conference of the Workers' Party. The Conference mandated that the ILD subsume the LDC and that the party should do all that was possible to help the organisation grow into a mass movement. Under Cannon's leadership, the ILD drew in non-Communist militants, including former Wobbly comrades such as Ralph Chaplin. Soon, the ILD also subsumed the FSR, and Karsner joined Cannon in day-to-day running of the group. One lesson from the LDC (and its disputes with Walsh) was that although the ILD cast a wide net in terms of who it defended, Communists kept control of the leadership to maintain a class-struggle approach.[36]

By January 1926, the ILD had grown to 120 branches and had begun to publish a monthly journal, *Labor Defender*. According to the first issue, in addition to several Communists including Bedacht, Cannon, Fort-Whiteman, Foster, Gitlow and Ruthenberg, the National Committee included non-Communist radicals such as Debs, Upton Sinclair, Robert Dunn and David Rhys Williams. The issue contained articles on Communists in the US, as well as defending Sacco and Vanzetti, Illinois miners, and an extended article defending Hungarian Communist Mátyás Rákosi. The ILD aimed to 'appeal to every class conscious worker regardless of affiliation', and initiated a monthly $5 stipend to 106 class-war prisoners. Perhaps reflecting the experience of the FSR, *Labor Defender* regularly published a list of receipts and, every several months, a balance sheet.[37]

35 There are various accounts of the meetings between Cannon and Haywood. See, for example, Harry Ring interview with Cannon, 15 August and 5 September 1973, in Cannon papers, reel 1; Cannon 1962, p. 163. In the Ring interview, Cannon mentions that Karsner was also present.

36 *Fourth National Convention* 1925, pp. 18–19; Syd Stapeton interview with Cannon, 20 October 1973, in Cannon 1974, pp. 24–6; Chaplin 1948, p. 333; 'Resolutions Unanimously Adopted by the National Defense Conference, Ashland Auditorium, Chicago', 28 June 1925, in Comintern archives, 539:3:1073. On the LDC and ILD, see Jenkins 1976; Jenkins 1978.

37 *Labor Defender*, January 1926; February 1926; May 1926. The January 1927 issue of the *Labor Defender* responded to allegations of mishandling money for Sacco and Vanzetti's defence.

The ILD was a good example of the united front. As Cannon wrote to Debs, his goal was to 'construct the ILD on the broadest possible base', making it 'non-partisan and non-sectarian'. 'The ILD is the defender of every worker persecuted for his activism in the class struggle', Cannon emphasised, 'without any exceptions and without regard to his affiliations'. Through it, the party joined with non-Communists to defend the common interests of the working class. Although the ILD defended Communists, most of the militants it defended were not Communists. These included well-known prisoners such as Sacco and Vanzetti, Mooney, Warren Billings and Centralia IWW militants, but also less known prisoners such as John Merrick, 'a shoe worker in Haverhill who was framed up in January, 1923, of placing a bomb in front of a shoe factory'. By the ILD's second conference, in 1926, it claimed 156 branches, comprising '20,000 individual members and a collective, affiliated membership of 75,000 workers'.[38]

The ILD raised funds, arranged legal help, and publicised prisoners' cases. By itself, this did not make the ILD unique; Baldwin's civil liberties union fulfilled this niche with more liberal support. The ILD was distinguished by its view that the state was the repressive apparatus used by the capitalist class to repress the working class. It saw defence work, including defending proletarian victims of repression in other countries, as basic working-class solidarity. The ILD tried to provide militants with the best legal representation possible, but as Communists, its leaders had no illusions that the American justice system could be fair to workers or leftists. Ultimately, the social power of the working class would be decisive, not legal briefs. Cannon underlined in the *Labor Defender*, 'Our policy is the policy of the class struggle' that, 'while favoring all possible legal proceedings … calls for agitation, publicity, demonstrations—organized protest on a national and international scale'.[39]

The ILD's first major campaign was in defence of the Passaic strikers in what Cannon, in the *Labor Defender*, labelled 'a historic battle in the class struggle'. Solidarity was key to the strike, he continued, since 'Everything that is alive in the labor movement is taking a hand in Passaic'. The ILD helped to provide defence lawyers and $83,150 in bail money to arrested strikers, and also undertook to organise a 'powerful, nation-wide and united defense and protest movement' for Weisbord and the strikers. The legal work was done in

38 J.P. Cannon to Eugene V. Debs, 15 July 1925, in Cannon papers, reel 3, frame 19; *Labor Defender*, January 1926; October 1926; On Merrick, see *Haverhill Frame-Up* 1923.

39 Cannon 1927. On the relationship between the Civil Liberties Union and the ILD, see minutes of Political Committee meeting number 31, 20 April 1928, in Lovestone papers, box 225, folder 11.

cooperation with Baldwin's American Civil Liberties Union. At the second ILD conference, in 1926, Weisbord described the organisation as 'a rear guard organization during strikes' and was added to the National Committee.[40]

The ILD's most famous campaign in the 1920s was to free Sacco and Vanzetti. Communists had long been dedicated to stopping the Italian anarchists' execution; for example, the founding convention of the Workers' Party in December 1921 pledged the party to their cause. The ILD, with backing from the Comintern and the IRA, mounted an international campaign. Even though the ILD failed to prevent their execution in August 1927, it made the names Sacco and Vanzetti synonymous with American class injustice throughout the world.[41]

In a reactionary period, with the party hobbled by factionalism, the ILD built a mass united-front movement under Communist leadership and underscored the Communist Party's potential. As part of an international movement, and under Comintern guidance, the party built upon its roots in American radicalism and deepened its role and influence in the labour movement. The ILD represented one fruit of Communists' approach to Wobblies. (Certainly, it was the most productive result of Haywood's affiliation with the Communist Party, often depicted as only negative).[42]

Like everything else in the party at the time, the ILD soon became embroiled in factionalism. On one level, for Cannon the organisation was a refuge from the endless factionalism, allowing him to engage in productive work among his comrades from his time in the Wobblies. Nonetheless, the ILD could not be separated from factional discord. At the ILD's inception in 1925, Cannon was still allied with Foster, so Ruthenberg opposed Cannon's leading the group. After Cannon split with Foster, his alignment with Ruthenberg shielded the ILD from attack. In a factional letter from February 1926, Lovestone defended the ILD from Foster's supporters who were 'trying to make a factional issue of the defense society' in order 'to kill Cannon'. He pledged to 'go out of my way to defend the general line of the ILD at the same time working for its improvement'. (At the same time, Lovestone, whom Cannon later claimed never entered the ILD headquarters, saw defence work as a way to divert Cannon

40 Cannon 1926; see also *Labor Defender*, June 1926; on Weisbord, see *Labor Defender*, October 1926.

41 *New York Times*, 27 December 1921; *Labor Defender* deals with Sacco and Vanzetti's case regularly in its first two years; the July 1926 issue is on the international campaign, see McGirr 2007. On the case in general, see Temkin 2009.

42 See Cannon to Draper, 17 April 1955, in Cannon papers, reel 25, on the ILD as an extension of Haywood's influence.

from factionalism). When Cannon's group became independent, the ILD was sufficiently well established to survive.[43]

In addition to many non-Communists, the National Committee drew members from all factions. Foster was included; so were Ruthenberg and his allies Gitlow, Lovett Fort-Whiteman (a leading black Communist) and Bedacht. Cannon and his supporters—especially Karsner and Shachtman—commonly had bylines, but not to the exclusion of non-Communists or members of other factions. By the summer of 1927, when the ILD once again became a factional football, it was flourishing and the Sacco and Vanzetti campaign was gaining Communists international attention. In mid-1928, the stylish *Labor Defender's* circulation reached 22,000.[44] The Passaic strike and the ILD demonstrate the potential of the Communist Party's mass work, even amid the conservative 1920s; at the same time, they demonstrate how factionalism and the accompanying political unclarity hindered this work.

43 Minutes of Political Committee, 26 June 1925, in Cannon 1992, p. 330; J [Lovestone] to 'Dear Comrades', 3 February 1926, in Lovestone papers, box 197, folder 4; Ring interview with Cannon, 5 September 1973, in Cannon papers, reel 1, frame 863.

44 Cannon 1992, p. 160; 'Dear Comrades', Lovestone factional circular, 11 June 1927; statement by Max Bedacht, attached to 11 July 1927 PolCom meeting, both in Prometheus Research Library collection; Drucker 1994, p. 27.

CHAPTER 10

The Death of Ruthenberg and the Ascension of Lovestone, 1926–7

In 1926–7, as the factional situation in the American Communist Party worsened, the Stalinist degeneration of the Soviet Union reached a crucial point. The Soviet bureaucracy became increasingly self-confident, and Stalin emerged as the dominant leader in the Soviet and international Communist movement. Stalin broke the 'troika' and allied with Bukharin on the right of the Soviet party, while Zinoviev and Kamenev formed the 'Joint Opposition' with Trotsky.

This opposition stressed industrialising Russia, gradually collectivising the countryside, and improving the condition of the working class. They counterposed revolutions in advanced industrial capitalist countries to Stalin's programme of socialism in one country, and fought for inter-party democracy. Followers of Stalin and Bukharin disrupted oppositionists' speeches and meetings, and removed them from responsible posts. In July 1926, Zinoviev was removed from the Soviet party's political bureau; in October, he was dismissed as head of the Comintern, and Trotsky was removed from the political bureau. By the end of 1927, Zinoviev and Kamenev had capitulated to Stalin, while Trotsky faced exile to Alma Ata.[1]

This chapter examines how simultaneous factional struggles in the American party and the Comintern deepened the Stalinisation of both. Although not directly related to the American party, this struggle changed the quality of the Comintern's intervention into the party, especially as Stalin sought loyal leaderships throughout the Comintern. He recognised the importance of keeping one set of possible allies in reserve for future use against current allies. Second, the leaders of the party viewed the struggle in Russia from the perspective of the factional battles at home, encouraging them to manoeuvre for support from Stalin and Bukharin. In late 1926, Lovestone wrote to his factional allies from Moscow, bemoaning that his faction was 'until recently … considered to be with Zinoviev'. Under Pepper's guidance, Ruthenberg and Lovestone quickly joined the anti-Zinoviev bandwagon, and the rival factions followed suit.[2]

1 Degras 1960, II, pp. 308–10; Deutscher 1959, pp. 275–97.

2 Draper 1986, pp. 237–40; see Bittelman's memoirs, 'Things I Have Learned', Chapter 15, p. 462 for a description of the way the factionalism of the Soviet party played out in a factional way in the US 'J' [Lovestone?] to 'Dear Friends', 26 November 1926, in Lovestone papers, box 212, folder 6.

By early 1927, Cannon's anti-factional perspective was paying off. William W. Weinstone, Jack Stachel and John J. Ballam, long-time Ruthenberg supporters in New York, had (in Weinstone's words) 'definitely separated from Ruth group and united with Cannon group on issues against factionalism and [for] unification [of] party'. In a factional circular, Cannon described this 'break with the Ruthenberg group' as 'absolutely definite on ideological and political grounds'. In New York City, he indicated, supporters of Foster were also open to joining the alliance.[3]

Cannon stressed that he was interested not in reconstituting the old Foster-Cannon majority group, but in ending factionalism altogether. Political issues, not factional manoeuvres, should be paramount, or as he put it, 'policy must be the decisive question governing all important action in the party'. A summary of the Cannon-Weinstone group's aims advocated the 'liquidation of factionalism and the unification of the Party on the basis of correct policy without factions'. All of the factions contained important elements to lead the party, but by itself, none could offer leadership. 'The dissolution of the existing factions is a necessary prerequisite for the unification of the Party', the document read, because 'Party leadership must replace faction leadership'.[4]

Cannon attempted to win leading elements of all factions to his perspective. In the unsigned notes of a meeting between Cannon and Ruthenberg, Bedacht and Lovestone, the stenographer noted that Cannon 'believes that factionalism is played out'. He did not think 'that [the] party [wa]s facing the alternative of the Ruthenberg group or the Foster group'. Instead, Cannon advocated 'collective leadership'. Factionalism was frustrating, because 'he must always convince four [members of the CEC] or lose' a vote. He told his counterparts that 'I cannot conceive a party leadership without you three comrades' and advocated 'a fusion of all those qualified for leadership in the party'. Ruthenberg appeared open to this perspective, and at the meeting outlined 'two roads before the party': either continued factionalism and 'a fight for power', or 'the group working together'. He warned that he was prepared to slug

3 W.W. [Weinstone], telegram draft 'For B' [William F. Dunne], no date [1927], in Cannon papers, reel 20, frame 16; [James P. Cannon], 'Dear Comrades', 10 January 1927, in Cannon papers, reel 3, frame 43. Ballam was 'Curtis' of the earlier Left Opposition who had split from the party over the question of legality.

4 [James P. Cannon] to 'Dear Comrades', 15 January 1927, in Cannon papers, reel 3, frame 52; Cannon and Weinstone group, 'Outline of Statement on the Liquidation of Factionalism and Unification of the Party' [Spring 1927], in Lovestone papers, box 204, folder 'General Reports on American Question, 1927'.

it out, but told Cannon that 'it would be a good idea to have you, Foster, and myself get together before a Polcom meeting and lay a basis of agreement'.[5]

Ruthenberg seemed to have been sincere. Bittelman recalled in his memoirs that incessant factionalism seemed to tire Ruthenberg. About a fortnight after this meeting, Ruthenberg sent a telegram to Minor, then in Moscow, about negotiations with Foster 'for possible convention and [to] head off factional struggle', and noted that one proposal had been a 3-3-3 political committee. In contrast, Lovestone seemed not to take such ideas seriously. A factional letter he wrote at the time accused Cannon of 'fulfilling his usual role of demagogy and hypocrisy'.[6]

Lovestone Takes Power Over Ruthenberg's Dead Body

On 2 March 1927, Ruthenberg, aged 44, suddenly died of acute appendicitis. All factions respected Ruthenberg, who had been active in the pre-war Socialist left wing, a founder of the party, a central party leader since 1919, and a member of the ECCI Presidium. He had been imprisoned twice, and at the time of his death the Supreme Court was deliberating his appeal against the conviction from the Bridgman raid. His death left a void, and created a stronger factional whirlpool. It slowed Cannon and Weinstone's attempt to forge a faction against factionalism, and allowed Lovestone to take the leadership of the Ruthenberg faction as a stepping-stone to controlling the party.[7]

---

5 Cannon 1992, pp. 387–91. The original is in Lovestone papers, box 200, folder 11.

6 [Lovestone] to 'Dear Comrades', 5 February 1927, in Lovestone, box 197, folder 10; Bittelman, 'Things I Have Learned', folder 15, pp. 429–30; 'Telegrams Submitted to C.I. About American Question' by Duncan [Minor], in Comintern archives, 515:1:948. Bittelman, one of the later official Communist chroniclers of the party's own history, solved the problem of explaining how the good Ruthenberg spawned the bad Lovestone by stressing the differences between the two leaders. In his memoirs, he implies that Lovestone was guilty of Ruthenberg's death for not having made him see a doctor; in a speech on the thirtieth anniversary of the party's founding, he asserted that Lovestone benefited from wrapping himself in the 'Ruthenberg tradition' even though 'Ruthenberg hated Lovestone; he despised him'; 'Speech of Alex Bittelman', [1949], in Bittelman papers, box 1, folder 'Writings, Clippings, Notes'. This is at least better than Oakley Johnson's biography of Ruthenberg, which merely ignores the factionalism altogether to assert that there was no link between Ruthenberg's and Lovestone's perspectives.

7 *New York Times*, 3 March 1927. On the Foster faction's respect for Ruthenberg, see Bittelman, 'Things I Have Learned', folder 16, p. 476. The Supreme Court had decided to reject

Taking a page from Stalin's manoeuvres after Lenin's death, Lovestone seized upon Ruthenberg's demise to create a cult of personality and depict himself as the departed leader's natural heir. Lovestone was the chair of the committee that took Ruthenberg's ashes from Chicago to New York after a 15,000-strong memorial featuring various Communist leaders. An honour guard of 1,000 Communists met the train at Grand Central Station, and took the ashes first to the Furriers' Union on East 22nd Street, then to ILGWU headquarters down the block, and finally to *Freiheit* offices at Union Square, before ending up at the Manhattan Lyceum on East Fourth Street. There some 5,000 mourners filed past the urn. After a memorial in Carnegie Hall, Ruthenberg's ashes were taken to Moscow. He was interred at the Kremlin Wall, as some 7,000 workers' delegates stood by, and after Bukharin, J. Louis Engdahl and black Communist Harry Haywood had spoken.[8]

Before Ruthenberg's death, Lovestone had sensed that his faction's leadership of the party was tenuous. In a factional letter written during the Seventh ECCI Plenum in late 1926, Lovestone complained that the faction's 'connections here are not very good', that they were seen as 'creatures of the Zinoviev cable', and that Stalin was 'not openly hostile' but did not 'go out of his way to be charmed by us'. Bukharin was more friendly, but more because he was 'a nice fellow than [because of] his conscious support for us'. While Pepper was 'our most powerful and effective friend' in the Comintern apparatus, the Ruthenberg-Lovestone faction was seen as 'illegitimate, a bastard CEC, given birth at a convention through a Caesarean operation, a convention at which we were a minority'. Since 'one cable can overthrow any kingdom', Lovestone urged his faction to build better connections in Moscow.[9]

On 6 March, he cabled Minor that 'Ruthenberg's request [was that] Lovestone succeed and that Central Committee's supporters should solidify their ranks'. He urged Minor to 'see Bucharin [sic] and Stalin' to discuss the

---

Ruthenberg's appeal, but did not issue a decision because of his death. Brandeis and Holmes dissented from the decision; see Meaks 2010, pp. 13–14; Collins and Skover 2011.

8 *New York Times*, 4 March; 7 March; 9 March; 27 April 1927; Haywood 1978, pp. 184–7. Several of the speeches at Ruthenberg's Moscow funeral are in the Comintern archives, 515:1:928. For the posthumous Ruthenberg cult, see the Ruthenberg papers, box 8, folders 1 and 2. In 1928, Lovestone wrote a short biography, *Ruthenberg: Communist Fighter and Leader* and edited a collection of his writings, which were made part of the 'Voices of Revolt' series, along with speeches by Robespierre, Marat, Lassalle, Wilhelm and Karl Liebknecht, Danton, Bebel, Lenin and Debs; see Lovestone 1928 and Ruthenberg 1928. In May, Weinstone accused Lovestone of distorting party history for factional advantage in his Ruthenberg hagiography; see Weinstone speech at Plenum, 27 May 1927, in Shachtman papers, box 1, folder 22.

9 [Lovestone?] to 'Dear Friends', 21 November 1926, in Lovestone papers, box 212, folder 6.

'situation regarding secretaryship', as well as Pepper's returning to America. He accused Cannon and Foster of factionalism and opposing the emerging cult of Ruthenberg. Several days later, Lovestone sent another cable to Minor: 'Because of the death of the Party's leader try to have the Comintern cable an appeal to membership against factionalism and support energetically the Central Committee', namely, Lovestone.[10]

When Cannon and Weinstone, along with Foster—together a majority of the CEC—proposed that Weinstone temporarily assume power and that the CEC meet within a week to prevent a 'disastrous' factional battle, Gitlow immediately nominated Lovestone for leadership. Lovestone advocated a delayed CC plenum, followed by a national convention, to allow him time to consolidate his power. Cannon, Foster and Weinstone then insisted on an immediate delegation to Moscow to decide leadership. The Comintern, however, supported Lovestone, opposed a delegation to Moscow and ordered the upcoming plenum to not discuss who should follow Ruthenberg.[11]

After Ruthenberg's death, 'Lovestone became Lovestone', as Cannon put it. He emerged as a factional leader in his own right, not just as a lieutenant for Ruthenberg. This gave free rein to his nasty personal characteristics and his increasingly rightist political impulses. Trained by Pepper in factionalism, and absorbing the degenerated culture of the Stalinist Comintern, Lovestone mixed ambition, arrogance and manipulation. His opponents despised him. According to Cannon, Foster 'remarked more than once that if Lovestone were not a Jew, he would be the most likely candidate for leadership of a fascist movement'. Bittelman in his memoirs three decades later claimed of Lovestone that 'had he been in possession of government power, he would have put his opponents in jail, most likely, to insure his victory'. He was 'ruthless, unscrupulous and iron-fisted'. Long after Lovestone had ceased to be any kind of leftist, an FBI agent described him as 'a very intelligent individual, a proficient con man, capable of intrigue and of assuming any role to fulfil an ultimate result'.[12]

10 Lovestone to Duncan [Minor], 6 March and 11 March 1927, in Comintern archives, 515:1:948.

11 Draper 1986, p. 255. The Presidium's cable, and three different cables (all dated 25 March 1927) by Cannon, Dunne, Swabeck, Abern and Reynolds; Aronberg, Bittelman, Foster, Johnstone and Krumbein; Weinstone, Ballam, Kaplan, Don and Tochey, all appealing for a delegation to Moscow, are in Comintern archives, 515:1:929.

12 Cannon 1962, pp. 156, 172; Bittelman, 'Things I Have Learned', folder 15, p. 430; folder 16, p. 474; Special Agent H.T. O'Connor to J.E. Hoover, 8 December 1948, in Lovestone FBI file, section 2.

Nor was Lovestone popular among his supporters. Gitlow recalled that he 'was a veritable Tammany chieftain among us Communists', and that Lovestone's own followers 'did not trust him and did not like him'. He not only attacked factional opponents (something all leading Communists did), but also took aim at his supporters. He once complained that 'Altogether too many of our boys are lazy, irresponsible and stupid'. Another letter bragged that when a supporter was too ill to come to the office, 'I bawled her out to the weeping point'.[13]

As Weinstone had warned, the frenzied factionalism after Ruthenberg's death stirred up ill will among the party leadership, consolidating factional divisions. Factional tactics became dirtier. For example, in April 1927, Foster supporter Jack Johnstone complained that his personal files, kept under lock and key inside the party headquarters, had been rifled. Gitlow later admitted that his faction had taken the documents. While Lovestone and Pepper were both masters of using quotations from internal documents to frame a personal polemic, all adopted this style.

This fighting angered the Comintern. In early April, the Comintern sent a curt cable to the party, denying the factions' request to once again send delegates to Moscow, citing the 'urgent necessity' of opposing US imperialism in China and Nicaragua and defending the party against attacks by the AFL and government. In late June, in response to an allegation by Lovestone that Foster had conspired to remove Ruthenberg from the Political Bureau, the American Commission refused to investigate factional hearsay, resolving that to do so would 'make the inner Party discussion more acute and unprofitable'. One can sense the frustration when Commission member Petrovsky told the American Commission in June that he refused 'to pass judgement upon all the mutual accusations' because 'all the groups are sufficiently clever and capable in finding fault with each other'.[14]

---

13 Gitlow 1939, pp. 320–5; [Lovestone] to 'Dear Boys', 6 March 1926, in Lovestone papers, box 197, folder 5; Lovestone to C.E. [Ruthenberg], 26 October 1926, in Lovestone papers, box 197, folder 9. Lovestone particularly disliked Robert Minor and John Ballam. For a biography of Lovestone, see Morgan 1999. See also the hostile remarks by Max Bedacht—who was an important leader in the Ruthenberg-Lovestone faction until its split in 1929—in Theodore Draper's interview notes, 1 February 1954, in Emory University Draper papers, box 10, folder 16; copy in Prometheus Research Library collection.

14 Johnstone's statement and the Comintern cable are included in Political Committee minutes, 8 April 1927, in Prometheus Research Library collection; 'Decision of the American Commission'; Petrovsky in American Commission, 10 June 1927; both in Comintern archives, 495:37:12. Petrovsky (real name Max Goldfarb, but also known as

In late April, the ECCI sent two cables to the American party. On 24 April, the ECCI ordered that 'Jack comma Ben and Bill'—Lovestone, Gitlow, and Foster—come to Moscow for the upcoming Eighth ECCI plenum. It added that 'Jim [Cannon] and Weinstone' would also be desirable if the Political Committee agreed. Only reluctantly did the Lovestone leadership accede. (The cable did not mention another Cannon supporter, Dunne, at all, even though unlike his allies, he did not need permission to attend because he had been made a candidate member of the ECCI at the Fifth Congress and thus had the right to attend its meetings. Lovestone claimed this omission indicated that the ECCI opposed Cannon and Weinstone; in Moscow, Kuusinen called it a mistake and denied any intended slight).[15]

Two days later, on 26 April, the ECCI sent another cable, directing that the CEC convene a plenum before the American delegation left for Moscow. At the same time, it ordered that this plenum's decisions not be considered final until endorsed by the ECCI. Thus the actual plenum, in late May, had little authority, and served as a stage for factional drama. There, Cannon and Weinstone (along with his fellow former Lovestone supporter, John Ballam) were allied. Prior to the plenum, Cannon had rejected alliances based on factional dominance, emphasising that the 'next period [will be] one of independent principle[d] struggle' and that cooperation with the other factions 'can ensure only when Jay[']s dictatorship and Foster[']s hegemony are smash[ed] by fight'.[16]

At the plenum, Weinstone denounced Lovestone for his post-Ruthenberg 'policy of "macht politik", to remain in power at all costs'. He added that this group 'is different today than it was before the death of Comrade Ruthenberg'. Ruthenberg 'tended to orient it to the left', while 'the policy of Comrade Lovestone today is an orientation to the right'. Weinstone emphasised 'the idea of collective leadership of the party', against Foster as well as Lovestone.[17]

Cannon, for his part, argued that attacks on the unions, and the union bureaucracy's attacks on leftists, marked 'a turning point in the American labor movement, and consequently a turning point in our party work in the

---

Bennett) was a prominent member of the Comintern's Anglo-American Secretariat. He had lived in New York City, where he supported the *Forward*.

15 Cable from ECCI/Kuusinen, 24 April 1927, Comintern archives, 515:1:929; copy in Shachtman papers, box 1, folder 23. On the omission of Dunne and Kuusinen's explanation, see the unsigned Cannon-Weinstone faction letter, 26 June 1927, in Shachtman papers, box 1, folder 24.

16 Cable from ECCI/Kuusinen, 26 April 1927, in Shachtman papers, box 1, folder 23; See William F. Dunne's 2 April 1927 cable to Cannon and Cannon's draft reply (written in longhand on back and also later typescript), in Cannon papers, reel 3.

17 Weinstone at Plenum, 27 May 1927, in Shachtman papers, box 1, folder 22.

unions'. He emphasised that right-wing bureaucrats—such as UMW leader John L. Lewis—could not reach a stable relationship with the capitalists, and that 'some of the bureaucrats, under the pressure of the masses, will be compelled to take part in the fight against the bosses to maintain the unions and even help us organize the unorganized'. However, 'the unstable situation in the party and the unstable leadership in the party ... cannot provide normal processes of discussion' on how to approach these changes. He warned of 'factional bankruptcy' and 'factional corruption and unprincipledness' caused by the 'heterogeneous composition of the factions and the stubborn maintenance of permanent factional organization'. He underlined:

> It is anomalous for a Bolshevik Party to have factional groupings within which there are political divisions on issues of prime importance, while the groups cross each other in support of major political questions, and yet these groups retain their separate factional identity, cohesion and discipline.

The TUEL demonstrated how factionalism hurt the party. The League was 'too narrow from the standpoint of the labor movement at present', but also 'too narrow from the standpoint of the party'. The Foster faction had 'a monopolistic attitude' towards the TUEL, while Lovestone's faction maintained a perspective of 'factional passivity'. Cannon and Weinstone's solution was not that one faction should destroy the others, but that factionalism itself should be liquidated through a collective leadership. 'Party leadership must replace factional leadership', as Cannon put it.[18]

Both Lovestone and Foster's factions reacted angrily, continuing to seek complete victory. Wolfe dismissed Cannon's 'empty speech absolutely devoid of content', full of 'goody, goody "sugar and spice and everything nice" '. Foster railed against Lovestone's 'insincerity, double dealing, campaigns of personal vilification and downright treachery'. He claimed to support 'collective leadership' as well, but on the basis of his own faction's rule, not on what he saw as Cannon's 'total political bankruptcy'. The party faced growing isolation from the working class, Foster argued. Lovestone's faction had no experience in mass work, while Cannon's had 'an appreciation for mass work but exhibit[ed] rightist deviations'. Lovestone emphasised the farcical quality of the plenum

18 Cannon's speech is reprinted in Cannon 1992, pp. 392–426. See also the documents: Weinstone, Cannon, Dunne, Ballam, Abern, Swabeck, Reynolds, and Gomes [sic], 'Outline Statement on Liquidation of Factions and Unification of the Party', no date [1927?], and 'The Middle Group and What it Stands For', no date [1927?]; both in Shachtman papers, box 1, folder 20.

when he snuck away to Moscow before it was over. His opponents soon followed, arriving just in time for the conclusion of the ECCI's plenum.[19]

In Moscow, Again

The Eighth ECCI Plenum (18–30 May 1927) was dedicated to issues more pressing than Lovestone's histrionics. In April, the Chinese Communist Party's entry into and subordination to Chiang Kai-shek's bourgeois-nationalist Goumindang had proven disastrous as Chiang's forces massacred tens of thousands of pro-Communist workers. Trotsky had opposed the alliance with Chiang, and denounced the policy at the Plenum as a betrayal. Then, days prior to the opening of the plenum, police and other government agents in London raided the offices of the All-Russian Cooperative Society, alleging subversive activity, leading to Britain's breaking diplomatic relations with Soviet Russia.[20]

The defeat in China confirmed Trotsky's criticisms, but strengthened Stalin's determination to defeat him. Zinoviev, the former head of the Comintern, was barred from entering the plenum. On the last day, American Communists, along with delegates from Britain, Czechoslovakia, France, Italy and Germany put forward a motion to expel Trotsky and Serbian Zinoviev supporter Voja Vujovič from the ECCI. With Stalin and Bukharin in control, the plenum passed this motion. (For its part, the American delegation issued a statement against the Opposition).[21]

Amid this, it is understandable that, as E.H. Carr put it, 'Nobody wanted to discuss the American factional quarrel'. Still, each faction tried to navigate the changing winds from the Soviet leadership, and lobby Comintern and Soviet leaders. In late May, Lovestone complained that the 'main office was totally uninformed' about American issues, and 'up to this point it has been absolutely impossible to see the biggest fellow or even talk at length with Bookman', evidently referring to Stalin and Bukharin. Lovestone and his supporters soon secured Stalin's audience for three hours. Lovestone reported in a letter to his co-factionalists that 'Steelman ... said after long session with him that even

19 Bertram Wolfe, Speech on Factionalism, 14 May 1927; William Z. Foster, 'Analysis of the Last Plenum of the CEC and the Conclusions We Must Draw From It', 12 May 1927, both in Wolfe papers, folder 4. See also Draper 1986, pp. 255–7.

20 For a description of Chiang's April coup, see Isaacs 2010, Chapter 10. On the English raid, see Flory 1977.

21 See Trotsky 1932 for his arguments at the time. On the plenum, see Pantsov 2000, Chapter 9.

with his eyes closed one can see the weaknesses of Zigzag', referring to Foster by his nickname.[22]

Cannon and Weinstone were also optimistic. An unsigned factional circular, reporting on discussions with Kuusinen and Arthur Ewert, a German in the Comintern apparatus, indicated that Kuusinen 'said Lovestone could not take the place of Ruthenberg and that collective leadership must be established'. There was 'much sentiment here for a bloc', the letter continued, between Cannon and Weinstone on the one hand and Foster's supporters on the other. The letter suggested a '3-3-3' leadership divided among the factions with the goal of eradicating factionalism.[23]

One issue bringing the Foster and Cannon groups together was the fear that Lovestone wanted 'to "unify" the party by smashing the opposition groups', as Cannon put it in a speech to the American Commission in early June. In his speech, Cannon addressed his comments 'in the most impersonal way and serious way about the question of Comrade Pepper, not as a person, but as a problem—as an artificially added problem to our other difficulties in America'. He complained that 'at several periods in the Party when the groups were moving towards unity, the Lovestone group would receive some letter from Comrade Pepper outlining some new manoeuvre, some new scheme whereby the factional fires were intensified'. When the Lovestone-dominated Political Committee recalled Robert Minor, its representative in Moscow, 'for Party work', it voted that Pepper 'act as representative of the American Party to the ECCI'. Foster and Cannon saw this attempt to 'inject Comrade Pepper actively into the American situation' as a 'clear declaration of uncompromising war against all the opposition groups' because Pepper had 'persistently kept alive factionalism'.[24]

In mid-June, Cannon, Weinstone and Foster submitted a document to the American Commission that defended the TUEL, especially in light of the Passaic strike. They criticised the lack of attention to 'the task of giving organised form to the left wing in the TUEL'. They called to broaden the TUEL beyond 'Party members and close sympathisers' and to embrace 'all honest elements willing to fight and preserve the unions as organs of struggle'. The league should stand on a programme to organise the unorganised, democratise

22 Carr 1976, III, p. 595; Jacko [Lovestone] to 'Dear Boys', 22 May 1927; 13 June 1927, in Wolfe papers, box 4. See also Draper 1986, p. 259 and Gitlow 1939, p. 431.

23 'Dear Boys', 26 June 1927, in Shachtman papers, box 1, folder 24.

24 On a Foster-Cannon bloc, see Lovestone to 'Dear Comrade', 21 June 1927 in Wolfe papers, box 4; untitled Foster document, 23 June 1927, in Wolfe papers, box 5; Cannon speech to American Commission, 10 June 1927, in Comintern archives, 495:37:12; PolCom minutes, 20 June 1927, in Prometheus Research Library collection.

the unions, amalgamate the craft unions, form a labour party, and struggle against capitalism. Despite Foster's history, the letter advocated a flexible approach to new unions. It warned against light-mindedly forming new unions in response to bureaucratic expulsions, and advocated that expelled militants and locals fight these attacks. At the same time, warning against illusions in the current unions, it argued: 'The actual formation of independent organisations in such cases has to be determined according to concrete circumstances'. The document concluded by calling for 'collective leadership … which includes the strongest forces of the three groups', concretely through a nine-member Political Bureau evenly divided among the three factions (the 3-3-3 solution). The main obstacle to party unity, it asserted, was Lovestone and his followers.[25]

On 1 July 1927, the American Commission issued its resolution on the American Question, divided into four sections. The first, 'the struggle against imperialism and the war danger', emphasised the need 'to form a broad united front to intensify the struggle against American imperialism', which was 'the mightiest imperialist power' in the world. This criticised the Lovestone majority for 'minimizing the predatory role of American imperialism in China and by representing it one-sidedly only as a tool for British imperialism'. The next section, 'the development of the revolutionary movement in America', cautioned that this movement would develop slowly and that 'a great rise' in class struggle 'is not to be expected in the nearest future'. Although there would be 'mass struggles of a predominantly economic character', American capitalism still provided workers 'a comparatively higher standard of living' than workers elsewhere. Furthermore, it was 'still on the upward grade of development', and this posed the danger of the 'bourgeoisification' of sections of the workers. Communists were instructed to struggle against the AFL bureaucracy and to 'create a basis for a Communist mass Party' in anticipation of a world capitalist crisis.

A third section on trade-union activity, 'the most important work of the Party', took much from Cannon, Foster and Weinstone's letter. Instead of discarding the TUEL, the party was instructed to broaden it and attract all 'Left Wing and genuine progressive movements'. The resolution continued:

> the TUEL must avoid any kind of rigid organizational forms, adapt itself to the special conditions in various trade unions and industries in order to prevent even in the most intense struggle against the trade union bureaucracy a split of the trade unions.

25 J.P. Cannon, Wm. Z. Foster and William W. Weinstone, 'Letter to the American Commission', 16 June 1927, in Lovestone papers, box 211, folder 1.

At the same time, 'The Party should not limit itself only to work in the existing trade unions', and 'every effort must be made to link these [new unions] up with the existing trade unions and at the same time to insist on the right of the workers themselves to administer the unions'. The resolution criticised adherents of each faction. Rose Wortis and Charles Zimmerman, Lovestone supporters in the needle trades, were guilty of 'Right deviations' and 'not develop[ing] sufficiently clear and decisive leadership in the mass struggles'. Cannon ally William F. Dunne and Foster supporter Joseph Zack were attacked, although the resolution stated that 'Comrade Foster and Weinstone fought these conceptions and that between them and the majority of the Polcom Committee [sic] no difference exists on these points'. The list of deviations is hard to follow without a roster of factional activists, but such a litany minimised differences among the factions.

The fourth section dealt with 'the inner Party situation', marked above all by factionalism, 'the existence and intensity of which we seek in vain to explain through serious differences of principles'. The resolution underlined the lack of political differences: 'A struggle of the majority of the Political Committee (Lovestone) against the groups at present in opposition (Foster, Weinstone, Cannon) would be justified if it were a question of anti-Communist comrades who threaten the further development of the Party (like Lore). This not so in the case of Comrades Foster, Weinstone and Cannon'. To 'facilitate unity with the majority of the Political Committee before and after the Party Conference', the opposition was ordered to 'cease their factional methods'.

The resolution ordered a late August conference; a 'commission for the preparation' of this convention, comprising three members from each faction with Foster and Lovestone as 'deputy chairmen' and a 'neutral comrade' as chairman; the election of a 'broad Party executive' with 'important representation' for Foster; naming Foster and Lovestone as co-secretaries of the party, and Gitlow and Foster as co-heads of trade-union work; and a transfer of the party headquarters from Chicago (an industrial city where Foster was popular) to New York (where Lovestone enjoyed wide support).[26]

Attached to the resolution, but not published in the party press, was an 'Agreement for the carrying out of the resolution of the American Question', signed by the leaders of the factions and the American Commission's head, Ewert:

---

26 'Resolution on the American Question', marked 'Final Text, Endorsed by the Presidium of the ECCI', 1 July 1927, in Comintern archives, 515:1:927; also in Shachtman papers, box 1, folder 24, and Wolfe papers, box 4. The resolution was printed in *Daily Worker*, 3 August 1927.

> The unity of the Party can be achieved only thru the liquidation of the existing groups and factions, the cessation of the factional struggle and the amalgamation of the Party into one unified whole. We pledge ourselves to work in this direction with all our power and without any reservations.

It called to 'merge' the factions, and spelled out the composition of the preparatory committee for the upcoming conference. Pepper (a signatory to the document) was to remain as representative to the ECCI until a new delegate could be selected by the Central Committee elected by the conference.[27]

Foster, Cannon and Weinstone also signed a separate 'declaration' that pledged support to the agreement, but stated that the cooperation among their two groups against Lovestone's faction was 'not in opposition to the general agreement for the unification of all the groups' but 'necessary for the merger of the groups and unification of the Party'. Despite the declared support by all factions for the resolution, they were incapable of passing a common motion on this at the Political Committee. Lovestone's supporters voted their 'complete acceptance' of the resolution, asserting that they did 'not hold the decision of the Communist International to be a victory of any group or combination of groups'. Cannon, Foster and Weinstone's supporters put forward a motion to endorse the decision 'without any reservations', but denounced the Lovestone faction's 'ultrafactional practice' designed to 'permanently maintain itself as a closed faction ... and exercise "hegemony" over the party'.[28]

This did not bode well for party unity. Nor did the fact that the same day the decision was released, Foster and Cannon's supporters in the US organised the 'National Committee of the Opposition Bloc'. They saw the Comintern decision as a mandate to wrest control from Lovestone, not to dismantle their factions.

27 'Agreement for the carrying out of the resolution on the American question adopted by the Presidium of the Executive Committee of the Comintern', signed by A. Braun [Ewert], Jay Lovestone, Benj. Gitlow, John Pepper, J.P. Cannon, Wm. Z. Foster and Wm. W. Weinstone', no date, in Shachtman papers, box 1, folder 24; also Wolfe papers, box 4. On Pepper's status as representative, see Jay Lovestone to the Comintern Presidium, 7 July 1927, and Jay Lovestone to OMS [Otdyel Mezhdunarodnoi Svyazi, International Liaison Section], 7 July 1927, both in Comintern archives, 515:1:929.

28 'Declaration', signed by Foster, Cannon and Weinstone, 7 July 1927, in Comintern archives, 515:1:943; 'Declaration of the Political Committee on the American Question Adopted by the Presidium of the Executive Committee of the Communist International', in Wolfe papers, box 5; see also *Daily Worker* 3 August 1927; 'Statement of the Minority of the Political Committee on the Resolution of the ECCI and the Question of Party Unity', Lovestone papers, box 211, folder 5.

(The name of the bloc, while logical, was maladroit, since it seemed to refer to Zinoviev and Trotsky's opposition against Stalin and Bukharin). Lovestone seized upon this bloc to paint his faction as loyal to the Comintern. His supporters cabled the Comintern, warning of the Opposition's alleged attempts to split the party, and requested the ECCI intervene.[29]

This tipped the Comintern in favour of Lovestone's faction. On 7 July, the Presidium cabled the party:

> The Comintern is categorically against the sharpening of the factional struggle … The Comintern recognizes that in many political questions the Ruthenberg group followed a more correct line in the past than the Foster group. On the other hand the executive is of the opinion that Ruthenberg group had not understood how to estimate sufficiently the full significance the trade union forces in the party and that Foster at the time was more correct on many trade union questions.

In general, the Comintern had supported Ruthenberg's faction, provided it corrected its errors on trade-union work and included Foster in the party leadership. But the cable continued:

> Now the previous political and trade union differences have almost disappeared. The Comintern condemns most categorically every attempt towards the sharpening of the situation as exemplified by the formation of a national committee of the opposition bloc. The Comintern considers factions without political differences the worse offense against the party.

The Presidium ordered the party's press reprint the cable (which the *Daily Worker* did, on its front page, along with an introduction against the 'Foster-Cannon-Weinstone Opposition Bloc').[30]

29 Alex [Bittelman] and Jack [Johnstone] to 'Dear Comrade', [1 July 1927], in Lovestone papers, box 211, folder 5; see also statement by 'National Committee of the Opposition Bloc', 1 July 1927, in Wolfe papers, box 4, 'position papers'; Cable from Max Bedacht to Comintern, 5 July 1927, in Wolfe papers, box 4, 'position papers'; for the Lovestone's group's reaction to the bloc, see 'The Meaning of the Formation of the National Committee of the Opposition Bloc', 6 July 1927, in Lovestone papers, box 204, file 'General Reports, American Question, 1927'.

30 Cable from ECCI Presidium, 7 July 1927, in Comintern archives, 515:1:929; also attached to PolCom minutes, 7 July 1927, in Wolfe papers, box 4, 'position papers'; reprinted in *Daily Worker*, 8 July 1927. See also Draper 1986, pp. 261–3.

Cannon, Weinstone, Foster and their supporters responded with a cable to the Comintern, complaining that 'Lovestone group [is] grossly misinterpreting Comintern cable [of] July Seventh' and using it to 'sustain hegemony claims'. In turn, the ECCI sent another cable, attempting to lessen the impact of its first cable. The previous cable 'did not aim at all to support the hegemony of one group ... but the merging of all groups'. The Presidium criticised all factions and noted the agreement among the factions, and 'condemned' any breaking of this agreement, 'no matter from which side it should come from'. Again, the party was instructed to publish the cable, which it did, on the front page of the *Daily Worker*. (Two days later, the paper published a correction, criticising the *Daily Worker* editors for having added an introduction to the 7 July cable).[31]

From the 'Brooklyn Bridge' to the Daily Worker

In private correspondence, Lovestone's followers greeted the decision as 'a complete *political* and *organizational victory for the Ruthenberg group*'. Lovestone's majority on the CEC issued a 'call upon the membership of our Party to support of the Communist International to close the ranks of our Party'. This statement closed by appealing to Ruthenberg's supposed last words: 'Tell the comrades to close ranks, to build the Party'. What followed was a series of manoeuvres by each group to court the Comintern, often through cables across the Atlantic, many dutifully published in the *Daily Worker*. A report on 'Directives from the ECCI to the American CP' from this period concluded that the increased traffic 'shows how carefully the Comintern has followed the American CP and how quick it has been to correct shortcomings or errors'. (This summer was also the height of the struggle to save Sacco and Vanzetti, who were executed on 23 August 1927).[32]

---

31 Cable from 13 Central Committee members, including Cannon, Foster and Weinstone, to Kuusinen, no date [8 July 1927?]; cable from ECCI Presidium, 9 July 1927, both in Comintern archives, 515:1:929. The Comintern cable was published in *Daily Worker*, 12 July 1927; the correction is in *Daily Worker*, 14 July 1927.

32 *Daily Worker*, 9 July 1927; Lovestone factional circular, 21 July 1927, in Prometheus Research Library collection; Bosse [A.J. Brooks], 'Directives from the ECCI to the American CP from the Sixth ECCI Plenum to Date', 25 November 1927, in Comintern archives, 515:1:934. According to Weinstone, Ruthenberg's last words 'were intrepreted by Lovestone: "Close the ranks of the Ruthenberg group and fight on against the other groups and leaders of the Party"'; Weinstone's speech at American Commission, Moscow, 13 June 1927, in Lovestone papers, box 204, folder, 'General Reports, American Question, 1927'.

At a meeting of the Political Committee on 11 July, Lovestone supporter Bedacht warned, 'our Party has never been nearer a split', and accused the Foster and Cannon groups of having 'deliberately lie[d] to the C.I. and deliberately misrepresent[ed] C.I. decisions' to the party's rank and file. The Foster-Cannon opposition in turn accused the Lovestone group of deceiving the Comintern through 'false cables' and misinterpreting Comintern cables for factional reasons. In the face of such a danger of a split, the Comintern sent another cable clarifying its previous cable, which 'did not aim to support the hegemony of one group in the Workers Party but the merging of all groups'. It emphasised that the agreement in Moscow had safeguarded the minority's 'right to express and defend in a non-factional comradely way its opinion in all meetings of the party units'.[33]

The opposition argued that they had dissolved their bloc, and stood for 'unity and collective leadership', while the 'Lovegroup is only party section which maintained hidebound faction since convention'. They cabled the Comintern, complaining of the Lovestonites' 'arrogance only explained by the petty-bourgeois intellectual composition of its leadership' in trying to 'give the impression that it has been selected by the Comintern as the permanent leadership of our Party'. Lovestone in turn sent a livid cable to Moscow. The ECCI then telegrammed:

> ECCI considers such methods as opposition group uses in statement impermissible factional. Such expressions styling majority of Polcom 'petty bourgeois intellectuals' as 'clique leadership' are opposed resolutions of ECCI. ECCI most decisively opposes these faction methods. On the other hand ECCI declares against any disciplinary measures against opposition.

The *Daily Worker* published this cable on its front page, without even turning it into Standard English. It added a 'Declaration of the Political Committee' that attacked factionalism.[34]

33 Statement by Max Bedacht, attached to 11 July 1927 motion on factionalism, in Prometheus Research Library collection; 'Statement of the CEC Majority Group in Exposing the Factional Irresponsibility of the Lovestone Group' [July 1927?], in Lovestone papers, box 204; ECCI cable, in PolCom minutes in Prometheus Research Library collection; see *Daily Worker*, 12 July 1927.

34 Aronberg, Abern, Bittelman, Dunne, Johnstone, Krumbein, Reynolds and Swabeck statement, in PolCom minutes, 11 July 1927, in Prometheus Research Library; PC minutes, 27 July 1927, in Prometheus Research Library; *Daily Worker*, 20 July 1927.

The final round of cables was about who could send cables. At a Political Committee meeting, Johnstone argued that both chairmen, Foster and Lovestone, must sign all cables. Lovestone responded that only one signature was needed, 'especially the signature of comrade Lovestone, who is named first in the order of the secretaries by the C.I.' On a vote split along factional lines, Lovestone's motion won, thus anointing him 'first secretary'.[35]

A national convention was still needed to fulfil the Comintern decision. Since Lovestone had control of the apparatus in the American party and the support of the Comintern, this was a formality and Lovestone could afford to follow democratic forms. The 'Committee for Preparation of the Party Convention' established strict guidelines for open discussion in the *Daily Worker*, and set up full membership meetings in ten major cities for each faction to present its case. Lovestone's message was that a vote for him was a vote for the Comintern, and a vote for the minority was a vote against the international leadership. A memorandum by the Foster and Cannon group from August 1927 indicated that Lovestone received 59 percent of the total votes, while the opposition gained 41 percent. Of 3,015 eligible voters in several large locals, some 400 members (13 percent) either did not vote or abstained. The circular claimed that this high rate of abstention indicated a lack of confidence in Lovestone's leadership, but it also represented a vote against factionalism itself.[36]

The convention itself, the party's fifth, met in New York City from 31 August to 6 September 1927. 'Braun' (Ewert), the Comintern representative, sympathised with Lovestone, although he was less dramatic than Gusev. One account (by Alfred J. Brooks, a New York schoolteacher who reported on American affairs for the Comintern) described it as 'far less factional than any other for years', and noted that thanks to the preparation of the ECCI's American Commission, 'there was comparatively little difference on the main political, economic and trade union problems facing the Party in the Convention'. The convention voted to move the party headquarters to New York from Chicago (which had been Foster's stronghold). It elected a new Central Executive Committee, comprising 74 people (including alternate and candidate members), of which 46 supported Lovestone. The convention was not free of factionalism, of course. Bittelman recalled a 'very intense' struggle for delegates, although Foster's

35 PC minutes, 28 July 1927, in Prometheus Research Library. Interestingly, in the summer of 1927, routine covering notes sent to the Comintern were signed by both Lovestone and Foster as 'General Secretaries'; see, for example, Jay Lovestone and Wm. Z. Foster to ECCI, 18 August 1927, in Comintern archives, 515:1:929.

36 *Daily Worker*, 5 August 1927 and 11 August 1927; Cannon 1962, pp. 173–4; 'Dear Comrade' minority circular, 8 August 1927, in Prometheus Research Library; see Draper 1986, p. 265.

faction did worse than expected because Lovestone had the Comintern's support. In electing the delegates, proportional representation was used to not undercount oppositional support; still, the credentials committee had been unable to come to agreement on deeper issues. Lovestone and Browder disagreed over the role of US imperialism in China. Cannon, according to the report, complained about Lovestone's aim of smothering opposition, and said he 'desired a free discussion of policies without this being characterised as factionalism'. Pepper, even in his absence, provoked rancour. He was voted onto the CEC as a Lovestone supporter, although, unlike for all other majority supporters, Cannon and Foster faction members abstained. Opposition was strong enough that Lovestone was forced to put forward a motion 'that no one shall either raise the issue of or make proposals for the return of Comrade Pepper to the US', and that 'only the ECCI has the power to deal with the question'.[37]

37 Bittelman, 'Things I Have Learned', box 1, folder 16, p. 478; Bosse [Alfred J. Brooks], 'The Convention of the Workers' (Communist) Party of America', 20 September 1927, in Comintern archives, 515:1:934. On Brooks, see Draper 1986, p. 167. On Ewert, see Hornstein 1993, pp. 80–1.

CHAPTER 11

Lovestone Between Bukharin and Stalin, 1927–8

Emerging from World War I as the strongest capitalist country, the United States in the 1920s experienced 'prosperity': increased production, mass credit, consumerism and apparent affluence. Accompanying this was an 'open shop' campaign against unions, great economic inequality, nativism and racism, as well as frequent imperialist intervention in Latin America and the Caribbean. From a high point in 1920, the unions declined (both as a percentage of the workforce and in absolute numbers) until the industrial union drives of the 1930s. The number of strikes fell, from an average of one hundred per year in 1916–21 to eighteen in 1926–30. The labour bureaucracy favoured class collaboration instead of class struggle, and drove many radicals from the unions. While much of Europe faced economic and political crisis, capitalism in the US appeared stronger than ever; although American workers received a smaller portion of the national wealth, there was little working-class militancy. Despite three minor recessions, American capitalism seemed robust, the Communist Party increasingly isolated, and revolution in the United States more distant than ever.[1]

It was a challenge to understand world capitalism in the 1920s. Ever since Lenin's *Imperialism, The Highest Stage of Capitalism* of 1916, Communists had held that capitalism was in decline, and that only socialist revolution could further develop society's productive forces. This was self-evident to Marxists during and after World War I, but the failure of revolutions in Finland, Hungary and above all Germany had allowed capitalism to survive. By 1921, the Third Comintern Congress recognised a temporary 'stabilisation' in world capitalism. If, from today's vantage point, the Great Depression illuminates signs of a future economic downturn, at the time the 1920s challenged the Communist understanding of capitalism in its 'highest stage'.[2]

1 Description of the 1920s is taken from Bernstein 1960; Dumenil 1995; Leuchtenburg 1958. There were recessions in January 1920 to July 1921, May 1923 to July 1924, and October 1926 to November 1927. See National Bureau of Economic Research 2010. See Laidler and Thomas 1927, p. iii, for an example of radicals' describing the limits of prosperity and predicting a downturn (although not so severe as the Depression turned out to be).

2 Shortly before his death in March 1927, Ruthenberg predicted 'an immediate danger of a depression or crisis'; see C.E. Ruthenberg, 'First Signs of a Downward Trend in Industry', undated [February 1927], in Comintern archives, 515:1:1221. Again, there is a temptation to see

The state of the American economy was a question not just for American Communists, but also for the entire international Communist movement, including the Russian party. Nor was it only an economic question, since it involved Communists in the Soviet Union, the United States, Europe and Asia. It also reflected factionalism in the Russian Communist Party and the deepening bureaucratic degeneration of the Soviet workers' state. As Richard B. Day has put it, the 'transition from the revolutionary internationalism of 1917 to Stalin's defiant nationalism of 1925 can be traced and explained in terms of changing Soviet estimates of the fate of capitalism'. Similarly, Stalin's break with Zinoviev and Kamenev in favour of Bukharin, and then his break with Bukharin, were reflected in the Comintern's analyses. With Bukharin, Stalin emphasised the strength of capitalism. In response to internal and external crises in 1927–8, Stalin underlined the instability of international capitalism; at first Bukharin went along with Stalin's move to the 'left', but by 1928–9, he balked. By the late 1920s, Stalin was the indisputable leader of the Soviet Union and the Comintern, and under the rubric of the 'Third Period' of imminent capitalist collapse he adopted 'left' measures, including collectivising agriculture and the Five Year Plan.[3]

While increasingly echoing the views of the Comintern leadership, the American comrades had trouble making sense of shifting alliances in Moscow. Stalin's move to the left and his fight against Bukharin was 'the least public and most covert' of internal party battles, 'virtually clandestine', according to Bukharin's biographer, and historians still disagree on the relative role of Stalin and Bukharin in the shift in Comintern perspective. Bukharin continued to play a role in shaping Comintern theory even after the beginning of 'Third Period' rhetoric. Compounding this, Stalin's theoretical defence of this lurch was after-the-fact, inconsistent and confusing. (Famously, regarding the collectivisation of agriculture, Stalin in 1930 lambasted 'our comrades [who] have become dizzy with success and for the moment have lost clearness of mind and sobriety of vision'). In the American Communist movement, it was even more dizzying because it was refracted through heated factionalism; although by this time there were few political differences dividing the factions, each faction tried to outmanoeuvre the others in courting Comintern approval and denouncing the other with insults imported from Moscow. In 1927–8, this drama played out in two main arenas: the fight against the Opposition in the Russian Communist Party and debates over the continued strength of US

this as a prediction of the Depression, but more realistically, it is a description of the then current recession.

3 Day 1981, p. 40. For a criticism of Day's analysis, see Kozlov 1990.

capitalism. This chapter attempts to give Lovestone the 'credit' due to him as a soldier of the *Stalinisation* of the American party (and, all proportions guarded, the Comintern itself), despite his later dramatic break with *Stalin*.[4]

Anti-Trotskyism in the American Party

In the Comintern, Lovestone was personally and politically sympathetic to Bukharin. The 'City College Boys'—college-educated intellectuals—at the core of the post-Ruthenberg Lovestone factional leadership were similar to the 'Bukharin school' of young party ideologues in Russia. While much would later be made of Lovestone's sympathies, his support for Bukharin also made sense as a matter of *realpolitik*; in 1926–7 Bukharin was the leading figure in the Russian and international Communist movements, and there was no open rift between him and Stalin yet. Seeking Comintern support meant courting Bukharin. As Stephen Cohen put it, 'Official Bolshevism in 1925–27 was Bukharinist', and, as in the earlier 'troika', Stalin was overshadowed by his more famous and respected partner. Only in retrospect can we call the degeneration of the Comintern 'Stalinisation'; as Trotsky observed later, 'the success which fell upon him was a surprise at first to Stalin himself'. There was no contradiction between Lovestone's support for Bukharin and his role in the Stalinisation of American Communism. At the same time, Lovestone's factional opponents also played a role in advancing Stalinism. Lozovsky, loyal to Stalin and head of the Profintern, favoured Foster and intervened on his behalf; several times Lovestone complained to the Comintern about this. Foster's connections to Stalin via Lozovsky (rooted in the common experiences in the pre-war syndicalist movement) by the late 1920s were more useful than Lovestone's connections to Bukharin via Pepper. But this was not clear in the mid-1920s.[5]

4 Cohen 1980, p. 277; on the dispute over Stalin and Bukharin's role, see Kozlov and Weitz 1989 and Draper 1972b; Stalin 1955, p. 205. The issue of China also divided the party. For a discussion of the role of China in the Russian Communist Party, see Pantsov 2000. For material on the work on China that Communists were doing in early 1927, including with the American representatives of the *Guomindang*, see Comintern archives, 515:1:1218 and 515:1:1219.

5 Cohen 1980; on the 'Bukharin school', see Cohen 1980, pp. 217–19; on Bukharin's commanding role in the Comintern, see Cohen 1980, pp. 214–15; Draper 1972b, pp. 101–3; Trotsky 1937, p. 93. An example of Lozovsky's attacks on the Ruthenberg-Lovestone faction can be found in his speech at the Seventh ECCI Plenum, in Lovestone papers, box 212, folder 7; For Ruthenberg-Lovestone factional complaints about Lozovsky, see Duncan [Robert Minor] to 'Dear CE [Ruthenberg]', 25 December 1926, in Lovestone papers, box 212, folder 6; [Jay Lovestone?] to 'Dear Comrade Stalin', 30 December 1927, in Comintern archives, 515:1:944; Jay Lovestone

Pepper, still in Moscow, helped Lovestone navigate the currents of Moscow politics; Lovestone described him as 'a tower of strength to us'. His faction wrapped itself in anti-Trotskyism and hostility to the Zinoviev-Trotsky Opposition. Although the Russian Opposition had no supporters among the party leadership, the party voted several motions and ran several articles against Trotsky and Zinoviev in 1926–7. In November 1926, Minor wrote to his factional allies from Moscow stressing the urgency of organising an anti-Trotsky and anti-Zinoviev campaign. In May 1927, the American delegation to the Eighth ECCI Plenum went on record against Trotsky and Zinoviev, described by Engdahl in a July article in the *Daily Worker*. In late September, Pepper advised the American Political Committee to escalate its anti-Trotsky and anti-Zinoviev campaign, stating that it was his 'personal opinion' that 'certainly it will be soon necessary to expel' Trotsky from the ECCI. The next month, when this happened, the CEC in turn passed a motion 'approv[ing] wholeheartedly' Trotsky and Vujovič's expulsion from the ECCI. The motion asserted: 'The time has come to take more energetic measures against an opposition which has so completely discredited itself'.[6]

to 'Dear Comrade Bukharin', 31 December 1927, in Comintern archives, 515:1:929. Lovestone's papers contain notes—apparently from 1928 or 1929—on the 'Relations of Profintern to American Party' that label Lozovsky an 'enemy of the Party' and 'factional agent of opposition'; in Lovestone papers, box 227, folder 13; Lozovsky was one of the first supporters of Stalin to openly challenge Bukharin and his allies in the run up to a final split; see Cohen 1980, pp. 267, 280. Lozovsky sided with Foster despite the fact that Lozovsky originally had severe criticism of Foster's policy in Passaic; in addition to Duncan's letter cited above and Lozovsky's speech, see Bittelman's speech at the Seventh ECCI Plenum, 1 December 1926 in Lovestone papers, box 212, folder 7.

6 J. [Lovestone] to 'Dear Friends', 26 November 1926, in Lovestone papers, box 212, folder 6; on Pepper's guiding role, see for example his 'Moscow Cable' [1927?], distributed by the party's national office and marked 'All Party Papers *Must* Publish', in Comintern archives, 515:1:925; Duncan [Minor] to 'Dear Friends', 6 November 1926, in Lovestone papers, box 212, folder 6; Duncan [Minor], 30 May 1927 note, in Prometheus Research Library collection; Engdahl 1927; Pepper to Political Committee of the Workers' (Communist) Party, 25 September 1927, in Comintern archives, 515:1:946; Bosse, 'The Workers' (Communist) Party on the Opposition', report to the Information Department of the ECCI, 27 October 1927, in Comintern archives, 515:1:934. For discussion against the Trotsky and Zinoviev oppositions, see minutes of Political Committee meetings number 3, 7 September 1927; number 8, 16 November 1927; number 9, 23 November 1927; and number 13, 14 December 1927, in Prometheus Research Library collection. Pepper's role in Moscow is explored in Sakmyster 2012, Chapter 7.

The Fight Against Max Eastman

With no significant pro-Trotsky group *within* the party, the party leadership continued to worry about Lore after his expulsion in 1925. They also worried about Max Eastman, the former editor of the *Masses* and the *Liberator* (which evolved into the Communist theoretical journal, *Workers Monthly*). He had travelled to Soviet Russia in 1922 and stayed for two years while writing a biography of Trotsky. This overlapped with the death of Lenin and the beginning of the struggle between Trotsky and the 'troika'. In 1925, after leaving Russia, he published the sympathetic *Leon Trotsky: The Portrait of a Youth* and *Since Lenin Died.* The latter was the first pro-Trotsky account of the struggle in the Russian party and Trotsky's fight against the troika. It contained extracts from unavailable Russian documents, especially Lenin's suppressed 'Testament', which included harsh words on Zinoviev, Kamenev and Stalin. Eastman argued that Trotsky stood in the tradition of Lenin, and denounced the troika's attacks as 'perfectly wanton distortion and misinterpretation and direct turning upside-down of every word written and every position taken by Trotsky', claiming that they 'would be thrown out of a prize essay contest in a school for defective children'.[7]

Eastman had been a brief marginal member of the American Communist Party. Nonetheless, unlike many foreign Communists he had learned Russian and, as he recalled, 'came much closer than most foreign visitors, even most delegates of the International, to the inner circles of the early Bolshevik regime'. Coupled with his authority on the left as former editor of the *Masses*, this made Eastman a threat to the Comintern leadership, even if he had no plans to organise a pro-Trotsky group. The Comintern attacked him constantly. He recalled in his autobiography: 'There is hardly a civilized language on the globe in which the party militants did not learn to pronounce, and execrate, my name'. In April 1925, Bittelman attacked Eastman in the *Workers Monthly*. Several anti-Eastman articles in English came from the British Communist Party (CPGB), where Trotsky had almost no sympathisers. American Communists took up these attacks: in June, the *Workers Monthly* reprinted a hostile review of the book by British Communist leader Andrew Rothstein, and in September, the journal published an attack on Eastman by Lenin's widow, Nadezhda Krupskaya. Meanwhile, under pressure from Stalin and Bukharin, and seeking

7 Eastman 1925a; Eastman 1925b, p. 51; 'Die New Yorker Volkszeitung Zur Opposition in Der WKP', Report for the Information Department of the ECCI, 3 August 1927, in Comintern archives, 515:1:934. On the importance of Lenin's 'Testament', see, for example, McNeal 1959. On Eastman's time in the Soviet Union, see Eastman 1964, pp. 408–28.

to buy time for the Left Opposition to organise in the Soviet party, Trotsky renounced Eastman's efforts, calling his book full of 'false and erroneous generalities' in the French Communist daily *l'Humanité*, and based on 'second hand and ... more indirect sources' in *International Press Correspondence*. The party monitored Eastman closely; for example, in October 1925, Lovestone wrote to Eastman's American publisher, requesting copies of all reviews of his books.[8]

In October 1926, the *New York Times* ran a front-page article by Eastman that began: 'The most important thing happening in the world today is the struggle between two groups of "Bolsheviki" for control of the Russian Communist Party, and thus for control of the entire territory of the former Russian Empire'. It contained Lenin's complete 'Testament' for the first time in English. In anticipation of the appearance of Eastman's article in the *New York Times* (of which Lovestone had received word), the Political Committee unanimously voted to prepare a response in the *Daily Worker*.[9]

The Lovestone leadership continued a steady anti-Trotsky campaign, supported by the other factions. Allies in Moscow reported on the struggle against the Russian Opposition. After Pepper sent his September letter urging the party to escalate its anti-Trotksy campaign, the Political Committee unanimously approved a motion by Wolfe favouring the 'strengthening of the criticism of the opposition of the CPSU' by Americans resident in Moscow. Wolfe also put forward a motion approving the expulsion of Trotsky and Zinoviev from the ECCI. Wolfe, director of the party's 'Agitprop Committee', also wrote

8 Eastman 1925a; Eastman 1964, pp. 344, 443; Goldner 2007; McManus 1925; Bittelman 1925; Roebuck 1925 (Roebuck was Rothstein's pen name); Krupskaya 1925. On the anti-Eastman campaign in the CPGB, see Upham 1980, pp. 9–10; the editorial note to Rothstein's article describes Eastman's marginal relationship to the party, as does Eastman 1964, p. 332. On Trotsky's denunciation of *Since Lenin Died*, see *l'Humanité*, 16 July 1925; *International Press Correspondence*, 3 September 1925. On Trotsky and Eastman in 1925–6, see Deutscher 1959, pp. 200–2; Eastman 1964, pp. 446–7; Trotsky 1934. The role of the French and British Communist parties in denouncing Eastman are probably due to the lack of significant support for Eastman in either party, and the fact that *Since Lenin Died* was first published in London while Eastman was resident in France. Jay Lovestone to Greenberg Publishing Company, 9 October 1925, in Comintern archives, 515:1:521. Lars Lih, editor of Stalin's correspondence with Molotov, argues that Eastman's book was 'an inaccurate, highly charged account that contrasts Trotsky, with his "saintly" devotion to the revolution, to all the other leaders of the party who are nothing more than unscrupulous usurpers', and that Trotsky's denunciation of Eastman was necessary to maintain his credibility within the party; see Lih 1995, pp. 18–24.

9 *New York Times*, 18 October 1926; Political Committee minutes, 16 October 1926, in Cannon papers, reel 47, frame 620 (Cannon was not present at this meeting).

to the ECCI in late October declaring that the leadership thought 'that at this time it is necessary to intensify its work of propaganda against the views of the opposition in the CPSU' and requesting more anti-Opposition propaganda. In mid-November, the CEC passed motions to publish an anti-Opposition bulletin, a collection of speeches by Stalin, and an anti-Trotsky article. Over the next fortnight, the CEC passed other motions against Trotsky and Zinoviev. It was no wonder that a November report to the ECCI stressed that 'there is practically no following of the Russian Opposition' in the American party. The next month, Lovestone wrote to Bukharin that support for Trotsky, 'inside the Party ... is insignificant in open form, altho [sic] there is some more covered strength', particularly in the Jewish federation.[10]

By early 1928, with Trotsky in exile in Alma-Ata, Kazakhstan, and his alliance with Zinoviev and Kamenev over, the Left Opposition seemed to be dwindling and in any case still claimed no organised supporters in the American party. This did not mean that the party leadership relaxed its attacks on Trotsky, Zinoviev and Kamenev. A report from early January described a series of 'discussion meetings' that were 'very carefully arranged under the direction of the American Party agitprop department' and 'a carefully planned campaign in the party press'. With satisfaction, the reporter asserted that 'not a single member of the Central Executive Committee is for the Opposition' and there was 'only slight support for the Opposition in the party's rank and file'.

At the same time, Trotsky was not without sympathy, including among those the report labelled 'Jewish business elements, who still cling to the fringe of the Party'. Gitlow, describing a tour through various branches in the winter of 1927–8, noted that 'the Russian controversy is being intensely followed in Minneapolis' and that 'among our Jewish sympathizers there is considerable warm feeling for Trotsky'. Gitlow complained that Vincent Dunne (William's younger brother) 'asked a very bad question', raising the possibility of 'the execution of Trotsky and Zinoviev if they continue their opposition'. Antoinette Konikow, a Russian-American medical doctor in Boston and

10 An example of the reports on the struggle in the Russian party is 'C' to J.P. Cannon, 4 July 1926, in Cannon papers, reel 3, frame 839; PC Minutes, 7 October 1927, in Comintern archives, 515:1:981; Bertram D. Wolfe to ECCI Agitprop Department, 28 October 1927, in Comintern archives, 515:1:929; PC Minutes, 16 November and 30 November 1927, in Comintern archives, 515:1:981; Jay Lovestone to 'Dear Comrade Bukharin', 31 December 1927, in Comintern archives, 515:1:929. Bosse, 'American Friends of the Russian Opposition', Report to the Information Department of the ECCI, 4 November 1927, in Comintern archive, 515:1:934.

long-time socialist, whose decades of militancy spanned back to Georgi Plekhanov's Emancipation of Labour group, also supported Trotsky.[11]

A report by Wolfe prepared about the same time described his anti-Trotsky presentation at the branch in Brownsville, Brooklyn; although nobody voted against an anti-Trotsky motion, 'many spoke against the resolution and made vicious speeches denouncing the government of the Soviet Union, etc.' and almost a quarter of the membership abstained from voting. (According to the first report, Lovett Fort-Whiteman, a prominent black Communist, also supported Trotsky, but a subsequent letter by Lovestone attested to Fort-Whiteman's anti-Trotsky credentials). There was enough opposition that in December the Political Committee passed a motion that active pro-Opposition members would be expelled from the party if they persisted, and that any party functionary who voted against or abstained on anti-Opposition motions would be removed from his post. The same meeting advised that the Boston district deal with Konikow without, however, expelling her.[12]

Most pro-Trotsky sentiment, then, came from former Communists like Lore and Eastman who, moreover, were neither willing nor able to forge an American Left Opposition. Eastman recalled a meeting during early winter 1928 that he and his wife attended in Lore's New York City flat, along with Soviet economist Eleazar Solntzev and Konikow. They agreed that Eastman would translate and publish various Trotskyist documents that had been smuggled out of Russia (published later that year as *The Real Situation in Russia*), but no organisation came out of the meeting. In late January, Eastman resigned from the Executive Board of the *New Masses* in protest at Communist control,

11 'Discussion on the Opposition in the CPSU by the American Party', stamped 16 January 1928, in the Comintern archives, 515:1:1235; Ben Gitlow to 'Dear Jay' [Lovestone], 1 January 1928, in Comintern archives, 515:1:1331. It is not clear why Trotsky would have been more popular among Jewish members. Although he was, indeed, Jewish, so too were Bittelman, Gitlow, Lovestone, Pepper, Wolfe and others; nor was the Left Opposition based on particular Jewish issues. Konikow (*née* Bucholz) was from a Lutheran family, but her first husband (whom she divorced in 1910) had been Jewish. Both had been active in Boston's radical Jewish community in the late 1890s and early 1900s; see Murolo 1994, p. 167. The Dunne brothers were of Catholic origins.

12 Bertram D. Wolfe, 'Report to the New York District of the Discussion on the Opposition in the CPSU in the Brownsville Sub-Section', 3 January 1928, in Comintern archives, 515:1:1241. Minutes of Political Committee meeting number 13, 14 December 1927, in Prometheus Research Library collection. For Lovestone's defence of Fort-Whiteman, see Jay Lovestone to 'Dear Comrade Engdahl', 15 April 1928, in Comintern archives, 515:1:1325. On Konikow, see Murolo 1994; Palmer 2007, pp. 332–4. According to the National Agitprop Committee minutes, 24 February 1928, in late January the Boston local had decided to expel Konikow; in Comintern archives, 515:1:1353.

and in early February he complained to his friend and fellow ex-Communist, Jamaican-American poet Claude McKay that Stalin was 'leading the Russian workers back to capitalism with the red flag flying'. Eastman observed that he was 'practically alone in this country, and there is practically nothing to do about it, unless I wanted to go for political leadership, which I don't. I dread that eventuality just as much as the party does, which, I am told, is a lot'. For Lovestone, there was no reason to believe that the Russian Opposition posed a threat to his control of the American party.[13]

Lovestone and the Genesis of American Exceptionalism

Lovestone is associated with what later became known as 'American exceptionalism', even though he did not use the term. For the official Communist historians—who also were Lovestone's factional opponents—this 'exceptionalism' posed a fundamental threat to Leninism. Foster, in his 1952 work *History of the Communist Party of the United States*, described Lovestone's supposed view that 'in its essence capitalism in the United States is different from and superior to capitalism in other countries and is, therefore, exempt from that system's laws of growth and decay'. Foster even claimed that Lovestone had argued that 'American capitalism, unlike capitalism elsewhere, was sound at heart; and that there was no prospect of economic crisis in the United States'. Bittelman recalled that Lovestone asserted that America 'was entering a new period of growth of expansion', a 'new "Victorian Age"', marked by the 'impregnable strength' of capitalism. 'It followed', according to Bittelman, 'from Lovestone's outlook that American Communism—our party—might as well go to sleep for all it could expect to do to influence American life for a whole historic period'. These attacks distort the historical record, including the fact that Lovestone's crime was not 'exceptionalism' but later running afoul of Stalin.[14]

13 On the meeting, see Eastman 1964, pp. 510–12 and Palmer 2007, p. 331; the resulting book was Trotsky and Eastman 1928; statement of resignation from *New Masses* by Max Eastman, 21 January 1928, attached to minutes of Political Committee meeting number 22, 20 February 1928, in Lovestone papers, box 225, folder 10; in a letter to J. Louis Engdahl in Moscow, Wolfe claimed that the party had 'driven Max Eastman off [the *New Masses*] editorial board'; Bertram D. Wolfe to J. L. Engdahl, 12 March 1928, in Comintern archives, 515:1:1355; Max Eastman to Claude McKay, 12 February 1928, Claude McKay papers, Yale University, box 3, folder 67.

14 Foster 1952, pp. 271–2; Bittelman, 'Things I Have Learned', box 1, folder 17, p. 484.

The standard historical view of 'American exceptionalism', while not so visceral, is similar: that Lovestone asserted that American capitalism was still growing and the American working class was backward politically, in part due to the wealth of US capitalism. Furthermore, according to this view, this was the reason for Lovestone's later downfall, since Lovestone's view contradicted Stalin's view.[15]

This is oversimplified. To begin with, it makes Lovestone's position more unique and coherent than it was. While Lovestone had a right-wing political tint, especially in the last portion of his tenure as leader of the party, his views were assembled from ideological components shared throughout the party and the Comintern; Lovestone (like his factional rivals) had argued contradictory views at different times. This is because, although the issues under discussion were real, the debate was not about developing a Marxist analysis of American society in the 1920s, but justifying the factionalism within the American and international Communist movements. As Bedacht recalled decades later, instead of a Marxist analysis of the rise of US imperialist strength, 'policies and tactics were based on momentary factional needs, or on passing momentary phenomena'.[16] For Stalin, Lovestone's sin was not arguing that America was different from Europe, but using this difference as a cover to challenge the Soviet leader. Indeed, the pressures arising from being Communists in the most successful capitalist country helped give rise to the Stalinisation of American Communism in the first place.

A 1928 document by Pepper and Engdahl spelled out the elements of 'American exceptionalism':

> Capitalism is still on its upward trend in America. The working class as a whole has a privileged position in the United States. America has the most powerful labour aristocracy. The bulk of the working class is still directly connected with the political parties of the bourgeoisie. America is the single big industrial country in which there does not exist a political mass party of the proletariat ... [T]he Communist Party is small and

15 An example of this is Ottanelli 1991, pp. 13–14. On the pre-history of American exceptionalism (and the development of the theory in general), see Draper 1986, Chapter 12; [James P. Cannon] to 'Dear Comrades', 10 January 1927, in Cannon papers, reel 3, frame 43; Lovestone, while referring to the US as an 'exception' to the general condition of world capitalism, did not use the actual term 'exceptionalism', which was first used in attacks against Lovestone. See the Oxford English Dictionary entry on 'exceptionalism'; see also Pease 2010 pp. 58–9.

16 Bedacht, 'On the Path of Life', folder 26, p. 311.

> there is no likelihood that it can, in the next period, directly reach the proletarian masses ...[17]

On the face of it, these are all true statements. There were four related but different questions that Lovestone tried to answer: 1) The peculiar nature of American society, especially its lack of a labour party; 2) the immediate state of the US economy, specifically whether it was facing continued 'prosperity' or downturn; 3) the role of American imperialism in the world capitalist system; 4) the way in which the first three features affected the perspectives and tasks of the Communist movement.[18]

America is a Strange Place

By the 1920s, leading Socialists—including Kautsky, Plekhanov and Lenin—had attempted to analyse the economic militancy and political backwardness of the American labour movement amid the strength of American capitalism. In fact, the role of Lovestone and other American Communists in the discussion within the Comintern was marginal and unoriginal. A Marxist examination of the specific nature and history of capitalist development in North America would be worthwhile, and, in the last analysis, necessary for would-be Communists. What follows does not do this. Nor does it even claim to trace the entire discussion among Communists; rather, it aims to show the relationship between the issue as it was posed in America and as it played out in Moscow.[19]

Lovestone, on the sesquicentennial of the Declaration of Independence, recognised that 'to speak of Americanizing our Party in the bolshevik sense of the word, means to speak of the Party adopting tactics based on the objective conditions in America'. Above all, the role of 'American exceptionalism' demonstrates how the Comintern had changed by 1926–7. A discussion of

17 Engdahl and Pepper, 'An Outline for the Labour Party Policy of the Workers' (Communist) Party of America' [1928], in Comintern archives, 515:1:1232.

18 According to Sakmyster's biograpy of Pepper, 'Pepper had dabbled with the idea [of American exceptionalism] as early as 1922' in his perspectives for a labour party; Sakmyster 2012, pp. 169–70.

19 The literature on 'American Exceptionalism' is too vast to cite here; the classic work is Sombart 1976. For an overview of the historical question of the lack of a labour party, see Foner 1984. Examples of Marx and Engels's attempts to analyse the US are collected in Marx and Engels 1953 and Marx 1972. See also Lenin 1980; Kautsky 1902; Kautsky 2009; Baron 1995. A useful study of Marx and Tocqueville's view of America, especially centred on race, is Nimtz 2003. A useful discussion of the debate over the role of capitalism in the 1920s is Day 1981.

America's relationship to Europe, and whether more general perspectives applied to the US, was necessary. At the Seventh ECCI Plenum, in late 1926, Bittelman noted:

> Some of these problems, the investigation of their nature and their relationship to our struggles, sometimes prove beyond the theoretical capacity of our own Party ... The Communist International must help and assist us in this as well as in many other respects.[20]

The Comintern had indeed helped 'Americanise' Communism before. But this is what neither the Comintern nor American Communist leadership attempted to do in the late 1920s. Instead, they seized upon elements of reality to justify their own factional positions. This was the opposite of classical Marxist and Bolshevik approaches, which had not attempted to shoehorn the world with its complexities into a schematic or dogmatic view of capitalist development.

In retrospect, the partial and simplistic nature of many of the arguments in the United States is obvious: in the 1920s, the US was the wealthiest capitalist country in the world, *and* it was nearing a massive economic crisis. Although the Communists cannot be blamed for not predicting the Great Depression, they can be faulted for confusing the long-term (secular) economic growth of American capitalism with the immediate possibility of cyclical crisis. Even taking into account the Great Depression of the 1930s and the cataclysm of the Second World War, the US would remain the strongest imperialist economic and military power for decades to come. The dogmatism, scholasticism and dishonest argument—of a piece with broader discussions within the Comintern at the time—were a product of the degenerating Comintern under the leadership of Stalin and Bukharin.[21]

Furthermore, the Communists did not pose the issues in debate in Marxist terms. First, they confounded *political* and *economic* stabilisation: the capitalists had not survived the post-war revolutionary wave because they had been able to stabilise their system economically, but rather because revolutionaries had not been capable of overthrowing them. Second, a period of 'prosperity' does not necessarily translate into political conservatism, nor does economic crisis automatically lead to revolutionary struggle. Third, momentary economic

20 Bittelman speech, Seventh ECCI Plenum, 25 November 1926, in Lovestone papers, box 212, folder 7.

21 Lovestone in Wolfe, Lovestone and Dunne 1926, p. 19. In addition to Draper, cited in note 15 above, see Klehr 1974 for a description of the development of the 'exceptionalism' dispute, albeit one marred by confounding the Comintern in the late 1920s with 'Leninism'.

growth or crisis is not the same thing as broader long-term economic growth or decline. Finally, befitting the epoch of 'socialism in one country', the discussion viewed American capitalism in isolation from the world economy. This national myopia is often carried over in the treatment of the debate by historians; for example, Harvey Klehr's article on the issue, while comprehensive, does not treat it as part of a broader debate within the Comintern.[22]

The Comintern Views the Rise of American Imperialism

After the defeat of revolutionary surges following the Bolshevik Revolution, the Comintern examined the role of US imperialism in 'stabilising' world capitalism. In the early 1920s, Comintern leaders (including Bukharin, Trotsky, Eugen Varga and Zinoviev) understood that American society was different from Europe, and that American capitalism was stronger than European capitalism. They differed over what conclusions to draw from this.

For the Third Comintern Congress of 1921, Trotsky and Comintern economist Varga prepared a report on 'The International Situation'. They observed that the World War 'gave a powerful impetus to the capitalist development of the United States and quickened the aggrandisement of Japan', so that 'the centre of gravity of world industry was shifted from Europe to America'. The report argued that while European capitalism could not regain its leading role, 'American capitalism to-day has also lost its balance', and predicted a crisis in the US. Later that year, Varga, a Hungarian exile, wrote an article in *Communist International* on the 'economic basis of imperialism in the US of North America', which highlighted the 'material prosperity' of 'American workers of the white race'. Varga underlined that 'the class consciousness of the proletariat of the United States has attained a very low level'.[23]

In May 1924, Zinoviev made similar points at the Comintern's American Commission. At the Fifth Comintern Congress a month later, Varga's report on international capitalism contrasted the 'isolated' strength of US capitalism to

22 As of today, US capitalism is undeniably in crisis and arguably in decline, but the lack of class struggle and absence of socialist politics is, if anything, greater than during the 'prosperity' of the 1920s. According to Richard B. Day, 'For Marx's followers, one of the difficulties created by *Capital* was that of distinguishing between *periodic* industrial crises and the *terminal* crisis, or "crash", of the capitalist system as a whole'; Day 1981, p. 2; Klehr 1974.

23 Trotsky and Varga 1921; Mommen 2011, pp. 57–8; Varga 1921.

the 'decaying capitalist world economy'. He stressed that American capitalism was 'still healthy' and 'certainly on the upgrade'.[24]

Trotsky also underlined the role of the United States. He called America 'the master of the capitalist world' and declared that 'American capitalism is seeking the position of world domination; it wants to establish an American imperialist authority over our planet'. American capitalists, he argued, wanted to 'put Europe on rations'. Trotsky predicted that the rise of American imperialism and the decline of British imperialism could lead to war between the two rivals.[25]

In a 1925 article in *Communist International*, Varga argued that American capitalism was 'still rising upon a capitalist basis' compared to capitalist Europe and Soviet Russia. He predicted that 'in the future the final struggle between bourgeoisie and the proletariat on an international scale will be carried out under the leadership of the United States and the Union of Soviet Republics'.[26]

E.H. Carr labelled this perspective 'unstable stabilisation', since the Comintern leadership predicted a crisis that would devastate the United States no less than Europe. The March 1925 *Workers Monthly* published an article by Browder called 'Industrial Depression or Prosperity?', which stressed that 'for the working class, capitalism is just one crisis after another, and prosperity is a reality only to those small sections whom the capitalists find it advantageous to corrupt by special privileges'. The article predicted that a 'breakdown of the capitalist system of production on a mass scale' was 'definitely in the near future for the United States', although Browder refused to forecast a date. Similarly, Kuusinen, at the ECCI's American Commission in April 1925, noted the strong position of American capitalism, but stressed that this was not permanent: 'And then, when it cannot remain at that height any longer, but begins a down-grade course and slides[,] then the higher it stood the worse it will be'. He added: 'it will be the great task of the American comrades of the Workers Party to assist in this downward trend of the most powerful finance capital of the world'.[27]

24 Zinoviev at American Commission of the ECCI Presidium, 20 May 1924, in Lovestone papers, box 210, folder 1.

25 Trotsky 1945b, pp. 191, 221.

26 Varga 1925; it is useful to keep in mind Trotsky's characterisation of Varga as 'the perfected type of theoretician *à la* Polonius, at the service of every leadership of the Communist International' by concocting economic analyses to justify a given political turn; Trotsky 1974a, p. 240.

27 Carr 1976, Chapter 67; Browder 1925, p. 219; Kuusinen at ECCI American Commission, April 1925, in Cannon papers, reel 47, frame 235. He did not elaborate how the small Communist Party should help create an economic crisis.

In 1925, Trotsky's *Where Is Britain Going?* was published. A colourful analysis of British capitalism, its core was a polemic against the alliance with left-wing Labour leaders that the Comintern and the British Communists were pursuing. Trotsky described US and British capitalism as 'twin stars, one of which grows dim the more rapidly as the brilliancy of the other increases'. The book's thesis was that British capitalism had lost its predominant role in relation to the United States, and as a result was 'headed toward an era of great revolutionary upheavals'. Trotsky's introduction to the American edition (published as *Whither England?*) asserted that 'in revolutionary development, America does not stand in the front rank', even though 'the inevitable hour will strike for American capitalism also'. In other words, for Trotsky, the decline of British capitalism in the face of American growth was a sign of imminent British revolution, not a reason to postpone revolution in the US.[28]

Lovestone then entered this debate. As the leader of the American Communist Party, it was natural that he would take a position on the relationship between America and Britain, although his contribution—a *Workers Monthly* review of Trotsky's book—seems sycophantic and too smart by half. While largely favourable, Lovestone's review argued that *Where Is Britain Going?* 'definitely indicates that [Trotsky] has had a change of mind on the subject', claiming that Trotsky's previous speech had predicted 'a period of peaceful Anglo-American' relations. According to Lovestone, in rejecting this, Trotsky now 'tend[ed] towards agreement on the most basic points with the estimate of this crucial point in the international situation made by Comrade Pepper'. Lovestone tried to parry Trotsky's polemic against the CPGB and Comintern leadership. He claimed that Trotsky 'underestimates the significance and the possible role of this movement towards the left wing' by British workers and confused 'the Left Wing leaders and the masses constituting the Left Wing'. Lovestone referred the reader to 'the illuminating analysis' of Pepper. Lovestone concluded with an attack on 'American comrades [who] opposed the establishment of a Labor Party in America' for similar reasons.[29]

28 Trotsky 1973b, pp. 23, 50. On the polemical purpose of the book, see Trotsky 1930, p. 527. According to Upham 1980, p. 13, the CPGB originally missed the polemical knife aimed at them in the book and saw it mainly as an attack on Labour leaders. Although it was not the book's purpose, it also illustrates that it is possible to analyse the 'exceptional' nature of a capitalist country without denying the general applicability of Marxism and the necessity of revolution: 'We do not mean to say that English imperialism and the English labor movement have not their "peculiarities"... But we explain these peculiarities on the basis of the objective conditions, of the structure of society and its changes'; Trotsky 1973b, p. 62.

29 Lovestone 1925b.

Trotsky responded in a speech in February 1926, one of his last to Soviet workers. This speech—published in a pamphlet under the title *Europe and America*—was his most sustained analysis of American capitalist development in the context of the post-war decline of European capitalism. In it, he dismissed Lovestone for his distortion: 'If any communist past the Pioneer age said this or something similar, one would simply have to expel him from communist ranks'. More stinging was Trotsky's emphasis on socialist revolution internationally, an implicit polemic against Lovestone's patrons in the Comintern, Stalin and Bukharin.

Analysing America's origin as 'a distant self-sufficient world, an immense, god-forsaken backwoods area nourished with the crumbs of European civilization', Trotsky argued that although World War I devastated European capitalism, it allowed the US 'to rise at one stroke above the whole world as the master of its destinies'. It became 'the principal factory, the principal depot and the central bank of the world'. Trotsky underlined: 'American capitalism is far stronger and stabler than European capitalism: it can look to the future with far greater assurance'. Yet the very strength of American capitalism was pushing Europe closer and closer to revolutionary upsurges, and since American capitalism was 'becoming increasingly dependent upon Europe' for markets, 'a victorious revolution in Europe and Asia would inevitably inaugurate a revolutionary epoch in the United States'. He emphasised: 'the power of the United States—such is the dialectic—is now the greatest lever of the European revolution'. For Trotsky, then, internationalism was the key to the puzzle of American exceptionalism: on its own, American capitalism was exceptional, but its role in the international capitalist system confirmed the Leninist understanding of the decline of capitalism.[30]

In this view, the British general strike in May 1926 (precipitated by attacks on coal miners' wages) confirmed his prediction of class struggle, as well as his criticism of the CPGB's seeking allies with the left wing of the union bureaucracy. In response to the strike—the nearest the English-speaking world had come to workers' revolution—the American Communist Party published two pamphlets, by Dunne and Pepper (then in Moscow). Dunne emphasised the 'decline' and 'decay' of British imperialism, and Pepper highlighted that 'American capitalism is still on an ascending curve' while 'present-day capitalist Europe, and primarily the British Empire, is being ground to dust'. While echoing Trotsky's prediction of massive class struggle in Britain, neither Dunne nor Pepper criticised the CPGB or Comintern perspectives. In the *Communist International* in December 1926, Pepper (who was then in charge

30 Trotsky 1943.

of British affairs in the Comintern) predicted a strengthened CPGB emerging from the strike, growing out of a labour 'Left Wing [that] will transform itself into a Communist one, which will stand not only under the influence, but also under the direct influence of the Communist Party'. (Pepper's meddling in the CPGB earned him the dislike of British Communists who successfully lobbied the ECCI to remove him from dealing with Britain). Writing from Moscow, Browder criticised Dunne's pamphlet for being soft on the Labour leaders who betrayed the workers, but never mentioned that the CPGB tailed those same leaders, or that in doing so, they were following Comintern policy.[31]

After the strike, the British *Communist Review* carried an article by Dunne on the American labour movement which described the US economy as 'still a rising capitalism' and noted the 'official Labour movement is going to the Right', even while noting a 'fairly strong drift to the Left' among rank-and-file workers. Months later, Ruthenberg attacked what he saw as right-wing deviations based on the unique strength of American capitalism, and criticised 'party members who are making excuses for lack of progress' and 'trying to excuse their own pessimism and lack of energy in the struggle by a theory which has no basis in fact'. Ruthenberg argued that economic crisis was not necessary to make workers more radical, but 'quite the contrary, it is exactly in such times of prosperity that demands for higher wages and better working conditions are made that movements for organization of the unorganized workers to attain better wages and improved conditions are developed'. In other words, capitalist growth could lead to class struggle. Ruthenberg's faction was not more defeatist than the others.[32]

31 Trotsky 1930, p. 257; Pepper 1926a, pp. 6–7; Dunne 1926a, p. 8; Pepper 1926b, p. 13; Earl Browder, 'How Not To Write About the British Strike', 7 August 1926, in Comintern archives, 515:1:924. For his part, Stalin, while labelling the CPGB 'one of the best sections of the Communist International' and its 'policy throughout the time of the strike' 'perfectly correct', concluded that 'there is ... no doubt that the weakness of the British Communist Party was of no small importance in the defeat of the General Strike'; Stalin 1926. After the strike, the ECCI Agitprop Department's 'Investigation into Campaigns Carried Out by Eight C.I. Sections During the British Mining General and Miners' Strike' criticised the American (and other) Communists for underestimating the betrayal of the left-wing Labour leaders and for initially characterising the conclusion of the strike a victory instead of a defeat; in Lovestone, box 209, folder 18.

32 Ruthenberg 1926a; Dunne 1926b; see also Klehr 1971, pp. 97–100. In December 1926, the situation between Pepper and the CPGB had become so dire that British Communist Tom Bell wrote to the ECCI complaining that the British Communist leadership 'had no confidence in Comrade Pepper's political discretion' and requested that the ECCI 'rearrange Comrade Pepper's work in such a manner as to ensure as far as possible that he shall

Both Ruthenberg and Foster's factions shared with the Comintern leadership a similar view of the strength of American capitalism. In November 1926, the American delegation to the Seventh ECCI plenum formally requested that Bukharin add a section 'on the conditions in America and the tasks of the American Party' to his report on world capitalism. In his presentation, Bukharin described the US as 'a country which expresses most sharply the upward curve of the capitalist economy'. This met with the approval of the two American delegates. Lovestone claimed that 'American imperialism has not yet reached its highest point of development', and Bittelman stated that 'American capitalism is still moving upwards'. None of these statements was noteworthy at the time.[33]

In the aftermath of the British general strike, Stalin's followers denounced Trotsky for denying the possibility of building socialism in Russia. At the Seventh ECCI Plenum, in November 1926, Lovestone attacked Trotsky; his comments were later reprinted in the March 1927 issue of the *Communist*. He denounced 'the theory of Comrade Trotsky that America is pursuing such a course as will subordinate completely European politics to American politics'. In a fanciful amalgam, Lovestone argued that Trotsky's perspective 'means that New York is today the decisive, the sole, primary obstacle to the proletarian revolution', that 'no revolution is possible in Europe without there first being a successful revolution in America' and thus 'the building of Socialism in the Soviet Union is out of the question'. (The original speech used the word *kaput*).

In the article, it is true that Lovestone repeated that 'beyond a doubt American capitalism is still on the upgrade'. But he also attacked Trotsky for 'exaggerat[ing] the weakness of European capitalism and overestimat[ing] the strength of American imperialism'. (During this time, the Lovestone faction emphasised the strength of *British* imperialism, for example, in China). Lovestone's vision of the strength of US imperialism, far from being a chal-

have no direct or indirect voice in British affairs'. By early 1927, Pepper was removed not only from overseeing British affairs but also from any specific role in the Comintern; see Sakmyster 2012, pp. 137–41.

33 On the Seventh ECCI Plenum, see Carr 1976, pp. 133, 594. On the request for a section on the US, see Minutes of the American Delegation to the Enlarged Plenum of the ECCI, 25 November 1926, in Lovestone, box 212, folder 7; see speeches by Bittelman, 25 November 1926; Birch [Lovestone], 25 November 1926, in Lovestone papers, box 212, folder 7. Interestingly, it was left to M. N. Roy, a future adherent of Bukharin's Right Opposition, to dissent, arguing that both the Comintern leadership and the American Communists were overly pessimistic about the strength of American imperialism and the weakness of American Communism; see his speech, 27 November 1926, in Lovestone, box 212, folder 7.

lenge to Stalinisation in this period, was formulated to defend Stalin's attacks on Trotsky.[34]

Much 'American exceptionalism' could be found in Comintern economist Eugen Varga's analyses. Like Lovestone, Varga stressed empirical data from bourgeois statistical sources. (The writings of both often drown the reader in statistics). On a theoretical level, Varga recognised that government policy in capitalist countries could offset, if only temporarily, the tendency to economic downturns. By 1927, Varga had distinguished himself in his attacks on Trotsky and fellow Oppositionist, economist Evgeny Preobrazhensky. He was the director of the Institute of World Economy and Politics in Moscow and advised Stalin on economic issues. His work focused on the tendency of capitalism to decline and the business cycle in capitalist countries.[35]

America's Upward Grade and Lovestone's Rightward Shift

Lovestone's role in developing what is seen as a right-wing deviation appears odd since Ruthenberg in the mid-1920s was seen as a 'leftist' within Communist politics, and many of the faction's earlier positions contradicted its future evolution. Pepper too (along with Béla Kun) had been a 'leftist', advocating a revolutionary offensive in the early 1920s; at the Third Comintern Congress, Pepper

34 Lovestone 1927a; for the original, see the speech of Birch [Lovestone] at the Seventh ECCI Plenum, 25 November 1926, in Lovestone, box 212, folder 7. On Lovestone's anti-British perspective, see Cannon 1992, pp. 440–1, n. 1. In the speech of 30 April 1927, Lovestone declared: 'We brought in the proposition that we must mobilize anti-British sentiment in this country. The opposition comrades said it is wrong; the comrades' duty is to fight American imperialism first and other imperialism second. They cannot see a situation dynamically. We said: What you said is correct but the fact of the matter is, it is not yet definite that America and Great Britain have [a] close alliance in China; it is not true that conflicts of interest have disappeared for good. Our job is to utilize ever[y] force in the U.S. which can be utilized to mobilize sentiment against British imperialism'; Lovestone papers, box 204, file, 'General Reports, American Question, 1927'.

35 Varga recognised something that was largely lost in the subsequent debate over the decline or growth of American capitalism: even though the early 1920s was 'the beginning of a *period of crises* for capitalism', as he put it, nonetheless, 'within this period of crises the course of business progresses in cycles, just as it did with the normal capitalism of pre-war days: *periods of booms alternate with periods of crises*. The principle question is that of placing an estimate *upon the whole period, and not upon the phase* of which it is made up'; Varga 1924, p. 5; Roh 2010, Chapters 1 and 3. On Lovestone's 'faith in statistics' to the point of 'virtual exclusion of Marxist economic theory', see Bittelman, 'Things I Have Learned', box 1, folder 17, p. 480.

had clashed with Trotsky and Varga's prognosis of capitalist stabilisation. In early 1926, Foster criticised Ruthenberg's faction, then in control of the Central Committee, for 'ultra-left sectarian tendencies' in trade-union work.[36]

However, by early 1927, with the defeat of the Zinoviev-Trotsky Joint Opposition, the Comintern had begun to shift to the left again. At the Seventh ECCI plenum, Bukharin introduced the idea of a new, 'Third Period' of imminent capitalist decline, although he drew no practical conclusions. The eighth plenum, in April–May, after the debacle of the anti-Communist bloodbath by Chiang in China, was marked by the 'disappearance of any reference to the stabilization of capitalism', according to Carr. At the Fifteenth Russian Communist Party Congress, in December, Stalin asserted that 'the stabilization of capitalism is becoming more and more rotten and unstable', and that 'Europe is now plainly entering the phase of a new revolutionary upsurge'. This weakened Bukharin's position, but he did not openly oppose this left turn at the time.[37]

The Ruthenberg faction supported this shift. In January 1927, Lovestone wrote to Stalin and Bukharin that 'it is obvious that the peak of the recent long prosperity wave has passed' even while 'it is true that capitalism in America is on the ascendancy'. He criticised Foster's alleged argument that imperialism was 'succeeding in corrupting the whole American working class'. In late February 1927, *Communist International* ran an article by Robert Minor, a Ruthenberg supporter, about the American labour movement. Not essentially different from Dunne's article from the previous May, this asserted that 'America is not Europe' because 'capitalist imperialism still continues to move upward'. Rather than being defeatist, however, Minor, citing the importance of Communists in the recent Passaic and Furriers strikes, argued for an increased Communist role in labour struggle. He predicted: 'The present period is shown to be one in which the Communist Party can make substantial strides forward in mass influence'. In fact, so far from being right wing was Ruthenberg's faction that, at about the same time, Cannon denounced the 'leftist factional regime of the Ruthenberg group'.[38]

36 Vargas 1924, p. 5, n. 1; Foster, speech to American Commission, 19 February 1926, in Comintern archives, 495:164:377. In a factional letter in February 1927, Lovestone complained of being depicted as a leftist by Foster and Cannon; see his letter to 'Dear Comrades', 5 February 1927, in Lovestone papers, box 197, folder 10. Bukharin, of course, had also been on the left wing of the Bolshevik Party after the Revolution, but moved to the right by the end of the decade.

37 Carr 1976, pp. 133, 143–8; Draper argues that Bukharin was the original author of this left turn, which Stalin later extended; Draper 1972b, pp. 104–6.

38 JL [Lovestone] to 'Dear Comrades Stalin and Bucharin', 23 January 1927, in Comintern archives, 515:1:944; Minor 1927; [James P. Cannon] to 'Dear Comrades, 10 June 1927, in

How did the Ruthenberg-Lovestone faction move from the left to the right of the party? The faction was defined not by a common political outlook, but by a desire to gain and maintain factional power in the party. In February 1927, Cannon described the faction as 'not a finished product'. Ruthenberg's death changed the political momentum of the faction, as did Stalin and Bukharin's fight against Zinoviev, Kamenev and Trotsky. Oakley Johnson is probably right in saying that Ruthenberg had nothing to do with Lovestone's view of American exceptionalism, but his implication that Ruthenberg and Lovestone were in the same faction as if by accident is not credible, since there was a political logic underlying the group. The faction was the most enthusiastic advocate of the farmer-labour and third-party perspectives. While based on an overestimation of the immediate revolutionary potential in the US, these positions highlighted an impressionism, a willingness to tail non-working-class forces, and a denigration and pessimism about steady, open Communist work—with Pepper's manoeuvring and wild theorising adding flare, like paprika in goulash. When this 'get rich quick' opportunism failed, the same methodology could easily lead to the conclusion that there were no longer opportunities for a strong Communist movement on the immediate horizon. In April 1927, Lovestone argued that although the strength of American capitalism created 'tremendous difficulties for the development of a mass communist party on a quick basis', the task was not hopeless. However, he concluded that a strong *Communist* programme was an obstacle to growth: 'To say that American imperialism has been able to buy out the working class is to be guilty of Bernsteinian

Cannon papers, reel 3, frame 43; Ruthenberg also described Cannon's denouncing his faction for 'ultra-leftist leadership', in a telegram from Ruthenberg to Duncan [Robert Minor], 6 February 1927, in Comintern archives, 515:1:948. The terms 'left' and 'right'—always used differently within the socialist movement from within society at large—were also abused in the mid-to-late 1920s, depending on factional alliances within the Russian party, undermining the definition of these terms and leading to more confusion. For example, in January 1926, Stalin declared 'that Rights and "ultra-Lefts" are actually twins, that consequently both take an opportunist stand, the difference between them being that whereas the Rights do not always conceal their opportunism, the Lefts invariably camouflage their opportunism with "revolutionary" phrases'. Bittelman, reading this speech in the 18 February *Pravda*, used it to attack Cannon and Ruthenberg at that evening's meeting of the American Commission; see Stalin 1954; Comintern archives, 495:164:375. See Halfin 2007 for a discussion of the use of language in the mid-1920s Soviet discourse (albeit one marred by a refusal to look at the *political* basis of the various disputes).

revisionism of the worst order, just as to say that if there is room for a communist party, then there is room for only a 100% pure communist party'.[39]

By the mid-1920s, Lovestone was, in Draper's words, 'the party's first anti-imperialist expert', and had published several pamphlets on this theme, including *American Imperialism: The Menace of the Greatest Capitalist World Power.* Lovestone and his ally, Bertram Wolfe, paid attention to Latin America, especially Mexico (where Wolfe had been a leading member of the Communist Party). Opposition to one's 'own' imperialism was a crucial part of Communism in the 1920s, but it could also slide into overestimating the power of imperialism to corrupt or 'embourgeoisify' the working class. In 1925, Lovestone had already described the strength of US imperialism, 'a world unto itself', as the basis for the 'great influence and power of the "bourgeoisified" strata of the American working class' that had 'infiltrated the ranks and manifested itself in countless ways in the activities of nearly every section of the American working class'. He called Latin America 'the natural economic hinterland for the Yankee capitalists'. Like much of Lovestone's theory, there was truth in these observations, but they also served to justify his factional positions, in this case a powerful imperialist bourgeoisie and a powerless proletariat.[40]

Finally, if Lovestone chose the wrong position in relation to Comintern politics, this was not clear at the time. In July 1927, the American Commission raised the spectre of 'bourgeoisification' and posited that American capitalism was still on an upward curve; this gave the outline of 'American exceptionalism' the Comintern's imprimatur. In fact, a prior draft of the resolution had gone further, declaring that 'In no other highly developed capitalist industrial

39 Cannon 1992, pp. 387–91. In this context, Foster's presentation to the ECCI American Commission, 4 March 1925, while focused on the FFLP and La Follette discussion, highlights important characteristics of the future Lovestone faction; in Lovestone papers, box 210, folder 3. Johnson 1957, p. 176. Johnson, although a founder of the party, left it for most of the 1920s before rejoining. His biography of Ruthenberg focuses on its subject's early years while all but ignoring the factionalism, of which it claims there was 'no point in going into it here'. According to Johnson, Ruthenberg's 'unwilling involvement [in factionalism] was, historically speaking, merely an incident in this difficult period of party history'; Johnson 1957, p. 174; Jay Lovestone speech on 30 April 1927, in Lovestone papers, box 204, folder 'General Reports, American Question, 1927'.

40 Lovestone 1924b; Lovestone 1925a, pp. 4, 12; 'Report of Jay Lovestone on the convention of the Communist party of Mexico, the establishment of a Pan-American Communist bureau, campaign against American imperialism and the party programme for the Philippine crisis' [1925?], in Lovestone papers, box 202, folder 26. On Wolfe's time in Mexico, see Taibo 2008, especially Part 7, Chapter 7.

country are the objective difficulties for the formation of a Communist mass Party so great as in America'.[41]

With few exceptions, the leadership of all the factions echoed this view. A document by Cannon and Weinstone in May 1927 on the 'economic and political situation' described the US as having 'a more and more prominent and in some way special position among the capitalist powers'. They claimed 'American capitalism still continues on the upward curve', even while predicting 'a period of either a short and sharp crisis or a deep-going and protracted depression'.[42]

A.J. Brooks's report to the Comintern on the Workers' (Communist) Party convention in the summer of 1927 noted that Lovestone had labelled 'the increasing bourgeoisification of the working class as a result of imperialism' one of the 'main problems facing the party'. Browder went further and asserted that 'Imperialism was not only bourgeoisifying the working class, but was also changing its organic composition, not through its propaganda or high wages for certain privileged sections, but through decreasing the number of industrial workers and increasing those in non-essential and luxury industries, those in offices, personal services, technicians, etc.' Only Cannon cautioned against the pressure of such pessimism, and 'spoke of the difficulties facing the Party and of the liberal and radical fringe surrounding and greatly influencing it'. All speakers agreed on the conservative period and lack of socialist consciousness among the mass of workers—something that no historian of the 1920s would contest.[43]

Much of Lovestone's analysis today seems obvious and trite. Lovestone asserted in 1927 that 'American capitalism is still on the upward grade—still in the ascendancy'. He added that 'the peak of American capitalism—of American imperialist development—has not yet been reached'. In another article, he explained that the 'upward trend' resulted in 'corrupting parts of the working class' by the capitalists, something that 'will continue and will drive parts of the working class to the right'. Yet Lovestone did not deny that downturns in the economy were possible. In late 1927, he wrote to Bukharin that

41 'Draft Resolution', 19 June 1927, in Comintern archives, 515:1:926.

42 Weinstone and Cannon, 'The Economic and Political Situation and the Tasks of the Workers' (Communist) Party of America', 6 May 1927, in Comintern archives, 495:37:16.

43 Bosse [Alfred J. Brooks], 'The Convention of the Workers' (Communist) Party of America', 20 September 1927, in Comintern archives, 515:1:934.

'the prosperity bugaboo has broken', and that unemployment was rising while wages were falling.[44]

In a speech published in the party's theoretical journal, Lovestone observed that in the US, 'the power of capitalism is today as supreme as it ever was'. The wealth of imperialism has 'split up the working class', dividing the 'labor aristocracy of skilled workers' from 'the semi-skilled and unskilled workers'. This damaged the labour unions, and undercut the labour-party movement. While denying pessimism, Lovestone asserted that 'the main task of the Party ... still is to hasten the development of the working class politically' through 'united front activities'. The main arena for this, he stressed, was the trade unions. Communists should join unions if they could, but above all, 'we must build the left wing' and 'not permit it to be narrowed down to an organization of Communist Party members with a narrow circle of Communist sympathizers'. In the *Daily Worker*, Lovestone wrote 'that the objective conditions prevailing today in the United States are not favorable for the development of a mass Communist Party and it would be a crime against the Party to develop such illusions among the members if we were to say that the conditions of a mass Communist Party are favorable'. As Draper put it, 'in its immediate effect, Lovestone's position was pessimistic'. However, as Draper emphasised, Foster's position was similar.[45]

Coupled to American exceptionalism was an apparent attempt to analyse the history of the United States from a Marxist perspective. Most early American Communists ignored American history, seeking inspiration from Europe, especially the Soviet Union. Communists were less interested in American history than American social democrats such as A.M. Simons or James Oneal; ironically, several European socialists, such as Marx, Kautsky, Plekhanov and Lenin, had analysed United States history more perceptively.

By 1926—the 150th anniversary of the Declaration of Independence—Communists had begun to examine American history. However, instead of making sense of this contradictory history, Communists wrapped themselves in the red-white-and-blue, celebrating the 'revolutionary tradition' of America—feeding into the anti-British tilt of the party. In a pamphlet, *Our Heritage from 1776* (reprinting articles from the *Daily Worker* under a cover bearing a 'Don't Tread On Me' flag), Wolfe declared that 'this year, the Workers' (Communist) Party intends to claim this inheritance on behalf of the American

44 Lovestone 1927b; Jay Lovestone to 'Dear Comrade Bukharin', 31 December 1927, in Comintern archives, 515:1:929.

45 Lovestone 1927b (a typescript is available in Comintern archives, 515:1:1221); Draper 1986, p. 278.

working class' and that the struggle against the British was 'our revolution'. In 1927, the *Daily Worker* sought lessons from the war against Britain and polemicised against radical historians (such as Oneal) who allegedly denigrated the Revolution. The same year, the *Communist* began running Marx and Engels's articles on the American Civil War, and carried a two-part study, 'Marx, Engels and America'.[46]

Lovestone's American exceptionialism synthesised the conservatising effects of a long, unprecedented capitalist 'prosperity', and the Comintern's shift from revolutionary internationalism under Bukharin and Stalin. In an article on this, while capturing the fatuous quality of this debate, Klehr argued that 'the Lovestoneite commitment to Leninism thus precluded a realistic assessment of America'. However, Lovestone was motivated not by Leninism, but by Stalinism. While Klehr argued that Lenin 'involved an insistence that monopoly capitalism had effaced all differences in the West', in fact Lenin (like Marx) recognised that different countries had different traditions and histories. In 1927, so did Stalin. Indeed, despite his later attack on 'exceptionalism', Stalin's 'socialism in one country' was based on the nationalist idea that somehow Russia was so exceptional that it alone could build socialism in isolation amid a revitalised capitalist world. As Trotsky quipped after Lovestone was expelled from the Comintern: 'Whatever exceptionalism Lovestone and Co. sought for the United States, it could not be higher than the one Stalin secured for the USSR by Comintern decree'. Lovestone could not assess American reality, not because he was a Leninist, but because he was not a Leninist. For him, sociology and history were only useful to justify the line from Moscow.[47]

In this, Lovestone reflected the Stalinist degeneration of the Comintern, and paved the way for the party's embrace of Stalinism. As Cannon stressed to Draper, 'the party became receptive to the ideas of Stalinism, which were

46 For social-democratic histories of the US, see Oneal 1912; Simons 1904; on earlier Marxist attempts to analyse the US, see Kautsky 1902; Kautsky 2009; Baron 1995; Wolfe, Lovestone and Dunne 1926, pp. 1, 2; see, for example, Kruse 1927; O'Flaherty 1927. While many of the writers in this genre were supporters of Lovestone, some (such as Dunne and O'Flaherty) were not; Landy 1927. On later Communist attempts to deal with the American Revolution from the perspective of the popular front, see David De Leon 1979. By way of context for the anti-British tilt, it is useful to keep in mind that, at about the same time, the Knights of Columbus, the American Legion, and the Daughters of the American Revolution, led a campaign against 'pro-British' school books, leading to legislation in several states; see Ginger 1974, pp. 10–11.

47 Klehr 1971; Trotsky 1973c, p. 41.

saturated with conservatism, because the party cadres were unconsciously yielding to their own conservative environment'.[48]

Thus, although exceptionalism would later be the crime for which Lovestone was driven out of the Communist Party, his advocacy of it in 1927 was in keeping with the perspectives of Moscow. By the end of 1927, although Lovestone was firmly in power (with the support of the Comintern), factionalism still divided the party and hamstrung the party's work. It disillusioned members and leaders alike. The party had proven itself incapable of ending factionalism and focusing on the issues the party confronted in such a reactionary period. In the past, the Communist International had intervened to help set the party on the right course. While the Comintern increased its interventions in this period, these were not designed to help the party solve these problems, but to create a leadership and party that supported the bureaucracy that was consolidating its strength in Moscow.

48 Cannon 1962, p. 25.

CHAPTER 12

The 'Third Period', the Sixth Congress and the Elimination of Opposition, 1928–9

The Comintern announced the 'Third Period' at the end of the 1920s. The first period had been after the Bolshevik Revolution, when revolution was possible in several countries. The second period, in the early 1920s, had been marked by the 'stabilisation' of world capitalism and the need for united-front tactics to gain influence among the working class. The Seventh ECCI Plenum in late 1926 declared that a new period of revolution had begun, and over the next several years Communist parties began to adopt 'left' tactics, including denouncing social democrats as 'social fascists' and refusing to work with or vote for them under the slogan 'class against class'. In many countries, Communists split from established trade unions with social-democratic leaderships, and formed 'red' unions.

The Third Period confused many Communists, and still confuses historians. While Stalinism, at bottom, was a right-wing development in the Communist movement, abandoning the perspective of world revolution, this was masked by 'leftist' Third Period rhetoric. For many Communists, the Third Period must have appeared to be a return to the militancy of the post-war revolutionary period, especially since Third Period concepts seemed to echo the language of early Communism, even if their application was different.[1] Like Stalinism as a whole, the ideology of the Third Period evolved to fit the needs of the Soviet bureaucracy, so that it meant different things at different times.

The origins of this turn are also hard to tease out. In domestic Soviet terms, it reflected Stalin's move against Bukharin and the 'right' in favour of industrialisation and collectivisation. It was also an attempt to deal with the danger posed by a growing layer of wealthy peasants ('kulaks') hostile to the Soviet government. The turn also undercut Trotsky's Left Opposition by adopting elements of its programme, usually in more extreme (and brutal) forms. By the end of the Third Period and the turn towards the 'Popular Front' (in 1934–5), Stalin was the unrivalled head of the Soviet Union.

On international terms, the Third Period reflected the failure of open class-collaborationism that had lead to disasters, such as the British general strike in May 1926 and the Shanghai massacre in April 1927. Although the Third Period

1 See Worley 2004, pp. 3, 6.

was ultimately aimed at the Bukharinite 'right danger', Bukharin remained the leading Comintern ideologue through 1929 and helped to lay the basis for the turn. This chapter does not intend to unpack all the nuances of the period.[2] Rather, it will examine how the rise of Third Period Stalinism affected the American Communist Party. The nature of the intervention of the Communist International—now more openly led by Stalin—was new. Instead of offering political guidance and trying to persuade dissident Communists, the Comintern insisted on 'subordination' and 'loyalty', and threatened harsh discipline against those who did not submit.[3]

In early 1928, Lovestone and his faction were in charge of the American party and enjoyed the apparent support of the Russian leadership. In the first portion of 1928, the party's main concerns were the coal miners' union, the needle trades unions, and the upcoming elections. In May, Pepper returned to the US, and (under the name Swift) resumed his place in the Political Committee.[4]

During this time, Trotskyism appeared to have no support in the party except for Antoinette Konikow in Boston, some Jewish leftists on the fringe of the party, and vilified ex-Communists such as Lore and Eastman. This did not stop Engdahl, in Moscow, from criticising the party's leadership for a tepid anti-Trotsky campaign. In response, the party stepped up its efforts, largely under the direction of Wolfe. In early 1928, he drew up a twenty-page outline of a presentation against Trotsky, along with a covering note requesting reports from branch meetings on how members voted on anti-Trotsky motions.[5]

At a February 1928 CEC plenum, Wolfe gave an hour-long presentation on the fight in the Russian party, and the plenum approved a two-and-a-half-page motion against the Russian opposition. This was not aimed at any

2 The scholarship on this is vast. On the Third Period, examples include: Draper 1972b; Kozlov 1990; Kozlov and Weitz 1989; McDermott 1995; McIlroy and Campbell 2002; Weitz 1990. On the impact of the turn on the internal factional situation of the Russian CP, see, for example: Deutscher 1959, Chapter 6; Gorinov and Taskunov 1991; Lewin 1974, Chapter 1. See Worley 2004 for a collection of studies on the Third Period in different countries.

3 One of few recent examinations of the Third Period and the American party is Ryan 2004.

4 On Pepper's return, see minutes of Political Committee number 27, 19 March 1928, in Lovestone papers, box 225, folder 11. See also unsigned draft Comintern letter to Political Committee, 6 March 1928, in Comintern archives, 515:1:1228, a version of which was read into the above minutes; see also Sakmyster 2012, Chapter 9.

5 For Engdahl's criticisms, see 'L' [J. Louis Engdahl] to Central Executive Committee, 17 February 1928; see also the official response by Wolfe, 12 March 1928, both in Comintern archives, 515:1:1253. On Wolfe's outline, see Bertram D. Wolfe to District Organizers [February 1928?], with attachment, in Comintern archives, 515:1:1358.

particular member of the leadership, but to keep the party in line with the broader Comintern effort against Trotsky. Cannon recalls feeling uneasy about the motion and not voting, even though Dunne urged him to. Perhaps because the point was interrupted with a discussion on the situation in the mine workers' union,[6] nobody seemed to pay attention to Cannon's lack of enthusiasm. The Canadian Communist representative to the plenum, Maurice Spector, evidently also had qualms about the situation in the Russian party. He and Cannon secretly shared their concerns, although with no plans of doing anything about them.[7]

The Sixth Congress of the Communist International

The Communist International held its Sixth Congress in Moscow from 17 July to 1 September 1928, four years after the Fifth Congress. Stephen F. Cohen described the Congress as 'in reality the occasion of two congresses'. The official purpose of the Congress was to finalise a programme for the Comintern. As head of the Comintern and author of its draft programme, Bukharin dominated this congress. Yet with Trotsky expelled from the Russian party and in exile in Alma-Ata, Stalin (and, more openly, his allies such as Lozovsky and Vissarion Lominadze) turned against Bukharin and his allies in a 'corridor congress'. As Trotsky observed in 1929, 'Outwardly, the leadership seemed to belong to Bukharin … His domination seemed complete. And in the meanwhile everybody knows that the real influence of Bukharin on the Congress was next to nothing'. At the close of the Congress, Bukharin was still in formal control of the Comintern, but Stalin was ascendant.[8]

6 Most likely, this was the 'Pittston Mine War' in Northern Pennsyvania in early 1928, which erupted in violence between pro- and anti-Lewis forces in the UMWA. Several dissidents were murdered, and others were charged with the death of a pro-Lewis 'bodyguard'; see Howard 2004, pp. 38–43; see also 'Workers Party Statement on Murder of Alex Campbell and Peter Riley', 28 February 1928, in Howard 2004, pp. 225–6.

7 See minutes of CEC Plenum, Seventh Session, 7 February 1927, in Comintern archives, 515:1:1256; the minutes, strangely, do not list the voting of the motion. See Cannon 1962, p. 185; Draper 1986, pp. 323–4; Palmer 2007, p. 323. According to Bryan Palmer, Spector nursed doubts about the Comintern leadership going back to the failed German revolution of 1923, although he did not become a Trotskyist until much later; see Palmer 2005, pp. 103–6. Others, for example Gary O'Brien, argue that 'From 1924 to 1928, Spector used his position as editor of *The Worker* and party chairman to advance Trotsky's ideas and defend the Left Opposition as best he could'; O'Brien 1974, pp. 4, 7.

8 Cohen 1980, pp. 291–2; Trotsky 1974a, p. 260.

This was the backdrop against which the American delegates continued their factional struggle. While the letters by American delegates indicate that all sides had some clue of the broader shift going on, there was no clear guide and each faction had to manoeuvre to better position itself. After some finagling by Engdahl in Moscow, the American Communists received 20 delegates to the Congress; other Americans then in Moscow, including several black members, were given fraternal (non-voting) status. About the only thing the faction-riven delegation could agree on was voting Foster and Lovestone to both the Congress Presidium and the Senioren Convent, which comprised leading members of the various delegations. (The same meeting also voted Cannon to the programme commission). Even before the Congress began, the Foster and Cannon groups unsuccessfully put forward a motion in the delegation assailing Lovestone as a rightist and calling for an American Commission.[9]

The Foster-Cannon groups submitted a common document for the Congress, 'The Right Danger in the American Party', which used the rhetoric of the developing 'left' turn in the Comintern to attack Lovestone. 'The main danger in the American Party comes from the right', the document began, contrasting this to the 'leftward drift of the masses'. It claimed that US capitalism was 'about to reach the apex of growth' that would reinforce 'a process of widespread and general radicalization among the most exploited sections of the workers'. Somewhat disingenuously, given Foster's historic positions and the experience of Passaic, the document attacked the Lovestone faction for its supposed 'failure to orientate towards new unions and the organization of the unorganized' and 'resistance to orientation of active struggle against [John L.] Lewis machine and for building new unions in the mining industry'. It also accused the leadership of 'opportunist mistakes in the election campaign',

9 The wrangling over the number of delegates is described in various letters by Engdahl, in Comintern archives, 515:1:1252, and is summarised in his letter to the Central Executive Committee, 22 February 1928, in Comintern archives, 515:1:1253; for the delegates, see [J. Louis Engdahl?] to the Mandate Commission, 3 July 1928, in Comintern archives, 515:1:1244 and J. Louis Engdahl to the Mandate Commission, 11 July 1928, in Comintern archives, 515:1:1248. A leading black Communist, Lovett Fort-Whiteman, was a voting delegate; Black Communists Roy Mahoney, James Ford, Harry Haywood, William Paterson, Edward Doty and Carl Jones were all present as well in various capacities, including students. The Minutes of the American Delegation are in Comintern archives, 515:1:1244; see description of the meeting in Cannon supporter's letter: Manny [Gomez?] to Marty [Abern?] and Max [Shachtman?], 8 July 1928; and an unnamed Lovestone supporter's letter, 15 July 1928, both in Comintern archives, 515:1:1248. (Cannon had not yet arrived in Moscow by the time of the meeting). See voting of commissions in Minutes of the Bureau Meeting of the American Delegation, 16 July 1928, in Comintern archives, 515:1:1244.

'opportunist mistakes in labor party work', 'failure to build the T.U.E.L.', 'pacifist and petty-bourgeois liberal tendencies in the anti-war and anti-imperialist work', 'underestimation and false conception of work among Negro masses', and other right-wing deviations.[10]

While the Cannon and Foster groups were working closely again, their leaders' control was weakening. Among Foster's faction, Bittelman was more prominent, reflecting not only his role as primary author of the 'Right Danger' document, but tensions over Foster's leadership style and the clash between a growing Comintern emphasis on organising new unions and Foster's historic advocacy of 'boring from within'. Cannon's problem was different. He had been ground down by the endless factionalism, and was disenchanted with the complex situation in the Russian party. According to a post-Congress letter by Dunne, Gomez and other co-factionalists, Cannon had 'signed the ["Right Danger"] document only after the greatest pressure had been exerted by us and after Dunne had agreed to withdraw as the nominee for candidate on the E.C.C.I. and we had agreed to support him (Jim)'. Nonetheless, Cannon had 'continued to resist and held back throughout the fight' and 'compromised the entire fight by remaining away from group meetings and refusing to take any leadership'. Frustrated, Cannon's supporters decided to support Dunne and Bittelman as ECCI candidates instead.[11]

This set the stage for the factional dispute. Foster and Cannon's supporters attacked Lovestone and Pepper for being rightists and for overestimating the strength of American imperialism. Lovestone and his allies stressed their support for the Comintern's leadership (Bukharin) and its analysis. Thus, Dunne described American capitalism undergoing a 'sharpening of class conflicts', predicted massive class struggle, and advocated 'the building of new unions in heavy industry'. Pepper, for his part, denounced Cannon and Foster supporters for having 'a basically different analysis of American capitalism and its role in the general world situation' than Bukharin's report, and in a lengthy exposition, explained the continuing growth, not decline, of American capitalism.

10 James P. Cannon, William Z. Foster, William F. Dunne, Alex Bittelman, J.W. Johnstone, Manuel Gomez and George Siskin, 'The Right Danger in the American Party' [Summer 1928], in Comintern archives, 515:1:1246. The most accessible version is serialised in the first four issues of *Militant*, 1 November and 1 December 1928; 1 January, and 15 January 1929.

11 Bill Dunne, C.A. Hathaway, D.A. Gorman, Sam Don, Max Salzman, Harry Haywood and Manuel Gomez, to 'Dear Comrades', 31 August 1928, in Comintern archives, 515:1:1248; Palmer 2007, pp. 321–2. See Trotsky 1974a. On tensions within the Foster group, see Bittelman, 'Things I Have Learned', folder 17, pp. 513–14.

Cannon predicted 'big objective possibilities' for American Communists and denounced Lovestone's 'over-cautious attitude' in the face of mass struggle and described his leadership as embodying the 'right danger'. This argument was continued throughout the Congress. The only novelty was that since the Comintern had begun to emphasise the 'Negro question', the two factions blamed each other for neglecting this issue, while several black Communists attacked factionalism itself for displacing work on fighting black oppression.[12]

Judging from the factional letters in the Comintern archives, each faction attempted to court the Comintern leadership, particularly Stalin and Bukharin. All agreed, as a Lovestone supporter put it, 'the Right wing danger ... is the main danger and so-called right wingers are not very popular at the present time'. Lovestone and the majority of the American leadership enjoyed the support of Bukharin and, apparently, Stalin. Lovestone bragged of a private meeting with Stalin, who said that Foster 'did not grasp political questions' and who 'asked me whether Foster ever reads any books'. (Lovestone responded: 'yes, some, but that he does not study any M[arxist] L[eninist] literature').[13]

According to Lovestone's circulars, the Cannon-Foster opposition 'tried to play upon differences real and imaginary between Steel [Stalin] and Book [Bukharin], hoping to win the former against the latter'. This reflected 'corridor' gossip of a break between the two Soviet leaders. Since it served both Stalin and Bukharin's interest to hide the growing split between their supporters, the Russian party issued a public declaration of support for Bukharin.[14]

For their part, the Foster and Cannon opposition continued to describe Lovestone's leadership as right wing. They pushed for an American Commission and continued to court support from the Comintern leadership; Foster secured an interview with Stalin, and Bittelman and Manuel Gomez obtained one with Stalin's ally, V.M. Molotov. Furthermore, they were bold enough to attack

12 Japanese Communist Sen Katayama, a long-time advocate of paying attention to black oppression in the US, blamed factionalism itself for the 'criminal neglect of the Negroes on the part of the American Party'. The fight on the 'Negro question' is examined in later chapters. On the delegates' jousting, see, for example, Communist International 1928c, pp. 772–3 (Ford); pp. 781–2 (Dunne); pp. 785–8 (Pepper); pp. 811–12 (Jones); pp. 840–1 (Cannon); pp. 844–6 (Bittelman); pp. 847–9 (Weinstone); pp. 850–1 (Wicks); pp. 856–7 (Katayama); pp. 875–6 (Dixon [Browder]); pp. 920–2 (Foster); pp. 934–6 (Lovestone).

13 Unknown Lovestone supporter to 'Dear Johnny', 21 July 1928; [Lovestone] to 'Dear Comrades', 6 August 1928; in Comintern archives, 515:1:1248.

14 Lovestone factional circular, 28 July 1928; see also letter from Jack Johnstone to 'Dear Comrades', 14 September 1928, complaining of Lovestoneite attacks on Minority for supposedly spreading rumours of divisions in the Russian party; both in Comintern archives, 515:1:1248.

Bukharin for supporting Lovestone. 'Comrade Bucharin made no mention whatever of the right danger in our Party', they wrote to the presidium, declaring their 'disagreement with the estimate of the American situation as given in the closing remarks by Comrade Bucharin'. Johnstone read this letter during the Congress proceedings. This approach seemed to pay off. A minority factional letter bragged in early August that Bukharin had backed off from his support for Lovestone and boasted of an interview with Stalin in which he 'was decidedly against the Lovestone group and in favour of us'.[15]

Concurrent with the Congress, the Comintern's Anglo-American Commission (which included Foster and Lovestone in addition to its twenty normal members) met, in part to discuss the criticisms of Bukharin's report. The non-American members seemed fatigued with the entire business. 'Long discussions haven't helped', Petrovsky quipped during a debate about speaking times, 'maybe short ones will'. That the meetings often started at 9pm, after Congress sessions, probably did not endear the American comrades to the commission, which included Lozovsky, Katayama and Ewert. At another point, Petrovsky argued against translating a huge number of documents, noting (in reference to the 26-page 'Right Wing Danger' document by Bittelman) that even were it translated, 'I give my word of honour ... comrades will read only the last two pages containing the final proposals'.[16]

Pepper and the Fight Against Bukharin

The official transcription of the debate in the Congress makes clear that while American delegates attacked one another, the American party served as a foil for Stalin's attacks on Bukharin. This was done obliquely, with pro-Stalin delegates Lozovsky and Lominadze attacking Bukharin (and Lovestone) allies such as Ewert and Pepper. According to historians, the Hungarian gained the

15 On painting the Lovestone group as rightist, see Alex Bittelman, Bill Dunne and Jack Johnstone to Bukharin and Molotov, 10 September 1928. The same Comintern folder contains the undated statements by the Lovestone majority and the Cannon-Foster minority on Bukharin's report; unsigned Foster factional letter, 2 August 1928; all in Comintern archives, 515:1:1248. See also Johnstone's speech at the 45th Session of the Sixth Congress, 29 August 1928, in which he read a statement signed by himself, Bill Dunne, Manuel Gomez, George Siskind, Schachmo Epstein and Alex Bittelman, in Comintern archives, 495:37:19. On the interviews with Stalin and Molotov, see Shipman 1993, p. 172 (Shipman was Gomez's real name.)

16 Protocol of the Enlarged Anglo-American Secretariat, 7 August 1928, in Comintern archives, 495:72:38.

nickname 'Der Tripper' (the clap). In his memoirs, Bittelman recalled how his faction had sensed this anti-Bukharin turn from 'the lobbies'—which 'was enough, of course, to encourage us to take a more or less challenging attitude to Bukharin—the head of the Communist International'.[17]

In a lengthy speech, Pepper defended Bukharin's presentation, attacked the Foster-Cannon opposition, and laid out a lengthy exposition of the unique nature of American capitalism. In his subsequent summary, Bukharin defended the positions of the Lovestone-Pepper leadership without naming them. He declared America 'a country that occupies an exceptional position in world economics', that 'the international possibilities of American capitalism' were not 'exhausted', and noted that he did 'not entertain hopes of a revolutionary situation arising in the United States in the near future' because 'in no country in the world is capitalism so strong as it is in the United States, where it has reached its zenith'. He also attacked the notion that the weakness of the AFL meant that 'we should abandon our work in the reactionary trade unions'.[18]

This apparently gave the Lovestone-Pepper leadership the Comintern's approval; in reality, Stalin's allies waged a sustained attack against Lovestone. Lozovsky (an ally of Foster) dedicated a significant portion of his speech to arguing that it was necessary to build new unions, including in the US, and that Lovestone and Pepper 'regarded the reactionary American Federation of Labour as a fetish'. Lozovsky singled out Pepper as 'occupy[ing] a special place in this muddle' for supposedly arguing that 'American capitalism is very strong, that the American working class is very poorly organised, that the party is weak, and that there are many difficulties in general'. Lozovsky ridiculed Pepper as the 'muddler of two hemispheres'.[19]

Lominadze was even harsher. He savaged Pepper for the 'dark perspective' that 'everything is hindering us' and that 'of perspectives, there are none at all'. In fact, Lominadze asserted that 'in America we have all the premises to make our Communist Party, which at the present time is a sect ... into a powerful force' because there were 'more favourable premises for the growth of the Communist Party in America than in a number of other countries'. For good measure, he also attacked Pepper for opposing Comintern policy in China, comparing his position to the Mensheviks' position in 1905. Later, in a

17 For the anti-Pepper campaign at the Congress, see Palmer 2007, p. 329; for the attacks on Ewert, see Hornstein 1993, pp. 83–5; Bittelman, 'Things I Have Learned', folder 17, pp. 488–90.

18 Communist International 1928c, pp. 869–74.

19 Communist International 1928c, pp. 913–16. Lozovsky repeated these criticisms in Lozovsky 1928b, p. 7.

discussion on the colonial question, Lominadze once again assailed the 'opportunism, lack of principle and narrow political sectarianism which Comrade Pepper personifies'. 'No one has ever seen or will see Pepper contend with any of the leading comrades … He always agrees with those who are his seniors even if a minute ago he defended an utterly different viewpoint'.[20]

These attacks worried Lovestone's supporters—and delighted his opponents, who celebrated that Lominadze 'took Pepper over his knee and gave him a thorough thrashing' and 'tore Pepper's position to pieces, stating that he underestimated the leftward drift of the workers'. No wonder one Lovestone factional letter from late July complained that Foster and Cannon 'have many friends here—some are not their friends but enemies of Pepper'.[21]

In itself, the Congress did not change much for the American party. In fact, as Bryan Palmer put it, American Communists were now 'more divided, and more precariously perched' vis-à-vis the Comintern than before. For the rank-and-file American Communist, Lovestone must have seemed firmly in control of the party, with this power based on his loyalty to Moscow—a situation Lovestone exploited. In December 1928, for example, a plenary meeting of the CEC passed, along factional lines, a motion criticising Foster's group and asserting that it 'accept[ed] all decisions of the Sixth World Congress of the Comintern without reservations'.[22]

Cannon and Trotsky

The most immediate fallout from the Congress was that Cannon, along with Spector, was won to the Left Opposition after reading a document by Trotsky. Trotsky and other expelled Left Oppositionists appealed their expulsions to the Congress, as was their right according to Comintern rules. They also submitted

20 Communist International 1928c, pp. 932–3, pp. 1461–2. Lovestone spoke immediately after Lominadze. He attacked many Foster-Cannon supporters, as well as Lozovsky for 'act[ing] in a factional, prejudiced manner against our C.E.C.' He did not criticise Lominadze, although it appears that he was preparing to when his time ran out; Communist International 1928c, pp. 934–8.

21 Unknown Lovestone supporter to 'Dear Johnny', 21 July 1928; Unknown Foster-Cannon supporter to 'Dear Comrades', 2 August 1928; Lovestone factional letter, 29 July 1928; all in Comintern archives, 515:1:1248.

22 Palmer 2005, p. 117. See Political Committee minutes No. 75, 25 December 1928, in Lovestone papers, box 220, folder 5. The only significant *official* change for the American Party was in viewing the oppression of black Americans as a national (and not racial) issue. This is examined in a subsequent chapter.

Trotsky's attack on the draft Comintern programme. According to Bryan Palmer, Cannon's biographer, there is still disagreement as to whether translated portions were circulated by mistake to the programme commission (Cannon's view) or more broadly as an anti-Bukharin manoeuvre by Stalin (as Isaac Deutscher implied). Harry Wicks, at the time a British Communist in the Lenin School and later a Trotskyist, recalled that it was carefully circulated to students, heads of delegations, and members of the programme commission.[23]

However it was circulated, the document, in the form of a criticism of the draft programme, attacked the entire basis of the post-Lenin Comintern, exposing the distance between revolutionary Bolshevism in Lenin's time and Stalin and Bukharin's policies. For Trotsky, 'socialism in one country' was a *betrayal* of Communism that would only result in more *defeats*, such as the aborted revolution in China. The Comintern's schizophrenic course over the last few years, the incessant attacks on people who had been leading Bolsheviks until recently, and the theoretical muddle in which it was all enveloped, Trotsky argued, was not a failure of analysis, but a programmatic reflection of the degeneration of the Russian Revolution itself.

In his memoirs, Bittelman claimed that 'how [Cannon] came to embrace Trotzkyism, I shall never be able to fully understand'; he believed that Cannon's support for Trotsky had nothing to do with the fundamental political issues, but came about because he felt mistreated by the Comintern and thought he deserved to be the leader of the American party. Since Spector was elected to the ECCI at the Congress, and the Cannon-Foster faction clearly believed power was in its grasp—in fact, Lominadze had favourably cited Cannon in his intervention at the Congress—Bittelman's explanation rings false.[24]

Rather, Cannon's decision—which he must have known would have resulted in his complete separation from the movement he had made his life's work, and perhaps isolation from most of his friends and comrades—was a *political* decision. Whatever opportunities Cannon and Spector enjoyed in their parties and the Comintern, they had already harboured doubts over the course

23 For the rejection of their appeal, see 'Resolution of the Sixth Comintern Congress on the Appeal of Trotsky, Sapronov, and Others', 1 September 1928, in Degras 1956, II, pp. 548–9; on the document's circulation, see Palmer 2007, p. 512 n. 16; Deutscher 1959, pp. 444–5; Wicks 1992, p. 102. Harry Wicks, the British Trotskyist, is not the same as the American H. M. Wicks. Much has been made of the fact that the document was hand-numbered and had to be returned; however, many documents circulated within the Comintern apparatus were treated similarly.

24 Bittelman, 'Things I Have Learned', folder 15, p. 509; Communist International 1928c, p. 932.

of the world Communist movement. As Palmer has pointed out, for Cannon and Spector, 'Trotsky's critique was so powerful because it brought together a forceful synthesis of what was wrong, programmatically, in the policies of the Communist International'. Cannon saw his support for Trotsky as a continuation of his original *political* allegiance to the international Communist movement, even as it led to his *organisational* break with the actual movement led by Stalin. Cannon recalled: 'It was clear as daylight that Marxist truth was on the side of Trotsky'.[25]

Cannon continued that he and Spector 'made a compact there and then ... that we would come back home and begin a struggle under the banner of Trotskyism'. Cannon's support for Trotsky was not so hidden as he had thought, since, according to Palmer, the Russian secret police supposedly began a dossier on Cannon. H. M. Wicks, a pro-Lovestone delegate, accused Cannon of lifting his denunciation of Pepper from Trotsky's document. Rather than fight at the Congress—which they thought would have been pointless—they smuggled Trotsky's document out of Russia. Upon returning to the US, Cannon first convinced his partner Rose Karsner, and then recruited a small number of his co-factionalists, including Abern, Shachtman and Swabeck. Soon rumours of Cannon's support for Trotsky circulated among the party's leadership.[26]

Cannon's Trotskyism provided Lovestone with a way to demonstrate his loyalty to Moscow, as well as weaken his factional opponents through guilt-by-association. This posed a threat to Foster; after temporising, Foster and his allies expelled Cannon and his supporters from their joint caucus and raised charges of Trotskyism against Cannon, Abern and Shachtman in the Political Committee. The three were removed from their positions in the ILD.[27]

25 Palmer 2005; Cannon 1972, p. 50.

26 Cannon 1972, p. 50; Communist International 1928c, p. 851; Palmer 2005, p. 115; in *I Confess*, Gitlow claimed that Bukharin had informed Lovestone that Cannon had Trotskyist sympathies, but advised him to use this information later for factional advantage; in the same book, however, Gitlow claims Cannon's support for Trotsky was 'a complete surprise to us'; Gitlow 1939, pp. 491, 558.

27 Minutes of Political Committee No. 58, 16 October 1928, in Lovestone papers, box 226, folder 1. These contain Foster, Bittelman and Aronberg's charges against Cannon, Abern and Shachtman, as well as the measures taken against the three. On the Foster group's moves against Cannon, see Foster caucus letter, undated [October 1928?] on discussions with Cannon, in Cannon papers, reel 47, frame 706; 'For a Correct Bolshevist Line in the American Party Against the Right Danger, and Against the Cannon Trotsky Opposition', document by Foster minority, appended to Political Committee minutes No. 70, 23 November 1928, in Lovestone papers, box 226, folder 4; Lovestone letter to ECCI,

Lovestone and his allies, relishing the fiasco among their opponents, called a 'trial' in the Political Committee over several meetings in October. In a statement, Cannon, Shachtman and Abern defended the 'Right Danger in the American Party' document, declaring that 'the present leadership of the Party, mechanically imposed upon the Party by the E.C.C.I. against the will of the membership, is a consciously developing right wing, whose course and actions are all in the direction of undermining the position of the Party in the class struggle'. More importantly, they proclaimed their support for Trotsky's Left Opposition and its struggle against the Stalinist degeneration of the Soviet Union and the Communist movement. Trotsky and the Opposition had 'been fighting for the unity of the Comintern and all its sections on the basis of the victory of Leninism'. (This declaration made Cannon's group the only tendency in the faction-ridden party that fought for an explicit *political* programme, not just party control).[28]

In the end, Cannon and his allies were expelled. In late October, the Political Committee passed a motion requiring that each current or past 'prominent member' of 'that section of the Opposition hitherto known as the Cannon group' for a 'statement on the document' by Cannon, Abern and Shachtman. Those who did not reply to the satisfaction of Lovestone were subject to expulsion. In addition, the party leadership convened meetings throughout

stamped 19 October 1928, in Comintern archives, 515:1:1241; [Tom?] Bell, 'The Situation in the Workers' (Communist) Party of America', submitted to the Comintern Secretariat, 5 December 1928, in Comintern archives, 515:1:1233. On the purge of the ILD, see Volksy [Stanislav Pestovsky] to 'Comrade Engdahl', 26 October 1928, and Engdahl's response, 1 November 1928, both in Comintern archives, 515:1:1252. On 20 October 1928, Cannon, Shachtman and Abern submitted a resignation letter to the ILD executive committee that obliquely referred to 'circumstances [that] arose on October 16, 1928 which obliged us to discontinue our duties'. On 25 October 1928, the party Political Committee met and voted to demand the resignation of the three Trotskyists from the ILD; see minutes No. 62, in Lovestone papers, box 226, folder 3; On 3 November 1928, the ILD national committee met, including Cannon, Shachtman and Abern, to finalise this purge. Although the now-expelled Trotskyists fought to maintain positions on the ILD executive committee, the political basis for the purge was avoided in the minutes. See minutes of the International Labor Defense National Committee, 3 November 1928, in Comintern archives, 515:1:1529. The Anglo-American Secretariat and the MOPR leadership adopted a 'Resolution on the Situation in the ILD of the U.S.A.' (19 November 1928) on the best way to purge the ILD of pro-Cannon and pro-Trotsky elements; in Comintern archives, 495:72:51a.

28 The 'trial' is contained in the Political Committee minutes Nos. 59–63; the combined minutes are more than 130 pages long; Statement by J.P. Cannon, Martin Abern and Max Shachtman, attached to Political Committee minutes No. 63, 27 October 1928, in Shachtman papers, reel 2.

the branches and the foreign-language federations to denounce Cannon and his supporters under the cloak of 'the struggle against the Right Danger and Trotskyism'. Thus, when the Connecticut district leadership had not endorsed the expulsions by early December, the Political Committee passed a motion (along factional lines) 'tak[ing] note' of this.[29]

Lovestone drew up guidelines on how to deal with members sympathetic to Trotsky or Cannon. 'Leading and responsible Party members and non-proletarian elements' would be expelled, while 'rank and file proletarian elements, who evidence lack of clarity on the issue and hesitate on it' would only be 'argued with and persuaded', unless they 'actively organize for Trotsky', in which case they too would be expelled. In all, some hundred members were expelled, either for open support of Cannon or for questioning his expulsion. For example, in November, when more than a dozen Minnesota Communists (including William F. Dunne's younger brother Vincent) objected to the expulsions, they were also expelled. Konikow was finally expelled when she refused to come to New York on short notice and defend herself in front of the Political Committee. Swabeck and Albert Glotzer were expelled in late November. In Canada, Spector was quickly expelled from the Canadian party after he refused to endorse Cannon's expulsion at a meeting of the Canadian Political Committee.[30]

29 Political Committee minutes No. 63, 27 October 1928, in Shachtman papers, reel 2; Shipman 1993, p. 174. Copies of the letters sent to 'prominent' Cannon supporters—both categories were interpreted broadly—can be found in Comintern archives, 515:1:1319. The series of meetings is described in detail in Palmer 2007, pp. 338–42. Discussion of the letters can be found in Political Committee Minutes No. 67, 8 November 1928, in Lovestone papers, box 226, folder 4. On the anti-Cannon, anti-Trotsky campaign, see, for example, Jay Lovestone to All Language Fraction Secretaries, 28 December 1928, in Comintern archives, 515:1:1329. The districts often used the Cannon expulsions as a basis to purge members thought to be sympathetic to Trotsky or queasy about the expulsions; see, for example, PolCom Minutes of District 7 [Detroit], 6 December 1928, in Comintern archives, 515:1:1408; Polcom Minutes District 5 [Buffalo], 1 November 1928, in Comintern archives, 515:1:1398; Minutes of Investigation Committee of Cannon-Trotsky Affair District 3 [Philadelphia], 3 November 1928, in Comintern archives, 515:1:1394; Minutes of the [Boston] District Control Commission, 17 November 1928, in Comintern archives, 515:1:1384; Political Committee minutes No. 72, 5 December 1928, in Lovestone papers, box 226, folder 5.

30 Jay Lovestone to All District Organizers, 1 December 1928, in Comintern archives, 515:1:1329. This letter reflects a motion from the Political Committee meeting No. 70, 23 November 1928, in Lovestone papers, box 226, folder 4; for a description of the expulsions, see 22 November 1928 statement by Arne Swabeck and Albert Glotzer (two Cannon supporters in the Communist youth organisation); Cannon, in a 20 December 1928 letter to Glotzer, claimed that some 70 members had been expelled from the US party and

Immediately after their expulsion, Cannon and his co-thinkers began to organise. With financial assistance from Eastman, they published a newspaper, the *Militant*, on 15 November, which contained 'a statement to American Communists' by Cannon, Abern and Shachtman titled 'For the Russian Opposition!' While openly supporting Trotsky's fight against the degeneration of the Russian Revolution, they appealed against their expulsion. Like the earlier 'trial', it was useful for the Lovestone leadership to waive the bloody shirt of Trotskyism against their opponents. At a 17 December CEC plenum, they were allowed to speak for two hours, before their appeals were denied. Soon, they allied themselves with Konikow's Boston supporters, and organised an American branch of the Left Opposition. In May 1929, the Communist League of America (Opposition) held its first convention, representing some 100 members determined to regain entry into the official party.[31]

After the expulsion of Cannon, Bittelman objected that Lovestone favoured a 'campaign of extermination and expulsion of the minority from the Party' by equating the Foster faction's objections to Lovestone with Trotskyism. Indeed, the Lovestone leadership continued to use Cannon's support for Trotsky as a cudgel against Foster and to bolster its position in the Comintern. For example, in a cable to Moscow shortly after the expulsions, Lovestone underlined that the *Militant* was running the Foster-Cannon document on the 'Right Danger'; 'Despite increasing Trotskyist menace', Lovestone wrote, 'Fosterites declare CEC greater menace than Trotskyism'. He continued: 'Some Fosterite functionaries developing dangerous tendency against expulsion [of] Cannonites [and] for tolerance and quote freedom [of] expression [for] opinions [of] Trotskyism unquote'. He ended with a request that the ECCI send a cable 'demand[ing]

about a dozen from the Canadian party; both in Glotzer papers, box 1. On the Minneapolis expulsions, see *Militant*, 1 December 1928. On Konikow, see Alex Bail to Antoinette Konikow, 30 October 1928 and Dr. A.F. Konikow to Jay Lovestone, undated, both reprinted in Konikow's *Bulletin*, December 1928, in Shachtman papers, reel 1; Alex Bail to Jay Lovestone, 2 November 1928, in Comintern archives, 515:1:1332; on Swabeck and Glotzer's expulsion, see Political Committee minutes No. 71, 1 December 1928, in Lovestone papers, box 226, folder 5; On Spector's expulsion, see report by [Tom] Bell, 'Expulsion of Comrade Spector from Canadian C.P. for Trotskyist Activities', appended to minutes of meeting of Anglo-American Secretariat, 22 December 1928, in Comintern archives, 495:72:43; *Militant*, 15 November and 1 December 1928; see also Angus 1981, Chapter 11; Palmer 2005, pp. 126–32; Rodney 1968, pp. 142–4. Spector's 6 November 1928 statement in support of Trotsky is reprinted in Angus 1981, pp. 356–62. According to one source, 'no more than seven comrades were expelled with' Spector; O'Brien 1974, p. 9.

31 Cannon 1972, pp. 54–8, 67; for Cannon's speech at the CEC plenum see *Militant*, 1 January 1929; Alexander 1991, p. 766.

Fosterites abandon their reservations' about the Sixth Congress thesis and 'acknowledge [the] correctness [of] polsect decisions' and 'repudiate common platform with Cannon'. In a letter to the ECCI, Lovestone reported on 'the existence of [an] additional Trotskyist group within the Party, working by Cannon's instruction within the Foster-Bittleman [sic] Opposition'. Foster and Bittelman complained in turn to the ECCI that Lovestone refused to publish their anti-Trotsky statement and 'carrie[d] on widespread campaign against us as Trotskyites'.[32]

The party's leadership reacted to Cannon with fury, fearing both the growth of an American Trotskyist group and the wrath of Stalin. A cable from the Comintern supported 'energetic measures taken against leaders of Trotskyist opposition', while calling 'on all workers who formerly supported the opposition to repudiate it publicly and definitely'.[33]

The American leadership slandered Cannon and his followers, and forbade comrades from talking with 'Trotskyites'. Cannon recalled: 'A wall of ostracism separated us from the party members', as 'people whom we had known and worked with for years became strangers to us overnight'. Most painful for Cannon was the hostility of William F. Dunne, who spent the period after the Sixth Congress in China and Mongolia. In late 1928, Lozovsky sent a cable to the American party containing a statement by Dunne ('now in Hankow') attacking Cannon. In April 1929, Dunne himself—no doubt under pressure because of his close alliance with Cannon and the Trotskyism of his brothers—sent a cable to the American party, declaring that the 'only connection of Cannon hyphen Trotzky counter revolutionary group with CPUSA is through the fist of our party under whose blows this collection [of] anti workingclass elements is disintegrating'.[34]

---

32 Minutes of Political Committee No. 68, 14 November 1928, in Lovestone papers, box 226, folder 4; Undated [Fall 1928?] cable from Lovestone [to ECCI?], in Comintern archives, 515:1:949; Lovestone, 'International Connections of Trotskyism in America', undated [December 1928?]; see also Lovestone cable, 'For Information of Political Secretariat', 7 December 1928; Foster, Bittelman, Aronberg, cable to Piatnitsky, 24 November 1928, all in Comintern archives, 515:1:1243. See also J. Louis Engdahl, 'American (U.S.A.) Party Fights Right Dangers and Trotskyism' [1928] that not only attacks the Foster group for supposedly being soft on Cannon and Trotsky, but also criticises Cannon for having (briefly) studied law and Weinstone for having graduated from university—without pointing out that Lovestone had attended the same law school as Cannon and the same university as Weinstone!

33 See undated [November 1928?] cables from Moscow, in Comintern archives, 515:1:1254.

34 Cannon 1944, pp. 63–4; cable from Lozovsky contained in Political Committee minutes No. 72, 5 December 1928, in Lovestone papers, box 226, folder 5; cable from Bill Dunne to WoPat [Workers' Party] New York, 28 April 1929, in Comintern archives, 515:1:1248.

In addition to shunning Cannon, the leadership carried out what Gitlow later termed a 'campaign of violence' that 'repeated the stupidest errors of the most provincial police department'. In Cleveland, Lovestone supporter Israel Amter, the district organiser, tried to prevent Cannon's holding a meeting. In New York City, party members attacked an all-woman *Militant* sales team outside the party's offices in Union Square. A block away at Irving Plaza, Manuel Gomez attended a meeting of his former factional ally to 'break it up'.[35]

Stachel, the Lovestoneite organisational secretary of the New York branch, directed the efforts against Cannon. He organised the burglary of Cannon's flat, stealing Opposition correspondence and subscription records. Reports of the correspondence were circulated throughout the party, as well as to the Canadian and Comintern leaderships. Branch and district leaders were given lists of people who had corresponded with Cannon, with the aim of purging anybody suspected of supporting him.[36]

These reports indicate the importance of Cannon's conversion to Trotskyism for the international Left Opposition. By late 1928, Trotsky and his followers, worn down after years of Stalinist attacks and slander, with its leaders in prison or exile, greeted the news joyfully. 'Overnight, the whole picture, the whole perspective of the struggle changed', Cannon later recalled, since 'the news of our fight reached the Russian comrades in all corners of the prisons and exile camps inspiring them with new hope and new energy to persevere in the struggle'. The *Militant*, a legal Trotskyist paper, was useful in publicising the Left Opposition's cause, helping to lay the basis for the sympathising groups internationally.[37]

35 Gitlow 1939, pp. 491–2; Cannon 1944, p. 70; *Militant*, 15 December 1928; Shipman 1993, p. 174.

36 See Political Committee minutes No. 75, 25 December 1928, in Lovestone papers, box 226, folder 5. This meeting passed a series of disciplinary motions against people whose names were found in the correspondence. Stachel's report to the Political Committee is printed in Cannon 1992, pp. 562–3; on the burglary, see Taber 1997; examples of reports included Janet Cork [Ella Wolfe], 'Summary of Correspondence between Maurice Spector of Canada and James P. Cannon of the U.S.A.', stamped 28 January 1929, and Janet Cork, 'Summary of Correspondence, Local and International Connections of the Cannon Trotskyist Group' undated, both in Comintern archives, 515:1:1235; Lovestone letter to ECCI, 'International Connections of Trotskyism in America', undated [December 1928?], 515:1:1243; the correspondence with the districts in late 1928 and early 1929 contains several examples of urging local leaderships to investigate people on Cannon's mailing lists. Typescripts of a large selection of the correspondence (including Spector) are in Comintern archives, 515:1:1492.

37 Cannon 1944, pp. 61–2.

Cannon was optimistic. Unlike Trotskyist sympathisers in several countries, Cannon left the Communist Party with an organised group of supporters. And the lack of influence of the official Communist Party in American society meant that the party had less weight to throw against Cannon—a point that Trotsky underlined a year later. Furthermore, Cannon hoped to capitalise on disgruntlement over Lovestone's leadership. In November 1928, for example, Shachtman wrote to a comrade that they had 'established fairly good contacts with some of the best New York comrades, formerly in our group, upon whom we are exercising a growing influence'. One important contact was Hugo Oehler, who would be a leader of the 1929 Gastonia, North Carolina, textile strike. Cannon advised Oehler 'to remain in [the Communist] party; to endeavor to build a fraction therein; to establish contacts with certain comrades in the Gastonia field; to try to build his way up into party ranks'. A month later, Oehler 'stated that the party was demoralized' under Lovestone and 'was ripe for our work'.[38]

38 Max Shachtman to Al [Glotzer], 24 November 1928, in Glotzer papers, box 1, Shachtman file; Cannon to Young [Oehler], 13 August 1929, reprinted in Cannon 1981, p. 201; Minutes of the Communist League of America National Committee, 24 September and 28 September 1929, in Glotzer papers, box 1; Leon Trotsky to *Militant*, 19 October 1929, in Exile Papers of Leon Trotskii, bms Rus 13.1 9068-72.

CHAPTER 13

Lovestone Becomes a Lovestoneite, 1928–9

Late 1928 to early 1929 was Lovestone's apex. The anti-Trotsky campaign was integral to his tenure as party leader. Many of the leaders of the campaign would soon be purged themselves. By supporting Bukharin at the same time as Stalin was preparing an attack on the head of the Comintern, Lovestone sowed the seeds of his own downfall. Lovestone had genuine affinities to Bukharin, but he also miscalculated in his attempt to position himself with the Comintern leadership. Lovestone had attacked Lozovsky, Stalin's ally, for 'making a muddle of nearly everything he has touched', and at the last meeting of the Senioren Convent (comprising high-ranking Comintern leaders), Lovestone attacked the 'corridor congress' against Bukharin, compelling Stalin to deny any breach between the two Russian leaders. Meanwhile the campaign against the 'right danger' in the Comintern increased; Lovestone's fixation with Cannon—and his attacks on Foster and Bittelman—left him open to criticism as a 'rightist'.[1]

Engdahl, in a cable from Moscow, indicated 'general approval here [about] Cannon expulsion', but stressed that the 'party must emphasize more however [the] struggle against right danger while fighting Trotzkyism'. Some in the Comintern attacked the *Daily Worker*'s coverage of the expulsions as 'mostly selfpraise and going [to] ridiculous extremes'. Couching himself in Comintern rhetoric, Lovestone argued that fighting Cannon and Trotskyism was part of the fight against the 'right danger'. According to a motion by the leadership of the Young Workers' (Communist) League: 'In the American Party at the present time, the Right danger is represented sharply by the Trotskyists'. In response, the Anglo-American Secretariat drafted a letter, which argued that 'such an exaggeration of the Trotsky situation as contained in the Majority resolution conceals the basic Right danger' and 'shows that the League majority has not yet a critical attitude towards the Right mistakes of the Party'. As Foster and Zack echoed in 1929, 'The Majority considered Trotskyism as the crassest expression of the Right danger because it does not want and is incapable to struggle against real Right danger'. The issue was not whether Trotsky was a 'right' or 'left' danger, but if Lovestone had the confidence of Stalin.[2]

1 Draper 1986, p. 309.

2 Engdahl, undated [3 November 1928?] cable to WoPat [Workers' Party], in Comintern archives, 515:1:1254; 'Resolution of the National Executive Committee of the Young Workers'

In November 1928, the ECCI sent a letter to the American leadership, criticising the *Daily Worker*'s reporting on the Comintern's view of the American party. It attacked the 'interpretation that the [Sixth] Congress has expressly declared its confidence in the majority, in contrast to the minority'. The letter insisted: 'this is not so'. It reiterated the 'Right danger is the main danger for the American Party', and ordered that the upcoming national convention 'investigate the objective sources of the Right danger and the struggle against it'.[3]

In early 1929, the Comintern leadership indicated its displeasure with Lovestone through a draft 'Open Letter'. Written by Gusev, the draft on the surface was directed to the party leadership to help prepare for the party's upcoming Sixth National Convention. This was one of several sent to Communist Parties that were having conferences. According to the *Communist International* these conferences were to take place 'during a time of struggle against the right-wing danger and against conciliatory attitudes of the right-tendency'. The letter reiterated the Third Period prediction of 'a growth of a leftward trend in the masses of the American proletariat' and 'great class conflicts' in the near future. The party was 'still inadequately prepared' for this radicalisation because of factionalism 'devoid of any political class content' that had degenerated into 'a struggle without principles and at times unprincipled'. The letter underlined that 'the existing groups must be *smashed, smashed and broken at all costs*' to create a 'mass Communist Party of the American working class'. It reiterated the Sixth Congress's conclusion that such right-wing errors 'cannot be ascribed to the majority leadership alone'. Still, the draft signalled the Comintern's lack of faith in Lovestone—and Gusev's role in writing it no doubt highlighted what happened to leaderships deemed deficient by the Comintern.[4]

(Communist) League of America Against the Trotskyist Danger'; Draft letter from Anglo-American Secretariat to America [December 1928], both in Comintern archives, 495:72:51; W.Z. Foster and J. Zack, 'Statement on the Situation in the Communist Party of the United States of America' [Spring 1929], in Comintern archives, 495:72:57. The statement that Trotskyism was the 'crassest manifestation' of the 'Right danger' is originally from the call for the sixth convention of the party, printed in *Daily Worker*, 10 November 1928. See also Bittelman's 'statement for record' in Political Committee minutes No. 68, 14 November 1928, in Lovestone papers, box 226, folder 4.

3 Letter from Secretary of the ECCI to the CEC of the Workers' (Communist) Party of America, 21 November 1928, attached to Political Committee minutes No. 75, 25 December 1928, in Lovestone papers, box 226, folder 5.

4 Martinov 1929. Comrade Gussiev, draft of 'Open Letter to the Convention of the Workers' (Communist) Party of America', [February 1929], Lovestone papers, box 198, folder 11; also in Comintern archives, 515:1:1547. At this point, it was common for the ECCI to write 'Open Letters' to parties; *International Press Correspondence* carried several examples.

Although on the surface neutral, this letter threatened the legitimacy that had helped Lovestone maintain control of the party since 1925: that his faction was more loyal to the Comintern. When Wolfe, whom Lovestone had sent to Moscow to better represent his factional interests, read the letter, he raised such a ruckus that the Comintern presidium convened a one-hour extraordinary meeting. As Wolfe later told the tale, he was forced to speak in German because of poor translation, and, with a 40-degree fever, denounced the Open Letter as ultraleft and sectarian. After the speech, he recalled: 'People whom I had known for years looked as if they feared contact with me'.[5]

The final version criticised both factions for an 'utter depreciation of the leftward trend of the working masses in other capitalist countries', right-wing errors rooted in misjudging the relationship 'between the American and world financial systems', and a tendency to overestimate the autonomy of US imperialism. Foster's faction had 'under-estimat[ed] the Trotskyist danger' and had 'form[ed] factional alliances' with 'openly right wing elements'. Lovestone's faction, however, had 'shown a tendency to underestimate the radicalization as well as the process of differentiation in the ranks of the working class' and thus had 'entirely ignore[d] the Sixth Congress's resolution on the advent of the Third Period' and 'great[ly] overestimate[d] the economic might and the powerful technical development of the United States'. The letter proposed to decapitate the factions by dispatching Bittelman and Lovestone to Moscow, and recalling Pepper. The letter emphasised 'the absence of substantial differences on points of principle' and that the factionalism 'was in the main not based on principle'. In order for the party to grasp the opportunities posed by the radicalisation of the working class, the letter argued, 'the factional struggle must be unconditionally stopped'.[6]

Wolfe's reports from Moscow upset Lovestone and his allies in the US. Nonetheless, Lovestone tried to brave it out, believing that, since 90 percent of the upcoming convention's delegates supported his faction, he was in a strong position to 'reach a satisfactory understanding with Stalin'. With chutzpah,

5 Wolfe 1981, p. 345, pp. 451–2; Gitlow 1939, pp. 512–22. The motion to replace Engdahl with Wolfe was voted at the 1 December 1928 Political Committee meeting; interestingly, Wolfe was the only Lovestone supporter who opposed it. See Political Committee minutes No. 71, in Lovestone papers, box 226, folder 5.

6 'Open Letter to the Convention of the Workers' (Communist) Party of America', 7 February 1929, in Lovestone papers, box 217, folder 1; also in Comintern archives, 515:1:1547; The letter was published in *International Press Correspondence*, 1 March 1929, and later, in Gruber 1974, p. 226; Degras 1956, III, pp. 9–16. Pepper's precarious situation in the US, in relationship to the Comintern, is detailed in Sakmyster 2012, pp. 188–9.

Lovestone's supporters wielded the Open Letter against Foster's allies and attacked them for 'speculating from the very beginning on the differences real or imaginary between the Bookman [Bukharin] and the Steelman [Stalin]'. Foster's allies criticised Lovestone for having (in the words of the California district organiser) 'organized the membership to carry on an open fight against the Comintern'. Both factions sought to benefit from the power struggles in Moscow. According to Gomez, the factions agreed to postpone the convention for months to 'see how the power struggle in Russia would end', although no doubt they were also waiting for the Open Letter. By the time that the party convened its Sixth National Convention on 1 March 1929, the factional machetes were drawn.[7]

Two ECCI representatives—Harry Pollitt from Britain and Philip Dengel from Germany—officially presented the Open Letter. Dengel later argued: 'Never in the history of the Comintern has there been a convention or a Congress of a Communist Party of such non-political, unprincipled and demagogical character'. For his part, Bittelman recalled that these representatives 'were frankly more sympathetic to our group than the Lovestone group'. By this time, Lovestone's supporters had reconciled themselves to the Open Letter's 'political line'—and even claimed it was 'obviously a repudiation' of Foster—but they rejected the recall of the leadership. Bedacht moved that the Convention appeal to the ECCI 'against some of the organizational proposals' as being 'not in harmony and not conducive toward' the dissolution of factionalism. This motion passed, against one by Browder to accept all the demands of the letter. Against Comintern advice that Foster be installed as secretary of the party, the Lovestone-dominated convention voted for Gitlow. (Pepper, secretly staying in a hotel in Westchester County, just outside New York City, refused to return to Moscow, prevaricating while secretly meeting with the Lovestone leadership).[8]

No doubt savouring the reversal of their misfortune in 1925, Foster and Bittelman's supporters denounced the Lovestone majority's 'open struggle

7 Unsigned Lovestoneite letter to 'Dear Comrades', 7 February 1929, in Lovestone papers, box 198, folder 11; J.G. Manus to 'The Members of the Party', 8 March 1929, in Lovestone papers, box 223, 'District 13 Correspondence'; Shipman 1993, p. 174. For the convention, see Draper 1986, Chapter 17. The convention renamed the party the Communist Party USA.

8 Dengel at Fourth Session of American Commission, 16 April 1929, in Comintern archives, 495:72:62; Bittelman, 'Things I Have Learned', folder 17, p. 525; unsigned Lovestoneite letter to 'Dear Comrades', 7 February 1929, in Lovestone papers, box 198, folder 11; Sixth W(C)P Convention minutes, 5 March 1929, in Lovestone papers, box 217, folder 3; Draper 1986, p. 399. On Pepper, see Gilbert Green, undated statement on John Pepper, in Comintern archives, 495:72:63; Sakmyster 2012, Chapter 10, describes Pepper's hiding during the convention.

against the Comintern' and demanded 'complete and unreserved acceptance of [the Open Letter's political and organisation proposals] as one individual whole'. Lovestone's opposition 'puts the Party in the camp of all those within the CI, the open Right wing and the conciliators, who are today waging a struggle against the CI and the line of the Sixth World Congress'. Such opposition was based on Bukharin's positions in Russia and expelled 'Rightists' such as Heinrich Brandler and August Thalheimer in the German Communist Party. 'Loyalty to the CI today', 67 leading Foster supporters declared, 'demands unqualified support for the line of its leading Party, the C.P.S.U. and its Central Committee led by Comrade Stalin'.[9]

In response, Lovestone and Gitlow introduced a motion calling for the end of Bukharin's leadership of the Comintern and accepting 'without reservations' the political perspective of the Open Letter. (This attack on Bukharin was too much for Pepper, who wrote to the Central Committee and the ECCI defending Bukharin and pointing out that 'up until the Party Convention it was only the privilege of the Bittelman Opposition to call Bukharin the head of the international Right wing', which no doubt undercut Lovestone's manoeuvre while diminishing Pepper's standing even more). For the first and only time, Stalin personally intervened by sending a cable that conceded the right of the convention to choose a CEC but insisted that the chief factionalists be put at the disposal of the Comintern:

> We cannot consent to your proposal that Comrade Lovestone should remain now at head of party ... Absolutely necessary that both Comrade Lovestone and Comrade Bittelman stand aside at present and be temporarily employed [in] Comintern work [in] other countries ... Organizational decision cannot be separated from political line ... ECCI can no longer tolerate unceasing factional struggle and is compelled to demand genuine elimination [of] all factors making for factional squablles [sic].

This was the most blatant attempt by the Soviet leadership to affect American Communist leadership.[10]

9 Bittelman, Browder, Dunne, Foster *et al.*, 'Statement to the Convention of the Workers' (Communist) Party of America', Lovestone papers, box 217, folder 4; the 67 signatories is significant because the Lovestoneites garnered 67 votes against the Open Letter.

10 Sixth W(C)P Convention minutes, 5 March 1929, in Lovestone papers, box 217, folder 3; John Pepper 'To the Central Committee of the CP of the U.S.A.', 31 March 1929; in Comintern archives, 495:72:63; cable from Presidium of ECCI 'For Victoria', during party convention. Lovestone papers, box 207, 'General Reports, 1929'. Although the cable is not signed, it

Against opposition by his co-factionalists, Bittelman put himself at the Comintern's disposal. He was assigned to the Far Eastern Secretariat, in Moscow, and was later sent to India, where he helped local Communists until he was expelled by British authorities in 1931. In his unpublished memoirs, Bittelman described his assignment as 'very exciting' and a promotion. Lovestone—whether expecting a more dangerous assignment or not wanting to forfeit control of the American party—travelled to Moscow to press his case. His supporters organised a ten-member delegation to Moscow. The only non-Lovestone supporter chosen was Foster; the others included Bedacht and Gitlow, and Huiswoud, as well as several 'proletarian' members. Since they were in Moscow, Bittelman (en route to his Comintern assignment) and Zack (a student at the Lenin School) also represented the opposition. Because Lovestone, Bedacht, Gitlow and Wolfe were all out of the country at once, the Political Committee (dominated by Lovestone supporters) elected Minor to be in charge of the Executive Department, and created a Secretariat of Browder, Minor and Stachel. (Foster and his supporters voted against this). Before he left, Lovestone took measures to maintain legal control of the party property.[11]

would appear to be the Stalin cable described in Draper 1986, pp. 401–2. According to Draper's interview notes with Bertram Wolfe, 22 January 1954, Wolfe claimed that he had cabled Lovestone during the convention that Bukharin had been removed, and Lovestone put forward the motion. Then, Wolfe complained, and Lovestone rescinded the motion; in Emory Draper collection, box 18, folder 20; copy in Prometheus Research Library collection. On Pepper's defence of Bukharin, see Sakmyster 2012, pp. 196–7.

11 See Political Committee Minutes, 21 March 1929, in Comintern archives, 515:1:1630. American Communists were often sent on Comintern assignments to Asia or Latin America: in the late 1920s, these included Browder (China); Darcy (Philippines); Dunne (Outer Mongolia); Johnstone (India and Mexico); Wicks (Australia and the Far East); Zack (Venezuela). See Draper 1986, pp. 170–1. On Bittelman's work in India—which resulted in his being expelled by the British—see his 'Things I Have Learned', folder 18. On the delegation, see Alexander 1981, p. 22; Gitlow 1939, p. 522. The representatives from the Lovestone group, in addition to Wolfe who was the party's representative in Moscow and Wicks who was the representative to the Profintern, comprised Bedacht, Gitlow, Huiswoud (a leading black Communist), William J. White, Ella Reeve Bloor, Edward Welsh, William Miller, Alex Noral and Thomas Myerscough; see 'American Delegates in Moscow', 9 April 1929, in Comintern archives, 495:72:59 and Draper 1986, p. 404.

Lovestone: Victim and Perpetrator

The Moscow trip would be a debacle for Lovestone, as Stalin pressed 'the entire weight of the Communist world superstructure' against him, according to Gitlow.[12] This poses two interrelated questions to the historian: first, why did Stalin—never active in the workings of the Comintern much less the American party—intervene forcefully in the arcane factionalism in one of the less significant Communist Parties? Second, why did Lovestone, usually so attuned to factional winds in Moscow and not one to put political principle over internal authority, press so hard in the face of such opposition by Stalin, provoking even harsher measures?

For Stalin, the American Commission came at a key moment in his campaign against Bukharin, and thus threatened to upset Stalin's plans while offering an opportunity to amplify his anti-Bukharin message. Going after Lovestone underlined his determination to purge Bukharin and his supporters from the Comintern, with the added benefit that the execrable Lovestone was an easier target than Bukharin (who was still, nominally, an important Bolshevik).

Nonetheless, this could not have caused Stalin to attack Lovestone by itself. The final reason that Stalin went after Lovestone was that once directly defied by Lovestone, the Soviet leader *had* to take him down. But why did Lovestone and his allies miscalculate and go after Stalin instead of taking their lumps and holding out for a better day? Anti-Communists like the *New York Times* later romanticised Lovestone as the man who 'once called Joseph Stalin a murderer to his face and lived to tell the tale'; Lovestone's arrogant resistance to Stalin was the homage that vice paid to virtue, especially given Lovestone's previous courting of Stalin and his record in the American party. Will Herberg, an important Lovestone supporter, claimed decades later that Lovestone supported Bukharin based on principle, not factional opportunism. It is true that on the spectrum of Communist politics, Lovestone was on the right and presumably preferred Bukharin's analysis to Stalin's. Yet Lovestone's actions were not as clear-cut as Cannon's support of Trotsky. Lovestone showed himself willing to throw both Bukharin and Pepper overboard when it suited him. Gitlow underlined this in a letter to a plenum of the Central Committee of the Soviet Party—which was dedicated to attacking Bukharin—highlighting the American party leadership's opposition to Bukharin.[13]

12 Gitlow 1965, p. 162.

13 Will Herberg interview notes by Robert Alexander, 12 December 1973, in Alexander papers, box 10, folder 50 (Herberg later became an important Jewish philosopher); *New York Times*, 21 December 1963; Benj. Gitlow, 'To the Plenum of the CPSU', 22 April 1921 [sic:

Lovestone was no innocent in Comintern intrigue, but he was handicapped by his loss of Pepper, his patron and one time 'tower of strength', in the Comintern apparatus. This left Lovestone on unsure footing; Dengel later reported to the American Commission that a leading Lovestone supporter reproached him for intervening strongly in the American party when 'one cannot tell . . . whether Stalin or Bukharin will win'. Foster's faction, on the other hand, was more sure, and counted on the protection of Lozovsky—something that Lovestone and his allies did not cease to bemoan. Second, although Lovestone's control of the party was based on what he himself termed an 'illegitimate, a bastard CEC, given birth at a convention through a Caesarean operation' in 1925, he had forgotten that the Comintern franchise could also be taken away. Foster and Bittelman, having lost power in 1925, were more flexible in accommodating themselves to Comintern demands.[14]

In Moscow, the issue became one of loyalty to the Comintern. 'No Convention of our Party has ever before rejected a decision of the Comintern and carried on such an utterly impermissible attack on the Comintern representatives', Foster charged in a document. Dengel attacked Lovestone's manoeuvring at the Sixth National Convention as 'an attempt to undermine the authority of the Comintern'. For their part, Lovestone and his supporters stressed how they had been loyal followers of the Comintern, and had been carrying out the perspective of the Sixth Congress. No longer able to bask in unquestioned support from the Comintern, they advocated 'Discontinuance of the practise of keeping the Party suspended on cables regarding the smallest matters, which serves as a decisive factor in the perpetuation of factionalism and the promotion of permanent instability in the Party'. They denounced Pollitt's and Dengel's roles at the past convention, and declared war on Lozovsky 'as the inciter, director and guiding spirit of the Opposition's continued faction struggle against

1929], in Comintern archives, 495:72:63. As will be discussed below, the significance of Gitlow's letter was not its anti-Bukharin tone, but its claim that the ECCI representatives supported it.

14 Dengel at Fourth Session of American Commission, 16 April 1929, in Comintern archives, 495:72:62; Tower of strength: J. [Lovestone] to 'Dear Friends', 26 November 1926, in Lovestone papers, box 212, folder 6; Caesarean operation: [Lovestone?] to 'Dear Friends', 21 November 1926, in Lovestone papers, box 212, folder 6. By this time, Pepper, facing expulsion, was resisting returning to Moscow, and the Lovestone leadership felt forced to support whatever discipline the Comintern meted out. See the various cables regarding Pepper in Comintern archives, 515:1:1550.

the American Party', while demanding that he be removed from the American Commission as a factionalist.[15]

The American Commission

In April and May 1929, the ECCI convened an American Commission. The Commission had twelve sessions and included Gusev, Kolarov, Kun, Kuusinen, Lozovsky, Manuilsky, Molotov, Walter Ulbricht and, several times, Stalin himself. 'The C.I. has seldom examined the situation of a party so carefully and in such detail', a leading member of the Anglo-American Secretariat claimed afterwards. During the meetings, the ire of the Comintern apparatus with the entire American leadership became clear.[16] Although the Open Letter and previous Comintern interventions had stressed the lack of political differences between the factions, speakers increasingly blamed Lovestone for 'right' deviations and for 'exceptionalism'.

At one point, Dengel described a stagnant party that had done little in important industrial areas. 'It is a shadow and has no roots in the American

15 W.Z. Foster and J. Zack, 'Statement on the Situation in the Communist Party of the United States of America' [Spring 1929], in Comintern archives, 495:72:57; Dengel at Fourth Session of the American Commission, 16 April 1929, in Comintern archives, 495:72:62; 'Proposals of the Delegation of the Sixth Convention of the Communist Party of the United States to the Comintern', 15 April 1929, signed by Bertram D. Wolfe, H.M. Wicks, Max Bedacht, Ella Reeve Bloor, Benj. Gitlow, Otto H. Huiswoud, Jay Lovestone, William Miller, Tom Myerscough, Alex Noral, Edward Welsh and W.J. White, in Comintern archives, 495:72:59. Attacks on Pollitt and Dengel can be found, for example, in Gitlow's 22 April 1929 letter to the plenum of the CC of the CPSU, in Comintern archives, 495:72:63; for examples of attacks on Lozovsky, see Gitlow's morning remarks at the American Commission, 12 April 1929, in Comintern archives, 495:72:61.

16 Mingulin 1929, p. 605. The first session met on the morning of 18 April 1929 and the 12th (presidium) session on 14 May 1929. Speeches were most often in English or German, with occasional Russian and French speeches. At times, sessions were almost a week apart. The stenograph of the commission is contained in the Comintern archives at various locations, including 495:37:32; 495:72:66; 495:72:62; the Russian stenographic report, comprising almost 200 pages, is in Comintern archives, 495:37:20. A list of all the speakers and all the sessions can be found in Comintern archives, 495:37:43. Some of the transcripts are also available in the Lovestone papers, box 211, folder 8. In addition, there are several contemporary accounts; these include a 15 May 1929 summary by an unnamed American, most likely a Lovestone supporter, in Lovestone papers, box 211, folder 8; a letter from H. M. Wicks to 'Dear Louis', 9 May 1929, in Draper papers, box 29; see also Draper 1986, pp. 406–23.

Labour Movement'. This was due to factionalism, since 'Everything is forgotten in the factional struggle, all Party work is in a morass'. Lovestone and his faction were only interested in destroying Foster's supporters instead of building the party. Going beyond the Open Letter, Dengel asserted that 'it has become clear to me that the political line of the Majority is the policy of conciliators' and 'has hitherto been an opportunist line'. He added: 'the present leadership must be replaced' since 'it will be impossible to carry through a new policy with these leaders'. At the same time, 'The minority comrades have not understood the Open Letter' and 'have misinterpreted both [the Open Letter and the organisational proposals] to suit themselves'.[17]

Lesser members of the American Commission also attacked Lovestone. Rafael Khitarov, a Russian leader of the Communist Youth International, accused Lovestone of having 'done everything to destroy the authority of the CI'. British Communist Thomas Bell raised rumours of a split in the party, stressing that if the Comintern 'decides on any particular decision it will carry it through no matter what the costs are'.[18]

Echoing these attacks, Weinstone and Bittelman attacked Lovestone and the leadership for disobeying the Comintern and for being 'rightists'. They attacked the factionalism of the recent CPUSA convention, which Weinstone described as an 'armed siege'. Bittelman accused Lovestone of having 'sabotaged' Comintern decisions because 'the Pepper-Lovestone leadership was against the CI line'. Lovestone, for his part, gave as good as he got. After dismissing Bittelman as 'one of the remnants of Trotskyism in our party', he termed the 'theory of exceptionalism charged against us' as 'exceptional nonsense'. Then Lovestone outlined several specific conditions of America capitalism. Calling his opponents liars, Lovestone dismissed Dengel as 'a sort of Red Columbus' who 'discovered America in four days'.[19]

On 6 May, Stalin spoke. He criticised both factions for 'right deviations', declaring that 'when the leaders of the majority and minority accuse each

17 Dengel at Fourth Session of the American Commission, 16 April 1929, in Comintern archives, 495:72:62.

18 Bell, morning session of American Commission, 25 April 1929.

19 See Weinstone at morning session of American Commission, 15 April 1929, in Comintern archives, 495:72:62; Bittelman and Lovestone at evening session of American Commission, 23 April 1929, in Comintern archives, 495:72:65. Whether consciously or not, Gitlow appropriated Lovestone's description of Dengel a decade later when he labelled Pepper 'the Hungarian political Christopher Columbus' who 'rediscovered America for the Communists'; Gitlow 1939, pp. 109–10. It is also possible that both were alluding to Russian poet Vladimir Mayakovsky's 1926 travelogue of his three-month trip to Mexico and the United States, *My Discovery of America*.

other of elements of a Right deviation, it is obviously not without some measure of truth'. Both factions—but 'particularly the majority'—were 'guided by motives of unprincipled factionalism' that 'place[d] the interests of their faction higher than the interests of the Party'. Both 'base[d] their relations with the Comintern, not on the principles of confidence, but on the policy of rotten diplomacy, a policy of diplomatic intrigue'. Thus, 'instead of a fight on principles you get the most unprincipled speculation on the differences within the C.P.S.U.' As a result, American Communism had degenerated into 'another game of rivalry—who can spit further'. Stalin characterised this attitude as follows: 'Let them know over there in Moscow that we Americans know how to play the stock market'. To behead the leadership of both factions, Stalin urged that Lovestone and Bittelman be required to stay in Moscow 'for a time'. He directed more fire at Lovestone, however, declaring that 'the actions of the majority at the [Sixth] Convention of the Communist Party ... must be condemned'.

Stalin's defence of the Comintern as the 'holiest of holies' against the noxious factionalism in the CPUSA must have appealed to many Communists, in the US and elsewhere. Stalin's opening of the speech in which he attacked Lovestone's supposed exceptionalism was also important. 'It would be wrong to ignore the specific peculiarities of American capitalism', Stalin conceded. He added:

> But it would be still more wrong to base the activities of the Communist Party on these specific features, since the foundation of the activities of every Communist Party, including the American Communist Party, on which it must base itself, must be the general features of capitalism, which are the same for all countries, and not its specific features in any given country.[20]

In other words, Stalin asserted the power of the Comintern, under his leadership, to set the policy and personnel issues of individual parties.

Molotov, who followed Stalin, spelled it out: Lovestone's error was that he and his supporters 'do not want to reckon with the will of the Comintern

20 Stalin's remarks are in the Comintern archives, 495:37:32 and 495:72:66, both marked 'Strictly Confidential: Not for publication, for the minutes only'. A typescript of Stalin's speeches is in the Communist Party USA. Collection, box 256, folder 22; and also the Daniel Bell papers, box 1, folder 'Expulsion of the Lovestoneites'; the party later published his speeches, in a slightly different translation, from which the above quotes are taken; Stalin 1929, pp. 11–15.

and … are concerned in turning the Comintern decisions into something that is favourable for their faction and not to take them as given by the Comintern'. Thus, Molotov added, 'what we have in America now is unreliable and unsound' and permeated with 'the spirit of absolute hostility towards the Comintern'.[21]

Speaking after Molotov, Foster attacked Lovestone for 'Right' errors, emphasising that one 'cannot simply consider the situation in the American party as a factional fight without any political differences'. He asserted that the Comintern 'must send one or two comrades, preferably two, to America to take over the Party, to correct its line, and to unify all those elements in the Party', underlining that this tutelage should last more than 'two or three months'. Between meetings, Gitlow drafted a defiant statement, asserting that 'the Executive Committee of the Communist International desires to destroy the [CPUSA] Central Committee' and accusing it of siding with the Foster opposition.[22]

The ECCI issued an 'address' to the American membership, singling out Lovestone and his supporters for 'methods and intrigues that cannot be tolerated in any section and which clearly bear the imprint of petty-bourgeois politiciandom'. These included organising the party's convention 'for factional purposes'; 'misleading honest proletarian members' into supporting Lovestone; 'unprincipled' speculation on differences in the Soviet party; 'inadmissible personal hounding of the delegation of the Comintern at the convention' and otherwise flouting Comintern authority. The letter called again for removing Bittelman and Lovestone from America, reorganising the American secretariat, rejecting the quick convention that Foster had advocated, and convening a Comintern control commission to decide the fate of Pepper.[23]

At an American Commission meeting on 12 May, Kuusinen denounced the Lovestoneites' resistance, comparing them to previous 'open oppositionists on the eve of a split'. He told Foster and Lovestone: 'We demand statements as to whether you will carry out the decision without reservations'. Foster supported the address, as did Weinstone and Bittelman. Gitlow prevaricated, 'ask[ing] for a little more time to draw up a statement of views on the letter', according to

21 Molotov, speech at American Commission, dated 2 July 1929 [6 May 1929?], in Comintern archives, 495:72:66.

22 Foster, speech at American Commission, 6 May 1929, in Comintern archives, 495:72:66.

23 'Address by the ECCI to All Members of the CP of the United States', 12 May 1929, in Gruber 1974, pp. 230–4. See also *International Press Correspondence*, 7 June 1929. In the upshot, Pepper was expelled from the Comintern in August 1929. He worked in various capacities for the Soviet government, until being readmitted to the Comintern in May 1932. In June 1937, he was arrested amidst the Stalinist purges. He was shot in February 1938. In May 1956, he was rehabilitated; see Sakmyster, pp. 205–15.

one witness. Molotov dismissed this, and Kuusinen denounced Gitlow's 'factional method'. Wolfe also asked for more time; Stalin called this 'shameful' and replied:

> The leadership of the faction is so illiterate, so backward, that they don't understand the significance of the letter. You are asked in different words: Do you recognize the discipline of the CI? Do you believe the part should obey the whole? There are statutes of the CI. If it is necessary for you to think this over, then who are you?

Béla Kun asked each Lovestone delegate if he would 'carry out the discipline without reservations'. One after another, the ten delegates refused to answer, trying to balance a rhetorical loyalty to the Comintern with a rejection of its dictates.[24]

Stalin and the Comintern leadership were enraged at the Lovestoneites. At a 14 May ECCI Presidium meeting, Stalin lashed out against them for 'non-submission to the decisions of the Presidium of the E.C.C.I.' and their 'path of insubordination, and hence of warfare against the Comintern'. He made it clear that failure to follow the Comintern's decisions would result in being purged. 'It is said that the Communist Party of America cannot get along without Comrade Lovestone, that the removal of Comrade Lovestone may ruin the Party'. Stalin added: 'That is not true, comrades'. He later asserted: 'I doubt it very much that at this stage Comrade Lovestone can be a Party leader'.[25]

The meeting lasted six hours; early in the morning, the Presidium endorsed the new address, against Gitlow's lone opposition. Stalin proposed that each American delegate declare his position on the decision. Two Americans—Bedacht, one of the most vehement Lovestoneites and Alex Noral—capitulated, but the others maintained opposition. When Gitlow declared he would resist the decision, Stalin became enraged and thundered (according to Wolfe):

> Who do you think you are? Trotsky defied me. Where is he? Zinoviev defied me. Where is he? Bukharin defied me. Where is he? And you? When you get back to America, nobody will stay with you except for your wives.[26]

24 This account is taken from the 15 May 1929 summary.

25 Stalin 1929, pp. 22, 32–3.

26 Stalin 1929, p. 33; Draper 1986, pp. 420–2 (Wolfe quote on p. 422). See also account by Charles Zimmerman, a Lovestone supporter present at the time, in interview notes by Robert Alexander 28 November 1973, in Alexander papers, box 10, folder 50; Theodore

On 15 May, Lovestone and his supporters drafted a cable to Minor and Stachel in New York. They protested against the decision, predicting that it meant 'destruction party unless firm solid front maintained'. Despite the 'desperate speculation on split [in] our ranks', the cable continued, 'entire delegation solid as one ... We can count on you all to show same splendid spirit'. Then, the cable urged their co-factionalists in America to secure 'all units all property all connections all mailing lists' and 'chek [sic] all checking accounts all organisations seeing that authorised signers are exclusively reliable'. Then it counselled to 'instantly finish preparations sell buildings' and remove Weinstone and others from trusteeship of the party's property. It concluded: 'Absolutely dont [sic] letter acknowledgement or cognisance this letter but guide thereby'.[27]

The speculation about a split in the Lovestoneite ranks was becoming real. According to Draper, the members of the delegation were 'subjected to a variety of bribes and threats' to keep them out of the US. On 17 May, the Comintern issued measures against Lovestone and his supporters. Lovestone and Gitlow were removed from the American Political Bureau and other members who 'refused to submit to ECCI decisions' were threatened with removal; the Political Bureau was reconstituted to comprise Foster, Weinstone, Minor and Bedacht, along with an ECCI representative with veto power; a CC plenum was ordered to discuss the Open Letter, among other measures. Bedacht cabled New York supporting the Comintern, contradicting the cable urging resistance, and urging his supporters to 'under no condition follow Majority delegation to fight Uncle'. Soon other important Lovestoneites, including Wicks, Bloor and Huiswoud decided to break ranks and capitulate to the Comintern, while, in New York, Stachel refused to split. Several black supporters of Lovestone had already capitulated and supported the new leadership. Faced with these defections,

Draper interview notes with Max Bedacht, 1 February 1954, in Emory University Draper papers, box 10, folder 16, copy in Prometheus Research Library collection.

27 'Unsigned Telegram Sent to New York from Moscow, May 15, 1929', in Comintern archives, 495:72:63. Draper quotes a slightly different version, from *Daily Worker*, 27 June 1929; he indicates that 'The message was taken out of Moscow by the American agent of the Soviet intelligence service at whose farewell party the arrangements had been made two days before, and was cabled by him in Berlin to New York on May 15'; Draper 1986, p. 416. The handwritten English title in the Comintern archives clearly indicates it was sent from Moscow, while the typed Russian title merely indicates it was sent to New York. The version in the Comintern archives appears to be a translation from German or a transcription by a German-speaker, using 'ZK' to refer to the Central Committee, for example.

Lovestone, Wolfe and Gitlow denounced the 'degenerated elements from the former Majority' who remained loyal to Moscow.[28]

Pravda devoted four columns to attacking Lovestone and his supporters; Walter Duranty quoted it in a snarky *New York Times* article. 'It has happened before that a foreign Communist party branch has claimed to know more about the affairs of its own country than the Kremlin', Duranty wrote, 'but to the best of your correspondent's knowledge, this is the first occasion on which the party linen has been washed so publicly'. (According to Wolfe, this article was the first that American Communists heard of anti-Lovestone measures).[29]

Perhaps sensing that he had gone too far, Lovestone tried to obtain leave to return to the US. He wrote to the presidium 'maintaining my disagreement with the Open Letter and its organizational instructions' while 'categorically repudiat[ing] and condemn[ing] all charges of resistance to Comintern decisions'. In late May, he wrote to Kuusinen requesting 'permission to leave for the United States immediately' for several weeks before putting 'myself at the disposal of the ECCI for the assignment of any work anywhere'. A week later he again requested a leave to the US, and 'strongly insist[ed]' that he 'be given work in some other country—outside Moscow and outside the United States'. The next day, the Comintern approved a fortnight's trip to the US, but the American leadership vetoed this. On 11 June, Lovestone sneaked out of Moscow (with

28 'Pour la Séance du Secrétariat Politique: Mesures Devant Etre Réalisées Immédiatement sur la Question Américaine', 17 May 1929, in Comintern archives, 515:1:1546. On Bedacht's role in writing the original cable, see *Militant*, 15 August 1929. Draft cables from Max [Bedacht] to Elizabeth Bedacht, Lydia Gibson Minor and Nancy Markoff, 18 May 1929, in Comintern archives, 495:72:63; Gitlow, Lovestone, Miller, Myerscough, Welsh and Wolfe, 'Appeal to the Comintern on the last Comintern Address and the Expulsions Now Taking Place in the Party', 10 July 1929, in Lovestone papers, box 209, folder 16; on black supporters deserting Lovestone, see Harold Williams 'To the Commission on the American Question', 22 March 1929 and John H. Owens, 'To the Commission on the American Question', 30 March 1929 , in Comintern archives, 495:72:63; Draper 1986, p. 425; Huiswoud's split with Lovestone appears to be part of his assuming more responsibilities within the Comintern and Profintern for work among black people internationally; see Enckevort 2001, pp. 50–1, pp. 89–90. In August 1929, an article denouncing Lovestone's 'open campaign against the C.I.' appeared in *International Press Correspondence* under Wicks's byline; see Wicks 1929. So strong were the feelings created by the split that in the autumn of 1930, when Robert Minor fell ill while in jail for political activity, his handwritten will took pains to swear loyalty to the Comintern and denounce Lovestone; Will by Robert Minor, 9 October 1930, in Communist Party USA. Collection, box 144, folder 18.

29 *New York Times*, 19 May 1929; Theodore Draper notes on interview with Bertram D. Wolfe, 22 January 1954, originally in Emory University Draper papers, box 18, folder 20; copy in Prometheus Research Library collection.

the aid of sympathetic workers in the Soviet Foreign Office). When he arrived at the party's office in New York, the surprised leadership sent him home and then, two days later, expelled him.[30]

Lovestone cabled the Comintern protesting that the leadership had 'expelled me without even hearing and launched [a] campaign [of] wholesale removals' and emphasising he had 'left Moscow [on] basis [of] permission [granted on] May thirtyfirst'. To no avail: the party leadership purged the organisation, for the second time in less than a year. In late July, the ECCI ordered that Lovestone return to Moscow in early August for a review of his expulsion; when he did not do so, he was expelled and the Political Committee issued an ultimatum to remaining Lovestone supporters to 'dissociate themselves from this renegade to Communism' within forty-eight hours or be expelled. So complete was the new leadership's anger with Lovestone that they did not even allow him and Gitlow to remove their personal possessions from the party headquarters, and claimed Lovestone had orchestrated a 'raid' to loot party files. The Tenth Enlarged ECCI Plenum, in July 1929, 'decided to relieve Comrades Bukharin, Gitlow, Serra and Humbert-Droz of their duties members of the Presidium', and 'excluded' Lovestone and Spector from the ECCI.[31]

30 Lovestone to 'Dear Comrades', undated [May 1929?]; Jay Lovestone to 'Dear Comrade Kuusinen', 22 May 1929, both in Comintern archives, 495:72:63; Lovestone to Political Secretariat, 30 May 1929, in Lovestone papers, box 198, folder 13; Cable from Communist International, 22 June 1929, in Comintern archives, 515:1:1549; the exchange of declarations and cables between Lovestone, the ECCI, and the American CP leadership are in an undated appeal signed by Ella Reeve Bloor, Gitlow, Lovestone, Tom Myerscough, William Miller, Edward Welsh, W.J. White and Wolfe, in Lovestone papers, box 207, file 'Reports 1929, Factional Disputes' (a covering note from 23 July 1929 from Bedacht to the ECCI indicates that Lovestone was circulating an appeal and that Bloor 'repudiate[d]' it; in Comintern archives, 515:1:1550). On Lovestone's arrival in the US and expulsion from CP, see cable from Secretariat to Moscow, 27 June 1929, in Comintern archives, 515:1:1550, as well as Charles Zimmerman interview notes by Robert Alexander, 28 November 1973, and Jay Lovestone interview notes by Robert Alexander, 28 December 1973, both in Alexander papers, box 10, folder 50. See also Draper 1986, pp. 425–9.

31 Lovestone cable to Piatnisky, [23 June?] 1929, in Comintern archives, 515:1:1550; *New York Times*, 7 July, 10 July and 30 July 1929; Undated cable [June 1929] from ECCI Presidium to WoPat [Workers' Party]; cable from ECCI to WoPat, 11 August 1929, both in Comintern archives, 515:1:1549; Max Bedacht for the Secretariat to Benjamin Gitlow *et al.*, 14 August 1929, in Gitlow papers, box 8, folder 6. On personal effects, see Gitlow 1939, p. 569. On the 'raid' of the party office, see *New York Times*, 28 August 1928 and the denial by Gitlow, Lovestone, William J. White and Wolfe, 'The Truth About the Raid on the Party Headquarters', 12 September 1929, in Lovestone papers, box 207. On the Tenth ECCI plenum,

The Expelled Lovestoneites: Three Who Didn't Make a Revolution

According to internal party reports, some 300 people were expelled in the aftermath of the Lovestone split, a large number in New York City. These included many functionaries: Political Committee and Central Committee members; the editor of *Communist*, district organisers in Boston, Seattle, and Detroit; lesser local leaders in California, New Jersey, New York and Pittsburgh; leading Communist youth league members; and important trade-union leaders, including Charles Zimmerman in the New York City ILGWU. Although a report to the Comintern claimed that the purges improved 'the vitality of the Party', it also indicated a shortage of trained functionaries in many districts.[32]

The expelled Lovestoneites organised the Communist Party of the USA (Majority Group) and began publishing a journal, *Revolutionary Age*. They criticised the 'Party-splitting and mass expulsion campaign, outrageous violation of the most elementary rights of Party democracy, [and] illegal expulsion' of Lovestone and his supporters. Unlike Cannon and Trotsky's Left Opposition, which had a clear programmatic difference with the Comintern leadership, Lovestone's goal was power in the American party. Thus, unwilling to attack the Third Period itself, *Revolutionary Age* argued that Stalin had perverted Bukharin's original understanding of the term. An early article denounced the 'course of revision away from the line of the VI Congress now carried through by the Ecci' in favour of the 'corridor congress'. Arguing that the 'actual decisions of the Congress ... are in the main generally correct', *Revolutionary Age* attacked the 'ultra-left line of the Ecci' as 'not a consequence of the line of the VI World Congress, but ... on the contrary a revision of that line'. Keeping the language of the Congress, Lovestone labelled Foster's supporters 'the traditional right wing in the American Party', and stressed that the expelled members were 'the banner bearers of the struggle against outright opportunism and Trotskyism'.[33]

see *International Press Correspondence*, 24 July and 9 August 1929. Serra was Angelo Tasca, an Italian supporter of Bukharin.

32 Smith, 'A Brief Balance of the Inner Party Situation in the CP of the U.S.A.', 5 November 1929, in Comintern archives, 515:1:1552; 'Summary Report on Organisation Condition of the CP U.S.A.', 18 February 1930, in Comintern archives, 515:1:1551; 'Mass Expulsions Begin in Every Party District' [pro-Lovestone circular, summer 1929], in Lovestone papers, box 207; Alexander 1981, p. 28.

33 *Revolutionary Age*, 1 November 1929; 15 July 1930. The first five issues of *Revolutionary Age* serialised an article by Will Herberg assessing the Tenth ECCI Plenum, as well as articles by Wolfe, Lovestone and Gitlow on the the Sixth Congress, the Comintern in general, and the party's trade-union work, respectively; 'The Traditional Right Wing in the American

In late 1930, Lovestone and his followers joined other expelled 'Right' Communists, including Thalheimer, Brandler and M.N. Roy, to form the International Communist Opposition. The Right Opposition had distinct politics from Stalin's faction in the CPSU, but (unlike the Left Opposition) lacked an explicit programme. They were hurt also by the fact that Bukharin had until recently been a key component of the consolidation of Stalinism in Russia and the Comintern, and that he now refused to forthrightly struggle for his own politics.[34]

It is useful to compare the development of Cannon and his followers with that of Lovestone. Despite their common opposition to the Comintern leadership, the two groups had counterposed perspectives. Shachtman, writing in the *Militant*, called Lovestone's group 'the banner-bearer in Russia of the Thermidorian elements' that 'represent[ed] the policy and interests of one class and we another'. Thus 'any collaboration or a common line between us is impossible' even if their 'demand for Party democracy, like Brandler's, may appear superficially to be similar to ours'.[35]

The Third Period affected each tendency differently. Cannon had hoped to capitalise on disgruntlement with the rightward drift of the party leadership under Lovestone; by getting rid of Lovestone and taking a 'left' perspective, the Third Period undermined one of the Trotskyists' main attractions. Nonetheless, with a programmatically forged cadre, Cannon's opposition grew into one of the larger Trotskyist groups in the world, with significant, if small, roots in the American labour movement (for example, leading a Teamsters' strike in Minneapolis in 1934). By the mid-1930s, the American Left Opposition became a key component of international Trotskyism.[36]

Party and Our Fight Against It', 17 August 1929, in Bell papers, box 1, file, 'Expulsion of Lovestoneites'.

34 On the December 1930 conference of the International Communist Opposition, see *Revolutionary Age*, 7 February 1931. On the lack of a role for Bukharin, see Charles Zimmerman interview notes by Robert Alexander, 28 November 1973, in Alexander papers, box 10, folder 50. See also Alexander 1981, pp. 278–9; Wheeler 1953, p. 133.

35 *Militant*, 15 August 1929. This was why Trotsky refused to make an alliance with Bukharin against Stalin, since he believed that while Stalin's policies were a degeneration of the Bolshevik Revolution, Bukharin's would have lead to rapid counterrevolution.

36 Cannon 1972, pp. 90–1. On the difficulties of recruiting left-wing Communists like William F. Dunne, see Cannon to Glotzer, 24 August 1929, in Cannon 1981, pp. 218–19. On the view of the Third Period among militants as a return to Communist fundamentals, see Worley 2004, p. 6. This is one of the reasons that Cannon considered the early 1930s the 'dog days' of Trotskyism in America; see Prometheus Research Library 2002.

Lovestone's group had several advantages. It offered a home to Communists disaffected by the Third Period; Gitlow recalled that it was 'certainly more sensible and had more reference to American conditions than the official Party's adventurist and ultra-Leftist "Third Period" nonsense'. Lovestone, Wolfe and Gitlow were bright and ambitious; historian Paul Buhle has labelled *Revolutionary Age* 'in some respects the most literate journal on the left'. Its weakness was that it found itself (in Gitlow's recollection) in the 'ridiculous position of both trying to reform the Communist International and declaring that Stalin's policies are one hundred percent correct'. An early document claimed that the new leadership was moving to the right, while 'comrades fighting for the line of the Sixth Congress are being expelled wholesale' and the party was supposedly becoming pro-Trotsky. The cynicism created by an opposition group based on factional pique might explain why none of the key Lovestoneite leaders remained on the organised left a decade after their leaving the party. In fact, Lovestone's group played a key role in the development of anti-Communism in the United States. Starting in the 1930s, its leaders began to act as braintrusters to the AFL bureaucrats' opposition to Communism and the CIO. Lovestone himself became a notorious anti-Communist operative of the AFL; Wolfe became a distinguished anti-Communist historian; Gitlow wrote two books defending his break with Communism and became a cooperative witness for the Congressional witch-hunt against Communists.[37]

The Post-Lovestone CP

Shortly after the expulsion of Lovestone, the party entered the height of the Third Period. In autumn 1929, the party replaced the TUEL with the Trade Union Unity League (TUUL) that, reversing years of Communist trade-union work, sought to create new unions under Communist leadership. In terms of the party's leadership, the Comintern did not just pass the baton back to Foster's faction; both Bittelman and Browder were in Asia on Comintern assignment. Foster, who had opposed the new unions, was denied the secretaryship and had to share power with three former Lovestone allies, with

37 Buhle 1999, p. 26; Gitlow 1939, pp. 327, 571; 'Mass Expulsions Begin in Every Party District' [summer 1929], in Lovestone papers, box 207; on the subsequent history of Lovestone and his followers, see Alexander 1981, pp. 133–4; Diggins 1994, pp. 128–59; Klehr 1971, pp. 176–8; Morgan 1999, p. 141. On the importance of the Lovestoneites in the AFL's anti-Communist campaigns, see Charles Zimmerman interview notes by Robert Alexander, 21 September 1976, in Robert Alexander papers, box 10, folder 46.

Bedacht as party leader. Bittelman later speculated that neither himself nor Foster became head of the party because Stalin was fearful of having a leadership that was too strong or independent.[38]

This configuration was temporary. In the summer of 1930, the party held its Seventh National Convention. Browder, recently returned to the United States, became head of the party, supported by Minor and Stachel; Bedacht was shunted to Workers' International Relief. (This was an assignment that 'fit neither my particular capabilities, nor my desires', he later recalled. In 1932, he became head of the IWO, where he met with some success). Thus the party was led by three competent figures who were important but not central leaders in their factions. At the same time, the new, thoroughly Stalinist, leadership finally put an end to factionalism.[39]

This intervention, by unifying the party, helped position the party to grow amid the Great Depression. During its 'heyday' in the coming decade, Communists gained a substantial following among intellectuals and artists, black Americans, the unemployed and, above all, in the industrial unions in basic industries. As the Great Depression underlined the bankruptcy of capitalism, between December 1929 and July 1930 more than 7,100 people joined the Communist Party. Although the party still experienced high turnover, by 1933 its membership reached 19,000, and it continued to grow over the next decade. The party became a real, if small, mass party with an influence unimagined in the 1920s. Communist union organisers led important strikes among textile workers in New Bedford, Massachusetts, and Gastonia, North Carolina, in 1928 and 1929. In the 1930s, Communists were key organisers in the new CIO unions, especially 'left-led' unions among transport, maritime and longshore workers.[40]

This intervention came at a steep cost. The Communist Party of the 1930s was not the same party as that of the 1920s, even if many of its leaders had been active in both periods. The party and its leadership had become 'Stalinised'. This could be seen in the different ways in which Lenin's Comintern had treated John Reed and Stalin's Comintern had treated Lovestone. Reed had differences with the leadership over work within the AFL. Lenin fought this 'left-wing infantilism', but he did so *ideologically* as a battle among comrades. Reed

38 Bittelman, 'Things I Have Learned', folder 17, p. 530; Draper 1986, pp. 430–5; Ryan 1999, pp. 37–8.

39 Bedacht, 'On the Path of Life', folder 26, pp. 315–16; on the TUUL, see Devintaz 2007; Draper 1972a; Green 1972; Johanningsmeier 2001; Ottanelli 1991, p. 21. On Gastonia, see Draper 1971; Salmond 1995. On the New Bedford strike, see Georgiana 1993.

40 Klehr 1984, p. 92; Ottanelli 1991, p. 43.

was not expelled; in fact, he was made a member of the ECCI and when he died shortly later, he was given a burial at the Kremlin wall.

In 1929, Lovestone also had differences with the Comintern, which by then was firmly in the hands of Stalin. His expulsion and the installation of a new leadership was the culmination of the party's Stalinisation, but this was not because Lovestone offered an alternative to Stalinism. As the present work has shown, the Stalinisation of the American party owed quite a lot to Lovestone; his differences with Stalin were in any case within the framework of Stalinism. Still, this did not stop Stalin from expelling his student from the Communist movement. By the time of his expulsion, Lovestone was an execrable figure, but his treatment by Stalin still demonstrated the degeneration of the Comintern. Lovestone's subsequent role in the labour movement testifies to both his training in the Stalinist Comintern and the calibre of cadres favoured by the Soviet leader.

CHAPTER 14

The 'Negro Question' to the Fourth Comintern Congress

During the Great Depression, the Communist Party became known for battling anti-black racism and discrimination. 'However one judges their motives', one historian wrote, 'Communists were often at the front in the battle for black rights'. In the South, Communists organised black and white workers and sharecroppers, and fought against Jim Crow racism and capitalist oppression. In the urban North, black and white Communists fought against eviction and for relief. Communists fought against the frame-up of the Scottsboro youths, exposing Jim Crow 'lynch law justice'.[1]

The party's approach to what it called the 'Negro question' during its first decade would not indicate the likelihood of such a development. At its founding in 1919, the CP had one black member and throughout the 1920s it counted fewer than 100 black members out of a total membership of at least 15,000. In 1929, it still had no more than 300 black members. Despite the Stalinist degeneration of Communism in the 1930s, the party became a real, if small, factor in the struggle for black liberation. By 1931, there were nearly 1,000 black Communists; in 1938, the Communist Party counted 3,000 members in Harlem alone. Given this, many of the historical studies of the intersection between blacks and Communists have dealt lightly with the 1920s and focused on the 1930s, leaving unanswered the question of how the party, starting from a position of such weakness, tapped into this historic substratum and ended up playing such an important role in black politics in the 1930s.[2]

The answer, the present study argues, lies in the combination of the intervention of the Communist International—which forced the (white) party

1 Kirby 1980, p. 153. On Communist work among blacks in the 1930s, see: Kelley 1990; Naison 2005; Solomon 1998; Storch 2009. More general studies on blacks and Communism include Hill 1951; Hutchinson 1995; T. Johnson 2010; Nolan 1951; Record 1951; Record 1964. Two recent studies that discuss the role of the Communist Party in the fight for civil rights in the North and South, respectively, are Sugrue 2008 and Gilmore 2008. Other studies of note include James 2003a, on the history of black Americans and the left; James 1998, on the importance of Afro-Caribbean radicalism on the American left; and Adi 2009, on the Comintern and blacks in the interwar period.

2 H.M. Wicks to 'Dear Louis [Engdahl?]', 9 May 1929, in Theodore Draper Papers, Hoover Institution, box 29; McDuffie 2011, pp. 87, 110.

leadership to address black oppression—and the efforts of the early black Communists to make the party assimilate the Comintern's directives. Black oppression offers the clearest example of the positive role of Comintern intervention in 'Americanising' the party. Left to their own devices, working within the social-democratic framework they had inherited, American Communists would have remained aloof from the struggle for black freedom.[3]

American Socialists and the 'Negro Question'

American capitalism has long rested upon a bedrock of black oppression, even after the Civil War smashed slavery. In the early twentieth century, the 'Great Migration' contributed to black people's economic integration into industrial capitalism, while remaining forcibly segregated at the bottom. Racial oppression became more central to American capitalism, and black workers became an important part of the working class, even as the labour movement in general remained at best indifferent to black workers. The foundation of the Communist Party in 1919 took place during the 'Red Summer', a tide of racism and violence, including 75 anti-black riots. In addition to the Great Migration, by the 1920s almost 30,000 black immigrants from the Caribbean had settled in Manhattan, comprising almost one out of every five black New Yorkers. From 1890–1930, the percentage of black people in the Northeast and Midwest increased from less than 10 percent to more than 20 percent of the total black population. What the Communists would call the 'Negro Question' was becoming central to American, and not just Southern, politics, making the role of black oppression in maintaining American capitalism ever more clear.[4]

These two migrations contributed to a new pride and militancy among Northern black people. This took various forms, including Marcus Garvey's movement, 'New Negro' radicalism, and, artistically, the Harlem Renaissance. World War I further changed race relations by providing blacks with industrial jobs in the North, and many blacks with military experience. Racist violence

3 The current work thus does not discuss much of the actual activity the party carried out. The studies cited in the first note above provide much more detail on this work, especially in the 1930s, the height of Communist activity in defence of black rights. Furthermore, given the importance of Manhattan both for the black left and the Communists, this chapter focuses on New York, while recognising that other Northern cities (especially Chicago) and the South are important in the evolution of black-Communist activity. Again, the reader is directed to the material cited in note 1 above.

4 Sitkoff 1978, p. 22; Domingo 2005, p. 176; Gibson and Jung 2002, tables 2., A-11 and A-15.

after the war contributed to militancy among black intellectuals and workers who refused to accept oppression.[5]

The Communist movement as a whole did not appreciate the importance of these developments. This reflected the fact that most American Communists were non-English-speaking immigrants dispersed among competing illegal groups concerned with other questions. That the role of blacks in the US was undergoing profound change made it harder to develop a cogent analysis. At bottom, though, Communist neglect of the Negro question was in keeping with the social-democratic framework of American Socialism, from which the Communists had emerged.

A review of American Socialist propaganda would reveal little about the oppression of black people, even though socialism in the US developed in the shadow of the defeat of Reconstruction in 1877 and the legalisation of segregation in the *Plessy v. Ferguson* Supreme Court decision in 1896. Some right-wing Socialists, like Victor Berger, were openly racist, supporting segregation and opposing Asian immigration. Most left-wing socialists were 'colour-blind': they opposed racism, but did not see black oppression as central to maintaining American capitalism.[6]

Eugene Debs is the best example: his hero was John Brown—the radical abolitionist who had given his life in the struggle to abolish slavery—and he opposed racial discrimination in his own railway workers' union. Debs saw blacks as suffering from extreme class exploitation, but not racial oppression. In a 1903 article in *International Socialist Review*, he wrote that 'The history of the Negro in the United States is a history of crime without a parallel'. Yet he maintained: 'There is no Negro question outside of the labor question'. He continued: 'The real issue … is not social equality, *but economic freedom*'. He advocated that Socialists simply 'say: "The class struggle is colorless". The capitalists, white, black and other shades, are on one side and the workers, white, black, and all other colors, on the other side'. Thus, the Socialist Party had 'nothing special to offer to the Negro, and … cannot make separate appeals to all the races'. Instead, it was 'the party of the whole working class regardless of color—the whole working class of the whole world'. In practice, this blindness towards the importance of racial oppression meant that the SP never attempted to fight for black liberation and tolerated racists like Berger.[7]

5 Reich 1996; Stephens 1999, p. 53. On the context of racial violence and self-defence, see King 2011.

6 See Miller 1984 and Miller 2003.

7 Ginger 1949, p. 8; Debs 1903. In a recent article, William P. Jones correctly points out that Debs's article was in fact anti-racist. However, the question was not so much about racism

There were a small number of black Socialists, primarily in New York City, who argued that Marxists should address racial oppression as a special issue. The most important black Socialist was the St. Croix-born Hubert Harrison. He failed to convince the SP, and split from the party during the factionalism of 1912–13, eventually becoming a black nationalist. Harrison influenced another generation of black Socialists, including black Caribbean immigrants like Otto E. Huiswoud (from Suriname, then a Dutch colony) and W.A. Domingo (from Jamaica), as well as American-born blacks such as Chandler Owen and A. Philip Randolph, who founded the *Messenger* in 1917. However, black Socialists could not counterbalance the indifference of the party as a whole. The only counterweight within the labour movement to the colour-blindness of American social democracy was the Industrial Workers of the World, who fought segregation and racism in their organising; at the IWW's height of one million members, some 10 percent were black.[8]

Early Black Communists

The early Communist movement continued this colour-blindness. James W. Ford, a long-time Communist leader and the first black man to run for Vice President (in 1932, 1936 and 1940) stated decades later that 'When the Communist Party of the U.S.A. was founded in 1919, it broke with social democratic rubbish in general, including especially its position on the Negro question. In its first conventions, the problems of the Negro people received special attention'. In fact, during the seminal 1919 faction fight, Domingo criticised the left wing for not paying more attention to black Americans:

> In order to accomplish world revolution the Bolsheviki have not hesitated to encouch in their platform statements that are calculated to attract and gain for them the support of all the oppressed peoples of the world...Since it is the avowed object of the Left Wing to establish

as it was about whether and to what extent Socialists should make fighting black oppression central to their work, including through 'special appeals' to blacks. Debs, while opposed to racism, did not believe this.

8 See Harrison's *International Socialist Review* article, 'Socialism and the Negro' (1912), reprinted in Perry 2001. On Harrison, see: Perry 2009; Hawkins 2000, Chapter 1; Samuels 1977. There is also an edited collection of Harrison's writings: Perry 2001. Black Caribbean radicalism is dealt with in James 1998; On Randolph's Socialism, see Bush 1999; Bynum 2010; Kornweibel 1971; Marable 1983. On the IWW, see Brown 1968; Spiro and Harris 1972, p. 331.

> Socialism through the medium of the dictatorship of the proletariat, how can they expect to accomplish it with a large portion of the American proletariat untouched by revolutionary propaganda?

Decades later, William Weinstone, a charter member of the party, noted the 'serious omission in the Left Wing Manifesto [of 1919] with regards to the Negro question'. Black Socialists, at least in Harlem, seem to have not been involved in the factional struggle. Randolph was the most prominent Harlem Socialist, but his 'ideological position' is 'difficult to firmly define', according to a recent study by Cornelius Bynum. Other black Socialists, including those who became Communists later, remained in the SP. Huiswoud was the only black charter member of the Communist Party; his left-wing activity owed much to the influence of S.J. Rutgers, a Dutch leftist then in the US.[9]

After the 1919 anti-black race riot in Chicago, the Chicago-based CLP published a front-page article that deplored the violence but offered no programme to fight black oppression:

> The workers, both negro and Caucasian, must realize the fact that their misery is not due to race antagonisms, but to *class* antagonisms; and the reason that the conditions of employment are becoming worse is because the capitalist class owns the means of production. The capitalist class—not the workers who belong to another race—is the only enemy of all the workers and workers' problems can only be solved through the elimination of the capitalist.

In a similar vein, the CPA's journal, *Revolutionary Age*, reduced the question of black oppression to exploitation in general under capitalism and denied its special nature: 'The Negro ... constitutes a vital problem of our revolutionary movement. The race problem is simply a phase of the general social problem,

9 James W. Ford, fragment of document on Negro Question draft for *Political Affairs* [1950s?], in James W. Ford papers, box 1, folder 'Writings on the Communist Party'; Domingo reprinted in *Revolutionary Radicalism* 1919, 1501–2; Berland 1999, p. 413; Bynum 2010, pp. 78–9; Makalani 2004, p. 46; Weinstone 1969, p. 11. On Huiswoud, see Enckevort 2001; Turner 2005, pp. 73–5. According to Hermina Dumont Huiswoud, Otto's wife, another black man was present at the founding of the CP: Arthur Hendricks, 'a theological student from British Guiana (present day Guyana) who influenced Huiswoud's early understanding of Communism' but who died of tuberculosis soon after. Hermina Dumont Huiswoud, letter to *Nationale Voorlichtings Dienst*, 20 November 1985, Hermina Dumont Huiswoud papers, box 1, folder 3. Mark Solomon, basing himself on Dumont Huiswoud, asserts that Hendricks, although a supporter of the left-wing, died *before* the founding of the Communist movement: Solomon 1998, pp. 3, 316.

which the Communist revolution alone can solve'. The *Revolutionary Age*'s editor, Louis Fraina, also edited (along with Debs and Ludwig Lore) *Class Struggle*. This latter journal argued that 'the white man must understand that there is but one alternative—either competition to the utmost or a common fight of all workers, without regard to color, race or creed, against the common enemy, the capitalist class'.[10]

To their credit, early Communists spoke out against anti-black racism in the shadow of this lynch-mob terror, but had nothing on offer other than anti-racist appeals. As opposed to their calls to turn a strike by Brooklyn transport workers into a proletarian insurrection, Communists did not advocate any concrete action against these pogroms and did not analyse the role of anti-black racism and black oppression beyond the most superficial level. Their failure to recognise the unique nature of the oppression of blacks within American capitalism underlined their distance from American social reality.

The Comintern and Special Oppression

Although the 'Negro question' was an American question, a result of US history, American Communists proved incapable of grasping its importance. James P. Cannon recalled decades later that the 'CP policy in the Negro question got its initial impulse from Moscow, and that all further elaborations of this policy ... came from Moscow'.[11]

Based on his experience in tsarist Russia—a 'prison house' of oppressed peoples—Lenin had long argued that the development of capitalism created deep divisions within the working class, including those based on national, racial, ethnic and religious oppression. Lenin's Bolshevik Party developed into a new type of party, based on the 'advanced' layers of workers and not, as had been the social-democratic norm, the entire working class. Social-democratic parties, embracing the entire working class, tended to downplay special oppression as a diversion from pure economic issues. Thus, in a famous passage in his *What Is to Be Done?* Lenin insisted that a Communist militant not be a 'trade-union secretary, but the tribune of the people' who would 'react to every manifestation of tyranny and oppression, no matter where it appears'. Much of the appeal of the Bolsheviks was their insistence on the right of

10 *Communist* (CPA), 9 August 1919; *Revolutionary Age*, 9 August 1919; see also 2 August 1919 and 23 August 1919; *Class Struggle*, August 1919.

11 Cannon 1962, p. 229.

self-determination—separation—of oppressed nations. According to one recent study, the Bolshevik's Central Committee between 1917–23 was between 58 and 70 percent non-Russian.[12]

Generalising from the Russian experience, the Bolsheviks emphasised anti-imperialism and anti-colonialism. Since special oppression often was integral to capitalism, struggling against it could spark broader social struggles. This understanding compelled the Bolsheviks to sense the importance of the 'Negro Question', although it did not substitute for specific knowledge of American conditions.[13]

While not experts, the Bolsheviks had some appreciation of the importance of racial oppression in the US. According to one study, Harriet Beecher Stowe's abolitionist *Uncle Tom's Cabin* had impressed Lenin as a youth, but in any case, as early as 1913, Lenin had noted the importance of the Negro question when he wrote: 'Everyone knows that the position of the Negroes in America *in general* is one unworthy of a civilised country—capitalism *cannot* give either *complete* emancipation or even complete equality'. Segregation in East St. Louis struck Alexandra Kollontai when she visited the US during the World War. Sen Katayama, a leading Japanese Communist who had attended university in the American South, appreciated the importance of black oppression in the US and would play an important role in getting the Comintern to address it.[14]

The Second Comintern Congress

The first Comintern intervention concerning racial oppression in the US took place at the Second Congress, in the summer of 1920. Lenin's 'Preliminary Draft Theses on the National and Colonial Questions' had solicited information on a number of national and colonial situations. He listed 'Negroes in America' between 'Turkestan, its experience' and 'Colonies'. (The final theses on the question mentioned 'the Negroes in America' as one of the 'nations that are dependent and do not have equal rights'). In the lead-up to the Congress, John

12 Lenin 1961, p. 423; On the Bolsheviks' composition, see Riga 2008; by the end of the nineteenth century, ethnic Russians comprised less than half of the population of the Russian Empire: see Freeze 2009, p. 152.

13 This helped make the Bolsheviks more sensitive to issues of racial oppression; see Matusevich 2008, p. 59.

14 Reynolds 2011, p. 175; Lenin 1975, pp. 543–4; Porter 1980, p. 229.

Reed wrote a five-page summary of the history and condition of black people in the US. He asserted that 'the war has put a new spirit into the Negroes'.[15]

Although the Second Congress's American Commission was occupied with factionalism, Lenin urged Reed to deliver a short presentation on the American black population. When Reed expressed reluctance, Lenin insisted that the report was 'absolutely necessary'. Reed's speech broke no new ground in analysing the Negro question and echoed Debsian colour-blindness. He argued that the 'only proper policy for the American Communist to follow is to consider the Negro first of all as a laborer'. Nonetheless, this was the first time an American Communist noted the unique features of black oppression. As an 'oppressed and downtrodden people', Reed argued, blacks combined 'a strong race and social movement' with 'a strong proletarian labor movement'. He stressed the lack of nationalism among blacks. Most importantly, Reed emphasised that Communists 'must not ... stand aloof from the Negro movement'. (However, immediately after Reed spoke, Fraina downplayed the significance of black oppression in the US, putting it on the same plane as anti-immigrant racism).[16]

During the Congress, the ECCI advised the American delegates that 'it consider[ed] it advisable to convene a 'Congress of the Negro Peoples of the World' and requested that the Americans come up with a plan to organise this. Joseph Zack Kornfeder decades later recalled that the party leadership received a letter from Lenin in the late autumn, demanding that the party address the issue as well as send a report on its work. The CEC assigned this task to Zack. Around this time, attention to the Negro question was transferred from the ECCI's 'American Agency' (led by Fraina and Katayama) to the newly unified American Communist Party.[17]

---

15 Lenin 1965a, pp. 141–51; Reed to 'Dear comrade Zinoviev', 25 February 1919, in Comintern archives, 495:155:1. The report is evidently misdated, since at this time Reed was facing trial in Philadelphia for inciting a riot: see *New York Times*, 27 February 1919; 28 February 1919.

16 Reed to Lenin with Lenin's handwritten reply, in John S. Reed papers, fms Am 1091:533; Reed's speech is in *Second Congress* 1977, I, pp. 120–4, as well as Foner and Allen 1987, pp. 7–8; Fraina's speech is in *Second Congress* 1977, I, pp. 124–6.

17 Undated note from the Secretary of the ECCI to 'Comrades Reed, Fraina, Gurvitch [Hourwich], Janson and Scott', in Comintern archives, 495:155:1 (Janson and Scott were in fact the same person); Joseph Kornfeder to Theodore Draper, 11 April 1958, in Solomon and Kaufman papers, box 1, folder 29. (The original letter is in Draper's papers at Emory University, box 21); Kat[ayama] and Fra[ina], 'To the Small Bureau' [after August 1921], in Comintern archives, 5:3:619. 'Lenin' was written across the top of the letter, indicating its importance.

In 1921, the Workers' Party of America advocated united black and white working-class struggle, and pledged to 'support the Negroes in their struggle for liberation', which included 'economic, political and social equality'. In the 1980s, James S. Allen and Philip S. Foner—both of whom sympathised with the Communist Party—claimed that this programme 'marks an important step forward' on the Communist position on the Negro question; in reality, this was a verbal concession unmatched by real activity. The same year, the Communist press began to stress fighting black oppression. *The Toiler* (10 December 1921) asserted that 'Every blow struck for Negro liberation will be a blow struck for the world Proletariat, since whether the Negroes consciously will it or not, the effects will be the weakening of the capitalist foe of both the "subject peoples" and the exploited white workers'. Nonetheless, the paper did not indicate that *Communists* should strike some of the blows.[18]

Early Black Response to Bolshevism

The Bolshevik Revolution resonated among black intellectuals and radicals. The Revolution intersected great ferment among black Americans, as 'New Negro' radical movements clashed with both the traditional liberal integrationists represented by W.E.B. Du Bois and nationalist followers of Garvey.

By 1919, the broader 'New Negro' movement rejected Du Bois and the NAACP, whom they now derided as 'Old Crowd Negroes'. During the war, Du Bois had supported the US as an opportunity for black Americans to prove their suitability for freedom. The optimism of the NAACP's *Crisis* about the improvement of the conditions of black people did not fit the terrorism of the 'Red Summer', and made the gradual, legal strategy for winning black rights less attractive. Haywood Hall, a returning black veteran who became a Communist (under the name Harry Haywood) later recalled thinking that the NAACP's 'reliance on white rulers' had 'let us down'. One reflection of this was the growth of Randolph and Owen's *Messenger*. At first, this paper was pro-Bolshevik, and ruthlessly criticised black leaders and called for 'a new leadership—a leadership of intelligent and manly courage'. This 'new crowd', wrote Randolph, 'must be composed of young men who are educated, radical and fearless'.

18 *Program and Constitution of the Workers Party of America* (1921), in Foner and Allen 1987, p. 9 (editorial comment on p. 8; *Toiler* quoted on p. 15).

The *Messenger* published articles by radicals including Huiswoud, Fort-Whiteman and Domingo.[19]

In addition to the NAACP and the left, an important factor in black politics was Marcus Garvey's Universal Negro Improvement Association (UNIA). The UNIA had up to a million members within the US and an equal number abroad, making it most likely the largest black organisation in history. In the early 1920s, Garvey's *Negro World* had a weekly press run of up to 200,000 issues. The UNIA linked the North American black population to the aspirations of blacks internationally, particularly in the Caribbean. Yet for its supporters in Jamaica, Central America, the US, Africa and Britain, the Garvey movement meant different things. Unlike the liberal-integrationist NAACP, or the pro-Socialist 'New Negro' movement, the back-to-Africa UNIA argued that black 'redemption' was possible only outside of the US and that it was futile to struggle to alter the oppression of black people in the US. Garvey's programme, such as the Black Star steamship line based on investment, was pro-capitalist. Since Garvey viewed the US as a 'white man's country', he was willing to appease the most reactionary elements of white supremacy.

At the same time, the movement's emphasis on strident race pride made the UNIA appear more militant than Booker T. Washington's abject accommodationism. This is one reason why Garvey was imprisoned for tax fraud in 1925 and deported to Jamaica two years later. By politicising blacks during the reactionary post-Reconstruction period, the UNIA and Garvey served as a transition from the bitter defeat of black people to the renewal of the struggle for equality. In some areas, such as the San Francisco Bay Area and among the West Indian diaspora in the Greater Caribbean, the Garvey movement had a large working-class base and intersected the black labour movement. At this time, there was no Chinese Wall between Garvey and more radical black nationalists, and important black radicals had been friendly to Garvey.[20]

Although in retrospect Haywood claimed that upon returning to the US he concluded that Communism was 'where the action was', few black militants noticed, and far fewer supported, the party. Not only did the party continue a colour-blind approach, but it was also illegal and comprised more than a dozen insular foreign-language groups. Although the *Messenger* was sympathetic

19 *Crisis*, July 1918; Ellis 1992; Lewis 1993, pp. 556–8; Harry Haywood dictation, 16 March 1970, Haywood Papers; *Messenger*, January 1918; July 1918; May/June 1919; December 1919. See also Bynum 2010, pp. 60–1.

20 Frederickson 1995, p. 153; Digby-Junger 1998, p. 268; Stein 1986, pp. 169–70. Jenkins 2008; Heideman 2008, pp. 66–7; Makalani 2011, p. 60. For a more detailed analysis of the contradictions of the Garvey movement (from which the above paragraph is adapted), see Zumoff 2007, p. 214. See also Fraser 1994, p. 8.

to Bolshevism, Randolph and Owens avoided the Communist Party. Lovett Fort-Whiteman was the only other black Communist, besides Huiswoud, recruited from the SP Left Wing, as well as the first US-born black Communist. Born in Dallas, Texas, a graduate of the Tuskegee Institute, and a former medical student in Tennessee, Fort-Whiteman had visited Mexico during that country's Revolution and then settled in Harlem. He had been a Socialist and supporter of the IWW before becoming a Communist.[21]

The Jamaican-born writer Claude McKay was another early black Communist with experience in the Socialist movement. McKay had written for Max Eastman's *Liberator*; he became a Communist in London. In late 1919, in a letter to Garvey, he argued that 'radical Negroes should be more interested in the white radical movements' in the British Empire because 'they are the great destructive forces *within*, while the subject races are fighting without'. He cautioned:

> I don't mean that we should accept them unreservedly and put our cause into their hands. No: They are fighting their own battle and so are we; but at present we meet on common ground against the common enemy. We have a great wall to batter down and while we are working on one side we should hail those who are working on the other.

The next month, the British Communist newspaper *Workers' Dreadnought* published a front-page article by McKay, 'Socialism and the Negro', which stressed that in the US 'the coloured workers are ready and willing to meet the white workers half-way in order that they might be united in the fight against capitalism' even while, due to racism, 'the whites are still reluctant to take the step that would win the [American] South over to Socialism'. McKay was briefly active in the US in 1922 between European sojourns. Nonetheless, he played a crucial role in making the early Communists address black oppression. The exceptional nature of these three black Communists—McKay and Huiswoud, two Caribbean immigrants, and Fort-Whiteman, an anarchist from Texas who had travelled to Southern Mexico—highlights the early CP's distance from black politics.[22]

---

21 Haywood dictation, 16 March 1970, Haywood papers; on Fort-Whiteman, see Gilmore 2008, pp. 32–7. In the minutes of the Communist Party, he is often referred to as merely 'Whiteman'.

22 Claude McKay to [Marcus] Garvey, 17 December 1919, Hubert Harrison, box 2, folder 66; *Workers' Dreadnought*, 31 January 1920. On McKay, see Cooper 1990, Chapter 4; Gosciak 2008; Holcomb 2007, Chapter 1; James 2003b; Turner 2005, pp. 85–90; Zumoff 2010.

The African Blood Brotherhood

The first breakthrough the Communists had in recruiting black cadres was the African Blood Brotherhood (ABB). The ABB—which counted among its members Fort-Whiteman, Huiswoud and McKay—had been organised by Cyril Valentine Briggs. He was an immigrant from Nevis who had been fired as editor of the *Amsterdam News* because he refused to tone down his criticism of racism and Jim Crow in the Army. In September 1918, he founded the *Crusader*, which mixed black nationalism, pan-Africanism and community news. The frontispiece declared 'Onward for democracy. Upward with the race', while the paper advocated 'Africa for the Africans' and argued that 'Victory for the allies must usher in Democracy for the people—regardless of race, creed or color ... We therefore look for a free Africa, as well as a free Poland, Serbia and Belgium as one of the guaranteed results of the Allied victory'. Free Africa meant 'Africa will no longer be exploited by a ruling caste of European overlords'.[23]

For Briggs, the fight against black oppression in the US was part of a global struggle against imperialism and colonialism. The *Crusader* carried articles about black people in New York City, but also in the American South, Latin America and the Caribbean, and Africa. In the early *Crusader*, the Irish fight against the British resonated more than the socialist fight against capitalism. The paper's emphasis no doubt reflected Briggs and other Caribbean blacks' dual perspective of opposing anti-black racism in the US and European colonialism in the Caribbean. The paper's international focus and pan-Africanism was informed by the history of anti-slavery and anti-colonial struggle in the region. It also reflected the felt need to transcend the many linguistic, ethnic and national barriers within the Greater Caribbean, and the history of massive migration within the region and between the islands and Central and North America. The *Crusader* sought an 'honorable solution of the "Negro Problem", and ... a renaissance of Negro power and culture throughout the world'. This meant 'achiev[ing] for Ethiopia a place among the nations'. In the US, the choice was 'complete equality or complete annihilation'. The journal advocated 'the creation and existence of an independent Negro Nation' and

23 Much of the following discussion is drawn from Zumoff 2007, which also contains a fuller bibliographic and historiographic treatment. Sources on the ABB include: Kuykendall 2002; Makalani 2011; Parascandola 2006; The best overall treatment of Caribbean immigrants in black radical politics is James 1998; see also Stephens 2005; Stevens 2010; C.V. Briggs to Oakley Johnson, 18 April 1962, Oakley Johnson papers; *Crusader*, September 1918.

'government of the Negro, by the Negro and for the Negro' which could 'best be attained and secured in our sunny motherland: *Africa*!'[24]

The November 1919 *Crusader* carried a small notice soliciting members to join 'The African Blood Brotherhood for African Liberation and Redemption'. Although the notice did not mention politics, much of the early leadership of the ABB were Socialists, including Domingo, Richard B. Moore and Grace P. Campbell. Domingo, born in Jamaica, had been close to Garvey, but gravitated to the Harlem Socialist Party in the late teens and twenties. Moore, born in Barbados, had been active in Harlem Socialist politics as well, before becoming a long-time Communist activist. Campbell, born in Georgia of a Caribbean-born father and an American mother, was likely the first black woman Socialist according to Winston James; she played a crucial role in organising the ABB. (None of these Socialists were active in the pre-Communist Left Wing).[25]

Although the next several issues of the *Crusader* carried positive letters from readers in Central America, the Caribbean and throughout the US, it is difficult to gauge the success of the ABB. A December 1919 British government report on 'revolutionary movements' throughout the world noted the ABB's formation. By the end of 1920, the *Crusader* claimed a distribution of '(on average) 33,000 copies per issue', while Winston James estimated a subscription peak of 20,000. Briggs later stated that the ABB had begun with 'less than a score' of members, all in Harlem, and did not even attain three thousand members at its peak. The credentials committee of the Fourth Congress of the Communist International in 1922 reported that the organisation had 500 members.[26]

The group entered public consciousness in 1921, after the Tulsa, Oklahoma, race riot was blamed on its members. During the three-day riot, a white mob destroyed the prosperous black section of Tulsa that left some 300 people dead and thousands homeless. The *New York Times* reported that Briggs claimed 50,000 members in 150 branches throughout the country and that 'several hundred members of the African Blood Brotherhood' turned out in Harlem to hear Domingo speak on 'race retaliation' after the riot. Clearly, the ABB did not

24 *Crusader*, April 1919, August 1919, November 1919. On the international perspective of the ABB, see Makalani 2011, Chapter 2; Zumoff 2007.

25 Biographical information on Domingo and Moore from Zumoff 2008a and Zumoff 2008b; on Moore, see also Lewis 1995; McClendon 2006, and Turner and Turner 1988, pp. 19–100; information on Campbell from James 1998, pp. 174–6; see also McDuffie 2011.

26 Directorate of Intelligence (British Home Office) 1919, p. 28; *Crusader*, December 1920; James 2003a, p. 370; C. Briggs to Theodore Draper, 14 April and 4 June 1958, Theodore Draper papers, box 31, folder marked 'Negro—Briggs'; Riddell 2011, p. 437.

foment the riot, but drew attention, from blacks and whites, for espousing the right of self-defence.[27]

The Politics of the African Blood Brotherhood

In June 1920, the *Crusader* urged: 'affiliate yourself with the liberal, radical, and labor movements. Don't mind being called "Bolsheviki" by the same people who call you "nigger". Such affiliation in itself won't solve our problems, but it will help immensely'. The article described the UNIA as 'the biggest thing so far effected in surface movements', while stressing that supporters should 'adopt the policy of race first, without, however, ignoring useful alliances with other groups'.[28] The ABB leadership was moving closer to the Communist movement, as the *Crusader* began to write in class terms. It also began to write favourably of the Soviet Union. In December 1921, a *Crusader* advertisement drafted by Briggs urged readers to '*stand by Soviet Russia* and thereby stand by your own and make it possible for her to give further aid to the *liberation struggle* of the darker people'.[29]

Several people around the ABB left the Socialist Party in this time. In May 1921, Harlem Socialists invited prominent Socialist Algernon Lee to speak; when he claimed that the SP did not have the resources or interest to organise blacks, several black Socialists quit the party. Briggs and the rest of the ABB leadership joined the CP in 1921. (The exception was Domingo, who never joined the Communist Party, and instead focused on importing Caribbean food to New York. In the 1930s, Domingo became active in Caribbean nationalist politics). By August 1921, Briggs was a member of the party's 'Negro Committee', and the party had begun to subsidise the *Crusader*. Briggs attended the conference that created the Workers' Party in late 1921. In June 1922, Briggs, Huiswoud and Moore were leaders in the West Harlem branch of the Workers' Party. Campbell, an important (if unrecognised) pioneer black Communist woman

27 *New York Times*, 5 June 1921 and 20 June 1921. On the Tulsa riots, see Madigan 2003; Ellsworth 1992. On the ABB and the riot, see Turner 2005, pp. 93–4. According to Gates 2004, pp. 87–8: 'On more than one occasion, [ABB] leaders had visited Oklahoma' before the riot, and had corresponded with black Oklahomans about racial violence there. Such correspondence 'brought members of the ABB to Tulsa before and after the riot. (Some black survivors say that a few got caught in Tulsa at the time of the riot).'

28 *Crusader*, June 1920.

29 *Crusader*, December 1921.

who had twice stood for the New York State Assembly as a Socialist, stood on the Workers' Party ticket in 1922. In late 1923, the CP absorbed the ABB, and in 1925 the ABB was dissolved.[30]

The ABB at its birth had no connection to the Communist movement.[31] Communism was not the 'logical' or inevitable conclusion to the ABB's politics. Indeed, the American Communists with their social-democratic colourblindness must not have appeared attractive; the Communist Party would have been unable to recruit the ABB on their own. Briggs and the ABB, like many throughout the colonial world, were attracted to the Communist International because of its anti-colonialism and anti-imperialism, as well as Lenin's emphasis on fighting special oppression. Briggs and the other ABB recruits did not want to join the American CP per se, but saw themselves as enlisting in the American branch of international Communism.[32]

For the CP, recruiting the ABB opened the door to increased black recruitment. In a letter to the Comintern, the American leadership was optimistic: 'With the winning of these black comrades and the consequent extension of the Communist Party into the "dark regions" of the Southern States which have hitherto been impenetrable to Socialist propaganda, the Communist Party feels that it has made a step toward the aim of becoming a mass party'. Although this was too optimistic, the ABB cadres in the 1920s provided the leadership that opened the road to recruiting larger numbers of black members—including women—in the 1930s. They served as a tribune for black concerns within the party by consistently pressing the issue of racial oppression and taking the Communist leadership to task for neglect of the Negro Question.[33]

30 Zumoff 2007, p. 210; Turner 2005, pp. 85–90. On Briggs and the formation of the WPA, see the reports by 'Agent 800' in December 1921, in Briggs's FBI file.

31 Draper asserted that the ABB and CP were 'organized ... in complete independence' of the Communists; Draper 1986, p. 326. But Robert A. Hill argued that the two were part of 'a simultaneous and organic process'; Hill 1987, p. xxiv. I have examined this controversy in more detail elsewhere; see Zumoff 2007, pp. 208–9. For his part, William Z. Foster describes the ABB as 'an offshoot of *The Messenger* group in New York during the early 1920's', attesting to his lack of intersection with the ABB cadres; Foster 1952, p. 268.

32 C.V. Briggs to Oakley Johnson, 3 October 1961, Oakley Johnson papers, reel 4/Box 8, folder 18.

33 Taylor 2009, p. 7; Griffler 1995, p. 44; on the recruitment of black women, see Harris 2009; McDuffie 2011, Chapter 1.

The ABB and the UNIA

Much of the activity of the now CP-aligned ABB was aimed at the Garvey movement. This may seem strange, given his pro-capitalist politics, but the UNIA was the largest black organisation in the world and had managed to recruit radicals. Both Domingo and Harrison had been editors of the *Negro World* and Garveyite workers were often quite militant, for example, in the massive Panama Canal strike in early 1920. Although Garvey's perspective was based on accepting the existence of white supremacy in the US, in the 1920s and 1930s, a number of former Garveyites would join the CP.[34]

In August 1921, Briggs sent a cordial letter to Garvey, inviting him to a 'conference on those major questions in the work for African liberation in which both yourself and I, and our respective organizations[,] are intensely interested'. The letter asserted that although the two groups were 'moving in different spheres', they shared 'the same aims and ideals' and were 'bound to help each other—and that whether we consciously co-operate or not'.[35]

After Briggs sent the letter, the ABB attempted to intervene at a UNIA 'Convention of the Negro Peoples of the World'. A manifesto, 'to New Negroes who really seek liberation', hailed the Bolsheviks' 'many acts in behalf of the liberation of the Darker Peoples' and called Soviet Russia 'to-day the greatest menace to Imperialism'. The manifesto called for 'a federation of all existent Negro organizations, molding all Negro factions into one mighty and irresistible force, governed and directed by a Central Body made up of representatives from all the major Negro organizations'. The conference received Stokes, a white Communist, warmly, if patronisingly—perhaps because her speech did not directly criticise the UNIA. But the conference tabled the motions prepared by the ABB.[36]

The falling out of Garvey and Briggs happened because Garvey's pro-capitalist black nationalism was incompatible with Communism. At the same

34 Storch 2009, pp. 95–6; McDuffie 2006, pp. 235–8. On the ABB and Garvey in general, see Vincent 1972; Vincent 1996. On Garvey's supporters and the Panama strike, see Burnett 2004; Maloney 1989. Foster's *History of the Communist Party* merely states that the Communists 'generally adopted a friendly, although critical, attitude toward the Garvey movement'; Foster 1952, p. 228.

35 *Crusader*, November 1921; the letter is also reprinted in Hill 1986, pp. 667–8.

36 Stokes's speech is in *Negro World*, 27 August 1921, and reprinted in Hill 1986, pp. 675–81; 'To New Negroes Who Really Seek Liberation: To the Delegates of the Second Negro International Convention and to the Negro Race in General', August 1921, and *Negro Congress Bulletin and News Service*, 6 August 1921, both in Briggs FBI file. See also Naison 2005, p. 8; Stephens 1999, pp. 71–87; Zipser and Zipser 1989, pp. 227–8.

time, the ABB's anti-Garvey campaign reflected broader anti-Garvey sentiment in Harlem and black America, caused by his disregard for established black leaders, pageantry and questionable financial methods. Garvey's June 1922 meeting with the leadership of the Ku Klux Klan (on the basis that both believed the US was a white man's country) further galvanised black public opinion against him. After the UNIA convention, Domingo wrote to Du Bois, calling the Black Star Line 'about as ill-conceived and dark a suggestion as any Negro-phobist like Clark [sic] of the Ku Klux Klan could devise for transferring the relatively small capital of Negroes from their race into the coffers of white capitalists for the purpose of reducing us to ridicule and finally impotency'. Anti-Garvey sentiment culminated in a 'Garvey must go' campaign, in which Randolph played a leading role. In August and September 1922, several mass meetings were held against Garvey. In 1922, Garvey was arrested; in 1923, he was convicted; in 1925 (after appeals were exhausted) he was imprisoned; and in 1927 (after his sentence was commuted) he was deported.[37]

The Briggs-Garvey feud was sordid. After the 1921 UNIA convention, the *Negro World* described (the light-skinned) Briggs as a 'white man' and a 'Negro for convenience' who had formed the ABB 'to catch Negroes'. Briggs sued Garvey for libel, and won. FBI records detail the work of a Department of Justice *agent provocateur* in stirring up animosity between the UNIA and the ABB. James Wormley Jones, known as 'agent 800', became the circulation manager of the *Negro World*, and a secret ABB member. His reports document how he anonymously gave UNIA membership information to the ABB, while 'telling Briggs that the article in the Negro World about Briggs being a white man was libel'. According to FBI records, Briggs also encouraged the government 'to take action against Marcus Garvey and the Black Star Line for having used the United States mail to defraud its shareholders'. In late October, the *New York Herald* reported that 'Cyril V. Briggs ... caused the arrest yesterday of Marcus Garvey'. While Briggs does not deserve the blame for the capitalist state's

37 On the anti-Garvey campaign, see *New York Times*, 7 August, 21 August, and 11 September 1922; W.A. Domingo (on ABB stationary) to Dr. W.E.B. Du Bois, 24 August 1922, copy in Solomon and Kaufman papers, box 3, file 10 (presumably Domingo was referring to Edward Young Clarke, then an Imperial Wizard in the resurgent Klan); Bynum 2010, pp. 76–7; Grant 2008, pp. 309–12; Heideman 2008, p. 90; Stein 1986, Chapter 8; Zumoff 2007, pp. 212–17; on Communist recruitment among former Garvey supporters, see Storch 2009, pp. 95–6. See also Cyril Briggs, 'Our Approach to the Garveyites', *Harlem Liberator*, 23 September 1933, in Hill and Bair 1991, pp. 561–2. There was also a xenophobic anti-immigrant aspect of the anti-Garvey campaign. For obvious reasons, the ABB did not participate in this; Domingo resigned from the *Messenger* to protest its anti-Caribbean sentiment.

hostility to Garvey, the claim by a Justice Department agent that 'Briggs promised to obtain the names of persons who could be used by this Department as witnesses' against Garvey, if true, would be indefensible.[38]

Briggs subsequently denied that he assisted the government. It would be foolish to take Agent 800's reports at face value, especially since some are absurd: in September 1921, for example, he claimed that Briggs was buying Thompson submachine guns with money from the Soviet and the Japanese governments, as well as seeking funding from 'the Turkish, Indian, and Egyptian Unionist' movements. What is not in dispute is that amid government surveillance and provocation, the Briggs-Garvey dispute descended into squalid intrigue.[39]

The Comintern Intervenes

The Comintern established a Negro Commission at its Third Congress in 1921 to deal with the Negro question in different countries. South African delegates had proposed an international commission to deflect criticism from their own problems intervening in the militant, yet racist, miners' strike. David Ivon Jones, a Welshman resident in the Soviet Union who represented South Africa at the Congress, argued that the international Negro Question was part of the colonial question, centred 'in South Africa', even if its 'most aggravating form ... is found in America'.[40]

38 *Negro World*, 8 October 1921; *New York Herald*, 21 October 1921; both clippings in Solomon and Kaufman papers, box 3, folder 10. On the Manifest of the SS *Trinidad*, arriving at Ellis Island on 3 July 1906, Briggs's 'race or people' was originally listed as 'white', but this was crossed out and 'West Indian' apparently written over. Available at <www.ellisisland.org>; Mortimer J. Davis, 'In Re: Black Star Line—Violation Section 215, U.S.C.C.—Using Mails to Defraud', 18 November 1921; 'Agent 800' [James Wormley Jones] to Geo. F. Ruch, no date [1921]; Mortimer J. Davis, 'In Re: Black Star Line—Alleged Violation of Section 215—Using Mail to Defraud', 8 December 1921, all in Marcus Garvey FBI file; 'Agent 800' to Geo. F. Ruch, 10 August 1921; 'Agent 800' to Geo. F. Ruch, 7 October 1921; 'Agent 800' to Geo. F. Ruch, 18 October 1921, all in Cyril Briggs FBI file; see also Kornweibel 1998, pp. 120–31.

39 Cyril Briggs to Theodore Draper, 17 March 1958; Cyril Briggs to Sheridan W. Johns III, 7 June 1961; both in Solomon and Kaufman papers, box 1, folder 16. The investment of resources by the government in spying on the UNIA and the ABB underlines the importance it saw in maintaining black oppression. The similiarities between the government's dirty tricks in this period and later 'Counterintelligence' (COINTELPRO) activities is also notable. For government spying on black militants in this period, see Kornweibel 1998.

40 Hirson and Williams 1995, p. 215. During the ten-week miners' strike on the Rand—which was at bottom an attempt by white workers to maintain the colour bar—the South African party urged white workers to be 'for the workers as workers, white, brown, yellow,

This underscored the international importance of the fight against black oppression. At the same time, the original Comintern perspective put oppression of black Americans together with the oppression of black Africans into *one* Negro question. In turn this Negro question was subsumed by the category 'toiling masses of the East'. According to Maxim Matusevich, this 'lumped Africa, Asia and the Middle East together with scant attention to regional, racial and religious distinctions'.[41]

The Commission charged with preparing the discussion at the Fourth Comintern Congress comprised Bunting, 'together with delegates from North America, Egypt, Tunis, Java, England, Holland, Belgium, Russia and Japan', although not all members consistently attended. At an ECCI Anglo-American-Colonial Group meeting in May, Katayama stated that 'the negroes would play a big part in the world revolutionary movement' and that 'the *Comintern* could tackle this problem better than the Communist Party, in America' which 'would suffer through the strong anti-negro prejudice of the people, especially in the South'. The meeting agreed that there should be black delegates to the upcoming Congress and that they should meet afterward.[42]

Jones advocated that the Congress deal with the Negro question. Noting the existence of racial consciousness among blacks in South Africa, he stressed that 'it remains to the *Comintern* to give this common feeling of the Negro race a proletarian content'. He highlighted the connection of the struggle for black liberation in the US with the fight against capitalism internationally: 'The South African delegates and negro masses generally would derive enormous benefit from intercourse at Moscow with the best proletarian Negroes of America, such as the African Blood Brotherhood'. There was strong opposition to this proposal; one Communist[43] wrote to Jones that 'The Negro race

black and all—and against the capitalists as capitalists—the *only real black man*'. Another article concluded: 'Communism alone can make South Africa a white man's country.' See Hirson and Williams 1995, pp. 228–9, 235. A 2007 article by Alison Drew makes the case that the South African Communists were not guilty of having raised the infamous banner calling for 'Workers of the World, Unite for a White South Africa'. Nonetheless, she still depicts a party having trouble coming to grips with the racial dynamics in South Africa. Documents reprinted in Davidson *et al.* 2003, reflect the attempts of South African Communists to grasp these changes.

41 Matusevich 2008, p. 59.

42 [S. P. Bunting] to Communist Party of South Africa [29 April 1923], in Comintern archives, 495:64:16, reprinted in Davidson *et al.* 2003, p. 130; ECCI Anglo-American-Colonial Group minutes, 10 May 1922, in Comintern archives, 495:72:2.

43 Davidson *et al.* reprint this document, noting that it 'is unsigned but the name "Amter" appears on the back of the original'; Davidson *et al.* 2003, p. 105.

question is of doubtful revolutionary value and can be of distinct counter-revolutionary value, like Zionism'. The writer defended the 'White Australia' policy (which limited immigration to Europeans) as a 'demand for the maintenance of decent standards of life' and criticised 'sectarian socialists' who opposed it. Jones disavowed his support for a Negro Congress.[44]

Jones was correct about the importance of the ABB cadres: McKay and Huiswoud played important roles in the Congress. While most American Communists were consumed with the debate over legalising the party, for black Communists the Congress presented an opportunity to highlight the party's problems with fighting black oppression. At bottom, these issues were different facets of the same problem: understanding American social reality. According to his wife, Huiswoud 'had gone to Moscow prepared to raise the issue'. As the *Amsterdam News* put it in the title of an article about the Congress: 'Negroes' Wrongs Aired at Moscow'.[45]

There appear to have been tensions between Huiswoud and McKay, in part because they disagreed over legality. The official delegation gave McKay the cold shoulder because he believed the party should become legal; Katayama, who had known McKay in the US, intervened to assure that McKay was seated as a special fraternal delegate. For his part, McKay criticised Briggs and other ABB leaders as 'the wrong horse at this juncture' for the Comintern to support. He argued that the party's illegal nature had prevented Communists from recruiting Domingo, whom he held in higher regard than Briggs.[46]

Huiswoud argued at the Congress that 'Although the black question is chiefly economic in nature, we nonetheless find that the problem is worsened and deepened by frictions between the white and black races'. He criticised the racist exclusionism of the AFL and the 'ultra-nationalist' UNIA, while

44 D. Ivon Jones, 'Remarks on Proposal to Call a Negro congress at Moscow', 2 January 1922, in Comintern archives, 495:155:3 (although note that Adi asserts that Jones did not think that the American Negro Question was key to Africa); see Adi 2009, p. 160; 'Discussion In Anglo-Saxon Group Meeting' (letter to Ivon Jones), 10 May 1922, Comintern archives, 495:155:3; D. Ivon Jones, 'Further Notes on Proposed Negro Congress', 23 March 1922, Comintern archives, 495:155:3; see also Weiss 2009, pp. 38–9.

45 Adi 2009, pp. 158–9; Turner 2005, pp. 99; Hermina Dumont Huiswoud to Philip S. Foner, 12 May 1970, in Dumont Huiswoud Papers, folder 7; *Amsterdam News*, 6 December 1922.

46 Turner 2005, pp. 100, 105–6, 109; Crusader/ABB press release, 11 December 1922, in Comintern archives, 515:1:91; Claude McKay to Com. Kolaroff, 23 December 1922, Comintern archives, 515:1:93; Solomon 1998, p. 41; In his autobiography, *A Long Way From Home*, McKay does not refer to Huiswoud by name but as 'the mulatto'; McKay 1937, p. 143. On McKay's difficulties being seated at the conference, see Claude McKay 'An das Sekretariat der K.I.' [1924?], in Comintern archives, 515:1:275.

describing its 'radical membership' who have 'awakened racial consciousness and utilised it on a broad scale, even into the interior of Africa, where one would hardly expect that an organisation formed in the United States would find a base of support'. Huiswoud compared the South to Dante's *Inferno* and argued that the Comintern address the issue: 'in the South, the lynching of a black is the occasion for enjoyment, as it is elsewhere to go to the cinema. When you grasp that the white population of the South is so imbued by this notion of white domination of the blacks, you will also understand that we must take up this question'.[47]

McKay, although not a full delegate, received the most attention of the two. He asserted that the 'black race at present has a special position in the economic life of the world' and argued that the condition of American blacks was worse than Jews in tsarist Russia. McKay condemned the traditional left-wing position, noting that the 'socialists and Communists conducted this struggle with great caution, because there are still strong prejudices of this kind among the American socialists and Communists. They do not want to take up the black question'. Although he supported the legalisation of the party, he noted that an integrated Communist Party 'would be illegal in the South'. In *International Press Correspondence* at the time of the Congress, he stressed that 'the future of the American Negro, whether they become the pawn of the bourgeoisie in its fight against white labor or whether they will become class conscious, depends on the nature of the propaganda that is conducted among them and the tactics adopted towards their special needs'. He warned, however, that 'the blacks are hostile to Communism because they regard it as a "white" working class movement and they consider the white workers their greatest enemy'. *Izvestia* also published an extensive article, based on an interview with McKay, on 'The Race Question in America'.[48]

The Congress stressed the international aspects of the struggle against black oppression. Jones, the South African delegate, wrote that black oppression was not an American question, but 'a question of Africa ... The status of the American negro cannot be raised without the awakening of Africa. But it is no less true that the European proletariat cannot obtain a real link with Africa except through the more advanced negroes of America'. This approach made the oppression of black people a *bona fide* political issue in the

47 Riddell 2011, pp. 800–5. Huiswoud used the name 'Billings'.

48 Riddell 2011, pp. 807–10; McKay 1922, p. 817; *Izvestia*, 16 November 1922; a translation of the article is in McKay's FBI file. Indicating McKay's significance, he and not Huiswoud was quoted in an Associated Press story on the discussion in the *New York Times*, 30 November 1922.

international Communist movement, drawing together the struggles of black people in Africa, North America, the Caribbean and North America. It made the Negro question a pressing issue for the Comintern as a whole and removed it from the narrow context of the United States (or South Africa) where the local Communist leaderships had proved incapable of dealing with it. But it confused different national contexts: racial oppression (and even the definition of race) took different forms in different countries and continents.[49]

The Negro Commission at the Fourth Congress made clear that fighting black oppression must be a key task of Communists in the US since 'The Negro problem has become a vital question of the world revolution'. The final resolution declared: 'The history of the Negroes in America qualifies them to play an important part in the liberation struggle for the entire African race'. The resolution 'recognize[d] the necessity of supporting every form of the Negro movement which undermines or weakens capitalism, or hampers its further penetration'. The Comintern pledged to 'fight for the equality of the white and black races, for equal wages and equal political and social rights'. It urged black workers to join unions, and for unions to organise them. Finally, it called for 'a world Negro congress or Conference'. This resolution, whatever its limitations, was a turning point in the Communist appreciation of the links between black oppression and capitalism. It also solidified the Comintern's reputation as a tribune of black concerns within the international movement. At the same time, it continued to confound the situation of black Americans with South Africans. Another South African Communist at the Fourth Congress, the English-born Sidney Bunting, criticised the resolution because it 'laid down as universal a policy which is chiefly applicable to conditions in the northern United States'.[50]

49 Hirson and Williams 1995, p. 249; Baldwin 2002, pp. 45–6. Later, this perspective would be enshrined in the 'Third Period' Communist perspective on the Negro Question; see Bergin 2006, pp. 100–1.

50 'Theses of the Fourth Comintern Congress on the Negro Question', 30 November 1922, in Degras 1956, I, pp. 399–401; 'Letter from SP Bunting to General Secretary, Comintern', 1 January 1923, in Comintern archives, 495:64:12, reprinted in Davidson *et al.* 2003, p. 117. On the importance of the Fourth Congress, see Cyril Briggs to Sheridan W. Johns III, 7 June 1961, in Solomon and Kaufman research files, box 1, folder 16; McDuffie 2011, p. 46.

Claude McKay and the Fight to Address the Negro Question

In his visit to Soviet Russia, McKay met a cross-section of society, from Bolsheviks like Trotsky to 'non-partisan and antibolshevist circles' of poets and 'young anarchists and menshevists'. Far from homogeneous, Russia was 'a country where all the races of Europe and of Asia meet and mix'. Unlike in West Europe or North America, McKay was not subjected to racism—further highlighting the pathological nature of black oppression in the United States.[51]

While in Soviet Russia, McKay wrote to Trotsky on the issue of Communist agitation against France's use of black colonial troops in occupying Germany and the ensuing racist backlash in Europe. Trotsky believed that 'The Negroes themselves must offer resistance to being so employed' by the French imperialists. It was in 'the most vital interests' of European workers to help 'enlighten ... the colored people'. Trotsky continued:

> The day of general resolutions on the right of self-determination of the colonial peoples, on the equality of all human beings regardless of color, is over. The time has come for direct and practical action ... A Communist Party confining itself to mere platonic resolutions in this matter, without exerting its utmost energies towards winning the largest number of enlightened Negroes for its ideas, within the shortest possible time, would not be worthy of the name of Communist Party.

This condemnation of the social-democratic approach must have seemed to McKay to be applicable in the American context as well.[52]

Trotsky commissioned McKay to write a study of the Negro Question. This study, published (in Russian) as *The Negroes in America*, argued that 'the whole American nation', pointedly including white workers, 'is, in a strange way, possessed by a Negro neurosis'. 'Labor', he wrote, 'is divided against itself. It conducts a shameful, half-hearted struggle against capitalism, since it does not extend a fraternal hand to the black working class, historically the most exploited class in American life'. McKay analysed the history of black people in America, and their contributions to labour, politics, sport and art. 'With the

51 See McKay 1923 and McKay 1924.

52 Trotsky to Claude McKay, 13 May 1923, in Trotsky 1945a, II, p. 354. On the racist furore see Levine 2003, pp. 168–71; in 1920, McKay objected to a racist article opposing the use of black troops by France in Germany by reformer E.D. Morel in the London *Daily Herald*; see McKay 1920; Derrick 2008, pp. 95–6; James 2003b.

birth of American democracy in 1776, the Negro question became the main question', according to McKay.

McKay did not pull any punches in his criticisms of the Communist Party leadership. He quoted an article in the *New York Times* about the founding convention of the Workers' Party, the legal arm of the Communist movement: 'Efforts by some delegates to make a fight for the social equality of the negro were overwhelmingly defeated'. McKay responded: 'If that report is accurate, then it only indicates once more the inability on the part of the vast majority of American revolutionaries to fully understand the Negro question'. The Communists would never recruit blacks by continuing to ignore the question, since 'every Negro worker knows ... whatever the party, when it refuses to take a stand on social equality, to that extent it also refuses to approach the Negro question'.[53]

The report *was* accurate. While the 1921 programme, quoted above, did call for social equality, the 1924 programme asserted only that 'The Workers Party will support the Negroes in their struggle for liberation and will help them in their fight for economic, political and educational equality'. Social equality—especially in sexual relations—was an explosive issue in the 1920s because it cut to the core of the definition of race in the US and emphasised what McKay had labelled a 'Negro neurosis'. The Communists' retreat perhaps was a reflection of the spectre of interracial sex that racists raised against Communists and all others who opposed segregation.[54]

McKay did not cease to criticise the weaknesses of American comrades on the Negro question. In a document he recalled that, arriving at the Fourth Congress, he 'found Comrade Carr [Ludwig Katterfeld], the leader of the American delegation very ignorant about the revolutionary trend of the American Negroes'. Other Communists were 'afraid of carrying on propaganda

53 McKay 1979, p. 38, p. 41; *New York Times*, 26 December 1922.

54 For the 1921 programme see Foner and Allen 1987, p. 9; the 1924 revised *Program and Constitution of the Workers Party of America* is in the Comintern archives, 515:1.188; section on racial equality on p. 9. On 'social equality', see Davis 2001, especially Chapter 4. According to Bergin (2006, p. 98), in the 1930s, 'The claim that the CPUSA recruited black men through the sexual availability of white Communist women was ... pervasive'. The Communists' retreat on the issue took place in the context of the furore caused in October 1921, when Republican president Harding spoke in Birmingham, Alabama, and stated his support for more rights for blacks, but opposed 'social equality'. NAACP activist Walter White responded in the *Liberator* that 'there can never be economic, political, educational and industrial equality without potential social equality'. For his part, Garvey supported Harding's position. See *New York Times*, 27 October 1921; *Liberator*, January 1922; Grant 2008, p. 304.

among the Negroes as Negroes, because they dread a racial uprising', even though 'racial riots and lynching and burning of Negroes are common occurrences in the United States, propaganda or no propaganda'. He attacked Rose Pastor Stokes—then married to millionaire James Graham Phelps Stokes—because 'she learns much of what Negroes were thinking from the ignorant Negro maid her bourgeois husband employs'. This was one example of 'many of the very excellent white comrades' who were 'woefully lacking in sympathy and understanding of the American Negroes'. Thus, 'after two years of talk about the Negro problem, the American Communists have little to show except bulky reports'.[55]

To the historian, more damning of the CP's indifference than McKay's polemics is the history of the book itself. Trotsky, not the American Communists, commissioned McKay to write it. In June 1923, McKay wrote to Karl Radek, claiming that 'It is of an importance, I think, that this book shoul[d] be given to the Negro public in America as soon as possible'. He added: 'The fact that I was officially asked to do it in Moscow will appeal to the general Negro public'. Yet the Communist Party never translated, published or distributed the book. While in Moscow, McKay also wrote a series of short stories, *Trial by Lynching*, which underscored the depth and depravity of black oppression in the US. These books remained only available in Russian until they were re-translated into English and published by small publishing houses in the 1970s.[56]

By 1923, then, the Communists had begun to transcend the social-democratic heritage on the issue of fighting black oppression, and had recruited important black militants. Rather than being based on an organic appreciation of black oppression, this was a result of prodding by the Comintern. This offers an illustration of the crucial role that the early Comintern played in 'Americanising' its American section.

55 Claude McKay, 'For a Negro Congress' [1922?], in Comintern archives, 495:155:43.

56 Claude McKay to 'Dear comrade Radek', 20 June 1923, in Comintern archives, 495:72:8; according to McKay's letter, when he departed Moscow, he had left his notes and research materials to be sent to him safely, and that this had not happened; McKay 1977; Baldwin 2002; Maxwell 1999, p. 75; Zumoff 2010. Interestingly, in William F. Dunne's two-part article on 'Negroes in American Industry' (*Workers Monthly*, March and April 1928), he discusses the 'false dogma' of black sexual obsession with white women, noting that 'in other countries where there are large Negro populations, the sexual question does not arrive', citing a statement by Lord Olivier, former governor-general of Jamaica. While it is impossible to prove what Dunne's inspirations were, his writing echoes McKay's book.

CHAPTER 15

The 'Negro Question' from the Fourth to the Sixth Congress

Following the Fourth Congress, the party made slow headway recruiting blacks. In March 1923, Israel Amter, American representative to the ECCI, complained of the lack of progress, noting that this was in part because the 'small number of Negro comrades in the Party makes this work difficult'. The party leadership also had differences with the Comintern's emphasis. Amter's next report stated that the 'Workers Party has started work among the Irish and Negroes', but added that 'the Party does not agree with the thesis adopted by the Fourth Congress on the Negro Problem'. Three leading Communists, including C.E. Ruthenberg and John Pepper, wrote to the ECCI, arguing that the 'resolution of the Fourth Congress does not give a satisfactory solution of this problem, especially from the trade union standpoint'. Nonetheless, a month later, in April, they claimed that the party had established a school 'for Negro propagandist[s]' and that a 'program of work among the Negroes has been prepared and this work will be pushed aggressively'.[1]

Tensions within the party continued. On one level, given the internecine factionalism, it was unlikely that 'Negro work' would escape. There is also evidence that leading members of the party, including Ruthenberg and Pepper, resented the ABB. In March 1923, the Organization Committee put Huiswoud in charge of a six-week course to train black propagandists, but refused to allocate a part-time stenographer. In July, Ruthenberg accused the ABB of supporting emigration from the South, touting blacks' scabbing against white strikers, and advocating 'race hatred of whites'. A month later, Briggs wrote to the leadership, complaining of rumours of his being a spy. The Political and Organization Committee refused to take action, claiming that it did not have enough information. In December, at Benjamin Gitlow's instigation, the executive council passed a motion that 'we will not in the future carry on any work among the Negroes thru Briggs and Huiswoud'. Huiswoud was evidently

1 Report by I. Amter to Comintern, 7 March 1923; I. Amter, 'Report on the United States to 20 March 1923', both in Comintern archives, 515:1:174; Pogány [Pepper], Ruthenberg, and Jakira to ECCI, 9 March 1923; Pogány, Ruthenberg and Jakira, 'Report on the American Party Situation to the Enlarged Executive Committee of the Communist International', 11 April 1923, both in Comintern archives, 515:1:201.

disturbed enough to write a document called 'The Negro Problem Is Important'. This tension would come to a head in May 1924. At a Farmer-Labor conference in Minnesota, Huiswoud denounced a Texas delegate's opposition to black equality. Since unity with the farmer-labour movement was more important than taking a forthright stand for black rights, the leadership suspended Huiswoud for a year.[2]

The differing conceptions of the Negro question can be seen from two documents written in 1923 by Amter and Katayama. Amter's document, 'The Negro and the World Revolution', called 'the Negro problem one of the burning issues of the day'. The nine-page document sketched out the state of black America; however, it repeated the Debsian argument: 'Although the Negro problem is a race problem, in the final analysis it is a class problem and can only be solved when the working class as a whole unites in the struggle for emancipation'. The document also connected the fight for black liberation in the US to a broader fight for African liberation. No doubt unconsciously, Amter echoed Garvey: 'The American Negro, by reason of his higher education and culture, his greater aptitude for leadership and because of the urgency of the issues in America, will furnish the leadership of the Negro race'. The document ended by stressing the importance of a 'Negro World Congress' to 'crystallize the Negro sentiment and create an organization that will be representative of the whole Negro race'.[3]

Katayama's document, on the other hand, asserted that 'The Negro problems differ from each other' in 'different countries', including the US, South Africa and the French African colonies. Katayama pointed out that 'The American representatives were generally against taking the Negro problem up by the Comintern' and 'wanted to minimize the problem as much as possible, putting obstructions at every step in the discussions on the Negro Commission'. 'If the American Communist Party had followe[d] faithfully the decisions of the II Congress and live[d] up to speech made so eloquently by its representative John Reed, instead of putting every obstruction on the work of the Comintern on the Negro problems, there might have been a strong Negro revolutionary movement in America today!'

2 Minutes of Organization Committee, 29 March 1923, in Comintern archives, 515:1:204; Minutes of Political and Organization Committee, 24 July 1923; Minutes of Political Organization Committee, 23 August 1923, both in Comintern archives, 515:1:197; Minutes of Executive Council, 14 December 1923, in Comintern archives, 515:1:190; Otto E. Huiswoud, 'The Negro Problem Is Important', Workers' Party press release, 30 April 1923, in Comintern archives, 515:1:211; Enckevort 2001, p. 35.

3 I. Amter, 'The Negro and the World Revolution', in Comintern archives, 495:155:17.

He attacked the social-democratic framework. 'The trouble is that the Negro problems [sic] can not be treated as simply an economic problem'. He returned to the issue later in the document:

> The American Negro question can not be solved simply on the economic ground. It is only a means of approach to the problem. On this ground only the whites are induced to take up the Negro problem. And perhaps it may be the best and the most convenient way of dealing [with] the question. But the American Negro problems are most complicated as I said already. They are above all racial which involves social, political and economic [problems] interwoven each and the other.

The Negro conference 'depends wholly on active support of the American Communists', Katayama concluded. 'We hope that they will [support it] without hesitation'.[4]

Around the same time, McKay advocated that the congress comprise 'representative American, South African, West African and West Indian Negroes of Revolutionary spirit'. It was to be 'a conference of the real Negroes to meet with members of the Comintern [to] plan a programme of action'. He stressed that the Comintern should 'not limit the task of getting the proper personnel to the Communist Groups'. He was 'opposed to the American and South African Parties having an altogether free hand in organizing the Conference as I do not think they are familiar or class-consciously enough interested in the Negro or revolutionary material'. He added: 'especially the U.S.A. (the C.P. may antagonise comrades who can reach the masses)'.[5]

'The World Negro Congress'

Amter was placed in charge of organising the conference. McKay's warning seems to have been justified. In November 1923, Max Bedacht, in a report to the Party's leadership, complained that the Fourth Congress resolution 'gives no analysis, contains only general phrases and ends with the proposal for a world negro congress'. As shown, the idea for such a Congress had been around

4 Sen Katayama, 'Negro Race as a Factor in the Coming World Social Revolution', 14 July 1923, in Comintern archives, 495:155:17.

5 Claude McKay, 'For a Negro Congress' [1922 or 1923], in Comintern archives, 495:155:156.

since at least the Second Congress, and paralleled the Profintern-organised conferences of radical unionists and an alternative to the various Pan-African Congresses and UNIA gatherings.[6]

American Communists faced several problems in organising a congress. There were very few black Communists; a 'report on individuals' drawn up at this time lists seven black Communists or sympathisers whom the party could draw on for a congress. Most were Caribbean immigrants; this recalled McKay's warning that 'the differences existing between the American and West Indian Negro may even spoil the preliminary arrangements [for a congress] if they are not tactfully worked out'.[7]

The biggest obstacle was the fact that leading Communists opposed a Negro Congress. After the Fourth Comintern Congress, the ECCI sent a letter to the American Central Committee, complaining that 'the question yet is too unprepared', and that the issue would be discussed at an upcoming April Moscow meeting dealing with the British Communist Party. The ECCI gave the American Party the responsibility to 'take care of the propaganda' and 'prepare the ground' for this Congress. In Moscow, South African and American representatives advocated postponing the Congress, and approved a proposal by Mikhail Borodin that there first be 'preliminary regional congresses'. Katayama objected that this 'would only cause delay and put the Congress back further and further'. In a document called 'Action for the Negro Movement Should Not be Postponed', Katayama sketched a history of a lack of interest in the Negro question by American Communists, arguing that 'The American C.P. never has done any marked effort to get the Negro masses to the Communist movement'. He accused the CP of not championing an anti-lynching bill in Congress, not making use of the Tulsa race riot to condemn American capitalism, and added that he had heard that the American Communists even had opposed a strong Japanese section of the CP because Japanese were discriminated against in the US. 'The Negro question is the American question chiefly', he stressed. 'And the Comrades of the American CP are [at] every [step] against the Negro Question; traditionally so, and the Negro Conference has been postponed again by the very suggestion of the American C.P.' His angry letter seems to have been

6 Max Bedacht, report to the Executive Committee of the Workers' Party, 30 November 1923, in Comintern archives, 515:1:201.

7 'Report on Individuals' [no date], in Comintern archives, 495:155:43. There are no names on this document, although some of the people referred to may be discerned, such as Huiswoud and Briggs; McKay, 'For a Negro Congress', in Comintern archives, 495:155:156.

drawn from discussion with McKay. He denounced the 'utter neglect and convenient excuses of [the] American C.P.' for this failure.[8]

The different Communist Parties treated the Congress as a hot potato. In March 1923, the American Communist leadership passed a motion that the Congress be held in London—that is, not in the US. Amter wrote to the American leadership, stating that a Negro conference at the same time as the Comintern Congress was impossible because of difficulties facing African delegates. He proposed convening the conference in London and not New York, given the former's proximity to Moscow. In August, the CP leadership passed another motion, proposing the Congress be postponed until the Fifth Comintern Congress. In a report on the Fourth Comintern Congress, Amter blithely mentioned that the Negro Congress was being scheduled for the Fifth Comintern Congress, ignoring the dispute. In October, Amter wrote to the presidium strongly advocating that the Negro Congress be held in London, not New York. Similarly, Tom Bell of the British CP argued that the Congress be held in Paris—that is, not in Britain.[9]

This planning for the conference, although ultimately futile, is notable because the Comintern tried to coordinate attention to black oppression in Africa, North America, Latin America and Europe. Amter wrote to the leading bodies of several Communist Parties, requesting to be sent Communist propaganda on the issue and 'the Negro papers that are published in your country, or slippings [sic] of articles in other papers pertaining to the Negro population or question', as well as reports on 'the situation of Negroes in your country'. Communists in Britain, France and Portugal, for example, were urged

8 O.W. Kuusinen to WPA CC, 23 February 1923, in Comintern archives, 515:1:164; Minutes of Commission Appointed by the Orgbureau to Prepare and Guide the Work for the Forthcoming World Negro Congress, [May?] 1923, in Comintern archives, 495:155:8; Sen Katayama, 'Action for the Negro Movement Should Not Be Postponed', 22 May 1923, in Comintern archives, 495:155:17; on the lack of enthusiasm among the American Communist leadership for organising this conference, see Baldwin 2002, pp. 46–7.

9 Minutes of Political and Organization Committee, 14 April 1923, in Comintern archives, 515:1:197; Minutes of Organization Committee, 29 March 1923, Comintern archives, 515:1:197; Amter to CEC of the WP, 16 July 1923, in Comintern archives, 515:1:176; I. Amter, 'The Communist International: The Emancipator of the Whole People', 1 August 1923 press release, in Comintern archives, 515:1:212; I. Amter, 'Negerkonferenz', to the Comintern Presidium, 15 October 1923, in Comintern archives, 515:1:176. On the preference to hold the conference in London and not the US, see also C.E. Ruthenberg to Grove, 22 August 1923, in Comintern archives, 515:1:201; Tom Bell to Israel Amter, in Comintern archives, 495:155:27, cited in Sherwood 1996, p. 140. See Adi 2009, pp. 160–1, for the broader international context.

to work among African sailors passing through Europe and carry out propaganda in the colonies. Information was solicited from South African and Latin American Communists on the conditions of black people there and the possibility of sending delegates.[10]

In the US, Communists' steps towards a preliminary conference began in the spring of 1923. Independent of Communist manoeuvring, this intersected plans for a conference of black leaders, the so-called Sanhedrin. In 1922 William Monroe Trotter, editor of the Boston *Guardian* and a co-founder of the Niagara movement with W.E.B. Du Bois, had called for a council of black leaders, and in 1923 Kelly Miller, Dean of Howard University, began organising such a conference. The *Amsterdam News* recalled similar meetings by European Jewry and Indians under British rule, stating that 'the Negro needs most of all the stimulation of race conscientiousness and the formulation of a race ideal' to 'furnish inspiration to every' black person. By 1923, many black organisations supported a conference.[11]

The Communists soon took up this call, seeing such a Congress as a vehicle to build support among blacks. An 8 April 1923 press release signed by W.A. Domingo, George S. Schuyler, James Weldon Johnson and William M. Trotter, among others, noted that the ABB, the NAACP and four other groups had met in New York in March and called for an all-race Congress by 1 April 1924. The minutes for that meeting show that Briggs called for a united-front federation of black groups, 'a purely Negro federation, made up of organizations that are purely Negro'. In April, the Workers Party issued a press release calling for 'an all-race conference [to] stimulate the confidence and powers of the Negro people' that would bring about 'the greater awakening of class consciousnesses'. In August, the ABB reported that its representatives had been expelled from the Second Garvey Convention after advocating the 'creation of a United Negro Front with which to meet the enemies of the race'.[12]

10 Draft letter from Secretary for Calling Negro Conference to Executive Committee of Communist Parties, 15 November 1923, in Comintern archives, 495:155:14. See letters to the central committees of various parties in the summer and autumn of 1923 in the same location.

11 *Amsterdam News*, 31 January 1923.

12 Jeanette D. Pearl, 'Negro Organizations Present United Front', Workers' Party press release, 27 April 1923, in Comintern archives, 515:1:210; 8 April [1923] press release; 'Minutes of United Front Conference', 24 April 1923; August [1923] press release; all three in Comintern archives, 495:155:11.

The Sanhedrin conference took place in Chicago, on 11–15 February 1924 (spanning Lincoln's birthday). Church, professional, fraternal and social organisations dominated the leadership. According to one historian, they contained the 'spirit of race assertiveness on the one hand, and race conservatism on the other'. Some 300 such delegates attended, representing more than a million people. Given this petty-bourgeois composition, the final agenda avoided incendiary, working-class or radical issues such as resisting lynching, peonage, or the Klan.[13]

In January, the party's Political Committee approved five Workers' Party members' attending the Sanhedrin conference, although initially the committee had balked at helping the delegates pay for transportation. In early February, the leadership discussed the motions that the delegates would be presenting, noting that the delegates must 'carry out the policies of the Party as determined upon by the Political Committee'. At the conference, Communists presented resolutions against segregation, anti-miscegenation laws and 'real estate sharks'. The *Daily Worker* described the Communists' intervention, as well as their hostile reception. They advocated a labour-centred perspective, which was not appreciated by the conference's leadership. The Communists were edged out of the movement, but they had made it clear to the conference why they thought Communism offered the only solution to the Negro question. This intervention, objectively speaking, was unimportant in American politics; the Negro Sanhedrin movement petered out within a few years. Nor did it serve as a springboard to a world Negro Congress—something that would only be organised, finally, in Hamburg in 1930. Nonetheless, the Communist intervention provided the Communists a public platform for their position on black oppression, putting themselves on the map.[14]

The Fifth Comintern Congress and Fort-Whiteman

At the Fifth Congress of the Communist International, held in June and July 1924, the party came under heavy criticism for its lack of 'Negro work'.

13 Hughes 1984, pp. 1, 9.

14 Minutes of the Political Committee, 22 January 1924; 31 January 1924; 8 February 1924; all in Comintern archives, 515:1:299. The Workers' Party published a pamphlet containing the resolutions its delegates raised. Copies exist in the Robert Minor papers, box 13, folder 'Negro Sanhedrin, 1924', and in the Comintern archives, 495:155:23; Foner and Allen 1987, pp. 53–65; Solomon 1998, pp. 29–33. See also Adi 2008.

Fort-Whiteman (under the name Jackson), who was studying in Moscow at the time, emphasised the *special* nature of black oppression: 'The negroes are not discriminated against as a class but as a race...The same newspapers do not satisfy the needs of the negro worker which suits the needs of the white'. He argued that the 'ideas of Marx have spread only slowly among the negroes, because the Socialists and even the Communists have not realised that the problem must be dealt with in a specialised way'. This contradicted the traditional colour-blind approach. 'The negroes are destined to be the most revolutionary class in America', Fort-Whiteman declared, 'But Communist propaganda among the negroes is hampered by the lack of publicity carrying a special appeal'.[15]

Fort-Whiteman repeatedly criticised the party on the Negro question. In the November 1924 *Communist International*, he argued that achievements among blacks 'are but slight' because 'the Communists have not recognized and accepted as a starting basis the peculiar social disabilities imposed upon the race'. The article ended by warning that 'the Communist Movement cannot afford to overlook the Negro in America'. The journal's editors added a note calling the article 'a testimony that our American comrades of the ruling race have not yet been able to approach the Negro question in a right and proper manner'.[16]

In private letters to the Comintern leadership, Fort-Whiteman's complaints were more forceful. He wrote to Zinoviev that 'The American Workers Party does nothing practically on the Negro race issue in America, nor has it made any serious or worth while efforts to carry communist teaching to the great masses of American black workers'. He complained that even though he was a 'full-fledged American delegate' to the Congress, the Party leadership had refused to pay for his trip, leaving this to 'individual Negro Communists'. He proposed an American Negro Labor Congress (ANLC) in Chicago. The Comintern Secretariat supported this since 'such an organisation...at once

15 Communist International 1924, pp. 200–1.

16 James Jackson [Lovett Fort-Whiteman], 'The Negro in America', *Communist International*, November 1924, in Foner and Allen 1987, pp. 86–9. Interestingly, the draft editorial note was much more critical of Fort-Whiteman, describing as 'very superficial' the argument that 'antagonism to negroes is not so much class antagonism, as racial antagonism'. However, this statement—which would have been an endorsement of the social-democratic 'colour blind' approach—was changed before it was published. It is not clear how it was changed; see James Jackson, 'The American Negro', with appended 'Editorial Note', in Comintern archives, 495:155:25.

brings into a medium in which our Negro comrades can work and through which the Workers' Party can be able to influence the Negro masses'.[17]

The American Negro Labor Congress

According to a plan by the Comintern's Negro Commission in January, the 'Negro Workers' Congress' was to draw black workers, unionists, farmers and 'eventually representatives of the existing semi-petty-bourgeois and semi-intellectual Negro organisations'. It was to discuss 'all problems of the Negro race in addition to all problems of the Negro workers'. One emphasis was the trade unions; the Congress should support black trade unions, advocate integrating white-only unions, and call for the amalgamation of white and black unions. Fort-Whiteman was put in charge of the Congress, but the 'Congress should not be officially convened by the Communists, but by active workers in the Negro movement'. Instead, 'Communists must work at this Congress as a *fraction* under the direction of the PolBureau of the American Party'. Interestingly in the light of subsequent developments, the Commission stressed that 'Our chief slogan: "The Right of Self-Determination even to Separation" must be complemented for America by the demand of *absolute social equality*'. These arguments were soon echoed in a two-part *Workers Monthly* article, 'Negroes in American Industry', by William F. Dunne. This announced that 'sometime this year will be held a conference of delegates from Negro working class organizations'.[18]

Some Communists resisted the ANLC. In February 1925, Fort-Whiteman (still in Moscow) complained to the Comintern's American Commission that 'there has developed some opposition to the plan proposed by the Comintern for calling the American Negroe [sic] Labour Congress'. While the Sanhedrin conference was 'an organ of the Negroe [sic] petty-bourgeoisie', it did not intersect

17 James Jackson [Fort-Whiteman] to Zinoviev, October 1924, Comintern archives, 495:155:27. Fort-Whiteman did not shy away from criticising what he saw as racism in Soviet Russia either. The Comintern archives contain a letter requesting an interview with the Comissar of Education, Anatoly Lunacharsky, to discuss 'peculiar and unfortunate conditions in regard to the Jewish schools' in Uzbekistan as well as caricatures of black people in advertisements; note by James Jackson, no date [1924], in Comintern archives, 495:155:27. Letter from Secretariat of Communist International to Central Executive Committee of the Workers' Party of America, December 1924, Comintern archives, 495:155:27.

18 Decisions of the Negro Commission, 16 January 1925, in Comintern archives, 495:155:30. The most comprehensive treatment of the rise and fall of the ANLC is Solomon 1998, Chapter 4; see also Makalani 2011, pp. 116–31; Dunne 1928, p. 259.

either the 'essentially proletariat' base of the Garvey movement, or the many black and integrated trade unions. To achieve this, Fort-Whiteman underlined the importance of the ANLC.[19]

One presumes that the resistance reflected differences on the Negro question itself, since the ANLC was a 'special appeal' to black workers. In March-April 1925, the American Commission passed another resolution on the Negro question. This stressed that:

> The Negro question in the U.S.A., representing the most characteristic form of national oppression in a capitalist state whose historic roots are connected with the birth of class society, is becoming in the present period of imperialism and social revolutions the most actual question for the American proletariat, in the sense of exposing the *class substance of racial antagonism* on the one hand, and of counteracting the emergence of racial prejudices in the Negro population as a result of national oppression, on the other hand.

The resolution continued, perhaps in response to McKay's book, that Communists 'should fight against all social restrictions imposed on the Negroes in the Southern and Northern states of America'.[20]

Like most of the party's activities in this period, the ANLC was drawn into factionalism. Since Fort-Whiteman (like most black Communists) supported Ruthenberg's faction, other factions were less enthusiastic. In August 1925 (when the Foster-Cannon groups together still controlled the party leadership), Fort-Whiteman complained that he had 'some strong enemies here among the Majority faction of the Party'. He recounted that he and co-factionalist Robert Minor were called before the pre-Conference Parity Commission and charged with 'stating that the Majority leaders were actuated by some degree of Race prejudice'. In the autumn of 1925, for example, A. Jakira, the pro-Ruthenberg Pittsburgh organiser, complained that factional

19 Jacks [Fort-Whiteman], 'To the American Commission' [6 February 1925], in Comintern archives, 495:155:33.

20 'Resolution on the Negro Question', in Comintern archives, 495:155:30. The French translation reads better than the English, but the English version is quoted above with one change. The English version describes the Negro question as 'the most characteristic form of national expression [sic]', but the French describes it as 'la forme la plus caractéristique d'oppression national'. The German uses the description, 'die als Produkt der am meisten charakteristischen Form nationaler Unterdrückung im capitalistichen Staate'. The German version is in the same location as the English; the French is in the Comintern archives, 495:37:5.

opponents were stacking the delegates to the ANLC. (This prompted Lovestone to reply that 'it is entirely asinine to send a big squad of delegates to the ANLC who are neither Negroes nor members of the Congress').[21]

Another dispute arose over how close the ANLC should be to the Communist Party. In the spring, Otto Huiswoud complained to the CEC 'that the Party in its anxiety to promise this work has given publicity of such a nature that would easily tend to linking the Party with the American Negro Labor Congress, the result of which is necessarily detrimental'. Ruthenberg responded that this criticism 'is of course a sound one'. In late May, Huiswoud, Moore and two other black Communists complained to the CEC that the *Daily Worker*'s coverage of the ANLC 'clearly identif[ied] both organizations'—the party and the ANLC—'as one'. This risked narrowing down the ANLC 'merely to communists and their close sympathizers' and alienating black trade-union leaders and workers. Ruthenberg wrote to Huiswoud again, assuring him that the party will 'avoid in any way establishing a close and formal connection between the Party and the American Negro Labor Congress'. This disagreement continued throughout the actual Congress.[22]

This reflected the tension between Fort-Whiteman and the ANLC and the ABB cadres. Harry Haywood recalled that Fort-Whiteman's 'selection was the cause for some disgruntlement among the Black comrades' since there were other black Communists with 'revolutionary records superior to Fort-Whiteman's'. In a December 1925 *Workers Monthly* article hailing the conference, for

21 Lovett Fort-Whiteman to 'Dear Comrade' [Pepper?], 6 August 1925, in Comintern archives, 495:155:33; Jack [A. Jakira] to 'Dear J' [Lovestone], no date [autumn 1925]; [Lovestone] to 'Dear Jack' [A Jakira], 6 October 1925, in Lovestone papers, box 221, folder 1.

22 Otto E. Huiswoud to Earl R. Browder, 12 May 1925, in Comintern archives, 515:1:513; C.E. Ruthenberg to Otto E. Huiswoud, 19 May 1925 in Comintern archives, 515:1:506; Richard B. Moore, Otto E. Huiswoud, August Warreno and A.C. Bailey to CEC of WPA, 31 May 1925, in Comintern archives, 515:1:504; C.E. Ruthenberg to Otto E. Huiswoud, 15 June 1925, in Comintern archives, 515:1:506. For this dispute during the Congress, see 'Statement on the American Negro Labor Congress by Lovett Fort-Whiteman, National Organizer', 24 November 1925, in Comintern archives, 495:155:34. On the other hand, Haywood Hall (Harry Haywood), criticised 'opportunism and unconscious Loreism' on the part of some black Communists at the Congress shown through 'the tendency of certain Party members ... to subject Party interests to those of their other affiliations'; see Haywood Hall, 'How Not to Bolshevise the Party' [1926?], in Comintern archives, 515:1:924. The archives also contain a letter from Ruthenberg, in response to a question about 'the work which our Party has undertaken in relation to the Negroes of the United States', directing the correspondent to the ANLC; C.E. Ruthenberg to Paul Benahand, 8 May 1925, in Comintern archives, 515:1:504. It is interesting to note that this criticism of the ANLC paralleled the Ruthenberg faction's criticism of the TUEL.

example, Robert Minor gave faint praise to the ABB, declaring that it 'had and still has a splendid "theoretical" program but … never attained mass influence'. According to Haywood, Moore and Huiswoud 'made no attempt to hide their contempt for Fort-Whiteman' at this time. Other Communists, including fellow supporters of the Lovestone faction, complained about Fort-Whiteman's organising efforts.[23]

In August, a 'committee of seven', including leading black Communists and Minor, wrote to Ruthenberg, requesting sufficient funds and support to build for the approaching ANLC. This included making Huiswoud and Briggs an organiser and editor, respectively. It also requested that the French Communists send a black Communist and the South African Communists send Clement Kadalie to the conference. They proposed that the party send Aaron Davis, 'a native of Mississippi and of the Peasant class', to tour the South to build support and 'organize groups among the Negro agricultural workers in the southern states'.[24]

The party's fractious Fourth National Convention in August 1925 (where a Comintern cable overturned the Foster-Cannon majority) passed an extensive resolution on the Negro question. A section on 'Social Demands' supported 'demands for political equality, the right to vote, social equality, "economic" equality, abolition of jim-crow laws and also jim-crow customs not written into law' as well as 'the abolition of all anti-intermarriage laws'. The party now dedicated itself to full racial equality.

The motion stressed the creation of a significant black component of the working class. This changed the Negro question:

> From being a sectional question, the Negro problem became a national question. From being a secondary factor in industrial labor, the Negro moves into [the] position of a great mass employed in basic industries, and already in notable strikes in the coal fields, etc., he has shown himself eminently fitted for the front ranks of militant organized labor.

23 Minor 1925, p. 68; Haywood 1978, pp. 139, 146; see also Makalani 2011, pp. 116–23. It would be tempting to view this dispute through the lens of factionalism. However, while Fort-Whiteman and Minor were Ruthenberg supporters, so was Huiswoud—as were 'most of the Party's black members' according to Haywood; Haywood 1978, p. 140. For examples of complaints about Fort-Whiteman, see Jack [A. Jakira] to 'Dear J' [Lovestone], no date [autumn 1925], in Lovestone papers, box 221, folder 1; I.A. [Israel Amter] to 'Dear Jay' [Lovestone], no date [fall 1925], in Lovestone papers, box 221, folder 1. At the time, Jakira was the organiser for Pittsburgh and Amter for Ohio.

24 Hall, Allen, Phillips, Doty, Whiteman, Minor and Henry to C.E. Ruthenberg, 7 August 1925, in Comintern archives, 515:1:504.

Noting the racism of the AFL bureaucracy, the motion stressed that 'the cause of the Negro in the labor movement is essentially a left wing fight and one which must energetically be championed by the Workers' (Communist) Party'. The resolution stated that 'in all of our party actions, all party units must make an especial effort to reach and enlist the most advanced Negro workers in our ranks'. The motion hailed the ANLC—which was scheduled to convene in Chicago the next month—as the centre of Communist 'work among the Negroes' and 'a genuine expression of the Negro workers and farmers of the United States'. The motion saluted the 'pioneer work' of the ABB, but commanded that 'local organizations merge' with the ANLC. (That this all but made the ANLC a Communist affiliate seemed not to be noticed).[25]

The ANLC, under Fort-Whiteman's leadership, was the first significant organised effort by the Communists to attract black workers. The ANLC reflected the Comintern's understanding that special organisational forms were needed to draw specially oppressed groups into the revolutionary movement; thus it broke with social-democratic colour-blindness. It underscored the *class basis* of black oppression without dissolving racial oppression into a purely class issue. Seventeen people, including at least six party members, signed its call in the spring of 1925 'to bring together the most potent elements of the Negro race for deliberation and action upon those most irritating and oppressive social problems affecting the life of the race in general and the Negro working class in particular'. The ANLC sought to attract black leaders to its conference in October. Du Bois, while guardedly positive, did not attend; Randolph (the most important left-wing black trade-union leader) refused to attend. William Green, the head of the AFL, denounced the meeting as a Communist plot, warning black trade unionists that it was 'a trap that will eventually be their undoing'. Another important black leader—Ben Fletcher, leader of the Philadelphia longshoreman and a former IWW member—did not attend, because Fort-Whiteman did not want him to. This undercut the possibility of the ANLC sinking roots in the black labour movement.[26]

In an accounting to the Comintern, the secretary of the ANLC organising committee claimed that 4,000 people attended the entire week of meetings, with an average attendance of 600 people per night, and that this represented

25 *Fourth National Convention* 1925, pp. 115–23.

26 'A Call to Action' [Spring 1925], in Foner and Allen 1987, pp. 109–11; Lovett Fort-Whiteman to W.E. Burghardt Du Bois, 23 September 1925 and Du Bois to Fort-Whiteman, 8 October 1925, in Du Bois papers, reel 14, files 1237–8; Bynum 2010, p. 114. On Green, see *New York Times*, 10 August 1925; on Fletcher, see Makalani 2011, p. 122; Palmer 2007, p. 213.

organisations of almost 35,000 members. Thirty-nine delegates attended the Congress, 'about 2/3 were Party members', according to a report by Ruthenberg. With the exception of a black longshoreman from Galveston, Texas, and a fraternal delegate from Oklahoma, all the delegates came from the North. A report by an undercover Department of Justice agent describes how between 500–600 people attended several 'mass meetings' at the Congress to hear speeches by various Communists. For example, on the second day, attendees listened to Moore denounce Booker T. Washington for 'continuing the policy of slavish submission of the Negro race and repudiating its demand for social equality'. At another meeting, Lucy Parsons—the widow of Haymarket martyr Albert Parsons—spoke. The hall itself was 'decorated with pictures of leaders of revolutions among colored peoples in different lands'. These included S.D. Saklatvala, the Indian-born Communist member of the British parliament who had been denied entry into the US the month before; Sun Yat Sen, the Chinese Nationalist; Abd el-Krim, who was fighting against the Spanish and French in North Africa; Toussaint L'Ouverture, the Haitian revolutionary; and Nat Turner and Denmark Vessey, slave rebels in the early US.[27]

Perhaps recalling the Farmer-Labor fiasco, the party did not inflate the size of the Congress. An 'outline for party speakers' on the Congress stated that it 'did not have a wide mass representation' and 'had for us significance only as a good beginning'. 'Never before', Minor wrote in the *Workers Monthly*, 'with the exception of the years just after the Civil War, has there been even a pretense of a big national congress of Negroes on the basis of their class character as workers'. Minor hailed the meeting as 'a breaker of traditions' and 'objectively and ultimately a danger to those who profit by things as they are', including the established black press such as the *Chicago Defender*. Still, Minor admitted that the ANLC was not 'as yet a mass movement'. He continued that the significance of the Congress was not its size, but that it 'resulted in forming a strong nucleus

27 'Report of H.V. Phillips, Secretary of National Committee Calling the American Labor Congress', with cover note by Jay Lovestone, stamped 4 December 1925, in Comintern archives, 495:155:34; C.E. Ruthenberg, note on ANLC 'To all DECs, City Executives, Section Executive Committees, and Sub-Section Executive Committees', 24 November 1925, in Comintern archives, 495:155:33; 'Statement on the American Negro Labor Congress by Lovett Fort-Whiteman', 24 November 1925, in Comintern archives, 495:155:33; Report on American Negro Labor Congress, 5 November 1925, in ANLC FBI file No. 61-5941-1. A. Rodríguez, a delegate from Brownsville, Pennsylvania, was subsequently expelled from the CP, in 1929, on charges of being a spy; see A. Jakira to 'Comrade Stachel', 4 April 1929, in Lovestone papers, box 221, folder 1. On Saklatvala, see *New York Times*, 17 September 1925.

for a mass movement which already has the beginnings of mass connections' as well as the 'formulation of a clear program'.[28]

The party leadership saw the ANLC as the vehicle to gain a substantial base in the black working class and the black population internationally. The Congress demonstrated to black Americans that (as Du Bois was quoted in the *New York Times*) 'the Russian Communists have gone out of their way to express sympathy with negro and colored workers all over the world'. In April 1926, Fort-Whiteman wrote to the Peasants' International (Krestintern) in Russia that the ANLC 'has had a favorable growth during the last six or seven months among the Negro Workers of the cities and we feel that the time has arrived when we can undertake a definite program of action among the Negro Farm Workers'. He wrote of plans for 'organizational work this summer in the cotton and sugar-cane fields of the South'. He added that the ANLC 'at this time has some very broad connections, particularly in West and South Africa and we would like to work out with the council of the Peasant's [sic] International a program of action embracing America, West and South Africa'. In September 1926, the Political Committee of the party approved fourteen proposals by William F. Dunne on 'broadening the work' of the ANLC through 'establishing a base' in 'heavy industry and bringing it into closer contact with militant Non-Communist elements among the young Negro intellectuals, the unorganized workers and the trade unions'. These included calling for a conference with the purpose of 'the organization of the Negro workers into trade unions'. No evidence exists of these plans being realised.[29]

The ANLC never fulfilled the hopes of its founders. Its Chicago membership, one of the largest branches, remained around fifty. Despite efforts by the TUEL, the ANLC never gained a following among black workers, reflecting the anti-black hostility of the AFL leadership, the anti-Communism of Randolph, and the opposition by the black petty bourgeoisie.

Nonetheless, in addition to its ideological importance, the organisation attempted to connect the struggle against black oppression in the US to the

28 C.E. Ruthenberg, note on ANLC 'To all DECs, City Executives, Section Executive Committees, and Sub-Section Executive Committees', 24 November 1925, in Comintern archives, 495:155:33; 'Outline for Party Speakers on Subject: The American Negro Labor Congress and Its Background', undated, in Robert Minor papers, box 12, folder 'Negro, 1924–25'; Minor 1925.

29 *New York Times*, 17 January 1926; Lovett Fort-Whiteman/James Jackson to Acting Secretary Dombal [Tomasz Dąbal?], International Farmer's Council, 16 April 1926, in Comintern archives, 495:155:37; Minutes of Political Committee No. 92, 21 September 1926, in Cannon papers, reel 47, frame 614–15.

fight against US imperialism and racial oppression throughout the world. Two important black Communists were recruited through the ANLC: James W. Ford and Malcolm Nurse, better known as George Padmore. Both had key roles in the Comintern's subsequent attempts to intersect black workers internationally. The ANLC was important for the party's continued work among Caribbean immigrants. Almost no early issues of the ANLC's paper, the *Negro Champion*, exist; the June 1926 issue indicates the breadth of its interest. Its headline dealt with black workers in the ongoing Passaic textile strike, and smaller articles were on the AFL bureaucracy's opposition to the ANLC; efforts by Pullman porters to organise; racist attacks in Florida; coverage of China, South Africa and Haiti; and an article critical of Marcus Garvey. The ANLC was serious enough that, in January 1926, the *New York Times* ran a front-page article, 'Communists Boring Into Negro Labor', that, after reassuring its readers that the ANLC was small, warned that 'in the event of industrial depression ... serious trouble might ensue'.[30]

Fort-Whiteman headed the ANLC until May 1927. By then, the criticism of his 'leftist sectarian policies and incompetent direction' became too strong and he was replaced by Moore. A report described the Congress as 'merely ... an office in Chicago' whose leadership was 'not in contact with the local organizations, and does not know that these exist, altho [sic] at one time there were at least twenty five local groups organized'. Although between 5,000 and 10,000 copies of the *Negro Champion* had been printed for more than a year, the paper had no more than 400 subscribers, 'no payments have been received, worth mentioning, for the bundles sent out', 'nor is there any assurance that the bundles sent out have been distributed'.[31]

According to the minutes of the Political Committee, the ANLC was guilty of a 'failure to initiate and develop concrete struggles of negro masses on the basis of immediate political issues'. It had been 'operating on too narrow a basis' and failed to 'draw in non-party left-wingers and progressives'. Bittelman, secretary of the CEC's subcommittee on 'Negro work', justified deposing Fort-Whiteman because the state of the ANLC was 'very bad'.

30 On the ANLC and the TUEL, see minutes of TUEL National Committee, 20 May 1925, in the Prometheus Research Library; Solomon 1998, pp. 57–9. On the international significance, see Eastern Department of the ECCI, 'Information Review No. 5: Negro Conference in Chicago', 19 September 1925, in Comintern archives, 495:133:34; Stevens 2008, p. 63; *Negro Champion*, June 1926 (copy in Tamiment Library); *New York Times*, 17 January 1926. On Padmore's recruitment and early Communist activity, see James 2012, pp. 55–9.

31 'Report on the Committee of Negro Work', no date [1927?], in Comintern archives, 515:1:207.

> Its organization is vague and indefinite. Its membership is negligible. There are barely more than about half a dozen local branches functioning and the membership is difficult to define, being not more than about 300.

From the complaints of various people, including fellow black Communists and fellow Ruthenberg factionalists, Fort-Whiteman's organisational style left something to be desired. However, it seems unfair to blame him for all the ANLC's difficulties, given the party leadership's longstanding problems with the Negro question, and the factionally poisoned atmosphere of the party. The Communists lacked sufficient black cadres for such an ambitious project, especially in the context of increasing Klan membership and declining unions. In 1928, Ford criticised the party leadership as a whole for the failure of the ANLC, which he argued 'was organised without sufficient *attention* and *guidance* in *methods* and *tactics*.' He noted that the party had given 'insufficient financial attention' to the ANLC, and assailed the 'tendency to view the organisation of Negro workers *arbitrarily* and *simply* as a *class problem*' while paying 'insufficient attention to the position of Negroes as an *oppressed minority*'. Katayama, writing at the same time, was more blunt: the ANLC's 'failure was entirely due to the lack of preparation and subsequent continued work on the part of the Party'.[32]

The ANLC, whatever its problems, underscores the importance of the Comintern in making the American party address black oppression. Not only was the plan developed at a meeting in Moscow, but Comintern appreciation of the importance of the Negro question gave Fort-Whiteman the tribune to push aggressively to organise a working-class struggle against black oppression. In a sense, then, the ANLC was a dress rehearsal for the work of the Communists in the next decade. At the same time, the difficulties with the ANLC emphasise the continuing problems of the party's 'Negro work'.

32 'Directions to the Party Fraction in the National Executive Committee of the American Negro Labor Congress'; Alexander Bittelman, 'Report and Recommendations on the Conference of the Party Fraction in the General Executive Board of the American Negro Labor Congress', both attached to PolCom minutes, 26 May 1927, in Comintern archives, 515:1:981; also in Comintern archives, 495:155:39. Solomon 1998, pp. 57–9; James W. Ford, 'Negro Work in America', 11 May 1928, in Comintern archives, 495:155:59; Katayama, 'Attitude of Party and Comintern Past and Present', 23 May 1928, in Comintern archives, 495:155:61.

(Meanwhile, for the next year Fort-Whiteman remained important enough that he was selected as a delegate to the Sixth Comintern Congress, in the summer of 1928. He stayed in Moscow afterwards, and died in the 1930s, a victim of the Stalinist purges).[33]

33 On the fate of Fort-Whiteman, see Klehr, Haynes and Andersen 1998, pp. 218–27.

CHAPTER 16

The Sixth Congress and the 'Negro Question'

The Sixth Congress (17 July to 1 September 1928) was a turning point in the Communist approach to the 'Negro Question'. A resolution passed shortly after the Congress established that the American black population was an oppressed *nation* with the right to self-determination, up to independence from the US. The Congress and its aftermath was also a turning point in the factionalism racking the party; this factionalism was not *about* black oppression, but in the atmosphere of 1928–9, the Negro question became intertwined with the struggle for control of the party.

Most black Communists supported the Ruthenberg-Lovestone faction. The Foster-Cannon group's emphasis on the trade unions, and Foster's dedication to working within the AFL, were not attractive to black militants given the racism of the trade-union bureaucracy (as Claude McKay had made clear in *Negroes in America*). After the 1925 convention, the Ruthenberg faction's claim to be more loyal to the Comintern must have played a role, since as William J. Maxwell has argued, 'indigenous black interests were sometimes better represented in Comintern directives than in U.S. Communism at its most national'. Pepper's role as the chairman of the first Comintern Negro Commission in 1925, and Minor's importance in 'Negro work' in America, buttressed their faction's credentials as well.[1]

Despite black Communists' support for the Lovestone leadership, the Negro question was not prominent in the party's work in 1927. In this period the struggle to save Sacco and Vanzetti consumed much of the party's external efforts. Black Communists, such as Moore, were active, although not more than other comrades. (Through this work, the Communists recruited a young black attorney, William L. Patterson). This is not to say that the party ignored the Negro question altogether: at the same time as the Commonwealth of Massachusetts was preparing to execute the two Italian anarchists, its legislature was debating a bill 'prohibiting the Intermarriage of whites and persons of African descent'.

1 Maxwell 1999, p. 72; McKay 1979, pp. 34–5. Bryan Palmer called 'race ... something of a factional preserve' and 'an almost wholly owned subsidiary' of the Ruthenberg-Lovestone faction; Palmer 2004, p. 198. On Pepper, see Saknyster 2012, Chapter 9.

The NAACP was active in mobilising against it; Communists also opposed the bill, even appearing before a legislative committee to denounce it.[2]

In February 1927, American Communists participated in the Brussels conference of the League Against Imperialism. Raised by the CPGB in 1925, and organised by German Communist Willi Münzenberg, the League was meant to attract Communist and non-Communist opponents of imperialism. (The culmination of seeking alliances with bourgeois nationalists was the alliance with the Goumindang; soon after the Brussels conference, this resulted in one of the bloodiest defeats for Communists as the Chinese nationalists turned on their erstwhile allies).[3] Several delegates—including Moore (representing both the ANLC and the UNIA) and representatives from South Africa and Francophone West Africa—drew up a resolution on the Negro question.

In presenting the motion, Moore called 'to unite the European workers with the workers in the colonies for a common fight against this monster' of world imperialism. Moore warned that 'the imperialists are concocting a new world war, a terrible war in which race will fight against race'. He added: 'It is conceivable that the despised Negro peoples will be instrumental in tipping the scale of freedom in favor of the oppressed classes against the imperialistic oppressors in the event of a war between the oppressed and the exploiters'. The resolution demanded withdrawal of imperialist troops from and independence for much of the Caribbean, and called for a 'Confederation of the British West Indies'. It demanded racial and national equality, free speech and press, and the right to form trade unions and the right to an education. In the US, the All-American Anti-Imperialist League, led by Manuel Gomez, focused on

---

2 For an example of Moore's activism, see *New York Times*, 17 April, 28 July, and 22 August 1927; on Patterson, see Patterson 1971; also see his obituary in *New York Times*, 7 March 1980. On the anti-miscegenation bill, see Miletsky 2008, pp. 127–8; for Communist opposition, see B.B. Rubenstein, 'Workers Party Opposes Intermarriage Bill in Mass'. [1927], in Comintern archives, 515:1:1224. The bill was ultimately defeated. On the rise of laws against intermarriage in the 1920s, see Mumford 1997, Chapter 9.

3 Sean McMeekin argues that Münzenberg's building of the conference was based on a double lie: to the Comintern, in that the various nationalists and 'anti-imperialists' were sympathetic to Soviet Russia, and to the attendees, in that the conference was not organised and financed by Moscow; McMeekin 2003, p. 196. However, the fundamental 'lie' of the League was that bourgeois nationalists (like Chiang Kai-shek) and Communists could form an anti-imperialist united front. On the League Against Imperialism, see Jones 1996; Melgar Bao 2008; Petersson 2007. See also the coverage of the conference in the special edition of the *Bulletin de la Ligue Contre l'Oppression Coloniale et l'Impérialisme* [1927], in Prometheus Research Library collection.

Latin America, but also demanded the 'complete abolition of economic, political and social discrimination against the Negroes in the United States'.[4]

The Lead-Up to the Sixth Congress

In early 1928, the Anglo-American Secretariat set up a subcommittee on the Negro question to draft a resolution for the upcoming Sixth Congress. This included several black students in Moscow (including the brothers Otto and Haywood Hall, known as Carl Jones and Harry Haywood, respectively), Clarence Hathaway (a white Foster supporter studying at the Lenin school), James Ford and William F. Dunne (both already in Moscow for the Fourth Profintern Congress), and Minor. Another member was Nikolai Mikhailovich Nasanov (known as Charlie), a former representative of the Young Communist International in Chicago and one of a handful of Soviet experts on race, colonialism and Africa (as well as a member of the Far Eastern Bureau). Petrovsky, as head of the Anglo-American Secretariat, also played a role.[5]

The Fourth Profintern Congress helped set up the Comintern Congress. It heralded the creation of new unions under Communist leadership. Ford raised the need to address black workers. Lozovsky (whose sympathies in America were with Foster) in his report highlighted the attendance of black workers,

---

4 Derrick 2008, pp. 172–82; Jones 1996, p. 8; the resolution is in Turner and Turner 1988, pp. 143–6; the programme of the All-American Anti-Imperialist League is in the League's FBI file. See also Ventadour [1927].

5 H. Haywood 1978, p. 227. On Nasanov, see Berland 2001; Solomon 1998, p. 70. Nasanov's full name (and role as one of a few Soviet Africanists) is mentioned in Filatova 2007, p. 206. In the text, Otto Hall is referred to as 'Hall' and his older brother as 'Haywood', the public names they used in the US. It is almost impossible to untangle the various committees, commissions, subcommittees and sub-commissions that met during this time. The Comintern, the Profintern and the Krestintern each had Negro Commissions, often sharing members. At times, these commissions delegated members to create sub-comissions. Further, the issue was discussed in different bodies, including the Anglo-American and Colonial Commissions, who also shared members. At times non-members would attend commissions and members would be absent. Complicating the matter further is the fact that the minutes are not precise in their names: the meeting on 2–4 August 1928 was referred to as both the 'Negro Commission' and 'the Anglo-American Secretariat Sub-Commission on Negro Work'. A complaint by Pepper indicates the absurdity of trying to formally separate the deliberations: 'From the Negro Committee we went to a meeting of the American Delegation, from there we went to the colonial delegation. From there, we went here'; Negro Commission transcript, 28 August 1928, in Comintern archives, 495:155:56. For a valiant attempt to explain the various committees, see Weiss 2009, pp. 10, 59–65.

'who in the so-called civilised countries are the pariahs among the proletariat'. Lozovsky also criticised the TUEL for supporting racial equality but not doing any 'concrete work'. According to John Ballam (a Lovestone supporter), Lozovksy argued that the party was infected by anti-black chauvinism and that 'this prejudice should be stamped out with a hot iron'. The Congress made Ford a member of the Profintern secretariat. The Congress also created the International Trade Union Committee of Negro Workers (ITUC-NW), which published a monthly journal, *The Negro Worker*, under Ford's leadership.[6]

During the Profintern Congress, Ford wrote a document that argued 'Negro workers have become an important industrial and labour factor in America, [and] also a political factor', especially with the growth of industry in the non-union South. This 'not only raises the question of labour organisation in the South', he wrote, 'but also has its effect (unemployment, etc.) on the organised and unorganised workers who are left in the North and East'. A large portion of the document, however, attacked the Communist Party for its 'little success in the organisation of Negro workers and Negro work generally'.

After explaining the failures of the ANLC (described in the previous chapter), Ford complained that 'the proper apparatus of our Party has not developed and initiated concrete methods and tactics for breaking down racial and colour bars in existing unions' and has 'not participated directly in the organisation of Negro workers nor worked within existing unions'. 'In spite of our correct attitude to the Negro question in general, our Party has no clear understanding of the question based on scientific analysis'. In fact, the party, he continued, still had 'some of the vestiges of racial narrowness and racial prejudices'. (In support of this, he cited problems in Gary, Indiana).

Ford criticised the party leadership's lack of attention to developing black cadres. Perhaps thinking of the ANLC, he wrote:

> Many capable Negro comrades who are constantly pointing out mistakes and errors are not given consideration but relegated to insignificant positions and even driven from the Party ... Our Negro comrades are allowed to make mistakes without any previous direction, mistakes which are inevitable as a result of incorrect policies. When a sufficient number have occurred the comrade is held up as incapable and useless. Then another comrade is brought forth to supersede him and so on. Negro comrades

6 Losovsky 1928a, p. 422. Remarks by Ballam at May [1928] plenum, in Lovestone papers, box 228, folder 11. On the International Trade Union Committee of Negro Workers, see Adi 2009, pp. 165–6; Davidson *et al.* 2003, p. 5; Edwards 2003, Chapter 5; Makalani 2011, p. 161; Stevens 2006; Weiss 2009.

> are pitted one against another, causing confusion in the pursuance of Negro work.

To help solve these problems, Ford urged 'that a delegation of Negro comrades composing 5 or 6 comrades be immediately (June 1st. 1928) brought to Moscow for a conference'. He proposed eight black Communists, including Briggs, Edward Dotty, Fort-Whiteman, Huiswoud, Moore and himself. 'All these comrades', he added, 'have maintained a stand which the CEC has not wanted exposed'. He predicted that the American leadership would block them from attending.

The Profintern Congress unanimously approved Ford's motion for 'a special conference of Negro delegates'. The Congress passed a resolution on America that 'steps must be immediately taken to set up special unions for Negroes', while also fighting for existing unions to organise black workers. A 'supplementary resolution' passed by the Profintern executive bureau stressed that new unions should be organised 'on the basis of complete equality of all the workers in the industry, irrespective of race, creed, colour, or sex'. It added, 'special emphasis' must be given to organising black workers.[7]

'Negro Work' in America

Back in the US, Pepper (using the name Swift) soon presented an extensive document on 'Negro Work' to the Political Committee. This acknowledged that 'the party as a whole has not sufficiently realized the significance of the work among the Negroes'. It underlined that 'the Negro question is a *race question*', while stressing that Communists should 'be the champion and organizer of the Negro *working class elements*'. After describing the creation of a significant black working class, Pepper's document urged connecting race and economic issues. Raising the necessity of 'intermediary organizations' and training black

7 James W. Ford, 'Negro Work in America', 11 May 1928, in Comintern archives, 495:155:59; *International Press Correspondence*, 12 April 1928; American resolution at Profintern Congress, attached to Political Committee minutes No. 35, 16 May 1928, in Lovestone papers, box 225, folder 12; 'Supplementary Resolution on the Tasks of the RILU Supporters in the United States of America', [1928] in Lovestone papers, box 227, folder 17. The original draft of the motion proposed by Lozovsky, along with inserts to address fears of appearing to support 'revolutionary "Jim-Crowism"', are in Zimmerman papers, box 1, file 'Sixth Session of the Central Council of RILU'. The final motions are printed in Red International of Labour Unions 1928, pp. 135–42.

Communist cadres, it also urged that 'comrades who play leading roles in non-party organizations should come out openly as Communists'. (Later the document specified Moore). Examples of intermediary organisations included a Negro youth organisation, a Negro miners relief committee, the Harlem Tenant League, and a revitalised ANLC. The resolution called for a 'Negro Race Congress' that would not be Communist, but have a heavy labour presence.

The document stressed that the Negro question should be a key part of the Nominating Convention in the 1928 Communist election campaign and that the party should stand black Communists as candidates. It called for a black member of the CEC; more black students at Communist training schools; a reinforced *Negro Champion*; and as many black delegates to the upcoming Sixth Comintern Congress as possible. The document urged that Fort-Whiteman be added to the *Daily Worker* staff; that Huiswoud become a party organiser; and that Briggs edit the *Negro Champion* and organise a black news service.[8]

Also in May, Fort-Whiteman, William L. Patterson and H.V. Phillips presented the CEC with a controversial 'Thesis for a New Negro Policy'. They argued: 'It is no longer possible to ignore the desperate need to formulate a new and constructive programme for work among the Negro masses'. Noting that there were fewer black Communists in 1928 than at the time of the first meeting of the ANLC, the document criticised the ANLC for having created 'a spirit of separatism from our Party' among black and white comrades. It warned of 'Jim Crowism in our revolutionary work in America', that 'the Negro members of our Party are to be regarded as something of appendages to our Party and that only [issues] pertaining to the American Negro Labour Congress and to the Race are of interest to them'. The document criticised the ANLC's emphasis on black oppression in the South, which could 'no longer be utilised as an issue for a Negro liberation movement'. The document stated: 'it is ideologically impossible to build a mass movement on a program oppositional to lynching, Jim Crowism, and political disenfranchisement'. Instead of focusing on the fight against Southern-style segregation, it was necessary to recruit blacks directly into the Communist Party.[9]

8 J. Swift [Pepper], 'Policies on Negro Work', attached to minutes of Political Committee No. 32, 30 May 1928, in Comintern archives, 495:155:64.

9 'Thesis for a New Negro Policy: Submitted by Negro Comrades of New York City to the C.E.C.', 8 May 1928, in Comintern archives, 495:155:64. A different version of the document, signed by Fort-Whiteman, William J. Patterson and Phillips, is in the Comintern archives, 515:1:1213. On this document, see Solomon 1998, pp. 64–5.

After the civil rights movement, it is easy to dismiss this argument. Still, the document highlighted the importance of connecting the fight for democratic rights to the struggle for socialism—raised by the ANLC and subsequent Communist work. It also highlighted the resentment of veteran black Communists over the perception that, in response to Comintern pressure, the party leadership had shunted 'Negro work' to black Communists instead of making it central to the work of the whole party.[10]

As the Sixth Comintern Congress approached, these tensions grew. The first dispute was over which black comrades to select as delegates. Against Ford's suggestion that five or six black Communists represent the party in Moscow, the Negro Commission suggested four: C.W. Fulp, a black mineworkers' leader; Moore, the head of the Negro Commission; Fort-Whiteman; and Ford. The Political Committee further narrowed it down. With Lovestone's support, the committee selected Fort-Whiteman and Phillips as delegates (with Ford as a fraternal delegate). Foster, Cannon and Bittelman voted for Moore, and nobody voted for Fulp.[11]

Moore protested to the ECCI that his 'exclusion' was a 'narrow manoeuvre to prevent thorough analysis [of] errors' and requested that 'ECCI require Moor [sic] be delegate'. Gitlow (who was the senior leader remaining in the US during the Congress), responding for the Political Committee, claimed that Moore had been rejected 'on ground of anti-party attitude', and that he was 'unworthy [of] such high confidence [of] American Party' because he had not been an open Communist and because of problems in the ANLC. (This was a peculiar argument, since Fort-Whiteman had been selected). In Moscow, Ford claimed that the dispute 'demonstrates very clearly the underestimation of Negro work' and argued again for five black delegates—Moore, Fulp, Edward Doty, Fort-Whiteman and himself. This was in addition to various black fraternal delegates: Phillips, a representative of the Communist youth, and nine black students at the Lenin School or the Communist University of Toilers of the East (KUTV). The Anglo-American Secretariat accepted Gitlow's arguments, and Moore did not attend the Congress; nor did many of those whom Ford had proposed to come to Moscow in the spring. Caribbean Communists—Briggs, Huiswoud, Moore—were edged out by American-born blacks. These pioneer black Communists, while less knowledgeable about the American South, tended to be more critical and independently minded than their recently recruited comrades. Those who did attend, in addition to Philipps, included

10 Enckevort 2001, p. 38.

11 Minutes of Political Committee No. 38, 13 June 1928, in Lovestone papers, box 225, folder 12. Fulp's role in the mineworkers' union is discussed in Nyden 1977, p. 86.

Fort-Whiteman and Ford; the nine black students (including the Hall brothers) were also present.[12]

'White Chauvinism' and 'Reserves of Reaction'

As the Congress opened, Lovestone's leadership faced challenges regarding the Negro question. Foster and Cannon's 'Right Danger' document charged that 'The Lovestone majority has systematically and continuously neglected work among the Negro masses' because 'for two and half years the Negro work of our Party has been bankrupt'. As a report drawn up by the party on its work since the Fifth Congress in 1924 stated in a section on 'Negro work': 'The Party has made a number of attempts to develop this work, [but] has not always met with any significant success'. The report lauded the party's activities in the UMWA intersecting black miners; failures included the 'little initiative' shown by the party in intervening in A. Philip Randolph's campaign to organise Pullman porters, and the party's lack of support in the South.[13]

At the Congress, two explanations were offered for these shortcomings. One was 'white chauvinism' and the other Lovestone's alleged view that black people in the rural South were 'reserves of reaction'. There were elements of truth in both explanations, but these were also used by Lovestone's opponents in

12 Moore, cable to ECCI, 28 February [June] 1928; Gitlow, cable to ECCI, 28 June 1928, in Comintern archives, 515:1:1241; J. Louis Engdahl to Anglo-American Secretariat, 16 July 1928, in Comintern archives, 515:1:1248. The question of Moore was discussed at a Political Committee meeting, which authorised Gitlow to respond. Most of the leading members were absent because of the Comintern Congress; see Political Committee minutes No. 41, 27 June 1928, in Lovestone papers, box 225, folder 12; Ford, 'Negro Delegates to the Comintern Congress' (memo to Petrovsky and the Anglo-American Secretariat), 28 June 1928, in Comintern archives, 495:155:66.The response of the Anglo-American Secretariat is attached to the Political Committee Minutes No. 45, 23 July 1928, in Lovestone papers, box 225, folder 13. On black American students at the KUTV, see McClellan 1993. On opposition to Huiswoud, Moore and Briggs as delegates, see Enckevort 2001, p. 44.

13 James P. Cannon, William Z. Foster, William F. Dunne, Alex Bittelman, J.W. Johnstone, Manuel Gomez and George Siskin, 'The Right Danger in the American Party', serialised in *Militant* in between 15 November 1928 and 15 January 1929; the section on the Negro question is in the 1 January 1929 issue; Communist International 1928a, p. 348. Reports from Lovestone supporters during the Congress indicate that they were attacked for problems in Negro work: see letters of 29 July and 31 July 1928; see also the 2 August 1928 minority faction letter, all in Comintern archives, 515:1:1248.

Moscow and New York to weaken his faction's control. 'White chauvinism' was a broad and malleable term, like 'rightism' and 'Trotskyism'.

Later, most notably in the 'trial' of Finnish Communist August Yokinen in Harlem in 1931, 'white chauvinism' became a synonym for anti-black prejudice. (During the Cold War, the campaign against 'white chauvinism' became a witchhunt). To be sure, black Communists complained of prejudice in the 1920s. One report noted that in the Harlem branch, 'we were making some progress in drawing Negroes into our party, and as soon as they began to come into the branch the white members of the branch who lived in that district began to transfer their membership to a down town branch which was very far away from their district'. The same report noted a segregated public meeting in Richmond, Virginia, in 1924; the lack of black recruitment in Washington, DC; 'condescension' towards black Communists in Detroit; among other things.[14]

As originally used, the term did not refer mainly to overt racism, but to neglect of the fight for black freedom. The clearest example was Huiswoud's suspension from the party for a year for having rebuked a racist Texan at the St. Paul Farmer-Labor convention in 1924. Events such as these indicated that the party did not make the Negro question so important as black Communists—and the Comintern—believed it should be.[15]

'White chauvinism' did not only mean racism, however, but a denigration of the fight for black rights. An oft-cited example was Lovestone's supposed argument that rural black Southerners were reactionary. At the time, this was seized upon to attack the Lovestone leadership. Subsequently, after Lovestone's expulsion and anti-Communist trajectory, Communists (and sympathetic historians) have used this to lay the party's problems on the Negro question on Lovestone's back and absolve the rest of the party. Consequently, it is worthwhile examining the issue in more depth.[16]

14 'The Party Attitude on Negro Work', in Comintern archives, 495:155:59. On the later 'white chauvinism' witchhunt, see Starobin 1972, pp. 198–201. According to the report, the situation in Virginia led to the expulsion of 'all the Negroes from this branch'. Among these was Abram L. Harris, then an undergraduate university student. Harris, the document notes, not surprisingly became bitter to the party.

15 Enckevort 2001, p. 34.

16 William Patterson claimed, long after Lovestone's expulsion, that Lovestone 'had strong overtones of racism' and was 'a racist'; Patterson 1971, pp. 95, 97. For an example of a historian's attack on Lovestone's position, see Johnson 2011, p. 459. After his expulsion, the Communist Party heaped every type of insult on Lovestone, much of which rang true given his odious personality, factionalism and later right-wing role in the labour movement. However, like Browder two decades later, he was also a scapegoat for broader political problems shared across the leadership.

In a report to the party's fifth convention in the autumn of 1927, Lovestone noted the continuing black migration to the North. This, he said, was leading to the break-up of the two-party political system, 'one of the basic obstacles to the development of a class party on a mass basis'. He called this migration 'another form of proletarianization', adding:

> consequently, the existence of this group as a reserve of capitalist reaction is likewise being undermined. The more we are able to reach the Negro masses with our propaganda, in their changed conditions, the more they can be a most valuable reserve for the revolutionary forces.

This passage's implication is that rural black Southerners were not a source of social struggle, an odd note against the Greek chorus attacking Trotsky for 'underestimating the peasantry'. That Lovestone was underestimating Southern blacks would be demonstrated by the party's work in the Depression. However, like most of Lovestone's thought, this was not original. It reflected the traditional Marxist emphasis on the urban working class and the 'New Negro' focus on the urban North. As Marx had stated in the *Communist Manifesto*:

> The bourgeoisie has subjected the country to the rule of the towns. It has created enormous cities, has greatly increased the urban population as compared with the rural, and has thus rescued a considerable part of the population from the idiocy of rural life.

In his study of agriculture in the United States, Lenin wrote of American Southerners who were:

> fleeing to other capitalist areas and to the towns, just as the peasantry in Russia is fleeing from the most backward central agricultural gubernias [provinces]... to those areas of Russia which have a higher level of capitalist development, to the metropolitan cities, the industrial gubernias and the South... The share-cropping area, both in America and in Russia, is the most stagnant area, where the masses are subjected to the greatest degradation and oppression... For the 'emancipated' Negroes, the American South is a kind of prison where they are hemmed in, isolated and deprived of fresh air.

In 1918, Socialist W.A. Domingo wrote a document called 'Socialism Imperiled, or the Negro—A Potential Menace to American Radicalism'. He stressed the necessity of recruiting blacks as a way of transforming the black population from a threat to the labour movement into allies. Likewise, in his speech at the Fourth Comintern Congress, Huiswoud had indicated the 'constant danger to white strikers' that black Southerners posed when hired by capitalists as strike-breakers.[17]

The immediate inspiration for Lovestone's formulation was probably Stalin's 1924 *Foundations of Leninism*. This described how imperialism, by exporting modern production into the colonial world, 'saps radically the position of capitalism by converting the colonies and dependent countries from reserves of imperialism into reserves of the proletarian revolution'.[18]

In a *Workers Monthly* article on 'The Great Negro Migration' in February 1926, Lovestone had set out his views in detail. He described the migration and the War as transforming black politics in the North and South. He described 'a deep going change in the ideology of the Negro masses called forth by the war' that 'created favorable opportunities for a wave of intense dissatisfaction among the Negro tenants and agricultural workers'. He described how 'The Negroes have begun to organize themselves' and were 'now taking up the struggle against their oppression in a more organized fashion'. Northern migration, by making black oppression a national issue, had *increased* the South's importance: 'the more the Negro problem takes on a national character the more important a role does the South begin to play in the economic and political life of the United States'. It was a tenet of the 'New Negro' movement from which most early black Communists had emerged that migration and industrialisation were transforming the Negro question.[19]

The real weakness indicated by Lovestone's position was not that he was a racist who hated black Southerners. Rather, it highlighted the lack of the party's connections in the South, still home to most American blacks. Lovestone opened himself up to charges of white chauvinism and underestimating the

17 *Daily Worker*, 22 September 1927; Marx and Engels 1975, p. 488; Marx 1979, p. 187; Lenin 1964b, pp. 26–7; Vincent 1994, p. 159. Huiswoud, however, also put the blame on the trade-union bureaucracy, something Lovestone did not mention in his speech. See Riddell 2011, p. 804.

18 Stalin 1953b.

19 Lovestone 1926. As Alec F. Hickmott recently put it: 'Imagining a black political modernity largely in terms of migration, the North, and urban life, New Negro political radicalism's most articulate spokesmen struggled to embrace popular movements rooted in the black-belt South, which in many respects contradicted the core of their ideological and programmatic goals'; Hickmott 2011, p. 397. There is no way to prove it, but it is likely that Lovestone's perspective was borrowed from his black co-factionalists; certainly its treatment of the South was no worse than Fort-Whiteman, Patterson and Phillips's document from the spring of 1928.

revolutionary potential of black 'peasants'; he also gave his factional opponents a convenient excuse to explain the problems the early Communists had with the Negro question.

The Sixth Congress

At the Congress, black Communists denounced the party for the neglect of 'Negro work'. Ford repeated his criticisms of the 'definite under-estimation of Negro work in general'. He argued that the 'inner Party struggle has hampered more than any other section of our work, the Negro work'. According to his count, the Comintern had already sent 19 resolutions on the Negro question to the American party, but nothing had been done. 'The few Negro comrades we have in the Party have been making a fight for years to bring the question before our party. And now we bring it before a Comintern Congress'. Again, he called for a Negro Commission.[20]

Hall emphasised organising unorganised workers, 'which includes the organisation of Negroes'. He claimed that there was 'more chauvinism in the American party than in any Party in the Comintern' and described a 'very unhealthy atmosphere in the party'. He denounced the 'failure to understand the potential revolutionary possibilities of the Negro masses' and an 'under-estimation of the necessity of work among the Negroes'. He emphasised that these 'mistakes in regard to Negro work have been made by the Party as a whole and not by any particular group'.[21]

The main (white) representatives of the two factions ignored the issue in their remarks, emphasising their argument over the strength of American imperialism. The exception was Dunne, the only leader of the Cannon-Foster opposition to have devoted serious attention to black oppression. He claimed that 'no serious Negro work has been done for two and one half years'—since the ANLC's Chicago meeting, but also since the ascendancy of Lovestone's faction. At one session, Katayama stated: 'The current neglect of the Negroes on the party of the American Party ... is solely due to the factional struggles in the American Party'.[22]

20 Communist International 1928c, pp. 772–3.

21 Communist International 1928c, pp. 811–12.

22 Communist International 1928c, pp. 781–2 (Dunne), pp. 856–7 (Katayama). On Dunne and race, see Palmer 2007, p. 217. Katayama's intervention must be read on two levels. On the one hand, he sincerely cared about racial oppression in the US. At the same time, it was also likely an attack on Pepper and his allies. In October 1927, Pepper had been assigned

'Self-Determination'

Katayama's speech reminded the delegates that 'Comrade Lenin considered the American Negroes a subject nation, placing them in the same category as Ireland'. Soon, this would become the official line of the Comintern: that black Americans were an oppressed nation with a 'right to self-determination', that is, to form their own nation state. Black nationalism was not new, but the Communist embrace was. According to Theodore Draper, by 1928 black nationalism 'had an ancestry going back at least a century but ... the American Communists had not known of it at the time and had not made use of such precedents until much later'. Communists had long rejected the form of nationalism familiar to them, Garveyism.[23]

In the early 1920s, Claude McKay contrasted black struggles in Africa, the Caribbean and the United States. In Africa, 'the natives are organising to defend their native rights against the growing encroachment of the Whites'. In the Caribbean, 'the movement is for independence'. But in 'the U.S.A. the big demand of the race as a whole is for full citizenship rights'. Fort-Whiteman, writing in the *Negro Champion* in June 1926, spelled out the Communist attitude:

> If the Negro is a lamb in America certainly he is not going to be a lion in Africa under France and England who hold large sections of Africa and are the main formidable powers in Europe ... Africa will be free but the initiative will come in Africa on the part of its native people ... The Negro in America is an American. He has grown up with American life. We must fight here for our place.[24]

At least one important black Communist had already entertained 'self-determination': before joining the Communist Party, Briggs and the African Blood Brotherhood had advocated a mixture of emigration, separatism and socialism. In retrospect, Briggs claimed to have not raised self-determination

to travel to Japanese-occupied Korea. Out of fear of state repression, Pepper seems never to have gone, but he submitted a falsified report and financial accounts. In early 1928, Katayama attacked both the political conclusions and the truthfulness of Pepper's report. See Sakmyster 2012, pp. 144–6.

23 Communist International 1928c, p. 856; Draper 1971a, p. ix.

24 Claude McKay, 'For a Negro Congress' [1922 or 1923], in Comintern archives, 495:155:43; Fort-Whiteman 1926, p. 2.

out of fear of not being taken seriously, but it is possible he had discarded it. Draper concluded that the ABB's leadership joining the Communist Party, 'which then strongly opposed any kind of African orientation for American Negroes, showed how superficial the Brotherhood's Africanism had been'.[25]

Important Soviet Communists had a proclivity to see American blacks as a national group. Lenin's remarks at the Second Congress have already been mentioned. Harry Haywood recalled that in 1925, Bob Mazut, a representative from the Young Communist International, had raised the idea on the behest of Zinoviev. Otto Hall recalled that he and other black KUTV students had met Stalin the same year. In the meeting, Stalin—considered an expert on the 'National Question' and ultimately responsible for the school—suggested that black Americans were a national minority. Only later did Stalin force this position, and then in the face of what Haywood described as 'the unanimous opposition of the American Party, including its Black members'. The initial reluctance to impose this position was in keeping with the Second Congress's theses on the national and colonial questions, which stressed that the Communist Party 'should not base its policy on abstract principles' but 'on an exact appraisal of specific historical and above all economic conditions'.[26]

In contrast to the 'social-chauvinists' of the Second International who supported colonialism, Lenin insisted that Communists in the imperialist world champion oppressed nations' right to self-determination, that is, national independence. The eighth condition (of twenty-one) for adherence to the Comintern required supporting anti-colonial liberation movements. Unlike the Irish, with a history of nationalist opposition to colonial subjugation, black people in the United States were oppressed by colour and race, not nationality. They were an integral part of American society, albeit forcibly segregated at the bottom. Black struggle since antebellum times had been focused on ending racial oppression and for full *integration* into American society, not separation. A separate black nation state seemed fantastical and contradicted Marxist theory. As even Stalin's own *Marxism and the National Question* (written in 1913 under Lenin's guidance) stressed, a nation was 'not racial or tribal, but a historically constituted community of people … formed on the basis of a common language, territory, economic life, and psychological make-up manifested

25 Cyril Briggs to Theodore Draper, 24 March 1958, in Draper papers, box 31, folder 'Negro-Briggs'; Draper 1971a, pp. 60–3; Draper 1986, p. 334.

26 Haywood 1978, pp. 219, 227; Riddell 1991, I, p. 285. In the 1930s, Trotsky also supported seeing black Americans as a nation; see Draper 1971a, p. 66, and Trotsky 1973d.

in a common culture'. The 'Great Migration' undercut the possibility of a black nation even more, while making black workers a key part of the proletariat.[27]

How did American Communists adopt a position Communists—black and white—had repeatedly rejected? The new line did not originate from within the American Communist movement. It was propelled by the Comintern leadership (and ultimately Stalin). This position was not in the draft programme adopted by the ECCI in late May.[28]

In fact, in August 1928, *Communist International* published an article by Endre Sik (a Hungarian exile and one of the first Soviet experts on Africa). Sik criticised the Fourth Congress resolution, emphasising that 'it is clear that it is impermissible simply to identify racial oppression and exploitation with national-colonial oppression', and that it was 'impermissible to deal with the racial under a clause on the national question'. Instead, Communists 'should put forward demands on behalf of the oppressed American negroes not as a nation but as a race'. Furthermore, 'they should demand not the right to national self-determination (self-determination has no practical meaning here!) but complete social and political equality'.[29]

27 Stalin 1953a, p. 307. See Dicken and Day 1969 for an (anti-Stalinist) criticism of using Stalin's definition in support for black nationalism. See also Shachtman 2003 for a contemporary criticism of the Communist position. My view on the role of black oppression in American capitalism is heavily indebted to Richard S. Fraser, particularly Fraser 1990. Susan Campbell, in her treatment of the issue, refuses to analyse whether black self-determination was 'realistic', and instead asserts that it 'should be respected' nonetheless; Campbell 1994, pp. 442–3. This diverges from the Marxist perspective that is based in material reality, not subjective desire.

28 The draft programme only said that the Comintern 'conducts propaganda against all forms of chauvinism and imperialist ill-treatment of great and small enslaved races (attitude towards Negroes, "yellow labour", etc.) and supports the latter's struggle against the bourgeoisie in the oppressing nation'; Communist International 1928b, p. 563. The 'self-determination' slogan is well covered in the historical literature; see, for example, Berland 2000; Campbell 1994; L. Carr 1981; Cruse 1967, pp. 140–6; Draper 1986 pp. 342–53; Enckevort 2001, Chapter 3; Gilmore 2008, pp. 61–6; Goldfield 1980; Haywood 1978; Hill 1951; T. Johnson 2010; T. Johnson 2011; Klehr and Thompson 1989; Record 1951; Record 1958; Solomon 1998, Chapter 5. The works written before the early 1990s did not have access to the Comintern archives; of the earlier works, Draper's study is the most valuable, given his research; Haywood's account is also important, while Goldfield's review establishes an important political framework, albeit without the aid of subsequent resources.

29 Shiek 1928. On Sik (who published the article as A. Shiek), see Darch and Littlejohn 1983.

This article, however, was only one of several in the *Communist International*. During the spring and summer of 1928, the Anglo-American Secretariat's commission on the Negro question discussed 'self-determination'. Katayama stressed that Communists must recognise 'Negroes' right to an independent existence' while the Comintern 'must support the revolutionary movement of subject nations' including black Americans. He asserted: 'The aim of the American Negro movement must ultimately be the establishment of the Soviet regime and the independent existence of the Negro people'. Katayama demanded 'the American Party to pay greater and more serious attention to the Negro work!' A report by J. Louis Engdahl on the history of the party's work among blacks, written shortly afterward, seconded Katayama's argument, adding (falsely) that John Reed had argued at the Second Congress 'to the effect that Negroes constitute a subject nation'.[30]

The International Context

The change in the Communist position towards black Americans in 1928 was informed by an earlier shift towards South Africa, the only other country that counted a Communist Party and significant black population. In March 1927, Bukharin had advocated that South African Communists adopt 'a demand for a Negro Republic independent of the British Empire'; in July, the ECCI resolved that Communists 'should put forward as [their] immediate political slogan an *independent black South African Republic* as a stage towards a Workers' and Peasants' Republic with full autonomy for all minorities'. This codified the two-stage approach to revolution advocated by Stalin, making national independence, and not socialism, the first goal of Communists. Although a political betrayal, this made some sense unlike the American slogan for 'self-determination', since South Africa was a majority-black country dominated by white imperialists. Nonetheless, the Comintern amalgamated

30 There were three additional articles in the German and Russian editions of *Communist International* in August and September 1928; see Draper 1986, p. 549, n. 84; Katayama, 'Attitude of Party and Comintern Past and Present', 23 May 1928, in Comintern archives, 495:155:61; J. Louis Engdahl, 'The Activities of the American Communist Party among the Negro Workers and Farmers', 11 June 1928, in Comintern archives, 495:155:59. In fact, Reed declared that 'every movement which has thus far been carried on among them [American blacks] with the aim of establishing a separate national resistance [existence?] ... has met with little, if any, success' since 'they consider themselves first of all Americans and feel entirely at home in the United States'; quoted in Foner and Allen 1987, p. 8. See Chapter 13 above.

black oppression in the two countries into one 'Negro question', and raised a similar demand in each country. (Underscoring the connection, in August 1928 the Sixth Congress's Negro Commission voted to 'confine its work to the work among Negroes in South Africa and the U.S.A.'; the same meeting voted to place Haywood and Bittelman on a commission to deal with South African Communist S.P. Bunting's opposition to the new South African line).[31]

The most active advocate of 'self-determination' for American blacks was Nasanov, who convinced Harry Haywood—whom he had met in Chicago. Haywood in turn argued this view in response to a presentation by his brother on the Garvey movement, which had stressed that black people were not a nation. Haywood declared: 'the Negro movement, which is nationalistic in character and based upon the peasantry, is a vital factor for the American [Communist] revolution and that this movement must be supported, utilised and directed by the American Communist Party, particularly since potentially revolutionary it is yet easily liable to be directed into reactionary channels'. Haywood acknowledged that black people in the US 'did not comply' with Stalin's definition of a nation, but 'nonetheless there are present among them many features in common with a nation'. American black people, Haywood insisted in an ambiguous formulation, 'are not a nation, but a racial minority which through historical development in the peculiar American environment has inevitably taken on certain nationalist features'.[32]

In response, Hall criticised his brother's 'sophomoric tirade' and 'amateur Marxian' use of 'hackneyed phraseology'. He attacked the idea that the existence of black 'peasants' proved that American blacks were a nation, since 'If a nationalist movement among the Jews was considered reactionary' by Stalin's book on the national question, 'then nationalist movement[s] among Negroes in America would be more so because they have less basis for nationalism than

31 'Remarks of N. Bukharin to Presidium, ECCI', 16 March 1927, in Comintern archives, 495:2:71a; 'Resolution of Politsecretariat of ECCI', 22 July 1927, in Comintern archives, 495:64:56. Both excerpted in Davidson *et al.* 2003, pp. 155, 161. On the adoption of the 'Native Republic' slogan, see also Hirson 1989 and Hirson 1992. South Africa after the end of Apartheid has become an 'independent black Republic', with the government in the hands of mainly black politicians (including South African Communists) who run the state in the interests of the white capitalists. Minutes on Negro Commission, 11 August 1928, in Comintern archives, 493:1:573 and 495:155:56. Note Bunting's warning on the difference between South Africa and the US, in 'Some Notes for S. African Delegate Report to Negro Sub-Commission', 9 August 1928, in Comintern archives, 495:155:56.

32 Hall 1978, pp. 228–30; Harry Haywood, 'The Basis for Nationalist Movements Among Negroes in the United States, and What Should Be the Attitude of Our Party Towards Them', 10 June 1928, in Lovestone papers, box 214, folder 3; see also Solomon 1998, p. 70.

the Jews in spite of the fact that they have a peasantry'. While Haywood had pointed to the Garvey movement as proof of nationalism, Hall argued that 'this movement attracted these masses in spite of its nationalist character and not because of it'. His brother had argued that the remnants of pre-capitalist conditions in the South made a national-bourgeois struggle necessary; Hall stressed that the US had no feudal history and that the Civil War had destroyed slavery.

> Today, the rapid advance of capitalist development is destroying the slave remnants. The introduction of new farm machinery, coupled with the migration of the Negroes from the farms are fast making these hangovers untenable. There is no need for another bourgeois-democratic revolution in America to destroy the remnants of feudalism. We know that America including the Negro population is ready for the proletarian revolution.[33]

In early August, there was an expanded Negro Commission comprising most of the American delegates. Haywood and Nasanov submitted a document for discussion.[34] This began with broad-sweeping criticism of recent attempts to deal with the Negro question, including Lovestone's assertion that rural black Southerners were a 'reserve of capitalist reaction'; Pepper's 30 April Political Committee resolution; Fort-Whiteman, Phillips and Patterson's document; and Moore's supposed neglect of black workers in favour of the petty bourgeoisie. They argued: 'Although there are some peculiarities in the Negro question in the United States which distinguish it somewhat from most *other national problems*, nonetheless the sum total of the economic, social and political relations existing between the Negroes and the white population make this question one of an oppressed national (or racial) minority'. Their document continued that 'in the South especially there are some pre-requisites which *may* lead to the future development of a national (racial) revolutionary movement among the Negroes'. These included a concentrated black population, 'the

33 [Carl Jones], 'Is There a Basis for the Nationalist or Separatist Movement in the United States?', 14 June 1928, in Comintern archives, 515:1:1239 and 495:155:56, and also Lovestone papers, box 214, folder 7. See also Carl Jones, 'Against the Slogan for Self-Determination Among American Negroes', 22 June 1928, in Lovestone papers, box 214, folder 11. These documents disprove L. Carr's argument that Stalin's definition of a nation was unimportant in the discussion; L. Carr 1981, p. 46.

34 Thus Klehr and Thompson's statement (made before the Comintern archives were opened) that self-determination 'had never been discussed in any American Communist meeting, whether of the Politburo or the Central Committee', while true, is misleading, since most key leaders of the party were present at this meeting; Klehr and Thompson 1989, p. 355.

semi-peasant character of that population, the slave remnants in agriculture (peonage, share-cropping, landlord supervision and marketing, etc.), political disenfranchisement, segregation and lynching'. Thus, 'it is the peasant question, which lies at the root of the Negro national (racial) question'.

While referencing the Second Congress resolution, the document did not mention self-determination as a solution to the vague 'national (racial) question'. It stressed 'that the Party must completely reorientate itself in regard to Negro work'. The document emphasised that the party should take up the fight for black liberation and purge itself of 'white chauvinism'. It underlined that Communists must pay attention to the South and organise black farmers. Noting the existence of a black industrial working class, the document stressed *'the principle emphasis of all our Negro work must be placed on these new forces'.* Communists should fight for unions to organise black workers without any discrimination. 'In order to start its work in the South', the document argued, 'the Party should establish a new district in Birmingham, Alabama'—the centre of Southern industry.[35]

In a lengthy rebuttal to his brother, Hall called the application of the right of self-determination for blacks in America 'nonsense'. Using population data, he showed that migration since the turn of the century had decreased the concentration of black Americans in the South and diminished blacks' percentage of the total Southern population. He also stressed class differences among American blacks, arguing that there was no separate black economy since most black capitalists and professionals were tied to the white bourgeoisie. Black people, he added, had no national culture that differentiated them from other Americans.

He criticised those 'comrades who see the American Negro problem only through the eyes of their experience with national minorities in Europe and the East'. In reality, 'The American Negro problem has many unique features which make it necessary to examine the special facts as they exist in the United States. In no other country in the world have we a parallel situation'. In the atmosphere of the late 1920s and early 1930s, with the battle against 'exceptionalism', such words could not have helped Hall's case.[36]

35 H. Haywood and N. Nassanoff, 'The Tasks of the American Communist Party Regarding Negro Work', 2 August 1928, in Comintern archives, 495:155:56.

36 Carl Jones, 'Nationalism Among American Negroes', 10 August 1928, in Comintern archives, 495:155:59 and 515:1:1233. Although the document was prepared after the earlier meetings, it reads as a transcript of a presentation directed against the Nasanov-Haywood document.

As Petrovsky (who chaired the meeting) complained at the end of the meeting, the 'participation of the comrades of the American delegation was not very helpful' since it reflected factionalism. Bittelman, Gomez, Dunne, Foster and Cannon praised Haywood and Nasanov's document, and emphasised the party leadership's neglect of the Negro question. Engdahl, Darcy, Wolfe, Kruse, Reeves, Wicks, Weinstone, Lovestone and Zam opposed the document. They stressed the importance of blacks in the working class, class divisions within the black population. For them (as Darcy put it), 'The main problem of the Negro question is, however, not the setting up of a separate independent republic, but of gaining social equality; the former would only lead to segregation'.

Pepper (under severe attack at the Sixth Congress) was more slippery, trying to straddle the question. Like his co-factionalists, he insisted that the 'Negro question is a race question' and emphasised class divisions among black Americans. He allowed, however, that 'Negroes are not a nation but are developing slowly towards a nation', and cited Czechoslovakia, Ireland and Hungary as examples of developing national questions. The party's 'general slogan must be full complete social equality of the Negroes' but 'in 4–5 states [where] Negroes are in majority of working population' he had 'no objection to raising issue of Negro Soviet Republic in certain parts of the U.S.' He stressed that 'such slogan does not slove [sic] problem for millions of Negroes in North and East', where the party must demand 'racial, social and political equality, also, as well as self-determination'. This was 'a typical Pepperism', as Draper put it. A 'Negro Soviet Republic' went beyond Haywood and Nasanov. They emphasised the *right* of black independence without *advocating* it. According to Petrovsky, 'It is one thing that the American working class give self-determination and another when the Negroes may want it or may not'.[37]

With the exception of Haywood, black Communists opposed the document, with Hall the most vociferous. Ford complained that 'the question for us at the present moment is merely an academic question'. He added: 'It would be of great importance if we had any serious contact with the Negro masses and any influence among them'. While Ford called Haywood's belief in a black nation 'wrong', he also described the debate as 'nothing more than a factional manoeuvre of the CEC majority, who try to utilize this theoretical discussion about Nation and Race as a means of putting aside all of the acute, practical

37 Minutes of Negro Commission, 2 August 1928; Minutes of Anglo-American Secretariat on Negro Work, 3 August 1928; Minutes of Meeting of Negro Commission, 4 August 1928; discussion in Negro Commission, 7 August 1928, in Comintern archives, 495:155:56; Draper 1986, p. 347. Pepper's position is dealt with in Sakmyster 2012, p. 180.

questions concerning Negro work'. Ford criticised Wolfe for proposing a study of black life and past party work. 'The conditions of the Negro masses are well-known. The achievements of our party in Negro work are also well known—they are practically nil'. It would be better to discuss 'concrete steps' to improve the party's Negro work instead of continuing 'the football play with the Negro question'.[38]

The commission approved Haywood and Nasanov's theses, on a vote of six to four. It also approved six motions put forward by Petrovsky. First, given Southern industrialisation and Northern migration, it was 'imperative to place greater emphasis on the working class character of the Negro work'. Second, since most American blacks lived in the rural South:

> The peasant question lies at the root of the Negro racial (national) problem. The task of the party is to transform these masses of the Negro population into the allies of the working class and the reserves of the revolutionary movement against American imperialism.

Third, the American Negro question was 'part and parcel of the general international Negro problem'. Fourth, the 'immediate tasks' of the party were to 'strengthen the Communist movement amongst the Negroes', organise black and white workers into integrated unions (and only in 'exceptional cases' into separate unions), and to intervene in 'the race organisations of the Negroes' to recruit blacks to the Communist Party. Fifth, the party should carry out 'a courageous campaign of self-criticism concerning the work among the Negroes' including fighting white chauvinism. Finally:

> While fighting the cause of the Negroes as an oppressed race, and while underlining the international race character of the Negro movement, the Party must also bear in mind that in the South of the USA there are certain prerequisites which lead to the future development of a national revolutionary movement among the Negroes. The Party must be prepared for this possible development of the Negro movement theoretically and politically.

Pepper submitted several amendments to Petrovky's resolution. The meeting approved one that stressed the need to struggle against the 'Negro bourgeoisie' and 'the influence of the petty-bourgeoisie'. Most were defeated. These

38 'Statement by Comrade Ford at Negro Commission, 3 August 1928', in Comintern archives, 495:155:56; also in Lovestone papers, box 224, folder 29.

included one that the party 'should consider the question of raising the slogan of a Negro Soviet Republic'. Petrovsky's resolution was carried unanimously, although three people—Sam Darcy, Hall and Wilson—objected 'to the part dealing with national question'. The meeting then elected a five-person sub-commission on the general Negro question, comprising Haywood, Nasanov, Petrovsky, Ford and Wilson. Hall was not selected. The preparatory work had been done, and 'self-determination' was ready for its debut at the Congress itself.[39]

39 Minutes of Meeting of Negro Commission, 4 August 1928, in Comintern archives, 495:155:56. A week later, Pepper again proposed an amendment calling for the right to form a 'Negro Soviet Republic', which was again defeated with only Pepper's support; see Minutes of Negro Commission, 11 August 1928, in Comintern archives, 493:1:573 and 495:155:56.

CHAPTER 17

'Self-Determination' and Comintern Intervention

By the Sixth Congress's colonial commission in mid-August 1928, Lovestone was on the defensive despite having the support of black Communists. The Foster-Cannon faction had seized on the issue to attack Lovestone for his leadership's supposed 'white chauvinism' and alleged overestimation of the strength of US imperialism. The commission's sessions focused not on American blacks, but rather India, China and Latin America. Discussion on black Americans was dispersed. Katayama, whose area of expertise was Asia, dedicated only a small amount of time to the issue. He noted that the Comintern's leaders 'generally do not call the American Negroes a colonial people'. Citing Lenin as an authority, he labelled black Americans 'a subject nation', and argued that American Communists 'should put up a propaganda slogan—self-determination and complete independence of the American Negroes, [and] point to the living example of the Soviet Union'.[1]

Gomez, a Cannon supporter and a specialist on anti-imperialist work, urged his party to 'link up the struggle of the Negroes as an oppressed minority in the United States with anti-imperialist struggles in Haiti, Santo Domingo, etc.' He added: 'This includes propaganda of the right of self-determination for the Negroes in the United States'. He attacked Lovestone for the party's lack of work among blacks, connecting it to the growing refrain that the then-dominant faction was soft on US imperialism.[2]

Petrovsky reported that the Negro commission had decided that a stronger fight against black oppression was necessary, and that the party should 'change to some degree the programme of the American Party on the question'. This meant that 'the American Party must come out openly and unreservedly for the right of national self-determination to the point of separation and the organisation of a separate state of the Negroes in the South'. Lovestone's supporters sidestepped the issue, discussing other aspects of the colonial question.[3]

Towards the end of the Sixth Congress, the American delegation adopted 'A Resolution on Work Among the Negro Masses of the United States of America'. The original version began with the following statement: 'Within the Negro population of the United States, the Negro working class is destined to

1 Communist International 1928c, p. 1313.
2 Communist International 1928c, p. 1320.
3 Communist International 1928c, pp. 1322, 1395.

be the vanguard of all liberation movements and may become the vanguard of the liberation movement of the Negro peasant masses on an international scale'. The first several pages of the resolution described the mechanisms of black oppression in the United States, including Jim Crow segregation in the South, lynch-law terror, and the creation of large black ghettoes in Northern cities. 'The racial caste system is a fundamental feature of the social, industrial and political organisation of the United States'. As a result, 'the oppression of the Negro race is one of the most important bases of the government apparatus of American capitalism'.

Repeatedly, the draft resolution referred to 'the Negro race'—although in the copy in the Comintern archives, 'race' was often crossed out and replaced with 'people'. The resolution labelled the 'central slogan' the *'abolition of the whole system of race discrimination, [and] full racial, social and political equality of the Negro people'.* It continued: 'But it is necessary to supplement the struggle for the full racial, social and political equality of the Negroes with a struggle for the right of national self-determination of the Negroes'. This meant 'the right to establish their own State, to erect their own government, if they choose to do so'. Later, the resolution added: 'the realisation of this self-determination cannot be secured under the present relations of power under capitalism'. As opposed to the earlier conception that black Communists did not have to advocate independence, the resolution stated that 'the Negro Communists must put in the centre of their propaganda on this point (self-determination) the establishment of a Negro Soviet Republic'.[4]

After discussion, the Negro Sub-Commission adopted a modified resolution. This eliminated the opening section about the international role of American blacks, and added more detail about the concentration of the black population in the Southern black belt. The document focused more on the role of the black 'peasantry' in the South. It also toned down the importance of self-determination and took out the demand for a Negro Soviet Republic. 'It is the duty of the Communist Party of the U.S.A. to mobilise and rally the

4 'Resolution on Work Among the Negro Masses of the United States of America, Adopted by the American Delegation', 25 August 1928, in Comintern archives, 495:155:49. Given the controversy over Lovestone's 'reserves of reaction' formulation, the following passage is notable: 'It is the basic duty of the Communist Party to develop all revolutionary possibilities of the Negro race [struck out and replaced with 'people'], to transform the "solid south" and the "black belt" from "reserve forces for the bourgeoisie into reserves of forces for the proletariat" (Stalin)'. This and the use of the Negro Soviet Republic slogan seem to indicate the hand of Pepper in writing this motion.

broad masses of the white workers' against black oppression. As part of this, Communists:

> must come out as the champion of the right of the oppressed Negro race for full emancipation. While continuing and intensifying the struggle under the slogan of full social and political equality for the Negroes, which must remain the central slogan of our Party for work among the masses, the Party must come out openly and unreservedly for the right of national self-determination to the point of separation and the organisation of a separate state for the Negroes.

Presumably to quell objections that 'separation' might be seen as Jim Crow with a Communist veneer, the resolution emphasised that 'Special stress must be laid on organising active resistance against lynching, Jim Crowism, segregation and all other forms of oppression of the Negro population'.[5]

In late October, after the Sixth Congress, the Comintern passed a final motion that declared: 'The various forms of oppression of the Negro masses, who are concentrated mainly in the so-called "Black Belt", provide the necessary conditions for a national revolutionary movement among Negroes'. It asserted that 'the agrarian problem lies at the root of the Negro national movement'. The programmatic punchline was that:

> While continuing and intensifying the struggle under the slogan of full social and political equality for the Negroes, which must remain the central slogan of our Party for work among the masses, the Party must come out openly and unreservedly for the right of the Negroes to national self-determination in the Southern states where the Negroes form a majority of the population.

Like the penultimate draft, the resolution did not emphasise this demand. It urged that 'the Party must consider the beginning of systematic work in the South as one of its main tasks'. The party must 'set up special unions for those Negro workers who are not allowed to join the white unions', while at the same time fighting 'for the inclusion of Negro workers in the existing unions'. It criticised the TUEL for having 'completely neglected the work among the Negro workers'. 'White chauvinism', the resolution continued, was not only present among workers, 'but is even reflected in various forms in the Party itself'. To 'reach the bulk of the Negro masses, special attention should be paid to the work

5 'Resolution of the Negro Sub-Commission on the Negro Question in the United States', 30 August 1928, in Comintern archives, 495:155:51.

among the Negroes in the South'. The party needed to train black Communist leaders. In short, 'The Party must link up the struggle on behalf of the Negroes with the general campaigns of the Party' so that 'the Negro problem' becomes 'part and parcel of all and every campaign conducted by the Party'.[6]

'Self-Determination' and Stalinisation

Before trying to determine why this new line was adopted, it is worthwhile understanding the role of Stalin. While it is impossible to deny that the slogan originated 'in Moscow' and not the US, this still leaves open how 'Moscow' developed the slogan. The intellectual history of the concept of a black nation in the United States goes back before Stalin; nor was Stalin the first Communist to pose the idea. Nonetheless, it is inconceivable that in 1928 'self-determination' could have been adopted without Stalin's support. Draper is correct that its 'Stalinist origins [are] unmistakable'.[7]

The new line reflected the Stalinisation of the Comintern—personally, and more important, politically. Debate over the South African 'Native Republic' slogan, discussed above, was still ongoing at the Sixth Congress; Comintern leaders used American Communists to attack Bunting and others who opposed it. Similar perspectives were proffered for black and indigenous populations in Australia, Brazil, Cuba, Ecuador and Peru. In Canada, Communists (mainly English-speakers and East European immigrants) raised the call for Québécois self-determination. In some cases, such as Quebec (where a Francophone nation was long oppressed by English Canada), referring to national self-determination was appropriate, but in other cases it was not. Forcing these divergent situations into the framework of a classic European national question offered Stalin the chance to bolster his 'theoretical' credentials and strengthen his ideological grip on the Comintern's sections.[8]

6 'Resolution on the Negro Question in the U.S.A. of the Political Secretariat', 26 October 1928, in Comintern archives, 495:155:51 and 515:1:1226; the resolution (along with an explanation of its subsequent publication in the US) is in Foner and Allen 1987, pp. 189–96.

7 Draper 1986, p. 350. The most forceful exponent of the view minimising Stalin's role is L. Carr 1981. On 'socialism in one country' and Vollmar, see Trotsky 1937, p. 293.

8 On Australia, see Bozinovski 2008, pp. 136–7; Cottle 2011; on Brazil, see Dulles 1973, p. 473; Graham 2010, Chapter 2; on Cuba, see B. Carr 1998, p. 99; on Ecuador, see Becker 2008, p. 36; on Peru, see Becker 2006. The attempt to call for an Indian Republic in Peru failed because the leading Peruvian Communist, José Carlos Mariátegui, opposed it and, unlike in South Africa or the US, the Comintern was too weak to force compliance. On Quebec, see Avakumovic 1975, p. 254; Lévesque 2006, Chapters 2 and 3; Lévesque 2008; Penner 1977, pp. 91–112. Maria Gertrudis van Enckevort argues that the 'new line allowed Stalin to gain

Although Harold Cruse is wrong that the 'self-determination' line led to Lovestone's expulsion from the American Communist Party, the discovery of a 'national question' was a tool against Lovestone's faction. In May 1929, Stalin attacked Lovestone for basing Communist work on 'specific features' of the United States, and argued that Communists should emphasise 'the general features of capitalism, which are the same for all countries, and not its specific features in any given country'. Opposition to framing black oppression as a national question was rooted in seeing race relations in the United States as different from European national oppression—as Hall had argued. Furthermore, since Lovestone came under fire for overestimating the strength of US imperialism, his faction's opposition to the new line—which argued that black oppression was a sort of domestic colonialism—made his position worse.[9]

Beyond the consolidation of Stalin's personal power, the new line reflected the political degeneration—Stalinisation—of the Comintern. According to Stalin's 'two-stage' theory of revolution—itself borrowed from Menshevism—Communists in backward or colonial countries must first unite with bourgeois liberals and nationalists to achieve national liberation and democratic reforms. Only later would Communists struggle for socialism.

In China in 1927 (and elsewhere), this led to massacres. In the US, the most developed capitalist country in the world, the 'two-stage' approach was absurd *and* a betrayal. By creating a national question in the US, Stalin could insist that this question be solved before socialist revolution was on the agenda. Although not explicit in 1928, this was spelled out in a 1946 resolution reasserting the 'self-determination' line: 'It is the bourgeois-democratic revolution which gives rise to sovereign nations, but the bourgeois-democratic revolution in the Black Belt was crushed after Reconstruction, and the slave South became instead the semi-feudal South'.[10] In other words, since the American South was still semi-feudal, it was necessary to first realise the bourgeois-democratic revolution in collaboration with bourgeois elements, and only later worry about social-

control over the American party leadership'; Enckevort 2001, p. 83. This seems too one-sided. The line cannot be disentangled from the drive by Stalin to gain control over the party leadership, but this is not sufficient to explain why it was adopted; Stalin could have asserted (and did assert) his control over the Comintern and its sections in any number of ways.

9 Cruse 1967, p. 141. Stalin's anti-Lovestone remarks (dealt with in detail in Chapter 13) are in the Comintern archives, 495:37:32 and 495:72:66.

10 'Draft Resolution of the Negro Commission of CPUSA on the Negro Question', 10 July 1946, in Weinstone papers, box 9, folder 1.

ism. In 1928, Hall, in his document quoted above, went against the Stalinist orthodoxy by insisting that the American South was ready for socialist, not bourgeois-democratic, revolution.

Resistance

This new line surprised most American Communists. In retrospect, its adoption was certain—especially after the ostracism of Bunting in South Africa for opposing the Native Republic slogan. This did not diminish the discussion's heat. The Foster and Cannon groups, with little black support, were happy to wield it against the Lovestone leadership. Lovestone supporters opposed it. Minor, the faction's leading (white) theoretician on the issue, exemplified this unease. A product of segregated Texas, before becoming a Communist, Minor had been a prominent cartoonist and still doodled notes. One read: '"National" Question—as a question of "Self-Determination["] for Slave States'. Another posited that if the new theory was correct, then 'Marx and Engels would have been wrong' and 'Jef. Davis, then, would have been right'. (Of course, Minor did not openly oppose the new line).[11]

The one exception was Pepper. Perhaps hoping to show his loyalty to the Comintern and escape the disdain that Stalin's allies had heaped upon him at the Sixth Congress, Pepper revised his *Communist International* piece into an article for the October *Communist*, later issued as a pamphlet. This argued that while Communists as a whole should support the right of 'self-determination' without advocating either assimilation or independence, 'The *Negro* Communists should emphasize in their propaganda *the establishment of a Negro Soviet Republic*'. Pepper had consistently held this line during the last months—and it had been consistently rejected. Presumably to atone for their opposition to the 'self-determination' line, Lovestone and his allies supported Pepper.[12]

Like much of what Lovestone-Pepper touched in late 1928, this slogan damaged the faction's position. Pepper's insistence that this be a *Soviet* republic went against Stalinist 'two-stage' dogma. An article by Haywood in 1933 denounced Pepper's slogan as 'an opportunist attempt to skip over the present

11 Minor papers, box 12, folder 'Negro New York, no. 7–9'. It is not clear when these doodles were made, but most likely it was shortly after the slogan was adopted.

12 Pepper 1928, p. 12. Sakmyster argues that Pepper took this position for 'pragmatic political reasons' since he did not believe it 'privately'; Sakmyster 2005b, p. 65. See also Saymyster 2012, pp. 179–80.

stage of preparation and organization of the Negro masses'. At the same time, by advocating a separate black society, the slogan could not have been appreciated by most black Communists.[13]

In late November, the Political Committee addressed the Negro question. It unanimously passed a motion by Weinstone 'to disapprove of any agitation against the slogan of self-determination in view of the fact that it is a decision of the World Congress and the Comintern, and at the same time the Polcom approves discussion on the question for the purpose of clarification and approves the discussions now going on in the Negro Commission'.[14]

Pepper introduced a motion against Moore for his membership in the church that 'instruct[ed] Comrade Moore to leave the church immediately' and called on all comrades to do the same. (Like W.A. Domingo and Grace Campbell, Moore had been an early member of the Harlem Unitarian church, led by the left-wing Jamaican Ethelred Brown and popular among 'free thinkers' in Harlem). Although it is striking that a leading Communist belonged to a church, one suspects that Pepper's motion had less to do with militant atheism than Moore's independence. The same motion demoted Moore by making Huiswoud head of the Negro Commission.[15]

Pepper's pamphlet proved controversial. Bittelman put forward a motion 'that the statement in Comrade Pepper's pamphlet urging the Negro Communists to agitate for a Soviet Negro Republic are Comrade Pepper's personal views and not the views of the Polcom, which stands on the position

13 Haywood 1933. Trotsky continued to believe that black Americans comprised an oppressed nationality; see Lehr 2001, pp. 7–9. While wrong (as Max Shachtman has demonstrated), this does not contradict Trotsky's concept of permanent revolution since the existence of a national question does not mean that socialist revolution is off the agenda. That Quebec (or Ireland) is an oppressed nation does not mean that Canada (or the British Isles) first must pass through a bourgeois-democratic revolution and then a socialist revolution *unless* one already accepts the Stalinist two-stage perspective. The strength of Trotsky's programme of permanent revolution consists in its ability to connect the fight for bourgeois-democratic demands to the struggle for working-class revolution. For Trotsky's view of the Negro question in the US, see Trotsky 1973d. Pepper's advocacy of a 'Negro Soviet Republic' unwittingly echoed the *Appeal To Reason*'s embrace of segregation under socialism, with 'black cities' as 'beautiful as those the whites live in'; quoted in Draper 1986, p. 315.

14 Polcom Minutes No. 69, 22 November 1928, in Lovestone papers, box 226, folder 4.

15 On Moore, see Makalani 2011, p. 153. According to Unitarian historian Mark D. Morrison-Reed, 'there was a strong political element ... incorporated into the Harlem Unitarian Church', which 'seemed to be caught between wanting a political dialogue and wanting a religious worship service'; Morrison-Reed 1994, pp. 91–2; on Brown, see also Floyd-Thomas 2008; K. Jones 2011.

of the Comintern'. This failed. Only Bittelman supported it, Foster and Aronberg abstained, and Lovestone's supporters opposed it. Stachel then put forward an abstruse motion to 'approve the formulation, in the pamphlet of Comrade Pepper, of the section dealing with the Negro Congress, [Negro] Champion, Tenants' League, etc., because it correctly stated "that we instruct the Communist factions in these organizations" etc. etc.' This passed, with Lovestone's supporters voting for it, and Foster's voting against.[16]

Although black Communists disliked the 'self-determination' slogan, no leading black Communist left the party over it. There are several reasons why black Communists did not fight the new line. In the Comintern of the late 1920s, any dissent from the official line would be taken as either support for 'Trotskyism' or the 'Right danger'. The expulsions of Cannon and Lovestone made clear that renewed factionalism would be treated harshly.

Several black Communists supported Lovestone's resistance to the Comintern in 1929—which was not, of course, centred on the Negro question. Two of the ten-comrade Lovestone delegation to Moscow in 1929 were black. These were Huiswoud and Edward Welsh, a member of the executive committee of the Harlem Tenants' League. Most black Lovestonenites—including Huiswoud, who soon transferred from the American party to international work under the ITUC-NW—chose remaining in the Comintern over loyalty to their factional leader when he was expelled in the spring of 1929; the two prominent exceptions were Welsh and Grace Campbell, probably the first black woman recruited to the party.[17]

For any Communist, splitting from the Comintern came with profound political and social implications; this was more so for black Communists, for whom the Comintern enjoyed special importance for having focused Communist attention on the Negro question. At the 1931 Yokinen trial, Moore claimed he 'would rather have my head severed from my body by the capitalist lynchers than to be expelled from the Communist International'. Finally, 'self-determination' was only one theoretical 'innovation' that Communists in this period had to swallow. A black nation in the American South was less difficult

16 Polcom Minutes No. 69, 22 November 1928, in Lovestone papers, box 226, folder 4.

17 On black supporters deserting Lovestone, see Harold Williams, 'To the Commission on the American Question', 22 March 1929 and John H. Owens, 'To the Commission on the American Question', 30 March 1929, in Comintern archives, 495:72:63. Huiswoud's split with Lovestone appears to be part of his assuming more responsibilities within the Comintern; see Enckevort 2001, pp. 50–1. On Campbell and Walsh's support for Lovestone, see McDuffie 2011, pp. 47–8; Naison 2005, p. 23. Campbell's FBI file suggests that as of March 1931 she was still a Lovestone supporter.

to accept than 'socialism in one country'—that a classless society of abundance could be built in an isolated peasant society surrounded by hostile imperialist countries. Remaining in the Comintern, however, did not mean that black Communists were enthusiastic about the new line. Huiswoud, for example, ignored it for two years; he only acknowledged it when he began working for the Profintern in 1929. Similarly, Otto Hall remained in the party until his death almost four decades later—even though he never accepted the line.[18]

Effects of 'Self-Determination'

How did the theory of 'self-determination' affect the party's 'Negro work'? Harvey Klehr and Mark Naison, from divergent perspectives, both referred to the theory as 'an albatross'. According to Klehr, it 'isolat[ed] the Party from virtually every Negro organization'; for Naison, it was 'a singularly poor mobilizing device in the North or the South'.[19]

The theory as such had little effect on the party's day-to-day work. As James S. Allen, one of the first Communists sent to the South in the 1930s and the editor of the *Southern Worker* acknowledged, 'the Party placed little emphasis on the goal of Black self-determination'. The resolution itself was not published until the *Daily Worker* did so on 12 February 1929. 'Self-determination' was not part of daily Communist 'Negro work'.[20]

No doubt the lack of emphasis on the slogan made it easier to accept, as did the party's increased emphasis on black equality in the late 1920s and early 1930s. In February 1929, party militants protested against an Upper West Side delicatessen's racist practices. Three black and three white comrades, along

18 Moore 1992, p. 59; Enckevort 2001, Chapter 3; Gwendolyn Midlo Hall to author, 2 May 2012; there is an announcement of Otto Hall's death in *New York Times*, 6 January 1968, by the furriers' union, which suggests that he was sympathetic to the Communist Party.

19 Klehr 1984, p. 343; Naison 2005, p. 18.

20 Allen 2001, p. 51. Timothy V. Johnson has published a fascinating study of Communist work among Alabama sharecroppers in the early 1930s. This argues that 'without the position of self-determination and the recognition of African American oppression as a national question, it is highly unlikely the Party would have devoted as much time and resources to organizing among sharecroppers in the South', as well as 'that the struggle of the sharecroppers was directly connected to the fight for self-determination'; Johnson 2011, p. 466. Although this falls outside the present study of the 1920s, it is my opinion that Johnson has not proven his case beyond showing that the party braved violent repression and that 'self-determination' was the official line of the party at this time.

with Briggs (as photographer), were arrested (in the *Daily Worker*'s words) for 'carrying placards denouncing the Jim Crow policy of the Tip Toe Inn and calling for full racial, economic, political, social equality for the Negro'. The *Daily Worker* did not mention 'self-determination'. According to one researcher, the party's *Southern Worker* contained twelve articles that mentioned 'self-determination' between November 1930 and October 1934, out of 52 editions comprising at least 1,000 articles.[21]

The *Red International of Labour Unions*, the Profintern journal edited by Stalin's ally Lozovsky, carried several articles on black oppression in the US, most critical of the leadership of the party. In August 1929, there was an article by Jack Johnstone, 'The Struggle for Social Equality for Negroes in [the] South', that did not mention 'self-determination'. The next issue carried a critical letter by Lozovsky to the TUEL that also ignored 'self-determination'. Two articles by Foster in the next issues about the newly founded TUUL mentioned the struggle against Jim Crow, but not 'self-determination'. Only in spring 1930, in the last two paragraphs of an article by Padmore about organising black workers in New York City, did the journal defend the slogan. Communists were so reluctant to emphasise the slogan that in 1930 the Comintern passed another resolution stressing it. Padmore's own 1931 *Life and Struggle of Negro Toilers*, an ambitious description of black oppression in the Americas, Africa and US colonies, refers only to 'national (race) oppression' and does not focus on self-determination for American blacks.[22]

The Comintern's intervention on 'self-determination' had three main effects on the party's work among blacks. First, it forced the party to redouble this work. Second, making the Negro question a national question underscored its special (that is, non-class) nature and its international importance, placing it on the same plane as the Irish or Jewish questions. Third, insisting that the black 'peasantry' was key to black liberation forced the party to go beyond its antipathy to the South and establish roots there. In the autumn of 1928, Foster, the party's presidential candidate, travelled several Southern cities and the

21 *Daily Worker*, 2 February and 5 February 1929; Briggs was released and the six protesters received suspended sentences; information on *Southern Worker* taken from Dick J. Reavis to the author, 25 December 2011. On the *Southern Worker* in general, see Reavis 2012. The paper has just been digitised and posted on the Internet: <www.marxists.org/history/usa/pubs/southernworker/index.htm>.

22 Johnstone 1929; Losovsky 1929; Foster 1929; Foster 1930; Padmore 1930, p. 23; Klehr and Thompson 1989; Padmore 1931.

party organised units in Richmond, Virginia; Birmingham, Alabama; Atlanta and Macon, Georgia; and Charlotte, North Carolina.[23]

As writers such as Naison and Robin Kelley have described, in the Third Period, Communists carried out courageous work in the North and South—organising tenants, workers, share-croppers, while demanding racial equality. In late 1928 and 1929, the party formed 'trade union schools' in the South Side of Chicago and Harlem to train black organisers, including classes on black and labour history. More than twenty years before the *Brown v. Board of Education* decision, the party defied segregation and embraced 'social equality'. In 1930, the *Liberator* and *Labor Unity*—the papers of the ANLC and the TUUL, respectively—held an 'Inter-Racial Dance' in Harlem, featuring modern dancer Edith Segal, Duke Ellington and William Z. Foster.[24]

By August 1930, the party counted more than 50 members in Birmingham, AL; in 1931, almost a quarter of the party's membership in Chicago were black—even though black people comprised less than seven percent of the city's total population. In Baltimore, the party emphasised black rights in the 1930s, becoming 'a major catalyst for the revival of the local Black freedom movement', according to Andor Skotnes. In 1930, there were some 75 Communists in Chattanooga, TN, and the party stood a black candidate for the state senate and a Jewish candidate for governor, on a platform calling for a 'workers' and farmers' government' and 'full equality for the Negro masses' and against 'lynching, jim crowism, and segregation'.

In Atlanta, under the leadership first of Otto Hall and then Angelo Herndon, Communists organised black and white unemployed in the face of massive state repression—and then led a national defence campaign when Herndon was arrested for 'insurrection'. The party's fight against the frame-up of the 'Scottsboro Boys'—nine black youths accused of rape in Alabama in 1931—highlighted the racist nature of the American justice system and emphasised the party's struggle for racial equality.

23 Goldfield 1980, p. 50; Hickmott 2011. On the party's Southern work in 1928, see Bass 2009, pp. 38–9. On the importance of the CP in the Southern struggle for black rights, see Gilmore 2008. The Comintern's intervention forced the party to grapple with the role of racial oppression in American history, and historians sympathetic to the Communist Party, such as Herbert Aptheker and Philip S. Foner, were pioneers in the study of black history. Their approaches were echoed (and transcended) in a later generation of historians such as Eric Foner, Herbert Gutman, Eugene Genovese and David Montgomery.

24 'On Trade Union Schools Among Negroes Conducted by RILU' [11 December 1928], in Communist Party USA collection, Tamiment, box 141, folder 13. On the party's work in this period, see Kelley 1990; Naison 2005. On the party's embrace of integrated dancing, see Graff 1997, pp. 35–8; Manning 2004, p. 71; Prickett 1990, p. 48.

In Western Pennsylvania, the Communist-led National Miners Union 'achieved some notable gains because it recruited a large number of exploited, defiant African American miners', according to historian Walter T. Howard. In East St. Louis, Illinois—the site of an anti-black riot in 1917—and across the Mississippi in St. Louis, Missouri, Communists braved police violence to fight for relief. The TUUL led a strike of some 1,400 largely black women workers in the Funsten nut pickers' strike in 1933. The 'black belt' theory played almost no role in these struggles, but repeated Comintern intervention was crucial.[25]

The theory, of course, was not a necessary *precondition* for the party's struggle against black oppression. No doubt the party would have been better served by a realistic understanding of the black oppression in America. The fact remains, however, that the party entered the 1930s with this theory, and its work was done *despite* it. What was crucial was not the theory itself, but the Comintern intervention that came wrapped in it. This contradicts Kate Baldwin's assertion that 'the Comintern was unwilling to do anything concrete to combat racism within [American] Party ranks', but 'deferred to what was perceived as Americans' superior grasp of racial matters'. In fact, the Comintern consistently intervened in the party. The salutatory nature of the Comintern's intervention is shown, in the negative, by comparison with the Communist Party of Costa Rica. Despite Costa Rica's important black minority (originating as Caribbean migrants who worked as banana workers), Communists there never put the fight for black rights at the centre of their work. This reflects the fact that the party affiliated to the Comintern during the popular-front era, and thus did not receive the same Comintern attention on this issue. More broadly, the Comintern's uneasy embrace of black nationalism, while not resonating much in the US, contributed to the growth of pan-Africanism in the 1930s.[26]

25 On Alabama, in addition to Kelley 1990, see T. Johnson 2011; on Atlanta, see Lorence 2006; Lorence 2009; on Baltimore, see Skotnes 1996; on Chicago, see Storch 2009; on Tennessee, see Bass 2009, p. 116; on Scottsboro, see Carter 1979; on Western Pennsylvania, see Howard 2001, p. 93; Nyden 1977; On East St. Louis and the Funsten strike, see Barber 2011; Fichtenbaum 1991. On Angelo Herndon, see Martin 1979. The party's work in the South during the Depression can also be ascertained by reading the *Southern Worker*.

26 Baldwin 2002, pp. 55–7. On Costa Rica, see Zumoff 2011. Brent Hayes Edwards, in *Practice of Diaspora*, argued that the Comintern's focus on international black oppression and training of black radicals like Padmore and West African Tiemoko Garan Kouyaté, enabled 'a collaboration, a nascent discourse of black internationalism, that is at once inside communism, fiercely engaged with its ideological debates and funneled though its institutions, and at the same time aimed at a race-specific formation that rejects the Comintern's universalism, adamantly insisting that racial oppression involves factors and forces that cannot be summed up or submerged in a critique of class exploitation';

By the Second World War, American Communists were known as fighters for black equality. Later, the party would squander much of its authority, as the Stalinised Comintern discarded Third Period militancy in favour of alliances with bourgeois liberals. In the late 1930s, the party supported the Democratic Party dominated 'New Deal Coalition', and during the Second World War, supported the war aims of American capitalism. As Norman Markowitz, a historian sympathetic to the Communist Party, admitted, during the war, 'determined Communist opposition to civil-rights militancy … bred hostilities that would compromise post-war Communist appeals to the Negroes'.[27] This does not undercut the importance of the Comintern's intervention, but it does underscore the Stalinist degeneration of the international Communist movement.

Edwards 2003, p. 245. Padmore and Kouyaté, of course, broke from the Comintern and became hostile to Communism. 'Black internationalism' is also dealt with in Featherstone 2012, Chapter 4.

27 Markowitz 1973, pp. 206–7.

Conclusion

This study ends with the expulsion of Lovestone in 1929 and the subsequent Browder leadership. In addition to ending the party's first decade, this marked a qualitative change in the party: the party leadership was now fully Stalinised. Any opposition to Stalin's leadership, be it from the right or left, was expelled. The party accepted without opposition Stalinist concepts such as 'socialism in one country' and the right of 'self-determination' for American black people, as well as the ideology of the Third Period.

In some ways, the Stalinist nature of the American Communist Party is obvious. Yet recall that Stalinism means more than loyalty to the dictates of Stalin. The Stalinisation of American Communism meant its transformation from a party dedicated to workers' revolution into a social-democratic party that sought to pressure the American government for policies benefitting the Soviet government. The reformist, social-democratic aspects of Stalinism were clear in the popular-front period in the mid-1930s. In the five years of the Third Period, however, this was not the case.

During this period, the CP's rhetoric was the most revolutionary it had ever been, at least since the heady days of the Red Scare. According to one study of Communist pamphlets: 'By January 1930 the American Communist Party had launched a propaganda campaign to convince Americans that the social and economic crisis of the Depression necessitated a communist revolution'. In 1932, Foster published a book, *Toward Soviet America*. No wonder one historian titled his study of this period 'A Final Stab at Insurrection'. (Although it should be noted that this 'insurrection' was more rhetorical than real: the CP never attempted to seize power, a move that would have been suicidal in the United States).[1]

Certainly, many Communists took the revolutionary rhetoric of the Third Period at face value. The study of Communist pamphlets identified several characteristics of this propaganda that must have appealed to revolutionaries: an emphasis on revolution and class struggle; a focus on Marxist theory (albeit as interpreted through Stalin); attacks on Democratic politicians (including President Roosevelt); polemics against Socialists and trade-union leaders for betraying the working class. Instead of trying to make alliances with liberals and petty-bourgeois intellectuals and professionals, the Communists stressed the need to destroy capitalism and replace it with socialism. In its actions too the party appeared revolutionary. Communists were at their most

1 Burgchardt 1980, p. 376; Foster 1932; Ryan 2004. See also Bellush and Bellush 1980.

heroic during this period, as they formed militant unions against the AFL, fought Jim Crow, and organised the unemployed. Although marked by ideological errors and eccentricities such as dual unionism, 'self-determination' for black Americans, and the belief that the collapse of capitalism was posed, the Third Period in the United States had more positive effects than in other countries. In fact, the problems with the Third Period were more immediate and more apparent for Communists outside the US. For example, the theory of 'social fascism' contributed to the German Communists' refusal to organise against the rise of Hitler, demonstrating that the Comintern in the early 1930s was anything but revolutionary. This illustrates the importance of viewing the American Communist Party within an international context: the anti-revolutionary nature of the Third Period is less obvious in the United States, where there was little chance of revolution, than in European countries that faced revolutionary situations.[2]

It may appear strange, then, to pose the Stalinisation of the CP in the early 1930s as an abandonment of a revolutionary perspective. This is one reason that Cannon and his Trotskyist followers had a hard time recruiting dissident Communists in this period. Communists believed that they were fighting for Communism. Nonetheless, many of the party's leaders had already accepted the idea that their role was to serve as a transmission belt between the Stalinist Comintern and the American party. Thus, when the Comintern officially abandoned the Third Period in favour of the popular front, the same leaders had no problem courting the same 'social fascists' whom they had opposed until recently. Above all, the contradictions of the CP in the early 1930s demonstrate that Stalinisation was neither an obvious nor smooth process. However, by 1929 the programmatic and organisational foundation had been laid for the party's subsequent social-democratisation.

This poses the issue of the main tragedy of the American Communist Party. Although the party was hindered by various internal weaknesses—especially factionalism—it is unlikely that anything the party could have done by itself could have broken through the conservatism of the period and 'made a revolution'. Intensive Comintern guidance, on a political and tactical level, helped the party hold out during this period. As Michael Goldfield has argued, in this context, the party's accomplishments in the decade, although disparaged by

2 Burgchardt 1980; like most scholars, Burgchardt is critical of the Third Period. The few sympathetic scholarly treatments of this period include R.D. Green and Isaacson 2012 and J. Green 1972; see also Devinatz 2007. Writers on the CP's work among blacks tend to be more sympathetic to the Third Period; see Goldfield 1980, Goldfield 1985; Kelley 1990.

historians, are significant.[3] By the time of the Great Depression, the Communists had already shown themselves to be the one significant opposition to capitalism, and in the context of a worldwide capitalist crisis, Communists built a mass party whose influence, especially in the labour movement and among black militants, extended far beyond its numbers. Yet shackled by Stalinism, the Communist Party squandered this influence and support. How this happened is another book. The roots of this betrayal have formed the subject of this study. Those who would build a revolutionary workers' movement in this country must assimilate the lessons of this failure.

3 See in particular Goldfield 1985, p. 327.

Bibliography and Works Cited

1 Archival Sources

(An asterisk indicates microfilm version was used)
Robert J. Alexander Papers, Rutgers University
American Fund for Public Service Papers, New York Public Library (*)
Charles Ashleigh, interviewed by Patrick Renshaw, 19 November 1965, Twentieth Century International History Archives, Nuffield College Library, Oxford University
Charles Ashleigh Papers, Wayne State University Library
Max Bedacht Papers, Tamiment Library, New York University
Daniel Bell Papers, Tamiment Library, New York University
Victor L. Berger Papers, State Historical Society of Wisconsin (*)
Alexander Bittelman Papers, Tamiment Library, New York University
Ella Reeve Bloor Papers, Smith College Library
Louis B. Boudin Papers, Columbia University
Earl Browder Papers, Syracuse University (*)
James P. Cannon Papers, Wisconsin Historical Society (*)
Communist International (Comintern) archives, Russian State Archive of Socio-Political History, Moscow; portions of archives also consulted in European Reading Room, Library of Congress; Prometheus Research Library; Schomburg Center, New York Public Library; Tamiment Library, New York University
Communist Party USA. Collection, Tamiment Library, New York University
Lewis Corey Papers, Columbia University
Sam A. Darcy Papers, Tamiment Library, New York University
Eugene Debs Papers, microfilm edition (*)
Theodore Draper Papers, Hoover Institution, Stanford University
W.E.B. Du Bois Papers, W.E.B. Du Bois Library, University of Massachusetts Amherst (*)
William F. Dunne Papers, Tamiment Library, New York University (*)
Elizabeth Gurley Flynn papers, Wisconsin Historical Society (*)
James W. Ford Papers, Tamiment Library, New York University
Benjamin Gitlow Papers, Hoover Institution, Stanford University
Albert Glotzer Papers, Hoover Institution, Stanford University
J.B.S. Hardman Papers, Tamiment Library, New York University
J.B.S. Hardman Reminiscences, Interview with Arthur A. Goren, 19 July 1966, in American Jewish Committee Oral History Collection, Dorot Jewish Division, New York Public Library
Hubert H. Harrison Papers, Columbia University
Harry Haywood Papers, Schomburg Center, New York Public Library

Morris Hillquit Papers, State Historical Society of Wisconsin (*)
Hermina Dumont Huiswoud Papers, Tamiment Library, New York University
Oakley Johnson Papers, Schomburg Center, New York Public Library (*)
David Karsner Papers, Tamiment Library, New York University
Jay Lovestone Papers, Hoover Institution, Stanford University
Claude McKay Papers, Beinecke Rare Book and Manuscript Library, Yale University
Robert Minor Papers, Columbia University
Passaic Strike Oral History Project, American Labor Museum/Botto House National Landmark, Haledon, New Jersey
Passaic Strike Vertical File, Julius Forstmann Public Library, Passaic, New Jersey
Prometheus Research Library Collection, Prometheus Research Library
John S. Reed Papers, Houghton Library, Harvard University
Morris Rosen Papers, Tamiment Library, New York University
C.E. Ruthenberg Collection, Ohio Historical Society (*)
Max Shachtman Papers, Tamiment Library, New York University (*)
Max Shachtman Reminiscences (1965), Socialist Movement Project, Oral History archives, Columbia University
Socialist Party Papers, Duke University (*)
Socialist Party Papers, Tamiment Library, New York University (*)
Mark Solomon and Robert Kaufman Research Files on African Americans and Communism, Tamiment Library, New York University
Rose Pastor Stokes Papers, Tamiment Library, New York University (*)
Arne Swabeck Memoirs, 'From Debs to Mao' (1975), copy in Prometheus Research Library, original in Hoover Institution, Stanford University
Charles E. Taylor Reminiscences (1965), Oral History archives, Columbia University
Exile Papers of Leon Trotskii, Houghton Library, Harvard University
William W. Weinstone Papers, Library of Congress
John Wiita Papers, Immigration History Research Center, University of Minnesota
Charles S. Zimmerman papers, Tamiment Library, New York University

2 Federal Bureau of Investigation Freedom of Information Act Files

All-American Anti-Imperialist League, File 61-6065-1
American Negro Labor Committee, File 61-5941-1
Cyril Briggs, File 61-826
Grace P. Campbell, File 61-6864-1
Marcus Garvey, File 190-1781-6
Jay Lovestone, File 61-1292
Claude McKay, File 61-3497

3 Personal Correspondence

Mark Donnelly (on Nicholas Hourwich), 23 June 2011
Samatha Fitzgerald (Harvard Law School Registrar's Office, on Albert Weisbord), 22 June 2011
Gwendolyn Midlo Hall (on Otto Hall), 2 May 2012
Dick Reavis (on *Southern Worker*), 25 December 2011

4 Newspapers and Periodicals

Amsterdam News, 1922–3
Class Struggle, 1917–19
The Communist (Communist Party of America), 1919–21
The Communist (Unified Communist Party), 1920–1
The Communist (Communist Party), 1922
The Communist (Left Opposition), 1922
The Communist (successor to *Workers Monthly*), 1928–9
The Communist International, 1919–29
Communist Review (London), 1925–8
Crisis, 1918–20
Crusader, 1918–20
Daily Worker, 1924–9
Farmer-Labor Advocate (St. Paul, Minnesota), 1923–4
Industrial Pioneer, 1921–2
Industrial Syndicalist, 1910
International Press Correspondence, 1922–9
International Socialist Review, 1903, 1912, 1916–17
Labor Defender, 1926–8
Labor Herald, 1922–4
Messenger, 1918–19
Militant, 1928–9
Negro Champion, June 1926
New Solidarity, 1919–20
New York Communist, 1919
New York Times, select issues
Ohio Socialist, 1918–19
One Big Union Monthly, 1920–1
Party Organizer, 1928–30
Passaic Daily Herald, 1926–7
Passaic Daily News, 1926–7

Red International of Labour Unions, 1928–30
Revolutionary Age (edited by Luis Fraina), 1919
Revolutionary Age (Lovestoneite), 1929–30
Solidarity, 1920–1
Voice of Labor, 1921–4
Workers' Council, 1921
Workers' Dreadnought (London), 1920
Workers Monthly, 1924–8
Workers World, 1919

5 References

Adi, Hakim 2008, 'Pan-Africanism and Communism: The Comintern, the "Negro Question" and the First International Conference of Negro Workers, Hamburg 1930', *African and Black Diaspora* 1, 2: 237–54.

——— 2009, 'The Negro Question: The Communist International and Black Liberation in the Interwar Years', in *From Toussaint to Tupac: The Black International since the Age of Revolution*, edited by Michael O. West *et al.*, Chapel Hill, NC: University of North Carolina Press.

The AFL Textile Workers: A History of the United Textile Workers of America 1950, Washington: Department of Research and Education, United Textile Workers of America.

Ahola, David John 1981, *Finnish-Americans and International Communism: A Study of Finnish-American Communism from Bolshevization to the Demise of the Third International*, Washington: University Press of America.

Albert, Gleb J. 2011, '"German October is Approaching": Internationalism, Activists, and the Soviet State in 1923', *Revolutionary Russia*, 24, 2: 111–42.

Alexander, Robert J. 1981, *The Right Opposition: The Lovestoneites and the International Communist Opposition of the 1930s*, Westport, CT: Greenwood.

——— 1991, *International Trotskyism, 1929–85: A Documented Analysis of the Movement*, Durham, NC: Duke University Press.

Allen, James S. 2001 [1984], *Organizing in the Depression South: A Communist's Memoir*, Minneapolis, MN: MEP Publications.

Alperin, Robert J. 1959, 'Organization in the Communist Party, U.S.A., 1931–1938', Unpublished PhD thesis, Northwestern University.

Amter, Israel 1924, 'The Communist International and the American Movement', *Communist International*, 5.

Anderson, Paul H. 1942, 'The Attitude of the American Leftist Leaders Toward the Russian Revolution, 1917–1925', Unpublished PhD thesis, University of Notre Dame.

Angus, Ian 1981, *Canadian Bolsheviks: The Early Years of the Communist Party of Canada*, Montreal: Vanguard Publishing.

Asher, Martha Stone 1990, 'Recollections of the Passaic Textile Strike of 1926', *Labor's Heritage*, 2, 2: 5–23.

Attempt by Communists to Seize the American Labor Movement 1923, Indianapolis, IN: United Mine Workers of America.

Avakumovic, Ivan 1975, *The Communist Party of Canada*, Toronto: McClelland and Stewart.

Avrich, Paul 1986, *The Haymarket Tragedy*, Princeton, NJ: Princeton University Press.

Azcárate, Manuel 1978, 'What is Eurocommunism?', in *Euro-Communism: Its Roots and Future in Italy and Elsewhere*, edited by G.R. Urban, London: Temple Smith.

Baev, Jordan and Kostadin Grozev 2008, *An Odyssey Across Two Worlds: George the Bulgarian and Soviet-American Relations During the First Half of the 20th Century*, unpublished revised English translation of Bulgarian original.

Baldwin, Kate A. 2002, *Beyond the Color Line and the Iron Curtain: Reading Between Black and Red, 1922–1963*, Durham, NC: Duke University Press.

Barbero, Andrew 2011, 'Riverfront Reds: Communism and Anti-Communism in East St. Louis, 1930–25', Unpublished Master's thesis, Southern Illinois University at Carbondale.

Baron, Samuel H. 1995 [1986], 'Plekahnov and American Exceptionalism', in *Plekhanov in Russian History and Soviet Historiography*, Pittsburgh, PA: University of Pittsburgh Press.

Barrett, James R. 1998, 'Boring from Within and Without', in *Labor Histories: Class, Politics, and the Working Class*, edited by Eric Arensen *et al.*, Urbana, IL: University of Illinois.

——— 1999, *William Z. Foster and the Tragedy of American Radicalism*, Champaign, IL: University of Illinois Press.

——— 2002, 'Revolution and Personal Crisis: William Z. Foster, Personal Narrative, and the Subjective in the History of American Communism', *Labor History*, 43, 4: 465–482.

——— 2003, 'The History of American Communism and Our Understanding of Stalin', *American Communist History*, 2, 2: 176–90.

Bass, John Lawrence 2009, 'Bolsheviks on the Bluff: A History of Memphis Communists and their Labor and Civil Rights Contributions, 1930–1957', Unpublished PhD thesis, University of Memphis.

Bassett, Michael E.R. 1964, 'The Socialist Party of America, 1912–1919: Years of Decline', Unpublished PhD thesis, University of Notre Dame.

Becker, Marc 2006, 'Mariátegui, the Comintern, and the Indigenous Question in Latin America', *Science & Society*, 70, 4: 450–79.

——— 2008, 'Indigenous Nationalities in Ecuadorian Marxist Thought', *A Contracorriente*, 5, 2: 1–46.

Beckner, Earl 1925, 'The Trade Union Educational League and the American Labor Movement', *Journal of Political Economy*, 33: 410–31.

Bedacht, Max 1926, *The Menace of Opportunism: A Contribution to the Bolshevization of the Workers' (Communist) Party*, Chicago, IL: Daily Worker Publishing Company.

Bekken, Jon E. 1992, 'Working-Class Newspapers, Community and Consciousness in Chicago, 1880–1930', Unpublished PhD thesis, University of Illinois at Urbana Champaign.

——— 1997, 'A Paper for Those Who Toil: The Chicago Labor Press in Transition', *Journalism History*, 23, 1: 24–33.

Bell, Daniel 1967, *Marxian Socialism in the United States*, Princeton, NJ: Princeton University Press.

Bellush, Bernard and Jewel Bellush 1980, 'A Radical Response to the Roosevelt Presidency: The Communist Party (1933–1945)', *Presidential Studies Quarterly*, 10, 4: 645–61.

Bengston, Henry 1999 [1955], *On the Left in America: Memoirs of the Scandinavian-American Labor Movement*, translated by Kermit Westerberg, edited by Michael Brook, Carbondale, IL: Southern Illinois University Press.

Berger, Victor L. 1913, *Broadsides*, Milwaukee, WI: Social-Democratic Publishing Company.

Bergin, Cathy 2006, 'Race/class politics: the *Liberator*, 1929–1934', *Race & Class*, 47, 4: 86–104.

Berland, Oscar 1999, 'The Emergence of the Communist Perspective on the "Negro Question" in America: 1919–1931, Part One', *Science & Society*, 63, 4: 411–32.

——— 2000, 'The Emergence of the Communist Perspective on the "Negro Question" in America: 1919–1931, Part Two', *Science & Society*, 64, 2: 194–217.

——— 2001, 'Nasanov and the Comintern's Negro Program', *Science & Society*, 65, 2: 226–8.

Bernstein, Irving 1960, *The Lean Years: A History of the American Worker, 1920–1933*, Boston, MA: Houghton Mifflin.

Bimba, Anthony 1936, *The History of the American Working Class*, New York: International Publishers.

Bittelman, Alexander 1924, *Parties and Issues in the Election Campaign*, Chicago, IL: Literature Department.

——— 1925, 'Max Eastman on Leninism', *Workers Monthly*, 4, 4: 255–6.

'Boring From Within: The Debate' 2001, *Anarcho-Syndicalist Review*, 31.

Bornet, Vaughn Davis 1964, *Labor Politics in a Democratic Republic: Moderation, Division and Disruption in the Presidential Election of 1928*, Washington: Spartan.

Boudin, Louis B. 1907, *Theoretical System of Karl Marx in the Light of Recent Criticism*, Chicago, IL: Charles H. Kerr.

——— 1916, *Socialism and War*, New York: New Review.

——— 1917a, 'The Emergency National Convention of the Socialist Party', *Class Struggle*, 1, 1: 41–50.

——— 1917b, 'The Tragedy of the Russian Revolution', *Class Struggle*, 1, 4: 85–90.

Boughton, Bob 2001, 'The Communist Party of Australia's Involvement in the Struggle for Aboriginal and Torres Strait Islander People's Rights 1920–1970', in *Labour and Community: Historical Essays*, edited by Raymond Markey, Wollongong: University of Wollongong Press.

Bozinovski, Robert 2008, 'The Communist Party of Australia and Proletarian Internationalism', Unpublished PhD thesis, Victoria University.

Braudy, Susan 2003, *Family Circle: The Boudins and the Aristocracy of the Left*, New York: Knopf.

Brody, David 1987, *Labor in Crisis: The Steel Strike of 1919*, Urbana, IL: University of Illinois Press.

Broks, Janis, Aivars Tabuns and Ausma Tabuna 2001, 'History and Images of the Past', in *National, State and Regime Identity in Latvia*, edited by Aivars Tabuns, Riga: Baltic Study Centre.

Brooks, Robert R.R. 1935, 'The United Textile Workers of America', Unpublished PhD thesis, Yale University.

Browder, Earl 1925, 'Industrial Depression or Prosperity?' *Workers Monthly*, 4, 5: 218–20.

——— 1936, *What Is Communism?* New York: Vanguard Press.

——— 1967, 'The American Communist Party in the Thirties', in *As We Saw the Thirties: Essays on Social and Political Movements of a Decade*, edited by Rita James Simon, Urbana, IL: University of Illinois Press.

Brown, Kathleen A. 1996, 'Ella Reeve Bloor: The Politics of the Personal in the American Communist Party', Unpublished PhD thesis, University of Washington.

Brown, Kathleen A. and Elizabeth Faue 2000, 'Social Bonds, Sexual Politics and Political Community on the U.S. Left, 1920s–1940s', *Left History*, 7, 1: 9–45.

Brown, Myland Rudloph 1968, 'The I.W.W. and the Negro Worker', Unpublished PhD thesis, Ball State University.

Buhle, Paul 1980, 'Jews and American Communism: The Cultural Question', *Radical History Review*, 23: 9–33.

——— 1987, *Marxism in the United States: Remapping the History of the American Left*, London: Verso.

——— 1995, *A Dreamer's Paradise Lost: Luis C Fraina/Lewis Corey (1892–1953) and the Decline of Radicalism in the United States*, Atlantic Highlands, NJ: Humanities Press.

——— 1999, 'Lovestone's Thin Red Line', *Nation*, 24 May.

Burgchardt, Carl R. 1980, 'Two Faces of American Communism: Pamphlet Rhetoric of the Third Period and the Popular Front', *Quarterly Journal of Speech*, 66, 4: 375–91.

Burnett, Carla 2004, '"Are We Slaves or Free Men?" Labor, Race, Garveyism and the 1920 Panama Canal Strike', Unpublished PhD thesis, University of Illinois at Chicago.

Bush, Rod 1999, *We Are Not What We Seem: Black Nationalism and Class Struggle in the American Century*, New York: New York University Press.

Bynum, Corenelius L. 2010, *A Philip Randolph and the Struggle for Civil Rights*, Urbana, IL: University of Illinois Press.

Camarero, Hernán 2007, *A la Conquista de la Clase Obrera: Los Comunistas y el Mundo del Trabajo en la Argentina, 1920–1935*, Buenos Aires: Siglo Veintiuno.

Camp, Helen C. 1995, *Iron in Her Soul: Elizabeth Gurley Flynn and the American Left*, Pullman, WA: Washington State University Press.

Campbell, Susan 1994, '"Black Bolsheviks" and Recognition of Africa-America's Right to Self-Determination by the Communist Party U.S.A.', *Science & Society*, 58, 4: 440–70.

Cannon, James P. 1924, 'The Bolshevization of the Party', *Workers Monthly*, 4, 1: 34–7.

——— 1926, 'The United Front in Passaic', *Labor Defender*, June.

——— 1927, 'Who Can Save Sacco and Vanzetti?', *Labor Defender*, January.

——— 1956, 'Early Years of the American Communist Movement', *Fourth International*, 17, 1: 25–9, 35.

——— 1962, *First Ten Years of American Communism: Report of a Participant*, New York: Lyle Stuart.

——— 1972 [1944], *The History of American Trotskyism: Report of a Participant*, New York: Pathfinder.

——— 1974, *James P. Cannon: A Political Tribute, Including Five Interviews from the Last Year of His Life*, New York: Pathfinder.

——— 1981, *Writings and Speeches: The Left Opposition in the U.S., 1928–31*, New York: Pathfinder.

——— 1992, *James P. Cannon and the Early Years of American Communism*, New York: Prometheus Research Library.

——— 2007 [1922], 'We Want the Comintern to Give Us Assistance: 1922 Speech by James P. Cannon', *Spartacist*, 60: 44–8.

Carr, Barry 1998, 'Identity, Class, and Nation: Black Immigrant Workers, Cuban Communism, and the Sugar Insurgency, 1925–1934', *Hispanic American Historical Review*, 78, 1: 83–116.

——— 2007, 'Hacia una Historia de los Comunismos Mexicanos: Desafíos y Sugerencias', in *El Comunismo: Otras Miradas desde América Latina*, edited by Elvira Concheiro, Massimo Modonesi and Horacio Crespo, Mexico City: UNAM.

Carr, Edward Hallett 1966 [1953], *The Bolshevik Revolution, 1917–1923*, Volume 3, Harmondsworth: Penguin.

——— 1967 [1961], *What Is History?*, New York, Knopf.

——— 1976, *The Foundations of a Planned Economy*, Volume 3, Part 1, London: Macmillan.

Carr, Leslie G. 1980, 'The Origins of the Communist Party's Theory of Black Self-Determination: Draper vs. Haywood', *Critical Sociology*, 10, 3: 35–49.

Carter, Dan T. 1979, *Scottsboro: A Tragedy of the American South*, Baton Rouge, LA: Louisiana State University Press.

Cascaden, Gordon 1922, *Shall Unionism Die? Report on 'Red' Union International Congress*, Windsor: Industrial Union League of Canada.

Chambelland, Colette 1964, 'Autour du Premier Congrès d l'Internationale Syndicale Rouge', *Le Mouvement Social*, 47: 31–44.

Chaplin, Ralph 1948, *Wobbly: The Rough-and-Tumble Story of an American Radical*, Chicago, IL: University of Chicago Press.

Cherny, Robert W. 2002, 'Prelude to the Popular Front: The Communist Party in California, 1931–35', *American Communist History*, 1, 1: 5–41.

Chester, Eric Thomas 2004, *True Mission: Socialists and the Labor Party Question in the U.S.*, London: Pluto.

Cochran, Bert 1977, *Labor and Communism: The Conflict that Shaped American Unions*, Princeton, NJ: Princeton University Press.

Cohalan, Florence D. 1983, *A Popular History of the Archdiocese of New York*, 2nd ed., Yonkers, NY: US. Catholic Historical Society.

Cohen, Stephen F. 1980, *Bukharin and the Bolshevik Revolution: A Political Biography, 1888–1938*, Oxford: Oxford University Press.

Coleman, Stephen 1990, *Daniel De Leon*, Manchester: Manchester University Press.

Collins, Ronald K.L. and David M. Skover 2005, 'Curious Concurrence: Justice Brandeis' Vote in Whitney v. California', *The Supreme Court Review*, 1: 333–97.

Communist International 1924, *The Fifth Congress of the Communist International (Abridged)*, London: Communist Party of Great Britain.

——— 1928a, *The Communist International between the Fifth and the Sixth World Congresses, 1924–1928*, London: Communist Party of Great Britain.

——— 1928b, 'Draft Programme of the Communist International Adopted by the Programme Committee of the E.C.C.I., 23 May 1928', *International Press Correspondence*, 8, 30: 549–64.

——— 1928c, 'Sixth World Congress of the Communist International, July–August 1928', *International Press Correspondence*, 8: 706–1772.

——— 1988 [1921], *Guidelines on the Organizational Structure of Communist Parties, on the Methods and Contents of their Work: Resolution of the Third Congress of the Communist International, 12 July 1921*, New York: Prometheus Research Library.

Conlin, Joseph R. 1967, 'The IWW and the Socialist Party', *Science & Society*, 31, 1: 22–36.

Conolly-Smith, Peter 2004, *Translating America: An Immigrant Press Visualizes American Popular Culture, 1895–1918*, Washington: Smithsonian.

Cooper, Wayne F. 1990, *Claude McKay: A Rebel Sojourner in the Harlem Renaissance*, New York: Schocken.

Cottle, Drew 2011, 'The Colour-Line and the Third Period: A Comparative Analysis of American and Australian Communism and the Question of Race, 1928–1934', *American Communist History*, 10, 2: 119–31.

Cruse, Harold 1967, *The Crisis of the Negro Intellectual: From Its Crisis to the Present*, New York: William Morrow.

Currell, Susan 2009, *American Culture in the 1920s*, Edinburgh: Edinburgh University Press.

Darch, Colin and Gary Littlejohn 1983, 'Endre Sik and the Development of African Studies in the USSR: A Study Agenda from 1929', *History in Africa*, 10: 79–108.

Darlington, Ralph 2008, *Syndicalism and the Transition to Communism: An International Comparative Analysis*, Aldershot: Ashgate.

Davenport, Tim 2007, 'Friends of Soviet Russia, 1921–1930', *Early American Marxism*, available at: <http://www.marxists.org/history/usa/eam/other/fsr/fsr.html>.

——— 2010, 'Formation of the Proletarian Party of America, 1913–1923: Part 1, John Keracher's Proletarian University and the Establishment of the Communist Party of America', unpublished paper.

——— 2012, 'Socialist Party of America Annual Membership Figures', *Early American Marxism*, available at: <http://www.marxisthistory.org/subject/usa/eam/spa membership.html>.

Davidson, Apollon, Irina Filatova, Valentin Gordodnov and Sheridan Johns (eds.) 2003, *South Africa and the Communist International: A Documentary History, Volume I, Socialist Pilgrims to Bolshevik Footsoldiers, 1919–1930*, London: Frank Cass.

Davis, Colin John 1997, *Power at Odds: The 1922 National Railroad Shopmen's Strike*, Urbana, IL: University of Illinois Press.

Davis, F. James 2001, *Who Is Black? One Nation's Definition*, University Park, PA: Pennsylvania State University Press.

Day, Richard B. 1981, *The 'Crisis' and the 'Crash': Soviet Studies of the West, 1917–1939*, London: New Left Books.

De Leon, Daniel 1966 [1907], *As to Politics*, Brooklyn, NY: New York Labor News.

De Leon, David 1979, 'The Popular Front CPUSA and the Revolution of 1776: A Study in "Patriotic Marxism"', *California Institute of Technology Humanities Working Paper* 39.

Debs, Eugene V. 1903, 'The Negro and the Class Struggle', *International Socialist Review*, 4, 5: 257–60.

Degras, Jane (ed.) 1956, *The Communist International. Documents*, London: Oxford University Press.

Derrick, Jonathan 2008, *Africa's 'Agitators': Militant Anti-Colonialism in Africa and the West, 1918–1939*, London: Hurst.

Deutscher, Isaac 1954, *The Prophet Armed*, London: Oxford University Press.

——— 1959, *The Prophet Unarmed*, London: Oxford University Press.

Devinatz, Victor G. 1996, 'The Labor Philosophy of William Z. Foster: From the IWW to the TUEL', *International Social Science Review*, 71, 1/2: 3–13.

——— 2007, 'A Reevaluation of the Trade Union Unity League, 1929–1934', *Science & Society*, 71, 1: 33–58.

Dicken, Nick and Leon Day 1969, 'The Secret War Between Brother Klonsky and Stalin (And Who Won)', *Spartacist*, 13: 4–7.

Digby-Junger, Richard 1998, '*The Guardian, Crisis, Messenger* and *Negro World*: The Early-20th-Century Black Radical Press', *Howard Journal of Communications*, 9, 3: 263–82.

Diggins, John P. 1994, *Up From Communism: Conservative Odysseys in American Political Development*, New York: Columbia University Press.

Directorate of Intelligence (British Home Office) 1919, *A Monthly Review of Revolutionary Movements in Foreign Countries* 14, December.

Domingo, W.A. 2005 [1925], 'Gift of the Black Tropics', reprinted in *'Look For Me All Around You': Anglophone Caribbean Immigrants in the Harlem Renaissance*, edited by Louis J. Parascandola, Detroit, MI: Wayne State University Press.

Draper, Theodore 1971a [1970], *The Rediscovery of Black Nationalism*, London: Secker & Warburg.

——— 1971b, 'Gastonia Revisited', *Social Research*, 34, 4: 3–29.

——— 1972a, 'Communists and Miners, 1928–1933', *Dissent*, 19: 371–92.

——— 1972b, 'The Strange Case of the Comintern', *Survey*, 18, 3: 91–137.

——— 1985 [1957], *The Roots of American Communism*, Chicago, IL: Elephant Publishers.

——— 1986 [1960], *American Communism and Soviet Russia: The Formative Period*, New York: Vintage.

Drew, Allison 2007, '"1922 and all that": Facts and the Writing of South African Political History', in *The Meaning of Collective Memory in South Africa*, edited by Hans Erik Stolten, Upsala: Nordiska Afrikaninstitutet.

Drucker, Peter 1994, *Max Shachtman and His Left: A Socialist's Odyssey through the 'American Century'*, Atlantic Highlands, NJ: Humanities Press.

Dubofsky, Melvyn 1969, *We Shall Be All: A History of the IWW*, Chicago, IL: Quadrangle.

——— 1987, *'Big Bill' Haywood*, Manchester: Manchester University Press.

Dubofsky, Melvyn and Warren Van Time 1986, *John L. Lewis: A Biography*, Urbana, IL: University of Illinois Press.

Dulles, John W.F. 1973, *Anarchists and Communists in Brazil*, Austin, TX: University of Texas Press.

Dumenil, Lynn 1995, *Modern Temper: American Culture and Society in the 1920s*, New York: Hill and Wang.

Dunne, William F. 1923, *Wm. F. Dunne's Speech at the A.F. of L. Convention*, Chicago, IL: Trade Union Educational League.

——— 1926a, *The British Strike: Its Background—Its Lessons*, Chicago, IL: Daily Worker Publishing Company.

——— 1926b, 'The Official Labour Movement in the U.S.A.', *Communist Review*, 7, 1: 10–15.

——— 1928, 'Negroes in American Industry', *Workers Monthly*, 4, 3: 206–8, 237; 4, 4: 257–9.

Dyson, Lowell K. 1972, 'The Red Peasant International in America', *Journal of American History*, 58, 4: 958–73.

——— 1982, *Red Harvest: The Communist Party and American Farmers*, Lincoln, NE: University of Nebraska Press.

Eastman, Max 1925a, *Leon Trotsky: Portrait of a Youth*, New York: Greenberg.

——— 1925b, *Since Lenin Died*, London: Boni and Liveright.

——— 1964, *Love and Revolution: My Journey through an Epic*, New York: Random House.

Ebner, Michael 1970, 'The Passaic Strike and the Two I.W.W.s', *Labor History*, 11, 4: 452–66.

Edwards, Brent Hayes 2003, *The Practice of Diaspora: Literature, Translation, and the Rise of Black Internationalism*, Cambridge, MA: Harvard University Press.

Eley, Geoff 1986, 'International Communism in the Heyday of Stalin', *New Left Review*, I/157: 90–100.

Ellis, Mark 1992, '"Closing Ranks" and "Seeking Honors": W.E.B. Du Bois in World War I', *Journal of American History*, 79, 1: 353–60.

——— 1994, 'J Edgar Hoover and the "Red Summer" of 1919', *Journal of American Studies*, 28, 1: 39–59.

Ellsworth, Scott 1992, *Death in a Promised Land: the Tulsa Race Riot of 1921*, Baton Rouge, LA: Louisiana State University Press.

Enckevort, Maria Gertrudis van 2001, 'The Life and Work of Otto Huiswoud: Professional Revolutionary and Internationalist (1893–1961)', Unpublished PhD thesis, University of West Indies at Mona.

Engdahl, J. Louis 1922, 'The Workers Party Is Launched', *Labor Age*, February.

——— 1927, 'The Drift of the Trotzky-Zinoviev Opposition', *Daily Worker*, 22 July.

Epstein, Melech 1959, *The Jew and Communism: The Story of Early Communist Victories and Ultimate Defeat in the Jewish Community, U.S.A., 1919–1941*, New York: Trade Union Sponsoring Committee.

Esposito, Anthony V. 1992, 'A Class to End Class: The Ideology of the Socialist Party, 1901–1917', Unpublished PhD thesis, University of Connecticut.

Executive Committee of the Communist International 1987 [1922?] 'To the Communist Party of America', *Spartacist*, 40: 27–8.

Falkowski, William G. 1994, 'Anna Reinstein', in *European Immigrant Women in the United States*, edited by Judy Barrett Litoff and Judith McDonnell, New York: Garland.

Featherstone, David 2012, *Solidarity: Hidden Histories and Geographies of Internationalism*, London: Zed.

Filatova, Irina 2007, 'Soviet Historiography of Anti-Colonial Struggle (1920s–1960)', in *The Study of Africa, Volume II: Global and Transnational Engagements*, edited by Paul T. Zeleza, Dakar: Council for the Development of Social Science Research in Africa.

Filene, Peter G. 1967, *Americans and the Soviet Experiment, 1917–1933*, Cambridge, MA: Harvard University Press.

Fine, Nathan 1928, *Labor and Farmer Parties in the United States, 1828–1928*, New York: Rand School of Social Science.

Firsov, Fridrikh 1989, 'What the Comintern Archives Will Reveal', *World Marxist Review*, 32, 1: 52–7.

Fitchenbaum, Myrna 1991, *The Funtsen Nut Strike*, New York: International.

Flory, Harriette 1977, 'The Arcos Raid and the Rupture of Anglo-Soviet Relations, 1927', *Journal of Contemporary History*, 12: 707–23.

Floyd-Thomas, Juan M. 2008, *The Origins of Black Humanism in America: Reverend Ethelred Brown and the Unitarian Church*, New York: Palgrave Macmillan.

Foner, Eric 1984, 'Why Is There No Socialism in the United States?' *History Workshop Journal*, 17, 1: 57–80.

Foner, Philip S. 1950, *The Fur and Leather Workers Union: A Story of Dramatic Struggles and Achievement*, Newark, NJ: Nordan Press.

——— 1964, *History of the Labor Movement in the United States*, Volume 3, New York: International.

——— (ed.) 1967, *The Bolshevik Revolution: Its Impact on American Radicals, Liberals and Labor, A Documentary Study*, New York: International.

——— 1988, *History of the Labor Movement in the United States*, Volume 8, New York: International.

Foner, Philip S. and James S. Allen (eds.) 1987, *American Communism and Black America*, Volume 1, Philadelphia, PA: Temple University Press.

Ford, Earl C. and William Z. Foster 1913, *Syndicalism*, Chicago, IL: William Z. Foster.

Fort-Whiteman, Lovett 1926, 'Garvey's Leadership Imperils Usefulness of UNIA', *Negro Champion*, June.

Foster, George 1985, 'British Communism Aborted: The Far Left, 1900–1920', *Spartacist*, 36/37.

Foster, William Z. 1920, *The Great Steel Strike and Its Lessons*, New York: Huebsch.

——— 1921a, 'What Ails American Radicalism', *Socialist Review*, April.

——— 1921b, *The Russian Revolution*, Chicago, IL: Trade Union Educational League.

——— 1922a, 'Dual Unions a Mischievous Idea', *Labor Age*, January.

——— 1922b, *The Bankruptcy of the American Labor Movement*, Chicago, IL: Trade Union Educational League.

——— 1922c, 'The Chicago Federation of Labor', *Labor Herald*, 1, 10: 8–11.

———, James P. Cannon and Earl R. Browder 1925, *Trade Unions in America*, Chicago, IL: Daily Worker Publishing Company.

——— 1929, 'The Convention of the Trade Union Unity League', *Red International of Labour Unions*, 1, 10: 417–20.

——— 1930, 'The Trade Union Unity League and the Jim-Crow System', *Red International of Labour Unions*, 2, 1: 548–51.

——— 1932, *Toward Soviet America*, New York: International.

——— 1937, *From Bryan to Stalin*, New York: International.

——— 1939, *Pages from a Worker's Life*, New York: International.

——— 1952, *History of the Communist Party of the United States*, New York: International.

Fourth National Convention of the Workers' (Communist) Party of America 1925, Chicago, IL: Daily Worker Publishing Company.

Fowler, Josephine 2007, *Japanese and Chinese Immigrants: Organizing in American and International Communist Movements, 1919–1933*, New Brunswick, NJ: Rutgers University Press.

Fraina, Louis C. 1919, 'The Attitude of Lenin', *Class Struggle*, 1, 2: 138–40.

Fraser, Richard S. 1990 [1954], 'The Negro Struggle and the Proletarian Revolution', in *In Memoriam: Richard S. Fraser*, New York: Prometheus Research Library.

——— 1994 [1955], 'For the Materialist Conception of the Negro Struggle', *Marxist Bulletin 5 (Revised)*, New York: Spartacist Publishing Company.

Fraser, Steven 1991, *Labor Will Rule: Sidney Hillman and the Rise of Labor*, New York: Free Press.

Frederickson, George M. 1995, *Black Liberation: A Comparative History of Black Ideologies in the United States and South Africa*, New York: Oxford University Press.

Freeman, Joshua B. 1989, *In Transit: The Transport Workers Union in New York City, 1933–1966*, New York: Oxford University Press.

Freeze, Gregory (ed.) 2009, *Russia: A History*, Oxford: Oxford University Press.

Gage, Beverly 2009, *The Day Wall Street Exploded: A Story of America in its First Age of Terror*, New York: Oxford University Press.

Gambs, John S. 1932, *The Decline of the I.W.W.*, New York: Columbia University Press.

Gardner, Virginia 1967, 'John Reed and Lenin: Some Insights Based on Mss. Collection at Harvard', *Science & Society*, 31, 4: 388–403.

Gates, Eddie Faye 2004, 'The Oklahoma Commission to Study the Tulsa Race Riot of 1921', *Harvard Black Letter Law Journal*, 20: 83–9.

Gedicks, Al 1976, 'The Social Origin of Radicalism Among Finnish Immigrants in Midwest Mining Communities', *Review of Radical Political Economy*, 8, 3: 1–31.

General Relief Committee of Textile Strikers [1926a], *Hell in New Jersey: A Story of the Passaic Textile Strike Told in Pictures*, Passaic, NJ: General Relief Committee.

——— [1926b], *Textile Strike of 1926: Passaic, Clifton, Garfield, Lodi, New Jersey*, Passaic, NJ: General Relief Committee.

George, Harrison [1918], *The Red Dawn: The Bolshevik and the I.W.W.*, Chicago, IL: IWW Publishing Bureau.

Georgiana, Daniel 1993, *The Strike of '28*, New Bedford, MA: Spinner.

Gibson, Campbell and Kay Jung 2002, 'Historical Census Statistics on Population Totals By Race, 1790 to 1990, and By Hispanic Origin, 1970 to 1990, For The United States, Regions, Divisions, and States', *U.S. Census Bureau Working Paper Series* No. 56, available at: <http://www.census.gov/population/documentation/twps0056>.

Gilmore, Glenda Elizabeth 2008, *Defying Dixie: The Radical Roots of Civil Rights, 1919–1950*, New York: Norton.

Ginger, Ray 1949, *The Bending Cross: A Biography of Eugene Victor Debs*, New Brunswick, NJ: Rutgers University Press.

——— 1974 [1958], *Six Days or Forever? Tennessee v. John Thomas Scopes*, New York: Oxford University Press.

Gitlow, Benjamin 1939, *I Confess: The Truth About American Communism*, New York: Dutton.

——— 1965 [1948], *The Whole of Their Lives*, Boston, MA: Western Islands.

Glazer, Nathan 1961, *The Social Basis of American Communism*, New York: Harcourt, Brace and World.

Going to the Masses! 1921, New York: Workers' Council.

Goldfield, Michael 1980, 'The Decline of the Communist Party and the Black Question in the U.S.: Harry Haywood's *Black Bolshevik*', *Review of Radical Political Economics*, 12: 44–63.

——— 1985, 'Recent Historiography of the Communist Party U.S.A.', *The Year Left*, 1: 315–58.

Goldner, Loren 2007, 'Max Eastman: One American Radical's View of the "Bolshevization" of American Radicalism and a Forgotten, and Unforgettable, Portrait of Trotsky', *Critique*, 35, 1: 119–39.

Goodall, Alex 2006, 'Aspects of the Emergence of American Anticommunism, 1917–1944', Unpublished PhD thesis, University of Cambridge.

Gorinov, M.M. and S.V. Taskunov 1991, 'Life and Works of Euvgenii Aleskseevich Preobrzhenskii', *Slavic Review*, 50, 2: 286–96.

Gosciak, Josh 2008, 'Most Wanted: Claude McKay and the "Black Specter" of African American Poetry in the 1920s', in *Modernism on File: Writers, Artists, and the FBI, 1920–1950*, edited by Claire A. Cullerton and Karen Leick, New York: Palgrave.

Graff, Ellen 1997, *Stepping Left: Dance and Politics in New York City, 1928–1942*, Durham, NC: Duke University Press.

Graham, Jessica L. 2010, 'Representations of Racial Democracy: Race, National Identity, and State Cultural Policy in the United States and Brazil, 1930–1945', Unpublished PhD thesis, University of Chicago.

Grant, Colin 2008, *Negro With A Hat: The Rise and Fall of Marcus Garvey*, Oxford: Oxford University Press.

Graziosi, Andrea 1988, 'Foreign Workers in Soviet Russia, 1920–40: Their Experience and Their Legacy', *International Labor and Working-Class History*, 33: 38–59.

Green, James 1972, 'Working Class Militancy in the Depression', *Radical America*, 6, 6, 1–36.

Green, Rodney D. and Michael Isaacson 2012, 'Communists and the Fight for Jobs and Revolution', *Review of Black Political Economy*, 38: 1–19.

Griffler, Keith P. 1995, *What Price Alliance? Black Radicals Confront Black Labor*, New York: Garland.

Gruber, Helmut (ed.) 1974, *Soviet Russia Masters the Comintern: International Communism in the Era of Stalin's Ascendancy*, Garden City, NY: Anchor.

Gurowsky, David 1978, 'Factional Disputes in the ILGWU, 1919–1928', Unpublished PhD thesis, State University of Binghamton.

Halfin, Igal 2007, *Intimate Enemies: Demonizing the Bolshevik Opposition, 1918–1928*, Pittsburgh, PA: University of Pittsburgh Press.

Hallas, Duncan 2008 [1985], *The Comintern: A History of the Third International*, Chicago, IL: Haymarket.

Halonen, Arne 1945, 'The Role of Finnish-Americans in the Political Labor Movement', Unpublished MA dissertation, University of Minnesota.

Hardman, Jacob Benjamin Salutsky (ed.) 1928, *American Labor Dynamics in the Light of Post-War Developments*, New York: Harcourt.

Hardy, George 1956, *Those Stormy Years: Memories of the Fight for Freedom on Five Continents*, London: Lawrence and Wishart.

Harris, LaShawn 2009, 'Running with the Reds: African American Women and the Communist Party during the Great Depression', *Journal of African American History*, 94, 1: 21–43.

Haupt, Georges and Jean-Jacques Marie (eds.) 1974, *Makers of the Russian Revolution: Biographies of Bolshevik Leaders*, Ithaca, NY: Cornell University Press.

The Haverhill Frame-Up 1923, Haverhill: Workers' Defence Conference.

Haverty-Stacke, Donna T. 2008, *America's Forgotten Holiday: May Day and Nationalism, 1867–1960*, New York: New York University Press.

Hawkins, Clifton C. 2000, '"Race First versus Class First": An Intellectual Odyssey of Afro-American Radicalism, 1911–1928', Unpublished PhD thesis, University of California at Davis.

Haynes, John Earl 1996, *Red Scare or Red Menace? American Communism and Anti-Communism in the Cold War Era?*, Chicago, IL: Ivan R. Dee.

——— 2000, 'The Cold War Debate Continues: A Traditionalist View of Historical Writing on Domestic Communism and Anti-Communism', *Journal of Cold War Studies*, 2, 1: 76–115.

——— 2003, 'Poison or Cancer: Stalin and American Communism', *American Communist History*, 2, 2: 183–92.

Haynes, John Earl and Harvey Klehr 2006, 'The Historiography of Soviet Espionage and American Communism: from Separate to Converging Paths', paper presented at European Social Science History Conference, Amsterdam, available at: <www.johnearlhaynes.org/page101.html>.

——— 2007, 'The "Mental Comintern" and the Self-Destructive Tactics of CPUSA, 1945–1958', available at: <www.johnearlhaynes.org/page65.html>.

Haywood, Harry 1933, 'The Struggle for the Leninist Position on the Negro Question in the U.S.A.', *The Communist*, 12.

——— 1978, *Black Bolshevik: Autobiography of an Afro-American Communist*, Chicago, IL: Liberator Press.

Haywood, William D. 1921, 'Revolutionary Problems in America', *Communist International*, 3, 16/17.

——— 1929, *Bill Haywood's Big Book*, New York: International.

Haywood, William D. and Frank Bohn 1911, *Industrial Socialism*, Chicago, IL: Charles H. Kerr.

Healy, Dorothy and Maurice Isserman 1980, *Dorothy Healy Remembers: A Life in the Communist Party*, New York: Oxford University Press.

Heideman, Paul 2008, 'Banquo's Ghost: The Russian Revolution and the Harlem Renaissance', Unpublished MA dissertation, University of Wisconsin.

Herreshoff, David 1967, *American Disciples of Marx*, Detroit, MI: Wayne State University Press.

Hickmott, Alec Fazackerley 2011, '"Brothers, Come North": The Rural South and Political Imaginary of New Negro Radicalism, 1917–1923', *Intellectual History Review*, 21, 4: 395–412.

Hill, Herbert 1951, 'The Communist Party: Enemy of Negro Equality', *Crisis*, 58: 365–71.

Hill, Robert A. (ed.) 1986, *The Marcus Garvey and Universal Negro Association Papers*, Volume 3, Berkeley, CA: University of California Press.

——— 1987, 'Racial and Radical: Cyril V. Briggs, *The Crusader* Magazine, and the African Blood Brotherhood', in *The Crusader: A Facsimile of the Periodical*, edited by Richard A. Hill, New York: Garland.

Hill, Robert A. and Barbara Bair (eds.) 1991, *The Marcus Garvey and Universal Negro Inprovement Association Papers*, Volume 7, Berkeley, CA: University of California Press.

Hillman, Sidney 1922, *Reconstruction of Russia and the Task of Labor*, New York: Amalgamated Clothing Workers of America Education Department.

Hillquit, Morris 1919, *The Immediate Issue*, New York: The Socialist.

——— 1965 [1909], *History of Socialism in the United States*, New York: Russell and Russell.

Hirson, Baruch 1989, 'Bukharin, Bunting and the "Native Republic" Slogan', *Searchlight South Africa*, 3: 51–65.

——— 1992, 'Trotsky and Black Nationalism', in *The Trotsky Reappraisal*, edited by Terry Brotherstone and Paul Dukes, Edinburgh: Edinburgh University Press.

Hirson, Baruch and Gwyn A. Williams 1995, *The Delegate for Africa: David Ivon Jones, 1883–1924*, London: Core.

Holcomb, Gary Edward 2007, *Claude McKay, Code Name Sasha: Queer Black Marxism and the Harlem Renaissance*, Gainesville, FL: University of Florida.

Holmes, John D. 2007, 'American Jewish Communism and Garment Unionism in the 1920s', *American Communist History*, 6, 2: 171–95.

——— 2008, 'The Life and Times of Noah London: American Jewish Communists; Soviet Engineer; and Victim of Stalinist Terror', Unpublished PhD thesis, University of California at Berkeley.

Holmio, Armas K.E. 2001, *History of the Finns in Michigan*, Detroit, MI: Wayne State University Press.

Hornberger, Eric and John Biggart (eds.) 1992, *John Reed and the Russian Revolution: Uncollected Articles, Letters and Speeches on Russia, 1917–1920*, London: Macmillan.

Hornstein, David P. 1993, *Arthur Ewert: A Life for the Comintern*, Lanham, MD: University Press of America.

House Immigration and Naturalization Committee Hearings 1920, Washington: General Printing Office.

Hoover, J. Edgar 1959, *Masters of Deceit*, New York: Pocket.

Howard, Walter T. 2001, 'The National Miners Union: Communists and Miners in the Pennsylvania Anthracite, 1928–1931', *Pennsylvania Magazine of History and Biography*, 125, 1: 92–124.

——— 2004, *Forgotten Radicals: Communists in the Pennsylvania Anthracite, 1919–1950*, Lanham, MD: University Press of America.

——— (ed.) 2004, *Anthracite Reds: A Documentary History of Communists in Northern Pennsylvania during the 1920s*, New York: iUniverse.

Hudelson, Richard 1993, 'The Scandinavian Local of the Duluth Socialist Party, 1910–1924', *Swedish American Historical Quarterly*, 44, 4: 181–90.

——— 2002, 'Duluth's Scandinavian Left, 1880–1950', *Swedish American Historical Quarterly*, 53, 3: 179–96.

Hughes, C. Alvin 1984, 'The Negro Sanhedrin Movement', *Journal of Negro History*, 69, 1: 1–13.

Hummasti, P.G. 1996, 'Ethnicity and Radicalism: The Finns of Astoria and the *Toveri*, 1890–1930' *Oregon Historical Quarterly*, 97: 362–93.

Hurewitz, Daniel 2007, *Bohemian Los Angeles and the Making of Modern Politics*, Berkeley, CA: University of California Press.

Hutchinson, Earl Ofari 1995, *Blacks and Reds: Race and Class in Conflict, 1919–1990*, East Lansing, MI: Michigan State University Press.

Isaacs, Harold R. 2010 [1938], *The Tragedy of the Chinese Revolution*, Chicago, IL: Haymarket.

Isserman, Maurice 1995 [1982], *Which Side Were You On? The American Communist Party During the Second World War*, Urbana, IL: University of Illinois Press.

——— 1999, 'They Led Two Lives', *New York Times*, 9 May.

Jaffee, Julian F. 1972, *Crusade Against Radicalism: New York During the Red Scare, 1914–1924*, Port Washington, NY: Kennikat.

James, Leslie Elaine 2012, '"What We Put in Black and White": George Padmore and the Practice of Anti-Imperialist Politics', London School of Economics, Unpublished PhD thesis.

James, Winston 1998, *Holding Aloft the Banner of Ethiopia: Caribbean Radicalism in Early Twentieth-Century America*, London: Verso.

——— 2003a, 'Being Red and Black in Jim Crow America: On the Ideology and Travails of Afro-America's Socialist Pioneers, 1877–1930', in *Time Longer than Rope: A Century of African American Activism, 1850–1950*, edited by Charles M. Payne and Adam Green, New York: New York University Press.

——— 2003b, 'A Race Outcast from an Outcast Class: Claude McKay's Experience and Analysis of Britain', in *West Indian Intellectuals in Britain*, edited by Bill Schwarz, Manchester: Manchester University Press.

Jansen, Steven D. 1985, 'Floyd Olson: The Years Prior to His Governorship', Unpublished PhD thesis, University of Kansas.

Jenkins, Glenn 1976, 'Labor Defense Activities and Organizations, 1919–1925', unpublished paper in Prometheus Research Library collection.

——— 1978, 'Frank P. Walsh and Labor Defense Activities, 1917–26', unpublished paper in Prometheus Research Library collection.

Jenkins, Robin Dearmon 2008, 'Linking Up the Golden Gate: Garveyism in the San Francisco Bay Area, 1919–1925', *Journal of Black Studies*, 39, 3: 266–80.

Johanningsmeier, Edward 1993, 'Philadelphia "Skittereen" and William Z. Foster: The Childhood of an American Communist', *Pennsylvania Magazine of History and Biography*, 117, 4: 287–308.

——— 1994, *Forging American Communism: The Life of William Z. Foster*, Princeton, NJ: Princeton University Press.

——— 2001, 'The Trade Union Unity League: American Communists and the Transition to Industrial Unionism, 1928–1934', *Labor History*, 42, 2: 159–77.

Johnpoll, Bernard K. (ed.) 1994, *A Documentary History of the Communist Party of the United States*, Westport, CT: Greenwood.

Johnson, Daniel J. 2000, '"No Make-Believe Class Struggle": The Socialist Municipal Campaign in Los Angeles, 1911', *Labor History*, 41, 1: 25–46.

Johnson, Oakley C. 1957, *The Day Is Coming: The Life and Work of Charles E Ruthenberg, 1882–1927*, New York: International.

Johnson, Timothy V. 2010, '"Death to Negro Lynching!" The Communist Party, U.S.A.'s Position on the African American Question', in *Red Activists and Black Freedom: James and Esther Jackson and the Long Civil Rights Movement*, edited by David Levering Lewis, Michael E. Nash and Daniel J. Leab, London: Routledge.

——— 2011, '"We Are Illegal Here": The Communist Party, Self-Determination and the Alabama Share Croppers Union', *Science & Society*, 77, 4: 454–79.

Johnston, Scott D. 1953, 'Wisconsin Socialists and the Conference for Progressive Political Action', *Wisconsin Magazine of History*, 37, 2: 96–100.

Johnstone, J.W. 1924, 'Two Battles Against Reaction', *Workers Monthly*, 4, 1.

——— 1925, 'The Carpenters Face Their Leaders', *Workers Monthly*, 4, 5: 228–9.

——— 1929, 'The Struggle for Social Equality for Negroes in [the] South', *Red International of Labour Unions*, 1, 6/7: 291–3.

Jones, Jean 1996, *The League Against Imperialism*, London: Socialist History Society.

Jones, Ken 2011, 'Rev. Ethelred Brown: He Mixed Religion with Politics', *Gleaner*, 4 September, available at: <http://www.jamaica-gleaner.com/gleaner/20110904/focus/focus11.html>.

Jones, William P. 2008, '"Nothing Special to Offer the Negro": Revisiting the "Debsian View" of the Negro Question', *International Labor and Working-Class History*, 74: 212–24.

Karni, Michael G. 1975, 'Yhteishyvä—or, for the Common Good: Finnish Radicalism in the Western Great Lake Region, 1900–1940', Unpublished PhD thesis, University of Minnesota.

Karsner, David 1964 [1924], 'The Passing of the Socialist Party', in *American Socialism, 1900–1960*, edited by H. Wayne Morgan, Englewood Cliffs, NJ: Prentice Hall.

Kautsky, Karl 1902, 'Socialist Agitation Among Farmers in America', *International Socialist Review*, available at: <http://www.marxists.org/archive/kautsky/1902/09/farmers.htm>.

——— 2009, [1906], 'The American Worker', in *Witness to Permanent Revolution: The Documentary Record*, edited by Richard B. Day and Daniel Gaido, Leiden: Brill.

Kazin, Michael 2011, *American Dreamers: How the Left Changed a Nation*, New York: Knopf.

Kearns, Michelle 2011, 'Red Hero, Black Sheep: The Boris Reinstein Story', *Buffalo News*, 11 November, available at: <www.buffalonews.com/spotlight/article628584.ece>.

Keeran, Roger 1979, 'Communist Influence in the Automobile Industry, 1920–1933: Paving the Way for an Industrial Union', *Labor History*, 20, 2: 189–225.

——— 1980, *The Communist Party and the Auto Workers Union*, Bloomingdale, IN: University of Indiana Press.

——— 1995, 'National Groups and the Popular Front: The Case of the International Workers Order', *Journal of American Ethnic History*, 14, 3: 23–51.

Keiser, John Howard 1965, 'John Fitzpatrick and Progressive Unionism, 1915–1925', Unpublished PhD thesis, Northwestern University.

Kelley, Robin D.G. 1990, *Hammer and Hoe: Alabama Communists during the Depression*, Chapel Hill, NC: University of North Carolina Press.

Kellogg, Paul 2009, 'Leninism: It's Not What You Think', *Socialist Studies*, 5, 2: 41–63.

Kendall, Walter 1994 [Review of Cannon 1994], *Journal of Trotsky Studies*, 2: 225–31.

Kero, Reino 1973, 'The Roots of Finnish-American Left-Wing Radicalism', *Publications of the Institute of General History, University of Turku*, 5: 45–55.

——— 1975, 'The Social Origins of the Left-Wing Radicals and "Church Finns" Among Finnish Immigrants in North America', *Publications of the Institute of General History, University of Turku*, 7: 55–62.

Kerssfeld, Daniel 2007, 'La Liga Antiimperialista de las Américas: Una Construcción Política entre el Marxismo y el Latinoamericanismo', in *El Comunismo: Otras Miradas desde América Latina*, edited by Elvira Concheiro, Massimo Modonesi and Horacio Crespo, Mexico City: UNAM.

Kimmeldorf, Howard 1999, *Battling for American Labor: Wobblies, Craft Workers, and the Making of the Union Movement*, Berkeley, CA: University of California Press.

King, Shannon 2011, '"Ready to Shoot and Do Shoot": Black Working-Class Self-Defense and Community Politics in Harlem, New York, during the 1920s', *Journal of Urban History*, 37: 757–74.

Kipnis, Ira 1972 [1952], *The American Socialist Movement, 1897–1912*, New York: Monthly Review.

Kirby, John B. 1980, *Black Americans in the Roosevelt Era: Liberalism and Race*, Knoxville, TN: University of Tennessee Press.

Klehr, Harvey 1971, 'The Theory of American Exceptionalism', Unpublished PhD thesis, University of North Carolina at Chapel Hill.

——— 1978, *Communist Cadre: The Social Background of the American Communist Party Elite*, Palo Alto, CA: Stanford University Press.

——— 1984, *The Heyday of American Communism*, New York: Basic.

Klehr, Harvey and William Thompson 1989, 'Self-Determination in the Black Belt: Origins of a Communist Policy', *Labor History*, 30, 3: 354–66.

Klehr, Harvey, John Earl Haynes and F.I. Firsov 1995, *The Secret World of American Communism*, New Haven, CT: Yale University Press.

Klehr, Harvey, John Earl Haynes and K.M. Andersen 1998, *The Soviet World of American Communism*, New Haven, CT: Yale University Press.

Klehr, Harvey and John Earl Haynes 2003, *In Denial: Historians, Communism, and Espionage*, San Francisco, CA: Encounter.

Kornweibel, Theodore J. 1971, 'The *Messenger* Magazine, 1917–1928', Unpublished PhD thesis, Yale University.

——— 1998, *'Seeing Red': Federal Campaigns Against Black Militancy, 1919–1925*, Bloomington, IN: Indiana University Press.

Kolehmainen, John I. 1952, 'The Inimitable Marxists: The Finnish Immigrant Socialists', *Michigan History*, 36: 395–405.

Kornbluth, Joyce (ed.) 1964, *Rebel Voices: An IWW Anthology*, Ann Arbor, MI: University of Michigan Press.

Kostiainen, Auvo 1978, *The Forging of Finnish-American Communism, 1917–1924: A Study in Ethnic Radicalism*, Turku: Turun Yliopisto.

——— 1983, 'Santeri Nuorteva and the Origins of Soviet-American Relations', *American Studies in Scandinavia*, 15: 1–13.

——— 1989, 'Radical Ideology vs. Ethnic Social Activities: The Finnish Americans and the Communist Party of the United States, 1923–1932', *American Studies in Scandinavia*, 21: 30–9.

Koviukngas, Olavi 2003, 'Finns Abroad: A Short History of Finnish Migration', Institute of Migration website, available at: <http://www.migrationinstitute.fi/articles/027_Koivukangas.pdf>.

Kozlov, Nicholas N. 1990, 'Bukharin, Eugen Varga, and the Comintern Debate on the Stablization of Capitalism', in *Nikolai Ivanovich Bukharin: A Centenary Appraisal*, edited by Nicholas N. Kozlov and Eric D. Weitz, New York: Praeger.

Kozlov, Nicholas N. and Eric D. Weitz 1989, 'Reflections on the Origins of the "Third Period": Bukharin, the Comintern and the Political Economy of Weimar Germany', *Journal of Contemporary History*, 24, 3: 387–410.

Krupskaya, Nadezhda 1925, 'Lenin and Trotsky', *Workers Monthly*, 4, 11: 516.

Kruse, William F. 1927, 'What is Marxian Interpretation of the American Revolution?', *Daily Worker*, 4 July.

Kublin, Hyman 1964, *Asian Revolutionary: The Life of Sen Katayama*, Princeton, NJ: Princeton University Press.

Kuusinen, Aino 1974, *The Rings of Destiny: Inside Soviet Russia from Lenin to Brezhnev*, New York: William Morrow.

Kuykendall, Ronald A. 2002, 'African Blood Brotherhood: Independent Marxists During the Harlem Renaissance', *Western Journal of Black Studies*, 26, 1: 16–21.

La Follette, Bella C. and Fola La Follette 1953, *Robert M. La Follette*, New York: Macmillan.

Laidler, Harry W. 1920, 'Present State of Socialism in America: Three Party Conventions', *Socialist Review*, January.

Laidler, Harry W. and Norman Thomas (eds.) 1927, *Prosperity? A Symposium*, New York: Vanguard.

Landy, Avrom 1927, 'Marx, Engels and America: Attitude Toward America in the Early Period', *Communist*, 6, 5: 295–309; 6, 6: 394–400.

Larkin, Emmett 1990, *James Larkin: Irish Labour Leader, 1876–1947*, London: Pluto.

Lasch, Christopher 1962, *The American Liberals and the Russian Revolution*, New York: Columbia University Press.

Lazitch, Branko and Milorad Drachkovitch 1986, *Biographical Dictionary of the Comintern*, Stanford, CA: Hoover Institution Press.

Leavell, John Perry 1962, 'The Socialist Party Conventions of 1919 and 1920', Unpublished MA dissertation, Duke University.

Le Blanc, Paul 1996, 'Leninism in the United States and the Decline of American Trotskyism', in *Trotskyism in the United States: Historical Essays and Reconsiderations*, edited by George Breitman, Paul Le Blanc and Alan Wald, Atlantic Highlands, NJ: Humanities Press.

Lehr, Quincy R. 2001, 'Black Liberation and Revolutionary Socialism: American Trotskyism and the Black Question, 1928–1963', unpublished paper in Prometheus Research Library collection.

Leinenweber, Charles R. 1968, 'Immigration and the Decline of Internationalism in the American Working Class Movement, 1864–1919', Unpublished PhD thesis, University of California at Berkeley.

Lendler, Marc 2012, *Gitlow v. New York: Every Idea an Incitement*, Lawrence, KS: University of Kansas Press.

Lenin, Vladimir I. 1961 [1903], *What Is to be Done?*, in *Lenin Collected Works*, Volume 5, Moscow: Progress.

——— 1964a [22 November 1915], 'Letter to the Secretary of the Socialist Propaganda League', in *Lenin Collected Works*, Volume 21, Moscow: Progress.

——— 1964b [1917], *New Data On the Laws Governing the Development of Capitalism in Agriculture*, in *Lenin Collected Works*, Volume 22, Moscow: Progress.

——— 1965a [1920], 'Preliminary Draft Theses on the National and Colonial Questions', in *Lenin Collected Works*, Volume 31, Moscow: Progress.

——— 1965b [18 June 1921], 'Speech on the Italian Question', in *Lenin Collected Works*, Volume 31, Moscow: Progress.

——— 1966a [22 November 1915], 'To Alexandra Kollontai', in *Lenin Collected Works*, Volume 36, Moscow: Progress.

——— 1966b [19 March 1916], 'To Alexandra Kollontai', in *Lenin Collected Works*, Volume 36, Moscow: Progress.

——— 1966c [1920], *'Left Wing' Communism. An Infantile Disorder*, in *Lenin Collected Works*, Volume 31, Moscow: Progress.

——— 1966d [13 October 1921], 'To Sidney Hillman', in *Lenin Collected Works*, Volume 35, Moscow: Progress.

——— 1969a [23 July 1920], 'Material for the Second Congress of the Communist International', in *Lenin Collected Works*, Volume 42, Moscow: Progress.

——— 1969b [10 June 1921], 'To Zinoviev', in *Lenin Collected Works*, Volume 42, Moscow: Progress.

——— 1972 [6 April 1907], 'Preface to the Russian Translation of *Letters by Johannes Becker, Joseph Dietzgen, Frederick Engels, Karl Marx and Others to Friedrich Sorge and Others*', in *Lenin Collected Works*, Volume 12, Moscow: Progress.

——— 1975 [1913], 'Russians and Negroes', in *Lenin Collected Works*, Volume 18, Moscow: Progress.

——— 1977 [18 July 1913], 'What Can Be Done for Public Education', in *Lenin Collected Works*, Volume 19, Moscow: Progress.

——— 1980, *Lenin on the United States of America*, Moscow: Progress.

Leonhard, Wolfgang 1979 [1958], *Child of the Revolution*, London: Ink Links.

Lesure, Michel 1965, 'Les Mouvements Révolutionnaires Russes de 1882 à 1910 d'après les Fonds f7 des Archives Nationales', *Cahiers du Monde Russe et Soviétique*, 6, 2: 279–326.

'Letter from American Workers to the Soviet Government' 1970 [December 1917/January 1918], *Political Affairs*, March.

Leuchtenburg, William E. 1958, *The Perils of Prosperity, 1914–1932*, Chicago, IL: University of Chicago Press.

Lévesque, Andrée 2006, *Red Travellers: Jeanne Corbin and Her Comrades*, Montreal: McGill-Queen's University Press.

——— 2008, 'The Weakest Link: French-Canadian Communists Before 1940', unpublished paper, available at: <http://www.library.utoronto.ca/fisher/kenny-prize/andree-levesque.pdf>.

Levine, Philippa 2003, *Prostitution, Race, and Politics: Policing Venereal Disease in the British Empire*, New York: Routledge.

Lewin, Moshe 1974, *Political Undercurrents in Soviet Economic Debates from Bukharin to the Modern Reformers*, Princeton, NJ: Princeton University Press.

Lewis, David Levering 1993, *W.E.B. Du Bois: Biography of a Race, 1868–1919*, New York: Henry Holt.

Lewis, Linden 1995, 'Richard B. Moore: The Making of a Caribbean Organic Intellectual, A Review Essay', *Journal of Black Studies*, 25, 5: 589–609.

Liberman, Esther E. 1963, 'The Influence of Left-Wing Radicalism in the Paterson Silk Strike of 1912–1913 and the Passaic Woolen Strike of 1926', unpublished paper in New Jersey Collection, Rutgers University Library.

Liebman, Arthur 1997 [1976], 'The Ties that Bind: Jewish Support for the Left in the United States', in *Essential Papers on Jews and the Left*, edited by Ezra Mendelsohn, New York: New York University Press.

Lih, Lars T. 1995, 'Introduction', *Stalin's Letters to Molotov*, edited by Lars T. Lih, Oleg V. Naumov and Oleg V. Khlevniuk, New Haven, CT: Yale University Press.

——— 2006, *Lenin Rediscovered: 'What Is To Be Done?' In Context*, Leiden: Brill.

——— 2009, 'V.I. Lenin and the Influence of Kautsky', *Weekly Worker*, 783, available at: <http://www.cpgb.org.uk/worker/783/vileninandtheinfluence.php>.

Lincove, David A. 2004, 'Radical Publishing to "Reach the Million Masses": Alexander L. Trachtenberg and International Publishers, 1906–1966', *Left History*, 10, 1: 85–124.

Liu, Jianyi 2000, 'The Origins of the Chinese Communist Party and the Role Played by Soviet Russia and the Comintern', Unpublished PhD thesis, University of York.

Lore, Ludwig 1917, 'To Make the World Safe for Democracy', *Class Struggle*, 1, 2: 1–8.

Lorence, James J. 2006, 'Mobilizing the Reserve Army: The Communist Party and the Unemployed in Atlanta, 1929–1934', in *Radicalism in the South Since Reconstruction*, edited by Chris Green, Rachel Rubin and James Smethurst, New York: Palgrave Macmillan.

——— 2009, *The Unemployed People's Movement: Leftists, Liberals, and Labor in Georgia, 1929–1941*, Athens, GA: University of Georgia Press.

Losovsky, A. 1928a, 'The Result of the IV. Congress of the Red International of Labour Unions', *International Press Correspondence*, 8, 22: 421–2.

——— 1928b, 'On Carrying Out the Decision of the R.I.L.U.: Opposition to the Fourth Congress Resolution Fixed on False Grounds', *Red International of Labour Unions*, 1, 1: 5–11.

——— 1929, 'Letter to the National Convention of the Trade Union Educational League', *Red International of Labour Unions*, 1, 8/9: 369–74.

Lossieff, V. 1921, 'Industrial Workers of the World', *Communist International*, 3, 16/17 [old series].

Lovestone, Jay 1924a, *The La Follette Illusion As Revealed in an Analysis of the Political Role of Senator Robert M. La Follette*, Chicago, IL: Workers' Party of America.

——— 1924b, *American Imperialism: The Menace of the Greatest Capitalist World Power*, Chicago, IL: Workers Party of America.

——— 1925a, 'American Imperialism To-Day', *Communist International*, 14.

——— 1925b, '"Whither England": A Review', *Workers Monthly*, 5, 1: 37–41.

——— 1926, 'The Great Negro Migration', *Workers Monthly*, 5, 4: 179–84.

——— 1927a, 'America Facing Europe', *Communist*, 6, 1.

——— 1927b, 'Perspectives for Our Party', *Communist*, 6, 4: 200–7; 6, 5: 287–94.

——— 1928, *C.E. Ruthenberg: Communist Fighter and Leader*, New York: Workers Library.

Lundberg, Ferdinand 1946 [1937], *America's 60 Families*, New York: Citadel.

MacKay, Kenneth 1947, *The Progressive Movement of 1924*, New York: Columbia University Press.

Mackson, Deborah 1996, 'Class-Struggle Defense Work in the United States', *Women and Revolution*, 45: 25–36.

Madigan, Tim 2003, *The Burning: Massacre, Destruction, and the Tulsa Race Riot of 1921*, New York: St. Martin's.

Makalani, Minkah 2004, 'For the Liberation of Black People Everywhere: The African Blood Brotherhood, Black Radicalism, and Pan-African Liberation in the New Negro Movement', Unpublished PhD thesis, University of Illinois at Urbana-Champaign.

——— 2011, *In the Cause of Freedom: Radical Black Internationalism from Harlem to London, 1917–1939*, Chapel Hill, NC: University of North Carolina Press.

Maloney, Gerardo 1989, *El Canal de Panamá y los trabajadores antillanos: Panamá 1920: cronología de una lucha*, Panama City: Universidad de Panamá.

Manning, Susan 2004, *Modern Dance, Negro Dance: Race in Motion*, Minneapolis, MN: University of Minnesota Press.

Manuilsky, D. 1925, 'The Bolshevisation of the Parties', *Communist International*, 10.

Marable, Manning 1983 [1980], 'A Philip Randolph and the Foundations of Black American Socialism', reprinted in *Workers' Struggles: Past and Present*, edited by James Green, Philadelphia, PA: Temple University Press.

Margulies, Sylvia R. 1968, *The Pilgrimage to Russia: The Soviet Union and the Treatment of Foreigners, 1924–1937*, Madison, WI: University of Wisconsin Press.

Markotich, Stanley 1992, 'International Communism and the Communist Party of Canada', Unpublished PhD thesis, Indiana University.

Markowitz, Norman 1973, *The Rise and Fall of the People's Century: Henry A. Wallace and American Liberalism, 1941–1948*, London: Collier-Macmillan Publishers.

Martin, Charles H. 1979, 'Communists and Blacks: The ILD and the Angelo Herndon Case', *Journal of Negro History*, 64, 2: 131–41.

Martinek, Jason D. 2010, 'Business at the Margins of Capitalism: Charles H. Kerr and Company and the Progressive Era Socialist Movement', *Business and Economic History Online*, 8: 1–8, available at: <http://www.h-net.org/~business/bhcweb/publications/BEHonline/2010/martinek.pdf>.

——— 2012, *Socialism and Print Culture in America, 1897–1920*, London: Pickering and Chatto.

Martinov, A. 1929, 'Comintern Instructions to Forthcoming Party Congresses', *Communist International*, 6, 8: 225–38.

Marx, Karl 1972, *Karl Marx on America and the Civil War*, edited by Saul K. Padover, New York: McGraw-Hill.

——— 1979 [1852], *The Eighteenth Brumaire of Louis Bonaparte*, in Marx and Engels *Collected Works*, Volume 11, New York: International.

Marx, Karl and Frederick Engels 1975 [1848], *Manifesto of the Communist Party*, in Marx and Engels *Collected Works*, Volume 6, New York: International.

——— 1953, *Letters to Americans, 1848–1895: A Selection*, New York: International.

Mason, Daniel and Jessica Smith (eds.) 1970, *Lenin's Impact on the United States*, New York: New World Review.

Matusevich, Maxim 2008, 'An Exotic Subversive: Africa, Africans and the Soviet Everyday', *Race & Class*, 49, 4: 57–81.

Maxwell, William J. 1999, *New Negro, Old Left: African-American Communism Between the Wars*, New York: Columbia University Press.

McClellan, Woodford 1993, 'Africans and Black Americans in the Comintern Schools, 1925–1934', *International Journal of African Historical Studies*, 26, 2: 371–90.

McClendon, John M. 2006, 'Richard B. Moore, Radical Politics, and the Afro-American History Movement: The Formation of a Revolutionary Tradition in African American Intellectual Culture', *Afro-Americans in New York Life and History*, 30, 2: 7–45.

McDermott, Kevin 1998, 'The History of the Comintern in Light of New Documents', in *International Communism and the Communist International, 1919–43*, edited by Tim Rees and Andrew Thorpe, Manchester: Manchester University Press.

McDermott, Kevin and Jeremy Agnew 1996, *The Comintern: A History of International Communism from Lenin to Stalin*, London: Macmillan.

McDonald, Verlaine Stoner 2010, *The Red Corner: The Rise and Fall of Communism in Northeastern Montana*, Helena, MT: Montana Historical Society.

McDuffie, Erik S. 2006, '"[She] Devoted Twenty Minutes Condemning All Other Forms of Government But the Soviet": Black Women Radicals in the Garvey Movement and in the Left during the 1920s', in *Diasporic Africa: A Reader*, edited by Michael Gomez, New York: New York University Press.

——— 2011, *Sojourning for Freedom: Black Women, American Communism, and the Making of Black Left Feminism*, Durham, NC: Duke University Press.

McEnroe, Thomas H. 1960, 'The Industrial Workers of the World: Theories, Organizational Problems, and Appeals, As Revealed in the *Industrial Worker*', Unpublished PhD thesis, University of Minnesota.

McGirr, Lisa 2007, 'The Passion of Sacco and Vanzetti: A Global History', *Journal of American History*, 93, 4: 1085–115.

McKay, Claude 1920, 'A Black Man Replies', *Workers' Dreadnought*, 24 April.

——— 1922, 'The Racial Issue in the U.S.A.', *International Press Correspondence*, 2, 101: 817.

——— 1923, 'Soviet Russia and the Negro, Part I', *Crisis*, 27, 2: 61–5.

——— 1924, 'Soviet Russia and the Negro, Part II', *Crisis*, 27, 3: 114–18.

——— 1977 [1923], *Trial by Lynching: Stories about Negro Life in North America*, Mysore: University of Mysore Centre for Commonwealth Literature and Research.

——— 1979 [1924], *The Negroes in America*, Port Washington, NY: Kennikat.

——— 2007 [1937], *A Long Way From Home*, New Brunswick, NJ: Rutgers University Press.

McManus, Arthur 1925, 'Since Lenin Lied: More Facts and Fiction', *Communist Review*, 6, 1: 35–41.

McMeekin, Sean 2003, *The Red Millionaire: A Political Biography of Willy Münzenberg, Moscow's Secret Propaganda Tsar in the West*, New Haven, CT: Yale University Press.

McMullen, David Lee 2005, 'The Elusive Ellen: Reconstructing the Life of Ellen Dawson and the World Around Her', Unpublished PhD thesis, University of Aberdeen.

——— 2010, *Strike! The Radical Insurrections of Ellen Dawson* Gainesville, FL: University of Florida Press.

McNeal, Robert H. 1959, 'Lenin's Attack on Stalin: Review and Reappraisal', *American Slavic and East European Review*, 18, 3: 295–314.

McNeal, Robert H. and Richard Gregors (eds.) 1974, *Resolutions and Decisions of the Communist Party of the Soviet Union: Volume 2, The Early Soviet Period, 1917–1929*, Toronto: University of Toronto Press.

Mears, Patrick E. 2010, 'From the Palmer Raids to the Bridgman Raid: The Trials of the Nascent American Communist Movement', *Stereoscope*, 8, 1: 1–20.

Melgar Bao, Ricardo 2008, 'The Anti-Imperialist League of the Americas between the East and Latin America', *Latin American Perspectives*, 25, 2: 9–24.

The Menace of 'Criminal Syndicalism' n.d., New York: Labor Defense Council.

Michels, Tony 2005, *Fire in Their Hearts: Yiddish Socialists in New York*, Cambridge, MA: Harvard University Press.

——— 2011, 'Communism and the Problem of Ethnicity in the 1920s: The Case of Moissaye Olgin', *Contemporary Jewry*, 25: 26–48.

Miletsky, Zebulon V. 2008, 'City of Amalgamation: Race, Marriage, Class and Color in Boston, 1890–1930', Unpublished PhD thesis, University of Massachusetts at Amherst.

Miller, Sally M. 1973, *Victor Berger and the Promise of Constructive Socialism, 1910–1920*, Westport, CT: Greenwood.

——— 1984, 'Socialism and Race', in *Failure of a Dream? Essays on the History of American Socialism*, edited by John H.M. Laslett and Seymour Martin Lipset, Berkeley, CA: University of California Press.

——— 1995, 'The Socialist Party Schism of 1919: A Local Case Study', *Labor History*, 37, 4: 599–611.

——— 2003, 'For White Men Only: The Socialist Party of America and Issues of Gender, Ethnicity and Race', *The Journal of the Gilded Age and Progressive Era*, 2, 3: 283–302.

Mingulin, I. 1929, 'The Struggle for the Bolshevisation of the Communist Party of the United States', *International Press Correspondence*, 9, 28: 605–8.

Minnesota Federal Writers' Project 1938, *Minnesota: A State Guide*, New York: Viking.

Minor, Robert 1925, 'The First Negro Workers' Conference', *Workers Monthly*, 5, 2: 68–73.

——— 1927, 'The Party and the Trade Union Front in the United States', *Communist International*, 4, 3: 39–42.

Mishler, Paul C. 1995, 'Red Finns, Red Jews: Ethnic Variations in Communist Political Culture During the 1920s and 1930s', *YIVO Annual*, 22: 131–54.

Mommen, André 2011, *Stalin's Economist: The Economic Contributions of Jenö Varga*, London: Routledge.

Montgomery, David 1987, *The Fall of the House of Labor: The Workplace, the State and American Labor Activism, 1865–1925*, Cambridge: Cambridge University Press.

Morgan, Ted 1999, *Covert Life: Jay Lovestone, Communist, Anti-Communist, and Spymaster*, New York: Random House.

Morray, Joseph P. 1983, *Project Kuzbas: American Workers in Siberia*, New York: International.

Morrison-Reed, Mark D. 1994, *Black Pioneers in a White Denomination*, Boston, MA: Skinner House.

Mumford, Kevin J. 1997, *Interzones: Black/White Sex Districts in Chicago and New York in the Early Twentieth Century*, New York: Columbia University Press.

Murolo, Priscilla 1994, 'Antoinette Konikow', in *European Women in the United States: A Biographical Dictionary*, edited by Judy Barrett Litoff and Judith McDonnell, New York: Garland.

Murphy, J.T. 1921, *The 'Reds' In Congress: Preliminary Report of the First World Congress of the Red International of Trade and Industrial Unions*, London: British Bureau of Red International of Trade and Industrial Unions.

——— 1941, *New Horizons*, London: John Lane.

Murray, Robert K. 1964 [1955], *Red Scare: A Study in National Hysteria, 1919–1920*, New York: McGraw-Hill.

Naison, Mark 1985, 'Communism From the Top Down' [Review of Klehr 1984], *Radical History Review*, 32: 97–101.

——— 2005 [1984], *Communists in Harlem During the Depression*, Urbana, IL: University of Illinois Press.

Narinksy, Mikhail and Jürgen Rojahn (eds.) 1996, *Centre and Periphery: The History of the Comintern in the Light of New Documents*, Amsterdam: International Institute of Social History.

Nash, Michael 1981, 'Schism on the Left: The Anti-Communism of V.F. Calverton and his *Modern Quarterly*', *Science & Society*, 45, 4: 437–52.

Nation, R. Craig 1989, *War on War: Lenin, the Zimmerwald Left, and the Origins of Communist Internationalism*, Durham, NC: Duke University Press.

National Bureau of Economic Research 2010, 'U.S. Business Cycle Expansions and Contractions', available at: <http://www.nber.org/cycles/US_Business_Cycle_Expansions_and_Contractions_20100920.pdf>.

Naumov, Oleg 1996, 'The Present Condition of the Comintern Archives', in *Centre and Periphery: The History of the Comintern in the Light of New Documents*, edited by Mikhail Narinksy and Jürgen Rojahn, Amsterdam: International Institute of Social History.

Nelson, Steve, James R. Barrett and Rob Buck 1981, *Steve Nelson, American Radical*, Pittsburgh, PA: University of Pittsburgh Press.

New York Times 2000, '1920 Election Results', available at: <http://www.tv.nytimes.com/learning/general/specials/elections/1920/featured_article3.html?scp=1&sq=election%20results%20christensen%201920&st=cse>.

Nimtz, August H. 2003, *Marx, Tocqueville, and Race in America: The 'Absolute Democracy' or 'Defiled Republic'*, Lanham, MD: Lexington.

Nolan, William 1951, *Communism Versus the Negro*, Chicago, IL: Henry Regnery.

Nyden, Linda 1977, 'Black Miners in Western Pennsylvania, 1925–1931: The National Miners Union and the United Mine Workers of America', *Science and Society*, 41, 1: 69–101.

O'Brien, Gary 1974, 'Maurice Spector and the Origins of Canadian Trotskyism', Unpublished MA dissertation, Carleton University.

O'Connor, Emmett 2002, 'James Larkin in the United States, 1914–23', *Journal of Contemporary History*, 37, 2: 183–96.

O'Donnell, L.A. 1997, *Irish Voice and Organized Labor in America*, Westport, CT: Greenwood.

O'Flaherty, T.J. 1927, 'The Day They Celebrate', *The New Magazine Section of the Daily Worker*, 2 July.

Olgin, Moissaye Joseph 1926, 'World's In the Making', *Workers Monthly*, 5, 11.

Oneal, James 1912, *The Workers in American History*, St. Louis, MO: National Rip-Saw.

Orenstein, Eugene Victor 1978, 'The Jewish Socialist Federation of America, 1912–1921: A Study of Integration and Particularlism in the American Jewish Labor Movement', Unpublished manuscript.

O'Riordan, Manus 1998, 'Larkin in America: The Road to Sing Sing', in *James Larkin: Lion of the Fold*, edited by Donal Nevin, Dublin: Gill and MacMillan.

Ottanelli, Fraser M. 1991, *The Communist Party of the United States: From the Depression to World War II*, New Brunswick, NJ: Rutgers University Press.

Ottini, Virginia 1948, 'The Socialist Party in the Election of 1920', Unpublished MA dissertation, Stanford University.

Padmore, George 1930, 'Some Shortcomings in Our Trade Union Work Among Negroes in the United States', *Red International of Labour Unions*, 2, 2/3: 20–3.

——— 1931, *The Life and Struggle of Negro Toilers*, London: RILU.

Palmer, Bryan D. 2003, 'Rethinking the Historiography of United States Communism', *American Communist History*, 2, 2: 139–73.

——— 2004, 'Race and Revolution', *Labour/Le Travail*, 54: 193–221.

——— 2005, 'Maurice Spector, James P. Cannon, and the Origins of Canadian Trotskyism', *Labour/Le Travail*, 56: 91–148.

——— 2007, *James P. Cannon and the Origins of the American Revolutionary Left, 1890–1928*, Urbana, IL: University of Illinois Press.

——— 2009, 'American Communism in the 1920s: Striving for a Panoramic View', *American Communist History*, 6, 2: 139–49.

Patterson, William L. 1971, *The Man Who Cried Genocide*, New York: International.

Pantsov, Alexander 2000, *The Bolsheviks and the Chinese Revolution*, Honolulu: University of Hawaii Press.

Parascandola, Louis J. 2006, 'Cyril Briggs and the African Blood Brotherhood: A Radical Counterpoint to Progressivism', *Journal of African American History*, 30, 1: 7–18.

Pasolini, Ricardo 2007, 'Immigrazione Italiana, Comunismo e Antifascismo nell' Entre-Deux-Guerre Argentino: l'Ordine Nuevo, 1925–1927', *Archivio Storico dell'emigrazione Italiana*, available at: <http://www.asei.eu/index.php?option=com_content&task=view&id=105&Itemid=250>.

Pease, Donald E. 2010, 'American Studies After American Exceptionalism? Toward a Comparative Analysis of Imperial State Exceptionalisms', in *Globalizing American Studies*, edited by Brian T. Edwards and Dilip Paramehwar Gaonkar, Chicago, IL: University of Chicago Press.

Pedersen, Vernon L. 2001, *The Communist Party in Maryland, 1919–1957*, Urbana, IL: University of Illinois Press.

Penner, Norman 1977, *The Canadian Left: A Critical Analysis*, Toronto: Prentice-Hall.

Pepper, John 1923, *'Underground Radicalism': An Open Letter to Eugene V. Debs and All Honest Workers Within the Socialist Party*, New York: Workers' Party of America.

——— 1926a, *The General Strike and the General Betrayal*, Chicago, IL: Daily Worker Publishing Company.

——— 1926b, 'Britain's Balance-Sheet for 1926', *Communist International*, 3, 5: 5–13.

——— 1928, *American Negro Problems*, New York: Workers Library.

Perry, Jeffrey B. (ed.) 2001, *A Hubert Henry Harrison Reader*, Middleton, CT: Wesleyan University Press.

——— 2009, *Hubert Harrison: The Voice of Harlem Radicalism, 1883–1918*, New York: Columbia University Press.

Peterson, Ellis 1927, 'Our Constitution and the Language Fractions', *Daily Worker*, 19 August.

Peterson, Larry 1984, 'Revolutionary Socialism and Industrial Unrest in the Era of the Winnipeg General Strike: The Origins of Communist Labour Unionism in Europe and North America', *Labour/Le Travail*, 13: 115–31.

Petersson, Fredrik 2007, 'In Control of Solidarity? Willi Münzenberg, the Workers' International Relief and League Against Imperialism, 1921–1935', *Comintern Working Paper*, 8, available at: <http://www.abo.fi/student/media/7957/cowopa12petersson.pdf>.

Pfannenstiel, Todd 2003, *Rethinking the Red Scare: The Lusk Committee and New York's Crusade Against Radicalism, 1914–1923*, New York: Routledge.

Porter, Cathy 1980, *Alexandra Kollontai: The Lonely Struggle of the Woman Who Defied Lenin*, New York: Dial.

Pratt, Norma Fain 1973, *Morris Hillquit: A Political History of an American Jewish Socialist*, Westport, CT: Greenwood.

Pratt, William C. 1988, 'Rethinking the Farm Revolt of the 1930s', *Great Plains Quarterly*, 8: 131–44.

Preston, William 1994, *Aliens and Dissenters: Federal Suppression of Radicals, 1903–1933*, Cambridge, MA: Harvard University Press.

Prickett, Stacey 1990, 'Dance and the Workers' Struggle', *Dance Research*, 8, 1: 47–61.

Prometheus Research Library (ed.) 2002, *Dog Days: James P. Cannon vs. Max Shachtman in the Communist League of America, 1931–1933*, New York: Prometheus Research Library.

Prusdon, David 1984, 'Communism and the Jewish Labor Movement in the U.S.A., 1919–1929', Unpublished PhD thesis, Tel Aviv University.

Rabban, David M. 1997, *Free Speech in its Forgotten Years*, Cambridge: Cambridge University Press.

Reavis, Dick 2012, 'In Introduction to the *Southern Worker*', available at: <http://www.marxists.org/history/usa/pubs/southernworker/reavis-introtosouthernworker.pdf>.

Record, Wilson 1951, *The Negro and the Communist Party*, Chapel Hill, NC: University of North Carolina Press.

——— 1958, 'The Development of the Communist Position on the Negro Question in the United States', *Phylon*, 19, 3: 306–26.

——— 1964, *Race and Radicalism: The NAACP and the Communist Party in Conflict*, Ithaca, NY: Cornell University Press.

Red International of Labour Unions 1928, *Report of the Fourth World Congress of the R.I.L.U.*, London: R.I.L.U.

Reed, John 1920, 'The Fighting I.W.W. in America', *Communist International*, 13, I: 88–98.

——— 1967 [1919], *Ten Days that Shook the World*, New York: New American Library.

Rees, Tim and Andrew Thorpe (eds.) 1998, *International Communism and the Communist International, 1919–43*, Manchester: Manchester University Press.

Rees, Tim 2009, 'Deviation and Discipline: Anti-Trotskyism, Bolshevization and the Spanish Communist Party, 1924–1934', *Historical Research*, 82, 215: 132–56.

Reeve, Carl 1972, *The Life and Times of Daniel De Leon*, New York: Humanities Press.

Reich, Steven A. 1996, 'Soldiers of Democracy: Black Texans and the Fight for Citizenship, 1917–1921', *Journal of American History*, 82, 4: 1478–504.

Reinstein, Boris 1929, 'On the Road to the First Congress', *Communist International*, 6, 9/10: 428–35.

Reis, Albert 1964, 'The Profintern: Origins to 1923', Unpublished PhD thesis, Columbia University.

Renshaw, Patrick 1968, 'The IWW and the Red Scare, 1917–1924', *Journal of Contemporary History*, 3, 4: 63–72.

Report of the Proceedings of the Second Conference for Progressive Action 1922, Cleveland, OH: CPPA.

Résolutions et Décisions du 1er Congres International des Syndicats Révolutionnaires 1921, Moscow: International Syndicats Rouge.

Revolutionary Radicalism: Its History, and Purpose and Tactics with an Exposition and Discussion of the Steps Being Taken and Required to Curb: Report of the Joint Legislative Committee Investigating Seditious Activities, Filed April 24, 1920, in the Senate of the State of New York 1920, Volume 2, Albany, NY: J.B. Lyon.

Reynolds, David S. 2011, *Mightier than the Sword: Uncle Tom's Battle for America*, New York: Norton.

Riddell, John (ed. and trans.) 1987 [1919], *Founding the Communist International*, New York: Pathfinder.

——— (ed. and trans.) 1991 [1920], *Workers of the World and Oppressed Peoples, Unite! Proceedings and Documents of the Second Congress, 1920*, Volumes 1 and 2, New York: Pathfinder.

——— (ed. and trans.) 2011 [1922], *Toward the United Front: Proceedings of the Fourth Congress of the Communist International, 1922*, Leiden: Brill.

Riga, Liliana 2008, 'The Ethnic Roots of Class Universalism: Rethinking the "Russian" Revolutionary Elite', *American Journal of Sociology*, 114, 3: 649–705.

Rodney, William 1968, *Soldiers of the International: A History of the Communist Party of Canada, 1919–1929*, Toronto: University of Toronto Press.

Roebuck, C.M. 1925, 'Since Eastman Lied', *Workers Monthly*, 4, 6: 369–72.

Roh, Kyung Deok 2010, 'Stalin's Think Tank: The Varga Institute and the Making of the Stalinist Idea of World Economy and Politics, 1927–1953', Unpublished PhD thesis, University of Chicago.

Ro'i, Yaacov 2010, 'Solomon Abramovich Lozovskii', *YIVO Encyclopedia of Jews in Eastern Europe*, available at: <http://www.yivoencyclopedia.org/article.aspx/Lozovskii_Solomon_Abramovich>.

Rojahn, Jürgen 1996, 'A Matter of Perspective: Some Remarks on the Periodization of the History of the Communist International', in *Centre and Periphery: The History of the Comintern in the Light of New Documents*, edited by Mikhail Narinksy and Jürgen Rojahn, Amsterdam: International Institute of Social History.

Rosenstone, Robert A. 1975, *Romantic Revolutionary: A Biography of John Reed*, Harmondsworth: Penguin.

Rosmer, Alfred 1974, *Lenin's Moscow*, London: Pluto Press.

Routsila, Markku 2009, 'Communism as Anarchism: The Pro-War Socialists, the Old Guard, and the Forging of Socialist Anticommunism in the United States', *International History Review*, 31, 3: 499–520.

Rutgers, Sebald Justin 1916, 'The Left Wing: An Actual Beginning', *International Socialist Review*, 16, 6.

Ruthenberg, Charles Emil 1917, *Are We Growing Toward Socialism?* Cleveland, OH: Local Cleveland Socialist Party.

——— 1922, 'Russian Revolution and U.S. Communist Movement', *Voice of Labor*, 3 November.

——— 1923, 'The Skirmish in Cleveland', *Liberator*, January.

——— 1924, *The Farmer-Labor United Front*, Chicago, IL: Literature Department of the Workers' Party of America.

——— 1925, *From the Third Through the Fourth Convention of the Workers' (Communist) Party of America*, Chicago, IL: Daily Worker Publishing Company.

——— 1926a, 'Do We Believe in the Theory of Misery?', *Daily Worker*, 3 September.

——— 1926b, 'Seven Years of the Communist Party of America', *Workers Monthly*, 5, 11.

——— 1928, *Voices of Revolt: Speeches and Writings of Charles E. Ruthenberg*, New York: International.

Ruthenberg, C.E., Alfred Wagenknecht and Charles Baker 1917, *Guilty? Of What? Speeches before the Jury in Connection with the Trial of C.E. Ruthenberg, Alfred Wagenknecht, Charles Baker*, Cleveland, OH: Ohio Socialist Party.

Ryan, James G. 1999, *Earl Browder: The Failure of American Communism*, Tuscaloosa, AL: University of Alabama Press.

——— 2004, 'A Final Stab at Insurrection: The American Communist Party, 1928–34', in *In Search of Revolution: International Communist Parties in the Third Period*, edited by Matthew Worley, London: I.B. Tauris.

Ryle, Martin 1970, 'International Red Aid and Comintern Strategy, 1922–1926', *International Review of Social History*, 15: 43–68.

Saknyster, Thomas L. 2005a, 'A Communist Newspaper for Hungarian-Americans: The Strange World of the *Uj Elore*', *Hungarian Studies Review*, 32, 1/2: 42–70.

——— 2005b, 'A Hungarian in the Comintern: Jozsef Pogány/John Pepper', in *Agents of the Revolution: New Biographical Approaches to the History of International Communism in the Age of Lenin and Stalin*, edited by Kevin Morgan, Gidon Cohen and Andrew Flinn, Oxford: Peter Lang.

——— 2012, *A Communist Odyssey: The Life of József Pogány/John Pepper*, Budapest: Central European University Press.

Salerno, Salvatore 1989, *Red November, Black November: Culture and Community in the Industrial Workers of the World*, Albany, NY: State University of New York Press.

Salmond, John A. 1995, *Gastonia 1929: The Story of the Loray Mill Strike*, Chapel Hill, NC: University of North Carolina Press.

Samuels, Wilfred D. 1977, *Five Afro-Caribbean Voices in American Culture, 1917–1929*, Boulder, CO: Belmot.

Saposs, David J. 1926, *Left Wing Unionism: A Study of Radical Politics and Tactics*, New York: International.

Schwantes, Carlos A. 1994, *Radical Heritage: Labor, Socialism, and Reform in Washington and British Columbia, 1885–1917*, Moscow, ID: University of Idaho Press.

Second Congress of the Communist International: Minutes of the Proceedings 1977 [1920], Volumes 1 and 2, London: New Park.

Second Year of the Workers' Party of America 1924, Chicago, IL: Literature Department of the Workers' Party of America.

Seidler, Murray B. 1967, *Norman Thomas: Respectable Radical*, Syracuse, NY: Syracuse University Press.

Seidman, Joel 1942, *The Needle Trades*, New York: Farrar and Rinehart.

Seretan, L. Glen 1979, *Daniel De Leon: The Odyssey of an American Marxist*, Cambridge, MA: Harvard University Press.

Seyler, William C. 1952, 'The Rise and Decline of the Socialist Party in the United States', Unpublished PhD thesis, Duke University.

Shachtman, Max 2003 [1933], *Race and Revolution: A Lost Chapter in American Radicalism*, London: Verso.

Shaffer, Ralph E. 1962, 'Radicalism in California, 1869–1929', Unpublished PhD thesis, University of California at Berkeley.

——— 1967, 'Formation of the California Communist Labor Party', *Pacific Historical Review*, 36: 59–78.

Shannon, David A. 1967, *The Socialist Party of America*, Chicago, IL: Quadrangle.

Shapiro, Stanley 1967, 'Hand and Brain: The Farmer-Labor Party of 1920', Unpublished PhD thesis, University of California Berkeley.

——— 1985, 'Hand and Brain: The Farmer-Labor Movement of 1920', *Labor History*, 26, 3: 405–22.

Sharp, Kathleen A. 1979, 'Rose Pastor Stokes: Radical Champion of the American Working Class, 1879–1933', Unpublished PhD thesis, Duke University.

Shchechilina, Valentina 1996, 'Creation and Activity of the Comintern Archives', in *Centre and Periphery: The History of the Comintern in the Light of New Documents*, edited by Mikhail Narinksy and Jürgen Rojahn, Amsterdam: International Institute of Social History.

Sherwood, Marika 1996, 'The Comintern, the CPGB, Colonies and Black Britons, 1920–1938', *Science & Society*, 60, 2: 137–63.

Shideler, James H. 1945, 'The Neo-Progressives: Reform Politics in the United States, 1920–1925', Unpublished PhD thesis, University of California.

Shiek, A. [Endre Sik] 1928, 'The Comintern Programme and the Racial Problem', *Communist International*, 5, 16: 407–11.

Shipman, Charles 1993, *It Had to Be Revolution: Memoirs of an American Radical*, Ithaca, NY: Cornell University Press.

Siegel, Morton 1953, 'The Passaic Textile Strike of 1926', Unpublished PhD thesis, Columbia University.

Siener, William H. 1998, 'The Red Scare Revisited: Radicals and the Anti-Radical Movement in Buffalo, 1919–1920', *New York History*, 79, 1: 23–54.

Simons, Algie Martin 1904, *Class Struggle in American History*, Chicago, IL: Charles H. Kerr.

Sitkoff, Harvard 1978, *New Deal for Blacks: The Emergence of Civil Rights as a National Issue*, New York: Oxford University Press.

Skotnes, Andor 1996, 'The Communist Party, Anti-Racism, and the Freedom Movement: Baltimore, 1930–1934' *Science & Society*, 60, 2: 164–94.

Solomon, Mark 1998, *The Cry Was Unity: Communists and African Americans. 1917–1936*, Jackson, MS: University Press of Mississippi.

Sombart, Werner 1976 [1906], *Why Is There No Socialism in the United States?*, White Plains, NY: International Arts and Sciences Press.

Soyer, Daniel 2005, 'Soviet Travel and the Making of an American Jewish Communist: Moissaye Olgin's Trip to Russia in 1920–1921', *American Communist History*, 4, 1: 1–20.

Spenser, Daniela 1999, *The Impossible Triangle: Mexico, Soviet Russia and the United States in the 1920s*, Durham, NC: Duke University Press.

——— 2011, *Stumbling Its Way Through Mexico: The Early Years of the Communist International*, Tuscaloosa, AL: University of Alabama Press.

Spiro, Sterling D. and Abram L. Harris 1972, *The Black Worker: The Negro and the Labor Movement*, New York: Atheneum.

Spolansky, Jacob 1951, *The Communist Trial in America*, New York: Macmillan.

Srebrnick, Henry 1999, 'Red Star Over Birobidzhan: Canadian Jewish Communists and the "Jewish Autonomous Region" in the Soviet Union', *Labour/Le Travail*, 44: 129–147.

——— 2010, *Dreams of Nationhood: American Jewish Communists and the Soviet Birobidzhan Project, 1924–1951*, Boston, MA: Academic Studies Press.

St. John, Vincent 1919, *The I.W.W.: Its History, Structure and Methods*, Chicago, IL: IWW.

Stachel, Jack 1927, 'How Communists Work Among the Foreign Born', *Daily Worker*, 2 February.

Stalin, Joseph V. 1926, 'The General Strike, 1926', available at: <http://www.marxists.org/reference/archive/stalin/works/1926/06/08s.htm>.

——— 1929, *Stalin's Speeches on the American Communist Party*, New York: Central Committee of the CPUSA.

——— 1953a [May 1913], 'Marxism and the National Question', in *Works*, Volume 2, Moscow: Foreign Language Publishing House.

——— 1953b [1924], 'Foundations of Leninism', in *Works*, Volume 6, Moscow: Foreign Language Publishing House.

——— 1954 [22 January 1926], 'The Fight Against Right and "Ultra-Left" Deviations', in *Works*, Volume 8, Moscow: Foreign Language Publishing House.

——— 1955 [2 March 1930], 'Dizzy With Success', in *Works*, Volume 12, Moscow: Foreign Language Publishing House.

Stark, Rodney and Kevin J. Christiano 1992, 'Support for the American Left, 1920–1924: The Opiate Thesis Reconsidered', *Journal for the Scientific Study of Religion*, 31, 1: 62–75.

Starobin, Joseph 1972, *American Communism in Crisis, 1943–1957*, Cambridge, MA: Harvard University Press.

State Department [of the United States] 1920, *The Second Congress of the Communist International, As Reported and Interpreted by the Official Newspapers of Soviet Russia*, Washington, DC: Government Printing Office.

Stein, Judith 1986, *The World of Marcus Garvey: Race and Class in Modern Society*, Baton Rouge, LA: Louisiana State University Press.

Stephens, Michelle Ann 1999, 'Black Empire: The Making of Black Transnationalism by West Indians in the United States, 1914–1962', Unpublished PhD thesis, Yale University.

——— 2005, *Black Empire: The Masculine Global Imaginary of Caribbean Intellectuals in the United States, 1914–1962*, Durham, NC: Duke University Press.

Stevens, Margaret 2006, 'A Bolshevik Current in the Black Caribbean Sea, 1929–1937', *Postamble*, 2, 2: xv–xx.

——— 2008, '"Hands Off Haiti!" Self-Determination, Anti-Imperialism and the Communist Movement in the United States, 1925–1929', *Black Scholar*, 37, 4: 61–70.

——— 2010, 'The Red International and the Black Caribbean: Transnational Radical Organization in New York City, Mexico and the West Indies, 1919–1939', Unpublished PhD thesis, Brown University.

Storch, Randi 2009, *Red Chicago: American Communism at its Grassroots, 1928–1935*, Urbana and Chicago, IL: University of Illinois Press.

Strouthous, Andrew 1996, 'A Comparative Study of Independent Working-Class Politics: The American Federation of Labor and Third Party Movements in New York, Chicago, and Seattle, 1918–1924', Unpublished PhD thesis, University of London.

——— 2000, *U.S. Labor and Political Action, 1918–1924*, London: Macmillan.

Sugrue, Thomas J. 2008, *Sweet Land of Liberty: The Forgotten Struggle for Civil Rights in the North*, New York: Random House.

Swabeck, Arne 1969, 'Let's Re-Write History: When History Collides With Facts' [Review of Weinstein's *Decline of Socialism in America*], *Progressive Labor Magazine*, May.

Sylvers, Malcom 1987, 'Pogàny/Pepper: Un Représentant du Komintern Auprès du Parti Communiste des Etats-Unis', *Cahiers d'Historie de l'Institut de Recherches Marxistes*, 28: 119–33.

Taber, Mike 1997, 'Papers Stolen 70 Years Ago Tell History of Communist Movement in United States', *Militant*, 61, 21, available at: <www.themilitant.com/1997/6121/6121_21.html>.

Taibo, Paco Ignacio II 2008, *Bolcheviques: Una Historia Narrativa de los Orígenes del Comunismo en México*, Mexico City: Ediciones B.

Talbert, Roy 1991, *Negative Intelligence: The Army and the American Left, 1917–1941*, Jackson, MS: University of Mississippi Press.

Taylor, Gregory S. 2009, *The History of the North Carolina Communist Party*, Columbia, SC: University of South Carolina Press.

Temkin, Moshik 2009, *The Sacco-Vanzetti Affair: America on Trial*, New Haven, CT: Yale University Press.

Third Congress of the Communist International 1922, London: Communist Party of Great Britain.

Thorpe, Wayne 1989, *'The Workers Themselves': Revolutionary Syndicalism and International Labour, 1913–1923*, Amsterdam: International Institute of Social History.

Tobias, Henry J. 1961, 'The Bund and Lenin until 1903', *Russian Review*, 20, 4: 344–57.

Tosstorff, Reiner 2000a, 'The Links Between the Comintern and the RILU', *Revolutionary History*, 7, 4: 68–75.

——— 2000b, '"Moscow" or "Amsterdam"? The Red International of Labour Unions', *Communist History Network Newsletter*, 8.

Trotsky, Leon 1918, *Our Revolution: Essays on Working-Class and International Revolution, 1904–1917*, edited and translated by M.J. Olgin, New York: Henry Holt.

——— 1925a, *Literature and Revolution*, New York: International.

——— 1930, *My Life*, New York: Scribner.

——— 1932, *Problems of the Chinese Revolution*, New York: Pathfinder.

——— 1934 [1928], 'On Max Eastman', *New International*, 1, 4: 125–6.

——— 1937, *The Revolution Betrayed: What Is the Soviet Union and Where is It Going?* New York: Doubleday, Doran and Company.

——— 1943 [1926], 'Europe and America', *Fourth International*, 4, 4: 120–4; 4, 5: 153–8.

——— 1945a [1924], *The First Five Years of the Communist International*, New York: Pioneer.

——— 1945b [1924], 'Perspectives of World Development', *Fourth International*, 6, 6/7/8.

——— 1973a [22 October 1922], 'The Fifth Anniversary of the October Revolution and the Fourth World Congress of the Communist International', in *The First Five Years of the Communist International*, London: New Park.

——— 1973b [1925], 'Where is Britain Going?', in *Leon Trotsky on Britain*, New York: Pathfinder.

——— 1973c [September 1930], 'Molotov's Prosperity in Knowledge', in *Writings of Leon Trotsky, 1930–31*, New York: Pathfinder.

——— 1973d, *Leon Trotsky on Black Nationalism*, New York: Pathfinder.

——— 1974a [1928], *The Third International After Lenin*, London: New Park.

——— 1974b [1935], 'The Workers' State, Thermidor and Bonapartism', in *Writings of Leon Trotsky, 1934–1935*, New York: Pathfinder.

——— 1975, *The Challenge of the Left Opposition, 1923–25*, New York: Pathfinder.

——— 1979 [1930], 'Discussions With Max Shachtman', in *Writings of Leon Trotsky, Supplement 1929–1933*, New York: Pathfinder.

——— 1980 [1921], 'Theses of the Third World Congress on the International Situation and the Tasks of the Comintern', in *Theses, Resolutions and Manifestos of the First Four Congresses of the Third International*, London: Ink Links.

——— 1987 [1924], *Lessons of October*, London: Bookmarks.

Trotsky, Leon and Max Eastman (ed. and trans.) 1928, *The Real Situation in Russia*, London: Allen & Unwin.

Trotsky, Leon and Eugen Varga 1921, 'The International Situation: A Study of Capitalism in Collapse', available at: <http://www.marxists.org/archive/varga/1921/x01/x02.htm>.

Turner, W. Burghardt and Joyce Moore Turner (eds.) 1988, *Richard B. Moore, Caribbean Militant in Harlem: Collected Writings 1920–1972*, Bloomington, IN: Indiana University Press.

Turner, Joyce Moore 2005, *Caribbean Crusaders and the Harlem Renaissance*, Champaign, IL: University of Illinois Press.

Uhlmann, Jennifer R. 2007, 'The Communist Civil Rights Movement: Legal Activism in the United States, 1919–1946', Unpublished PhD thesis, University of California at Los Angeles.

——— 2009, 'Moving On—Towards a Post-War Historiography of American Communism', *American Communist History*, 8, 1: 24–5.

United Brotherhood of Carpenters and Joiners of America, 'UBC History: Beating the Open Shop, 1900-1930', available at: <http://www.carpenters.org/WhoWeAre/History/1900-1930.aspx.>

United States Census Bureau 1921, *Fourteenth Census of the United States*, Washington, DC: Government Printing Office.

United States Commission on Industrial Relations 1916, *Final Report and Testimony Submitted to Congress by the Commission on Industrial Relations*, Volume 3, Washington, DC: Government Printing Office.

Upham, Martin R. 1980, 'The History of British Trotskyism to 1949', Unpublished PhD thesis, University of Hull.

VanGiezen, Robert and Albert E. Schwenk 2001, 'Compensation from before World War I through the Great Depression,' *Compensation and Working Conditions*, available at: <www.bls.gov/opub/cwc/print/cm20030124ar03p1.htm>.

Varga, Eugen 1921, 'Economic Basis of Imperialism in the U.S. of North America', *Communist International*, 1, 16/17.

——— 1924, *The Decline of Capitalism*, London: Communist International.

——— 1925, 'Ways and Obstacles to the World Revolution', *Communist International*, 2, 18/19.

Ventadour, Jacques [1927], 'Le Congès Anti-Impérialiste de Bruxelles', *Bulletin de la Ligue Contre l'Opression Coloniale et l'Imperialisme*, 6–10.

Vilkova, Valentina (ed.) 1996, *The Struggle for Power: Russia in 1923*, Amherst, MA: Prometheus.

Vincent, Theodore 1972, *Black Power and the Garvey Movement*, San Francisco, CA: Ramparts.

——— 1994, 'Evolution of the Split Between the Garvey Movement and the Organized Left in the United States, 1917–1933', in *Garvey: Africa, Europe, the Americas*, edited by Rupert Lewis and Maureen Warner-Lewis, Trenton, NJ: Africa World Press.

Voerman, Gerrit 2007, 'Proletarian Competition: The Amsterdam Bureau and its German Counterpart, 1919–1920', *Jahrbuch für Historische Kommunismusforschung*.

Walker, Thomas J.E. 1982, 'The International Workers Order: A Unique Fraternal Body', Unpublished PhD thesis, University of Chicago.

Ware, Clarissa S. 2005 [1923], *The American Foreign-Born Workers*, Corvallis, OR: Thousand Flowers Publishing.

Waterhouse, David L. 1991, *The Progressive Movement of 1924 and the Development of Interest Group Liberalism*, New York: Garland.

Weiner, Tim 2012, *Enemies: A History of the FBI*, New York: Random House.

Weber, Hermann 2008, 'The Stalinization of the KPD: Old and New Views', in *Bolshevism, Stalinism and the Comintern: Perspectives on Stalinization, 1917–1953*, edited by Norman LaPorte, Kevin Morgan and Matthew Worley, London: Palgrave Macmillan.

Weigand, Kate 2001, *Red Feminism: American Communism and the Making of Women's Liberation*, Baltimore, MD: Johns Hopkins University Press.

Weinstein, James 1967, *The Decline of Socialism in America, 1912–1925*, New York: Vintage.

Weinstone, William 1969, 'Formative Period of the CPUSA', *Political Affairs*, 48: 9–10.

Weisbord, Albert 1926, *Passaic: The Story of a Struggle against Starvation Wages and for the Right to Organize*, Chicago, IL: Daily World Publishing Co.

——— 1976, *Passaic Reviewed*, San Francisco, CA: Germinal Press.

Weisbord, Vera Buch 1977, *A Radical Life*, Bloomington, IN: University of Indiana Press.

Weiss, Holger 2009, 'The Road to Hamburg and Beyond: African American Agency and the Making of a Radical African Atlantic, 1922–1930', Part One, *Comintern Working*

Papers, 16, available at: <http://www.abo.fi/student/media/7957/cowopa16weiss.pdf>

Wetzel, Kurt 1970, 'The Making of an American Radical: Bill Dunne in Butte', Unpublished MA dissertation, University of Montana.

What's Wrong in the Carpenters' Union? 1925, Chicago, IL: Progressive Building Trades Worker.

Wheeler, Robert H.L. 1953, 'American Communists: Their Ideology and Their Interpretation of American Life, 1917–1939', Unpublished PhD thesis, Yale.

Where La Follette Stands on Fifty Living Issues 1924, Los Angeles, CA: La Follette-Wheeler Headquarters.

Whitney, Richard Merrill 1924, *Reds in America*, New York: Beckwith.

Wicks, Harry 1992, *Keeping My Head: The Memoirs of a British Bolshevik*, London: Socialist Platform.

Wicks, H.M. 1929, 'The Anti-Comintern Opposition in the American Party', *International Press Correspondence*, 9, 37: 801.

Williams, George 1922, *The First Congress of the Red Trade Union International in Moscow, 1921*, Chicago, IL: Industrial Workers of the World.

Wise, Andrew Kier 2011, 'An American Bolshevik: The Evolution of Boris Reinstein's Political Ideology', paper presented at 61st Annual Meeting of the New York State Association of European Historians.

Wolfe, Bertram D., Jay Lovestone and William F. Dunne 1926, *Our Heritage from 1776: A Working Class View of the First American Revolution*, New York: The Workers School.

Wolfe, Bertram D. 1981, *A Life in Two Centuries*, New York: Stein and Day.

Wolff, Frank 2012, 'Eastern Europe Abroad: Exploring Actor-Networks in Transnational Movements and Migration History, The Case of the Bund', *International Review of Social History*, 57, 2: 229–55.

Worley, Matthew 2004, 'Courting Disaster: The Communist International in the Third Period', in *In Search of Revolution: International Communist Parties in the Third Period*, edited by Matthew Worley, London: I.B. Tauris.

——— (ed.) 2004, *In Search of Revolution: International Communist Parties in the Third Period*, London: I.B. Tauris.

Yamanouchi, Akito 1989, '"Internationalized Bolshevism": The Bolsheviks and the International, 1914–1917', *Acta Slavica Iaponica*, 7: 17–32.

——— 1996, *S.J. Rutgers and a Case Study of the International History of Socialism: Association with Sen Katayama, the Bolsheviks and the American Left Wing*, Kyoto: Minerva Shobo.

——— 2009, *The Early Comintern and Japanese Socialists Residing Abroad: A Transnational Network*, Kyoto: Minerva Shobo.

Zake, Ieva 2010, *American Latvians: Politics of a Refugee Community*, New Brunswick, NJ: Transaction.

Zaretsky, Eli 2012, *Why America Needs a Left: A Historical Argument*, Cambridge: Polity.

Zimmerman, Joshua D. 2010, 'Makysimillian Horwitz', *YIVO Encyclopedia of Jews in Eastern Europe*, available at: <www.yivoencyclopedia.org/article.aspx/Horwitz_Maksymilian>.

Zinoviev, Grigory, Joseph Stalin and Lev Kamenev 1925, *Bolshevism or Trotskyism?* Chicago, IL: Daily Worker Publishing Company.

Zinoviev, Grigory 1973 [1923], *History of the Bolshevik Party from the Beginnings to February 1917*, London: New Park.

Zipser, Arthur and Pearl Zipser 1989, *Fire and Grace: The Life of Rose Pastor Stokes*, Athens, GA: University of Georgia Press.

Zucker, Bat-Ami 1991, 'The "Jewish Bureau": The Organization of American Jewish Communists in the 1930s', in *Modern History*, edited by Michael J. Cohen, Ramat-Gan: Bar-Ilan.

Zumoff, Jacob A. 2007, 'The African Blood Brotherhood: From Caribbean Nationalism to Communism', *Journal of Caribbean History*, 41, 1: 200–26.

——— 2008a, 'Domingo, Wilfred Adolphus', in *African American National Biography*, edited by Henry Louis Gates and Evelyn Brooks Higginbotham, New York: Oxford University Press.

——— 2008b, 'Moore, Richard Benjamin', in *African American National Biography*, edited by Henry Louis Gates and Evelyn Brooks Higginbotham, New York: Oxford University Press.

——— 2009, 'The Americanization of the American Communist Party in the 1920s', *Cercles*, 19: 183–95.

——— 2010, 'Mulattoes, Reds, and the Fight for Black Liberation in Claude McKay's *Trial by Lynching* and *Negroes in America*', *Journal of West Indian Literature*, 19, 1: 22–53.

——— 2011, '"Ojos Que No Ven": The Communist Party, Caribbean Migrants, and the Communist International in Costa Rica in the 1920s and 1930s', *Journal of Caribbean History*, 45, 2: 212–47.

Index

Note: The American Communist movement underwent several splits in its early years. When unified in the early 1920s, it was first called the Workers' Party and then the Workers' (Communist) Party; in 1929 it became the Communist Party, USA. This work uses the term Communist Party (CP) to describe the party from 1922 on, and references are indexed in a single category here. [However there were other, distinct organizations with similar names; there are separate index entries for the Communist Party of America (1919–21), the Communist Labor Party (1919–20), the United Communist Party (1920–1) and the Communist League of America (Opposition) (1928–34).]

ABB See African Blood Brotherhood
Abd el-Krim 325
Abern, Martin 138n2, 139n1, 156, 169–170, 209n2, 212n, 220n2, 252n, 259–260, 262
ACWA See Amalgamated Clothing Workers
AFL See American Federation of Labor
Africa 296, , 298–299, 304–308, 313–317, 323, 325–327, 331–332, 342–346, 355, 357, 361, 363n2
French colonies 313, 325
See also pan-Africanism; South Africa
African Americans See blacks, American
African Blood Brotherhood (ABB) 23, 298–304, 306, 312, 317, 322–324, 343
See also Briggs
African sailors, Communist work among 317
agricultural workers, Communist work among 95, 287, 323, 326, 340, 348, 360n3
Alabama 5, 11, 348, 360n3, 362, 363n1
See also Scottsboro Boys
All-American Anti-Imperialist League 187, 331–332
Allen, James S. 295, 360
All-Russian Cooperative Society 213
Amalgamated Bank 181
Amalgamated Clothing Workers (ACWA) 104, 107–108, 122, 124, 148–149, 181, 188
See also textile workers
American Civil Liberties Union (ACLU) 72, 198n3, 202–203
American Communist Party (CP) See Communist Party
'American exceptionalism' 231–234n, 238, 241–248, 274–276, 348
American Federationist 125, 126n1
American Federation of Labor (AFL)
and FFLP 124, 126
and immigrant workers 76, 107, 193
and IWW 88, 92
and Passaic strike 190–193, 195–197
and Profintern 87, 91–92
and TUEL 106–108, 118
and women workers 193
anti-Communism 21, 83, 91, 112, 125–126, 148, 191, 193, 196, 210, 284, 324, 326
anti-strike activity 193
bureaucracy 75n2, 106, 118, 211, 215, 284
bureaucracy, racism of 102, 306, 324, 326–327, 330
Comintern on 21, 83–84, 87, 91–92, 109, 210, 256, 285
Communist work in 14, 21, 75–76, 83, 85, 115, 215
dissent within 75, 100, 108, 113
expulsion of Communists 110, 125–126, 149, 196–197
Foster in 98, 100–102, 106–107, 109, 192–193, 330
lack of militancy 2–3, 75, 100–101, 195–196
left opposition to 25, 76, 85, 115, 285, 366
Lenin on 83, 285
Lovestoneites and 284
membership figures 74, 114
racist policies 102, 107, 306, 324, 326–327, 330
support for bourgeois politicians 3, 113
support for La Follette 146–147
support for Socialists 25
support for WWI 100

American Federation of Labor (AFL) (*cont.*)
 unorganised workers 25, 84–85, 193, 195–197
 See also CFL; dual unionism; Fitzpatrick; Gompers; Lewis; UMWA; UTW
American Fund for Public Service 72n2, 181
Americanisation, Comintern role in 5–6
Americanisation, of Communist Party 1, 5–7, 70, 172
American Labor Alliance 59, 198
American Labor Monthly 124n2
American Legion 247n1
American Negro Labor Congress (ANLC) 23, 187, 319–328, 331, 333–336, 341, 362
American Revolution 246–247
American Workers' Party
 See Communist Party
Amsterdam News 298, 306, 317
Amter, Israel 73, 104, 119, 122n3–123, 132, 141–143, 185, 264, 305n4, 312–314, 316, 323n1
anarchists
 and Comintern 80
 and Profintern 87, 94
 arrests 2
 Cannon on 94
 deportations 50
 in Soviet Union 309
 in TUEL 105
 recruited to Communism 79, 89, 96, 297
 See also Haywood, William D.; Industrial Workers of the World; Sacco and Vanzetti case; Wobblies
anarchy, criminal, charges of 35n2, 51, 66
Anderson, John 44
Andreytchine, George 11, 12n1, 81, 88–90, 93, 96, 177
ANLC See American Negro Labor Congress
anti-colonialism 293, 298, 301, 304–305, 309, 331–332, 340, 342–343, 352, 355–356
anti-Communism, former
 Lovestoneites 123, 272, 284, 338
 See also Gitlow; Lovestone; Wolfe
anti-imperialist united front 213, 331, 356
anti-Trotskyism
 in Bolshevik Party 159, 163, 205, 227
 in Communist International 136–137, 152–153, 159, 213, 226–227, 229, 240–241, 263, 266–268, 359
 in Communist Party 136–137, 142, 154–158, 186, 225–230, 237, 250–251, 259–264, 266, 282, 338
 See also Engdahl; Gusev; Lovestone; Pepper; Ruthenberg; Stalin
anti-Trotskyist violence 12–13, 229, 264
Appeal to Reason 28, 173, 358n1
Aptheker, Herbert 362n1
Arbeter Ring (Workmen's Circle) 184
Argentine Communist Party 45, 91
Armenian federation 45n1
Aronberg, Philip 209n2, 259n3, 359
Asher, Martha Stone 191
Ashkenudzie, George 62, 66
Ashleigh, Charles 79, 88, 89n1, 90n1, 96
Asian immigration 289
Askeli, Henry 139
Atlanta 362
Australia 84n1, 271n2, 306, 355

back-to-Africa movement 296
 See also Garvey movement
Baker, Charles 33
Baldwin, Kate 363
Baldwin, Roger 72, 181, 198n3, 199–200, 202–203
Ballam, John J. (Curtis) 38–39, 62–64, 66, 139, 206, 209n2, 210n1, 211, 333
Ballister (Minor) See Minor, Robert
Baltimore 362
Barrett, James 4n2, 10, 14, 16, 19, 99n1, 105, 109, 124, 150
Bebel, August 208n2
Bedacht, Max 15, 18n2, 28n1, 41, 51–52, 54, 63, 68–70, 91, 143, 155n1, 158, 164, 169–170, 184, 201, 204, 206, 210n1, 220, 232, 269, 271, 274n1, 278–281, 285, 314
Belgium 298, 305
Bell, Thomas 239n2, 260, 262n2, 275, 316
Bennett, A.J. (Petrovsky)
 See Petrovsky
Berger, Victor 25, 27, 35–36, 55, 57, 116, 130–131, 150, 173, 289
Berkman, Alexander 50
Berlin syndicalists 93
Bernstein, Irving 74
Biedenkapp, Fred 199
Billings, Warren 202

Bimba, Anthony 149, 199
Birmingham AL 310, 348, 362
birth control 77
Bittelman, Alexander
and Cannon 69–70, 133, 155–156, 243, 253, 258–259
and Comintern 53, 69, 151, 157, 166–167, 222, 234, 240, 253, 256, 268–271, 273, 277
and Foster 76n2, 126n3–127, 155–156, 166, 168–169, 189, 222, 253, 262–263, 273
and Jewish Communists 69, 76, 155, 230n1
and Liquidators 52–53, 61, 69–70
and Negro work 327, 336, 346, 349, 358–359
and 'Right Danger' document 253, 255–256
background in Russian unions 133
Comintern assignment in India 270–271, 284
in SP left wing 56
on factions in CP 133, 139, 143, 155, 166–169, 205n2, 207, 222, 243, 262
on FFLP 127–128
on foreign-language federations 179, 183
on La Follette movement 132–133, 147, 151
on Lovestone 205, 207n2, 209, 222, 231, 241n2, 255n1, 262–263, 266, 269–270, 275
on Pepper 122–123n3, 127, 132–133, 138–139, 142, 169, 189, 275, 358
on Ruthenberg 205, 207, 243
on Stalin 166, 169, 285
on strike wave 76
on Trotsky 137–138, 142, 156–157, 258, 263
Stalin on 270, 276, 285
support for Stalin 155n2–156, 231, 243, 254
vs dual unionism 76n2, 189
vs Eastman 227
See also Foster-Cannon faction; Foster faction
black agricultural workers, Communist work among 323, 326, 339–340, 346–348, 350, 362
'Black Belt' (in US South) 340n3, 353–354, 356, 360–361, 363
black Caribbean Communists 23, 297–300, 307–308, 315, 336
See also ABB; Briggs; Huiswoud; McKay; Moore; Padmore
black Caribbean radicals 23, 287n1, 290, 296, 298n-300, 303n, 339–340
See also ABB; Domingo; Randolph
black Communists 4n2, 5, 15, 23, 71, 145, 208, 230–231, 252, 254, 271n2, 279–280n1, 287–288, 290, 295, 297–338, 340–343, 346–353, 355–363 See also ABB; ANLC; Ford; Fort-Whiteman; Haywood, Harry; Huiswoud; McKay; Moore; Padmore
black equality
and Communists 293, 295, 298, 308–310, 313, 320, 323, 325, 331, 333–334, 344, 349, 353–354, 360–364
and IWW 102
fight for 102, 296, 298, 308–310, 323, 353, 360–362, 364
See also black oppression; Jim Crow; racial discrimination; racial segregation; Socialist Party, 'colour-blindness'
black internationalism 297–298, 301, 307–308, 325–327, 331, 363n2–364n1
black migration to North 288, 312, 339–340, 344, 347–348, 350
black nationalism 290, 294–296, 298, 302, 306–307, 342–349, 363
See also Garvey movement
black oppression
class basis of 288, 291, 294, 305, 321, 324
Communist fight vs 6, 15, 20, 23, 254, 287–288, 291–292, 294–295, 306–311, 318, 321, 328, 330–332, 336, 341, 352–353, 360–364
compared to tsarist Russia 293, 307, 346–347
international nature of 297, 304–305, 307–308, 316, 326–327, 331, 350, 352, 361, 363n2
special nature of 307, 309, 314, 319, 328, 334, 342–344, 346–348, 353, 356, 361, 363n2
See also black self-determination; Jim Crow; lynching; 'Negro question'; racial discrimination; racial segregation; racist violence

blacks, American
and Bolshevik Revolution 295, 300, 302
and 'colour-blindness' on left 23, 288–290, 300–301, 309, 311, 314, 319, 324
and Communist International 292–294, 301, 304–314, 318–321, 324, 326, 328, 330, 336–339, 342–351, 352–359, 363
and IWW 102, 290, 297, 324
and Socialist Party 23, 288–291, 295–297, 299–301, 303, 307, 309, 319, 324, 339–34
Communist influence among 20, 287, 296, 326, 367
Communist work among 4, 11, 287, 290–291, 295, 300, 310–312, 318–320, 324, 327, 333, 337, 341, 345, 349–350, 352, 360–362
in Communist Party 4n2, 5, 15, 23, 71, 145, 208, 230–231, 252, 254, 271n2, 279–280n1, 287–288, 290, 295, 297–338, 340–343, 346–353, 355–363
See also black oppression; black separatism; Jim Crow; 'Negro question'; racial discrimination; racial segregation; racist violence
black self-determination 23, 309, 320, 330, 342–361, 365–366
black separatism 303, 306, 335, 342–343, 345n, 347n1, 349, 354, 358
See also Garvey movement; UNIA
Black Star Line 296, 303–304n
black trade unions 320–321, 334, 350, 354
black workers, unionization 308, 320, 326, 334, 348, 350, 354
Blatt, Dennis 42
Bloor, Ella Reeve 11, 45, 77, 98, 199, 271n2, 274n1, 279, 281n1
Bolshevik Central Committee, ethnic composition 293
Bolshevik Party See Bolsheviks; Russian Communist Party
Bolshevik Revolution
and American Communists 1, 3–4, 6, 50, 56, 76, 102–103
and SPL 31–33
and US blacks 300, 302
and US left 33–34
degeneration of 13, 112, 136, 152, 224, 258, 262
impact in US 34–35, 76, 149
impact on Socialists 31, 33–35, 37–38, 55–56, 104, 149
IWW view of 79–82, 88–91, 93, 95
Lenin on 6, 15
See also Soviet Union
Bolsheviks
and Comintern 1, 14, 16, 17, 24, 35, 49, 55, 66, 69, 72, 83, 141
and IWW 40, 78–82, 85, 88–94, 96
and left Socialists 29, 31–32, 35–37, 40, 55–57, 61–62, 104, 172
and SLP 40
and SPL 31–33
and Stalin 13, 136–137, 140
and trade union question 83–86, 91–92, 103
and Trotsky 33–34, 136–138, 156–157, 228
influence on American Communists 4, 6, 15, 48, 56, 69, 72, 97, 103, 172, 227
internationalism 1, 5, 17, 24, 49, 137, 172, 301
on La Follette movement 140–141
on national question 175, 290, 292–293, 301
on 'Negro question' 292–293, 326, 339
opposition to 34, 56–57, 61, 80–82, 88, 90, 92, 94, 107, 123
origins 163
underground work 53, 67n1
vs syndicalists 79, 82, 89, 91, 103
within Russia 13, 49, 136
See also Bolshevik Revolution; Bukharin; Lenin; Russian Communist Party; Stalin; Trotsky
Bolshevisation
and anti-Trotskyism 153–159
and factionalism in CP 14, 153–154, 187–188
and foreign-language federations 172, 175–176, 182–186, 190
and Stalinisation 22, 152–153
of Communist Party 136, 152–153
Bolshevism
black response to 295, 297, 300–302, 309
converts won to 17, 21, 23–24, 32, 35, 56, 61, 66, 79, 96, 103–104
Pepper vs 120, 131

principles of 5, 14–15, 24, 40, 46–47n1, 49, 55, 143n1, 156, 175, 292–293
vs Bukharinism 225, 258
vs Stalinism 258
See also Bolsheviks; Lenin; Leninism; Trotsky; Trotskyism
Book (Bukharin) See Bukharin, Nikolai
Bookman (Bukharin) See Bukharin, Nikolai
Borodin, Mikhail 315
Bouck, William 145–146, 148n2
Boudin, Louis 27, 33–34, 150, 154
Brandler, Heinrich 63, 270, 283
Brazil 45, 355
Bridgman MI convention (1922) 41n5, 65–66, 68–69n1, 105–107, 120–121, 163
Bridgman raid (1922) 41n5, 65, 72, 199, 207
defence campaign 199
Briggs, Cyril Valentine 298–304, 306, 312, 317, 323, 334–336, 342–343, 361
See also African Blood Brotherhood
Britain 213, 215, 236–238, 240–241n, 246–247, 296–299, 317, 342, 345, 358n1
British Communist Party
and 1926 General Strike 2, 20, 238–239, 249
Lovestone on 237
membership figures 18
on 'Negro question' 297, 305, 315–317
Stalinisation of 17
sterility of 16
Trotsky on 237–238
vs Pepper 238–240n
vs Trotsky 213, 227–228n1
British Communists 76, 78, 84, 94, 96, 115, 258, 269, 275, 316
British General Strike (1926) 2, 20, 238–239, 249
British Labour Party 56, 71, 84, 112–113, 115, 160, 189, 239
British Socialists 29, 47, 96
British syndicalists 86, 94, 98
British West Indies 331
Brook, Michael 186n1
Brooklyn transit workers strike (1920) 50, 76–77, 292
Brooks, Alfred J. (Bosse) 221, 245
Browder, Earl 10–11, 14, 23, 53, 66, 74, 77, 90, 98, 102, 119, 134n1, 138, 143, 151, 156, 163, 168, 222, 236, 239, 245, 269–271, 284–285, 338n3, 365
Brown, John 289
Brown, Rev. Ethelred 358
Brown, Roy 96
Brownsville, Brooklyn branch 230
Brown v. Board of Education decision 362
Brussels conference (1927) 331
Buck, Robert 100
Buhle, Paul 9, 30, 174, 284
building trades workers 109–111
See also UBCJA
Bukharin (Bookman) See Bukharin, Nikolai
Bukharin, Nikolai
and Pepper 225, 253, 255–256, 270, 272
and Lovestone 13, 22, 208, 213, 225, 229, 238, 242, 245–247, 253–256, 259n2, 266, 270, 272
as Comintern leader 159, 224–225, 235, 250–251, 254–256, 266, 271n1, 281
bloc with Stalin 205, 213, 218, 224–227, 234, 238, 242–243, 247, 258, 266
break with Stalin 224, 226n1, 249, 251, 254–255, 258, 266, 269–273, 278, 283
fall of 22, 271n1, 281
in America 29–30n, 32n2–33
intervention into American CP 53, 59, 69, 169, 173, 240, 255
on AFL 91–92
on 'Negro question' 345–346
on party legality 53, 59, 69, 91–92
on third party question 141–142
on Third Period 242, 249–250, 282
Right Opposition 240n2, 249–250, 270, 283
role in Stalinisation 13, 283
vs Trotsky 213, 238, 243, 258–259n2, 283n3
Bunting, Sidney P. 305, 308, 346, 355, 357
Bureau of Investigation See Federal Bureau of Investigation
Burman, Fahle 139n1
Butte Daily Post 125
Bynum, Cornelius 291

Cahan, Abraham 56, 108, 173, 198
Campbell, Grace P. 299–300, 358–359
Campbell, Susan 344n1

Canadian Communist Party 17–18, 45, 184, 251, 261–262n, 264, 355
Cannon faction 13, 127, 167, 169–171, 206, 222, 252–253, 259–261, 263–265, 283, 352, 357
  See also Cannon-Foster faction; Communist Party, factionalism; Foster faction; Lovestone faction; Ruthenberg faction
Cannon-Foster faction 126n3–128, 133–134n1, 138, 141, 143–145, 154–156, 158–170, 203, 206, 214, 217–222, 252–259, 262, 321, 323, 330, 337, 341, 352
  See also Cannon faction; Communist Party, factionalism; Foster faction; Lovestone faction; Ruthenberg faction
Cannon, James P.
  and Abern 138–139, 156, 169–170, 209, 212, 259–260, 262
  and Americanisation of CP 15, 38, 53, 67, 69–70, 98, 200
  and Bittelman 69–70, 133, 155–156, 243n, 253, 258–259, 263, 336
  and Comintern 15, 53, 60, 69–71, 73, 115, 121–122, 141, 143–144, 153, 159–162, 165–170, 209, 211, 214–222, 243n, 252–254, 257–259, 263, 266, 283, 292, 323, 336–337, 349, 352
  and Dunne 98, 164, 169, 171, 188, 211, 216, 251, 253, 263, 283n4, 341
  and farmer-labour movement 119–120, 122, 127, 132–133, 141, 144–147, 155, 161
  and FFLP 127–128, 146–147, 155
  and foreign-language federations 70, 120n3, 155, 172–173, 261
  and IWW 71, 77, 94–97, 197, 199n2–203
  and Lenin 15, 69
  and Lore 127, 132–133, 142–144, 154–158
  and Oehler 265
  and Pepper 120–122, 127, 132–133, 138–139, 143, 155, 158–160, 162, 169–170, 209, 214, 222, 253, 256, 259
  and Profintern 98
  and Rose Karsner 198, 201, 204, 259
  and Ruthenberg 122, 132–133, 169–171, 203, 206–207, 209, 242–243
  and Shachtman 164, 169, 204, 259–260, 265, 283
  and Socialists 36–38, 41, 58, 201–202
  and Spector 251, 257–259, 261, 264n2
  and Swabeck 70, 127, 158, 169–170, 259, 261
  and Trotsky 70, 73, 257–261, 264–265, 272, 282
  and Trotskyism 13–14, 22, 103, 138n2, 153–158, 228n2, 250–251, 257–266, 272, 282–283, 366
  and WP founding 60
  arrests 65, 72
  as CP leader 68–69, 206, 212
  as ILD leader 96, 197–204, 259–260n1
  as Trotskyist leader 13, 22, 153, 155n2, 257–260, 262–266, 282–283, 366
  biographies 11–12, 258
  bloc with Foster 127, 133, 141–142, 144–145, 154–156, 158–162, 164–165, 167–168, 203, 206, 209, 214, 216–222, 252–254, 256, 262–263, 321, 323, 330, 336–337, 341
  bloc with Weinstone 171, 206–207, 209, 211–212, 214, 216–219, 245
  break with Foster 166–170, 203, 211–212, 259
  defence work 72, 96, 197–204
  expulsion from CP (1928) 12–14, 23, 260–262, 266, 359
  in Moscow 69–71, 115, 120, 141–143, 159, 170, 252–254, 256–259, 341, 349
  on Bolshevisation 153
  on factionalism 159, 169–171, 187, 203, 206–207, 212, 222, 253
  on Foster 103, 119, 133, 203, 206–207, 209, 211
  on labour party 71, 115
  on legality of CP 15, 53, 60, 66–67, 69–71, 73, 115
  on 'Negro question' 254, 292, 321, 323, 330, 336–337, 341, 349, 352, 358
  on Passaic strike 195, 202
  on Pepper 5, 259
  on Stalinisation 16, 247–248
  on syndicalism 94–97
  on trade union work 106, 188, 195, 211–212, 215
  on TUEL 106, 127, 188, 194, 214–215
  recruitment to Communist Party 96

support for capitalist politicians 132–133
trade union background 74, 133, 197
vs Lovestone 170–171, 203–204, 207–209, 211, 214, 217, 219–222, 242n1, 252–254, 257, 259–266, 283, 337, 352, 357
writings 11, 97n1, 283n4
See also Cannon faction; Cannon-Foster faction
Caribbean 116, 296–298, 304n1, 308, 314–315, 331, 342
imperialism in 116, 223, 298, 331
Caribbean black Communists 23, 287, 290, 297–300, 315, 336
Caribbean immigrants, Communist work among 298, 327
See also African Blood Brotherhood
Caribbean immigration 288, 296, 323
Carney, Jack 37n1, 81
carpenters union 109–111
Carr, Barry 10
Carr, E.H. 120n2, 137n2, 213, 236, 242
Carr, J. (Katterfeld) See Katterfeld, Ludwig
car workers, CP work among 4
CCE See Central Cooperative Exchange
CCLP See Cook County Labor Party
Central Cooperative Exchange (CCE) 184
Centralia IWW militants 202
CFL See Chicago Federation of Labor
Chaplin, Ralph 79, 201
Charles H. Kerr & Co. 25, 26n1, 173
Charlotte NC 362
Chase, Stuart 181, 198
Chattanooga TN, Communist election campaign 1930 362
Chester, Eric Thomas 150
Chiang Kai-shek 213, 242, 331n2
Chicago
Communist work among blacks 288n1, 326–327, 341, 362
Communist work in unions 188
repression in 51, 65, 107, 125, 196
CP branch 10, 216, 221, 362
race riot (1919) 291
Chicago Defender 325
Chicago Federation of Labor (CFL) 75, 100–101, 113, 122
See also Cook County Labor Party; Fitzpatrick
China
1927 uprising 20, 213, 242, 258, 331, 356
Comintern policy in 210, 213, 215, 256, 258, 331, 352, 356
Communist work in 2, 210, 213, 225n1, 263, 271n2
Lovestone on 222, 240–241n
Chinese Communist Party 2, 20, 213, 258, 331, 356
Chinese immigrants, and Communists 11
CIO See Congress of Industrial Organizations
circulation, of Communist press 43, 109, 120–121, 173, 187, 204
Citizens' Committee (Passaic strike) 193, 196
Civil War (Soviet Union) 49, 136, 163
Civil War (US) 247, 288, 325, 347
Clarke, Edward Young 303n1
Class Struggle 27, 33–34, 154, 173, 292
class-war prisoners 79, 81n1, 93, 96, 197, 199–202
See also International Labor Defense; legal repression; Sacco and Vanzetti case
Cleveland Press 32
CLP See Communist Labor Party
coal miners See miners, United Mine Workers of America
Cohen, Maximilian 36
Cohen, Stephen F. 225, 251
COINTELPRO 304n2
collectivisation, in Soviet Union 13, 224, 249
Colonial Commission 332n2, 352
Comintern See Communist International
Comintern archives 7–8, 11–12, 30n1, 98, 107, 143, 168n2, 274n2, 344n2, 347n2, 353
Comintern jewels 44n
Committee for the Third International 57
Communism, regional studies of 11
Communist Caucus 90–91
Communist (CP) 41, 48, 59–60, 240, 247, 282, 357
Communist (CPA) 41, 61
Communist International 18, 78, 82, 85, 152, 235–236, 238, 242, 267, 319, 344–345, 357
Communist International
and American blacks 292–294, 301, 304–314, 318–321, 324, 326, 328, 330, 336–339, 342–351, 352–359, 363

Communist International (*cont.*)
and Dunne 211, 216, 251, 253, 263, 271n2, 332, 341, 349
and Foster 73, 103, 119, 127, 138–141, 143–144, 156, 161–170, 194–195, 209–222, 225–226, 240, 254–257, 262–263, 268–271, 273–275, 277, 284, 323, 330, 336
and Lovestone 22, 143, 159, 165–169, 179, 192, 205, 208–222, 225–226, 228, 231–233, 237–238, 240, 244, 247–248, 252–257, 259, 262, 266–282, 285–286, 336–337, 352, 359
and Pepper 120–122, 138–144, 156, 159–162, 165–170, 177, 194, 205, 208, 217, 222, 238–242, 255–257, 268–270, 273, 277, 330, 332n2, 341–342, 347, 349–351, 357–359
archives 7–8, 11–12, 30n1, 98, 107, 143, 168n2, 274n2, 344n2, 347n2, 353
birth of 24
Bukharin in 159, 224–225, 235, 250–251, 254–256, 266, 271n1, 281
intervention into CP 1, 4–6, 11, 13–16, 19–24, 39–40, 46–48, 59, 63–73, 75, 83, 103–104, 112, 141–144, 150, 153, 159–168, 205, 210, 215–219, 234, 248, 250, 267–281, 285–288, 293–294, 304–316, 323, 328, 343–344, 356n3–357n1, 362n1–366
IWW affiliation 80, 83, 93
Negro Commission 304, 308, 313, 320, 330, 332, 336, 341, 345–356, 358
'Negro question' 6–7, 254, 292–294, 301, 304–314, 323, 328, 331–332, 339, 341–359, 363
on La Follette movement 16, 22, 141–142, 146–148, 150–151, 156, 161
Stalin in 6, 12–13, 137, 152, 166, 205, 213, 234, 247, 250–251, 276
Stalinisation of 13–14, 17, 20–23, 152–154, 187–188, 205, 225, 240–243, 247, 355–356, 364
Trotsky in 1, 22, 69–70, 73, 107, 112, 136, 140–142, 159, 213, 226–229, 235–238, 258
Twenty-One Conditions (for Comintern adherence) 55–56, 343
Zinoviev in 69, 152, 159, 161, 166, 205, 213, 235
See also Bolsheviks; Bolshevisation; Comintern archives; *Communist International*; Krestintern; Profintern
Communist International congresses
First Congress (1919) 40, 83
Second Congress (1920) 49, 55, 83–87, 176, 293–294, 313–315, 343, 345, 348
Second Congress Theses on National and Colonial Questions 293, 343
Third Congress (1921) 6, 15, 49–50, 53–54, 86–87, 92, 137, 176, 198, 223, 235, 241–242, 304
Fourth Congress (1922) 23, 69–71, 73, 115, 299, 305–308, 310, 312, 314–316, 340, 344
Fifth Congress (1924) 23, 136–137, 152–153, 197, 211, 235–236, 316, 318–319, 337
Sixth Congress (1928) 22–23, 197, 251–259, 262–263, 267–268, 270, 273, 282, 284, 329–330, 332, 335–337, 341–342, 346–355, 357–358
Communist Labor Party (CLP) 40–44, 47n2, 74, 78, 199, 291
Communist League of America (Opposition) 262, 267n1
Communist (LO) 62–63
Communist Manifesto 339
Communist parties (besides American and Russian)
and Communist International 1, 13, 17, 20, 49, 71
and Negro World Congress 316–317
and Soviet Union 7, 17–18
compared to American CP 2, 16–18, 24, 45, 68, 78, 363, 366
Eurocommunism 7
foreign-language federations 45–46
membership figures 2, 18
repression of 2
role in class struggles 2, 18, 20
Stalinisation of 17, 20
See also Argentine CP; British CP; Canadian CP; Chinese CP; French CP; German CP; Mexican CP; Spanish CP
Communist Party (CP)
Americanisation of 1, 6–7, 10–11, 15, 52–53, 72–73, 97–98, 104, 233–234, 288, 311

and African Blood Brotherhood 298–302, 312, 317, 322–324, 343
and American Negro Labor Congress 23, 187, 319–328, 331, 333–336, 341, 362
and Debs 36–37n1
and émigré groups 29–34, 39, 176–178, 184, 298
and farmer-labour movement 16, 21, 112, 117–119, 122–124, 129, 131–136, 139–142, 144–150, 155–156, 158, 160–161, 313, 325
and FFLP 123–131, 134–135, 140, 146, 155
and labour party movement 21, 114–117, 119, 122, 160–161
and Soviet Union 3–5, 7–8, 205, 224, 280, 309, 320
and Third Period 16, 250, 267–268, 282–284, 308n1, 362, 364–366
anti-British tilt 241n1, 246–247
anti-Trotskyism in 12–13, 22–23, 155–159, 186, 213, 226–230, 237, 240–241, 250–251, 259–266, 268, 282, 338–339, 359
birth of 1–2, 18, 21, 24, 40, 50, 60–62, 108, 154, 203, 288, 290–291, 300, 310
black CP candidates 300–301, 335, 362
black members 4n2, 5, 15, 23, 71, 145, 208, 230–231, 252, 254, 271n2, 279–280n1, 287–288, 290, 295, 297–338, 340–343, 346–353, 355–363
black oppression, fight vs 6, 15, 20, 23, 254, 287–288, 291–292, 294–295, 306–308, 310–311, 318, 321, 328, 330–332, 336, 341, 352–353, 360–364
black women members 300–301, 359
blacks, work among 4, 11, 287, 290–291, 294–295, 300, 310–312, 318–320, 324, 327, 333, 337, 341, 345, 349–350, 352, 360–362
Bolshevik Revolution's influence on 1, 6, 21, 23, 34, 102–104, 137
Bolshevisation of 22, 136, 152–159, 172, 175–176, 182–188, 190
capitulation to racism 145, 310, 313, 315, 333, 338, 363
'colour-blindness' 23, 288, 290, 292, 296, 301, 310, 319, 324, 328
Comintern intervention 1, 4–6, 11, 13–16, 19–24, 39–40, 46–48, 59, 63–73, 75, 83, 103–104, 112, 141–144, 150, 153, 159–168, 205, 210, 215–219, 234, 248, 250, 267–281, 285–288, 293–294, 304–316, 323, 328, 343–344, 356n3–357n1, 362n1–366
defence of immigrants 175, 197
defence work 22, 53, 72, 96, 110, 187, 197–204, 219, 287, 330, 362
election campaigns 147–148, 300–301, 335
electoral participation 58, 84, 114–115, 147
expelled from trade unions 110, 125–126, 149, 196–197, 215
factionalism 15–18, 22–23, 42, 62–63, 148, 155, 158–161, 167–170, 188, 191, 194, 205–220, 224, 232, 244n1, 248, 254, 267–268, 272, 275, 285, 312, 321–323, 328, 330, 341, 349, 359, 366
farmers, work among 118, 126, 128, 135, 140, 324, 348
finances 181, 183–185, 198, 279
foreign-language federations 6, 11, 22, 39, 44–47, 52–53, 62, 67, 69, 96, 120, 153, 155, 172–186, 190, 192, 261, 296, 315
histories of 1–5, 8–12, 17, 19, 21, 66n2, 94, 98, 231, 302n1
in 1930s 2, 4–5, 10, 20, 23, 74, 151, 186, 283n4, 285, 287–288n1, 301, 328, 338, 348, 360, 362–367
in labour movement 2–4, 6, 17, 20–22, 50, 74–112, 117, 148–150, 187–197, 203, 242, 249, 274, 283–284n, 285–286, 363, 367
isolation of 2, 4, 19, 21–22, 53, 68, 74, 77, 104, 111–112, 124, 126–127, 129–130, 140, 148–150, 160, 195, 223, 265, 274–275, 360
IWW influence on 76
IWW stance towards 79–82, 86, 88, 90, 92–95, 203
'Jim Crowism' in 333–335, 338, 354, 358n1
legality, debate over 6, 14–15, 21, 50, 52–55, 58–63, 65–73, 92, 289, 296, 306–307
membership figures 2, 18, 45, 59, 183, 285, 287, 362
'Negro question' 6–7, 23, 254, 287, 289–292, 294–295, 301, 309–313, 315, 318–323, 328, 330–341, 343–344, 347–359, 363, 366
on American capitalism 233–246, 252, 256

Communist Party (CP) (*cont.*)
opposition to 3, 8–9, 19–21, 52, 61–63, 80, 82, 88–90, 92–94, 112, 117, 125, 144, 146, 149, 192n1, 194, 284
Pepper's interventions 18, 21, 119–123, 130–133, 137–139, 142–143, 158–162, 165–166, 188–189, 222, 226, 228, 232–233, 243, 256–257, 269–270, 277, 330, 334–335, 349–351, 353n, 357–359
popular frontism 2, 10, 16, 20, 112, 141, 151, 364–365
press of 15, 80–81, 89, 92, 121, 154–155, 158, 173–174, 181, 185–187, 266–267, 295, 319, 322, 327, 335, 361
recruitment from IWW 21, 25–26, 77–79, 81, 83, 88–89, 92, 94–98, 102–103, 200, 297, 324
recruitment from labour movement 24, 74, 77, 122
recruitment of Socialists 25–27, 29, 36, 39–41, 45, 56–58, 61–62, 70, 77, 91, 96–98, 102–103, 133, 154, 163, 190, 198, 207, 229–230, 291, 297, 299–301
regional studies 11–12n
repression against 3, 35n2, 42–43n5, 50–52, 65–66, 72–74, 76, 107, 125, 149–150, 197, 199–200, 202, 207, 213, 280n1, 304, 360–363, 365
social-democratisation of 16, 20–21, 175, 182, 365–366
splits from 62–64, 111, 184, 265, 282–284, 359
Stalinisation of 12, 16, 22–23, 152, 205, 225, 232, 240–241, 266, 272, 275–278, 285–286, 355–356, 364–367
theft of documents 210, 264, 281
trade union question 21–22, 50, 53, 71, 76, 83–88, 91–92, 98, 105–106, 115, 188–189, 192–196, 215–216, 242, 246, 252, 284
Trotskyists 257–265, 282–283, 366
Trotsky on 69, 140–141, 309–311
vs IWW 93–95, 97
'white chauvinism' 333, 337–338, 340–341, 348, 350, 352, 354
Workers' Party name 1n1, 73–74
work in South 23, 287–288n, 301, 307, 321, 323, 326, 333, 335, 337, 339–340, 348, 350, 352, 354–355, 360–363
See also dual unionism; FFLP; Geese faction; ILD; individual CP leaders; LDC; Liquidator faction; Stalinisation; TUEL
Communist Party of America (CPA) 40–48, 50–51, 61, 63–64, 76–77, 172, 199, 291–292
See also *Communist* (CPA); National Defense Committee, *Revolutionary Age*; workers government slogan
Communist Party of Argentina See Argentine Communist Party
Communist Party of Canada (CPC) See Canadian Communist Party
Communist Party of the USA (Majority Group) 282
Communist Party USA (CPUSA) 9–11, 263, 269n1, 275–277, 310n2, 356n3
See also Communist Party
Communist Review 239
Communists
personal experiences 4, 9–10
religious background 230, 358
repression of 3, 35n2, 42–43n5, 50–52, 65–66, 72, 76, 107, 197, 199–200, 202, 207, 213, 304, 360–363
See also Bolsheviks; British Communists; Caribbean black Communists; German Communists; Hungarian Communists; Italian Communists; Japanese Communists; Latin America, Communists; South African Communists
Communist University of Toilers of the East (KUTV) 336
Communist youth group 191, 261n2, 282, 336
Communist Youth International 275
Conference for Progressive Political Action (CPPA) 114, 116–117, 124, 134–135, 146–147
Congress of Industrial Organizations (CIO) 16, 74, 111n2, 197, 284–285
Congress of the Negro Peoples of the World 294, 302
Connecticut branch 261
construction workers 77, 109–111
Convention of the Negro Peoples of the World 302
Cook County Labor Party 113–114
Coolidge, Calvin 3, 130, 147, 149

Corey, Lewis (Fraina) See Fraina, Louis
Costa Rica, blacks in 363
CP See Communist Party
CPA See Communist Party of America
CPC See Canadian Communist Party
CPGB See British Communist Party
CPSU See Russian Communist Party
CPUSA See Communist Party USA
criminal anarchy, charges of 35n2, 51, 66
  See also legal repression
Crusader 298–300
Cruse, Harold 356
Cuba 355
Curtis (John J. Ballam) See Ballam, John J.
Czech federation 182
Czechoslovakia, national question 349

Daily Forward 198
Daily Worker 3, 10, 146, 156–157, 164–165, 174, 181, 184–186, 218–221, 226, 228, 246–247, 266–267, 318, 322, 335, 360–361
Damon (Ruthenberg) See Ruthenberg, C.E.
Darcy, Sam 90n-91n, 121, 271n2, 349, 351
Darlington, Ralph 80, 90, 97
Daughters of the American Revolution 247n1
Davenport, Tim 8n1, 26n1, 43n3, 125n2
Davis, Aaron 323
Davis, John W. 130, 147
Day, Richard B. 224, 235n1
Deak, Gustave 190, 192–193, 197
Debs, Eugene V.
  and Communists 36–37n1, 40, 72, 111
  and SP left wing 36–37n1, 40, 102
  election campaigns 113
  formation of SP 25
  founder of IWW 25
  in International Labor Defense 201–202
  in Labor Defense Council 72, 199
  on 'Negro question' 23, 289–290n, 292, 294, 313
  prosecution of 28, 36
De Leon, Daniel 25, 40, 41, 83, 90, 100, 154, 190n1, 247n1
  See also Socialist Labor Party
democratic-centralism 31, 46–47
Democratic Party 16, 20, 364
  See also popular front; Roosevelt, Franklin D.
Dengel, Philip 269, 273–275
Department of Justice (US) 50, 51n3, 82, 303–304, 325
Detroit MI 57, 90, 192n1, 261n1, 282, 338
Deutscher, Isaac 258
dictatorship of the proletariat 35, 40, 55, 57–59, 78, 80–81, 114–115, 291
  See also workers government slogan
Dirba, Charles (Dow) 62, 66
Domingo, W.A. 290, 296, 299–303, 306, 317, 339, 352, 358
Don, Sam 209n2, 253n2
Dorsey, John (Foster) See Foster, William Z.
Doty, Edward 252n, 336
Dow (Dirba) See Dirba, Charles
Drabkin, Yakov Davidovich (Gusev) See Gusev, Sergei Ivanovich
Draper, Theodore 3–5, 7–8, 10–12, 14, 38n2, 40, 42n3, 68, 73, 122, 151, 155, 162, 165, 170, 187, 192n1, 210n1, 242n2, 244, 246–247, 271n1, 279, 301n2, 342–344n2, 349, 355
dual unionism 25, 75–76, 83–85, 90–91, 93, 98, 101, 105–108, 115, 189, 196, 249, 366
Dubofsky, Melvyn 77
Du Bois, W.E.B. 295, 303, 317, 324, 326
Duncan, James A. (Seattle Central Labor Council) 75
Duncan (Minor) See Minor, Robert
Dunne brothers 77, 230n1, 261
Dunne, Vincent 229, 261
Dunne, William F.
  Americanisation of CP 98
  and Comintern 211, 216, 251, 253, 263, 271n2, 332, 341, 349
  and Pepper 126, 138–139, 238–239
  anti-Trotskyism 156, 251, 263, 270, 283n4
  break with Cannon 263, 283n4
  Cannon supporter 98, 126n3–127, 133, 164, 169, 171, 209n2, 211–212n, 216, 220, 251, 253, 341, 349
  criticism of 239
  expulsion from AFL convention 125–126
  on British General Strike 238–239
  on CP trade union work 188, 253, 326
  on 'Negro question' 311n2, 320, 326, 332, 337, 341, 349
  trade union background 77, 125, 127, 133
  vs Lovestone 255n1, 269–270, 341

Dunne, William F. (*cont.*)
vs Ruthenberg faction 164
vs trade union bureaucracy 125
Dunn, Robert 201
Duranty, Walter 280
Dutch Marxists 27, 32, 291

Eastman, Max 70, 154, 227–228, 230–231, 250, 262, 297
East St. Louis IL 293, 363
Ecuador 355
Egypt 304–305
Eley, Geoff 10
Ellington, Duke 362
emigration, to Soviet Union 177
Engdahl, J. Louis 55–57, 59, 61, 164, 192, 208, 226, 232–233, 250, 252, 266, 268n1, 345, 349
Engels, Friedrich 45, 47, 233n3, 247, 357
England See Britain; British General Strike; British Communist Party
English-language branches 47, 172, 177
English-language press 34, 53–54, 92, 173–174, 176
Epstein, Melech 60, 77
Epstein, Schachmo 255n1
espionage, accusations of 8, 192n1
Espionage Act prosecutions (1918) 28, 89
Ethiopia 298
Eurocommunism 7
Ewert, Arthur (Braun) 214, 216–217, 221, 255, 256n1

factional representation 159, 164–165, 167, 180, 216, 222
factory nuclei 180–181
famine, in Soviet Union 104, 198
Farmer-Labor Advocate 146
Farmer-Labor Party (FLP)
and Pepper 120–123, 138–144, 158, 160
Communist policy towards 112, 115, 118–119, 122–123, 129–130, 134–135, 139, 142–148, 150–151, 158, 160–161, 187, 243, 325
election campaigns 113–114, 147n1
racism in 313, 338
See also Minnesota Farmer-Labor Party
farmer-labour movement 4, 14, 21–22, 106, 112–113, 117–119, 125, 130–132, 142–146
See also Farmer-Labor Party; Federated Farmer-Labor Party; La Follette movement; Pepper
farmers, Communist work among 118, 126, 128, 135, 140, 324, 348
FBI See Federal Bureau of Investigation
February Revolution, in Russia (1917) 33–34
Federal Bureau of Investigation (FBI) 2–3, 11, 30n-32n, 40n2, 50, 52, 65, 177n1, 209, 303, 359n2
Federated Farmer-Labor Party (FFLP) 123–128, 130–135, 140–142, 145–147, 155, 160, 244n1
Federated Press 102
Ferguson, Isaac Edward 81
FFLP See Federated Farmer-Labor Party
Fifth Comintern Congress (1924) See Communist International congresses
Finland, failure of revolution 79
Finnish Americans, Communist influence among 177–178
Finnish American Socialists, support for Communists 62
Finnish American Wobblies 96
Finnish federation 121n1, 132, 173, 176–179, 182–185
Finnish language federation See Finnish federation
Finnish Socialist Federation (FSF) 61–62, 178
Finnish Workers Federation (FWF) 185
First Comintern Congress (1919) See Communist International congresses
First International 45
First World War See World War I
Fischer, Ruth 169n1
Fitzgerald, F. Scott 2
Fitzpatrick, John
and AFL 75, 100, 108, 118
and CPPA 114, 117
and FLP 113, 118–119, 123
and labour party 113–114, 117–119
and TUEL 108, 117
anti-Communism 123, 125
campaign for mayor of Chicago 113
Communist split with 123–124, 126–128, 139, 141, 148, 195
relationship with Communists 101, 108, 113, 117–119, 122–123, 125

suppport for strikes 101
See also Chicago Federation of Labor
Five Year Plan 224
Fletcher, Ben 324
Florida 327
FLP See Farmer-Labor Party
Flynn, Elizabeth Gurley 72, 77, 96, 195, 199
Foner, Eric 362n1
Foner, Philip S. 295, 362n1
Ford, James W. 252n, 290, 327–328, 332–334, 336–337, 341, 349–351
foreign-language federations
in IWW 45
of Communist Party 6, 11, 22, 39, 44–47, 52–53, 62, 67, 69, 96, 120, 153, 155, 172–186, 190, 192, 261, 296, 315
of CPA 44, 46, 172
of Socialist Party 29, 31, 36, 44–47, 56, 61–62, 172–175, 178, 184
press of 121, 154–155, 157–158, 173–174, 179, 181
Fort-Whiteman, Lovett (James Jackson) 187, 201, 204, 230, 252n, 296–298, 318–329, 334–337, 340n3, 342, 347
Forward 56, 108, 148, 173, 211n1
Foster-Cannon faction See Cannon-Foster faction
See also Cannon faction; Communist Party, factionalism; Foster faction; Lovestone faction; Ruthenberg faction
Foster, William Z.
and 'Americanisation' of CP 15, 38, 53, 66, 98, 104, 111
and Bittelman 76n2, 126n3–127, 155–156, 166, 168–169, 189, 222, 253, 262–263, 266, 269, 273, 285
and Bolshevik Revolution 102–105, 137n3
and Bolshevisation 182
and Bridgman convention 65, 72, 105–107
and CFL 100, 117
and Comintern 73, 103, 119, 127, 138–141, 143–144, 156, 161–170, 194–195, 209–222, 225–226, 240, 254–257, 262–263, 268–271, 273–275, 277, 284, 323, 330, 336
and CP black work 301n2, 302n1, 321, 323, 330, 336–337, 341, 349, 352, 357–359, 361–362
and CP trade union work 95, 98, 100, 104–107, 127–128, 140, 145, 169, 179, 188–189, 191–195, 214–216, 218, 242
and defence work 72, 201, 203–204, 259
and farmer-labour movement 119, 122, 127–128, 132–133, 140–141, 144–146, 149, 151, 160–161
and foreign-language federations 179, 181–183
and John Fitzpatrick 100–101, 108, 113, 117–119, 122, 127
and Lenin 103, 137n3
and Lozovsky 119, 225–226n1, 256, 273, 332
and Passaic strike 189, 191–193, 195, 214, 226n1, 252
and Pepper 119, 121–122, 127–128, 132, 134n1, 138–141, 143, 158–162, 165–166, 168–170, 194, 205, 214, 217, 222, 253, 256–257, 269, 357–359
and Profintern 102–103, 108, 225
and steel strike (1919) 101, 104, 107
and Trotskyism 137–138, 154–156, 158, 259, 262–263, 266, 268, 282
and TUEL 95, 101–102, 104–111, 148–149, 188–189, 193–195, 212, 214–215
arrests and prosecution 65, 72
as CP candidate 146–147, 361
as CP leader 66, 95, 98, 104, 109, 145, 162, 164–167, 169, 181, 188, 192, 195, 207, 212, 214–215, 221, 269, 279, 284, 365
as labour leader 21, 98, 100–101, 103–104, 117, 125, 127, 133, 189, 192–193
as Socialist 98, 102
as Stalinist 155n2–156, 225, 254–255, 270
as strike leader 101, 104
as syndicalist 98–103, 134n1, 225
biographies of 11, 98–99n1, 103
black radicals' view of 102
break with Cannon 166–167, 169–170, 203, 211–212, 259
Cannon on 103, 203, 206–207, 209, 211
criticism of 102, 106–107, 141, 160–161, 165, 194, 213–214, 218, 226n1, 242, 254
expulsion of Cannon 259, 262
in AFL 98, 100–102, 104, 106–107, 109, 125, 148–149, 192–193, 330
in CPPA 116–117

Foster, William Z. (*cont.*)
in IWW 96, 98–102
in Moscow 102–104, 108, 140, 159–164, 166, 168–169, 179, 181, 188, 192, 212, 252, 255, 271, 277, 279, 341, 349
on Bolshevik Revolution 102
on British CP 16
on FFLP 127–128, 140, 160
on IWW 95, 105–107
on La Follette movement 132–133, 140–141, 144, 151, 158, 244n1
on legality of CP 66–67, 72–73
on 'socialism in one country' 137n3
on Trotsky 137
outed by Pepper 119
political background 96, 98–102, 105, 111, 133, 225
political pessimism 246
recruitment to Communist Party 21, 65n2, 96, 98, 102–104, 109, 111
Stalin on 'Zigzag' (Foster) 213–214, 254–255, 285
support for capitalist politicians 132–133, 140–141, 151
support for WWI 100
violent attack on 125
vs dual unionism 76n2, 98–101, 103, 105–107, 189, 193, 195, 215, 252–253, 284
vs Gompers 100, 103, 107, 128
vs Lovestone 166, 209–211, 221, 225, 231, 242, 252–254, 259, 262–263, 266, 277, 282, 352
vs Lovestone faction 163–164, 169–170, 192, 209–210, 212–215, 218–221, 244n1, 252, 269–271, 273, 275, 277, 284, 337, 352, 357–359
vs Ruthenberg faction 140, 158–162, 164–167, 182, 189, 192, 194, 203, 206–207, 210, 242
See also Cannon-Foster faction; Foster faction; Labor Defense Council, *Labor Herald*; Liquidator faction, TUEL
Foster faction 126n3, 132, 138, 144, 151, 159, 162–163, 165, 169–170, 182, 188–189, 192, 194–195, 203, 206–207, 210–218, 222, 240, 242, 252–253, 222, 257, 259, 262–263, 268–269, 271, 275, 282, 284, 357
See also Cannon-Foster faction; Communist Party, factionalism; Lovestone faction; Ruthenberg faction
Fourth Comintern Congress (1922) See Communist International congresses
Fraina, Louis (Lewis Corey) 27, 30n-36, 38–40, 46, 76, 81, 85, 114, 154, 172, 177n1, 292, 294
France
Bolshevik supporters 24
Comintern delegates 91, 213
use of black colonial troops in Germany 309
See also French Communist Party; French Revolution
Fraser, Richard S. 344n1
Fraser, Steven 149
Freiheit 173, 183–184, 186
French Communist Party 18, 45, 228, 316–317, 323
French Revolution 131, 137n2
Friends of Soviet Russia 198, 200–201
FSR See Friends of Soviet Russia
Fulp, C.W. 336
Funsten nut pickers strike (1933) 363
Furriers strike 242
fur workers union 108, 208, 242, 360n1
FWF See Finnish Workers Federation

Garland Fund 72n2, 181
garment trades, Communist work in 77, 104, 108, 127–128, 148–149
See also ACWA; fur workers; Hillman; ILGWU; needle trades unions; Passaic NJ textile strikes; textile workers
Garvey, Marcus 296–297, 299, 302–304, 310n2, 313, 327
Garvey movement 288, 295–296, 300, 302–304n, 306, 315, 317, 320–321, 331, 342, 346–347
See also *Negro World*
Gary, Indiana 107, 333
Gastonia NC textile strike (1929) 265, 285
Gastonia NC textile workers 3, 265
Geese faction 66–69, 71, 73, 133
general strike, Britain (1926) See British General Strike
general strike, Seattle (1919) 76–77
general strike, Winnipeg (1919) 76
Genovese, Eugene 362n1
George, Harrison 78, 95–96
Gerisch, Grigory M. 169n1
German American socialists 27, 47, 154

German Communist Party 12, 14, 18, 183, 198, 270, 366
German Communists 35, 18, 55, 96, 169n1, 213–214, 269, 331
See also German Communist Party; Liebknecht, Karl; Luxemburg; Spartakists
German federation 28n1, 54, 127, 132, 154, 156, 174, 182–183, 190
See also Lore, Ludwig
German Revolution (1923) 20, 55, 136, 160
German Revolution, defeat of 13, 120, 136, 152, 223, 251n2
German Social Democracy 12, 24, 31, 38, 113, 154, 156, 366
Germer, Adolph 36–38, 46
Gitlow, Benjamin
and Bolshevisation 182
and *Revolutionary Age* 282n-284
and Stalin 272, 278, 284
as CP candidate 146–147, 149
as Lovestone lieutenant 209–211, 216–217n, 269–275, 277–284
break with Communism 284
election to NY Assembly 28–29
expulsion from ACWA 149
in Communist Labor Party 40, 78
in ILD 201, 204
in Ruthenberg faction of CP 134n1, 182, 188
in Socialist Party left wing 28–29, 38–40
later anti-Communism 66n2, 123
on Cannon 259n2, 264
on Negro work 312, 336–337n1
on Pepper 123, 139, 167–168, 275n3
on Trotsky 229, 259n2
prosecution of 35, 51, 200
removal from PB 279, 281
split with CPPA 146
trade union background 108, 134
vs Bukharin 270, 272–273n
work in needle trades 108, 149, 188, 192
See also Lovestone faction; Ruthenberg faction
Glotzer, Albert 261–262n
Goldfarb, Max (Petrovsky) See Petrovsky
Goldfield, Michael 11, 344n2, 366–367
Goldman, Emma 50, 94
Gomez, Manuel (Shipman) 187, 253–255n, 264, 269, 331, 337n2, 349, 352
Gompers, Samuel
anti-Communism of 107, 125–126, 144
Communists on 83, 88, 91–92, 103, 115
pro-capitalism of 25, 75, 100
opposition to within AFL 75, 124
support for WWI 100
vs Fitzpatrick 108, 118
vs Foster 100, 103, 107
vs TUEL 106–107, 118
'Great Migration' See black migration to North
Greek federation 173
Green (Gusev) See Gusev, Sergei Ivanovich
Green, W.H. (FFLP) 126
Green, William (UMWA & AFL) 125, 193, 324
Grove (Amter) See Amter, Israel
Guardian (Boston) 317
Guomindang (Kuomintang) 213, 225n1, 331
See also Chiang Kai-shek; China
Gurvitch (Hourwich) See Hourwich, Nicholas
Gusev, Sergei Ivanovich 163–169, 188, 194, 221, 267, 274
Gutman, Herbert 362n1
Gyptner, Richard 169n1

Haiti 325, 327, 352
Hallas, Duncan 152
Hall, Gus (Arvo Holberg) 185n2
Hall, Haywood (Harry Haywood) See Haywood, Harry
Hall, Otto (Carl Jones) 332, 337, 341, 343, 346–349, 351, 356–357, 360, 362
Halonen, Arne 175–176
Harding, Warren 69, 113, 310n2
Hardman, J.B.S. (Salutsky) See Salutsky, Jacob
Hardy, George 78, 80–82, 88, 94, 96
Harlem
ABB in 23, 299, 303
black Communists in 4n2, 287, 291, 297, 299, 362
black Socialists in 291, 299–300
See also African Black Brotherhood
Harlem branch(es) of CP 287, 300, 338
Harlem Renaissance 288
Harlem Socialist Party 299–300
Harlem Tenants League 335, 359
Harlem Unitarian church 358
Harriman, Job 25, 27

Harris, Abram L. 338n1
Harrison, Caleb 198
Harrison, Hubert 290
Harvey, Harold 96
Hathaway, Clarence 144, 332
Haymarket police riot (1886) 51n3–52, 325
Haynes, John Earl 8, 14–15, 17, 19
Haywood, Harry (Haywood Hall) 208, 252n, 295–296, 322–323, 332, 337, 343–344n2, 346–351, 357
Haywood, William D. 25–26, 28, 78–80, 82, 89–91, 94, 96, 100, 102–103, 106–107, 200, 203
Healy, Timothy 198n3
Heimo, Mauno 169n1
Henderson, Arthur 115
Hendricks, Arthur 291n
Henry (George Ashkenudzie) See Ashkenudzie, George
Herberg, Will 272, 282n3
Herndon, Angelo 362–363n1
Hill, Joe 99
Hillman, Sidney 104, 108, 124, 148–149
Hillquit, Morris 25–28, 35, 37–39, 55–57, 114, 116, 150
historians, anti-Communist 9, 284
historiography
  of American Communism 3–7
  post-Soviet 7–9
Hitler, Adolf 366
Holberg, Arvo (Hall) See Hall, Gus
Holland 305
Holmes, Rev. John Haynes 199
Hoover, Herbert 3, 198
Hoover, J. Edgar 3–4, 8, 52
Horthy, Miklós 155
Horwitz, Maksymilian (Valetski) See Valetski, Henryk
Hourwich, Isaac 29, 172n1
Hourwich, Nicholas 15, 29–30n1, 39, 54, 90, 172, 176–177n
Howard University 317
Howard, Walter T. 363
Howe, Frederic C. 116
Huiswoud, Hermina Dumont 291n, 306
Huiswoud, Otto
  and ANLC 322–323
  and CP factionalism 312, 323
  at 4th Comintern Congress 71, 306, 340
  at Minnesota FLP convention 313
  black Communist 71, 145, 291, 297, 300, 312, 334–336, 358
  black Socialist 290–291, 296–297
  break with Lovestone 279–280n1, 359
  head of Negro Commission 358
  immigrant background 290, 297, 336
  in African Blood Brotherhood 298, 306
  influences on 290–291
  in Lovestone faction 271n2, 279, 323, 359
  in Moscow 71, 271, 273–274n1, 306
  on legalisation 71, 306
  on 'Negro question' 306–307, 312–313, 338, 360
  on trade union bureaucracy 306, 340n1
  stand vs racism in FLP 144, 313, 338
  suspension from CP 145, 313, 338
  work within Comintern 280n1, 359–360
Humbert-Droz, Jules 159, 163, 169n1, 281
Hungarian Communists 190, 201, 235, 344
  See also Hungarian federation; Kun; Pepper
Hungarian federation 120–121, 173, 182, 190
Hungarian federation, and Pepper 66, 120–121, 182, 192
Hungarian Revolution (1919) 35, 55, 66, 120
Hungary 155, 223, 349
Hutcheson, William 109–110

IFWU See International Fur Workers Union
ILD See International Labor Defense
ILGWU See International Ladies' Garment Workers' Union
illegality, debate over 6, 14–15, 21, 50, 52–55, 58–63, 65–73, 92
  See also Geese faction; Liquidator faction; underground CP
immigrant workers, defence of 175, 197
India 271, 304, 317, 325, 352
Indonesia, Communists in 2
Industrial Pioneer 88–89
industrial unionism 30, 107, 125
Industrial Unionist 88–89n
Industrial Worker 78, 82, 98
Industrial Workers of the World (IWW)
  affiliation with Comintern 80, 83, 93
  affiliation with Profintern 90–91

and Socialist Party 26, 76
anti-Communism in 80–82, 87–92, 94
black members 102, 290, 297, 324
Communist fractions in 88, 94–95
Communist orientation to 21, 40, 75–76, 78, 80, 83–88, 93–97, 107
Communist recruitment from 21, 25–26, 77–79, 81, 83, 88–90, 92–98, 102–103, 200, 297, 324
decline 93–95
dual unionism 75, 83–84, 87, 90, 98–99, 107
expulsion of Communists 94
foreign-language federations 45, 96
Foster's history in 98–102
immigrants in 178
political program 25
press of 79–82, 88–89
repression of 26, 28, 78–82, 89–90n1, 93–94, 96–97, 100, 197, 199–200, 202
stance towards Communists 79–83, 86–90, 92–95, 203
strikes, involvement in 26, 90, 101–102, 190
See also anarchists; Haywood, William D.; syndicalists; Wobblies
Institute of World Economy and Politics 241
intermarriage See interracial marriage
International Communist Opposition 283
International Fur Workers Union (IFWU) 108
internationalism 5, 30, 224, 238, 247, 363n-364n
International Labor Defense (ILD) 90n1, 96, 187, 193, 197–204, 259–260n1
International Ladies' Garment Workers' Union 108, 125–126, 148–149, 188, 208, 282
International Left Opposition 22, 143, 213, 264, 282–283
See also Left Opposition (Trotskyist)
International Press Correspondence 228, 267n3, 280n1, 307
International Publishers 157n1
International Red Aid (IRA) 198, 200
International Socialist Review 25, 26n1, 28, 30, 289
International Trade Union Committee of Negro Workers 333, 359
International Trade Union Educational League 99
International Workers Aid 198
International Workers Defense Committee 200
International Workers Order (IWO) 184–185, 285
interracial dancing 362
interracial marriage 314, 318, 323, 330–331
interracial sex 310, 311n2
IRA See International Red Aid
Ireland 76, 84n1, 298, 342–343, 349, 358n1, 361
Irish American workers, in AFL 76
Irish, CP work among 312
Isserman, Maurice 4n2, 8
Italian Communists 6, 24, 213, 282n1
Italian federation 173, 183
Italy 6, 198
ITUC-NW See International Trade Union Committee of Negro Workers
IWO See International Workers Order
IWW See Industrial Workers of the World
Izvestia 307

Jakira, A. (Jack) 321, 323n1
Jamaica 296, 311n2
James, Winston 299
Japan 235, 304
Japanese Americans, in Socialist Left Wing 33n2
Japanese Communists 305, 315
See also Katayama, Sen
Japanese immigrants, and CP 11–12n1
Japanese section of CP 315
Java 305
Jewish Americans, radicalism among 178
Jewish Bund, in Russia 47, 65, 172
Jewish Communists 65, 69, 76, 120, 174, 178–179, 184, 209, 230n1, 362
support for Trotsky among 229–230n1, 250
Jewish federation, of Communist Party 132, 155, 173, 177, 183, 190, 229 6, 7, 8, 11
See also Yiddish federation
Jewish federation, of Socialist Party 31, 46, 56, 175
See also Yiddish federation

Jewish garment workers 108, 127, 174, 188, 190
Jewish People's Fraternal Organization 184
Jewish question 307, 317, 346–347, 361
Jewish schools in Uzbekistan 320n1
Jewish Socialist Federation (JSF) 56–61
Jewish Socialists 27, 56, 108, 174–175
Jewish workers, in AFL 76
Jews
  Communist support among 174, 178
  European 317
  in Russia 307, 346–347
Jim Crow, fight against 287, 298, 323, 335, 353–354, 360–362, 366
'Jim Crowism' in Communist Party 334n, 335, 354
Johnstone, Jack 102, 126n3, 188, 209n2–210, 221, 254n3–255, 271n2, 361
Johnson, James Weldon 317
Johnson, Oakley 207n2, 243
Johnson, Timothy V. 360n3
Joint Opposition (Zinoviev, Kamenev, Trotsky) 205, 218, 226, 229, 242–243
Jones, Carl 252n, 332, 347n1, 348n2
Jones, David Ivon 304–307
Jones, James Wormley 303

Kadalie, Clement 323
Kamenev, Lev 13, 136, 141, 156, 205, 224, 227, 229, 243
Kane, H.F. 82
Karsner, Rose 198, 201, 204, 259
Katayama, Sen 19n2, 33, 71, 177, 254n1–255, 293–294, 305–306, 313–316n1, 328, 341–342, 345, 352
Katterfeld, Ludwig 37, 60, 71, 73, 310
Kautsky, Karl 19n3, 24, 55, 79, 113, 233, 246
Kazin, Michael 10
Keiser, John 104
Kelley, Robin D.G. 5, 362
Kellogg, Paul 153n1
Kendall, Walter 153n1
Keracher, John 42
Kerr, Charles H. & Co. See Charles H. Kerr & Co.
Khitarov, Rafael 275
Klehr, Harvey 5, 8–9n1, 19, 234n2, 235, 247, 347n2, 360
Knights of Columbus 246n1
Kolarov, Vasil 274
Kollontai, Alexandra 29–30n1, 32n2–33, 40, 293
Konikow, Antoinette 229–230, 250, 261–262
Korea 342n1
Kornfeder, Joseph Zack 204
Kouyaté, Tiemoko Garan 363n2
Krasnoschekov, A.M. 96n3
Kravitz, Duddy 2
Krestintern 126, 326, 332n2
Krumbein, Charles 119, 209n2
Krupskaya, Nadezhda 227
Kruse, William F. 56–57, 61, 169, 192, 349
Kuhn, Henry 41
Ku Klux Klan 91, 131, 303
Kun, Béla 120, 169n1, 241, 274, 278
Kuomintang See Guomindang
KUTV See Communist University of Toilers of the East
Kuusinen, Aino 184
Kuusinen, Otto 53, 63, 69, 79, 91, 159, 163, 166, 169n1, 173, 179, 184, 211, 214, 236, 274, 277–278, 280

Labor Defender 96, 201–204
Labor Defense Council (LDC) 72, 110, 199–201
Labor Herald 105–106, 109, 117–118, 144
Labor Monthly 174
Labor Unity 362
labour movement
  and black workers 288, 290, 296, 324, 339–340
  and defence work 72, 197, 199
  and language 47, 67, 69, 172
  and TUEL 118, 161, 194–195
  Communist influence in 2, 20, 22, 67, 117, 187–189, 195, 197, 203, 367
  Communist work in 6, 17, 21, 50, 69, 74–111, 242, 283, 286
  Communist isolation from 21–22, 112, 124, 126–127, 129, 148, 150, 195, 274–275
  Communist recruitment from 24, 122
  Jewish leftists in 172n1, 178
  political consciousness of 8, 189, 233, 239
  repression of 34, 130

See also AFL; individual unions; Passaic NJ textile strikes; trade union bureaucracy; trade unions; strike wave
labour party movement 21, 70–71, 112–119, 122, 128, 141, 160–161, 189, 215, 233, 246
La Follette movement
Bittelman on 132, 151
Bolshevik debate over 136, 139–141
Browder on 151
Cannon on 146, 158
Comintern on 16, 22, 141–142, 146–148, 150–151, 156, 161
Communist support for 14, 22, 112, 131–135, 140–141, 144–146, 150, 161, 187 decline of movement 147
Foster on 140, 144, 151, 158, 244n1
left support for 114, 130, 134–135, 145–147, 149–150
Lore on 154
Lovestone on 131n1, 147
Lozovsky on 141
Pepper on 131, 142, 158
Ruthenberg on 132, 135, 147, 155, 160–161
Trotsky on 22, 140–142
Zinoviev on 141
La Follette, Robert M. 22, 112–113, 130
campaign 130, 146–147
vs Communists 144–145
language federations See foreign-language federations
Larkin, James 19n2, 35n2, 36, 38–39, 51, 74, 76, 200
Latin America
Communists 78, 244, 271n2, 316–317, 332, 352
imperialism in 223
Lovestone on 244
Latvia, and Rozins 30n2, 32
Latvians in Socialist Propaganda League 30, 46
Lauki, Leo 96
Lawrence MA textile strike (1912) 26
LDC See Legal Defense Council
League Against Imperialism 331
League for Industrial Democracy 198n3
League for Socialist Propaganda 40
Lee, Algernon 300
Left Opposition (CPA, 1921–22) 62, 64, 66, 68–69, 71, 206n1
Left Opposition (Trotskyist) 22, 136, 143, 153–154, 157, 213, 228–231, 249–251n2, 257, 260–264, 282–283 See also International Left Opposition; Trotsky; Trotskyists
Left Wing Manifesto (1919) 35, 291
left wing, of Socialist Party See Socialist Party, left wing
legal defence work See class-war prisoners; ILD; LDC; Sacco and Vanzetti case; Scottsboro Boys
Legal Defense Council 110
legal repression
against strikers 81n1, 195, 199
of anarchists 50
of blacks 296, 303–304, 362
of Communists 35n2, 42–43n5, 50–52, 65–66, 72, 74, 76, 107, 197, 199–200, 202, 207, 213, 303–304, 360–363
of IWW 28, 78–82, 89–90n1, 93–94, 96–97, 100, 197, 199–200, 202
of labour movement 26n1, 35, 100, 107, 195, 199–200, 202, 362
of Socialists 28, 32–33, 35–36, 199
See also class-war prisoners; criminal anarchy; Debs; Department of Justice; FBI
legality of Communist Party 6, 14–15, 21, 50, 52–55, 58–63, 65–73
See also Geese faction; Liquidator faction; underground CP
Leninism 5, 19–20n, 143n1, 153, 156, 159, 231, 234n2, 247, 260, 340
See also Bolshevism; Trotskyism
Leninism vs Stalinism 6, 17, 19, 234n2, 247, 258, 260
Lenin school (Moscow) 169, 258, 271, 332, 336
Lenin, V.I.
and Comintern 1, 5–6, 54, 86
and IWW 78–79, 81, 86, 88–89, 94, 97
and left Socialists 29–34, 40, 104
and Reed 86, 137n3, 285–286, 294
and Stalin 17, 227–228, 343
and Trotsky 1, 5, 227
arguments with American Communists 15, 47, 54, 84, 86, 103, 173, 285

Lenin, V.I. (*cont.*)
death of 136, 152, 208, 227–228
in United States 29, 40
on British Labour Party 84, 115
on capitalism/imperialism 223, 238, 247
on critical support 115
on democratic-centralism 31, 173
on English language 29, 47, 54, 84, 173
on national question 292–293, 343
on need for legal party 54, 69
on 'Negro question' 293–294, 301, 339, 342–343, 352
on NY Public Library viii, 6n2
on SPL 30–34
on trade unions 47–48, 83–84, 86, 103, 233
on united front tactic 50
opponents of 56
'Testament' 227–228
vs reformism 6, 79
vs syndicalism 79, 86, 97
vs ultraleftism 31, 49–50, 83–85, 115, 285–286
Leonhard, Wolfgang 7n2
Lettish federation 121n1
Lewis, John L. 3, 74–75, 109n2, 125n2–126, 212, 251–252
See also United Mine Workers of America
l'Humanité 228
Liberator 34, 79, 174, 227, 297, 310n2, 362
Liebknecht, Karl 12, 208n2, 55
Liebknecht, Wilhelm 208n2
Lih, Lars T. 19–20n, 228n1
Liquidator faction 66–73
Lithuanian federation 173, 183
Lominadze, Vissarion V. 13, 251, 255–258
longshore workers 285, 324
Lore, Ludwig
and CP language federations 127, 132, 155, 174
and FLP 127, 132–133, 156, 182
and 'Negro question' 292, 322n2
and Trotsky 33, 138, 143, 154, 157, 230
and Trotskyism 138, 142–143, 154–158, 250
campaign against in CP 144, 154–158, 161–162, 164, 216, 227, 250
in Socialist Party left wing 27, 33, 154
purged from CP 157–158, 227
Lossieff, Vladimir 82, 89–90n, 96
L'Ouverture, Toussaint 325
Lovestone faction
anti-Trotskyism 226, 228–231, 237, 260, 262, 264, 266, 283
black supporters 279–280n1, 323, 330, 336, 340, 352, 359
defections from 278–280, 359
expulsions from CP 282, 276, 281–282
later anti-Communism 284
on 'Negro question' 254, 341, 349, 352, 357–359
on TUEL 194, 212
purged from CP 278–271
Right Opposition 283
supporters of 209–211, 216, 220, 225, 244, 247n1, 257, 259, 264, 268, 271–272, 278, 284, 333
vs Foster faction 163–164, 169–170, 192, 203, 209–210, 212–215, 217–221, 244n1, 252–253, 257, 262, 269–271, 273–275, 277, 284, 337, 352, 357–359
See also Lovestone; *Revolutionary Age*
Lovestone, Jay
and 'American exceptionalism' 231–233, 241, 243–248, 274–276, 356
and Bolshevisation 180–181, 183, 185
and Comintern 22, 143, 159, 165–169, 179, 192, 205, 208–222, 225–226, 228, 231–233, 237–238, 240, 244, 247–248, 252–257, 259, 262, 266–282, 285–286, 336–337, 352, 359
and death of Ruthenberg 22, 207–209, 219, 243
and farmer-labour movement 122, 126, 131n1, 143, 147, 158
and Passaic strike 192n2
and Stalin 22, 213, 225, 231–232, 238, 240, 242, 247, 254–256, 266, 268, 270, 272–273, 275–276, 278, 282, 284, 286, 356
and Stalinisation of CP 22, 225, 232, 240–241, 247–248, 283, 286
and 'white chauvinism' 337–338, 340–341, 352
anti-Trotskyism 156–157, 226, 228–231, 237–238, 240–241, 259–263, 266, 282–283, 285, 339

as CP leader 12, 22, 68, 165, 207–209, 211, 216, 219, 221, 231–232, 237, 248, 250, 257, 260–262, 265–266, 270, 273, 278
as factionalist 133, 156–158, 163–164, 168, 171, 192n1, 207–212, 215–222, 228, 232, 243–244, 259–262, 266, 271, 275, 284, 338n3
as Pepper supporter 122, 126, 143, 156, 158–159, 166–168, 205, 208–210, 214, 222, 225–226, 232–233, 237, 241–243, 253, 255–257, 269–270, 272–273, 275, 357
as 'Right Danger' 252–255, 260, 262, 266, 337
as Ruthenberg supporter 122, 126, 157–159, 164–166, 169, 171, 183, 194, 205–209, 219, 241–243
background 134, 230, 263n1
biographies 11
bloc with Bukharin 22, 225, 238, 229, 240, 242, 245–247, 253–256, 266, 270–273, 282–283
expulsion from CP 13–14, 248, 276, 280–282, 284, 286, 338, 356, 359, 365
fall of 23
later anti-Communism 209, 272, 284, 338
on American capitalism 22, 215, 231–233, 237, 240–247, 253, 268, 275, 340
on CP black work 322, 330, 337–341, 352
on foreign-language federations 179–181, 183
on ILD 203–204
on Latin America 244
on legality of CP 53, 66–67
on 'Negro question' 338–341, 347, 349, 353n2, 356–357
personal nastiness 209–210, 212, 286, 338n3
purged from CP 278–282, 284, 286, 338, 356, 359–360
purged from Comintern 281
vs Cannon 169–171, 203–204, 206–209, 211–212, 214, 217, 219–222, 242n1, 252–254, 257, 259–266, 283, 337, 352, 357
vs Foster 166, 209–212, 221, 225, 231, 242, 244n1, 252–254, 259, 262–263, 266, 277, 282, 352
vs Trotsky 229, 237–238, 240–241, 247, 266, 284, 339
vs Trotskyists 156–157, 259–263, 266
vs Weinstone 211, 275, 277, 279
See also Lovestone faction; Ruthenberg-Lovestone faction
Lovett, Robert Morss 198n3f
Lozovsky (Solomon Abramovich Dridzo) 13, 80, 87, 90, 119, 141, 225–226n, 251, 255–257n, 263, 273–274n, 332–334n, 361
Lundberg, Ferdinand 130
Lusk Committee 52
Luxemburg, Rosa 12, 55
lynching 307, 311, 315, 318, 335, 348, 354, 362

MacDonald, Duncan 145–146
Macon GA 362
Mahoney, Roy 252n1
Mahoney, William 134, 146
Manley, Joseph 123, 139, 145
Manner, Kullervo 184
Mann, Tom 87, 98
Manuilsky, Dmitry 163, 274
March Action (Germany 1921) 120
Mariátegui, José Carlos 355n3
maritime workers 95, 285, 316–317
Markowitz, Norman vii, 364
Marshall, James (Max Bedacht) See Bedacht, Max
Marxist economics 241n2
Marx, Karl 47, 233n3, 235n1, 246–247, 339, 357
Massachusetts 30, 37, 174, 197, 199, 285, 330
Masses 28, 227
Matusevich, Maxim 305
Mauer, George 199
Maurín, Joaquín 87
Maxwell, William J. 330
Mazut, Bob 343
McDermott, Kevin 17, 152
McKay, Claude 71n2, 231, 297–298, 306–307, 309–311, 314–316, 321, 330, 342
McNamara case (Los Angeles) 26n1
Medical Relief Committee for Soviet Russia 198
membership dues 2n2, 43, 45, 108, 173, 180, 183, 184n
membership figures, Communist 2, 18, 41–43, 45, 62, 64, 96, 109, 120, 126, 173, 177, 183, 285, 287, 362

membership figures, Socialist 26n1, 29, 37, 39, 41, 45
Mensheviks 29, 140, 163, 256, 309, 356
Merrick, John 202
Messenger 290, 295–296, 301n2, 303n
Mexican Communist Party 157, 244, 271n2
Michels, Tony 173, 175
Militant 120n2, 253n1, 262, 264, 283, 337n2
Miller, Bert (Benjamin Mandel) 191–192
Miller, Kelly 317
Miller, William 271n2, 274n1, 280n–281n
Milwaukee Leader 173
miners
  black miners 335, 337, 363
  British miners 238–239
  Communist work among 3, 189, 250, 337, 363
  imprisoned 200–201
  in Communist Party 77
  South African racist mine strike 304–305
  See also British General Strike; Lewis; National Miners Union; United Mine Workers of America
Mink, George 96
Minneapolis Teamsters strike (1934) 283
Minnesota Communists 132, 261
Minnesota convention (FFLP, 1924) 131, 134, 140, 142, 144–146, 160, 338
Minnesota Farmer Labor Party 134, 146, 313
Minnesota FLP See Minnesota Farmer-Labor Party
Minnesota mine strike (1916) 81
Minor, Robert (Duncan) 66, 68–69, 89–90, 108, 139, 143, 207–210n1, 214, 226, 242, 271, 279–280, 285, 321, 323, 325, 330, 332, 357
Molotov, V.M. 13, 228n1, 254–255n1, 274, 276–278
Monatte, Pierre 134n1
Montgomery, David 362n1
Mooney, Tom 46n2, 200, 202
Moore (Ballam) See Ballam, John J.
Moore, Richard B. 299–300, 322–323, 325, 327, 330–331, 334–337n, 347, 358–359
MOPR See International Red Aid
Morrow, Fred 69n1
Mother Jones 122
Münzenberg, Willi 198, 331
Murphy, J.T. 78, 85, 87
Murray, Phil 125
Murray, Robert 51
Myerscough, Thomas 271n2, 274n1, 280n1, 281n1

NAACP See National Association for the Advancement of Colored People
Naison, Mark 360, 362
Napoleon, Trotsky compared to 137n2
Nasanov, Nikolai Mikhailovich (Charlie) 332, 346–351
National Association for the Advancement of Colored People (NAACP) 295–296, 310n2, 317, 331
National Committee of the Opposition Bloc 217–218
National Defense Committee (of CPA) 199–200
National Left Wing Conference, of SP (1919) 38
National Miners Union 363
national question
  and 'Negro question' 323, 343–344, 346, 349–351, 355–358, 360n3–361
  Bolsheviks on 292, 343
  in tsarist Russia 292, 307, 346
  Stalin on 340, 343–344, 346–347n, 355–356
  See also Quebec; self-determination
National War Labor Board 34
'Native Republic' slogan (South Africa) 346n1, 355, 357
Naye Welt 56
Nearing, Scott 28
needle trades unions 77, 106, 108, 125, 127, 148–149, 174, 179, 188, 216, 250
  See also ACWA; fur workers; garment workers; Hillman; ILGWU; textile workers
Negro Champion 327, 335, 342, 359
Negro Commission of Comintern 304, 308, 313, 320, 330, 332, 336, 341, 345–356, 358
Negro Congress 294, 305–306, 308, 313–318, 359
'Negro nation' See ABB; 'Black Belt'; black nationalism; black self-determination; 'Negro Soviet Republic' slogan

'Negro question'
and Comintern 6–7, 254, 292–294, 301, 304–314, 323, 328, 331–332, 339, 341–359, 363
and Socialists 23, 288–291, 300–301, 307, 309, 319, 339–340
in Communist Party 6–7, 23, 254, 287, 289–292, 294–295, 301, 309–313, 315, 318–323, 328, 330–341, 343–344, 347–359, 363, 366
Lenin on 293–294, 301, 339, 342–343, 352
Pepper on 312, 330, 332n2, 334–335, 341–342, 347, 349–351, 353, 357–359
Trotsky on 309, 309–311, 343, 358n1
See also black oppression; black self-determination; racial discrimination; racial segregation
'Negro Race Congress' 335
'Negro Republic' slogan (South Africa) 345
Negro Sanhedrin 23, 317–318, 320
'Negro Soviet Republic' slogan 349, 351, 353, 357–359
Negro Workers' Congress See American Negro Labor Congress
Negro World 296, 302–303
Negro World Congress 294, 305–306, 308, 313–318, 359
Nelson, Steve 4
New Bedford MA textile strike (1928) 197, 285
New Bedford MA textile workers 3
New Deal, Communist support for 2, 20, 151, 364
New Left historians 4–5, 7–9
New Majority 100, 113
New Masses 230, 231n1
'New Negro' movement 288, 295–296, 339–340
New Republic 198n3
New Solidarity 79, 82n2, 88n3
New York Call 34, 37n2
New York City 28–29, 35n2, 50–52, 88–89, 137, 240, 288, 290
New York Communist 35
New York, Communists in 11, 60, 108–109, 134n1, 171, 177n2, 179, 181–182, 186, 188, 191, 206, 208, 211n1, 216, 221, 261, 264–265, 281–282, 298, 316–317, 335n2, 338, 361
New Yorker Volkszeitung 154–155, 157–158, 173–174
New York Herald 303
New York left wing, of Socialist Party 28–29, 32, 35–38, 56
New York Review of Books 4n2, 5
New York Times 51, 56–57, 102, 107, 228, 272, 280, 310, 327, 360n1
Niagara movement 317
Nicaragua 210
Nín, Andrés (Andreu Nin) 87
Nockels, Edward 100
Non-Partisan League 116, 135n2, 145
Noral, Alex 271n2, 274n1, 278
North Africa 325
Northern migration See black migration to North
Nourteva, Santeri 62
Novy Mir 33
Nurse, Malcolm (Padmore) See Padmore, George

October Revolution See Bolshevik Revolution
Oehler, Hugo 265
Ohio Socialist 42
Oklahoma See Tulsa race riot
Olgin, Moissaye J. 11, 56–57n1, 61, 127, 132–133, 137n3, 139–140, 142, 154–157n1, 173, 175n2
Oneal, James 246–247
One Big Union Monthly 81–84, 88–89n
Orenstein, Eugene 56–57n
organising the unorganised 84–85, 110, 175, 189, 194–196n, 212, 214, 239, 252, 333, 341
Owen, Chandler 290

Padmore, George 327, 361, 363n-364n
Palmer, A. Mitchell 50, 52
Palmer, Bryan 11–14, 16, 60, 120, 150, 164, 197–198, 251n2, 257–259, 330n
Palmer raids 50–52
pan-Africanism 298, 315, 363
See also Briggs; *Crusader*
Panama Canal strike (1920) 302
Pankhurst, Sylvia 16
Paris Commune (1871) 88
Parity Commission 162–164, 167, 321

Parker, Parley P. 113
parliamentarism 1, 5, 38, 40n1, 41, 52, 78–80, 84
  See also Socialist Party, electoral reformism
Parsons, Albert (Haymarket martyr) 325
Parsons, Lucy 325
Party Organizer 186
Passaic NJ textile strike (1912) 90, 190
Passaic NJ textile strike (1926–27) 22, 90, 189–193, 195–197, 199, 202–204, 214, 226n1, 242
  AFL role in 192–193, 196
  black workers in 327
  See also United Front Committee; Weisbord
Passaic NJ textile workers 3, 189–191
Paterson NJ silk workers strike (1912) 190–192
Patterson, William L. 252n, 330–331n, 335, 338n3, 340n3, 347
peaceful coexistence 137
peasantry 34, 141, 156, 249, 339, 341, 345–348, 350, 353, 360–361
Peasants' International See Krestintern
Pennsylvania 11, 363
Pepper, John (József Pogány)
  and British Communist Party 238–240n1
  and Bukharin 225, 253, 255–256, 270–272
  and Cannon 120–122, 127, 132–133, 138–139, 143, 155, 158–160, 162, 169–170, 209, 214, 222, 253, 256, 259
  and Comintern 120–122, 138–144, 156, 159–162, 165–170, 177, 194, 205, 208, 217, 222, 238–242, 255–257, 268–270, 273, 277, 330, 332n2, 341–342, 347, 349–351, 357–359
  and Foster 119, 121–122, 127–128, 132, 134n1, 138–141, 143, 158–162, 165–166, 168–170, 194, 205, 214, 217, 222, 253, 256–257, 269, 357–359
  and Stalin 142, 255–256, 357
  and Trotsky 137–138, 142–143n, 156, 226, 228, 237–238, 240–242, 259
  anti-Trotskyism 137–138, 142, 156, 226, 228, 241–242
  as CP leader 121–122, 159, 217, 222, 250, 250
  as factionalist 121, 127, 133, 138–139, 143, 158–160, 165–168, 182, 205, 209, 214, 222, 226, 256–257, 269
  background 120, 230n1
  biographies 11, 120–121, 123, 165
  Bittelman on 122–123n3, 127, 132–133, 138–139, 142, 169, 189, 275, 358on
  Pepper bloc with Lovestone 122, 126, 143, 156, 158–159, 166–168, 205, 208–210, 214, 222, 225–226, 232–233, 237, 241–243, 253, 255–257, 269–270, 272–273, 275, 357
  bloc with Ruthenberg 121–123, 126, 128–129, 131–133, 144, 156, 158–161, 166, 169–170, 182, 188–189, 194, 205, 208, 312
  expulsion from Comintern (1929) 273n2, 277n3
  Gitlow on 123, 139, 167–168, 275n3
  in Germany 120
  in Hungarian federation 120–121, 182, 192
  in Hungarian Revolution 120n2, 241
  interventions in CP 18, 21, 119–123, 130–133, 137–139, 142–143, 158–162, 165–166, 188–189, 222, 226, 228, 232–233, 243, 256–257, 269–270, 277, 330, 334–335, 349–351, 353n, 357–359
  on 'American exceptionalism' 232–233, 256
  on CP work among farmers 139–140
  on farmer-labour movement 21, 119, 122–123, 127–130, 139–142, 144, 160
  on FFLP 123, 126–131, 140
  on labour party slogan 160, 189, 233n2, 237
  on La Follette movement 131–133, 139
  on 'Negro question' 312, 330, 332n2, 334–335, 341–342, 347, 349–351, 353, 357–359
  on 'Negro Soviet Republic' 349, 351, 353, 357–359
  on TUEL 188–189, 194
  opportunism and adventurism 120, 122–123, 128, 131, 151, 243, 256–257
  opposition to 127–128, 133–134n1, 138–139, 143, 159–162, 222, 239, 253, 255–256, 341n3–342n1, 349
  personality 121, 133, 341n3–342n1
  readmission to Comintern (1932) 277n3

supporters in CP 139, 143, 167–168
support for capitalist politicians 131–133
trial and execution (1937–38) 120, 277n3
vs Finnish federation 182
vs Lore 132, 142–143, 154–155, 182
permanent revolution 49, 137, 156, 358n1
Peru 355
Peterson (Allan Wallenius) 186n1
Petrograd Pravda 176
Petrovsky (Max Goldfarb, A.J. Bennett) 17, 19n2, 56–57n, 176, 210, 255, 332, 349–351, 352
Philadelphia dockers union, expulsion of IWW 81
Phillips, H.V. 325n, 335–336, 340n3, 347
Piatnitsky, Osip 263n1
Plekhanov, Georgi 230, 233, 246
Plessy v. Ferguson 289
Pogány, József (Pepper) See Pepper, John
Polish federation 173, 190
political prisoners 79, 81n1, 93, 96, 197, 199–202
See also International Labor Defense; legal repression; Sacco and Vanzetti case
Pollitt, Harry 269, 273–274n
Popular Front 10, 20, 140, 151, 247n1, 249, 363, 365–366
Post Office, anti-leftist actions 28
Pravda 280
Preobrazhensky, Evgeny 241
press, Communist 15, 80–81, 89, 92, 121, 154–155, 158, 173–174, 181, 185–187, 266–267, 295, 319, 322, 327, 335, 361
press, foreign-language See foreign-language federations, press of
Profintern (Red International of Labour Unions)
and 'Negro question' 280n1, 315, 332–334, 360–361
and TUEL 106, 108
CP factionalism in 225–226n1, 271n2
founding 86, 98
First Profintern Congress 87, 89–91, 102, 134n1
Fourth Profintern Congress 332–334
IWW hostility 92–94
Second Profintern Congress 93, 102
syndicalists in 87–94, 96, 103, 134n1
See also Lozovsky
Progressive movement 22, 112–113, 128–129, 130, 141, 144
See also farmer-labour movement; Federated Farmer-Labor Party; La Follette movement
Proletarian Party 42
Prometheus Research Library 7n2, 11, 97n1
Prusdon, David 174
pseudonyms, use of 7n2–8n1, 110
Pullman porters 327, 337

Quebec, national question 355, 358n1

racial discrimination See black oppression; Jim Crow; lynching; racial segregation; racist violence
racial segregation 287, 289, 293, 298, 304n3–305n1, 318, 320, 323, 333–335, 338, 348–349, 353–354, 358n1, 361–362, 366
See also Jim Crow
racist violence 287–289, 291–292, 295, 299–300, 307, 311, 315, 318, 335, 348, 353–354, 362–363
See also lynching
Radek, Karl 53–54, 69, 83–86, 89–91, 97, 102n3, 124, 141, 156, 173, 311
railway strike (1922) 65, 107, 114
railway unions 108, 114, 130, 289
See also railway strike (1922)
Rákosi, Mátyás 63, 201
Randolph, A. Philip 290–291, 295, 297, 303, 324, 326, 337
Rand School 56
Rebel Worker 79
Reconstruction 289, 296, 356
Red Army 80, 136, 156–157
Red International of Labour Unions (RILU) See Profintern
Red Peasant International See Krestintern
Red Scare 2, 15, 21, 40, 50–52, 66, 74, 197, 199, 365
See also class-war prisoners; legal repression
red unions See dual unionism
Reed, John
and Comintern jewels 44n
and Communist Labor Party 40, 44
and IWW 78–82, 84–86

Reed, John (*cont.*)
and Lenin 86, 285, 294
CLP-CPA unity talks 44, 47
death of 286
in Socialist Party 35–36, 38, 40, 172
nominated to ECCI 86, 286
on AFL 84–86
on Bolshevik Revolution 1, 34–35, 79, 137n3
on 'Negro question' 84, 293–294, 313, 345
on Trotsky 137n3
on trade union question 84–86
trial (Philadelphia, 1919) 294n1
Reinstein, Anna 66
Reinstein, Boris 17, 19n2, 40–41, 63, 65–66, 71, 83, 90, 120, 169n1, 176
repression See legal repression
Republican Party 3, 52, 75, 114, 130–131, 133–135, 142, 144, 147, 160, 310n2
See also La Follette
retail clerks union 134n1
Revolutionary Age 32n2, 34, 38, 46, 114, 282–284, 291–292
Richler, Mordecai 2
Richmond VA 338, 362
'Right Danger' document 252–255, 260–262, 337
Right Opposition (Bukharin) 240n2, 283
See also Bukharin
RILU See Profintern
Rojahn, Jürgen 16
Roosevelt, Franklin D.
Communist attacks on 365
Communist support for 151
Rosen, Morris (Mike Ross) 109–110
Rosmer, Alfred 86–87, 103, 134n1
Ross, Mike (Rosen) See Rosen, Morris
Rothstein, Andrew (Roebuck) 227–228n1
Roy, M.N. 19n2, 240n2, 283
Rozins, Fricis 30, 32
Russia See Bolshevik Revolution; famine; Lenin; Soviet Union; Stalin; Trotsky
Russian Communist Party
and American CP 136
anti-Trotsky fight in 136–138, 140, 153–159, 163, 205, 224–231, 242–243n, 250–251, 253–254, 262–264
ethnic composition of CC 293
farmer-labour debate 140–141, 156
Stalin vs Bukharin 242n, 266, 269–270, 283
See also Bolsheviks; Bukharin; Lenin; Stalin; Trotsky; Zinoviev
Russian federation, of Communist Party 15, 172, 176–177, 182, 190
Russian federation, of Socialist Party 39
Russian immigrants, in Communist Party 15, 19n2, 27, 29–33, 40, 47, 53–54, 56, 65–66, 70, 82, 96, 133, 156, 163, 176–177, 229–230
Russian Revolution (February 1917) 33–34, 67n1, 131
Russian Revolution (November 1917) See Bolshevik Revolution
Rutgers, S.J. 19n2, 27, 30, 32, 291
Ruthenberg, Charles Emil (C.E.)
and Cannon 122, 169–171, 203, 206–207, 242–243n
and CPPA 117, 135
and FFLP 122–123, 126, 128–129, 131–132, 134–135, 142, 155
and Lovestone 122, 126, 157, 159, 165–166, 169, 207–211, 214, 219, 225, 241–243
and Passaic strike 189–192
and Pepper 121–123, 126, 128–129, 131–133, 144, 156, 158–161, 166, 169–170, 182, 188–189, 194, 205, 208, 312
anti-war stance 32
arrests and imprisonment 65, 72, 200, 207–208n1
death of 22, 72, 207–211, 223n1, 243
defence of immigrants 175
election campaigns 32
formation of CPA 40
formation of UCP 42–43
fusion of CPA & UCP 47–48
in Cleveland elections 32, 117
in ILD 201, 203–204
in Socialist Party left 27–28, 32, 36, 38–39, 41n5, 172
on ABB 312
on ANLC 322–323, 325
on Bolshevik Revolution 6
on Bolshevisation 182–183
on economic crisis 223n-224n, 239
on foreign-language federations 182–183, 190

on La Follette movement 131–132, 134–135, 140, 142, 145, 147, 151, 155, 160–161
on legality of CP 53, 66–68, 73
on 'Negro question' 312, 322
on recruiting farmers 126
political history 172, 207
split with CPA 42–43
vs Foster-Cannon faction 128, 133, 138, 144, 158–170, 203, 330
vs Foster faction 170, 182, 188–189, 192, 194–195, 206–207, 210, 218, 240, 242
vs foreign-language federations 45
vs IWW 81, 95
vs Trotsky 138, 156–158
Ruthenberg faction 133–134n1, 138, 155, 157–171, 182, 187–192, 194–195, 206–207, 218–219, 239, 242–243n, 321–323, 328–330
See also Gitlow; Lovestone; Pepper; Ruthenberg; Ruthenberg-Lovestone faction; Weisbord
Ruthenberg-Lovestone faction 157–158, 194, 205, 207–211, 214, 219, 225, 241–243, 330
Ryan, James 153

Sacco and Vanzetti case ix, 3, 22, 187, 201–204, 219, 330
Sacco, Nicola 3, 187, 201–204, 219, 330
sailors, Communist work among 95, 285, 316–317
Saklatvala, S.D. 325
Sakmyster, Thomas 121, 165, 226n2, 233n2, 349n, 357n2
Salutsky, Jacob (J.B.S. Hardman) 31, 35, 56–57, 60–61, 68, 108, 111, 121, 124, 148n3–149
Sandgren, John 80, 82, 88
Sanhedrin conference (1924) 23, 317–318, 320
Santo Domingo 352
Saposs, David 125
Sapronov, Timofei 258
Scandinavian federation 45n1, 183
Scheidemann, Philipp 38
Schuyler, George S. 317
Scottsboro Boys 287, 362
Seattle Central Labor Council 75
Seattle general strike (1919) 76–77
Second Comintern Congress (1920) See Communist International congresses
Second International 1, 24, 26, 29, 31, 39, 55, 343
sedition 199
Segal, Edith 362
Seidman, Joel 149–150
self-determination
and 'Negro question' in US 23, 309, 320, 330, 342, 344–361, 365–366
and Stalinisation 355–356
right of 292–293, 309, 320, 330, 343–345, 352, 355–356
See also black self-determination; national question; 'Negro question'
Serra (Angelo Tasca) 281–282n
Serrati, Giacinto 6, 19n2
sexism, in Communist Party 9
Shachtman, Max 51, 76, 164, 169, 204, 259–262, 265, 283, 344n1, 358n1
Shanghai massacre (1927) 20, 213, 258, 356
Shatov, Bill 96, 176–177
shop nuclei 180–181
Sigman, Morris 188
Simons, A.M. 246
Sinclair, Upton 201
Siskind, George 255n1
Sixth Comintern Congress (1928) See Communist International congresses
Sixth National Convention of CP (1929) 267, 269, 273
Skotnes, Andor 362
slaughterhouse workers strike (Chicago) 101, 193
slave rebellions 325
slavery 288–289, 298, 347
Slavic federations, of Socialist Party 29
Slovakian federation 182–183
Slovenian federation 45n1
SLP See Socialist Labor Party
Smith, Alfred 114
Smith, Vernon 96
social-chauvinism 1, 5, 15, 24, 343
Social Democratic Publishing Co. 173
Social Democrats See German Social Democracy; Second International; social democracy; Socialist Party; Socialists

social democracy 1, 5, 12, 19, 24, 26, 29–30, 32, 49–50, 52, 55, 75, 79–80, 112, 133, 154, 156–158, 184, 246–247n, 249, 290, 292, 343
See Communist Party, social-democratisation of; German Social Democracy; Second International; social democracy; Socialist Party; Socialists
'social fascism' 249, 366
'socialism in one country' 13, 17, 136–137, 140, 156, 205, 235, 240, 247, 258, 355n2, 360, 365
Socialist Cooperative Publishing Association 155
Socialist Labor Party (SLP) 25, 40–41, 43, 65, 77, 98, 174
Socialist Party (SP)
and Comintern 1, 29, 55–56
and Communist Party 2, 4, 16, 37, 58, 63, 78, 82, 150, 365
and needle trades unions 149, 188
anti-Bolshevism 55, 57
anti-war stance 24, 26–29, 55
black members 290–291, 297, 299–300, 339
'colour-blindness' 23, 288–290, 300–301, 309, 311, 314, 319, 324
election campaigns 28–29, 150, 300–301
electoral reformism 24–25, 41, 114, 130–131, 150
ethnic composition 45
foreign-language federations 29, 31, 36, 44–47, 56, 61–62, 172–175, 178, 184
in CPPA 114, 117
left wing 21, 25–30, 32, 34–41, 55–58, 76–77, 102, 114, 131, 154, 172–173, 175, 199–200, 289, 297
membership figures 26n1, 29, 41, 43n3, 45
'Negro question' 23, 288–291, 295–296, 300–301, 303, 307, 309, 319, 339–340
purges of left wing 26, 37–40, 55–56, 58
right wing 25–27, 31–32, 37, 39, 46, 56, 130–131, 150, 173, 289
splits from 2, 14, 26, 30–34, 37–40, 56–58, 61–62, 98, 150, 175, 300
support for La Follette 131n1, 146–147, 150
youth organisation 56
See also Berger; Debs; Hillquit; Workers' Council
Socialist Propaganda League (SPL) 30–34, 46
Socialists
and Comintern 1, 29, 39
and IWW 26, 83
and 'Negro question' 23, 288–291, 296, 300–301, 306, 309, 311, 314, 319, 324
and US history 233, 246–247
Communist recruitment of 41, 56–58, 61–62, 70, 77, 91, 96–98, 133, 154, 163, 190, 198, 207, 229–230, 291, 297, 299–301
Jewish Socialists 108, 174
repression of 28, 32–33, 35–36, 199
See also Second International; social democracy; Socialist Labor Party; Socialist Party; Socialist Propaganda League; Workers' Council
Society for Technical Aid for Russia 198
Solidarity 81–82, 88n2
Solntzev, Eleazar 230
Sombart, Werner 154, 233n3
Sorge, Friedrich 45
South Africa
Communist debates on 304–305, 307–308, 313–314, 345–346, 355, 357
'Native Republic' slogan 345–346, 355, 357
South African Communists 304–305, 307–308, 315, 317, 323, 326, 331, 345–346
South African (racist) mine strike 304
Southern Worker 360–361, 363n1
South Slav federation 183
Souvarine, Boris 63, 90n2, 134n1
Soviet bureaucracy 136–137, 140, 205, 249
See also Stalin, Joseph; Stalinism
'Soviet Negro Republic' See 'Negro Soviet Republic' slogan
Soviet Russia See Soviet Union
Soviet Russia Pictorial 174
soviets (workers councils) 33, 40, 55, 79, 160
Soviet Union
and US blacks 300, 302, 309, 320, 352
Bolsheviks in 17
collapse of 7–8, 103
degeneration of 1, 11, 13, 112, 120, 136–137, 205, 224, 260, 262, 283

famine relief for 104
impact on IWW 95
influence on American Communists 3–4, 15, 56, 104, 176, 227, 246, 309, 320
recognition of 106, 110
relations with Britain 213
Stalinism in 12–13, 240
See also Bolshevik Revolution; Comintern archives; Russian Communist Party
SP See Socialist Party
Spanish Communist Party 152
Spartakists, in Germany 12, 55
special oppression 292–293, 301
See also black oppression; 'Negro question'; racial discrimination; racist violence; women's oppression
Spector, Maurice 251, 257–259, 261–262n, 264n2, 281
SPL See Socialist Propaganda League
Spolansky, Jacob 65
Stachel, Jack 169, 185, 206, 264, 271, 279, 285, 359
Stalinisation
of American CP 12, 16, 22–23, 152, 205, 225, 232, 240–241, 285–286, 365–366
of Comintern 13, 17, 20–23, 152–154, 187–188, 205, 225, 240–243, 247, 355–356, 364
See also Bolshevik Revolution, degeneration of; Soviet Union, degeneration of
Stalinism
and 'Negro question' 23, 287, 340, 343–344, 355–358
in American CP 12–13, 17, 20, 188, 225, 247, 285–286, 365–367
in Comintern 13, 17, 187–188, 209, 247, 283, 286, 366
in Soviet Union 13, 120, 152, 205, 224, 260, 283
popular-frontism 10, 16, 20, 140, 151, 213, 249, 356–357, 364–365
Third Period 16, 224, 249–250, 282, 365
vs Leninism 6, 17, 19, 247, 260
vs Trotskyism 140–141, 249, 260, 264, 358n1
See also Bolshevik Revolution, degeneration of; 'socialism in one country'; Soviet Union, degeneration of; Trotskyism
Stalinist purges in Soviet Union 15n, 120, 177n1, 277n3, 329
See also anti-Trotskyism; Bolshevik Revolution, degeneration of; Soviet Union, degeneration of
Stalin, Joseph
and China 20, 213, 225n1, 242, 258, 356
and degeneration of Bolshevik Revolution 1, 13
and Lovestone 22, 213, 225, 231–232, 238, 240, 242, 247, 254–256, 266, 268, 270, 272–273, 275–276, 278, 282, 284, 286, 356
and 'Negro question' 23, 287, 340, 343–344, 346–347n, 353, 355–358
and Pepper 142, 255–256, 357
as Comintern leader 6, 12–13, 137, 152, 166, 205, 213, 234, 247, 250–251, 276
bloc with Bukharin 205, 213, 218, 224–227, 234, 238, 242–243, 247, 258, 266
bloc with Zinoviev and Kamenev 136, 140–141, 227
break with Bukharin 224, 226n1, 249, 251, 254–255, 258, 266, 269–273, 278, 283
break with Zinoviev & Kamenev 205, 224, 243
intervention in American CP 1, 18–19, 166, 169, 224, 254–256, 270–272, 274–278, 285, 355n-356n
on British General Strike 239n1–240
opponents of 154–155n, 205, 227, 230–231
political views 6, 17, 136–137, 224–225, 232, 242–243n, 247, 345, 355
rise of 13, 16, 22, 66n1, 136, 152, 205, 224–225, 249
supporters of 13, 16–17, 23, 155n2–156, 163, 205, 225–226n, 241, 251, 254–256, 263, 266, 270, 361
vs Lenin 6, 17, 247, 258
vs Trotsky 10, 136–137, 156–158, 163, 205, 213, 229, 238, 240–241, 278
Stationary Firemen's Union 198n3
Steelman (Stalin) See Stalin, Joseph
Steel (Stalin) See Stalin, Joseph
steel workers strike 35, 101–102, 104, 107

St. John, Vincent 25, 77, 97, 98
St. Louis Manifesto (1917) 27–28
St. Louis MO 363
Stokes, James Graham Phelps 311
Stokes, Rose Pastor 28, 36, 37n1, 77, 302, 311
Stoklitsky, Alexander 29–30n1, 39, 81, 177n1
Stowe, Harriet Beecher 293
St. Paul Farmer-Labor convention (1924) 142–146, 160, 338
street nuclei 180–181
strike wave (1919) 34–35, 76, 101, 223
Strouthous, Andrew 113
Sullivan (Alfred S. Edwards) 71
Sun Yat Sen 325
Supreme Court (US) 50, 72, 89, 207, 289
Swabeck, Arne
  and Farmer-Labor Party 119
  and FFLP 127–128
  and Seattle general strike 77
  and Trotskyism 158, 259
  Cannon supporter 70, 158, 169–170, 259
  expulsion from CP 261–262n
  on AFL 76
  on Bolshevik Revolution 35
  on Comintern and CP 48, 166, 169–170, 209n2
  on La Follette 132
  on legality 70
  on Pepper 121, 128
Swedish press, of IWW 80
Swift (Pepper) See Pepper, John
syndicalism 4, 25, 78–79, 89, 98–100
  See also Industrial Workers of the World; Wobblies
Syndicalist League of North America 99, 102
syndicalists
  and Comintern 78–80, 83, 86, 94, 97
  and Bolshevik Revolution 79, 81, 89
  and Profintern 87, 90–91, 93, 103, 134
  recruitment of 97
  repression of 199

Tamiment Institute, NYU viii, 7n2
Tanner, Jack 94
Tanner, William 96
Taylor, Charles 135, 145–148n
Teamsters strike (Minneapolis, 1934) 283
Textile Committee, of CP 188, 192
textile strikes See Gastonia NC textile strike; New Bedford MA textile strike; Passaic NJ textile strikes; Paterson NJ silk workers strike
textile workers, Communist work among 3, 77, 188, 191–193, 195–197, 265, 285
  See also garment workers; Gastonia NC textile workers; ILGWU; needle trades; New Bedford MA textile workers; Passaic NJ textile strikes
textile workers union See United Textile Workers. See also ACWA; ILGWU
Thalheimer, August 270, 283
The Negro Worker 333
Thermidor 13, 152, 283
The Toiler 295
The Workers' Council 57–58
Third Comintern Congress (1921) See Communist International congresses
Third International See Communist International
third-party movement 14, 112, 130–132, 136, 139–141, 150n2–151, 156, 243
  See also Farmer-Labor Party; farmer-labour movement; labour party movement; La Follette movement
Third Period 16, 224, 242, 249–250, 267–268, 282–284, 308n1, 362, 364–366
  See also dual unionism; ultraleftism
Thomas, Norman 198n3
Titus, Herman Franklin 98
Tocqueville, Alexis de 233n3
Townley, A.C. 116
Trachtenberg, Alexander 56, 61
trade union bureaucracy 16, 70, 75n2, 83–84, 100, 106, 110, 112–114, 117–118, 124, 130, 147–150, 194, 196–197, 211–212, 215, 223, 238, 284, 289, 324, 327, 330, 340n1
  See also ACWA; American Federation of Labor; Gompers; Hillquit; Lewis
Trade Union Educational League (TUEL) 95–96n1, 101–102, 104–112, 117–118, 125–126, 148–149, 151, 161, 174, 188–189, 192–195, 212, 214–215, 284, 322n2, 326, 333, 354, 361
trade union movement See AFL; Communist Party, in labour movement; individual trade unions; labour movement

Trade Union Unity League (TUUL) 284, 361–363
transport workers 50, 65, 76–77, 107–108, 114, 130, 285, 289, 292
troika (Zinoviev, Kamenev, Stalin) 136, 141, 152, 157, 186, 205, 225, 227
Trotsky Circle 51
Trotskyism 137–138, 154, 158, 250, 259
  See also permanent revolution; Trotsky
Trotskyist Left Opposition See International Left Opposition; Left Opposition (Trotskyist)
Trotskyists 51, 120n2, 142, 147, 156–157, 229–230, 250–251, 257–260, 264–265, 283, 366
  expulsions of 13, 230, 260–262
  See also Abern; Cannon; Eastman; Karsner; Konikow; Lore; Shachtman; Spector; Swabeck
Trotsky, Leon
  and Bolshevik Revolution 34, 137n3
  and Cannon 70, 257–259, 265
  and Eastman 227–228, 230–231
  and international revolution 137, 156, 238, 258
  and IWW 80
  and McKay 309, 311
  and Pepper 137–138, 142–143n, 156, 226, 228, 237–238, 240–242, 259
  and Red Army 136, 156–157
  bloc with Zinoviev 205, 218, 226, 229, 242–243
  exile 205, 229, 251
  expulsion from CPSU 251
  expulsion from ECCI 213, 226, 228
  in Comintern 1, 22, 69–70, 73, 107, 112, 136, 140–142, 159, 213, 226–229, 235–238, 258
  in United States 33–34, 137
  Jewish support for 229–230n
  on American capitalism 69, 235–238
  on Bolshevism 5–6
  on Britain 236–238
  on Bukharin 251, 283
  on China 213, 258
  on Communist Party (US) 70, 112, 140–142, 265
  on draft Comintern program 257–259
  on La Follette movement 22, 140–142
  on Lovestone 247
  on 'Negro question' 309, 309–311, 343, 358n1
  on Stalin 10, 13, 137, 225, 238, 251, 283
  on Valetski 66n1
  removal from Soviet PB 205
  vs popular front 10, 140–142
  vs Stalinist bureaucracy 136–137, 152–153, 227, 258, 260, 262, 283
  See also anti-Trotskyism; International Left Opposition; Left Opposition (Trotskyist); permanent revolution; Trotskyism; Trotskyists
Trotter, William Monroe 317
TUEL See Trade Union Educational League
Tulsa race riot (Oklahoma 1921) 299–300, 315
Tunis 305
Turner, Nat 325
TUUL See Trade Union Unity League
Twenty-One Conditions (for Comintern adherence) 55–56, 343
Two and a Half International 144
two-stage revolution, theory of 345, 356–358n
  See also anti-imperialist united front; permanent revolution; Stalin; Stalinism

UBCJA See United Brotherhood of Carpenters and Joiners of America
UCP See United Communist Party
UFC See United Front Committee
UFEL See United Farmers Educational League
Uhlmann, Jennifer 9
Ukrainian federation 173, 190
Ulbricht, Walter 274
ultraleftism 16, 54, 176n1, 241–243n, 249, 268, 282, 284–285, 327
  See also dual unionism; Third Period
UMWA See United Mineworkers of America
underground Communist Party 14, 18, 21, 40, 51–53, 58–61, 66–67, 71–73, 77, 93, 105, 174, 198–199
unemployed 92, 160, 285, 362, 366
UNIA See Universal Negro Improvement Association

union bureaucracy See trade union bureaucracy
Union of Russian Workers 50
unions See labour movement; trade union bureaucracy. See also individual trade unions
United Brotherhood of Carpenters and Joiners of America 109–111
United Communist Party (UCP) 42–44, 46–48, 81–82, 114–115, 172
United Farmer 126
United Farmers Educational League (UFL) 126
united front against imperialism 331
United Front Committee (UFC), Passaic strike 190, 193, 196
united front tactic 50, 92, 95, 106, 118–119, 194, 200–203, 246, 249, 317, 331n2
United Mineworkers of America (UMWA) 75, 109, 125–127, 145, 189, 212, 251n1, 337
United Negro Front 317
United Textile Workers (UTW) 190, 193, 196–197
Unity Bulletin 94
Universal Negro Improvement Association (UNIA) 296, 300, 302–304n2, 306, 315, 331
Uruguay Communists 45
USSR See Soviet Union
UTW See United Textile Workers

Valetski, Henryk 65–68, 120
Vanzetti, Bartolomeo 3, 187, 201–204, 219, 330
Varga, Eugen 155n2, 235–236, 241–242
Vessey, Denmark 325
Voice of Labor 60n3, 87n2, 93
Volkszeitung See *New Yorker Volkszeitung*
Volodarsky, V. 33
Vujovi
Voja 213, 226

Wagenknecht, Alfred 27, 33, 36–39, 66, 198
Walecki (Valetski) See Valetski, Henryk
Wallace, Charles 54
Walsh, Frank 72, 199–200
Washington, Booker T. 296, 325
Washington DC 338
WC See Workers' Council
W(C)P [Workers' (Communist) Party] See Communist Party
Weber, Hermann 12, 14
Weinstone, William W. 171, 206–212, 214–219, 245, 263n1, 275–279, 291, 349, 358
Weisbord, Albert 189–193, 196, 202–203
Welsh, Edward 271n2, 274n1, 281n1, 359
West Africa 314, 331, 363n2
West Indies See Caribbean
Wheeler, Burton K. 135
White Australia policy 306
'white chauvinism' in Communist Party 333, 337–338, 340–341, 348, 350, 352, 354
White, Walter 310n2
White, William J. 271n2, 274n1, 281n1
Wicks, Harry (British Communist) 258
Wicks, Herbert Moore (US Communist) 259, 271n2, 279–280n, 349
Wiita, John (Henry Puro) 179, 182, 185
Williams, David Rhys 201
Williams, George 90–93
Williams, J.D. 33
Wilson, Woodrow 56
Winitsky, Harry 35n2
Winnipeg general strike (1919) 76
Wirtanen, Atos 169
Wobblies 25–26, 78–99, 134n1, 156, 197, 199–203
See also Industrial Workers of the World
Wolfe, Bertram D. 29, 38–40, 165, 212, 228–231n, 244, 246, 268, 271, 278–280, 284, 349–350
on Trotsky 156–158, 228–230, 250–251
women's oppression, Communists on 9n3
See also sexism
Worker 119, 174
Workers Clubs 174, 185
Workers' (Communist) Party
See Communist Party
Workers' Council (WC) 55, 57–59, 61–62, 68, 74, 108
Workers Defense Committee 199–200
Workers Defense Union (WDU) 77, 199
Workers' Dreadnought 297
workers government slogan 50, 76–77
Workers' International Industrial Union 40, 90

Workers' International Relief 285
Workers Monthly 157n1, 174, 227, 236–237, 320, 322, 325, 340
workers republic, slogan 59
Workers' Party of America (WPA) See Communist Party
Workers' Party (WP) See Communist Party
Workers' Red International 80, 95
See also Communist International; Profintern
World Negro Congress 294, 305–306, 308, 313–318, 359
World War I 1–2, 5, 24–26, 27n1, 29, 100, 199, 223, 235, 238, 288
World War II 4, 7n2, 8, 16, 234, 364
Wortis, Rose 127, 188, 216
WPA (Workers' Party of America) See Communist Party
WP (Workers' Party) See Communist Party
WWI See World War I

Yamanouchi, Akito 33
Yiddish federation 46, 56, 127, 132, 155, 173–178, 183, 229
Yiddish-language press 108, 173, 183–184, 186
Yiddish-speakers, and CP 11, 47, 56, 108, 172
Yokinen, August 338, 359
Yokinen trial (Harlem, 1931) 338, 359
Young Communist International 71n1, 332, 343
Young Workers' (Communist) League 266

Zack, Joseph (Kornfeder) 67, 196n3, 216, 266, 267n1, 271, 274n1, 294
Zam, Herbert 349
Zimmerman, Charles S. 77, 149, 188, 191, 216, 278n3, 281n1, 282
Zimmerwald manifesto 56
Zinoviev, Grigory
and Bolshevisation 152–153, 159
and Comintern 69, 152, 159, 161, 166, 205, 213, 235
and FFLP 124
and Joint Opposition 205, 218, 226, 229, 242–243
and La Follette debate 140–141, 147–148
and Lenin 49, 86, 88–89, 227
and 'Negro question' 319, 343
and Pepper 121–122, 138–139, 143, 154, 226
and Stalinisation 13, 153
anti-Trotskyism 154, 158
appeals to IWW 80–81n, 83, 97
bloc with Stalin 136, 140, 158, 227
break with Stalin 224, 278
campaign against in CP 226, 228–229
capitulation to Stalin 205
debates with IWW 84, 97
expulsion from ECCI 213, 228
fight vs Lore 154–156, 158
on American CP 18, 44, 47n, 86, 162–164, 167, 169
on legal party 53–54, 69
removal from Soviet political bureau 205
See also Russian Communist Party; troika
Zionism 306

CPSIA information can be obtained
at www.ICGtesting.com
Printed in the USA
LVOW08s1937281016
510693LV00003B/9/P

9 781608 464876